HUMANITY

HUMANITY

An Introduction to Cultural Anthropology

James Peoples

Garrick Bailey
University of Tulsa

West Publishing Company

St. Paul   New York   Los Angeles   San Francisco

COPYRIGHT ©1988   By WEST PUBLISHING COMPANY
COPYRIGHT ©1991   By WEST PUBLISHING COMPANY
50 W. Kellogg Boulevard
P. O. Box 64526
St. Paul, MN 55164-1003

Copyediting   Chris Thillen
Artwork   Alice Theide
Cover image   Suzanne and Nick Geary:
TSW-Click/Chicago

Library of Congres Cataloging-in-Publication Data

Peoples, James G.
  Humanity : an introduction to cultural anthropology / James
  Peoples, Garrick Bailey.--2nd ed.
  p.   cm.
  Includes bibliographical references.
  ISBN 0-314-77277-4
  1. Ethnology. I. Bailey, Garrick Alan. II. Title.
GN316.P384 1991
306—dc20   90-39183
                                                     CIP
                                                     ⊗

Text Photo Credits

Credits continued following last index page

To Deborah and Roberta.

ABOUT THE AUTHORS

James Peoples has taught at Southern Illinois University, the State University of New York at Plattsburgh, the University of Tulsa, and the University of California at Davis, from where he received a Ph.D in 1977. He currently teaches at Ohio Wesleyan University. His main research interests are in human ecology, economic and development anthropology, sociocultural evolution, and the peoples of Oceania. The author of several articles, he also has published *Island in Trust*, a book about the impact of American policy on the economy of a Micronesian island.

Garrick Bailey received his undergraduate degree in history from the University of Oklahoma, and his Ph.D. in anthropology from the University of Oregon. His primary research interests are in historic changes and contemporary sociocultural systems of Native American peoples. Although most of his field research has been among Native Americans in the Southwest and Oklahoma, he has also worked in Western Samoa. Presently Professor of Anthropology at the University of Tulsa, his publications include *changes in Osage Social Organization: 1673-1906, Historic Navajo Occupation of the Northern Chaco Plateau,* and *A Hisotry of the Navajo: The Reservation Years,* the latter two coauthored with Roberta Bailey.

CONTENTS

■ *Boxes in*
HUMANITY

PREFACE

Our main intention in the second edition of *Humanity* is to provide introductory level students with an overview of the discipline of cultural anthropology. We hope to provide all our readers with a sense of the excitement of discovering other ways of human life, with all their variety. We also hope to convince students of the value of learning to understand and tolerate other cultural traditions—for both humanitarian and practical reasons.

As in textbooks in other disciplines, in *Humanity* we try to introduce the key concepts, assumptions, methods, and major theoretical orientations of anthropology, which are the main subjects of parts 1 and 2. We think that the main empirical contribution anthropology has made to the understanding of the human species is its documentation of the sociocultural diversity of the world's peoples. Accordingly, the description of this diversity in part 3 takes up most of the book. Part 4 discusses the contemporary world—how it was affected by the expansion of the West and some of its major political and economic problems. The text concludes with an epilogue on the survival of indigenous peoples.

Changes in the Second Edition

This edition retains the design and content features of the first edition. We have added even more maps, especially in the new chapter 18. Some boxes have been replaced, and a few new boxes have been written. New text illustrations have been added. We are pleased to be able to include four inserts with color photos, briefly describing the peoples of Asia, Oceania, Africa, and the Americas. Again, we have limited in-text citations to quotations and have put detailed references at the end, organized by chapter and major heading. To give full credit to the scholars whose ethnographic descriptions and ideas we discuss, we have worked their names into the chapter text whenever possible.

Although some chapters (1, 4, 5, 7, 9, 12, 13, 15, and 19) are much the same, substantial changes appear in this edition. Chapter 2 has been reworked to sharpen the distinctions and definitions, and the discussion of social learning is moved to chapter 3. Half of chapter 3 has been deleted;

this chapter now deals exclusively with the relationship between human biology and sociocultural diversity. Chapter 6 has been reorganized and new material has been added on diachronic comparisons. In chapter 8, we redefined cultivation systems to bring them more into line with the most common terminology. Chapters 10 and 11 contain several clarifications and corrections that, we hope, make their technical portions less tedious. Extensive new material on castes has been added to chapter 14. We added information on male initiation rituals in New Guinea to chapter 16, to strengthen its factual components. The final section of chapter 17 has been placed into a new chapter 18, which discusses ethnicity and ethnic conflict in the modern world. This chapter is the only entirely new one in the book. The numerical data on population growth in chapter 19 (old 18) has been updated, in this chapter as in others. The epilogue (old 19) contains recent materials on the survival of indigenous peoples. In our judgment, *Humanity* is a much better book because of these changes. We hope our readers agree.

ACKNOWLEDGMENTS

We thank everyone who has contributed to the writing and production of this book. Our greatest intellectual debt is to those who have reviewed various chapters of the second edition. These include the following colleagues and friends of the authors: Mary Howard (who contributed Box 18.1), Lamont Lindstrom, William Davis, Henry Rutz, Peter Stromberg, George Odell, Annette Fromm, Donald Henry, Kathryn Meyer, Jan Smith, Ted Cohen, David Epstein, Jean Blocker, Blake Roxlau, Tim O'Meara, Pam Quagiotto, Doug Raybeck, A. J. Singh, David Boyd, Joe Kestner, Tom Love, Pat Blessing, and Richard Curley.

West Publishing Company had the first edition reviewed by the following scholars: Nancy Leis, John Reibsamen, Leslie Sponsel, Don Merten, James Flanagan, Gretchen Siegler, Norbert Dannhaeuser, Walter R. Adams, Michael Rhum, Donald Brown, Dianne Smith-Benson, and Elliott Fratkin. Their comments were invaluable in correcting and adding to the first edition. In addition to serving as a reviewer, Nancy Leis also authored the Instructor's Manual, and her input in both editions has substantially improved the book. The authors also wish to thank Michael Freedman for his helpful comment on the text.

We thank our friends Annette B. Fromm, David Boyd, Michael Whalen, Lamont Lindstrom, Victoria Lockwood, and Donald Henry for photographic materials. John Wilson loaned us an ogre kachina for an illustration, as well as prints from photos from the Jo Mora collection at the University of Northern Arizona. We thank Dan McPike at the Gilcrease Museum in Tulsa and the University of Northern Arizona for allowing us to reproduce negatives in their possession at minimal cost.

The entire project has been treated attentively and competently by West Publishing Company. Tom LaMarre has been with us through both editions, and we hope through many more. Tom Hilt's patience and competence has been enormously helpful. Copyeditor Chris Thillen is the most thorough editor either of us has worked with.

J. P. acknowledges the contributions of his parents, who waded through all nineteen chapters of the first edition—with no college credit earned! This meant a lot.

Last, but most, we thank our wives, Deborah Carter Peoples and Roberta Bailey. Second editions demand as much patience from one's spouses as do first editions. Without their willingness to tolerate our long hours and absentmindedness, the writing would have proceeded even more slowly.

THE STUDY
OF HUMANITY

■ Contents

■ (Above) *Cultural anthropology is the study of the customs and beliefs of living peoples, such as these South Asians.*

Where did the human species come from? How have we changed over time, both biologically and culturally? Is there a common human nature and, if so, what is it like? In what ways do humans who live in various times and places differ? How can we explain why cultures vary in their economic systems, religious beliefs, family relations, and artistic styles? Such questions are the concern of anthropology, the study of humanity.

Anthropologists are interested in almost everything about people. We want to know when and where the human species originated, how and why we evolved into our present form, and the ways in which this biological evolution continues to affect us today. Anthropologists want to know about the technological, economic, political, and intellectual development of humanity. We want to know the extent to which different human populations vary in their biological and social characteristics and to understand why these differences exist.

Anthropologists try to explain why people in some places believe that sickness is caused by dead ancestors, whereas others claim that tarantulas throw magical darts into their bodies, and still others tell you that the spirits of evil humans leave their bodies at night and seek out the internal organs of their victims, which they devour from the inside out. We want to understand the rules that you know unconsciously that instruct you when to bow your head and speak reverently, when to sound smart, when to act dumb, and when to cuss like a sailor. Anthropologists are interested in why Americans eat beef but devout Hindus do not, and in why some New Guinea people periodically engorge themselves with pork but some Middle Easterners regard pig flesh as unclean. We want to know why Balinese are fascinated by cock fights, Span-iards by bull fights, Thais by fish fights, and North Americans by people fights. In short, anthropologists are liable to be curious about practically everything human: our evolution, our genes, our bodies, our emotions, our behaviors, and our thoughts.

If you already have the impression that anthropology is a broad field and that anthropologists have quite diverse interests, you are correct. In fact, it is commonly said that the main distinguishing characteristic of anthropology—the thing that makes it different from the many other fields that also include people as their subject matter—is its broad scope. A good way to emphasize this broad scope is to say that anthropologists are interested in *all* human beings—whether living or dead, "primitive" or "civilized"—and that they are interested in many different *aspects* of humans, including their skin color, family lives, political systems, tools, personality types, and languages. No place or time is too remote to escape the anthropologist's notice. No dimension of humankind, from genes to art styles, is outside the anthropologist's attention.

The Subfields of Anthropology

Anthropology as a discipline, then, is enormously wide ranging. Of course, no single individual can be equally expert in all of humanity nor in all aspects of humans. Although the field is diverse, as a practical matter individual anthropologists narrow the scope of their interests. During their academic training, anthropologists today nearly always specialize in one of four subdisciplines, each of which focuses on only one or a few dimensions of humankind. One subfield is concerned primarily with the evolutionary origins and biological diversity of the human species. Another deals mainly with the technological and cultural development of humanity over long time spans. The other two focus on the languages and cultures of contemporary and historically recent human populations.

■ *Physical Anthropology*

As its name implies, the subfield of **physical anthropology** deals with the physical and biological aspects of the human species. It is concerned with topics such as the biological evolution of humankind; the social behavior and ecology of our closest living relatives, monkeys and apes; and the physical variation of living populations.

One subject investigated by physical anthropology is the emergence of *Homo sapiens* (the scientific name of humanity) from prehuman, apelike ancestors. This specialization is known as **paleoanthropology.** Throughout decades of tedious searching and painstaking excavations, paleoanthropologists have traced the outlines of how humans evolved anatomically and behaviorally. Although our knowledge remains incomplete, most paleoanthropologists presently believe that the divergence between the evolutionary lines leading to modern species of African apes (chimpanzees and gorillas) and to modern humans occurred at least five million years ago.

Other physical anthropologists, called **primatologists,** specialize in the evolution, anatomy, social behavior, and ecology of primates, the taxonomic order to which humans belong. Through studying fossils of extinct primates and comparing the anatomy of living species, primatologists can establish the evolutionary relationships between various primate species. By conducting field studies of how living primates forage, mate, move around, and interact socially, primatologists hope to shed light on the forces that affected early human populations, and thus help us understand how and why we evolved. Studies conducted of ground-dwelling monkeys and apes, such as baboons, gorillas, and chimpanzees, have been especially fruitful in this regard.

Another type of biological anthropologist studies how and why human populations vary physically. All humans are members of a single species. Nonetheless, the residents of different continents once were more isolated from one another than they are today, and during this separation they evolved differences in height, overall bodily form, skin color, blood chemistry, and other physical traits. Anthropologists who study human physical variation seek to measure and explain the biological differences between human populations.

■ Archaeology

Along with physical anthropology, **archaeology** is probably the subfield that most people associate with the word *anthropology*. Archaeologists study the ways of living of past peoples by excavating and analyzing the

■ *Physical anthropologists investigate the biological dimensions of humans, including our evolution, physical diversity, and the behavior of primates, our closest nonhuman relatives. Here primatologist Sarah Blaffer Hrdy weighs a langur, a species of monkey that lives in India.*

physical remains they left behind. Tools, ornaments, pottery, animal bones, human skeletal material, and even plant pollen all provide the archaeologist with evidence of how people lived in the distant past. Modern archaeology is divided into two major kinds of study, "historic" and "prehistoric."

Historic archaeologists use the evidence provided by excavated remains to enhance our understanding of historic peoples—that is, peoples who had writing and about whom written records are available. For example, historic archaeologists might work in an early colonial settlement and use the artifactual materials they discover to supplement historical records such as diaries, letters, land records, and tax-collection documents. One type of historic archaeologist, the *classical archaeologist*, deals primarily with the ancient civilizations and empires of Europe and the Middle East, including Egypt, Greece, Rome, and Persia.

In contrast, *prehistoric archaeologists* investigate human prehistory—that is, the periods of time in a region before writing developed. The painstaking excavation and careful interpretation of these remains are often the only scientific means available to discover how people lived in the prehistoric past. Archaeological research also is the only way to trace the outlines of human technological and cultural change over the many thousands of years before written records were made.

An *archaelogical field crew under the direction of Michael Whalen excavates a site in the American Southwest. Prehistoric archaelogists attempt to reconstruct the past by careful and systematic excavation of the material remains of prehistoric peoples.*

Modern prehistoric archaeologists attempt to learn more than merely "what happened in prehistory." Reconstructing the ways of living of long-extinct peoples is only one of the aims of this subfield. Archaeologists want to know not only what happened, but also why particular things happened at particular times and places. One major question, for example, is why people gradually began to cultivate plants, when the hunting and collecting of wild animals and plants seemed to suffice for tens of thousands of years. Another important question is why civilization developed not just once but a minimum of three or four times in various parts of the world. In the attempt to answer casual questions such as these, archaeologists have developed highly sophisticated methods of excavation and laboratory analysis.

■ Anthropological Linguistics

Linguistics is the scientific study of language. Linguists describe and analyze the sound patterns, combinations of sounds, meanings, and structure of sentences in human languages. They also attempt to determine how two or more languages are related historically. Modern linguists are especially interested in whether all human languages share any universal features. Some recent work suggests that human infants are born with knowledge of a set of generalized rules that allow them to discover the specific rules of the language around them and to formulate new sentences by applying these rules.

Not all linguists consider themselves anthropologists. Anthropological linguists usually focus on unwritten languages and are especially concerned with relations between language and other aspects of human behavior and thought. An anthropological linguist might describe and analyze a language hitherto unknown to linguistic science, but he or she is likely also to be interested in how the language is used in various social contexts. For example, what speech style must one use with people of higher social standing? How does a local political leader use language to earn people's allegiance? What can the naming of various parts of the natural and social environment tell us about people's perceptions of these environments?

Anthropological linguists also investigate the similarities between the structure of language and culture. Language is one kind of shared knowledge: speakers know unconsciously how to combine sounds into sequences that can be interpreted correctly by others. It is likely that we can learn much about culture—another kind of shared knowledge—by studying language. We return to this subject in chapter 4.

■ *Cultural Anthropology*

Cultural anthropology (also called *social* or *sociocultural anthropology*) is concerned with the cultural and social dimensions of contemporary and historically recent human populations. Cultural anthropologists conduct studies of living peoples, most often by visiting and living among a particular people for an extended

■ *Anthropological linguists focus mainly on nonwritten languages and on the interrelations between language and culture. Here linguist Francesca Merlin studies a language of highland Papua New Guinea.*

■ *Cultural anthropologists usually collect data on contemporary peoples by living with them, often in much the same way as the people themselves. Here fieldworker Richard Lee socializes with the San, a southern Africa people who until recently lived by hunting and gathering.*

period of time, usually a year or longer. During these periods of *fieldwork*, most cultural anthropologists attempt to learn and communicate in the local language and to live in close contact with the people. Their aim is to learn how the local society is organized, how people customarily behave in certain situations, how they stage their rituals, how the local political system works, and so forth. Fieldworkers usually report their findings in books or scholarly journals, so that the information collected becomes part of the accumulated knowledge about humanity. These written descriptions of how a single human population lives are called *ethnographies* (**ethnography** means "writing about a people").

Through their own fieldwork and through reading ethnographies, cultural anthropologists hope to gain a knowledge of the enormous social and cultural variation that exists among the many human populations of the world. (An introduction to this diversity in human ways of living is found in part 3 of this book.) But documenting cultural diversity is not the only interest of this subfield. We attempt to do more than merely record and describe the ways of life of peoples of various regions. We want to know not just *how* humanity is diverse but also the *reasons* for this diversity. We seek explanations of differences as well as similarities between the world's peoples.

When cultural anthropologists attempt to analyze and explain the way of life of the people of a region, or to compare a variety of ways of living in order to test hypotheses about the causes of human lifeways in

general, they are practicing **ethnology.** Ethnologists seek to discover the causes of the differences and similarities between the customs and beliefs of diverse human populations. As we shall see in the following chapters, ethnologists have proposed and attempted to test a great many hypotheses about the causes of differences and similarities between peoples, and about how one custom or belief is related to other customs and beliefs.

Perspectives of Cultural Anthropology

Taken as a whole, then, anthropology is indeed a very broad discipline. One or another kind of anthropologist studies human biology, prehistory, language, and contemporary ways of life. Even by itself, cultural anthropology, which is the main subject of this text, greatly overlaps with other disciplines that study people. For example, fieldworkers are likely to collect information on a society's agriculture, leadership patterns, beliefs about the cosmos, music, and art forms. They might therefore find it useful to be acquainted with the work of economists, geographers, political scientists, philosophers, musicologists, and artists or art historians. Likewise, a sociocultural anthropologist interested in some region may read the works of historians, sociologists, novelists, economists, psychologists, and political scientists who also write about the region. Cultural anthropology thus cuts across many disciplines, encompassing many of the subjects that other scholars consider their special province—law, religion, politics, literature, art and so on.

Do cultural anthropologists then regard their field as the "master science" of humanity? Indeed, some do. But there is no need for such academic imperialism. Researchers in other social sciences and the humanities investigate some subjects better than do anthropologists, just as anthropologists have their own unique contribution to make to studies of other kinds. Most cultural anthropologists believe that the main difference between their discipline and other human sciences lies not so much in the subjects they investigate as in the approach they take to their studies. This approach involves analyzing human ways of life holistically, comparatively, and relativistically. These three elements of the anthropological perspective on humanity together make up the unique contribution of anthropology, so it is worthwhile introducing each in some detail.

■ Holism

Cultural anthropologists believe that whatever they are investigating in some population is only a small part of a total system of customs, values, beliefs, and attitudes. They have found that any particular aspect of this system cannot be understood in isolation from others. This **holistic perspective** means that no single aspect of the lifeway of a population makes sense unless its relationships to other aspects are explored. Holism requires, for example, that an anthropologist studying the religious beliefs and rituals of a population must investigate how the religion is influenced by family life, the economy, the pattern of political leadership, the relationship between the sexes, and a host of other factors. This effort to study everything about a population in order to gain full insight into anything about their way of life is one reason why ethnographic fieldwork requires extended visits and close contact with the local people.

Why do cultural anthropologists adopt a holistic perspective when studying a society? First, various aspects of the way of life of a people do influence one another, so it is important to look for these interconnections. Second, cultural anthropologists have most often studied non-Western, preindustrial societies—those that are known popularly as *tribal* or *primitive*. Because such cultures differ in many respects from our own, we cannot assume that their family, religion, economy, political life, and so forth fit together in familiar ways. Finally, some exotic customs or beliefs seem strange or puzzling considered in isolation, but we often can make sense of them by understanding their context, or the role or function they fulfill in some larger system.

■ Comparativism

In the early decades of its existence, cultural anthropology was concerned mainly with the non-Western peoples of the world, who often acted and thought quite differently from members of "civilized" nations. Anthropologists soon learned that ideas and concepts that applied to their own societies often did not work elsewhere. For example, they learned to mistrust opinions espoused by French scholars about human nature when the only humans the scholars had ever encountered lived in western Europe. Indeed, a favorite

exercise of anthropologists in the early part of the twentieth century was to use their knowledge of non-Western peoples to shoot holes in theories of human nature and of human society formulated by scholars in other disciplines. Anthropologists believe that any valid theories about humans must be formulated and tested with a **comparative perspective.** The ways of life of human beings in different times and places are far too diverse for any theory to be accepted unless it has been tested in a wide range of human populations.

The failure to adopt such a comparative perspective continues to afflict popular ideas about humanity. We can best understand the kinds of dead ends to which such ideas can lead by an example. In the 1960s an eminent zoologist wrote a book that became enormously popular. One of the "facts" about people he tried to explain is why we are pair bonded—that is, why one human male establishes and maintains sexual and marital relationships with one human female, and vice versa. He believed this pair bonding was rooted in our biological makeup, which in turn was caused by the way our ancestors had to adapt to male hunting in open country some million or so years ago. The problem is that the behavior that was supposedly rooted in our common biology—the pair bond—is in fact a characteristic of only *some* humans. In only some societies do men and women establish a pair bond (of course, the zoologist lived in one such society). Because anthropologists are likely to know—or at least to take the trouble to find out—about the diversity of human societies, they are less likely to make the mistake of believing that the behaviors found in their own society are natural to humankind. They know that such "universal characteristics of human nature" usually turn out not to be universal at all. They know that facts must be validated and theories tested with a comparative perspective.

■ Relativism

The concept of **cultural relativism** (or relativity) is an important one to anthropologists. It has two meanings. The first refers to an attitude about the relative worthiness of ways of life. The second refers to a methodological approach to studying societies that differ from our own.

First, cultural relativism means that we view other ways of acting, thinking, and feeling as just as valid as those of our own cultural tradition. Relativism means that we do not view foreign lifeways as inferior to our own; that is, we do not take an ethnocentric attitude toward members of other cultural traditions. **Ethnocentrism** is the opinion that the moral standards, values, manners, knowledge, and so forth of one's own culture are superior to those of other people.

Viewing other people's customs, moral standards, religious practices, and so on relativistically is an idea that is easy to grasp but difficult to put into practice. Most of our readers are brought up in societies that value the right of people to elect their own political leaders; that allow freedom of speech, religion, assembly, and so on; that give lip service to equality of opportunity regardless of race and sex; and that allow individuals to choose their own spouses. Hereditary privileges, suppression of what we conceive to be individual rights, racism and sexism, arranged marriages, and other practices may be as abhorrent to anthropologists as individuals as to any other member of a democratic society. Anthropologists are as entitled to be as personally offended by such practices as anyone else. Thinking relativistically, then, does not mean that one should have no personal opinions and make no moral judgments. Rather, it means that we realize that each human group's ways of acting, thinking, and feeling are the result of its long history, and that we see the full implications of this fact: the present generation (you and I) did not think up values like democracy, freedom, and equal opportunity, but inherited these values from our past. As individuals, you and I deserve no more credit for these ideas than we do blame for the actions of some of our ancestors who enslaved Africans and massacred Native Americans. If we find cultural attitudes and practices such as male dominance and authoritarianism morally abhorrent, we have no right to feel morally superior, for we as individuals did not create the standards that allow such judgments to be made.

Relativism obviously implies toleration between the peoples of the world, a toleration that comes from the knowledge that all of us are largely a product of the traditions into which we happen to have been born and of the conditions under which we happen to be living. The value of a relativistic attitude toward other ways of life is one of the main practical lessons of anthropology. Understanding and even appreciation of people who do not act or think the way we do certainly becomes more valuable as improved communication and transportation bring the various peoples of the world into frequent contact with one another.

In addition to teaching tolerance between members of different cultural traditions, relativism is an approach to the scientific description and understanding of different ways of life. This approach—the second meaning of relativism—requires that the anthropologist search for the sensibility and rationality of actions and beliefs that seem puzzling. A good deal of sociocultural anthropology tries to make sense out of the behaviors and beliefs of other people that, at first glance, seem nonsensical or irrational. Why do some hungry people refuse to eat things they know are edible? Why do some people believe that others have the supernatural power to make them sick, when in fact no one has such powers? Why in some societies is it customary for well-to-do families to give away their possessions? Why are there customs such as human sacrifice, infanticide, cannibalism, self-torture, painful initiation rituals, and amputation of fingers when a relative dies? Approaching the explanation of such behaviors and beliefs relativistically means assuming that they are not attributable to simple ignorance, blind superstition, or collective perversion, but that they are sensible and intelligible once we understand enough about them and their causes and effects. In part 3 of this text, we explore numerous examples of attempts to interpret strange customs and beliefs relativistically.

The Contributions of Anthropology

What unique insights does anthropology offer about humanity? Of what practical use is the information that members of the various subdisciplines have gathered about the past and present of humankind? At one level, such questions are irrelevant. The accumulation of scientific knowledge about the natural and human world is valuable in its own right. The investigation of a particular subject need have no immediate practical use; its value may come both from its satisfaction of human curiosity and from its possible future applications to problem solving. Could Darwin—or mid-nineteenth-century English society—have known that his theory of natural selection would be useful a century later to the solution of environmental problems? We may not be able to see any apparent immediate practical value of the knowledge we gain about the world, but we cannot know the uses to which it might be put in the future.

At another level, however, these questions demand an answer. The resources that any modern nation is prepared to devote to research are limited, and it is perfectly valid to ask why they should be used to support one kind of study rather than others. In part 4 we say a great deal more about the specific contributions of knowledge derived from anthropological research to the solution of human problems. For now, we want to note some of the most general insights that anthropology offers.

First, because of its broad scope, anthropology allows us to understand the biological, technological, and cultural development of humanity over long time spans. Most of the scientific data that we currently have about human biological evolution, prehistoric populations, and tribal peoples were collected by anthropologists. Because much of this knowledge has become a part of the cultural heritage of industrialized nations, where it is recorded in textbooks and taught in schools, it is easy to forget that someone had to discover and interpret it. For example, only in the late nineteenth century did scientists generally accept that people are related to apes, and only in the late twentieth century did some of the details about the closeness of this relationship become apparent.

But it is not just facts that anthropology has contributed to our storehouse of accumulated knowledge. Theoretical ideas and concepts from anthropology have been incorporated as well. For example, most people in modern nations are aware of the concept of *culture*—shared and socially transmitted habits and beliefs—and use the term in their everyday lives. They are not aware that the scientific meaning of this word, as used in the phrase "Japanese culture," is not very old. Into the nineteenth century it was popularly believed that the varying ways of acting, thinking, and feeling of different human populations were transmitted across the generations not by learning but by biological heredity. Patterns of behavior and thought were believed to be rooted in an individual's biological constitution. Because there were easily observable differences in the physical appearances between members of different races, it was thought that physical differences also accounted for differences in behaviors and beliefs. In other words, differences that we now know are due largely to cultural inheritance were confused with racial differences caused by biological inheritance. Although they were not solely responsible for clarifying the distinction between culture and race, anthropologists such as Franz Boas, Margaret Mead, and Ruth Benedict made major contributions by showing that differences in culture cannot be attributed to biological heredity. Again, we see that anthropology

already has added to our accumulated knowledge of humankind but that most people are not aware of this contribution.

A second contribution of anthropology, and especially of the cultural subfield, is that it helps us to avoid some of the misunderstanding that commonly arises when individuals of different cultural traditions come into contact. As we shall see in future chapters, our upbringing in a particular society influences us in subtle ways of which we are not aware. North Americans generally know how to "read" each other's actions on the basis of speech styles or body language, but these cues do not necessarily mean the same things to people from different traditions. A North American trying to appear competent to a Latin American may come across instead as arrogant and egotistical. A Canadian businessman peddling his wares in Turkey may wonder why his host will not cut the chitchat and get down to business, whereas the Turk wonders why the visitor thinks they can do business before they have become better acquainted. Anthropology can help make us aware that when we interact with people from other cultural traditions, their actions are not always intended to mean what we take them to mean, and therefore much miscommunication can be avoided. This is a lesson that diplomats and corporations engaged in international business are beginning to learn (see Box 1.1).

Third, the holistic, comparative, and relativistic approach of anthropology offers members of industrialized societies their best hope of discovering how the quality of their lives compares to that of preindustrial people. The popular stereotype of "tribal" or "primitive" people—a stereotype derived partly from Tarzan and cowboy movies—is somewhat contradictory. We "civilized" folk usually see "savages" as either dirty or noble. When we see them as dirty savages, we imagine them in caves or grass huts, grubbing out a meager living with only the bare rudiments of technology, ignorant even of the fact that they could grow crops from seeds. Their long hours of drudgery are interrupted only by their bodily wants for sleep, sex, and sustenance, and by the periodic frenzied ritual dances required by their superstitions. The men beat "their" females, kick their dogs, and steal one another's property when they get the chance. As we turn on our TVs, sip our Perrier, and kick back in our recliners, we are glad we were born into the material comforts and security of the twentieth century.

Box 1.1

CULTURAL BLUNDERS KILL SALES

As the world's nations become increasingly interdependent economically, a greater sensitivity to cultural differences becomes necessary. The following newspaper article illustrates why those engaged in international business need to develop more understanding of cultural differences.

By SEHYON JOH, *Associated Press Writer*

NEW YORK (AP)—A woman executive, on the brink of clinching a big business deal, abruptly called off negotiations with Arab businessmen who had persistently ignored her and talked only to her subordinates.

"I don't care how much money I'm going to lose by walking out on them like this," she fumed. "I just cannot stand this humiliating male chauvinist game any more. I'm through."

The woman, vice president of a large U.S. company, got so angry she forgot it was only a game, says Ellen Raider, who counsels U.S. firms in international negotiation tactics.

"But if she couldn't tolerate the chauvinistic attitude of some men in a classroom, what would happen when she has to face 'real' Arab businessmen?" Ms. Raider said in a recent interview.

It's a game business needs to learn to play. The U.S. trade deficit hit a record $148.5 billion in 1985, as imports in December alone exceeded exports by $17.4 billion, the Commerce Department reported Thursday.

Ms. Raider is one of half a dozen "cross-cultural consultants" offering advice and training in dealing with foreign buyers.

"There was a time when we sold our goods on world markets with conviction that they were the best—if not the only—products in the world," Ms. Raider said. "But a strong competition from foreign countries in recent years has changed all that.

"We are now forced to scramble like everybody else in order to sell our goods overseas."

That takes more than a good product, and a skilled negotiator.

"You have to know local customs, business practices," says Clifford Clarke of the Intercultural Relations Institute, Palo Alto, Calif.

He told of a large electronics firm which has lost hundreds of thousands of dollars because its president misunderstood Japanese etiquette.

After long, hard bargaining, the U.S. firm had landed a large contract. At the signing ceremony, however, the Japanese executive began reading the contract intently. His scrutiny seemed endless.

The American panicked and offered to take $100 off each item.

What the U.S. executive didn't know, Clarke said, was that the Japanese president was merely demonstrating his authority, not backing out.

With more than 4 million Americans going abroad on business trips each year, even little mistakes add up. Not even the giant companies are immune.

When Coca-Cola Co. finally got an entree into China's vast market, its local sales people came up with four Chinese characters for a phonetical equivalent of the softdrink: "Ke Kou Ke La."

That translated as, "Bite the wax tadpole."

Coke tried again, and found a closer equivalent with a better meaning: "Ko Kou Ko Le," which translates: "May the mouth rejoice." Sales rose sharply, according to Lewis Griggs, producer of "Going International," a film pitched at large corporations and business schools.

In a series of four films, Griggs makes the point that fundamental cultural differences are important in business negotiations.

"In Saudi Arabia, you should never inquire about one's wife [sic] while in Mexico, it's essential that you do so," Griggs says. "And in Japan, small gifts are almost obligatory in business situations whereas giftgiving is prohibited in China."

George Renwick of Renwick Associates of Scottsdale, Ariz., says that minor misunderstandings and irritants can snowball into lost opportunities.

"Cultural differences don't cause a trade deficit," he said, "but understanding them can help reduce it." ∎

Source: Copyrighted by the Associated Press. Reprinted by permission.

When we see preindustrial people as noble savages, we imagine them living in harmony with their environments, apologizing to the spirit of each deer they are forced to kill to survive. Their wants are simple: food, family, and fire are all they need and all they desire. Women are equal to men, the elderly respected.

Neither anthropologists nor anyone else knows how to solve worldwide problems such as overpopulation and hunger. But the comparative, holistic, and relativistic perspectives of modern anthropology can lead to fresh insights on such problems.

Private property is unknown, sharing universal, conflict rare, murder unimaginable. As we return from a hectic day at the office and lock the doors and windows behind us to keep everybody else out, we wish we could trade our lives for theirs, or at least that we could recover the essence of humanness that we seem to have lost.

We imagine life in a natural state, then, as either hell or paradise, perhaps depending mainly on how we feel about our own lives at the moment. Neither of these images of preindustrial peoples is accurate. The truth about such either/or stereotypes often is somewhere in between the two extremes, but not in this case. The truth is that our knowledge about preindustrial peoples shows that their ways of life are too diverse to fit either of our contradictory images of them and too complex to say that they simply fall somewhere in the middle. We attempt to convey some of this diversity and complexity in part 3. Anthropology can offer no final answer to questions like, Is civilization worth it? or Has the quality of our lives improved?

What anthropology—and anthropology alone—can do is to reveal the alternate ways of living developed by diverse segments of humanity. Barring global catastrophe, we are unlikely to return to any of these alternatives, but at least the information reported by past and present ethnographers allows each of us individually to judge the benefits against the costs of life in an industrialized world.

Fourth, because of its comparative approach to humanity, anthropology allows us to identify which aspects of our own way of life are amenable to change. For example, we often hear statements like "Men have been going to war since the beginning of time," the implication being that men have always fought each other and are doomed to continue to do so. Or we used to hear that women are unsuited to hold high political offices or managerial jobs because of their physiology, which supposedly gives them nuturing personalities and makes them unwilling to make the tough decisions. Or we often hear that the profit motive is universal, racial hatred is innate, people are basically lazy, all societies are divided into haves and have-nots, and all humans need to believe in a god.

Without a comparative perspective on humankind, we have no way of judging the truth of such ideas. Unless we look beyond the boundaries of our own nations, we cannot separate what is unique to our way of life from what is general to all people. And if we cannot tell what is unique from what is general, we do not know our chances of eliminating warfare, sexism, racism, poverty, and crime. If these problems turn out to afflict all peoples, then they may indeed be difficult to solve. If, on the other hand, they turn out to afflict only some societies, then we can be fairly confident that we can change them through public policy or private actions.

Fifth, many cultural anthropologists use their expertise in particular subjects to formulate practical ways of coping with immediate social problems. *Medical anthropologists,* who investigate the interrelationships between human health, nutrition, and cultural beliefs and practices, have helped hospitals and agencies deliver health care more effectively to many people throughout the world. Because the spread of pathogenic organisms is affected by things such as a people's eating patterns and sexual behavior, medical anthropologists also work with epidemiologists in identifying the effects of such cultural practices on the transmission of disease. *Applied anthropologists* bring a holistic approach to development agencies and other groups attempting to introduce planned changes to the hundreds of thousands of small villages in the world. Applied anthropologists may work as consultants for institutions such as the U.S. Agency for International Development, UNESCO, the World Bank, and the Rockefeller Foundation. Two of their major roles are to provide information on target populations and to advise agronomists, engineers, and other experts on how to adapt their projects to local conditions and local needs. The ethnographic information gathered by *economic* and *ecological anthropologists* on preindustrial agricultural and herding practices, land-ownership customs, technological efficiencies, settlement patterns, and so forth, have proven useful to both indigenous people and outside experts in designing changes compatible with a region's cultural and economic conditions. These and other practical uses of anthropology are discussed further in part 4 of this text.

Summary

Anthropology studies human beings from a very broad framework. It differs from other disciplines in the social sciences and humanities primarily because of its very broad scope. The field as a whole is concerned with all human beings of the past and present, living at all levels of technological development. Anthropology is also interested in all aspects of humanity: biology, language, technology, art, politics, religion, and all other dimensions of human ways of living.

As a practical necessity, however, anthropologists must specialize. Traditionally, the field is divided into four subdisciplines. Physical anthropology studies the biological dimensions of human beings, including our biological evolution, the physical variations between contemporary populations, and the biology and behavior of nonhuman primates. Prehistoric archaeology is concerned with human prehistory, investigating topics such as technological development, long-term changes in social and political organization, and the evolution of agriculture and civilization. Anthropological linguistics studies language, concentrating on nonwritten languages and investigating the interrelationships between language and other elements of a people's way of life. Cultural anthropology, the main subject of this book, is concerned with the social and cultural dimensions of contemporary and historically recent populations. Cultural anthropologists conduct fieldwork among the people they study and describe the results of their investigations in books and articles called *ethnog-*

raphies. Cultural anthropology is more than an empirical study, for the field is also concerned with making generalizations about and seeking explanations for similarities and differences among the world's peoples. Those who conduct comparative studies to achieve these theoretical goals are known as *ethnologists*.

Cultural anthropologists are different from other scholars who study living people not so much by what they study as by their approach to their studies. There are three main characteristics of this approach. Holism is the attempt to discern and investigate the interrelationships between the customs and beliefs of a particular society. The comparative perspective means that any attempt to understand humanity or to explain some element of human societies or behavior must consider a wide range of human ways of life. Anthropologists have learned that most customs and beliefs are products of cultural tradition and social environment, rather than of a universal human nature. Relativism is partly an attitude of toleration that cultural anthropologists try to adopt when studying other peoples. It requires that anthropologists not be ethnocentric in their research, for each peoples' way of life has its own history and its own standards of morality and decency. In addition to being an attitude, relativism is an approach to the scientific description and analysis of societies. It requires researchers to search for the sensibility and rationality behind customs or beliefs that seem ridiculous, inhuman, or the product of silly superstitions.

Anthropology has practical value in the modern world, and it is not as esoteric as many people think. Only anthropology allows us to see the development of human biology and culture over very long time spans. Most of the knowledge we have about human evolution, prehistoric populations, and modern tribal societies was discovered by anthropologists. Early anthropologists were instrumental in popularizing the concept of culture and in showing that cultural differences are not caused by racial differences. The value of inculcating understanding and tolerance between citizens of different nations is another practical lesson of anthropology, one that is increasingly important as the economies of the world become more interdependent and as the development of weaponry makes the consequences of international misunderstanding more serious. The information that ethnographers have collected about alternative ways of being human allows us to judge the benefits against the costs of industrialization and progress. The comparative perspective of anthropology helps us to see which elements of our societies are amenable to change and what the consequences of these changes might be. Finally, specific anthropologists apply their expertise directly to the solution of medical, economic, social, environmental, and other problems.

Key Terms

physical anthropology
paleoanthropology
primatologists
archaeology
linguistics
cultural anthropology
ethnography

ethnology
holistic perspective
comparative
  perspective
cultural relativism
ethnocentrism

Suggested Readings

■ Fagan, Brian M. *People of the Earth: An Introduction to World Prehistory*. 6th ed. Glenview, Ill.: Scott, Foresman, 1989.
  An overview of what archaeologists have learned about prehistoric humans and about the development of technology, agriculture, and civilization in various parts of the world.

■ Farb, Peter. *Word Play: What Happens When People Talk*. New York: Knopf, 1974.
  A highly readable introduction to language and how it is used in social life.

■ Fromkin, Victoria, and Robert Rodman. *An Introduction to Language*. 4th ed. New York: CBS College Publishing, 1988.
  Witty and thorough introduction to linguistics.

■ Jurmain, Robert, Harry Nelson, and William A. Turnbaugh. *Understanding Physical Anthropology and Archaeology*. 4th ed. St. Paul, Minn.: West, 1990.
  A thorough textbook covering human genetics, racial classification, primate taxonomy and behavior, and human biological and sociocultural evolution.

■ Spradley, James P., and David W. McCurdy. *Conformity and Conflict: Readings in Cultural Anthropology*. 7th ed. Glenview, Ill.: Scott, Foresman, 1990.
  A collection of popular articles on a variety of topics, all related to cultural anthropology.

■ Wenke, Robert J. *Patterns in Prehistory: Mankind's First Three Million Years*. New York: Oxford, 1989.
  Covers the same ground as Fagan's text, but more thoroughly and technically.

■ Whitten, Phillip, and David E. K. Hunter. *Anthropology: Contemporary Perspectives*. Boston: Little Brown, 1987.
  A collection of readings covering all four subfields of anthropology.

The following ethnographies are excellent for introducing the ways of life of various peoples around the world. All are highly readable.

■ Balikci, Asen. *The Netsilik Eskimo*. Garden City, N.Y.: Natural History Press, 1970.
  A well-rounded description of an Eskimo people.

■ Fernea, Elizabeth. *Guests of the Sheik*. Garden City, N.Y.: Anchor, 1969.
  A writer, journalist, and academician's account of her experiences in an Iraqi village with her anthropologist husband.

■ Kluckhohn, Clyde, and Dorothea Leigton. *The Navaho*. Garden City, N.Y.: Anchor, 1962.
  A classic account of the most well studied Native American tribe.

■ Liebow, Elliot. *Tally's Corner*. Boston: Little, Brown, 1967.
  An account of streetcorner blacks in an American city.

■ Malinowski, Bronislaw. *Agronauts of the Western Pacific*. New York: E. P. Dutton, 1922.
  An account of the people of the Trobriand Islands in the southwest Pacific, which practically every cultural anthropologist has read. It was instrumental in establishing the importance of fieldwork as part of the professional training of anthropologists.

■ Service, Elman. *Profiles in Ethnology*. New York: Harper & Row, 1978.
  One of the best resources for one who wishes a short comparative overview of the way of life of diverse peoples. Contains short sketches of the life of twenty-three societies found on all continents.

■ Shostak, Marjorie. *Nisa: The Life and Words of a !Kung Woman*. New York: Vintage, 1983.
  An outstanding biographical account of a San woman.

■ Thomas, Elizabeth Marshall. *The Harmless People*. New York: Vintage, 1959.
  A wonderfully written account of the customs and beliefs of the San (formerly called "Bushmen" of southern Africa.

■ Turnbull, Colin. *The Forest People*. New York: Simon & Schuster, 1962.
  A readable and sympathetic ethnography, although the information presented in this book about the BaMbuti pygmies of the African rain forest has been challenged.

Part One

ESSENTIALS

cholars who work in any field of study consider certain knowledge to be essential in understanding the field and its subject matter. In this first part of the book, we introduce certain essential concepts used by cultural anthropologists (chapter 2). We also discuss the ways in which humankind's biological imperatives do and do not affect the various ways of human life that exist (chapter 3). Finally, we introduce the subject of language (chapter 4), for the knowledge and use of language is an important capability of humans that is part of the uniqueness of our species.

■ (Facing page) *This Buddhist priest from Tibet is officiating at a cremation. Different societies handle death in different ways.*

CONCEPTS

■ *Contents*

■ (Above) *As this religious ceremony illustrates, the culture of a society is passed down to new generations in a variety of subtle ways.*

If you were to ask a hundred cultural anthropologists what their field is all about—what, more than anything else, is its subject matter—most would answer "culture." If you were to find another hundred and ask them what characteristic of humanity most distinguishes us from other animals, probably seventy or eighty would respond "the capacity for culture." In this chapter we define culture in a special way, discuss its main components, and show how it relates to behavior. We also introduce the related concept of sociocultural system.

What Is Culture?

■ *Culture as "The Way of Life"*

In anthropology, the term *culture* generally refers to the way of life of some group of people. So we can speak of Chinese culture, meaning the way the Chinese people live—their religion, marital and family life, values, the organization of their economy and government, and so forth. Often the word *culture* emphasizes the unique or distinctive aspects of a peoples' customs and beliefs.

The definition of culture as the whole way of life of some people was proposed by E. B. Tylor in 1871, when scientific anthropology was in its infancy. He wrote, "Culture . . . is that complex whole which includes knowledge, belief, art, morals, law, customs, and any other capabilities and habits acquired by man as a member of society." This definition is still quoted widely as a useful way of looking at culture. The main thing to notice about it is that it defines culture as including almost everything about a people—their thoughts about the world, their beliefs about how people should live, their actions, and all other "capabilities and habits" that they acquire while growing up in a particular society.

Since Tylor's day, numerous anthropologists have tried to improve on this definition of the key concept in their discipline. Ralph Linton, writing in 1940, defined culture as "the sum total of knowledge, attitudes and habitual behavior patterns shared and transmitted by the members of a particular society." This way of looking at the concept rightly draws attention to two major characteristics of culture: it is shared by

some group, and it is passed down through the generations. Linton's definition is also quite broad. Notice the inclusion of all "knowledge, attitudes and habitual behavior patterns."

Knowledge and attitudes are things people carry in their minds—they are mental phenomena. We cannot observe knowledge, attitudes, and other kinds of mental phenomena directly. We can ask people what they think or how they feel about someone or some event and thus find out about their knowledge and attitudes. But we have no way of knowing by direct observation what is in their minds.

Behavior, in contrast, is directly observable. Of course, behaviors are strongly influenced by the knowledge, attitudes, and other things stored in peoples' minds. Information (including knowledge and attitudes) underlies behavior, which means that we can infer something about how a person thinks and feels by watching what he or she does in certain situations.

In sum, culture often is defined broadly as the whole way of life of a people. It consists both of the shared information stored in people's brains and their behavior. By this definition, culture includes both mental phenomena (ideas, including ways of thinking and feeling) and behavioral phenomena (ways of acting).

■ *The Ideational Conception of Culture*

Recently, influential anthropologists such as Roger Keesing, Ward Goodenough, and Clifford Geertz have proposed a narrower, less inclusive definition of culture. It is useful for some purposes to make a distinction between the shared information (ideas) people carry in their heads and the way they actually behave. We have just seen one reason why this distinction is useful: the information stored in someone's brain cannot be observed directly, but behavior is observable. Another reason is that people everywhere have notions about how they should behave, but their actual behavior does not always reflect their shared ideas. People can agree, in principle, that some things ought to be done in certain ways, and yet large numbers of individuals may not abide by these agreements. Finally, the more broadly we define a concept, the more confusion its use can cause. If culture is defined as the whole way of life of a people, then mental and behavioral phenomena tend to get lumped together and confused, and for some purposes it is useful to distinguish them.

For these and other reasons, in this book we use the term *culture* to refer to mental phenomena rather than to behavior. This way of conceptualizing culture often is called the **ideational definition of culture.** Culture consists not of activities—not of what Linton called "habitual behavior patterns"—but of shared and learned ideas. Of course, shared ideas influence behavior profoundly. But they are not the only influences on how individuals act, for shared ideas generally provide only guidelines for behavior, as we shall see.

If we define culture to include only learned and shared ideas, we need another concept that encompasses other aspects of how a people live. Unfortunately, no such single word now exists. The phrase most commonly used is **sociocultural system.** *Sociocultural* is a composite word, made up of *social* and *cultural*. *Social* refers mainly to patterned interactions between individuals, to the many kinds of groups that are found in diverse societies, and to the variety of relationships between these groups.

The word *system* emphasizes that the various aspects (subsystems) of a way of life are **integrated,** meaning that they mutually affect one another. To say that a way of life is integrated means that each of its elements is tied up with the others, so that many elements fit together to make up a sociocultural whole. For example, the economic, religious, and kinship subsystems all affect one another. The holistic perspective of anthropology is derived from the assumption that sociocultural systems are integrated.

System and *integration* are important concepts for two major reasons. First, sometimes we can make puzzling beliefs and practices intelligible by seeing them as parts of a system, when we cannot understand them in isolation. Second, integration implies that changes introduced in one component of a sociocultural system may have impacts on other components that are unintended, hard to foresee, and often undesirable or harmful to a people and to the persistence of their customs and beliefs.

Ordinarily the group that shares a sociocultural system is called a **society,** or a territorially distinct group whose members speak a common language and share a feeling of common identity relative to other societies. (However, some societies—notably many modern nations—include ethnic or racial minorities who share a sociocultural system that differs in some respects from that of the so-called mainstream.)

Behavior refers to what individuals actually do. In most of their behavior, individuals are influenced by other people with whom they interact socially and with whom they form groups. The behavior of any individual also is influenced by the ideas (culture) he or she shares with other people in the society. Because the behavior of individuals is so greatly affected by culture and by the existing relationships between individuals and groups, most individuals adopt similar behaviors in similar circumstances. We therefore speak of **patterns of behavior,** meaning what most people tend to do when they are in certain situations (e.g., in church, at a wedding or funeral, at a convention). So the phrase *sociocultural system* encompasses the patterns of behavior, the shared ideas, and the prevalent relationships between individuals and groups of a society. In this book, we use *sociocultural system* and *way of life* (or *lifeway*) interchangeably. To avoid tedious repetition, we sometimes use the phrase "customs and beliefs" to mean the same thing. *Culture*, however, always means shared ideas.

A Formal Definition of Culture

The concept of culture is so important that we need a formal definition of what we mean by the term:

> **Culture** is the socially transmitted knowledge shared by some group of people.

This definition is used partly because it is easy to break up into components that can be discussed separately.

■ *Socially Transmitted . . .*

To say that culture is socially transmitted is to say that it is learned in a special way. Two kinds of learning can be distinguished. The first is called **trial-and-error learning.** With this type, found even among many relatively simple animals such as snails, an animal tries out a behavior without any preconceptions as to whether it will work—that is, bring a reward. If it does not work, another behavior is tried, and so on until one trial works, after which it is repeated. By trial-and-error learning any animal, including a human, can acquire behaviors that work. But the trials are costly: they require time and energy that could be spent on behaviors that are rewarding. If there were a way to avoid the erroneous trials, learning would be more efficient.

The second kind of learning does away with the necessity to engage in costly trials that do not work, and is therefore more efficient. It is called **social learning** because an individual learns by imitating or communicating with other individuals, thus benefiting from their experience. Information that some individuals have accumulated about what works in some situation is socially transmitted to other individuals. So if you have learned through trial and error that some food is good to eat, I do not have to learn about it on my own; instead, I can profit from the knowledge you have gained through experience. If you and I are contemporaries, and if previous generations have learned about this food, both of us can benefit from their experience if they teach us their food habits.

Social learning not only spares each individual the costs of trial-and-error learning, but the knowledge that each generation acquires through its experience can be passed on—socially transmitted—to future generations. Social learning provides a mechanism by which the knowledge that underlies and guides behavior (i.e., culture) is transmitted between generations.

The process of cultural transmission from one generation to the next is called **enculturation.** Because of enculturation, the younger people in a society share the culture of the older people. When rapid change occurs, there may be generation gaps, in which members of a younger generation do not share—or have consciously rejected—some of the culture of their elders. Generation gaps can appear large to members of different generations in the same society. The youngsters frequently think they have little in common with their elders, and the elders may wonder how future generations will fare with such low standards of, say, sexual morality. But actually the widest generation gaps in a society are insignificant when compared to the much larger gaps between the sociocultural systems of different peoples. If your parents or grandparents are outraged at the number of opposite-sex people in their early twenties living together, think how both of you would react if large numbers of girls in their early teens married men in their sixties, or if a typical young man's first marriage was to an elderly widow. Yet these are common marriage patterns among the Tiwi people of Australia. In spite of generation gaps, you and your elders are a lot more alike culturally than either of you care to admit! (Besides being socially transmitted "down" through time to new generations, sociocultural elements can also be transmitted "out" spatially to other societies, as discussed in Box 2.1.)

■ . . . Knowledge . . .

Members of the same culture share basic beliefs about reality, take certain "facts" for granted, accept common standards of behavior, and revere similar values.

These and other kinds of ideas acquired during enculturation make up the cultural knowledge of a people.

By cultural *knowledge* we certainly do not mean truth. What matters about cultural knowledge is not its correctness by some objective standard of truth. What is most important is that

■ individuals share enough of it that they are capable of behaving in ways that are acceptable and meaningful to others; that is, individuals do not constantly misunderstand one another's behavior;
■ it leads to behavior that works at least well enough to allow the population to survive and perpetuate itself;
■ it is to some extent consistent; that is, it makes logical sense at least to the degree that actual events in the world can be interpreted in such a way that they do not disconfirm the facts and assumptions of cultural knowledge.

To put this in a few words, cultural knowledge must lead to behavior that is meaningful and adaptive, and the knowledge itself must not be so out of tune with reality that it is constantly falsified. On the last point, it is important to add that an event that would falsify some cultural assumption or belief to an outside observer does not necessarily disprove the belief to one who believes it. To an outsider, the fact that a particular rain dance does not bring immediate rain shows that rain dances do not work. But those who believe in rain dances are more likely to reason that perhaps this one was performed incorrectly; or maybe an enemy is performing more powerful magic to make the drought continue; or, more likely, the dance will bring rain later, as rain dances have in previous years. To take a more familiar example, we quote a minister one of us knows: "God always answers prayer; sometimes the answer is no."

■ . . . Shared by Some Group of People

Culture is an attribute of some kind of human group; it is shared by some kind of collectivity. *Shared* is a deliberately vague term meaning that, although all individuals differ somewhat in the ideas they acquire during enculturation, they largely agree on certain fundamental kinds of knowledge, which we shall describe shortly.

We often call the group that shares a common culture a society, but many societies exhibit internal sociocultural differences within their boundaries. Most modern nations, for instance, include people of many

Box 2.1

ONE HUNDRED PERCENT AMERICAN

Those who think their own society leads the world in technological genius should ponder the following article by Ralph Linton that appeared in 1937. It shows that, like other people, Americans rely on objects first invented long ago and far away.

There can be no question about the average American's Americanism or his desire to preserve this precious heritage at all costs. Nevertheless, some insidious foreign ideas have already wormed their way into his civilization without his realizing what was going on. Thus dawn finds the unsuspecting patriot garbed in pajamas, a garment of East Indian origin; and lying in a bed built on a pattern which originated in either Persia or Asia Minor. He is muffled to the ears in un-American materials: cotton, first domesticated in India; linen, domesticated in the Near East; wool from an animal native to Asia Minor; or silk whose uses were first discovered by the Chinese. All these substances have been transformed into cloth by methods invented in Southwestern Asia. If the weather is cold enough he may even be sleeping under an eiderdown quilt invented in Scandinavia.

On awakening he glances at the clock, a medieval European invention, uses one potent Latin word in abbreviated form, rises in haste, and goes to the bathroom. Here, if he stops to think about it, he must feel himself in the presence of a great American institution; he will have heard stories of both the quality and frequency of foreign plumbing and will know that in no other country does the average man perform his ablutions in the midst of such splendor. But the insidious foreign influence pursues him even here. Glass was invented by the ancient Egyptians, the use of glazed tiles for floors and walls in the Near East, porcelain in China, and the art of enameling on metal by Mediterranean artisans of the Bronze Age. Even his bathtub and toilet are but slightly modified copies of Roman originals. The only purely American contribution to the ensemble is the steam radiator, against which our patriot very briefly and unintentionally places his posterior . . .

Returning to the bedroom, the unconscious victim of un-American practices removes his clothes from a chair, invented in the Near East, and proceeds to dress. He puts on close-fitting tailored garments whose form derives from the skin clothing of the ancient nomads of the Asiatic steppes and fastens them with buttons whose prototypes appeared in Europe at the close of the Stone Age. . . . He gives himself a final appraisal in the mirror, an old Mediterranean invention, and goes downstairs to breakfast.

Here a whole new series of foreign things confronts him. His food and drink are placed before him in pottery vessels, the popular name of which—china—is sufficient evidence of their origin. He will usually begin the meal with coffee, an Abyssinian plant first discovered by the Arabs. . . . If our patriot is old-fashioned enough to adhere to the so-called American breakfast, his coffee will be accompanied by an orange, domesticated in the Mediterranean region, a cantalope domesticated in Persia, or grapes domesticated in Asia Minor. He will follow this with a bowl of cereal made from grain domesticated in the Near East and prepared by methods also invented there. From this he will go on to waffles, a Scandinavian invention, with plenty of butter, originally a Near-Eastern cosmetic. As a side dish he may have the egg of a bird domesticated in Southeastern Asia or strips of the flesh of an animal domesticated in the same region, which have been salted and smoked by a process invented in Northern Europe.

Breakfast over, he places upon his head a molded piece of felt, invented by the nomads of Eastern Asia, and, if it looks like rain, puts on outer shoes of rubber, discovered by the ancient Mexicans, and takes an umbrella, invented in India. He then sprints for his train—the train, not the sprinting, being an English invention. At the station he pauses for a moment to buy a newspaper, paying for it with coins invented in ancient Lydia. Once on board he settles back to inhale the fumes of a cigarette invented in Mexico, or a cigar invented in Brazil. Meanwhile, he reads the news of the day, imprinted in characters invented by the ancient Semites by a process invented in Germany upon a material invented in China. As he scans the latest editorial pointing out the dire results to our institutions of accepting foreign ideas, he will not fail to thank a Hebrew God in an Indo-European language that he is a one hundred per cent (decimal system invented by the Greeks) American (from Americus Vespucci, Italian geographer). ■

Source: Linton (1937).

ethnic backgrounds among their citizenry. These ethnic groups, which usually are defined on the basis of racial type, national origin, or native language, may share some customs and beliefs that differ in some respects from those of the majority population. However, because they usually live and work among the population at large, they also share a great many sociocultural elements with other citizens. To recognize at one and the same time their distinctiveness from the majority and their cultural similarity with other citizens, the term **subculture** is applied to members of such categories. Nations that contain people of many subcultures are paid to be **pluralistic** or are said to exhibit *subcultural variation.*

In the modern United States, several subcultures can be identified, including Hispanics, Blacks, Jews, WASPs, and Native Americans. The term *subculture* sometimes is used to refer to less noticeable differences in values and lifestyle among the majority population. The southern, northern, midwestern, and southwestern subcultures of white Americans differ in some respects (regional subculture). So do the subcultures of Protestants versus Catholics, working-class people versus professionals, preppies versus students in public schools, and yuppies versus farmers. Some anthropologists consider religious communities such as the Amish, the Hutterites, the Moonies, and the Hari Krishnas to be subcultures. Others consider them sufficiently different from the American mainstream to warrant being called separate cultures. Obviously, the term *subculture* can be used in many ways, and whether one wishes to apply the term to some particular category of people depends very much on one's interests at the moment.

Defining culture as the shared knowledge that results from social learning is certainly a more narrow conception of culture than defining it as a whole way of life. When we say a culture is shared by a group, we obviously mean that the members of the group agree on certain fundamental kinds of knowledge. What specifically do we mean by cultural knowledge?

Components of Cultural Knowledge

Even by the relatively narrow ideational definition, culture includes a lot, for the term refers to all the information people acquire while growing up in a particular society. This includes language; learning to make and use tools and other material objects; attitudes about family, friends, and enemies; general ideas about right and wrong (morality) and about proper and improper behavior (decorum); notions of dress, hygiene, and personal ornamentation; conceptions about males and females and their proper roles in society; beliefs about the supernatural; and ideas about sexual activity. The list could be expanded indefinitely.

Here we only wish to identify and explicate five broad components of cultural knowledge: norms, values, collective understandings, classifications of reality, and world views. These are not necessarily more important than others, but they do require some discussion because they are not entirely commonsensical.

■ Norms

A **norm** is a shared ideal (or rule) about how people ought to act in certain situations, or about how particular individuals should act toward particular other individuals. The emphasis here is on the words *ideal, rule, ought,* and *should.* To say that norms exist, it is not necessary for everyone to follow them all the time; indeed, some norms are violated with great regularity. *Norm* implies, rather, that (1) there is widespread agreement that people ought to adhere to certain standards of behavior, (2) other people judge the behavior of an individual according to how closely it adheres to those standards, and (3) individuals who repeatedly fail to follow the standards face some kind of negative reaction from other members of the group. We are able to make collective judgments about someone's personal morality because we share common norms. The ethical codes of some professions, such as medicine or law, are essentially norms that have been debated upon by some authority and then formalized. A law is a special kind of norm, one that is formulated and enforced by a governmental authority.

It sometimes seems to people that norms are irrational rules that stifle their creativity or keep them from doing what they want for no good reason. Individuals may feel that some norms about proper conduct are confining, such as norms about how to dress correctly for special occasions, or about when and to whom we must give gifts, or about fulfilling familial obligations, or about when to have sex. But in fact norms are quite useful to us as individuals. It is mainly because we acquire norms during enculturation that we know how to behave toward others and that we have expectations about how others should act

■ *Most modern nations are pluralistic. Shown here are a few of the subcultures represented in only one American city—Cleveland, Ohio. Clockwise from upper left: Americans of German ancestry dance at German American Day; a folk drama is performed annually in the Hungarian community; at the St. Vladimir Ukranian Orthodox Church, dances are held on Easter Monday; Hispanics sing at the Feast Day of St. John the Baptist; the Obun festival is held at the Japanese Buddhist Temple; Palm Sunday is celebrated by children of Slovenian extraction at St. Vitus Church.*

toward us. For example, when you enter a roomful of strangers at a party, you are somewhat uncertain about how to act. But everyone knows how to go about getting acquainted in your cultural tradition, so you soon are introducing yourself and shaking hands and asking the other guests how they make their living or what they are studying or—under some circumstances—finding out whether they are married, single, available, or willing. Here, and in many other cases in everyday life, norms are not felt to be constraining but serve as useful instructions on how to do something in such a way that others will know what you are doing and accept your actions as "normal".

■ Values

Values consist of shared ideas about the kinds of goals or lifestyles that are desirable or worthwhile for individuals, groups, or society as a whole. Values have a profound, although partly unconscious, effect on individuals. The aims we pursue, as well as our more general ideas about "the good life," are influenced by the values of the society into which we happen to have been born. Values also are critical to society as a whole, for they represent the qualities that a people believe are essential to maintaining their way of life. It is useful to think of values as the ultimate standards that a people believe must be upheld under practically all circumstances. An excellent example of values as ultimate standards is the American emphasis on certain rights of individuals as embodied in the Bill of Rights in the Constitution. No matter how much Americans hate what the press prints, what the right or left wing says, or what the Hari Krishnas preach, few of them believe that the offending newspaper should be outlawed or that the fanatic organization should be suppressed, so long as they do not engage in or advocate violence. Freedom of the press, of speech, and of religion are ultimate standards that take precedence over the opinions and interests of the moment.

■ Collective Understandings

Members of a single culture know how to interpret one another's behavior. Our understanding of what some behavior means allows us to interact with one another without the constant necessity to explain what we are doing. Such collective understandings seem to be among the most unconscious of all components of culture. It is possible to talk about and explain to a foreigner the norms and values of one's own cultural tradition and to give reasons (which of course the stranger might find strange) for why we think people ought to act in certain ways or why we think certain standards are important to uphold. We cannot, however, explain why a wink or a tone of voice or certain gestures or words mean what they do; we "just know" what meaning they convey but cannot say why they mean this rather than something else, or even how we know their meanings.

The feeling that we "just know" what some things mean—that they are "common knowledge"—is attributable to an enormously important characteristic of much cultural knowledge. Some things and behaviors carry meanings that have no obvious and necessary relationship to their physical properties; that is, the meanings of some things and behaviors are arbitrary. *Arbitrary,* in this context, means that there are no inherent qualities in the object or action itself that lead some human population to attribute one meaning to it, rather than some other meaning. The meaning exists only because of shared conventions and collective understandings.

Objects and actions whose meaning is arbitrary and conventional are called **symbols.** The twitch of an eyelid muscle that causes a momentary closing of the eye, which we call a wink, carries a flirtatious significance in some cultural traditions and is meaningless in still other traditions. The shared meaning of an upraised middle finger can result in a brawl in a few societies, but the same movement in other parts of the world elicits no reaction. To the Ndembu people of Zambia, the white secretions of a certain sacred tree carry connotations of womanhood, fertility, nourishment, and sexual maturity, although to most other people in the world it is merely tree sap. To the Christian the cross arouses deep emotions of reverence, but to many other people it stands for oppression and imperialism. All these objects and actions are examples of symbols.

· There is another important characteristic of symbolic behaviors and objects. The meaning of an action depends on the actions that preceded and followed it and on the total situation in which the action occurred. Similarly, the meaning of an object depends on the objects with which it is associated and on the surrounding circumstances. Simply stated, meaning varies with *context.* A wink is only sometimes flirtatious; in other situations, it means "just kidding," or "right on!", or something else. The cross at the altar means one thing; the cross on the grave, another. An upraised middle finger in the right place and situation is a joke rather than an affront. (And, as Sigmund Freud is reputed to have remarked: "sometimes a cigar is just a cigar.")

The meaning carried by symbolic objects and actions, then, is arbitrary and contextual. In these respects, symbols in general are like words, which of course are one particular kind of symbol. In English, the word for a certain kind of large mammal is *horse*, but in Spanish it is *caballo*, in German it is *pferd*, in Arabic it is *hisanun*, in French it is *cheval*, and so on for other languages. There is nothing about the animal itself that makes some combination of sounds better than others to stand for it; the relation between sounds and the meanings they convey is arbitrary. But *horse* does not always mean that animal, even in English; sometimes it means a hard worker or a large person— its meaning depends on context. We can instantly figure out the meaning the speaker intends by the words that surround *horse* (how it is used in the sentence) and by the total situation in which the sentence is spoken. Because the meanings people associate with symbolic acts and objects share the characteristics of arbitrariness and dependence on context with sounds, words, phrases, and sentences, language provides enormously helpful clues to the analysis of symbols. We discuss the analogies between language and culture in chapter 4.

■ Classifications of Reality

The carriers of a single cultural tradition share ideas of what kinds of things and persons exist. They have similar "cognitive categories," meaning that the human and natural environment are divided up according to common principles.

For example, people everywhere recognize a category of persons that are related to them biologically— their kinfolk, as we call them. But the principles by which certain kinds of relatives are placed into cultural categories vary between different kinds of kinship systems. Thus, we think of the sisters of both our mother and father as a single kind of relative, and we call them by the same kinship term, *aunt*. But there are some cultural traditions in which the sister of one's mother is considered to be one kind of relative, and the sister of one's father quite a different kind, and each is called by a separate kinship term. As we shall see in chapter 11, these various ways of classifying kin into

different categories or kinds of relatives is related fairly consistently to other characteristics of a people's kinship system. The general point for now is that people of different cultural traditions have different ideas about social life, and the way they conceive of their societies as divided up into kinds of people varies.

The same applies to the way a people classify their natural environment. Culture not only provides the categories by which we classify kinds of people but also categories by which plants, animals, phases of the moon, seasonal changes, and other natural phenomena are classified into kinds. Of course, the way people classify the things in their natural environment both affects and is affected by how they relate to it.

For example, on the island of Mindoro in the Philippines live a people known as the Hanunóo. These people grow most of their food by a method called *shifting cultivation*. This method, described further in chapter 8, involves farming a plot for a year or two, abandoning it for a number of years until some of the natural vegetation has regrown and it has recovered its potential to yield a crop, and then replanting it. It therefore is useful for the Hanunóo to be able to tell when a plot they abandoned some years previously has recovered enough to make it worthwhile to replant it. They judge this by the quantity and kind of natural vegetation that has recolonized the plot. The need to assess the degree of readiness of a plot for recultivation has led the Hanunóo to develop an extremely complex classification of the plants found in their habitat. They are able to identify over 1,600 different "kinds" of plants, which exceeds by over 400 the number of species that a scientific botanist would distinguish.

Which classification is right, that of the Hanunóo or that of the botanist? Both (or is it neither?). The point is not that the Hanunóo are right and the botanist wrong, or vice versa. Rather, the botanist uses one set of criteria to decide whether two individual plants belong to the same kind, and these criteria have been adopted because they have proved useful to science. The Hanunóo use a different set of criteria that, over the course of many generations, they have developed for their specific needs. The criteria by which various realms of nature are carved up and assigned to categories are important components of cultural knowledge, for they influence the way a people perceive the natural world.

They also influence how a people use the resources that occur in their environments. Plants and animals are classified not just into various kinds but also into

■ *Different kinds of plants and animals are regarded as edible and inedible by various peoples. These Yanomamö of the Amazon Basin are preparing a tapir.*

various categories of usefulness. Members of different cultural traditions perceive nature in different ways, and what one people consider to be a resource is not necessarily a resource for another people. For example, Muslims and Orthodox Jews consider pork to be unclean and traditional Hindus refuse to consume the flesh of cattle, their sacred animal. The fact that a given animal or plant is edible does not mean that people will *consider* it edible (had any boiled dog or roasted beetle larvae lately?). The same principle applies to other resources besides food. For example, the gold and silver metals that led Europeans to conquer the Americas were not valued to the same extent by most North American Indians.

Taking this one step further, cultures have different ideas about the kinds of things that do and do not exist. For instance, many cultures think that some individuals (called *witches* and *sorcerers*) use malevolent spiritual powers to harm their enemies. Traditional Navajo believe that witches can and do change themselves into wolves, bears, and other animals. The Tukano of the Bolivian rain forest think that a spirit of the forest controls the game animals they depend on for meat. So a Tukano group's shaman periodically makes a supernatural visit to the abode of the forest spirit. He promises to magically kill a certain number of humans, and to send their souls to the forest spirit in return for the spirit's releasing the animals so the hunters can find game. As a final example, in cultures that practice ancestor worship, the family group that gathers for the rituals genuinely believes that the ghosts of their deceased relatives partake of the food and other offerings made to them. In sum, not only do different cultures classify objective reality in different ways but they differ on what reality *is;* one culture's reality may be another's superstitions.

■ World Views

The **world view** of a people is the way they perceive and interpret reality and events, including their images of themselves and how they relate to the world around them. World views are affected by how people classify the social and natural world, which we have just discussed. But world views include more than just the way people and nature are carved up by a culture. People have opinions about the nature of the cosmos and how they fit into it. All systems of cultural knowledge distinguish physical bodies from spiritual souls and have beliefs about what happens to the latter after the former dies. People have ideas about the meaning of human existence: how we were put on earth, who put us here, and why. They have a notion of what evil is, where it comes from, why it sometimes happens to good people, and how it can be combated. They have beliefs about what supernatural powers or beings are like, what they can do for (or to!) people, and how people can worship or control them. Everywhere we find myths and legends about the origins of living things, objects, and customs.

These examples of various aspects of world view all come from religion. But it is important not to confuse world view and religion, and especially not to think that religion and world view are synonymous. Although religious beliefs do influence the world view of a people, cultural traditions vary in aspects of world view that we do not ordinarily think of as religious.

For instance, the way a people view their place in nature is part of their world view: do they see themselves as the masters and conquerors of nature, or as living in harmony with natural forces? The way people view themselves and other people is part of their world view. Do they see themselves, as many human groups do, as the only true human beings, and all others as essentially animals? Or do they see their way of life as one among many equally human, but different, ways of life? Most modern scientists share a similar world view: they believe all things and events in the universe have natural, discoverable causes that we can know through logic supported by certain procedures of observation and experimentation.

A people's conception of time and space is also part of their world view. Westerners are so used to thinking of time in arbitrary units—for our seconds, minutes, and hours are not natural segments of time—that we forget that other people do not share our ideas of how important these units are. North Americans frown on "wasting time" and on "living in the past," for our "period" in this world is "limited," so it is important to "make the most of our time here" by—among other things—eating "fast foods." This view of time as a resource that, like money, can be spent wisely or foolishly is not present in many other cultural traditions. Similar considerations apply to space. In a North American house, unused space—that is, areas in which little activity occurs or that are not filled up to the culturally appropriate degree with our possessions—is "wasted" space.

To a large extent, such views of time and space are understandable given other dimensions of the American way of life. They are connected to various American values, such as progress and the work ethic. They also are connected to certain economic conditions not found in many other places in the world. We must pay, and pay dearly, for the space of earth enclosed by the walls of our dwellings; in general, the larger the space, the more we pay; so unused space truly is wasted space, for we have paid for something we are not using. If, on the other hand, spaces of earth are freely available to all who wish to use them, the notion of wasting space is less likely to be strong. The same applies to time. We can waste it because it is possible for us to use every bit of it in some way. Time not spent sleeping, eating, and maintaining our bodies can be spent earning money or enjoying the things that money allows us to possess or participating in social activities that we barely can "find the time for." If, on the other hand, we were to stop working whenever we satisfy our bodily needs, as was once common among humanity, we would find ourselves with "time on our hands," and the view of time as a resource that can be wasted and used wisely or foolishly would be less developed.

In summary, cultural knowledge includes shared, socially transmitted norms, values, meanings, categories for classifying reality, and world views. You can see why this definition of culture is often called the ideational view, and why from this perspective culture is a mental phenomenon, and not a behavioral or physical thing. You also can see why not everything an individual knows should be considered "cultural." Technically, knowledge that you acquire on your own and do not pass along to other people is not cultural, because it is neither shared nor socially transmitted. If you have learned on your own to be a beetle-larvae eater but have kept the knowledge to yourself, then it does not become part of the cultural tradition of your group. On the other hand, you certainly by now can appreciate that much of what you consider to be common knowledge, or just plain common sense, is in fact socially learned and hence is cultural knowledge.

Culture and Behavior

Earlier, we noted the usefulness of distinguishing culture (as an unobservable mental phenomenon) from behavior (as an observable physical phenomenon). By defining culture as a mental phenomenon that consists of shared norms, values, understandings, views of reality, and the like, we exclude behavior as part of culture. We see culture rather as the system of shared knowledge that *underlies* behavior. How then shall we conceptualize the relationship between culture and behavior?

We might conceive of culture as rules that serve as instructions for behavior, telling individuals how to act in specific situations and how to relate to other people. We might imagine, for example, that culture instructs its "carriers" how to plan and carry out a wedding, how to wrest a living from the environment, how to settle a quarrel, and how to act toward their mothers-in-law. There is a fairly tight relationship between the unconscious rules and how real people act, according to this approach. Those individuals who do not act according to the rules are classified as deviants, but all cultures have procedures for handling deviant behavior. By some means those who deviate are brought back into conformity with the rules or eliminated or ostracized.

This way of conceptualizing the relationship between culture and behavior is the way most people think of the problem. To state this view somewhat baldly: Culture tells us what to do, and we generally do it; if we deviate, we are punished.

There is a growing trend among anthropologists against this approach. For one thing, cultural knowledge consists of more than just rules or instructions for behavior. It consists also of values, which provide only rough (sometimes conflicting) guidelines for behavior. It includes shared categories and views of reality that certainly influence behavior, but only indirectly (by affecting how we perceive the world) rather than directly (as rules). Finally, culture includes attitudes, shared understandings, and other kinds of knowledge that affect how we act, but not in the same way as rules. The effects of these other components of culture on behavior are too subtle and complex to call them "instructions."

For another thing, a large number of anthropologists now believe that culture provides a great deal of leeway for individuals to choose between alternative courses of action. Even most of the rules that people are said to "obey" do not specify how they should act in great detail, but provide only general guidelines. In their everyday lives, most people do not blindly follow the dictates of culture; they plan, calculate, weigh alternatives, and make decisions on what they think is best for them or for those they care about. They consider (or often consider, at any rate) the possible consequences of alternative courses of action in their minds before actually acting. Indeed, this ability—which we call thinking ahead—is one capacity that humans seem to have developed to a higher degree than other animals. Undoubtedly it is one of the secrets of our evolutionary success. In deciding how best to approach the relation between culture and behavior, we must take into account humanity's ability to plan and choose.

How shall we build planning and choosing into the relation between culture and behavior? One way is to begin with the realization that formulating plans and making choices are mental processes, and therefore they rely on and work within the framework of knowledge that individuals acquire culturally. To make a decision about how to behave involves at least the following procedures: choosing one's goals (or ends); determining the resources (or means) available to attain these ends; considering which specific actions are likely to be most effective; calculating the relative costs (in resources) and benefits (in rewards) of these alternative behaviors; and, finally, choosing between these behaviors. We can call these mental procedures **strategizing,** and the overall plan of behavior an individual has decided upon may be called a **strategy.** As a result of choosing between alternative strategies, individuals adopt particular behaviors (or series of behaviors) that they believe will help them effectively attain their ends.

What affects the strategies individuals choose and, thus, the behaviors they perform? All the factors and forces that affect the choices made and the strategies adopted are called **constraints.** Constraints include the information available to the chooser, subjective perceptions of costs and benefits, anticipated actions and reactions of other people, the individual's access to resources, and so forth. Constraints narrow the range of possible strategies that individuals can adopt, so that some behaviors are more likely to occur than others in a population. By channeling the behavior of many individuals into certain paths, constraints lead many individuals to do the same kinds of things in similar situations. Constraints therefore are partly responsible for the patterning of behavior in a sociocultural system.

Some, but not all, constraints arise from the system of shared knowledge that we call culture. Norms and values, for instance, constrain choices by forcing individuals to take into account how others will react to their behavior, and to consider whether some possible behavior will violate deeply held values or whether the chooser himself will feel guilty for trespassing on the legitimate rights of others. Choices also are constrained by cultural categories of persons and things, world views, and the chooser's anticipations of how others will interpret the meanings of his or her actions. We can see, at least roughly, how important culture is for the decision making of individuals: it affects goals, perceptions of resources, availability of means, relative weighting of costs and benefits, and so on. So important is the effect of culture on decisions that one influential anthropologist has defined cultural knowledge as "standards for deciding what is, . . . what can be, . . . how one feels about it, . . . what to do about it, and . . . how to go about doing it" (Goodenough 1961, 552). We therefore can say—and this is a useful way of conceptualizing the relation between culture and behavior—that one way culture affects behavior is by providing some of the most powerful constraints on choice making.

There are two other ways to state this perspective. The first is to say that behavior is patterned and that culture consists of mental patterns *for* behavior, rather than of actual patterns *of* behavior. Culture is sometimes said to be a code for behavior: we know how to encode our intentions into the behavior we perform, and we know how to decode the intentions of others from their behavior. An analogy with language will help in understanding this perspective. Like other cultural elements, knowledge of language profoundly affects behavior—how we send messages to one another, in this case. But when you actually use language (i.e., when you speak) language itself does not tell you what to say. Rather, it provides you with a way of putting your message into a form that others can understand—a means of encoding the message. Likewise, it provides your listeners with knowledge that allows them to know what you mean—a means of decoding the message.

The second way of stating this perspective emphasizes the normative components of culture: culture supplies the boundaries of behavior by determining which behaviors are proper or acceptable or understandable to others. People generally do not step outside these cultural boundaries because they fear negative reactions from others, or because doing so would involve actions that others might misinterpret. In this respect, culture is like the rules of chess and other games of strategy. The rules determine the moves that are and are not permissible (the "boundaries"), without actually determining which specific moves ("behaviors") players must make.

Why is it so important to distinguish between culture and behavior? One reason is that culture does not always predict behavior very well. We cannot necessarily say what someone will do in a given situation even though we know what other people expect the individual to do, and even though cultural requirements (norms) are fairly clear. Thus, many industrialized societies have an explicit norm that the only thing an employer should take into account in deciding whom to hire for some job is the relative qualifications of applicants. There is little doubt that this norm is frequently violated; it may even be violated more often than it is followed. Even norms that are powerful (in the sense that violations are considered serious breaches of morality and usually are punished in some way if detected) are not honored. For example, the norm against adultery is widely accepted and powerful; yet, in the United States in

the 1970s, almost half the married population committed adultery.

The same thing applies to the relation between values and behavior. It is agreed widely that equality of opportunity for all is one of the most cherished values of North Americans; society should be set up so that all individuals can do as well for themselves as their abilities and energies allow. Yet there is no doubt that some people have a head start in life's competition, and others must possess truly unusual talent or ambition to "make it" because of their ethnicity or impoverished background. Such distinctions between the ideal and the actual—between the "oughts" and the "ares" of a society—make it essential not to confuse culture with behavior.

At any rate, norms and values are not always consistent and so may not provide clear guidelines for behavior. (You should not lie, but sometimes a small lie is necessary to preserve a relation or avoid hurt feelings, or is so useful to you personally that you violate this—rather weak—norm.) In situations in which pursuing one worthwhile goal or upholding one value conflicts with pursuing another goal or value, individuals must choose between them. (Most North Americans simultaneously believe in the work ethic, in materialism, and in what recent political leaders call "family values." But jobs and career pursuits necessarily detract from the time we devote to our spouses, children, and parents, so we must decide how to allocate our time between activities that are all culturally defined as worthwhile.) Violations of rules and standards for behavior often are rationalized by believing that the person harmed by one's actions deserved it because of their own past violations. (You might justify stealing from your employer because you are underpaid.) Finally, individuals receive contradictory messages about acceptable behavior. Sometimes the official norms that are supposed to serve as models for behavior are contradicted by messages and models people receive from their friends' actions or from the popular media. (Adultery is wrong, but we gain the impression from television and movies that it is common and almost to be expected.)

There is a final reason for distinguishing between culture and behavior. Cultural systems change, and sometimes this change is partly caused by the contradiction between existing rules and standards and what many people actually are doing. There was a time in Medieval Europe when usury—the earning of interest from loans—was considered to violate the teachings in the Bible, and was prohibited by the Catholic church. To make money off of money without being excommunicated, Catholics lent such large sums that the borrower could not possibly repay when the loans came due. They then charged damages for failure to pay. Technically, the norms of Catholic interpretations of the scriptures were not violated, and of course money could always be borrowed from Jews, for their Torah contained no such restrictions. Later, with the Protestant Reformation and the beginnings of capitalism, the norms against usury became so burdensome even to Catholics that they disappeared. Here we see that strategies developed to get around an inconvenient norm without punishment, and as economic conditions changed, the norm itself eventually disappeared. This example shows how a change in behavior caused by a change in conditions can result in a change in norms, and hence why it is necessary to distinguish between the two.

On Sociocultural Systems

Thus far we have presented a narrow, ideational definition of culture, identified its major components, and shown how shared and socially learned ideas affect the behavior of individuals. We need also to be a little more explicit about the meaning of the phrase "sociocultural system."

As we use it, *sociocultural system* is a broad term referring to the way of life characteristic of some particular society. The phrase is meant to emphasize the interrelatedness of the shared ideas and patterns of behavior found among a people. It also emphasizes the "social" and "organizational" dimensions of life in a particular society: the kinds of relationships that prevail between individuals who hold different roles, the kinds of groups that organize various activities, how people become members of these groups, how groups control their members, and the like. *Patterns of behavior* refers mainly to the regularity and predictability of peoples' relations with one another in a particular society: for instance, how family members and other relatives typically relate to each other, how political leaders deal with subordinants, and how females and males usually interact.

The main practical difficulty with studying any sociocultural system is that we must divide it up in some way to observe, discuss, and analyze it. Here most an-

thropologists simply use their common sense. We speak of a people's "economic system," "family life," "political system," "religion," and so on. Essentially, we define *subsystems* based on the main purposes and functions of various organized activities. (We sometimes use *institution* to mean the same thing.) Thus "economy" refers to the patterned ways a people produce, distribute, and consume goods; "family life" includes things like relations between wives and husbands, how children are brought up, and the kinds of relatives who live and cooperate together in a single household; "political system" implies how a society maintains orderly relationships among its members and how it deals with its external friends and enemies; "religion" includes the nature of conceptions about the supernatural and rituals that people use to deal with spiritual powers; and so forth for other organized activities. Each subsystem or kind of institution is underlaid by a set of beliefs, norms, values, attitudes, and other cultural knowledge that profoundly affects it.

In part 3 of this book, we introduce the diversity found among humankind in these various dimensions of sociocultural life. Although it is practically necessary to divide a people's way of life into these components, we need to keep in mind that each component is related to the others (i.e., that the entire system is integrated).

As a final review of the two essential concepts used in this book:

- *culture* refers to the shared, socially learned ideas that underlie and profoundly constrain behavior;
- *sociocultural system* refers to the whole way of life of a people, especially to social relations between individuals who have various roles, the kinds of groups that exist, the organization of diverse activities that serve different purposes and functions, and the common ideas (culture) that underly these relations, groupings, and organizations. Because individuals are involved in relationships, are members of groups, participate in organized activities, and share common ideas, their behavior tends to be patterned.

Summary

Culture is one of the key concepts used by anthropologists. Although the term popularly means the whole way of life of some human society, in this book we define it more narrowly as shared and socially learned ideas. This view, often called the *ideational definition of culture*, sees culture as a mental phenomenon, not as objects and not as behavior. Culture is the shared knowledge that underlies and guides behavior. We define sociocultural system as the whole way of life of a people, including especially their behavioral patterns, their culture, and prevalant relationships between individuals and groups.

Culture is socially learned, meaning that it can be transmitted from one group or individual to another. Enculturation is the transmission of culture to new generations. Cultural knowledge is not true in any objective sense, but it must at least allow a society to persist in its environment and must be enough in tune with reality that actual events are not perceived as constantly falsifying it.

There are many components of cultural knowledge, some of which are norms, values, collective understandings (including the common understanding of the meanings of symbols), classifications of reality, and world views. Because these and other components of cultural knowledge are products of social learning—not inborn—we must learn them during enculturation, no matter how natural or commonsensical they seem.

As we use the word, *culture* does not include behavior. It is not really rules for behavior, for the relation between behavior and values, common understandings, classifications of reality, and world views is too complex to be captured by the term *rule*. Rather, culture is an enormously important constraint on behavior, for it affects how people plan to achieve their goals and how they choose between alternative strategies.

The concept of sociocultural system refers to the way of life of a people, and thus is encompassing. It is meant to emphasize social phenomena like relations between role-playing individuals, the kinds of groups that exist and how they are formed, the organization of common activities that have different purposes and serve different functions, and the patterns of behavior that are prevalent in a society.

Key Terms

ideational definition of culture	subculture
sociocultural system	pluralistic
integrated	norm
society	values
patterns of behavior	symbols
culture	world view
trial-and-error learning	strategizing
social learning	strategy
enculturation	constraints

Suggested Readings

■ Barclay, Harold B. *Culture: The Human Way.* Calgary: Western Publishers, 1986.
   A brief book about culture, its characteristics, its components, and the forces that change it.

■ Barrett, Richard A. *Culture and Conduct.* Belmont, Calif.: Wadsworth, 1984.
   In addition to serving as a short text, this book summarizes many issues in contemporary anthropology.

■ Gamst, Frederick, and Edward Norbeck. *Ideas of Culture: Sources and uses.* New York: Holt, Rinehart and Winston, 1976.
   A collection of articles arranged according to approaches taken by their authors.

■ Geertz, Clifford. *The Interpretation of Cultures.* New York: Basic, 1973.
   Collected articles by a leading American anthropologist who favors the ideational definition of culture. Two articles are especially well known: "Thick Description: Towards an Interpretive Theory of Culture" and "The Impact of the Concept of Culture on the Concept of Man."

■ Goodenough, Ward H. *Culture, Language, and Society.* Menlo Park, Calif.: Cummings, 1981.
   Views culture as a mental phenomenon that guides behavior. Includes a useful discussion of the relationship between individual and culture.

THE ROLE OF BIOLOGY

■ *(Above) Most cultural anthropologists believe that physical differences between human populations have little relevance for explaining sociocultural variations. These young Polynesians would be dancing differently if they had been born in the United States.*

The ways the members of a society satisfy their biological imperatives—their bodily needs for food, water, shelter, and the like—are largely determined by their sociocultural system. Thus, our hunger dictates that we eat but not whether we satisfy our appetites with rice, potatoes, cassava, or roasted beetle larvae. Similarly, our sexual urges have a biological basis, but what "turns us on"; who are and are not legitimate sexual partners; and when, where, and how we satisfy our desires all depend largely on which sociocultural system we happen to have been brought up in. How can we understand the relationship between human biological needs and drives and sociocultural systems?

———

Two issues need to be discussed, if not entirely resolved. The first issue has to do with whether the diversity of human ways of life can be explained partly by biological (that is, genetic) differences between human populations. Are there any biological differences between human populations that are consistently associated with the sociocultural differences between them? The second issue has to do with the degree to which humanity's common biological heritage influences the ways of life that exist. Are there any inherited biological drives or instincts, common to all of humanity, that are expressed in all sociocultural systems everywhere?

These two questions are quite distinct. It is essential not to confuse them. The first asks if sociocultural *differences* are correlated with, or partly caused by, biological *differences* between human populations. The second asks how the *common* biology of all of humanity affects human ways of life *in general*. Cultural anthropologists generally agree on the answer to the first question; they do not agree on the answer to the second.

Sociocultural Systems and Genetic Differences

The answer to the first question—are sociocultural differences caused by biological differences?—appears to be a qualified no. It did not, however, always appear

to be no. Before the twentieth century, many scholars assumed that differences in thought and behavior between humans are caused by inborn biological differences. Within a single society, some individuals are innately more intelligent or hard-working than others, for example. Because of their greater abilities, biologically superior persons inevitably tend to rise to the top of the social ladder. So class differences (especially differences in wealth and "breeding") were thought to be caused by differences in inborn aptitudes, diligence, and so forth.

What was true for the various individuals and groups in a single society surely also applied to the individuals in different societies. If particular individuals and classes within Britain, France, or Germany were innately superior to other citizens of these countries, and if their natural superiority led them to win the struggle for existence in these countries, the same must be true for the struggle for existence between different groups of people—between nations or ethnic groups, for instance. Taken one step further, why did people who looked dramatically different physically (i.e., members of different races) also often differ in their thoughts and actions? To many, the answer seemed obvious: Race, it was said, accounts for differences in customs, ways of thinking, and, especially, intelligence.

What a convenient idea! It relieved the members of the upper crust—who of course were largely responsible for the dissemination of this notion—of their social responsibility toward the poor in their own countries. If the masses are poor because they are dumb or lazy, or both, then what is to be done about it? Nothing can be done about it in the long term. For if their working conditions and wages are improved, or if the unemployed are provided for, then—like rats—they will only reproduce more unfortunates just like themselves, and the problems will be perpetuated indefinitely. Notice how this idea justifies the position of the well-to-do in society: unusual intelligence, diligence, or God-given talents allowed them to acquire their status. As in milk, so in society: the cream rises to the top!

These notions are known as **social Darwinism** (after Charles Darwin, whose theories social Darwinists mistakenly believed supported this political ideology.) As a theory about why groups of people differ in their thoughts and behaviors, it is a seductive idea. Not only is it easy to understand, but it is reassuring to you if your family is near the top of the social or economic ladder. It provides a handy rationalization for certain actions, such as slavery, towards members of so-called lower races. It can be used to justify colonialism as well: if you couple social Darwinism with *ethnocentrism* (the belief in the superiority of one's own way of life), you can legitimately go to the uttermost parts of the earth in search of natural resources, or cheap labor, or lost souls, or for the noble cause of bringing the "natives" up to whatever level of civilization they are mentally capable of attaining.

Social Darwinist thought is largely rejected today. Even *if* biological differences between individuals and races do have some effects on their relative degree of success in societies, other variables, such as decades of oppression and frustration and lack of opportunity, seem to be far more important.

However, it remains possible that significant differences in thoughts and actions—in sociocultural systems—between groups and races are caused *in part* by genetically inherited differences between them. We call this idea **biological determinism**, the notion that certain groups or races have an inborn predisposition to adopt some ideas or behaviors and to reject others. This means that some groups of people are more likely to believe certain things and act in certain ways than others, because of their genes.

As a theory of why human populations differ in their sociocultural systems, biological determinism almost certainly is wrong. One of the most notable achievements of early anthropologists, such as E. B. Tylor and Franz Boas, is that they helped to uncover some of the ethnographic evidence that shows why this notion is wrong. This evidence is worth presenting briefly.

We begin by noting that the most significant physical differences between groups of people are differences that we usually call racial. (Gender is equally or perhaps more significant, but because we discuss the degree to which differences between the sexes might be biologically determined in a later chapter, we shall ignore gender for now.) If biological heredity accounts to any significant degree for the kind of sociocultural system a society or ethnic group "carries," then we would expect to find some kind of correlation between race and sociocultural systems. Do we? Three major findings of ethnography, archaeology, and history show that we do not.

First, members of any race are equally capable of learning any cultural tradition. North America, for example, contains people whose ancestors came from various parts of the world and who differ genetically in observable ways. Suppose you are a black American. The Asian Americans you know resemble yourself in how they speak, think, and act more than they do the Asians who still live in Asia. And you yourself are

culturally less like the black people of Africa, your biological homeland, than you are like white Americans. African, Indian, and Vietnamese children adopted by American or European parents have no trouble learning and living in the Western sociocultural system—providing they do not face prejudice and discrimination because of their appearance or national origins. So members of various races can be and often are as alike in their thoughts and actions as people of the same race. So far as is known, one's race has no bearing on the ease or difficulty of acquiring any given cultural tradition. The evidence that any normal human can acquire any known cultural tradition is fairly conclusive. (The existence of subcultural diversity in North America based on race and ethnicity does not alter this evidence, incidentally. Although some blacks, Native Americans (Indians), and Asians do differ from mainstream white Americans in how they speak and act, others are culturally assimilated.)

Second, a full range of sociocultural variety occurs today or has occurred in the past among the members

◼ *Individuals of different races are able to socially learn any cultural tradition. These black children could grow into adults sharing the same ideas, attitudes, and behaviors of their white countrymen (at least they could if they did not live in Soweto, South Africa).*

of a single race. In future chapters we discuss the diversity of sociocultural systems—different ways of organizing economic activities, family life, political decision making, and the like. To take just one example, we shall see that political systems can be classified into types, called *bands, tribes, chiefdoms,* and *states.* Each type occurs, today or in the past, on every continent and among every race.

Third, different political (and economic, religious, and other) systems succeed one another in time within the same race and, indeed, within the same biological population. This sociocultural change occurs far too rapidly to be explained by genetic changes.

In short, we find—and these are simply empirical facts—that identical sociocultural systems can be and are learned by members of any racial category. Conversely, we find that a variety of sociocultural systems exists among members of the same racial category. Finally, enormous sociocultural changes occur among the same biological population in one or a few lifetimes, far too rapidly to be caused by genetic evolution.

We can conclude that biological/genetic factors do not predispose a human population to adopt one sociocultural system rather than another, at least in any significant way. For cultural anthropology this has an important implication: Because almost all cultural anthropologists agree on this issue, *in general* we do not resort to biological or genetic explanations for differences between human societies in ways of thinking and acting. (One popularly held biological explanation of social differences is explored in Box 3.1) Sociocultural differences and sociocultural changes can be explained by natural environment, by technology, or by historical accidents. They can also be explained by things inside the sociocultural system itself (such as conflicts or inconsistencies). But diversity in customs and beliefs, and change in behaviors and ideas, are *rarely* explained by biological/genetic differences and alterations.

We say "in general" and "rarely" because there are some exceptions. One of the best documented exceptions is the biological difference among human populations in lactase production. Lactase is an enzyme produced in the small intestine of infants that allows them to digest fresh milk. Like almost all other mammals, as they grow into adulthood most humans lose the ability to produce lactase and, hence, to digest milk effectively. Most adult Asians, Africans, Near Easterners, southern Europeans, and Native Ameri-

cans have intestinal problems (sometimes severe) when they drink milk. In northern and western Europe, however, most individuals retain the capacity to produce lactase into adulthood. This ability to use fresh milk probably developed as a result of natural selection that allowed northern and western Europeans to obtain calcium from herd animals. (Note, incidentally, that a biological capacity most of our readers have taken for granted all their lives—the ability to digest fresh milk into adulthood—is relatively unusual.)

In the case of variations between adults in lactase, we see how biological differences among human populations do influence their behavior by affecting their ability to digest milk into adulthood. If we were ignorant of these biological influences, we might explain the failure of some hungry Africans to drink milk as due to irrational cultural conservatism, mistrust of outside innovations, or some other cultural factor. Thus, in this case, and in a few others, biological differences do account for differences in behavior.

Sociocultural Systems and Humanity's Common Biological Heritage

There remains an enormous amount of disagreement over our second question: How does humanity's universal biological nature affect us? It is important not to confuse this question with the one just discussed. The first issue was whether there are any significant biological *differences,* especially between races, that are important in explaining differences in human ways of life. With minor qualifications, the answer is no. Notice that a yes to this question potentially supports racist ideas.

The second issue is how or whether the biological drives or predispositions shared by *all* people channel our culture and behavior into certain paths. For example, do modern humans make war because our early ancestors evolved an instinct for aggression? Are there innate differences in behaviors and emotional responses between females and males that are caused by biological differences between them?

Notice that yes answers to such questions also have important consequences. If the propensity for aggression is biologically inherited from our evolutionary past, then it is part of "human nature" today, and we may find it difficult to eliminate it. We need to be content with merely trying to control and channel it. Similarly for differences between the sexes: If males were the hunters, the protectors, the decision makers, the dominant sex during the evolution of our species, then they may have evolved more biological capacities for these behaviors than females. Men therefore may be better suited than women to fill comparable roles in modern societies.

What do anthropologists have to say on the issue of how humanity's common biology affects our thoughts and actions? Into the 1960s it was almost a dogma in anthropology that all human infants came into the world with a mental blank slate. That is, humans were born with only the most general drives and genetic predispositions. We had to eat, but we did not know what, when, or how. Children everywhere seemed to enjoy play, but the games they learned depended on the cultural tradition around them. Later in life, adolescents developed a sexual urge, but they did not know who to do "it" with, or how to get "it" started. Boys had to learn to play whatever roles the group assigned to men; girls had to learn to act like women, in whatever ways were approved by their cultural norms. The main thing individuals inherited biologically was the capacity to learn how people around them did things. Within the very broad limits of the imperatives to eat, sleep, have sex, and so on, culture wrote whatever it wished on the blank blackboards of our minds. Even the incredibly complex knowledge needed to speak a language was totally learned. "Human nature" was nearly irrelevant; "cultural nurture" was supreme.

In the late 1960s and early 1970s some anthropologist began to question the view that culture/learning overwhelms biology/instinct. Two well-known specialists in animal behavior, Konrad Lorenz and Desmond Morris, published popular books (*On Aggression* and *The Naked Ape*, respectively) on how humankind's animal nature affects our behavior today. In *African Genesis* and *The Territorial Imperative*, playwright Robert Ardrey championed the idea that people are aggressive today because our ancestors were territorial yesterday. These and other writers argued that because humans are a kind of primate, our primate nature predisposes us to learn some things more easily than others. This nature influences what we are and what we can become, so we should pay attention to what these biological constraints might be. (Ironically, two of the anthropological leaders of this people-as-animals school are named Tiger and Fox.)

In 1975, E. O. Wilson, an eminent biologist, published *Sociobiology: The New Synthesis*. This book summarized a wealth of data and hypotheses on the genetic basis of social behavior in assorted animals. Its first and last chapter argued that the general theories developed by biologists to explain the diversity of social behavior in animals would prove useful also in explaining human sociocultural systems. Like the behavior of all other animals, Wilson argued, human behavior has been molded by natural selection acting on genes and therefore has a biological basis. In particular, he thought that a good part of our behavior enhances our *inclusive fitness*—the number of genes we transmit to future generations through our personal reproduction and the reproduction of our close relatives.

A good number of anthropologists thought this made sense. However, most branded Wilson and his anthropological followers as biological determinists. The idea that the great diversity in human ways of living could be explained by a common human nature seemed ludicrous to many. Human sociocultural systems vary enormously, they argued; all humans share a common biological inheritance, so how can you explain something that is variable with something that is the same everywhere? This is one objection. Another is that the new field of **sociobiology** unintentionally (some say intentionally) provides support for racism, sexism, social and economic inequality, and other attitudes and social conditions that its critics do not like. A third objection simply returns to the old position that nurture rules over nature in human beings: whatever our biological nature might be, cultural nurture is far more important.

The debate over how sociocultural systems are limited by humanity's shared biological nature is far from over, and certainly cannot be settled in this text. For now, a compromise solution is in order. We can recognize the possibility that some behaviors have a genetic basis and at the same time acknowledge that cultural traditions may nurture these behaviors to a greater or lesser degree. Even the hard-line sociobiologists say that genetically determined drives are only released under certain conditions. And even critics of sociobiology acknowledge that something must be inborn; otherwise, as one sociobiologist notes, rat genes would work as well as human genes in making a person.

A clue to how our species' common biological endowment affects all ways of living is suggested by the existence of **sociocultural universals,** or elements that

ARE BLACKS NATURAL ATHLETES?

n interesting exploration of the notion that racial differences are important influences on differences in behavior and performance of skills is the overrepresentation of black Americans in the nation's three most popular spectator sports: baseball, football, and basketball. Over one-fifth of professional baseball players are black, nearly half of National Football League players are black, and blacks comprise nearly three-fourths of all players in the National Basketball Association. A high percentage of boxers and track and field athletes also are black. Since only 12 percent of Americans are black, black men are doing exceptionally well in these sports—certainly better overall than whites. Why?

One possible reason is biological factors. There may be something about the bone structure, stamina, strength, coordination, or size of blacks that makes them better natural athletes than whites. If so, then blacks do so well in these sports because they have greater natural talents than whites. Less skilled athletes are eliminated as they pass through increasing levels of competition in high school and college, so that by the time one has made it as a pro, only the very best are left. The fact that so many of these are black must mean that the best blacks are better endowed biologically for sports than the best whites.

Sensible as this argument seems, it does not show that the overrepresentation of blacks in American sports is explained entirely or even to any sig-

nificant degree by biological factors. First, notice that blacks are successful in only a few sports. Why are there so few black figure skaters, tennis players, gymnasts, skiers, swimmers, divers, and golfers? Whatever biological factors make blacks so successful at baseball, basketball, football, boxing, and track and field would be expected to carry over into other athletic competition. Yet blacks are underrepresented in these sports.

Second, notice that hardly anyone uses physical differences to explain why people of different nationalities perform well or poorly at particular sports. Physical factors do not explain why Germans do so well in swimming; Canadians in ice hockey; Swiss in skiing; Russians in gymnastics; Brazilians or Argentinians in soccer; British in cricket; Taiwanese, Koreans, and Japanese in the martial arts; or Cubans in boxing. Minnesota and Maine produce more hockey players than Florida and Texas—is this because of biological differences between residents of northern and southern states?

Third, notice that there was a period when various immigrants into the United States were overrepresented in sports. Contemporary Americans know that boxing today is dominated by blacks and Hispanics. How many of us know that other ethnic groups once dominated this sport? Large numbers of Irish came to the United States in the late nineteenth century following the potato famine in their homeland. In the first two decades of the twentieth century most of the great boxers were of Irish extraction. Later, Jews and Italians arrived in large numbers, and from the 1920s through 1930s, Jews and Italians did very well in boxing. An observer during the early decades of the twentieth century might have concluded that Irish, Jews, and Italians were naturally well-equipped for fighting, based on their dominance of professional boxing. But this statement

sounds silly today, for now most descendants of these immigrants are so assimilated that we do not think of them as different from other whites.

For these and other reasons (see Edwards 1971 and 1973) there is no solid evidence that blacks dominate certain kinds of professional athletics because on average they are better natural athletes than whites. Then why do blacks perform so well? Part of the reason is the past and present racial discrimination experienced by blacks who pursue other lucrative careers. Sports offers young blacks the opportunity to become rich and famous in a country in which they have few other chances to make it really big. So they work harder at sports than at other things, since it offers them their best opportunity. In addition, young blacks have plenty of role models. Talented and highly visible men who have escaped the poverty of the inner cities by means of sports are bound to serve as examples for other blacks.

But the existence of opportunities in sports and athletic role models cannot alone explain why blacks do so well in certain sports. Before there can be viable role models, a fair number of blacks must already have done well in college and pro sports. Why should they have done so well in such large numbers of not because of biological factors? And before they could have done well, they must have had the opportunity to participate. Why should they have had such opportunities, when they have been denied equal opportunity in so many other professions? Is there anything special about sports that would lure blacks into it over other potential careers? Specifically, is there anything about sports that would make it especially likely for blacks to be able to overcome the effects of poverty, poor education, and racial prejudice that hamper their achievement in other careers?

At root, racial prejudice means that an individual is evaluated negatively because of his or her perceived membership in racial category. It means that individual blacks are not judged on the basis of their merits and abilities, for whites' perceptions of blacks' merits and abilities are clouded by whites' prejudices. Members of an ethnic or racial minority can overcome prejudice by pursuing careers in which their performance can be evaluated easily and objectively, so that to some degree their performance overcomes the perceptual barrier of prejudice. In sports, statistics are kept that identify the better players in a relatively objective way. Batting average, rushing yardage, points per game, speed for the 100 meters, number of knockouts—such numbers allow fans, coaches, owners, and other players to judge individual performance accurately. Many fans in Brooklyn, and many fellow major-league players, did not like it when Jackie Robinson broke the "color barrier" in major-league baseball in 1947. But his ability was obvious from his record.

There are other special features of sports that explain why blacks are better able to overcome prejudice in athletics than in most other occupations. Teams are small groups, so the presence or absence of even one star player can make the difference between success and failure. The skills necessary for success are so rare that owners compete for the best talent. Any owner or coach who refused to hire or play a skilled black player would be at a competitive disadvantage with those teams who did not discriminate. For the same reason, white players are less likely to reveal overtly any prejudice they may harbor, since the success of the whole team (and their prestige and next year's contract) may be affected. Blacks therefore

experience less overt prejudice from their co-workers (teammates).

Further, teams are organized in such a way that cooperation generally takes precedence over competition. More than in most other occupations, the success of an athlete is not achieved at the expense of his co-workers, for success does not lead to promotion to a position of authority. White teammates therefore do not have to worry about taking orders from successful blacks, since all team members are subject equally to the authority of coaches or managers. And, significantly, there are few blacks in managerial roles in which they would be making important decisions and issuing commands, for this would threaten whites. The one exception, college and professional basketball, has such a high percentage of black players that black coaches are giving orders to mostly black teams.

In sum, blacks suffer from less overt prejudice and discrimination in athletics than in most other lucrative careers, so they are more attracted to and more likely to succeed in such careers. They experience less discrimination because

their abilities can be objectively measured and compared, because their bosses and teammates recognize that they need their skills to succeed, and because getting ahead need not be at the expense of someone else on the team. So it is the special nature of sports and of athletic competition, and not biology, that explains blacks' overrepresentation in sports.

This analysis also explains why blacks are overrepresented only in certain sports, which the natural-athlete explanation does not do. The sports in which blacks do well are cheap sports, meaning that free public facilities are available and equipment is inexpensive and durable. This contrasts with sports like golf and skiing, which require high expenses. With the exception of boxing, the sports in which blacks do well do not require expensive private coaching to acquire professional status (unlike gymnastics and tennis).

Although the claim that blacks are naturally better athletes than whites seems to be antiracist and even pro-black, a subtle form of racism is involved. For example, whites who do well at basketball are sometimes said to have worked hard and to be "thinking players," whereas blacks are said to have great "instincts" and to be "natural athletes." Implicitly, to claim that blacks are physically superior is to deny them equal intellectual abilities. Finally, and more importantly, to use black biology as the explanation for superior athletic performance results in channeling the energies of black youngsters into sports careers for which they are held to be naturally suited. But only a tiny fraction succeed in these careers; for most blacks, sports offers a false hope. ■

Sources: Blalock (1962), Coakley (1978), Edwards (1971, 1973), Figler (1981).

are found in all human societies. Some universals are obvious, because they are requirements for long-term survival or living in groups in a species that relies on technology. These include tools, methods of communicating, organized patterns of cooperation used in acquiring food and other essential resources, sexual habits, ways of caring for and enculturating children, and so forth.

However, other sociocultural universals do not seem to be absolutely necessary for survival of individuals or groups, but are nonetheless present in all known ways of life. Among these are a division of labor based partly on gender; incest taboos; organized ways of exchanging goods; beliefs about supernatural powers and rituals that are used to communicate with and influence them; recognition of obligations to relatives beyond one's own offspring and immediate family; ways of classifying these relatives into categories; and rites of passage that ceremonially recognize the movement of individuals through certain stages of life.

The very existence of these and other nonobvious sociocultural universals suggests that our biological makeup has strong effects on the kinds of lifeways we are able to develop and live in. At the very least, our genetic endowment makes it very hard (probably impossible) for humans to develop sociocultural systems with no rules about sexual intercourse with relatives, no religion of any kind, no recognition of kinship beyond the nuclear family, no organized exchanges, and so forth. Such systems are "probably impossible" because, despite all the variety in human ways of living, they have never been known to exist in the human species.

On the other hand, our genes do not "hard-wire" into us any *particular* variety of any of these universal elements. All societies have a sexual division of labor, but the specific tasks allocated to females and males vary, as we shall see in chapter 12. All sociocultural systems include prohibitions on incest, but anthropological research has revealed surprising variety in the kinds of relatives to whom the prohibition applies (chapter 10). All societies practice religion, but their beliefs about what spiritual powers are like and the rituals they employ are diverse (chapter 15). Everywhere the physical maturity and resulting status changes of individuals are marked by rites of passage, but what particular changes are marked and how they are marked varies from people to people (chapter 16). The general principle is that—although it sounds contradictory—universals vary, meaning that all peo-

ples exhibit sociocultural elements that are recognizably "the same thing," yet the specific forms these elements take differ from people to people.

This general principle applies specifically to aggression, another sociocultural universal that some have claimed to be rooted in instinct. Does the fact that aggression is universal mean that humans possess an instinctive need to act aggressively, or at least that we have genetically inherited a predisposition to engage in aggressive behavior? If it does, anthropologists know that this drive or instinct or gene(s) can be expressed to a greater or lesser degree according to the sociocultural conditions under which particular humans live. Under the right circumstances, the hypothetical predisposition can be suppressed, sublimated, or left dormant. Anthropologists know this because we have found that some human populations exhibit less aggressive behavior than others. We know also that people in different societies find different things worth fighting for. We know that people react to other people's aggressive behavior in different ways. We know, in short, that aggression varies in its manifestations from place to place, time to time, circumstance to circumstance.

The same general argument can be made for practically all other inborn drives or behavioral predispositions. If the tendency to behave in some way is, in fact, innate to all humans, it manifests itself in many different ways and to many different degrees in various sociocultural systems.

How, then, does humankind's common biological heritage influence sociocultural systems? It seems unlikely today that the mind of newborns is a blank slate on which culture can write any behavioral instructions whatsoever. At the very least, our genes endow us with the propensity to learn some behaviors more easily than others. But most cultural anthropologists believe that, whatever the nature of the human genetic program, it is not detailed enough to allow survival and reproduction without social learning. As Clifford Geertz suggested in the 1960s, individuals who do not learn a culture are incomplete human beings, unable to communicate, behave adaptively, interact with others, and perhaps even to think coherently. If this statement is correct, then the acquisition of some system of cultural knowledge is necessary to complete us as biological organisms. Without culture, we would only look human; socially, mentally, and behaviorally, we would be unfinished. On this point, at least, there seems to be broad agreement.

Two Channels of Transmission

It might be useful to summarize our points. At present, we cannot state precisely how humankind's common biological heritage affects ways of life (at least not in any way that very many other scholars will agree on!). But we can agree that the beliefs and behaviors of human individuals are determined by information that is transmitted to them from two sources, or through two channels.

First, we are born with genetic information that we receive from our two biological parents. Genes provide the information that programs the development of an individual's body (although even bodily development is not determined completely by one's genes, for environmental influences such as nutrition and exposure to disease interact with heredity in development). There is little agreement about the specific ways in which genes program the contents of our minds and behaviors.

Second, other members of the group into which we are born provide us with a culture. Cultural knowledge certainly influences the way any individual thinks, feels, and acts. How knowledge learned culturally interacts with information inherited genetically to make each person a unique individual is largely unknown and must be very complex.

All the genes in a population make up its gene pool. All the socially transmitted knowledge in a human group makes up its culture. So far as is known, these two channels of transmission of information across generations in a society are separate from one another.

Separate, however, does not mean that genes and culture have no influences on one another. It means only that genes and culture are transmitted from one generation to the next through different mechanisms: genes through biological reproduction, culture through social learning. Because the channels of transmission are separate, two individuals can be similar genetically, yet they can acquire vastly different cultures; conversely, two individuals can be as different genetically as is possible for two human beings, yet they can acquire identical cultures. Culture is transmitted socially, not genetically; it is a product of social learning, not of genetic inheritance. Therefore, in explaining sociocultural *differences* between groups of people, we can generally ignore the genetic differences between them. The existence of sociocultural universals suggests that the common genetic endowment of all humans constrains the kinds of sociocultural systems human populations can acquire, but we do not agree on how broad or narrow these constraints are.

Social Learning Again

Perhaps the most important single characteristic distinguishing the human species from other mammals is our dependence on social learning. Behavior in some animals is largely genetically determined; many other animals—including most primates—also rely heavily on learning, but humans depend almost entirely on the social learning of their group's accumulated cultural knowledge for their very survival. We conclude this chapter by discussing the benefits humans gain from social learning and the extent to which human social learning is unique.

What advantages does our reliance on social learning give to humanity? First, consider the benefits of trial-and-error learning (see chapter 2) over the genetic determination of behavior. If behavior is entirely genetically determined, organisms can do only what their parents did, since parents are the only source of genetic instructions. Trial-and-error learning allows an organism to experiment with novel behaviors and adopt them for future use if they somehow aid survival and reproduction. It thus allows individuals to find solutions to new problems, to discover better solutions to old problems, to adapt to environmental changes, and so forth. It does so by making behavior flexible throughout an individual's lifetime, rather than determined and fixed at birth. This advantage is no great mystery.

But trial-and-error learning is not culture. As we have seen, cultural information is transmitted from one generation to the next through social learning (enculturation). What are the benefits of social learning, as opposed to trial-and-error learning? They are primarily two. First, as mentioned in chapter 2, each member of a new generation is spared the costs of trials that do not work. Individuals can adopt behaviors that seem to work for others. The learners must, of course, assume that the behavior around them is tried and true. This is unlikely to be the case for all behaviors in the group, but on average making this assumption surely beats trail and error.

Second, social learning allows a group to accumulate useful information at a comparatively rapid rate. With trail-and-error learning, it might be possible for each individual to achieve successful solutions in his or her lifetime, but—assuming there is no social learning at all—a person cannot pass these solutions along to his or her offspring, nor to others in the group. Each generation cannot profit from the experience of its ancestors, but must learn again for itself. Nor can each individual learn from the experience of others in his or her group.

With social learning, in contrast, members of each generation have access to the knowledge of previous generations, which they learn from their parents and other older people, or in formal educational institutions. In addition, useful information that anyone in the group has acquired may be socially transmitted to others in the group, and thus become shared among the group-at-large. Assuming that the information becomes incorporated into the group's cultural tradition and is passed down to future generations, knowledge will accumulate over time. Current generations thus live largely by the technological know-how, values, norms, collective understandings, and other cultural knowledge they acquired from past generations. This is surely an enormous advantage: whatever technological and social progress has occurred would be impossible without social learning. (Incidentally, note that formal education in schools and universities is partly an attempt to teach younger generations what previous generations have thought and learned—or think they have learned—about the world.)

Are humans the only animal capable of social learning? No. Other animals can also learn by observing and imitating their parents or peers. For example, many canine and feline carnivores teach their young to hunt. Some primates even learn tool use from others. A Japanese macaque (a species of monkey) learned to remove dirt from her food by dipping it in water. This behavior was observed and copied in the troop and transmitted to future generations of monkeys. Wild chimpanzees throw things at predators. They also fashion a simple tool called a *termite probe* out of a stick, which they trim to the proper length and insert into a termite nest. When the insects latch their jaws onto the intruding object, the chimpanzees withdraw the stick and lick off the tasty bugs.

These examples are undoubtedly more complex than "monkey see, monkey do." Still, this kind of social learning occurs largely by means of imitation: the unexperienced individual observes an experienced individual successfully doing something, and tries out the

■ *Anthropologists used to believe that humans are the only animal to make tools and to pass a tool-making tradition along to future generations. As we see in this photo of a female wild chimpanzee probing for ants with a stick while her offspring looks on, both beliefs are now known to be mistaken.*

same thing itself. By definition, this "observe and imitate" learning is a form of social learning, for one animal learns from another. It is sometimes called *protoculture*. How does social learning in humans differ from this? Is there anything special about the social learning of humans?

We cannot go into this question deeply, but an enormously important ability of humans—lacking or quite undeveloped in other animals—is the ability to communicate information by means of a system of arbitrary symbols (see chapter 2). Human children do not need to learn solely by observing and imitating, although of course they do learn in this way. One individual can teach another by using meaningful symbols that are understood by both. The same applies to members of one group wishing to learn from members of another group, if the symbols of the teachers are also meaningful to the learners.

The mutually intelligible symbols are, of course, the individual sounds, words, and sentences of a language. And language, above all else, is the mental and physical capability of humanity that allows us to realize the full potential of social learning. Because we share a language, the knowledge that each generation possesses is communicated with amazing efficiency and precision to new generations. Such knowledge is communicated orally, by means of mutually intelligible sounds, among all human populations. Since the development of writing, much of the knowledge has been passed down in the form of marks on tablets, parchment, paper, or some other medium. Because of language, people can believe in the existence of things (such as ghosts, wereanimals, and souls) they have never actually seen. Because of language, people can hear about events (such as the tearing down of the Berlin walls, drug wars in Latin America, and student deaths in Beijing, China) remote from them in space. Because of language, people can learn about events (such as worldwide depressions and French revolutions) that happened long ago and far away. Because of language, people who learn something new can pass this knowledge along to others in their group and to future generations.

We see then that cultural knowledge is cumulative largely because language makes it possible to store information in our brains, on paper, or on floppy disks, and to communicate it to others. All culture therefore relies on language, for it provides the code by which information is transmitted between individuals and generations. It is no wonder that language is the first sophisticated knowledge children learn: practically all the subsequent culture they acquire relies on their understanding of language. In the next chapter, we consider this remarkable capability of humans in more detail.

Summary

How do biological factors affect human ways of life? Two separate questions are central to this subject. One is whether there seem to be any systematic relationships between genetic differences and sociocultural differences. Does the fact that each individual has a unique biological makeup affect the type of culture and behavior that individual is capable of acquiring? Does the fact that some populations differ biologically from others mean that they are better able to acquire some sociocultural systems than others?

In the nineteenth century social Darwinists justified inequality, slavery, colonialism, and other conditions and behaviors by claiming that biological differences were responsible for differences in patterns of thought and behavior (including intelligence). But much evidence suggests that biological determinism is wrong: it does not appear that any normal person or any population has any inborn propensity to acquire any particular set of customs and beliefs, with some notable exceptions such as lactase deficiency. So far as we know, any individual is capable of learning to behave in whatever sociocultural environment he or she happened to have been born into, just as any population is able to acquire any sociocultural system. This is mainly because genes and culture are transmitted through two distinct channels: genes through biological reproduction, culture through social learning. Because the channels are separate, cultural anthropologists generally ignore the possibility that biological differences between individuals and populations have an important role in explaining sociocultural differences between them.

There is much less agreement on the answer to the second question, How do biological features that are common to all humanity affect our thoughts and behavior? Into the 1970s the most widespread opinion of social scientists was that human individuals were born with no particular instincts or strong predispositions. Cultural and social environment (nurture) could mold us into practically any shape. In the 1970s an increasing number of scholars came to believe that biology (nature) sharply limits what we are able to become. Sociobiologists argued that humanity's biological nature makes us more likely to believe and act in some ways than in others, and that this explains why there are certain basic similarities in all sociocultural systems. If biology does provide us with certain instincts and strong behavioral predispositions, most anthropologists feel that the degree to which they are expressed as well as the form they will take are greatly influenced by the sociocultural environment of an individual.

So the existence of sociocultural universals and the possibility that they are explained by the common biological inheritance of humanity does not lessen the importance of social learning. Social learning is beneficial both because it is more efficient than trial-and-error learning and because it makes it possible for useful knowledge to accumulate in a cultural tradition, and thus allows what we call "progress" to occur. Although rudimentary imitative forms of social learning exist among other animals, humans are unique in our capacity to communicate information by the system of symbols known as language.

Key Terms

social Darwinism

sociobiology

biological determinism

sociocultural universals

Suggested Readings

■ Barash, David. *The Whisperings Within: Evolution and the Origin of Human Nature.* New York: Penguin, 1979.

Well-written book on the possible biological basis for sexism, parenting strategies, altruism, competition and warfare, and psychological processes. The author, a sociobiologist, is careful not to claim that sociocultural differences are caused by biological differences. Makes a good introduction to human sociobiology.

■ Gould, Steven Jay. *The Mismeasure of Man.* New York: W. W. Norton, 1981.

Summarizes nineteenth- and early-twentieth-century attempts by scientists to prove the inferiority of some races and nationalities by measuring their skulls. Informative, yet highly readable, this book shows the errors in the assumptions of biological determinism, including the notion that intelligence is genetically determined.

■ Lewontin, R. C., Steven Rose, and Leon J. Kamin. *Not in Our Genes: Biology, Ideology, and Human Nature.* New York: Pantheon, 1984.

Another argument against biological determinism, this book analyzes the social roots of the idea that differences between individuals, sexes, and races can be explained genetically.

■ Sahlins, Marshall. *The Use and Abuse of Biology: An Anthropological Critique of Sociobiology.* Ann Arbor: Michigan, 1976.

The most widely read critique of sociobiology written by an anthropologist. Questions the fundamental assumptions of sociobiology and uses anthropological data in the critique.

■ Wilson, E. O. *On Human Nature.* Cambridge: Harvard University Press, 1978.

A readable book by the most influential sociobiologist. Argues that human behaviors such as aggression, homosexuality, altruism, and religion have a biological basis.

LANGUAGE

Contents

■ (Above) *Using language to communicate complex messages is one of the main abilities that sets humans apart from other animals.*

What mental capability of humans most profoundly distinguishes us from other animals? In all probability, the answer is language, for many of the unique properties of our minds are related to the great advantage that communication by means of speech gave us in the course of our evolution.

Why are humans, so far as we know, the only creatures with myths, literature, beliefs in supernatural powers, and jokes? The answer is that we are able to communicate by spoken and written language, and without this one ability these and most of our other creative mental powers would not exist.

What, above all else, allows the things one generation has learned to be transmitted to future generations? Enculturation and formal education also are made possible by language, which probably explains why the ability to understand language is the first sophisticated subset of cultural knowledge children learn.

In short, language provides humanity with those mental and social learning capabilities that set us apart from other animals. Language, as we shall see, may be the most complex knowledge any human being possesses. Any discussion of humanity would therefore be incomplete if it omitted *linguistics*, the science of language.

We first describe some features of language that distinguish it from other systems of communication, such as the singing of birds and the tail wagging or howling of canines. We then show how people communicate with one another by combining sounds into words and words into sentences. Finally, we discuss how the way of life of a people and their language are related, and how people use speech in their everyday lives.

Some Properties of Language

Language is a specialized and extremely complex form of communication. Communication occurs when two things happen. First, one organism perceives through its senses some attribute or result of the action of another, such as a physical feature, a movement, a sound, an odor, or a touch. Second, the receiving organism decodes (understands) the attribute or action, usually showing a visible reaction to it. The information communicated from the sender to the recipient is known as the *message*. In human languages, before the development of writing, messages were usually communicated through speech. Knowing a language implies mastery of the rules by which messages can be spoken (put into words) and understood.

We can introduce language by describing some of its key properties. In 1960, Charles Hockett identified thirteen features shared by all human languages. We describe only the five that most sharply distinguish language from other systems of communication.

■ *Multimedia Potential*

All communication occurs by means of messages passed through some medium. When someone shouts "fire!" a distinctive pattern of sound waves is created in the air. These waves strike the ear drums of those present. If they know what this particular pattern of sound waves means (i.e., if they understand the English language), they will respond to the message. In this case, sound is the medium through which words, as well as cries, growls, barks and purrs, are transmitted. Similarly, light is the medium through which gestures are transmitted, and chemicals are the medium through which communication by means of the sense of smell occurs.

Unlike most other ways of communicating, language has **multimedia potential,** meaning that messages communicated with language can be transmitted through several mediums. Ordinarily, language messages are spoken (the medium is sound), but they may also be written or signed with movements of the hand (the medium is, respectively, marks on an object and light). Humans can even send language messages through touch (the medium is nerve signals; Helen Keller, blind and deaf, communicated this way).

■ *One key property of language is its multimedia potential, which makes it possible for messages to be communicated by several different mediums. This deaf couple uses American Sign Language. Their sense of sight allows them to understand by reading lips, although they cannot detect the sound waves most of us rely on for understanding messages.*

We can understand the message "I love you" whether it is spoken, written, or signed, assuming we know the language—that is, how to interpret the sounds, marks, or gestures made by the speaker, writer, or signer. The fact that humans are able to learn to transmit messages through several mediums is related to another fundamental characteristic of human language known as **arbitrariness.**

■ Arbitrariness/Conventionality

Language relies on arbitrary symbols. Consider what happens when children learn the words used by their community. During his or her first and second years of life, the child masters many words that refer to objects (*ball*), persons (*mama*), qualities (*blue, hot*), commands (*no, go to sleep*—with luck, she learns these two early!), actions (*eat, run*), emotions (*love*), and so forth. The specific words that stand for these objects, persons, qualities, commands, actions, and emotions have no inherent relation to the things themselves. The child must learn to pair up words with what they stand for,

which is to say that the child must learn the meanings that speakers assign to words. The feelings sometimes aroused by the sounds that make up "I love you" to an English speaker are also aroused by *te amo* to a Spanish speaker, although the sounds that communicate the message are completely different.

To say that linguistic messages are communicated by means of arbitrary symbols is to say that understanding is based entirely on conventions shared by both the sender and the recipient of the message. Analogously, it is because of shared conventions that one drives on the left side of the road in Britain and on the right side in North America. So long as drivers know and agree to abide by the convention, either side works as well as the other.

■ Discrete and Recombinable Elements

All languages are made up of discrete units or elements that are combined in different ways to communicate different messages. We can introduce the discreteness and recombinability of these elements by noticing that an alphabet is possible because of this property. In writing, the letters of an alphabet are strung together to symbolize words. What do these letters stand for? Originally, they symbolized discrete sounds—each letter represented a single recognizable sound, which was produced in a similar way in all the words in which it appeared. For example, the letter *b* appears in *bat, able, mob,* and *textbook,* and so does the sound we write as *b* in our alphabet. The same applies to all other letters in an alphabet.

(Incidentally, in the English alphabet, most single letters no longer represent a single sound. The letter *a,* for example, is pronounced differently in the words *act, father, warden, assume,* and *nature.* The same is true for other English vowels. Some single sounds in English are rendered in spelling as two letters, such as *th, ou,* and the *gh* in *rough.* Why does the spelling English now uses for certain words not reflect the way these words are pronounced? Basically, because the way words are spelled became standardized after the invention of the printing press, but the pronunciation of many English sounds has changed since then.)

Alphabets are possible because words are composed of discrete sounds. These sounds can be seen as the building blocks of language. By themselves, most of the sounds of a language carry no meaning: the three English sounds in the word *cat,* for example, are meaningless when pronounced by themselves. But by combining this limited number of sounds in different ways, words are formed, and words do communicate meanings. Thus, the same three sounds in *cat* can be put together in different sequences to form the words *act* and *tack*. Words, then, are composed of sound combinations that have recognized, conventional meanings in a speech community. And all languages use a small number of sounds to make a large number of words.

Sounds are not the only units of language that people recombine when speaking with one another. Words are combined according to the rules of the language to convey the quite complex messages carried by sentences. Sentences carry a message "greater than" the words that make them up. (This is seen clearly by contrasting the meaning of the following sentences composed of the same five words: This dog bit a man. This man bit a dog.) By mastering their language's **lexicon,** or its words and their meanings, and its **syntax,** or rules for combining words into sentences, speakers and hearers can send and receive messages of great complexity with amazing precision (e.g., "In the basket of apples on your left, hand me the reddest one on the bottom").

Because language is composed of **recombinable elements**, it is the most precise and complete system of communication known, as seen in the next important property of language.

■ *Productivity*

Also known as *creativity,* **productivity** refers to a speaker's ability to create totally novel sentences (and to a hearer's ability to comprehend them). Consider the following sentence: "A garden spider ate the mayfly on my shoulder." Neither you nor I have previously heard this precise message; indeed it is unlikely that it has ever been sent until now. Yet I formulated the sentence without consciously thinking about how to put the words together; and you understand it well enough to wonder why I allowed bugs on my body, even though you may not know what garden spiders or mayflies are.

Productivity means that a language's finite number of words can be combined into an infinite number of meaningful sentences by applying the rules of syntax. The sentences are meaningful because the speaker and hearer know what each word means individually and the rules by which they may be meaningfully com-

bined. The amazing thing is that individuals are not consciously aware of their knowledge of these rules, although they routinely apply them each time they speak and hear.

■ *Displacement*

Displacement refers to our ability to talk about objects, people, things, and events that are remote in time and space. Language has this property because of the symbolic nature of words and sentences, which means that things do not have to be visible to communicate about them. We can discuss someone who is not immediately present because the symbols of language call that person to mind, allowing us to picture and think about him or her. We can speculate about the future because, although its events have not happened and may never happen, our language has symbols that stand for future time and more symbols that allow us to form a mental image of events that are only possible. Displacement makes it possible for us to talk about things that do not even exist, such as goblins, ghosts, and ghouls; indeed, we can give these imaginary things detailed characteristics in our mind's eye, although our real eyes have never seen them. Because of displacement, we can tell each other stories about things that never happened, and thus create myths, folklore, and literature. Obviously, much of culture depends on this very important property of language.

Grammar

When we learn a language, we master the sounds used in that language, how the sounds can be combined into words, the meanings of words and idiomatic expressions, and the rules that govern how words are combined to form sentences. The elements (sounds, words) and the rules for combining these elements make up the total system of linguistic knowledge called a **grammar.** The term *grammar* refers to all the knowledge shared by those who are able to speak and understand a language: what sounds occur, how they may be properly combined into sequences that carry meaning, how words may be formed out of these sequences, and how new sentences may be constructed by stringing words together according to precise rules. The grammatical knowledge we share gives us the ability to speak to and understand one another—it is the basis of our linguistic *competence.*

Knowledge of grammar underlies our speech, or linguistic *performance*—what we actually say, when we say it, and how we say it.

Grammatical knowledge is *unconscious*, meaning that those who share a language cannot verbalize the nature of the knowledge that allows them to speak and comprehend one another. It also is *intuitive*, meaning that speaking and understanding are second nature—we ordinarily do not need to think long and hard about how to transform the message we wish to communicate into a sentence, nor how to decode a sentence we hear into a message.

This scientific, technical use of *grammar* differs from the common use of the term. In everyday speech we judge individuals partly on the basis of whether we consider their grammar proper. In the United States there are several dialects, or regional variants of English. One, called *Standard American English* (SAE)—the dialect we usually hear in the national news media—is culturally accepted as most correct. Other dialects, especially those spoken by many blacks and by southern or Appalachian whites, are looked down upon by many of those whose dialect is SAE.

But we need to realize that there is no such thing as superior and inferior dialects (or languages) *in the linguistic sense.* That is, each language, and each dialect, is equally capable of serving as a vehicle for communicating the messages its speakers need to send and receive. So long as an individual successfully communicates, there is really no such thing as "bad grammar," or people who " don't know proper grammar." The exchange of messages

> *Merle*: I ain't got no shoes.
>
> *Pearl*: I ain't got none neither.

is perfectly good English—to members of certain subcultures who speak one English dialect. So long as speakers communicate their intended meaning to hearers, then the words they use or the way they construct their sentences is as valid as any other. The evaluations we make of someone else's grammar or overall style of speech, then, are cultural evaluations. Culturally, people define some dialects as more correct than others. But if the history of the United States had been different, some other dialect of American English might have become standard, and the sentences

> *Amy*: I have no shoes.
>
> *Donald*: Nor do I.

might have become one of our cultural markers of ignorance or lack of sophistication.

This point is so important that it is worth saying another way. Many languages are not uniform but have variations based on region, class, ethnicity, or some other difference between people. These variations in the grammar of a single language are called **dialects.** The speakers of a language or dialect share a complete knowledge of its grammar. When linguists try to discover this grammar, they call what they are investigating a *descriptive grammar*: they are simply trying to describe completely and objectively the elements and rules that underlie communication in some particular language or dialect. The descriptive grammar a linguist would write of black English would differ slightly from that of SAE. But a linguist would never describe the differences between the two dialects in terms of relative superiority, since each dialect is capable of conveying the same messages.

In contrast, when some speakers of SAE label black or southern dialects as substandard English, they are basing their judgments on their cultural assumptions about the relative correctness of dialects. But this judgment is entirely *cultural. Linguistically,* all languages and all dialects work as well as others, meaning that all languages and all dialects have equal ability to communicate the messages their speakers need to send and receive.

With this point about the relativity of all languages and dialects in mind, we can discuss three areas of the study of grammar. The first, known as **phonology,** deals with the sounds of a language and how they are patterned into a consistent system. The second, called **morphology,** deals with how sounds are put together to form words and other sound sequences that carry meaning. The third field of study, *syntax,* which we defined earlier, deals with the unconscious rules of a language that the speakers use to string together a series of words to create a sentence or other utterance that conveys a complex meaning.

■ *Phonology*

As we have seen, any act of speech can be broken down into a string of sounds. The sounds of a language, together with the way these sounds occur in regular, consistent patterns, make up the *phonological system* of the language.

For example, if you hear the word *debt* you hear a sequence of sounds that you have learned to associate with a certain meaning. You do not consciously think, and may even be unable to recognize, that *debt* consists of three distinguishable sounds, /d/, /ɛ/, and /t/. (The slash marks / / denote sounds recognized as distinctive in a single language.) In fact, if someone asked you, "How many sounds are there in 'debt'?", you might say "four," because you would confuse the sounds in *debt* with its number of letters in English spelling.

But actually, you do know what the three sounds in *debt* are, although you might not know that you know. You know because you recognize that the word *pet* is a different word from *debt*, although only its initial sound, /p/, is different. You know because you recognize *debt* and *date* as different words, although they differ only in their second sound. And you know because you recognize the profound contrast in meaning between *debt* and *dead*, although this difference is caused by a single sound at the end of the two words. If English speakers did not know, at an unconscious level, that *debt* must be pronounced /dɛt/, rather than /pɛt/, /dayt/, or /dɛd/, they would mispronounce it, and their listeners would be unable to distinguish *debt* from these other words. Conversely, if a hearer did not know that /dɛt/ is different from /pɛt/, she or he might expect to receive a cat or a dog when the speaker said, "I'm repaying my debt to you."

The particular sounds that the speakers of a language recognize as distinct from other sounds are called the **phonemes** of the language. Phonemes are the atoms or minimal bits of a language that make a difference in the meanings of its words. For example, we can break up the word *brought* into four phonemes: /b/, /r/, /ɔ/, and /t/. The substitution of any other phoneme for any of the phonemes in the word *brought* would either change the word into another word (e.g., *bright*, in which a different vowel sound, /ay/, is substituted for /ɔ/) or make it unintelligible (e.g., *blought* or *broughk*).

Different languages have different phonemes, and the phonological systems of different languages are patterned somewhat differently. This means that different languages recognize and distinguish between sounds based on different sound qualities, and that each language has its own logic and consistency in making these distinctions.

As an example of the patterning of the phonological system of one language, compare two phonemes of English: /b/ and /p/. The phoneme /b/ appears in *boy*, *able*, *probation*, and *flab*. It is made by putting the lips together and then releasing them while making a slight vibration with the vocal cords. The phoneme /p/ appears in *pat*, *approach*, *mop*, and *example*. We make

the /p/ sound the same way as /b/, except that we do not vibrate our vocal cords.

You can hear the vibration of your vocal cords in /b/ by placing your hands over your ears while saying the word *bat* slowly and listening for a slight buzz during the pronunciation of /b/. This buzz is the sound your vocal cords make when your lungs force air through them while they are constricted, or tightened and brought nearly into contact with one another. All sounds in which the vocal cords vibrate are called *voiced*. Examples of other voiced consonants in English are /d/, /z/, and /j/ (/j/ is the first and last sound in *judge*.). All vowel sounds also are voiced in English.

Now place your hands over your ears while saying the word *pat*. You will not hear a buzz during the pronunciation of /p/. This is because your vocal cords are completely open, so the flow of air from your lungs is unimpeded and no buzzy sound is created. All sounds in which the vocal cords are open, so that their vibration does not contribute to the sound, are called *voiceless*. Other voiceless phonemes in English are /t/, /s/, and /č/ (/č/ is the first and last sound in *church*).

The only difference between *bat* and *pat* is this first sound, and the significant difference between the sounds /b/ and /p/ is that the vocal cords vibrate during /b/ but are open during /p/. Stated technically, the only difference between the two phonemes is that /b/ is voiced, whereas /p/ is voiceless.

We discussed these two English phonemes in some detail to make a general point: our understanding of words is based on our shared ability to hear *distinctions* between their constituent sounds and to recognize these distinctions as *significant*. People who speak English have no difficulty hearing the distinctions between the first sounds of *bill* and *pill*, although they do not consciously know what qualities make these sounds different. We also recognize the distinctions between the two sounds as significant—that is, as making a difference in the meanings of the words in which they appear. If the difference between /b/ and /p/ were not significant, we would not recognize any difference between words that differ only in these sounds—*pill* and *bill* would have the same meaning and hence would be the same word! Further, the one sound that makes *bill* and *pill* different itself differs only in whether it is voiceless (/p/) or voiced (/b/). Now, if *pill* and *bill* have different meanings, but the only difference between them is whether the initial sound is voiceless or voiced, then it must be the voiceless/voiced distinction that makes the words different.

In fact, the voiced/voiceless distinction matters for all English consonants. The distinctions that speakers make between phonemes tend to be consistent across phonemes of a language. In other words, the features of sounds that the speakers of a language recognize as significant are *patterned*. If a distinction (e.g., voiced/voiceless) is recognized for some sounds, the same distinction tends to be recognized for other sounds that differ in the same way. Thus English speakers recognize the differences between /f/ and /v/ (as in *feel* versus *veal*), between /s/ and /z/ (as in *peace* versus *peas*), between /k/ and /g/ (as in *curl* versus *girl*), and between other consonants that differ only in whether they are voiced or voiceless.

■ *Some Variations in Phonology*

So what? All we have done is put into words what every speaker of English unconsciously and intuitively knows: that we detect the difference between sounds such as /t/ and /d/ and /f/ and /v/ and that we recognize this difference as significant. Can't everyone in the world hear this difference, and doesn't everyone recognize this difference as significant?

No, they can't and don't. Although it may seem incredible to those who speak English, there are a great many languages in which sounds that differ only in whether they are voiced or voiceless are not recognized as different sounds. In fact, the speakers of one of these languages may not be able to hear the difference between sounds that differ only in whether they are voiced or voiceless. For instance, in Kosraen, a Micronesian language, the distinctions between the sounds /t/ and /d/, /p/ and /b/, and /k/ and /g/ make no difference in meaning. So the two alternative pronunciations of the following words make no difference in meaning to Kosraens:

kɨp and *gɨp* mean "satiated," "full from eating"

tʌn and *dʌn* mean "color"

pʌk and *bʌk* mean "sand"

It is as if English-speaking people made no distinction between *cot* and *got*, between *tan* and *dan*, and between *pig* and *big*. This does not mean, of course, that Kosraen ears are not as sensitive as Canadian, Australian, or English ears; it certainly does not mean that Kosraen is an inferior language to English. It means only that the Kosraen and English languages do not recognize the same distinctions in similar sounds as making a difference in the meanings of words. In

English, /k/ and /g/ are different phonemes; in Kosraen, they are alternative ways of pronouncing the same phoneme.

So differences between sounds that are meaningful in one language's phonological system do not always have meaning in another's. Conversely, one language may recognize distinctions between similar sounds that the speakers of another language do not detect. For example, we have referred to the English phoneme /p/ as if it is always pronounced the same way. In fact, we use two pronunciations for /p/, depending on the sounds around it. Consider the words *pit* and *spit*. You might think the only difference between the two is the sound /s/. If so, you are wrong. The /p/ in *pit* is followed by a short puff of air (called *aspiration*) between it and the vowel; the /p/ in *pit* is said to be aspirated. The /p/ in *spit* is not followed by such a puff; it is unaspirated. (You cannot hear this difference, but you may be able to feel it: put your hand immediately in front of your mouth while saying the two words, and you may feel the aspiration after the /p/ in *pit*, but not after *spit*.)

Surely such a slight difference cannot matter, but in many languages it does. In Thai, for example, /p/ and /pʰ/ (the ʰ stands for aspiration) are separate phonemes, which means that those who speak Thai detect the difference between many aspirated and unaspirated sounds and recognize it as changing the meaning of many words. This is seen in the following Thai words:

paa	"forest"	*pʰaa*	"to split"
tam	"to pound"	*tʰam*	"to do"
kat	"to bite"	*kʰat*	"to interrupt"

Note that a difference in sound that is nearly inaudible to a speaker of English actually changes the meanings of the paired Thai words just listed. Hindi, the language spoken by many Asian Indians, also recognizes the difference between aspirated and unaspirated sounds.

One of the most interesting ways in which languages differ in their phonological systems is the way the pitch of the voice is used to convey meaning. (The pitch of a voice depends on how fast the vocal cords vibrate: the higher the frequency of vibration, the higher the pitch of the voice.) English speakers use pitch to convey different meanings, as you can see by contrasting the following sentences:

She went to class.

She went to class?

The first statement is turned into a question by altering the pitch of the voice: in the question, the pitch rises with the word *class*. Now contrast these sentences:

What did Mary hit, a ball?
What, did Mary hit a ball?

Here, pitch is used together with slight pauses to convey questions with a different sense. Parents also use high pitch—often together with loudness—to scold their children. Consider the following statements by one mother to her son:

"You're playing with the ball in the house, Matthew." (*implication:* "how cute!")

"YOU'RE PLAYING WITH THE BALL IN THE HOUSE, MATTHEW." (*implication:* "which I've told you a zillion times not to do!")

Matthew may respond to the second sentence—the scold—with:

"I never get to do anything!"

Assuming, as is likely, that Matthew says this with a whine in his voice, he also uses pitch to show his displeasure.

Speakers of English use the changing pitch of their voice over the whole sentence to communicate a message—that is, the voice pitch falls or rises mainly from word to word, rather than within a word. There are many other languages in which a high, medium, or low pitch used within an individual word, or even in a syllable, changes the fundamental meaning of the word.

Languages in which the pitch (or tone) with which a word is said (or changes in the voice pitch during its pronunciation) affects the meaning of a word are known as **tone languages.** Tone languages occur in Africa and southeastern and eastern Asia. Chinese, Thai, Burmese, and Vietnamese are all tone languages, which is why they have a musical quality to ears accustomed to English. As an example of how pitch can affect meaning, consider these words from Nupe, an African tone language:

bá (high tone) means "to be sour"
bā (mid tone) means "to cut"
bà (low tone) means "to count"

Here, whether the two phonemes in *ba* are pronounced with a high, mid, or low tone changes their meaning. The same principle can apply to syllables within a word—how the pitch of the voice changes between the

Languages vary in the use of voice pitch to convey meaning. In tone languages, such as that spoken by these Chinese, voice pitch affects the basic meaning of words.

syllables alters the meaning. This is exemplified by the following Thai words:

nâa (tone of voice falls on second vowel) means "face"

nǎa (tone of voice rises on second vowel) means "thick"

Because the tone with which a word is pronounced, or changes in the tone within the word, can change its meaning, the pitch of the voice is a kind of phoneme in tone languages. It has the same effect as adding /s/ in front of the English word *pot*, which totally alters its meaning to *spot*.

■ *Morphology*

Morphology is the study of meaningful sound sequences and the rules by which they are formed. In the preceding section we used *word* to refer to any sequences of phonemes that carries meaning to speakers and hearers. In morphology we need a more precise concept than *word*. To see why, ask yourself if you know the meaning of the following sound sequences, none of which qualifies as a word:

un	ed
pre	s
non	ing
anti	ist

You do, of course, recognize these sound sequences. Those in the first column are prefixes, which change the meaning of certain words when placed before them. Those in the second column are suffixes, which alter a word's meaning when they follow the word.

Sound sequences such as these are "detachable" from particular words. Take the words *art* and *novel*, for example. By adding the suffix *-ist* to these words, we make new words meaning something like "a person who creates art" or "one who writes novels." That *-ist* has a similar meaning whenever it is attached to other words is shown by the made-up word *crim*; you don't know what this word means, but by adding *-ist* to it, you instantly know that a *crimmist* is "a person who crims." We need a concept that will include prefixes and suffixes such as *uni-*, *-ing*, *-ly*, and so forth in order to analyze such compound words and their meanings.

Any sequence of phonemes that carries meaning is known as a **morpheme**. There are two kinds of morphemes in all languages. **Free morphemes** are any morphemes that can stand alone as words, for example, type, walk, woman, establish. **Bound morphemes** are morphemes that are attached to free morphemes to modify their meanings in predictable ways, for example, *dis-*, *bi-*, *-er*, *-ly*. Thus, by adding suffixes to the example free morphemes, we get:

typist	typed	typing
walked	walking	walks
womanly	womanhood	womanish
established	establishment	establishes

Both prefixes and suffixes—which in English are the two kinds of bound morphemes—can be attached to a free morpheme to change its meaning, as shown in the following examples:

desire	desirable	undesirable
excuse	excusable	inexcusably
possible	impossible	impossibility
health	healthy	unhealthful
complete	completely	incompletely

Note that both free and bound morphemes carry meaning (although the meaning depends on the context in which they are used), unlike most phonemes such as /l/, /g/, /n/, and so on. Just as phonemes are the minimal units of sound, morphemes are the minimal units of meaning of a language. Thus, we cannot break down the free morphemes *friend*, *possible*, *man*, or *run* into any smaller unit that carries meaning. Nor can we break down the bound morphemes *non-*, *-ish*, *-able*, or *tri-* into any smaller units and still have them mean anything in English.

There is no doubt that the speakers of a language learn its rules for forming compound words by combining free and bound morphemes. That is, people learn how to make new compound words by applying a rule of compound-word formation, not by learning each compound word separately.

For instance, take the English rule for forming a plural noun from a singular noun. It can be done by adding the bound morpheme /z/, thus: *beads*, *apples*, *colors*, *eggs*. (Incidentally, /z/ represents one of only a few cases in English in which a phoneme is also a morpheme. When used as a bound morpheme at the end of a noun, /z/ usually carries the meaning "more than one"). Children learn the morphological rule for plural formation at an early age, but it takes them a while longer to learn the many exceptions to the rule. They apply the rule consistently to all words, saying "childs," "mans," "foots," "mouses," and so on.

The same is true for the English rule for forming the past tense of a verb. Generally, the bound morpheme /d/ is added as a suffix to the verb, as in *formed*, *bored*, *loaded*, and *included*. Again, children learn this rule for past-tense formation early, and they apply it consistently. We hear children say "goed," "runned," "bringed," and "doed."

Thus, one of the many things people unconsciously know when they know a language is its rules for changing the meaning of free morphemes by the addition of bound morphemes. We do not have to learn *tree* and *trees* as separate words. We need only apply a general morphological rule (i.e., add /z/ as a suffix to make a noun plural) to *tree*, or to many other nouns.

■ *Syntax*

Syntax refers to the unconscious rules that instruct speakers of a language how to combine words into meaningful sentences and listeners how to decode the string of words into a message. Each speaker-hearer of a language has a knowledge of syntactic rules and knows intuitively whether a particular sentence is said in a grammatical way. Yet, just as with phonology and morphology, untrained individuals are unable to describe (verbalize) these rules, although they apply them each time they speak or listen, and although they can tell when some particular utterance violates the rules.

As anyone who has tried to master a foreign language knows, languages vary in their syntactical rules. To give a brief impression of the range of this variability, consider these short sentences from four languages:

English: You are a beautiful person.

Spanish: *Usted es una persona bonita.*
(You are a person beautiful.)

Tannese: *Ik iema amasan.*
(You person good/beautiful.)

Kosraen: *Mwet kato se pa kom.*
(Person beautiful one equals you.)

As these simple sentences demonstrate, one way in which the syntax of languages varies is in the permissible order of morphemes. But this is by no means the only way. The Spanish example used the formal word *usted* for *you*, but it would also be possible to use the informal *tú*. Which form of *you* a speaker used would depend on whom she was addressing and the precise kind of message she wished to convey. In English and Spanish, to speak grammatically it was necessary to use some form of the verb *to be*. In this sentence, *are* is the correct form. Most English speakers would consider "You is a beautiful person" to be ungrammatical, although "He is a beautiful person" is acceptable. In contrast, Spanish has no different form of *to be* that needs to be used in this context: *es* is used regardless of whether the subject is *you* or *he*. Tannese lacks the verb *to be* altogether: it is simply understood that *amasan* refers to *ik*. Kosraen also has no verb *to be*, but one must use *pa* (meaning roughly "equal to" or "equivalent to") when two noun phrases (*you* and *beautiful person*) are being equated. If a Kosraen wished to communicate "You are beautiful," he would say merely *Kom kato*, omitting the *pa* that is required in "You are a beautiful person."

To sum up, the speakers of a language possess detailed unconscious knowledge that provides them with rules for combining words and other morphemes into meaningful sentences. Languages differ in these syntactic rules. We already have seen that languages also differ in their sound inventories, in which features of sound they consider significant, in their rules for combining sounds into morphemes, and in their rules for forming words out of free and bound morphemes. Do these facts together mean that human languages have little in common? Is all this diversity in phonology, morphology, and syntax unlimited?

Universal Grammar

The answer to the questions just posed is no, according to most modern linguists. In spite of their variability—which we have merely introduced—all human languages share many important features. All include both vowels and consonants among their phonemes. Every language has a way to discuss events that occurred in the past, a way to form negations, ask questions, make requests, give commands, express emotions, and so forth. Similar syntactical categories (or parts of speech, such as nouns, verbs, adverbs, and adjectives) occur in all languages. The speakers of all languages can discuss not just events, persons, qualities, things, and actions, but also abstract concepts similar to our notions of good and evil, souls, spirits, love, and beauty.

These and other universals suggest that languages are not as different as they initially appear to be. Is there other evidence that human languages share certain universal rules? Indeed, there is. It comes from an unexpected source: children.

Parents know the joy of experiencing their children's language learning. We try to coax them into saying their first word, which happens at about one year of age. We anxiously wait for them to put several words together, which most are able to do consistently at around two years. Some of us wonder about the best way to teach them to speak. We may compete with our friends to see whose child will advance fastest, believing that rapid learning of language is correlated with high intelligence.

Yet we do not teach language to our children at all, at least not in the sense that schools teach them to write, read, do arithmetic, memorize dates, and recite poetry. Adults cannot possibly teach children the rules of a language the way a third-grade teacher teaches them multiplication tables, for adults do not consciously know the rules themselves. An English-speaking person cannot teach a child who does not already know the English language grammatical rules such as "the adjective goes before the noun," that "/z/ after a noun means 'more than one'," that "voiced stops are unaspirated," that "a sentence consists of a noun phrase plus a verb phrase," and so on.

Further, even if we could agree on what *intelligence* means, the ability of children to learn language seems to have no relation to it. By the time they are five, most normal children have a complete knowledge of the grammar of the language to which they have been exposed. They can formulate sentences as well as any adult, although, of course, they continue to add vocabulary for many more years. A child who has been regularly exposed to two or more languages soon learns to distinguish them when speaking and rarely confuses their phonology, morphology, or syntax.

Obviously, children do learn language, but they do not do so in the same way they learn most other things—by imitation and memorization. At an early age they use language productively, uttering and comprehending sentences they have never heard. They do not merely copy adult models of speech. Children of English-speaking parents are most unlikely ever to have heard sentences like

Want other one spoon.
Oh, nobody don't like me.
I goed to the store.
You hurted me.

So where do children learn the grammar that produces such utterances, since they did not hear similar sentences from adults? Apparently, speech like this is characteristic of a certain period of language acquisition, during which the child is able to put together multiword sentences that express complex and comprehensible meanings but has not yet mastered the grammar used by adults.

This and other evidence suggests that children master the language of their community by a process of successive approximation: at different stages of the process of language learning, children deduce a set of grammatical rules from the speech around them, which they use to form novel sentences. (We say "deduced" because no adult could have told the child these rules; the child must figure them out from the evidence of adult speech.) The grammar of one stage is superseded as the child moves into the next stage, acquiring a closer and closer approximation of adult grammar.

Finally, and significantly, there seems to be little variation in the speed with which children who are exposed to different languages learn to speak. It might seem that some languages would be harder for children to learn—certainly some languages are more difficult to master than others for adults who already know one language. Yet children around the world show little variation in the rate at which they develop linguistic competence.

■ *Children learn to speak the language of their society by hearing adults talk. These Fijian women are doing just that. As the children listen, they are acquiring an unconscious knowledge of the grammar of Fijian.*

In short, normal children

■ learn language without formal instruction, for no one is capable of teaching them which of all possible phonemes their language uses, nor the rules for how these phonemes can be combined into meaningful morphemes and sentences.

■ learn language in a remarkably short period of time that varies surprisingly little from language to language.

■ learn language almost regardless of how well they perform other mental tasks.

■ learn language by a process of deduction rather than imitation and memorization.

The ability of children to learn language in this way is truly astounding. As we have already tried to make clear, the knowledge of the grammar of any language is incredibly complex—so complex that some of the best minds in the world are unable to give a complete account of it. Children under the age of five, however, learn it routinely, easily, and at nearly the same rate everywhere. How is this possible?

It would seem to be possible only if all children are born with a knowledge of *human language*. Noam Chomsky, probably the world's most influential linguist, was asked, "How could anyone possibly learn enough about the English language to possess the rich and exotic grammatical knowledge that we all seem to possess by the time we are five or six years old?" Chomsky replied:

The knowledge is built in. You and I can learn English, as well as any other language, with all its richness because we are designed to learn languages based upon a common set of principles, which we may call universal grammar . . . [which is] the sum total of all the immutable principles that heredity builds into the language organ. The principles cover grammar, speech sounds, and meaning. Put differently, universal grammar is the inherited genetic endowment that makes it possible for us to speak and learn human languages. (Gliedman 1985, 371)

Notice that Chomsky is not merely claiming that children are born with the capacity to learn language. Rather, he and many other linguists claim that there is an inborn human language, which consists of a set of grammatical rules—**universal grammar**—that do not have to be learned and that guide children's discovery and mastery of the grammar(s) to which they are exposed at the proper time in their lives. Children are born with a LAD (Language Acquisition Device), which provides them with a genetically programmed plan to discover and replicate the elements and rules of the specific language spoken around them. We do not know what this plan looks like, but it or something very like it seems necessary to account for the speed and ease with which children around the world master their native language.

And What About Culture?

Linguists debate the nature (and even the existence) of a universal grammar. But assume for the moment that children are indeed born with some set of grammatical rules. What implication would this have for the study of human cultural knowledge? It might mean that much of the diversity in the world's cultures is only superficial, only local variations on a panhuman culture.

But is culture really modeled on language? Is cultural knowledge built up out of elements related to one another in patterns and rules in a manner similar to grammatical knowledge?

Certainly it is useful for some purposes to conceptualize culture and language in similar terms. After all, both language and culture are systems of shared knowledge. It is plausible (which does not mean it is correct) to assume that the human brain organizes cultural knowledge in much the same way as it does grammatical knowledge.

Notice also that grammar consists of unconscious rules by means of which the messages speakers want to transmit are transformed into speech hearers can under-

derstand. Likewise, much of culture consists of rules, by means of which its individual carriers know how to behave in meaningful and appropriate ways.

Further, some anthropologists have proposed that language is to speech as culture is to behavior. That is, linguistic performance (meaningful speech) is possible because of linguistic competence (shared knowledge of grammar). Similarly, cultural performance (meaningful behavior, as in proper performance of roles) is possible because of cultural competence (shared knowledge of culture).

Along these same lines, cultural knowledge underlies behavior in much the same way that grammatical knowledge underlies speech. Grammar greatly influences how people say what they want to say, because serious violations of grammatical rules lead to miscommunication. But grammar does not determine what the speakers of a language say to one another. Individuals decide what messages they wish to communicate based on the situation in which they find themselves, what goals they seek, whom they are addressing, and many other factors. Analogously, many factors influence an individual's nonverbal behavior besides the cultural knowledge he or she shares with others. Grammar and culture underlie and constrain—yet do not determine—speech and nonverbal behavior.

Despite these analogies, there is no agreement that language serves as a useful model for all of culture. It may be, however, that some subsystems of cultural knowledge are organized the same way as language. If so, some of the understanding that linguists have gained of grammar will help us to understand at least these subsystems of culture.

In the 1960s many anthropologists came to believe that at least one subsystem of cultural knowledge—namely, classifications of reality (see chapter 2)—was closely analogous to the phonological system of languages. Known as *cognitive anthropologists* or *ethnoscientists*, these scholars applied the sophisticated methods of linguistics to the study of culture. They noted that a culture's classifications of reality are built up and organized into consistent patterns much like those of the phonological system of a language.

To glimpse the organization of these patterns, we return for a moment to phonology. As we have seen, English recognizes the difference between voiced and voiceless consonants as significant. On the other hand, many other languages do not recognize this distinction between sounds, for the meaning of a word in these languages is not affected by whether certain of its consonants are voiced or voiceless. The distinctions between the same sounds are objectively present in all languages, but they are not necessarily perceived and made significant.

Now recall that one difference between cultures is how they classify reality into categories of objects, people, and events. This is done by perceiving or not perceiving different features of things and by recognizing or not recognizing these differences as important (just as the speakers of a language do or do not perceive or recognize differences between sounds). On the basis of these perceptions and recognitions of contrasts and similarities between things, humans define categories of reality. We classify specific objects, people, natural phenomena, and so forth into one or another category, depending on which of their many features we notice and view as significant. And, of course, members of different cultural traditions do not necessarily base their categories on the same contrasts and similarities (just as speakers of different languages do not distinguish phonemes based on the same contrasts and similarities—recall, for example, that aspiration is not a difference that matters in English phonology, although it is the only difference between some phonemes in Hindi).

An example sheds light on how the "cognitive categories" of a people can be built up in much the same way as elements of language. Take three kinds of livestock: cattle, horses, and swine. How do North American farmers categorize and classify these animals? Consider the following list:

Cattle	Horses	Swine
cow	mare	sow
bull	stallion	boar
steer	gelding	barrow
heifer	filly	gilt
calf	colt	shoat

(Unless you have a farming background, you will not recognize some of these terms. Farmers need to discuss cattle, horses, and swine more than do suburban or city folk, so they use a rich lexicon to talk about livestock.) Note that the same features are used to contrast the different categories of cattle, horses, and swine. *Cow* and *bull* contrast in the same way as *mare-stallion* and *sow-boar*: the first is female; the second, male. There is a special term for each kind of male animal that has been neutered: *steer, gelding,* and *barrow*. And there are separate terms for female and male immature animals: *heifer-calf, filly-colt,* and *gilt-shoat*. Each kind of live-

stock then is divided into categories based on gender (female, male, neutered male) and age (adult, immature). And each category can be described by the features that distinguish it in the farmers' classification of livestock: a *filly* is an "immature female horse," a *barrow* is a "mature castrated male swine," and so on.

These are the features of animals that farmers find important enough to make the basis of their classification of livestock. Notice that this classification rests on contrasts and similarities between *selected* characteristics of the animals—just as the speakers of a language recognize only *some* features of sounds as significant. Notice also that the classification is patterned: the same contrasts and similarities (gender, age) are used to distinguish kinds of cattle, horses, and swine. Similarly, the phonological rules of a language are patterned: if a feature (e.g., voicing) of one class of sound (e.g., stop) is recognized as significant for one member of the class, it tends to be recognized as significant for other members of the class as well.

As this example shows, the way a people culturally classify things is built up out of selected features of the things, and these same features tend to be the basis for distinguishing between other, similar things. This subsystem of culture appears to be organized much like the knowledge speakers have of their language's phonology: potential differences and similarities between things are perceived as significant, and cultural conceptions of reality are constructed from these selected differences and similarities. This makes sense, for a people classify reality, at least in part, by assigning labels (words) to things, and it is hard to imagine any other criteria for placing things under one or another label besides the recognition of differences and similarities between them.

But are other subsystems of culture organized the same way? Are they also modeled on language? Anthropologists debate the extent to which norms, values, world views, attitudes, and the like rest on the languagelike patterning of differences and similarities. It is possible that at some deep level our knowledge of the cultural norms that instruct us in how to behave towards our mothers is organized in the same way as our knowledge of how to construct a sentence. But so far, no one has ever been able to describe the grammar of this knowledge. And whether efforts to describe such a *cultural grammar,* as some anthropologists call it, are even worthwhile is debatable. So it may be that the cognitive dimensions of culture are more like language than other dimensions.

Whatever the answer to the exceedingly difficult question of whether cultural knowledge is organized in the same way as grammatical knowledge, anthropologists do have some ideas on how the language a particular people speak is related to other aspects of their sociocultural system. We focus on this topic in the rest of this chapter.

Language and Sociocultural Systems

How do the language and sociocultural system of a people mutually affect one another? Hardly anyone doubts that there is some kind of relationship between a language and other elements of the way of life of those who speak it. But what is the nature of this relationship?

On the one hand, the language of a people mirrors (reflects) their lifeway. People encode lexically (i.e., they name or label) some objects, qualities, and actions rather than others; they have specific ways of discussing the social relationships that are important to them; they may develop a specialized vocabulary or speech style used in religious ceremonies; and so on. How the sociocultural system of a people affects their language in these and other ways in one issue.

On the other hand, it is possible that language helps to create a people's sociocultural system, as well as mirroring it. For instance, the language people share might influence the way they perceive reality, and hence shape their world view.

In this section we consider both ideas: first, that the language a people speak reflects their way of life; and, second, that language is a creative force, shaping perceptions and views of natural and social reality.

■ *Language as a Mirror*

Many elements of a language reflect its speakers' way of life. For example, a complex lexicon develops around things that are especially important to some group of people, as we saw with the farmers' classification of livestock. This makes it easier for them to communicate effectively about the social relations, actions, natural phenomena, and other subjects that matter most to them.

A simple example of how vocabulary reflects peoples' needs to communicate about certain subjects is found among individuals of different subcultural, oc-cupational, and gender categories in North American society. Take automobile tools, for example. A professional mechanic can identify hundreds of kinds of tools; the Saturday-afternoon home mechanic can identify perhaps several dozen; and the rest of us don't know a ring compressor from a hub puller, or a compression tester from a feeler gauge. The same idea applies to color: all else equal, American women label more colors than do men, presumably because they more often discuss shades such as taupe, mauve, and lavender. Numerous other examples cold be cited to show that a language's lexicon responds to the needs of people to discuss certain topics easily.

But not all specialized vocabularies are developed entirely to meet an objective need of the members of some group to converse easily or precisely among themselves. Specialized vocabularies also serve as status markers for professions and other groups. Lawyers speak "legalese" only partly because they need to make fine distinctions between points of law that are obscure to the rest of us. Legalese is a secret—as well as a specialized—vocabulary. Entry into the select group of attorneys depends in part on mastery of the vocabulary with all its nuances. And of course it does not hurt the profession as a whole that the general population cannot understand bills of sale or many other contracts written by attorneys. Many of us feel compelled to pay for the specialized knowledge of an attorney to interpret important documents.

In a similar manner, we are familiar with "bureaucratese," a special vocabulary bureaucrats use to put us off (or down). Unfamiliar words are sometimes used to *avoid* communicating information, to obscure messages intentionally, to direct questioners to someone else, or simply to say go away. (But we shouldn't be too hard on bureaucrats, for, as we shall see, we all routinely use language for similar purposes.)

In sum, in a diverse society, groups often develop specialized speech to facilitate communication among themselves, to mark themselves off from the rest of us, to help achieve their private goals, and so on. What about differences *between* whole languages, spoken by members of *different* sociocultural systems? Similar ideas apply. To understand them, the concept of **semantic domain** is useful. A semantic domain is a set of words that belong to a more inclusive class. For example, *chair, table, ottoman,* and *china cabinet* belong to the semantic domain of "furniture." "Color" is another semantic domain, with members such as *violet, red,* and *yellow.*

Semantic domains typically have a hierarchical structure, meaning that they have several levels of inclusiveness. For instance, two colors the English language distinguishes can be further broken down:

Blue	Green
aqua	kelly
sky	mint
royal	forest
navy	avocado
teal	lime

We divide the semantic domain of color into specific colors (e.g., blue, green), each of which in turn is divided into "kinds of blue" and "kinds of green," and even into—for some of us—"shades of sky blue" or "tones of kelly green."

By now you can see where this discussion is headed: Different languages spoken by members of different sociocultural systems vary in the semantic domains they identify, in how finely they carve up these domains, and in how they make distinctions between different members of a domain. Some of these differences are rather obvious. For instance, the semantic domain of "fish" is unlikely to be as elaborate among desert dwellers as among coastal or riverine peoples. Tropical lowland peoples are not likely to have the semantic domain we call "snow" in their native language, whereas some Arctic peoples discuss it so much that they have an elaborate vocabulary to facilitate communication about snow conditions. Further, the degree to which some semantic domain has a multilevel hierarchical structure tends to depend on the importance of the objects or actions in peoples' lives: island, coastal, or riverine people dependent on fish are likely to have many categories and subcategories of aquatic life, fishing methods, and flood and tide stages, for instance. Can we go beyond such fairly obvious statements?

For some domains we can. There are some things or qualities that seem to be "natural domains," meaning that the differences between their members seem to be obvious to anyone. In fact, they seem to be inherent in the things themselves. We therefore would expect that people everywhere would carve up these domains in similar ways. For instance, color is an inherent (natural) quality of things, which can be measured by instruments that determine the wavelength of light reflected from an object. Surely anyone can recognize that blue and green are different colors, and surely this recognition is reflected in separate terms for the two

colors! Likewise, biological kinship is a natural relationship, in the sense that who an infant's parents are completely determines who will and will not be his or her closest genetic relatives. What human cannot recognize that his or her aunts and uncles are fundamentally different kinds of relatives than parents?

However, although blue and green are objectively different colors, and aunts are objectively different relatives from mothers, people are not obliged to recognize these differences and make them culturally significant. The semantic domains of color and relatives are in fact divided up differently by different cultures, and these divisions are not self-evident.

The domain of "relatives" or "kinfolk" is an excellent example of how members of different cultural traditions divide up an apparently natural domain according to different principles. Because we return to this subject in chapter 11, here we want only to show that different sociocultural systems do not in fact make the same distinctions between relatives as we do—that is, the way relatives are culturally classified is variable.

Consider the relatives that English-speaking people call *aunt*, *first cousin*, and *brother*. An aunt is a sister of your mother or your father; a first cousin is a child of any of your aunts and uncles; and a brother is a male child of your parents. These individuals are all biologically related to you differently, so "of course" you place them in different categories and call them by different terms.

But notice that other distinctions are possible that you do not recognize as distinctions and that are not reflected in the kinship lexicon of English. Your aunts are not related to you in the same way: one is the sister of your mother, one the sister of your father. Why not recognize this distinction between them by giving them different terms? Similarly, your first cousins could be subdivided into finer categories and given special terms, such as *child of my father's sister*, *child of my mother's brother*, and so on. And, since we distinguish most other categories of relatives by their gender (e.g., brother versus sister, aunt versus uncle), why does gender not matter for any of our cousins?

We know it is possible to divide up the domain of relatives differently because other sociocultural systems do not identify the same categories of relatives as speakers of English. People in many societies, for instance, call their mother's sister by one term and their father's sister by another term (although we collapse both into one term, *aunt*). It is also very common for a people to distinguish between the male children of their father's sister and their father's brother, calling the first by a term that we translate as "cousin," the second by the same term as they use for their own brother! (These various ways of carving up relatives, by the way, are not haphazard. Anthropologists have discovered that these terminological systems are related to other aspects of a people's way of life, as we discuss in chapter 11.) So the ways people divide up members (specific kinds of kin) of the seemingly "natural domain" of biological relatives is not the same the world over.

The same applies to color, our other example. Brent Berlin and Paul Kay found great diversity in color terms among various human populations. Some had only two terms for, roughly, "light" and "dark." Others had terms for other wavelengths of the color spectrum, which, however, do not always translate neatly as our words *red, blue, green,* and so forth. This does not mean, of course, that members of other cultural traditions are unable to see differences between what we call, for example, "green" and "yellow." It does mean that any differences they perceive are not linguistically encoded, presumably because speakers do not need to convey precise information about colors to hearers.

A fascinating, and unexpected, result of these investigations about differences in color lexicons is that color terminology seems to have a regular evolutionary development. New colors are incorporated into the color lexicon in the same order everywhere. If a language has terms for only two colors, they will be *light* and *dark.* If a language has only three colors, the third will be *red,* although the term does not correspond to our *red,* since it may also include our *orange* and *pink.* Languages that have four primary color terms add either *green* or *yellow.* Languages with five terms add either *green* or *yellow,* depending on which they already had. If there is a sixth term, it refers approximately to our *blue.* Our *brown* is the seventh term, assuming there is a seventh term in the language. Only a few languages have more than seven primary terms, and they always add *pink, orange,* and *purple.*

Other examples could be cited, but the overall point is clear. Cultures divide up the world differently, forming different categories and classifications of natural and social reality out of the objective properties of things. These differences are reflected in the language of the bearers of the culture.

■ *Is Language a Creator?*

There is another possible relation between a people's way of life and their language. As we have just seen, some elements of a language mirror the lifeway of its speakers. Is this relation also reversed? Does a language predispose its speakers to perceive the world in certain ways? Does language have a role in creating the system of knowledge we call culture?

Language could shape perceptions and world views both by its lexicon and by its syntax. Any language's lexicon assigns labels to only certain things, qualities, and actions. It is easy to see how this might encourage people to perceive the real world selectively. For instance, as we grow up, we learn that some plants are "trees." So we come to think of *tree* as a real thing, although of course there are so many kinds of trees that there is no necessary reason to collapse all this variety into a single label. But we might perceive the plants our language calls *trees* as more similar than do people who speak a language that makes finer distinctions between these plants.

As for syntax, it might force people to communicate about time, space, relations between individuals and between people and nature, and so forth in a certain kind of way. Potentially, this constraint on the way people must speak to be understood by others can shape their views of what the world is like.

The idea that language influences the perceptions and thought patterns of those who speak it, and thus conditions their world view, is known as the **Whorf-Sapir hypothesis,** after two anthropological linguists who proposed it. One of the most widely quoted of all anthropological passages is Edward Sapir's point, written in 1929:

> [Language] powerfully conditions all our thinking about social problems and processes. Human beings do not live in the objective world alone, nor alone in the world of social activity as ordinarily understood but are very much at the mercy of the particular language which has become the medium of expression for their society . . . . The fact of the matter is that the "real world" is to a large extent unconsciously built up on the language habits of the group . . . . The worlds in which different societies live are distinct worlds, not merely the same world with different labels attached. (Sapir 1964, 68–69)

Sapir and Benjamin Whorf believed that language helps define the world view of its speakers. It does so, in part, by providing labels for certain kinds of phenomena (things, qualities, and actions), which different languages define according to different criteria. Some phenomena are therefore made easier to think about than others. The attributes that define them as different from other similar things become more important than other attributes. So the lexicon of our language provides a filter that biases our perceptions. It digs grooves in which our thought patterns tend to roll along.

But the Whorf-Sapir hypothesis is more subtle than this. In the 1930s and 1940s, Whorf suggested that language conditions a people's conceptions of time and space. Whorf noted that English encourages its speakers to think about time in spatial metaphors (e.g., "a long time" and "a long distance"), although time cannot really be "long" or "short" in the same sense as distance. Also, English-speaking people talk about units of time using the same concepts with which we talk about numbers of objects (e.g., "four days" and "four apples"), although it is possible to see four objects at once, but not four units of time. Finally, English-speaking people classify events by when they occurred: those that have happened, those that are happening, and those that will happen.

Because they share a certain kind of language, however, the Native American Hopi must speak about time and events differently. With no tenses exactly equivalent to our past, present, and future, and no way to express time in terms of spatial metaphors, Hopi speak of events as continuously unfolding, rather than happening in so many days or weeks. Whorf argued that the Hopi language led the Hopi people into a different perception of the passage of time.

What shall we make of the Whorf-Saphir hypothesis? None of us as individuals creates the labels our language assigns to reality, nor do we create the way our grammar constrains the way we talk about time and space. We must adhere to certain rules if we are to be understood. Surely this necessity biases our perceptions to some degree. It is therefore likely that language does affect ways of perceiving, thinking about, classifying, and acting in the world. To some degree, language then does "create" views of reality. The question is, how much? More precisely, how important is language as opposed to other things that also influence perceptions and views of reality?

Although intriguing, the Whorf-Sapir hypothesis is not widely accepted, for several reasons. First, if a language greatly shapes the way its speakers perceive and think about the world, then we would expect a people's world view to change only at a rate roughly comparable to the rate at which their language changes. Yet there is no doubt that world views are capable of changing much more rapidly than language. How else can we explain the fact that the English language has changed little in the past 150 years compared to the dramatic alteration in the world views of most speakers of English? How else can we explain the spread of religious traditions such as Islam and Christianity out of their original linguistic homes among people with enormously diverse languages? (This is not to suggest, however, that these traditions have remained unchanged as they diffused.)

Second, if language strongly conditions perceptions, thought patterns, and entire world views, we should find that the speakers of languages that have a common ancestor show marked cultural similarities. More precisely, we would expect to find the cultural similarities between speakers of related languages to be consistently greater than the cultural similarities between speakers of languages that are less closely related. Sometimes we do find this; unfortunately, we often do not.

For these and other reasons the Whorf-Sapir hypothesis is not highly regarded today by most scholars. But research on this very intriguing idea is continuing, and future results may show some unexpected effects of language on perception, cognition, and world views.

The Social Uses of Speech

During enculturation, humans learn how to communicate and how to act appropriately in given social situations. They learn that different situations require different verbal and nonverbal behavior, for how one speaks and acts varies with whom one is addressing, who else is present, and the overall situation in which the interaction is occurring.

To speak appropriately, people must take the total context into account. First, they must know the various situations, or social scenes, of their sociocultural system: which are solemn, which are celebrations, which are formal and informal, which are argumentative, and so on. Cultural knowledge includes knowing how to alter one's total (including verbal) behavior to fit these situations. Second, individuals must recognize the kinds of interactions they

Speech can be used to emphasize the relative social rank of individuals. These two Columbian men seem to be social equals.

are expected to have with others towards whom they have particular relations: should they act lovingly, jokingly, contemptuously, or respectfully and deferentially towards someone else? Cultural knowledge thus also includes knowing how to act (including how to speak) toward others with whom an individual has relations of certain kinds.

These two elements—the particular situation and the specific individuals who are parties to the interaction—make up the *context* of verbal and non-verbal behavior. Enough linguists have become interested in such topics that a special field of study has been devoted to them: **sociolinguistics,** the study of how speech behavior is affected by the sociocultural system, especially by context.

How the speech of the parties to a social interaction reveals and reinforces the nature of their relationship is seen clearly by terms of address. In some parts of the United States, unless instructed otherwise, Americans usually address those of higher social rank with a respect term followed by the last name (e.g., Dr. Smith or Mr. Jones). Those with higher rank are more likely to address those with lower rank by their first name, or even by their last name used alone (e.g., "You were in charge of that, weren't you Smith?") This nonreciprocal use of address terms often not only expresses a social inequality; it also reinforces it each time the individuals address one another. When address terms are used reciprocally—when both individuals call each other by their first names, for example—their relation is likely to be more equal. "Call me by my first name" often carries a meaning beyond mere instruction.

Spanish-speaking people have a similar understanding with polite address terms such as *Don* or *Señora*. They also have to choose between two words for *you*: the formal (*usted*) versus informal (*tú*). *Tú* is used between occupants of certain statuses, such as between intimate friends and relatives and to address children. In parts of Latin America, the informal *tú* is also a marker of rank, used by landlords, officials, and some employers towards their tenants, subordinates, servants, and employees. Here the fact that a social subordinate uses *usted* with a higher ranking person, while the latter uses "*tú*," symbolizes and reinforces the social differences between them.

Speech style and habits depend on status and rank in other ways. For example, there used to be greater differences between the speech of men and women in North America than there are today. Because of their enculturated fear of being considered unladylike, women were less likely to use profanity, at least in public. Men likewise were expected to avoid profanity in the presence of women, to avoid offending the ladies. Certain words were (and to some extent still are) regarded as more appropriate for women's use than men's such as *charming, adorable,* and *lovely.* More emphasis was placed on women using "good grammar" than on men doing so. Even minor differences in sentence construction existed between the genders. Women were more likely to show uncertainty and desire for approval and permission. When her husband asked, "What time is dinner?", a wife often responded with, "Is six o'clock all right?" Linguist Robin Lakoff suggests that such "half-declarative" sentences indicate a lack of self-confidence and an unwillingness to state an opinion, which are related to the cultural value on women being (overtly) submissive to men. (Box 4.1 discusses gender bias in English).

Other societies exhibit customs in speech behavior with which most English-speaking people are unfamiliar. Here are a few examples:

■ Some languages accentuate the difference between the sexes far more than English does. In languages such as Gros Ventre (of the northeastern United States) and Yukaghir (of northeastern Asia) men and women pronounced certain phonemes differently, which led to differences in the pronunciation of the words in which these phonemes appeared. In Yana, an extinct language spoken by a people who formerly lived in northern California, many words had two pronunciations, one used by men and one

Box 4.1

GENDER IN THE ENGLISH LANGUAGE

lthough English does not accentuate the differences between males and females as much as some other languages, it is in some respects a male-biased language. This bias is seen—and heard—in sentences such as

Man is the only animal with language.

A customer can't write a check when he shops at that store.

There are man-eating sharks in the water.

The man on the move has no time for leisurely lunches.

In these examples the use of the masculine noun or pronoun implicitly excludes women, although, of course, each sentence is meant to include both sexes. The same applies to terms like *chairman, spokesman, policeman, busi-nessman,* and *statesman,* all of which are statuses women are equally capable of holding in modern society. And what about *manmade, man-hours, man-sized,* or *talking man to man?*

In other sentences, masculine terms or male-biased phrasing implicitly gives men more importance in a relationship:

I now pronounce you man and wife.

I don't work; I'm just a housewife.

You guys need to work harder. (to a mixed-sex gathering)

I'd like to introduce Mrs. Bill Jones.

Other terms make unnecessary distinctions between men and women involved in a similar career: *actor* versus *actress, waiter* versus *waitress.*

Feminists have proposed various ways for speakers of English to make their speech less sexist by using terms and phrases that do not perpetuate pejorative attitudes and stereotypes toward women. For example, some have proposed the invention of a new, gender-neutral pronoun to be used in sentences like "A person must watch what he is doing." *Heesh* or *heshe* could substitute for *he; hiser* or *hes* for *his;* and *herm* or *hehm* for *him.* Thus, we might someday hear in a classroom: "If only each student would do hiser reading for hermself, heesh would get a good grade." (These, by the way, were serious proposals.)

More realistically, each time a pronoun is required, we could use *he/she, him/her,* or *his/hers.* This would result in statements like "Every human normally learns the language of his/her community while he/she is growing up." Other feminists believe that we should use *he* and *she, him* and *her,* and *his* and *hers* interchangeably, which is the approach we often take in this book. Whether such proposals, even if widely or universally adopted, would have much effect on improving women's status or removing stereotypes about women is subject to debate. (Note, incidentally, that if the Whorf-Sapir hypothesis is correct, then eliminating the gender biases in English would have some impact.) However, the proposals certainly have symbolic value. Given our present speech habits, avoiding words and phrases that are implicitly biased against females requires a special effort that is usually noticed by readers and listeners. ∎

---

by women. In a few languages the vocabularies of men and women differ, with men using one word for something and women quite a different word. In a language spoken by the Carib Indians, who formerly inhabited the West Indies, the vocabularies of men and women differed so much that early European explorers claimed (mistakenly) that the sexes actually spoke different languages! In many languages, the speech of the sexes differs in other respects, such as the degree of forcefulness of their speech, the degree to which they avoid confrontational speech, and the tone of voice.

■ In parts of Polynesia and Micronesia there used to be a special language, sometimes called a *respect lan-guage,* with which common people had to address members of the noble class. On some islands this was much more than a difference in speech style, for completely different words were used. Often, there were severe penalties for commoners who erred in addressing a noble.

■ On the Indonesian island of Java, there are distinct "levels" of speech, involving different pronouns, suffixes, and words. A speaker must choose between the three levels—plain, more elegant, and most elegant. The speech style the parties to the interaction use depends on their relative rank and on their degree of familiarity with one another. In choosing which style to use with a specific person, a Javanese thus communicates more than the message encoded in the utterance. He or she also imparts information about the quality of their relationship. Accordingly, changes in the relationship between two individuals are accompanied by changes in speech style.

- In Japanese, a complicated set of rules (called *honorifics*) governs the degree of formality and politeness people normally use to show respect to those of higher social position. For instance, verbs and personal pronouns have several alternative forms that speakers must choose between in addressing others. The main determinant of which forms are used is the relative status of the parties. One form of the verb is used when the speaker is of higher status than the listener, another form when the two are of roughly equal status, and yet another when the speaker is a social inferior. Women, who to some extent even today are considered "beneath" men, would generally be obliged to address men with honorific verb forms that symbolically express the superiority of the addressee. The same applies to personal pronouns (*I, you*), different forms of which are used to reflect the relative status of the parties. In fact, when a social superior is addressing an inferior, he or she often does not use the pronoun *I* as a self-reference, but refers to his or her status relative to the person being addressed. For instance, a teacher says to a student, "Look at teacher" instead of "Look at me"; a father says to his son, "Listen to father" instead of "Listen to me"; and so forth. Reciprocally, one usually does not use the pronoun *you* with one of higher status, but replaces it with a term denoting the superior's social position. This yields sentences like: "What would teacher like me to do next?" and "Would father like me to visit?" Confused foreigners trying to learn the subtleties of Japanese speech etiquette are usually advised to use the honorific forms to avoid giving offense unintentionally. (Fortunately for the rest of us, most Japanese are tolerant of our inability to master the nuances of their honorifics!)
- All societies have customs of taboo, meaning that some behavior is prohibited for religious reasons or because it is culturally regarded as immoral, improper, or offensive. It is fairly common to find taboos applied to language: some words cannot be uttered by certain people. For instance, the Yąnomamö Indians of the Venezuelan Amazon forest have a custom known as *name taboo*. It is an insult to utter the names of important people and of deceased relatives in the presence of their living kinfolk. So

the Yąnomamö use names such as "toenail of sloth" or "whisker of howler monkey" for people, so that when the person dies they will not have to watch their language so closely. Other name taboos are enforced only against specific individuals. Among the Zulu of southern Africa, for example, a woman was once forbidden to use the name of her husband's father nor any of his brothers, under possible penalty of death.

Most modern societies have stringent word taboos prohibiting the use of certain kinds of profanity in newspapers, magazines, and radio and television. People are paid to guard against taboo violations—we call them *censors*. Curiously, many popular TV shows now leave no doubt about what goes on in bedrooms, but to say "screw"—much less the other word—is prohibited. Figurative ass kicking—violence—has long been portrayed on prime time. Yet to say "kick your ass" is tabooed.

So speech is influenced by social context, including the culturally defined situations in which it is used and the individuals who are engaged in conversation. But there is still more to speaking: it also is a strategy, or a behavioral means by which individuals get what they want out of others. It is, as social scientists say, part of our "presentation of self." By speaking in a certain way, we communicate the image of ourselves we want others to see.

In everyday life we want to present ourselves properly, meaning that we want someone else—a potential employer, a suitor, a pastor or priest, a co-worker, even a parent—to gain a favorable impression of us. Our speech habits, or our speech style, are an important part of our presentation of ourselves to others (as are the ways we dress, sit, stand, walk, comb our hair, and do many other things). Almost without knowing it, we adjust our speech style and mannerisms to fit the context by our use and avoidance of certain words, by our enunciation, by the degree of formality of our speech, by whether we try to hide or accentuate our regional accents or dialect, and so forth.

When we play this "language game," we attempt to use our speech habits to manipulate the ways others see us. Most politicians have mastered the art of creating favorable impressions of themselves through their public speeches. This is done, as we know, by telling particular audiences what they want to hear without at the same time alienating other audiences (i.e., voters) who are not present. We are often critical of our elected officials for this "wishy-washiness," but in fact we all use speech as a strategy to manipulate the way others perceive us.

We said early in this chapter that language is composed of arbitrary symbols that convey conventional meanings. We can now add that the act of speaking itself is symbolic in another way. Recall that any behavior (including speech habits such as word choice, overall style, conformity to cultural notions of proper syntax, mannerisms, and so on) has a symbolic component if it stands for something else. Our speech habits are symbolic in this sense. Like the clothes we wear, the foods we eat, and the cars we drive, the way we speak is part of the way we represent ourselves to others. Because we know that others will read meanings into our speech habits, we can adjust our style of speaking and to some extent control the implicit messages we communicate about ourselves. In other words, we change our speech habits from situation to situation, context to context, when it is to our advantage to do so.

Summary

Language is the single most important capability of humans that distinguishes us from other animals. Five properties of language make it different from other systems of communication: its multimedia potential; its reliance on the conventional, shared understanding of arbitrary symbols; the fact that it is composed of elements (sounds, words) that can be combined into different sequences that convey different meanings; the fact that its speakers regularly and unconsciously use these recombinable elements creatively to send an infinite number of messages; and the fact that it allows humans to communicate about things remote in time and space.

Grammar refers to the elements of language and the rules for how these elements can be combined to form an infinite number of meaningful sentences. Grammatical knowledge is enormously complex, yet it is both unconscious and intuitive. Linguists divide the study of language into several fields, including phonology, morphology, and syntax.

Phonology is the study of the sounds and sound patterns of language. The basic meaningful sounds are called *phonemes*. Languages differ in the phonemes they recognize as distinctive and significant. Only some of the sounds humans are able to make with their vocal tract are recognized by any given language. Qualities or features of sounds that the speakers of one language recognize as significant—that is, as making a difference in the meanings of words in which they appear—vary from language to language. Languages also vary in the way they use the pitch of the voice to convey meanings, as shown by tone languages.

Morphology studies meaningful sound sequences and the rules by which they are formed. Any sequence of phonemes that conveys a standardized meaning is a morpheme. Free morphemes can stand alone as meaningful sequences, whereas bound morphemes are not used alone but are attached to free morphemes during speech. When people learn a language, they learn its free and bound morphemes and their meanings. They also learn the rules by which bound morphemes can be attached to free morphemes.

Syntax refers to the unconscious rules that tell speakers how to combine words into meaningful sentences. Although languages vary in their syntax, most modern linguists believe that this variation is limited—that all languages are variations of a single basic design, or universal grammar, that underlies apparent diversity. Research on how children learn language seems to support this conclusion.

Language, like culture, is a shared and socially learned system of knowledge. Cultural anthropologists have turned to linguistics as a source of ideas and models that might have value in the description and analysis of culture. Cognitive anthropologists propose that cultural classifications of reality are built up and organized in the same way as language.

The sociocultural system of a people is related to their language. Some aspects of language, particularly lexicon, reflect the sociocultural importance of subjects, people, objects, and natural phenomena. The need to converse easily about some subject leads to the elaboration of semantic domains connected to the subject, as seen in the domain of color. In other domains, such as relatives, anthropologists have discovered surprising diversity in how various peoples divide kin into kinds and give them different labels according to different principles.

Some anthropologists have argued that the language a people speak predisposes them to see the world in a certain way by shaping their perceptions of reality. This idea, known as the *Whorf-Sapir hypothesis*, argues that the lexicon of a language influences perceptions by leading its speakers to filter out certain objective properties of reality in favor of other properties. Syntax can also affect perception, and even world view, by forcing people to talk about time and space in a certain way if they are to be understood. The Whorf-Sapir hypothesis is not highly regarded by most modern scholars, although there has been a recent revival of interest in it.

Sociolinguistics is the study of how speech is influenced by sociocultural factors, including culturally defined contexts and situations, the goals of the speaker, the presence of other parties, and so forth. Speech can be used in subtle ways to mark differences in rank and status, as between ethnic groups, classes, and males and females. Because it is part of the way we present ourselves to others, control of the way we speak is one way we influence how others perceive us. Speech, then, is often part of our strategy for getting what we want out of others.

Key Terms

multimedia potential	morphology
arbitrariness (conventionality)	phonemes
	tone languages
lexicon	morpheme
syntax	free morpheme
recombinable elements	bound morpheme
productivity	universal grammar
displacement	cognitive anthropologists (ethnoscientists)
grammar	
dialects	
Whorf-Sapir hypothesis	semantic domain
phonology	sociolinguistics

Suggested Readings

■ Berlin, Brent, and Paul Kay. *Basic Color Terms—Their University and Evolution*. Berkeley, Calif.: University of California Press, 1969.
Summary of empirical cross-cultural studies on the semantic domain of color.

■ Escholz, Paul, Alfred Rosa, and Virginia Clark, eds. *Language Awareness*. New York: St. Martin's Press, 1982.
Thirty-six short articles dealing with various elements of English-language use. Contains sections on political speech, advertising language, jargon, prejudice, and taboos.

■ Farb, Peter. *Word Play*. New York: Knopf, 1974.
Readable, enjoyable introduction to anthropological linguistics.

■ Frank, Francine, and Frank Anshen. *Language and the Sexes*. Albany, N.Y.: SUNY Press, 1983.
How linguistic patterns and speech reflect and contribute to sexist attitudes. Contains an appendix on nonsexist language for speech and writing.

■ Fromkin, Victoria, and Robert Rodman. *An Introduction to Language*. New York: CBS College Publishing, 1983.
Excellent textbook, thorough in its coverage, readily understandable, with many excellent examples.

■ Hickerson, Nancy Parrot. *Linguistic Anthropology*. New York: Holt, Rinehart and Winston, 1980.
Textbook on anthropological linguistics.

■ Hymes, Dell, ed. *Language in Culture and Society: A Reader in Linguistics and Anthropology*. New York: Harper & Row, 1964.
Nearly seventy articles, many of them classics, on the subject of language and culture and the social uses of language.

■ Trudgill, Peter. *Sociolinguistics: An Introduction to Language and Society*. Middlesex, England: Penguin, 1983.
Excellent short book that summarizes sociolinguistic research on distinctions of class, ethnicity, and gender. Also has chapters on how speech varies with context and on the use of speech in everyday social interaction.

Part Two

THEORIES AND METHODS OF CULTURAL ANTHROPOLOGY

ny discipline asks certain kinds of questions about its subject matter. During the century of its existence as a separate field of study, the kinds of questions asked by anthropology have changed somewhat, but the answers different scholars have offered for these questions have changed much more dramatically. One goal of this part (chapter 5) is to trace the history of these answers, to show our readers how anthropological thinking about humanity has altered. This process is always useful, for many popular ideas about humanity have long been abandoned as inadequate by anthropologists.

Just as scholars ask certain questions, so do they develop a set of methods that they feel allow them to investigate these questions. Most nineteenth-century anthropologists sat in their offices and put together information about preindustrial peoples supplied by travelers, missionaries, colonial officials, and various ne'er-do-wells. Modern anthropologists generally conduct fieldwork to acquire their information about particular peoples. To analyze human lifeways comparatively, a sophisticated set of cross-cultural methods have been developed. Our second goal in this part (chapter 6) is to describe some of the methods used by modern ethnographers and ethnologists and to discuss some of the problems they face.

■ (Facing page) *Cultural anthropologists acquire most of their information about other peoples from first-hand fieldwork. Shown here is Napoleon Chagnon, working among the Yanomamö.*

Chapter 5

THE DEVELOPMENT OF ANTHROPOLOGICAL THOUGHT

Contents

■ (Above) *This famous anthropologist, the late Margaret Mead, was a student of Franz Boas, an early twentieth Century anthropologist who influenced modern thinking.*

The way anthropologists approach the study of humanity has undergone many changes since the discipline originated in the nineteenth century. Some ideas held by most scholars a century ago have been discarded today; others are still with us. In this chapter, we discuss some of the important scholars and schools of thought that shaped the way modern anthropologists approach their studies. For each approach, we emphasize its assumptions, its basic questions, its errors, and its contributions to the theoretical ideas of modern anthropology.

Theoretical Orientations and Questions

We shall use the term *theory* in this and future chapters, but be aware that this term is used rather loosely in the social sciences. In the physical sciences, a theory is a precise (often mathematical) statement about how some kinds of phenomena are related to other kinds of phenomena. For example, many modern physicists are searching for a single unified theory that will show the relationships between all the physical elements of nature—from the inside of atoms to the inside of stars. Genuine theories are constructed in such a way that experimentation can determine with a high degree of confidence whether phenomena are in fact related in the way the theory specifies.

In the social sciences, theories are rarely stated with mathematical precision and are generally not tested through experimentation. For these and other reasons, we prefer the more encompassing phrase *theoretical orientation* to the term *theory*. A theoretical orientation refers to the questions asked and to the concepts, assumptions, and methods used by a scholar or school of thought—more like an "approach" or a "way of thinking" about humankind than like the physicist's theory. Theoretical orientations guide research by asking questions and suggesting ways to answer them, but they cannot be shown to be right or wrong by seeing how well they "fit the facts." Rather, they are judged by their usefulness: Do they ask fruitful questions? Do their methods give reliable results? Do their concepts and assumptions take us very far in understanding humanity and specific sociocultural systems?

A given theoretical orientation suggests that some elements of human lifeways are more important than others, and so scholars who work from different orientations often focus on completely different subjects, as we shall see.

To focus our presentation of the major theoretical orientations of anthropology, we address three questions that have interested important thinkers.

■ Some anthropologists believe that the explanation of sociocultural differences and similarities is the major theoretical goal of their discipline. As documented in part 3, human lifeways vary geographically—they differ from place to place. They also vary temporally—they change over time. Many anthropologists want to explain these spatial and temporal differences found among humanity. Underlying this variability are certain common features, which also interest us. These similarities presumably result partly from humanity's common biological nature. They also exist because of the common problems faced by humans everywhere: wresting a living from nature; developing orderly social relations with one another; and establishing a system of cultural knowledge that guides behavior, allows communication, provides a meaningful and satisfying world view, and so forth. The first question, then, is How can we explain the differences and similarities in human ways of life?

■ Most anthropologists also are interested in another, related, theoretical problem: How are the various aspects of the way of life of a people related to one another? How do the many subsystems of an entire sociocultural system fit together and affect one another? For example, some anthropologists argue that the economic subsystem has great causal impact on other subsystems, affecting family life and kinship, gender roles, politics, religious beliefs, world views, and so on.

■ Finally, most theorists have something to say about the relationship between individuals and their sociocultural systems. Some give primacy to the biological and psychological needs of individuals, arguing that any sociocultural system exists primarily to fulfill these needs. Other scholars hold that the needs and wants of individuals are influenced, or even largely determined, by the overall nature of the sociocultural system, which molds the desires, thoughts, and responses of individuals. How do individuals and sociocultural systems affect one another?

Not all the scholars we discuss attempted to answer all three basic questions, but most did have something to say about one or more of these issues. It will be useful to keep them in mind throughout this chapter.

Nineteenth-Century Origins

As a separate field of scholarly study, anthropology arose in the nineteenth century. There is little point in trying to pin down exactly when and where anthropology originated. We can learn more (and be somewhat less bored!) by showing why interest in other ways of life became especially strong in the 1800s.

Early in the nineteenth century, at several places in England and France, crude axelike stone tools were found in association with extinct mammals. Influenced by the Judeo-Christian world view, many claimed that Satan had buried the stones in the earth to cause confusion and doubt. But others concluded (correctly) that the early, "prehistoric" inhabitants of Europe had once used stone tools and lived at the same time as extinct animals. For them, the problem was interpreting the significance of the remains for human history. How, and how long ago, did these ancient people live?

Meanwhile, several centuries worth of written records had accumulated about the strange ways of life of people of other lands. Beginning in the 1500s, Europeans increasingly came into contact with folk who differed from themselves in physical appearance, language, beliefs, and habits. European explorers, priests, fortune hunters, scientists, and other travelers reported on the customs and beliefs found among the inhabitants of the Americas, Africa, Asia, and the Pacific Islands. Who were these people (if, in fact, they were people at all)? How could they believe such fantastic things and engage in such "savage" practices? How were they related to Europeans and other "civilized" people? For that matter, how were they related to one another?

Answers to such questions varied, but again most were within the range of permissible interpretations of the Bible. Some intellectuals concluded that "natives" were so very different from Europeans that God must have made them separately from civilized man, during some creation event not mentioned in Genesis, and placed them on other continents. Others argued that they did in fact come from the same ancestor as ourselves. But then the problem was explaining (within the biblical world view of possible events) how they became separated from us and how they came to

■ In part, anthropology arose out of curiosity about the residents of other continents that Europeans encountered in the fifteenth through the nineteenth century. The Englishman James Cook explored the northwest coast of North America in the late 1700s. The caption on this lithograph from his voyage reads: "A Savage of Prince Williams Sound on the North West Coast of America."

have such depraved customs and false beliefs. Were they modern-day remnants of one of Israel's lost tribes? Could they be descendants of Noah's son Ham?

Until the early 1800s the dominant interpretation of these exotic peoples was that they had fallen from a previous higher state of civilization. Living without knowledge of the Creator, and ignorant of the true path to salvation, their ancestors had fallen under the influence of Satan. (Today this notion is known as *degenerationism*—the idea that contemporary "primitives" are descendants of peoples who had once been more advanced, but lost knowledge of the teachings of God, knowledge that all of humankind once possessed.) Most intellectuals who bothered to wonder about the "savage" residents of other continents agreed with this interpretation.

Thus, the customs and beliefs of other peoples were interpreted in terms of the biblical account of human history. Two elements of this account lost credibility among most scientists in the nineteenth century. One was the age of the earth, which generally was believed to be only a few thousand years old. New geological theories demolished this estimate and established that the earth has existed for many millions of years. The other was the belief that divine creation accounted for all life on earth. A new biological theory showed how the history and diversity of life were caused by naturalistic, rather than supernaturalistic, forces. Both these changes in the way scientists interpreted the world contributed to the beginnings and growth of anthropology.

First, let us consider geology. In 1795, James Hutton proposed that the physical features of the earth were formed by gradual processes, such as erosion of rock caused by winds and waves, and slow deposition of sediments in the bottom of ancient seas and lakes. These natural forces operated so slowly that they were scarcely noticeable in a human lifetime, but over many thousands of years their effects accumulated. Large-scale geological features result from the actions over very long time spans of imperceptible natural processes; thus, major changes result from the cumulative effects of a multitude of minor changes. In the 1830s, Charles Lyell popularized this **uniformitarian theory.** He amassed evidence that the processes responsible for the formation of the earth occur at steady ("uniform") and gradual rates. If uniformitarianism was correct, this meant that the earth must be incredibly old—millions of years rather than the few thousands of years previously believed.

These ideas about the history of the earth influenced the ideas of biologist Charles Darwin about the history of life. In turn, Darwin's ideas about the history of life influenced, and continue to influence, anthropology's ideas about humanity.

Darwin's *Origin of Species* appeared in 1859. Darwin presented evidence that natural species have changed, or "evolved," over long time spans. He also argued that radically new forms of life develop out of existing species. The reason we do not observe this transformation of one life form into another is simply that human lifetimes are too short for the slow changes to be perceptible to our senses. Darwin gave much evidence in support of this view of life's history. One form of evidence is the great diversity of domesticated animals and plants produced by intentional breeding. In each generation, breeders select for breeding those individual animals and plants that have the characteristics their human masters find desirable. Given enough time, new varieties are produced by this selection,

■ *Charles Darwin's theory of evolution influenced anthropology as well as biology. It suggested to some that preindustrial lifeways could be arranged into a sequence of progressive stages.*

although in each generation the differences are scarcely noticeable.

Darwin proposed a mechanism by which these changes occur. He noted that organisms compete with one another over space, mates, food, and other things needed for survival and reproduction. Those individuals who are most successful in this competition have the greatest chance of reproducing. The characteristics that give them greater success are passed along to their offspring. In each generation organisms encounter "natural" conditions that "select" for those individuals best able to compete, avoid being eaten, resist diseases and parasites, find and hold mates, and so on. Darwin called this process **natural selection.** He realized that it would favor the survival and reproduction of those organisms that are "most fit," or better adapted to the conditions of their environments.

Because of natural selection, each generation is slightly different from the previous generation. Over hundreds or thousands of generations, one form of life evolves into one or more other forms. The present diversity of life is explained partly by the fact that environments vary from place to place and time to time. For example, some individual members of a species periodically move into new environments, where their offspring encounter new conditions that make new characteristics useful. They gradually change into new varieties and, eventually, into new species. Two or more new forms of life can arise out of a single "parent" species by this process of adaptation.

Darwin's theory had many implications for the study of humanity (aside from the obvious one—that humanity itself had evolved out of other life forms). First, it was a theory that *explained* the diversity of species by a purely natural process. Like the movements of the moon, the history of life was subject to natural laws. No creation or supernatural intervention was required to account for the origins of species. This is, of course, the main reason that Darwin's theory was (and is) so strongly resisted by many fundamentalist religious leaders.

In addition, Darwin's ideas seemed to many to support the idea of overall progress in the history of life. This progress resulted mainly from competition. It came from the struggle for survival, in which "higher," "more complex" forms appeared successively. (Note, however, that many modern biologists prefer to speak merely of *diversification* or *change,* terms that carry fewer value judgments than *progress*.) In the fossil record, it was possible to see complex forms evolving out of simpler forms, to observe the evolutionary "stages" through which present-day organisms changed into their modern forms.

Most important to the development of anthropological thought, evolution provided a concept that suggested how the "natives" of other continents were related to one another, to the early residents of Europe who left behind those mysterious artifacts, and to Western civilization itself. The answer seemed to be that the prehistoric residents of Europe who made stone tools had not progressed to our level of technological, social, and moral advancement. They were still living in the "early stages" of evolution. What were these stages like? What were the customs and beliefs of these extinct people? It was impossible to know very much about them from the tools buried in the earth, for in those days scientists could infer little about the religion, marriage, and so forth of long-dead peoples from artifacts alone.

But there was a way to find out more about how ancient humans lived: by studying the customs and beliefs of those curious Indians, Africans, Polynesians, and other "primitives," who still retained many characteristics of the early stages of humankind's evolution. The thinking at the time was as follows: We can use the reports on these people to reconstruct the stages through which our own civilization passed in its progress toward the pinnacle of human achievement, that is, nineteenth-century Western civilization. To do so, we need to study these people scientifically, using our knowledge of them to advance our understanding of our own past. They are not "degenerated" folk whose barbaric customs prove that they have come under the iron grip of the Devil. They are, rather, merely "undeveloped"—their minds have not yet attained the level of scientific understanding of the world, their morals and manners remain rude, and so forth. By comparing them to one another and to Western civilization, we can reconstruct the sequence of stages through which our own civilization passed.

Such is the intellectual climate that gave rise to anthropology. To trace the development of humankind, scholars felt they had to study the nearest thing they could get to the ancient ancestors of civilization—namely, surviving "primitive" ways of life. Anthropology had its beginnings as the discipline that described and explained the sequence of stages through which humanity progressed along its long road to civilization.

The theory that nineteenth-century anthropologists developed to account for sociocultural development is known as **unilineal evolution.** Unilineal evolutionists believed that all human ways of life pass through a similar sequence of stages, or grades, as they evolve. These stages explained why various peoples around the world differ in their ways of life: different peoples are representative of different grades of development. Stages also accounted for why some customs and beliefs were scattered around the world among people who could not have had any contact with one another: regardless of their location in space, two or more peoples with similar lifeways had developed up to the same stage. Favored names for the stages were savagery, barbarism, and civilization.

So if we want to know why the Iroquois of North America had different habits from the native peoples of Australia, the answer, according to unilineal evolutionists, is that the Australians were arrested in their development at the stage of savagery, whereas the Iroquois had progressed into barbarism. If we want to find out how the earliest humans lived, we should study the surviving representatives of the stage of savagery. If we want to know what the immediate ancestors of civilized folk were like, we must examine the representatives of barbarism who have persisted into modern times.

Unilineal evolutionists differed in the criteria they used to define the stages of progress. One influential scheme was that of Lewis Henry Morgan, a lawyer from New York State. In *Ancient Society*, published in 1877, Morgan identified seven stages:

I. Lower Savagery
II. Middle Savagery
III. Upper Savagery
IV. Lower Barbarism
V. Middle Barbarism
VI. Upper Barbarism
VII. Civilization

Morgan defined these stages by what he called "inventions and discoveries" (today we would call them 'technological and economic innovations'). For example, Middle Savages had fire but lacked the bow and arrow, Upper Savages had invented the bow and arrow but still lacked pottery, Lower Barbarians had discovered pottery but did not know about the domestication of animals and plants, Middle Barbarians kept animals and grew their own food but had no knowledge of smelting metals, and Upper Barbarians had advanced enough to use iron but had no alphabet and hence no writing. Only the representatives of the final stage, Civilization, were literate.

Generally, unilineal evolutionists defined their stages on the basis of relative complexity. Just as the evolution of forms of life proceeded in orderly fashion from relatively simple to increasingly complex, so did the evolution of sociocultural forms. The stages could be ranked in an orderly sequence, with the simplest stages at the bottom and the most complex at the top. Various peoples then could be fitted into the sequence, as appropriate to their relative level of progress.

Unilineal evolutionists believed they had "discovered" the stages through which sociocultural systems develop. They did so by comparing the reports on primitive peoples around the world written by explorers, missionaries, colonial administrators, traders, and other untrained and frequently biased observers. By comparing and contrasting these accounts, they decided whether the customs and beliefs of one people were more or less complex than those of another people, and hence whether people A belonged to a higher stage than people B. Later scholars correctly objected to the ethnocentrism of this method. But the

unilineal evolutionists did recognize that human ways of life had to be compared if any "laws of progress" were to be discovered. As discussed in chapter 1, this comparative perspective on humanity became an enduring hallmark of anthropological thought.

Many unilineal evolutionists were unclear about whether those humans who still lived in the lower stages differed psychologically from civilized peoples. Was their progress arrested because their reasoning powers were inferior to our own? At least some scholars claimed that Savages and Barbarians were as capable of rational thought as ourselves, but their cultures were not developed enough to free their minds from erroneous logic. At birth, all peoples possess the same mental capacities and potentials; it is the degree of progress of their sociocultural system that determines how well they will reason. This idea of *psychic unity*—the doctrine that the human mind works the same way everywhere—is still an assumption of many sociocultural anthropologists.

The unilineal evolutionists felt that different people are at different levels of development because some peoples' ways of life have changed, whereas others' have altered little over many centuries. What made some ways of life change at faster rates than others? What is the "engine" that powers progress? Unilineal evolutionists were unclear about this. Morgan seemed to believe that technological and economic discoveries provided the impetus for progress into a higher stage. And once a new technology was invented, other aspects of a peoples' way of life had to undergo change as well. For example, some Lower Barbarians developed into Middle Barbarians once they learned to grow crops. This discovery led to progress in their property, institutions, family and marriage relations, and systems of government. So as new inventions and discoveries occur, other aspects of a sociocultural system are "pulled" into a new stage of progress as well. Notice that this notion implies a holistic perspective: things do not change piecemeal, but changes in one element lead to changes in other elements. Morgan realized that sociocultural systems are *integrated*, as we would say today.

Other scholars believed that progress occurred mainly because people gradually improved their abilities to reason from evidence. From long experience a few peoples managed to rid their minds of erroneous beliefs, and their improved ability to think clearly propelled them into a new stage. For example, in *Primitive Cul-*

ture, published in 1871, E. B. Tylor investigated the origins and development of religion. He proposed that religion had passed through three stages. The earliest was *animism*, defined as the belief that the world is populated by spiritual beings such as ghosts, souls, and demons. How can we explain the origins of such beliefs?

Tylor believed that people everywhere sought explanations for things and events. Two questions puzzled primitive peoples: (1) What is the difference between a live body and a dead one? (2) What is the origin of things seen in dreams, trances, and visions? Primitive peoples reasoned (falsely but nonetheless logically) that (1) living people have a spiritual essence—a soul—that leaves the body and thus causes death, and (2) the things people see in their dreams and fantasies are real, not the products of their imaginations. Souls must live on after death, since people sometimes see dead people in dreams and visions. Eventually, early peoples viewed the whole world as inhabited by supernatural beings. Later, some of the beings became elevated to a higher position than others, to become gods of the sun, moon, sky, earth, and so forth. The next stage of religion—*polytheism*—was thus born. Finally, one god acquired dominance over all the others; the others became "false gods," and the final stage—*monotheism*, Westerners' belief—came into existence. Religion thus originated from intellectual puzzlement, and it evolved as people gradually learned to reason correctly from evidence, according to Tylor.

From today's perspective the unilineal evolutionists were mistaken about many things. But they did make several enduring contributions to anthropological thought. They helped to establish two important perspectives of anthropology: holism and comparativism. (Relativism—the third hallmark of anthropology—did not come into vogue until the early twentieth century.) Unilineal evolutionists also had great faith that the application of scientific methods and reasoning would lead to the discovery of natural laws that govern humanity's development. The "history of mankind is part and parcel of the history of nature, . . . our thoughts, wills, and actions accord with laws as definite as those which govern the motion of waves, the combinations of acids and bases, and the growth of plants and animals," wrote E. B. Tylor (1871, 2). Many later anthropologists were not so sure about the existence of "laws of culture"; but the search for general causes of sociocultural systems, and for lawlike regularity in sociocultural change, remains a strong current in much modern anthropological research.

Diffusionism (ca. 1900–1930)

The unilineal evolutionists described many similarities between peoples who lived in widely scattered regions of the earth. For example, numerous societies from various continents were reported to practice worship of the sun. Why should tribes living far away from one another share such striking similarities in customs? There seemed to be two alternative answers. First, the custom had spread from one place to another through either movement of or contact between peoples. Migration or **diffusion** (the spread of customs and beliefs through contact between peoples and subsequent imitation of one people by another) thus might account for the widespread distribution of some sociocultural element. Second, the various peoples that practice the custom had "thought it up" independently, on their own. This second alternative, called **independent invention,** is a possibility because of the assumed psychic unity of humanity. Given that human minds everywhere work the same way, and that like minds must often encounter similar circumstances and problems, then naturally the same customs and solutions will occur again and again among assorted peoples who have never had contact with one another. If similar sociocultural elements occurred among widely scattered peoples, then unilineal evolutionists generally explained the similarities as due to independent invention rather than diffusion.

Around the turn of the century, many scholars in Europe doubted that people—at least "primitive people"—were sufficiently innovative to have independently invented most of their own customs. Instead, they argued that most sociocultural "traits" (as they came to be known) originated among only a few societies, from whence they diffused outward to less innovative peoples. For instance, in this view if you wish to explain why the Crow have clans, you must consider the history of their contact with other Indians from whom they "borrowed" the idea of clans. This meant also that most similarities between peoples resulted from diffusion, rather than from independent invention. These scholars became known as **diffusionists.**

One school of diffusionism arose in Germany around 1890. German diffusionists believed that most of the traits of assorted primitive peoples originated in only a few parts of the world and then spread outward from these geographic centers through diffusion and migration. In England in the early twentieth century, W. R.

■ *On the left is an early Egyptian stepped pyramid. On the right is a similar-looking "pyramid" from Palenque, of the Maya civilization of Mexico. On the basis of such apparent similarities, some diffusionists mistakenly believed that "higher" architectural forms, and indeed all of civilization, had diffused from Egypt to the rest of the world.*

Rivers and Elliot Smith held that most of the "higher," "advanced" elements of human lifeways arose in ancient Egypt. They were most impressed by the fact that architectural styles and megalithic constructions greatly resembling the Egyptian pyramids also occurred among certain North American Indians, such as the Maya and Aztec civilizations of Central America. It seemed to them unlikely that the Indians discovered such advanced architectural skills on their own. They never satisfactorily solved the problem of how the Egyptians managed to cross the Atlantic Ocean to plant the idea of pyramids into the "less-developed minds" of the American Indians!

Although it is well established that sociocultural elements are transmitted from place to place, diffusionism leaves numerous questions unanswered. First, examples abound of peoples who have been in contact with one another for decades or even centuries, yet each people often retain their own distinctive way of life. Obviously, diffusion is not an inevitable result of contact between societies. Under what conditions will a people adopt elements of the sociocultural system of another people with whom they have been in contact? Little attention was given to this very fundamental question by the diffusionists.

Second, diffusionists made little effort to account for why traits arose in the first place. Even granting that diffusion accounts for the present geographic distribution of a trait, its origination among a particular people at a particular time still must be explained.

Third, there is a subtle kind of cultural prejudice, or even racism, in the diffusionist assumption that there are human populations who acquired the bulk of their "higher" customs from more "advanced" peoples. The evidence is overwhelming that many of the world's people "progressed" into higher "stages"—whatever those terms may mean—whenever conditions were ripe, quite without the help of ancient Egyptians or any other higher civilizations. Yet even today diffusionist ideas are very much alive in the popular writings of Thor Heyerdahl and Eric Van Daniken, who trace those elements of "primitive" sociocultural systems that they regard as "developed" back to ancient Egypt or ancient astronauts.

Historical Particularism (ca. 1900–1940)

In the early twentieth century, another approach developed in the United States. Known as **historical particularism,** it arose as a reaction to the unilineal evolutionary sequences of the late 1800s. Historical particularism assumes that each way of life is the product of the many things that affected it in the past. Because each people have their own "particular history," every way of life is unique.

Such an emphasis on the differences between peoples has two implications. First, the search for general laws that explain sociocultural systems and why they change may be futile. If each lifeway is unique, how can we generalize? How, in fact, can we even compare them? Second, we must make every effort to free ourselves from our own culture's moral standards and assumptions when we study another way of life. This is because these assumptions and standards come from our own unique history and therefore may not apply elsewhere in the human world. We must therefore study each way of life on its own terms, rather than imposing our culture's judgments (e.g., "progress") upon it; that is, we must adopt a *relativistic* perspective toward other ways of life.

More than anyone else, American anthropologist Franz Boas formulated this approach. Around the turn of the century Boas concluded that the developmental sequences of the unilineal evolutionists were ethnocentric, speculative, and based on unproven assumptions. Let's look briefly at his objections and at the alternative he offered.

As we have seen, unilineal evolutionists defined their stages on the basis of relative complexity. But what does "complex" mean? We *might* agree that some peoples possess simpler tools than others: propelling a projectile (spear) with human arms may be simpler than with a bow (arrow), which in turn is simpler than with barrels and gunpowder (bullets). But what do we mean by "simple" in the context of religious beliefs? In what respect is animism "simpler" than monotheism? The same applies to many other aspects of human life: What does it mean to claim that one marriage or family form, or one way of holding property, is more complex than another? Boas realized that these things are merely different from people to people. One is not more simple, nor does one represent "progress" over the other, at least by any objective criterion.

If there is no objective way to judge the relative complexity of institutions, then how did the unilineal evolutionists develop their stages? Boas saw that the stages were defined using ethnocentric assumptions. Take our own marriage form, for instance: one woman married to one man who is not her close relative. Call this marriage "complex." Imagine its opposite: several women married to several men, with all the marital partners being close relatives. Call this marriage "simple." Then search through reports on hundreds of primitive peoples, looking for marriage forms that fall somewhere between the forms labeled simple and complex: e.g., one woman married to several men who are brothers. Arrange the intermediate forms into a sequence of stages, in order of how closely they resemble our own. You then have defined "grades of progress" and have assigned particular peoples to one or another grade.

But these grades exist only on paper. Boas saw that the unilineal evolutionists had not "discovered" developmental stages; they had made them up. Indeed, only by assuming that our own marriage form is the end point of evolution can the stages be ranked in order of increasing complexity. In other words, ethnocentric assumptions underlaid the arranging of ways of life into a sequence of progress. If the stages themselves are invalid, then obviously the notion that all cultures pass through them on their road to civilization is invalid as well. Sociocultural evolution therefore is not unilineal. Lifeways change along many narrow paths, not one wide road. Further, the direction in which any one lifeway changes depends on its own characteristics and on the external influences that affect it.

Boas also felt that the unilineal evolutionists were much too speculative in their theorizing. For example, since no one had ever observed one marriage form evolving into another, it was certainly sheer speculation to claim that one could arrange all marriage forms into a sequence of development. Boas believed that anthropologists must rid themselves of all speculative schemes of progress, for only by doing so can they rid their minds of preconceived ideas and assumptions.

Accompanying Boas' call for "less speculation" was his demand for "more facts." One reason the unilineal evolutionists had been led astray was that they had little firsthand knowledge of the peoples they so readily placed into the slots of their theory. They had only read reports written by other observers, who themselves were mostly untrained and ethnocentric. (One notable exception to this generalization is Lewis Henry Morgan, whose ethnography of the Iroquois is still an important source of information on these people.) Boas was scornful of such "armchair theorizing." He felt that to understand another way of life one must have the familiarity that can only come with long personal experience with it. Therefore, Boas contended that anthropologists need to leave their armchairs and immerse themselves in the direct observation of other societies. They need to do fieldwork among a people, to experience their customs and understand their beliefs from an insider's perspective, before engaging in idle speculation about "how all cultures develop."

Two benefits would follow from more firsthand experience with other cultural traditions. First, "primitive cultures" were already disappearing at a rapid rate (especially in North America, where Boas did his own work). Boas believed it was the duty of anthropology to record their traditional ways of life before they were

PEOPLES OF
SUB-SAHARAN AFRICA

The peoples of sub-Saharan Africa were historically divided into five major groupings: Black Africans, pygmies, Khoisans, The Peoples of the Horn, and Malagasy.

BLACK AFRICANS   Although highly diverse, Black Africa may be divided into two broad groupings based on linguistic relationships: Niger-Congo peoples and Nilo-Saharan peoples.

The hundreds of related languages spoken by Niger-Congo peoples are subdivided into seven linguistic subfamilies, of which Bantu is the most widespread. Originally occupying only West Africa, around A.D. 100 speakers of the Bantu subfamily began to expand to the southeast, displacing or absorbing indigenous peoples. By the seventeenth century Bantu speakers had reached the southern coast, and they occupied most of sub-Saharan Africa by the time of European contact. Predominantly settled village farmers, they cultivated rice, sorghum, and millet and herded cattle. Divided into hundreds of distinct polities, their political organization ranged from egalitarian tribes to multiethnic empires. Although most practiced unique religions many northern and eastern Niger-Congo peoples converted to Islam.

Nilo-Saharan peoples occupied most of the arid grasslands of north-central and eastern Africa, from Chad to the Sudan and Tanzania. Most were pastoralists, subsisting mainly from their herds of cattle and other livestock and living in scattered, seasonally nomadic camps. Most Nilotic peoples were politically organized as tribes, with cattle the focus of much of their ceremonial as well as secular lives.

PYGMIES Physically as well as historically distinctive, the pygmies were the original inhabitants of the tropical forests of the Congo Basin. Most of these remarkable jungle foragers were displaced by the Bantu expansion. Many bands attached themselves to Bantu village farmers, with whom they exchanged game and other forest products for produce and iron tools.

KHOISANS The Khoisan peoples (formerly pejoratively called *Bushmen* and *Hottentots*) are linguistically and physically distinct from other Africans. Formerly living by hunting and gathering, at one time they occupied most of the grasslands, savannahs, and deserts of eastern and southern Africa. Displaced by the expansionist Bantu, by the time of European contact Khoisan groups survived mainly in the most arid regions of southern Africa. Although some Khoisan peoples adopted cattle from the Bantu, most remained foragers into the twentieth century.

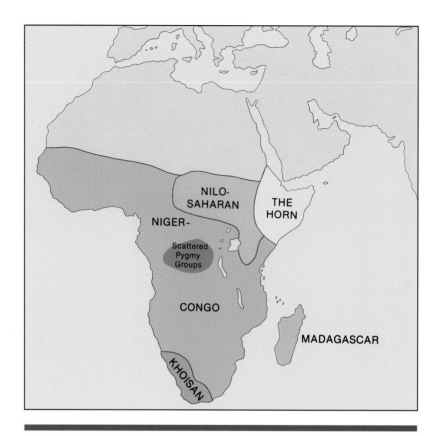

THE PEOPLES OF THE HORN

The Horn of Africa includes essentially the modern countries of Ethiopia and Somalia. Here sub-Saharan Africa and the Middle East greatly overlap, physically, linguistically, and socioculturally. Most languages were Afro-Asiatic, the large linguistic grouping that also includes Hebrew and Arabic. Almost half of Horn peoples were Ethiopean Orthodox (a variety of Coptic christianity). Moslem groups were equally numerous. A small group of Ethiopian Jews (Bete Israel) lived there. Most residents of the Ethiopian highlands lived in permanent farming villages, and the lowland deserts were occupied by nomadic pastoralists.

MALAGASY

The Malagasy people of Madagascar reflect their dual African and South East Asian heritage both linguistically and culturally. Originally settled from Southeast Asia, Madagascar's languages are related to those of Asia and Oceania. Later, African and Arab immigrants mixed with the first inhabitants to form a sociocultural mosaic. Though most Malagasy people on the wet (east) side are village farmers many Malagasy people are herders.

NEW PEOPLES

Freed slaves from England and the Americas resettled at Freetown, Sierra Leone, starting in 1788. In 1822, freed slaves from the United States settled at Monrovia, Liberia. Although the modern-day descendants of these peoples are a minority in both countries, they tend to dominate other ethnic groups politically. The most numerous Euro-African people are the Boers (or Afrikaners) and the British of South Africa. Other European settlements exist in the more temperate climates, such as the highlands of Kenya and Tanzania. Many East Indians and Arabs have settled inland in Tanzania, Kenya, and Uganda as merchants and civil servants.

■ (Above) Until recently, most Khoisan peoples of southern Africa got most of their food by foraging.

■ (Above) Like many other indigenous people of the world, West Africans face the psychological and sociocultural dilemma of maintaining their traditional lifeways in the face of influences from those more wealthy and powerful than themselves.

■ (Left) The largest group of the Niger-Congo category are the speakers of the Bantu subfamily, including these musicians of the Ivory Coast.

■ *(Left) Like these Masai of Kenya, most of the Nilo-Saharan peoples of north-central and east Africa were egalitarian and predominantly pastoral.*

■ *(Above) Many pygmies still live in the forests of Zaire by a combination of foraging and trading. This Efe man is making an arrowhead from scrap iron.*

■ *(Right) People who speak one of the Niger-Congo languages had spread over most of sub-Saharan Africa by the eighteenth century. Most were farming people, and many lived in highly organized states with an hereditary elite.*

Sources for the creation of this insert: Murdock (1959), Lipsky (1962), Davidson (1969), Grove (1971).

gone forever. Many anthropologists trained by Boas did just that; much of the knowledge we have about Native Americans was obtained by his students. Second, Boas believed that in his day the immediate need of the infant science of anthropology was more data. He stressed the need to know more about specific other societies and their particular histories before speculating further about laws that supposedly apply universally. Boas approached science *inductively*: he believed that—insofar as possible—facts should be gathered without the preconceived notions that always lead to bias in observation. Anthropologists should construct theories to account for the facts only after obtaining an unbiased record of the facts.

How can we obtain such an unbiased account? By approaching the study of another cultural tradition relativistically, we can come close to objectivity. Thinking relativistically, for Boas and for most contemporary anthropologists, means not judging other peoples' religions by our own religious beliefs, nor their morality by our own moral codes, nor the overall worth of their way of life by our standards of worthiness. The relativistic approach requires a temporary suspension of the beliefs, morality, and value standards of the anthropologist's own sociocultural system. It requires that we judge the behavior of individuals who belong to another way of life by their own standards. In this way we might avoid the mistake of the unilineal evolutionists: "grading" (with both meanings) other peoples by how closely they approximate us. More than any other single individual, Boas imparted into anthropology the doctrine of cultural relativism, which he believed was essential for scientific detachment and objectivity.

Boas was enormously influential. He trained most of the best-known American anthropologists of the twentieth century, including Margaret Mead, Ruth Benedict, Alfred Kroeber, and Robert Lowie. Most of his objections to unilineal evolutionism still seem valid. The evolutionists' stages were indeed ethnocentric and speculative; it seems certain today that all peoples do not pass through the same unilineal sequence of development. More fieldwork was indeed urgently needed in the early twentieth century, and today fieldwork is part of the professional training of most sociocultural anthropologists. By and large, it is still carried out in a relativistic manner—although modern fieldworkers recognize that it is impossible to work without preconceptions.

Another of Boas' enduring contributions was summarized in chapter 3: he and his students promulgated the idea that biological/racial differences between hu-

■ *Franz Boas is best known for his insistence on relativistic studies of other peoples and for his research on Native Americans.*

man populations do not explain the sociocultural differences between them. (As we have seen, this idea was foreshadowed by the psychic-unity doctrine of some unilineal evolutionists.) Historical particularism thus almost eliminated biological differences as a potential explanation for differences in sociocultural systems—at least, it did so in anthropology!

From a modern perspective, historical particularism has shortcomings of its own. Consider the claim that each culture is unique. Certainly, if differences between ways of life are what we are interested in, we can find them, and we can then go on to prove that no two ways of life are identical. Certainly, too, each society has its own past, and the precise events that shaped its history happened nowhere else. So, *to some extent*, no sociocultural system is like any other, and no line of historical development is duplicated anywhere else; but also, *to some extent*, there are similarities between human ways of living. Historical particularists tended to overlook the similarities and to neglect the study of factors that might explain them. The interest of American anthropologists returned to similarities—and to evolution—in the 1940s. Meanwhile, another theoretical orientation developed in Great Britain.

Functionalism (ca. 1920–1950)

At about the same time that historical particularism dominated American anthropology, an alternative approach was popular in Great Britain. Its basic tenet was that the sociocultural characteristics of a people should be explained by the useful functions they perform for the well-being of individuals or of society as a whole.

These scholars, known as *functionalists*, were critical of the American historical particularists. One criticism was that particularists believed that the way of life of a people was explained by their unique history, so one had to investigate the past of a people to understand their present. Functionalists believed that it was futile to investigate the histories of preindustrial peoples. They argued that without written records, reconstructions of the past are so speculative that they have little scientific value. One should ignore the historical *origins* of sociocultural systems and simply study how they *work*, or how their various elements "function."

Two varieties of **functionalism** developed in Britain during the early decades of the twentieth century: **biopsychological functionalism** and **structural functionalism.**

■ *Biopsychological Functionalism*

Biopsychological functionalism is associated most strongly with Bronislaw Malinowski, a man well known to all anthropologists because of his magnificent ethnographies of the Trobriand Islanders of the Pacific. Malinowski believed that sociocultural features exist to meet certain biological and psychological needs of humans. These needs, or "basic imperatives," are nutrition, reproduction, shelter from the elements and from enemies, and health (or maintenance of the body in good condition). The primary function of all society and culture is to fulfill these requirements for survival and well-being. The basic imperatives themselves are essentially constant across all populations, but the sociocultural mechanisms a people develop to fulfill them vary from place to place and time to time.

Humans, however, do not meet their needs in isolation from other humans. They organize cooperative groups to meet their basic imperatives more effectively. They develop institutions to give their need-serving activities regularity and predictability. People therefore must maintain the groups and institutions that serve their biopsychological needs: the behavior of group members must be regulated, statuses must be doled out to individuals, access to natural resources must be assigned, and so forth. Malinowski called these "derived needs"—in essence, the needs of groups and institutions to be maintained and perpetuated over time.

Finally, Malinowski argued that a people will adhere to the requirements of their groups and institutions only if they become committed to the norms and standards that guide behavior. This commitment is achieved through creating emotional attachment to the whole way of life. For example, attachment is achieved by enculturating individuals to value their way of life in its own right and by providing symbolic acts and objects that lend meaning and purpose to human life. Thus, other elements of the sociocultural system, notably cultural values and religion, are explained by their functions in creating sentimental attachment to the whole sociocultural system.

For anthropological thought, the important thing about Malinowski's approach is that it considers individuals as the starting point for explanation. Directly or indirectly, all sociocultural elements function to meet the biopsychological needs of individuals. The main problem with such an approach is that, *by themselves*, individual needs provide no explanation for why sociocultural systems *differ* in the way they meet basic imperatives. Why do different peoples fulfill their needs in different ways? For example, unless we know why some peoples satisfy their nutritional needs by eating beef, whereas others refuse to consume cattle flesh even though they are hungry, we have not explained a population's food-getting behavior. To generalize this point: human biological and psychological needs are relatively constant across societies and therefore cannot by themselves explain sociocultural variation.

■ *Structural Functionalism*

The second variety of functionalism that arose in Great Britain takes the needs of society, not the needs of individuals, as its starting point. Its adherents became known as *structural functionalists*, for they believed that the function of some particular sociocultural element is the contribution it makes to the persistence of social structure. *Social structure* refers to the enduring pattern of relationships between individuals and groups.

The leading proponent of structural functionalism was A. R. Radcliffe-Brown, who imagined that human societies are in some ways like living organisms. Organisms are composed of cells and organs that perform essential functions that maintain the body. Living things have a bodily structure: each organ plays a role in maintaining the whole body, and the functions of one organ complement the functions of others. We study the physiology of the organism—or how the organism stays alive through its life process—by analyzing how all its parts work together to maintain the body as a living whole.

For Radcliffe-Brown, the functions of the various parts of a sociocultural system are analogous to the functions of the body's various organs, namely, to maintain the whole "social body." If a social body is to be maintained, the relationships between the individuals and groups that are its parts must be orderly and predictable. The parts must perform their functions adequately, just as with real organisms. If some relations cause conflict, this conflict must be regulated in some way. And if some part fails to work properly (analogous to disease), compensating mechanisms must correct the malfunction and restore its essential activities on behalf of the whole.

Structural functionalists believed that the normal state of human societies is *equilibrium*, or the steady state of orderly relations between individuals and groups. After a disturbance, societies ordinarily return to equilibrium. Many puzzling customs were explained by their functions in maintaining this steady state, partly by regulating any potential conflict that might disturb it.

For example, Radcliffe-Brown noted that in any society there are certain social relationships in which conflict is especially likely to occur. To minimize this conflict, and the disruption in equilibrium that accompanies it, societies have developed norms of how the occupants of certain statuses ought to relate to one another. One such norm is obligatory *avoidance:* the individuals are obliged to avoid direct contact or communication with one another; in some cases, they are forbidden to even look at one another. Obligatory avoidance sometimes occurs between individuals and their parents-in-law, a relationship often fraught with conflict over the husband or wife or over the children of the marriage. Another widespread norm is *joking relationships,* in which one individual is permitted to poke fun at another with whom he or she has a certain relation. Quite often, brothers-in-law are expected to joke with one another. This is because, Radcliffe-Brown argued, their relationship contains contradic-

tory elements: they are united by their common interest in the wife-sister and her children, yet they are divided because they usually belong to different kinship groups that may be in conflict with one another. By giving a definite form to the brother-in-law relationship, the norm of joking resolves the contradictory aspects of the relation between these statuses and reduces the potential conflict between the individuals involved. Both obligatory avoidance and joking relationships function to reduce conflict between the occupants of statuses who are especially likely to have reasons to quarrel with one another.

More than any previous approach, structural functionalism contributed the notion that the various customs and beliefs of a people form an integrated system. Institutions and cultural norms cannot be understood in isolation from each other or from the whole system, for each has definite relations to the others and each has its function to perform on behalf of the social body. (Incidentally, structural functionalists disliked the diffusionist term *trait,* for it implies that elements of a sociocultural system are sufficiently independent from one another that they can be passed around freely from people to people.) By emphasizing the integration of the various aspects of human lifeways, structural functionalism strengthened the holistic perspective of anthropological thought.

Despite this contribution, the structural functionalists failed to answer many questions adequately. First, because of their emphasis on steady states, they did not produce an adequate theory of why sociocultural systems change. Such a theory is certainly a reasonable requirement of any approach, because change occurs everywhere at varying rates.

Second, because they mistrusted historical investigations, they paid little attention to the origins of sociocultural elements. An emphasis on how sociocultural systems work is fine, but we would also like to know how they come to possess their characteristics.

Third, most structural functionalists treated widespread conflict as an abnormal state: if individuals and groups regularly quarreled or fought with one another, structural functionalists believed that something had gone wrong with the mechanisms that restored equilibrium. Most anthropologists of today recognize that conflict is a normal condition of almost all peoples. Divergent interests, competition over resources (or desirable statuses, or mates), disagreement over how group activities should be carried out, and violation of the culturally legitimate rights of others are all sources of conflict that exist to varying degrees among all peoples. We would like to know the conditions under which dispute, feud, and outright warfare are most likely to occur in human societies; but structural functionalism by and large only tells us how these conflicts are regulated and resolved, not why they occur to different degrees among different peoples.

Later Evolutionary Approaches (ca. 1940–1960s)

In the United States the historical particularists' attack on the unilineal evolutionists led to the virtual abandonment of studies of sociocultural evolution for almost forty years. The particularists did indeed demolish the notion that all peoples pass through a single sequence of sociocultural evolution, but one need not adhere to a one-line view of progress to adopt an evolutionary perspective on sociocultural systems.

In the 1940s two new evolutionary approaches emerged, both of which survive in modified form in contemporary anthropology. One is known as **general evolution.** The other is called **specific evolution.**

■ *General Evolution*

General evolution was first championed by Leslie White, who did most of his important writings between the 1940s and 1960s. White agreed with the nineteenth-century evolutionists' claim that there was an overall direction to sociocultural change. He argued that the development of human ways of life was propelled forward by technological advances—by what Morgan called "inventions and discoveries." According to White, to speak of *progress*, one must define the word on a purely technological basis. The major purpose of technology, he contended, is to capture the energy locked up in the environment of a people. White therefore proposed that levels of evolution be defined by energy capture and use: systems in which more energy is captured and used per person per year are more evolved.

White went further. As technology advances, and as more energy becomes available to a people, other changes in their way of life necessarily occur as well. Their family forms, economic organization, and polit-ical structures change to enable people to use the new technology effectively. Finally, to strengthen and reinforce the new social relations, groups, and organizing principles created by technological advances, ideas and beliefs eventually changed as well. New classifications of the natural and social world, norms of behavior, values, world views, symbolic systems, and so forth (which we call *culture*) developed.

White thus argued that not everything is equally important in sociocultural systems or in sociocultural evolution. Technology is the "prime mover" of change, and is the "prime determinant" of both the social and cultural dimensions of human life. (White adapted these ideas from Karl Marx, whom we discuss later.)

As evidence of his theory, White noted that throughout the *general* course of human history, major changes in technology were soon followed by changes in other elements of the sociocultural system. Until about 10,000 years ago, all peoples lived in small bands and ate only wild plants and animals. After certain peoples began to cultivate crops and keep domesticated animals—that is, after a new source of food was developed—they settled down into larger and relatively permanent villages. As the food-growing methods improved, more food energy could be produced on a given area of land, which meant that more people could be supported in a region. Villages gradually grew, until people eventually began living in cities; and grand architectural styles, writing, specialization of labor, large-scale political organization—in a word, civilization—developed. These changes occurred in only a few areas of the world: ancient Mesopotamia, the Nile valley, the Indus valley, eastern China, Central America, and the western highlands of South America. Other peoples remained relatively undeveloped and continued to live by hunting and gathering of wild foods, or by simple cultivation.

These technological conditions continued, essentially unchanged, for several thousand years. Human sociocultural systems could not evolve further, according to White, until some fundamental technological innovation led to the discovery of a new source of energy to thrust development onward. Beginning in the late eighteenth century, and continuing into the present, the industrial revolution unleashed this new source of energy: first steam, then fossil fuels and electricity, and most recently the power of the atom. The changes that this latest revolution in technology will cause in human lifestyles have not yet had time to work themselves out, which is why modern societies experience so much turmoil.

White believed that the historical particularists were so involved with the intricate details of particular cultures, and with tracing out their unique histories, that they could not discern this general sequence of change. We need to take a bird's eye view of changes in human ways of life on the whole planet to see the overall evolution of sociocultural systems. White's brand of evolution is called "general" because it largely ignores specific variations among sociocultural systems. This is one of its major weaknesses, according to some scholars.

■ Specific Evolution

Taking off from this criticism, Julian Steward, a contemporary of White, developed another evolutionary approach. Steward noted that White's grand theory, although useful for some purposes, revealed little about specific peoples. He agreed with White that technology is an important influence on how human populations *in general* live, but he thought that White paid insufficient attention to the influence of the local environment on the way *specific* populations live. If we wish to explain why *a* people live the way they do in a particular place and time, we must understand how technology and environment interact to influence their sociocultural system, said Steward.

In the 1930s and 1940s, Steward proposed an approach that has become known as specific, or multilineal, evolution. Two key concepts underlie his approach. The first is *adaptation*, or the relations between humans and their natural environments. Many, but not all, aspects of a human way of life are greatly influenced by a population's need to exploit its environment for food and other materials. The way a population adapts is generally determined by the environment itself, and by the technology the people have developed to exploit it.

Like White, Steward divided sociocultural systems into parts, some of which are more important than others in affecting a population. He called one part the *culture core*, or those aspects of a people's whole way of life that allow them to exploit nature effectively. Culture core—which is Steward's second key concept—includes sociocultural features such as technology, patterns of settlement, ways of dividing up tasks, groups that cooperate in exploiting resources, and methods of regulating access to land. Steward believed that technology and environment together determine the core elements of a people's way of life. Other elements of their sociocultural systems are far less influenced by how they relate to their environment, such as legends, dances, art styles, and folklore. He applied the term *secondary features* to those sociocultural elements that are largely irrelevant for adaptation.

Despite their differences, White and Steward agreed that many aspects of sociocultural systems are related (directly or indirectly) to the need of all populations to exploit nature. They believed that a people's needs for food, water, shelter, fuel, and other material things took precedence over, and to some extent determined, other aspects of their way of life.

One contrast between the two men was the relative emphasis they gave to the influence of technology and to local environments. Whereas White argued that technological improvements powered sociocultural changes through the centuries, Steward argued that local environments also greatly influenced particular lifeways in specific places and times. As you might guess, the two approaches are complementary, not contradictory. Humans can only apply technology to the raw materials available in the environments in which they live; yet any population's ability to exploit an environment varies with the technology to which it has access. Technology (including technical knowledge as well as physical tools themselves) and environment interact; neither exerts its impact in isolation from the other.

The influence of White and Steward is still apparent. Modern sociocultural anthropologists such as Elman Service and Richard Adams still investigate the overall course of sociocultural evolution. They thus follow the path laid down by White, although contemporary general evolutionists do not necessarily agree that technology is the prime mover of sociocultural change. Other scholars, called *cultural ecologists*, are more concerned with showing how the way of life of particular peoples is influenced by the way they relate to their environments. Cultural ecologists thus follow in Steward's footsteps, although modern adaptive studies are more sophisticated and quantitative than those conducted by Steward.

The intellectual heirs of each school we have discussed so far are well represented in modern anthropological thought. Contemporary theorizing is enormously diverse—far too diverse to summarize here. However, a great many contemporary anthropologists can be "fit into" one of two general theoretical orientations, which we shall call *materialism* and *idealism*.

Modern Materialist Approaches

Modern anthropology includes several varieties of **materialism.** Although they differ greatly, they share a common theme: the way a human population acquires life-sustaining materials and energy is the most important influence on other aspects of its way of life. The harnessing of nature's resources influences the patterned relations individuals have with one another, the kinds of groups they form, and ultimately the cultural norms, attitudes, values, categories, world views, and so on that a people acquire.

Two influential modern varieties of materialism are historical materialism and cultural materialism. Historical materialism traces its roots to the nineteenth-century writings of Karl Marx. Cultural materialism, which also owes much to Marx, is similar to general and specific evolution. We now look briefly at each variety.

■ *Historical Materialism*

Although best known as the "father of communism," Karl Marx was also a brilliant theorist who influenced the thinking of future scholars about humankind. Marx proposed a theory—called **historical materialism**—that he thought explained history by peoples' striving to meet their material needs and wants. His theory is much more complex than we can summarize here, but its basic tenets can be presented simply.

Marx believed that two important forces determine a human way of life and, indeed, all of human history. First is a population's *mode of production*, which consists of the "forces," "relations," and "means" of production. The *forces of production* include, essentially, the technology used in the process of production. To employ the productive forces, people form *relations of production* with one another. For example, in societies in which the forces of production are relatively undeveloped, tasks are assigned on the basis of age and gender, so that individuals work on tasks they can do best. Land and other resources are owned communally

by the group, which cooperates in work and shares the products among all members on the basis of need. Everyone has access to all the tools and resources he or she needs to survive. Conflict is minimal, for communal control over resources leads to an emphasis on cooperative labor and sharing of products.

But people everywhere seek to master nature, according to Marx, and in some places this striving results in the development of the forces of production. These developments make labor and land more productive, but the benefits of this productivity are not equally distributed to all. Once the productive forces have developed enough to allow workers to produce a great surplus over their needs, a few people manage to acquire ownership over the *means of production;* that is, over land, resources, tools, and other things used in production. Society then becomes divided into two classes: those who own the means of production and those who are forced to work for the owners. The interests of the two classes are always opposed: the owners make their living by exploiting the nonowners, whereas nonowners resist the exploitation.

The opposing interests of the classes lead to conflict between them. This class conflict results from exploitation, which is made possible by one class's control over the means of production. Class conflicts are the second important force in human history, for they lead to revolutions. Revolutions create new relations of production and new classes, which create new forms of exploitation and inevitable conflicts, which breed new revolutions. This process, in which one mode of production and its class system breed conflicts, which produce a new mode and a new class system, Marx called the "dialectic." The struggle between classes for control over the means of production (and over the material rewards of such control) thus drives change in human history.

The owners of the means of production attempt to protect their privileged position by forestalling the threat of revolution. They use some of their wealth to control laws and government, which become instruments to protect their property rights and maintain law and order. The ruling class also controls the religious ideas of society, and it uses this control over religion to reinforce its own wealth and power—by, for example, offering heavenly rewards for earthly submission to authority or for placid acceptance of one's worldly poverty.

Marx lived in the nineteenth century, and we have learned much about humanity since his day. Few anthropologists—including those who call themselves Marxians—accept his theory in total. (Remember that the preceding description is greatly simplified.) But like Marx, modern Marxians tend to believe that conflict between classes is the major source of change in human ways of life. When they study a particular society, Marxians often focus on questions such as: What groups control productive resources? To what extent do they use this control to exploit others? How do existing ideas and beliefs reinforce and justify class relations? How are prevalent patterns of conflict influenced by the class structure? Marxian anthropologists often investigate colonialism, for colonial situations create periods of rapid change in which new classes arise and achieve control over the production process.

Modern Marxians generally agree also that control over the means of production is a major influence on the legal and political system and on the religious beliefs of a society. They view laws not as rules that benefit everyone in society equally but as enforced edicts that protect the property and privilege of the wealthy. They view governments not as impartial "dispensers of justice" and "protectors of the public welfare" but as formal social groups that "dispense" the wishes of the wealthy and "protect" the interests of the ruling class. Also, they generally agree with Marx's view of religion as a set of ideas that increases conformity with the status quo and submission to authority.

■ Cultural Materialism

Another modern variety of materialism is called **cultural materialism.** Cultural materialists believe that the way a people exploit nature using their tools and technical knowledge is the most important aspect of their sociocultural system. In this respect they agree with White and Steward; however, they recognize the influence of more than just technology and overall environment on human lifeways. The density of the human population in a region greatly affects the way a people can exploit its resources. For example, with very dense populations, some ways of acquiring life-sustaining materials are not viable. The presence of other human populations with whom a people trade, fight, or have other kinds of relations likewise affects a way of life. If a people are engaged in warfare with their neighbors, then they must adapt themselves to the military threat, which will affect the ways in which they exploit their own territory.

Cultural materialists also recognize a *feedback* relationship between a society and its environment; that is, as they interact with nature, people change it, and this change "feeds back" to affect the people themselves. For instance, as people exploit a resource, they often deplete its supply to themselves and to future generations. They must then work harder to acquire the resource in the future, or develop a new method of acquiring it, or switch to an alternative resource. Other sociocultural changes accompany these changes in adaptation.

Following this line of argument, one leading cultural materialist, Marvin Harris, proposes that many important changes in human lifeways result from a process known as *intensification.* Although human societies develop various ways of limiting their population growth, over the long term the population in a region increases. As population grows, people tend to over-exploit resources, which leads to degradation of their natural environment. This forces them to use their environment more "intensively": they turn to resources they previously ignored, which requires them to expend more labor in acquiring energy and materials, which leads them to develop new technologies to harvest and process resources. As human numbers continue to increase, the environment continues to deteriorate because of overexploitation, so people must continue to intensify their use of it. Both population growth and intensification lead to new social relations and organizations, which develop to facilitate the new ways of exploiting nature. In turn, new social arrangements require new world views, values, norms—a new *culture,* as we use the term—to reinforce them.

Notice how similar this line of reasoning is to both White's and Marx's: Exploitation of nature (adaptation and production, using technology) lies at the base of human lifeways; social relations, groups (including classes), and other social arrangements develop to facilitate the acquisition of resources; and the mental dimensions (culture) of human life exist to provide ideational support for social arrangements.

Modern Idealist Approaches

A great many (possibly most) modern cultural anthropologists do not accept any variety of materialist explanation. They believe that materialism gives insufficient attention to the causal influence of what is most unique about humanity: our minds and ideas. We next consider contemporary approaches that emphasize the importance of culturally determined perceptions and classifications of the world. A good way to introduce these approaches is to contrast them with materialism.

■ *Materialism Versus Idealism*

Much controversy in contemporary anthropology revolves around the relative influence of material conditions versus mental perceptions on human life. As we have seen, materialists emphasize the *objective conditions* under which people live. They believe that the need to exploit nature is a hard fact—an "iron law"—that no people can escape.

Other scholars question whether this iron law has much significance in determining the specific way in which any given people live. They believe that the way a people *subjectively perceive* the hard facts of their material conditions is as important as the objective reality of the conditions. This approach is often known as **idealism.** It holds that the ideas of a people are more than reflections of and justifications for the way they acquire resources or for the exploitation of one class by another. Cultural perceptions and classifications of reality have a life of their own. They affect, and are affected by, material forces.

As we have seen, materialists generally assume that the needs and wants of people for shelter, nutrition, fuel, items of wealth, and so forth take priority over other satisfying things. They take priority in the sense that the human desire for material satisfactions is more important than other needs and wants. The desire for "nonmaterial satisfactions"—such as for emotionally rewarding social relations, intellectually satisfying views of reality, or a meaningful as well as a prosperous existence—are less important or are acted upon only after material needs and wants are met.

Idealists, in contrast, place more emphasis on what goes on in human minds than on what goes into human stomachs. Idealists assume that humans require more than material satisfactions for contentment, and even for survival. Like all life forms, we do have bodily needs for food, water, and so forth. But idealists hold that humans do not live by wheat and meat (or rice and fish) alone: we need social relationships, symbols, satisfying world views, ultimate values, a sense of belonging, and so forth, to lend meaning to our lives.

Idealists also believe that materialists are mistaken when they take resources as a natural and given condition of the environment—as a hard fact of nature. Idealists think that resources are always culturally defined: Hindus do not consume their cattle, Moslems and Orthodox Jews refuse pork, Americans shun dog and horse flesh (not to mention beetle larvae), and so on. All these animals are perfectly edible and available, yet members of many traditions refuse to consume them because of religious or other cultural beliefs. (For an example of the contrast in how materialists and idealists explain a specific food prohibition, see Box 5.1).

This also implies that the materialists' belief that the local environment, population size and density, and technology interact to determine the basic organization of society is wrong. Obviously, if only some of the raw materials objectively present in nature are subjectively perceived and culturally defined as resources, then culture itself helps to determine the social arrangements that organize the exploitation of nature. Idealists believe that culture does not just reflect and support the organization of society but also shapes this organization.

Idealists also argue that the material needs of a people impose only very broad constraints on their actions, for these needs can be satisfied in a multitude of ways. No human population adapts to its environment in a historical vacuum. That is, any people carry their long history with them into their habitats. This history influences not only how they define *resource* but also which of the many possible ways of exploiting nature they will adopt. The particular way in which any given population satisfies its material wants depends on its unique history and on its specific cultural tradition, according to idealists.

Many idealists regard the materialists' effort to reduce ideas to mere reflections or justifications of material conditions as little more than Western ethnocentrism. Because Western culture places such a high value on material welfare and consumption, materialists mistakenly see "primitive economic men" everywhere else, idealists claim.

In contemporary anthropology there are two major varieties of idealist thought. One, called **structuralism,** emphasizes the universal pattern of human thinking. Structuralists believe that underneath the apparent diversity of human lifeways lies the human mind, which unconsciously manipulates ideas, themes, sym-

Melanesians make pigs the focus of much of their cultural as well as material existence. These men from the island of Tanna, Vanuatu, are preparing a pig for a feast. Moslems and Jews, on the other hand, consider pork to be unclean and unfit for consumption (see Box 5.1).

bols, and relationships. The other popular variety of idealism is sometimes known as **interpretive anthropology.** Unlike structuralists, interpretive anthropologists emphasize sociocultural diversity and, in fact, argue that the aim of cultural anthropology itself is to document and interpret the various ways of "being human." We conclude this chapter with an overview of these two varieties of idealism.

◼ *Structuralism*

Structuralism is one of the most controversial approaches of contemporary anthropological thought. Originating in France from the writings of Claude Lévi-Strauss, structuralism also is popular among English-speaking anthropologists. The term *structure* as used by Lévi-Strauss should not be confused with Radcliffe-Brown's "social structure." Whereas social structure refers to the pattern of social relations between individuals and groups, Lévi-Strauss is concerned with the structure of the human mind. His goal is to show how the structure of the mind unconsciously rearranges available ideas, themes, symbols, and objects into patterns, and thus creates culture itself.

What is this structure like? How does the human mind work? Lévi-Strauss believes that our thought is patterned in dual contrasts—the mind works by "binary oppositions." When we think about something, we unconsciously oppose it to something else with which it contrasts in some respect. The mind imposes a logical order on natural and social phenomena by opposing certain qualities to other qualities. Such binary oppositions are not real or objective characteristics of reality; actual objects and qualities in the real world grade into one another. But because the mind thinks in dual contrasts, it makes reality intelligible by breaking it up into pairs of opposites, then rearranging the opposites into a pattern. This structure of thought, which is common to all humanity, underlies culture, for culture results from the unconscious activity of the mind, according to Lévi-Strauss.

Notice the similarity between these ideas and the way linguists analyze language (chapter 4). Indeed, the inspiration for structuralism came from linguistics: just as a grammar selectively recognizes and makes patterns, structures, and meanings from distinctions between sounds and morphemes, so does the mind impose patterns, structures, and meanings on phenomena of all kinds. Further, like Noam Chomsky's universal grammar, which underlies a linguistic diversity that is only superficial, Lévi-Strauss believes that cultural diversity is more apparent than real. In many of his (quite complex) empirical studies of myth he tries to show that some myths are merely transformations of other myths, the same themes rearranged in new ways.

If structuralists are correct, the apparent diversity of human ways of life is superficial, for underlying all the variation are a few simple principles that combine and recombine to produce one lifeway here, another there. Whether these underlying principles are in fact principles of human thinking is—to say the least—debatable. But the notion that sociocultural diversity can be explained by a few common elements combining and interacting with one another is a respectable idea in modern anthropology—although by no means accepted by all.

◼ *Interpretive Anthropology*

Anthropologists are famous for pointing out the sociocultural differences found among humanity. This emphasis on human sociocultural diversity goes back to

Box 5.1

The Case of the Unclean Pig

Members of the Jewish and Islamic faiths regard the flesh of the pig as unclean and unfit for human consumption. In Judaism, two of the books of Moses—Leviticus (chapter 11) and Deuteronomy (chapter 14)—provide a long list of mammals, birds, fishes, and insects whose consumption was forbidden to the ancient Israelites. Among the list of forbidden animals was the pig. The prophet Mohammed also forbad the eating of pork in the Koran, the holy writings of members of the Moslem faith. Why?

Several explanations have been offered. Here we concentrate on only two, one idealist and one materialist. We do need to note, however, that one popular explanation for the prohibition is inadequate. It holds that pork that is not cooked thoroughly transmits a disease (trichinosis) to people, so both religions forbid the eating of pork to avoid this danger to human health. But this explanation is inadequate: pork is such an excellent source of protein that both Moses and Mohammed should have merely admonished their followers to cook it well. Forbidding its consumption altogether is unnecessary. Besides, pork is consumed avidly by other peoples, especially in Asia and Oceania. These people are not free from the danger of trichinosis, so the health explanation alone cannot explain why Jews and Moslems abhor pig flesh—otherwise Asians and Pacific Islanders would loathe it as well.

In her book *Purity and Danger*, Mary Douglas proposed an idealist explanation for the prohibition on eating pork among the ancient Israelites. (She says nothing explicitly about the Islamic taboo on pig flesh.) Douglas begins her analysis by asking: What do humans everywhere consider "dirty"? Dirt is simply anything that is out of place—that is not where it belongs—according to local cultural ideas. For instance, when we say "my house is dirty," we do not just mean that soil is on our floors. We also mean that our clothes are in the living room, our books are on the kitchen table, and our dishes are in front of the TV—rather than, respectively, in the closet, on the shelf, or in the dishwasher where they should be. Dirt is "matter out of place," Douglas (1966, 48) believes. Her idea is exemplified by "dirty dishes"—you've just eaten what was on your plate (it was "food" a few minutes ago), but now that you've finished eating, the dishes are unclean ("food" has become "dirt"). So something is considered dirt because it contradicts people's cultural ideas about where things properly belong. This means that dirt implies (1) a notion of where things should be (an order) and (2) something out of place (a violation of the order).

The preceding notion of dirt refers to things regarded as *physically* unhygienic or disgusting. But the same logic can apply to things regarded as *spiritually* unclean or unholy. Any culture includes a classification of animals and other things in nature. Humans always classify things by putting them into distinguishable conceptual categories—into "mental boxes." But, no matter how a culture classifies things, some things fall in between the categories: they do not belong clearly to any existing category but are unclear, ambiguous, or anomalous. Douglas believes that members of a culture regard these anomalous things as supernaturally unclean, unholy, polluting, or defiling because they fail to conform to existing classifications of reality. They are permanently "out of place," for they have no category in the existing cultural classifications.

What does all this have to do with pigs? Douglas argued that all the prohibited animals share one characteristic

---

historical particularism, which was based on the opinion that each human way of life was unlike any other, for each was a product of a particular history that was shared by no other people.

If a theoretical orientation emphasizes the differences between people, then generalization across the boundaries of sociocultural systems is difficult. If we view each way of life as unlike any other—if we believe that each must be analyzed entirely on its own terms—then we must seek a separate understanding for each sociocultural system, with its unique and idiosyncratic features. (Note what this says about materialist approaches, with their universalistic attempts to explain lifeways through material forces.)

An emphasis on the uniqueness of each human lifeway also makes comparison between two lifeways misleading, partly because elements that seem similar often are quite different. Elements that are superficially alike actually have different meanings or significance in various populations, for they occur in different socio-

that led the Children of Israel to regard them as unclean: they violated the Israelites' cultural conceptions of the order of creation. Their classification of the natural world is given in Genesis, where God created animals with certain characteristics to soar in the sky (birds with feathers); to swim in the water (fish with scales and fins); and to walk, hop, or jump on the land (creatures with four feet). But some animals did not conform fully to their category, for they had anomalous characteristics. These animals were declared to be unholy and unfit for eating. For example, terrestrial animals that moved by "swarming upon the earth" were unclean (Leviticus 11:41–42), since they did not move around by walking, hopping, or jumping.

As for the pig itself, it was considered unclean because it too failed to conform to any existing class, according to Douglas. The biblical text specified that clean, edible animals to the Israelites should chew the cud and have cloven hoofs; so domesticated animals such as cattle, sheep, and goats were edible. Although they do have cloven hoofs, pigs do not chew the cud; therefore, they were anomalous in the order of creation and were considered unclean and bad to eat. In this idealist explanation, the pig was unclean because it failed to fit into a particular cultural classification of reality—or so Mary Douglas argued.

Contrast this idealist explanation with the materialist explanation offered by Marvin Harris. Harris argues that people accept or reject ideas or behaviors on the basis of cost/benefit ratios. That is, before a sociocultural element will be found among a population, its material benefits must exceed its costs. Pigs yield returns (in calories and protein), but they also are costly (in time and energy required to feed and breed them). Because cost/benefit ratios can change over time, what once was useful often becomes harmful. Harris thinks that religious prohibitions are most likely to be applied to foods that once were useful but have become expensive in material cost/benefit ratios. A supernaturally based food prohibition serves to reduce the eating of things that previously were beneficial.

Applying this logic, Harris argues that swine have biological requirements that made them a poor animal for the inhabitants of the ancient Middle East to raise for food. Wild pigs are creatures of woodland habitats. This means that they cannot tolerate high heat well and that they thrive best when foraging on the forest floor. Because of human agricultural activity, the formerly extensive forests of the eastern Mediterranean shrank dramatically beginning about 7,000 years ago. As the forests declined, grasslands expanded, and the pig lost both the shade and the food of the forest. This meant that favorable habitats for pigs were rare by the time Leviticus and Deuteronomy were written. It was still *possible* to keep pigs, of course, but their food habits are so similar to those of humans that they became competitors with people. This changed environment made pigs too costly to raise, although pork was formerly important in the diet of most Middle Eastern peoples.

Further, unlike cattle, goats, and sheep, pigs are useful to humans only as food. Pigs do not pull plows or provide milk, wool, or hide. Their flesh alone is valuable to people. Since cattle, goats, and sheep thrived in the changed environment, and could be used to pull plows and to provide milk, clothing, and fertilizer as well as meat, there was no material benefit in continuing to raise pigs. It became "forbidden flesh" because it had an unfavorable cost/benefit ratio.

In sum, Douglas argues that the pig's physical features violated the Israelite cultural classification of reality. Harris argues that the pig's physical requirements violated their material interests. There is no better example of the contrast between idealist and materialist analyses than the case of the unclean ("unclear" or "unuseful"?) pig. ■

Sources: Douglas (1966), Harris (1977).

cultural contexts. We distort sociocultural systems when we rip their elements out of their contexts, call them "like" another element from another context, and search for a single explanation for their occurrence in both systems. (Analogously, translations from one language to another are misleading, for words in many languages have no equivalent words conveying the exact meanings in other languages.)

One of the leading contemporary theoretical orientations builds on such considerations. Because its aim is to interpret the meaning of customary behaviors and ideas, it is called *interpretive anthropology.* For interpretive anthropologists, all social behavior has a symbolic component, in the sense that participants constantly must behave in ways that others will understand. All social interaction therefore is symbolic and meaningful. Meanings exist only by virtue of common agreement among the parties to the interaction—whether the interaction is making conversation, making change in a store, making bumpers in an auto factory, or making time at a party. Neither participant can tell an observer how he or she knows what the other participant "means" by this or that behavior. Yet the participants consistently behave in ways that others understand, and they consistently interpret the behavior of others correctly.

The job of the anthropologist is not to explain elements of a sociocultural system but to explicate one element through others. That is, the anthropologist shows how one thing in a sociocultural system makes sense in terms of other things in the same system, for interpretation is seeing how things make sense when understood in their context. (Analogously, a dictionary explicates the meanings of words in terms of other words. Only if one knows the meaning of many words in the dictionary can one use it to decipher the meaning of unknown words.) We seek to understand a people's way of life as they understand it. In the words of one interpretivist, Clifford Geertz, we seek to grasp "the native's point of view," "to figure out what the devil they think they are up to" (Geertz 1983, 58).

According to many interpretive anthropologists, the search for generalized explanations of human ways of life is futile. So many factors contributed to the formation of a sociocultural system, and these factors interacted in such complex and unpredictable ways, that we must concentrate on understanding the unique elements of each way of life. In this respect, interpretive anthropologists share the assumptions of historical particularism more than any other body of thought we have discussed.

Either/Or?

There are other theoretical orientations in modern anthropology. However, the leading debate today is probably between materialists and idealists, which is why we chose to organize our discussion of modern thought around this theme.

No one has yet been able to resolve this issue—certainly not the authors of this textbook! Here we simply note that material forces such as technology, available raw materials, and population densities certainly influence all sociocultural systems. The question is, How much? More precisely, How important are material forces as opposed to other kinds of forces?

Most modern materialists are careful not to imply that material forces determine everything else in detail. They claim that technology, environment, and so forth determine other elements in a general way. They also insist that the determination is *probabilistic* rather than absolute; that is, more often than not, material conditions broadly determine social arrangements, which in turn broadly determine values, norms, world views, symbols, and other elements of cultural knowledge. (As you might guess, idealists respond that terms such as *probabilistic* and *broadly determine* water down materialist theory so much that hardly any theoretical power is left.)

The argument is not likely to end in any of our lifetimes. For this book, a sensible solution is to adopt a way of looking at the problem that avoids the either/or dilemma. First, we can treat the material conditions faced by any human population as important constraints (see chapter 2) on its way of life. Like other constraints, material conditions narrow the range of possibilities. For example, because a people live in a certain environment which they exploit with a given technology, a great many options are not available to them. Within the material constraints, people can develop a variety of social arrangements and can elaborate their cultural knowledge in ways that we cannot predict—ways that may be determined by their particular history or by their desire for nonmaterial satisfactions.

Second, we should recognize (as Steward did) that different elements of a human lifeway are influenced to different degrees by material conditions. Certainly, the way an economy is organized is greatly influenced by the local environment, by technology, and by the size and density of the human population. But the way a people resolve their disputes, raise their children, perform their rituals, or act toward their fathers-in-law is less influenced by material conditions or is influenced by them only indirectly. The legends they recite, the specific natural objects they use as religious symbols, or the styles they use to decorate their bodies may have very little to do with material conditions. Such elements of a sociocultural system may be only very loosely tied to material forces and to desires for material things. If so, we cannot expect to account for them without considering people's desires for a meaningful existence, for an emotionally gratifying social life, for an intellectually satisfying world view, and so forth.

Summary

This chapter discusses some of the past and present schools of thought in cultural anthropology. Today, as in the past, anthropological research is guided by a variety of theoretical orientations—questions, concepts, assumptions, and methods used to study particular societies or humanity in general. Three kinds of questions have been addressed by most of the major thinkers: (1) How can we explain the geographic and temporal differences and similarities between human populations? (2) How do the different subsystems of sociocultural systems mutually affect one another? (3) What is the relationship between individuals and the sociocultural system?

Anthropology originated as a separate academic discipline in the late nineteenth century. Colonialism brought people of European ancestry into increasing contact with the native inhabitants of Africa, Asia, the Americas, and the Pacific. The changing intellectual climate associated with the rise of uniformitarianism in geology and evolution in biology provided theories that led scholars to try to explain scientifically the customs and beliefs of people of other continents. Evolution was the key. These scholars' argument was that because such people remain at an early stage of sociocultural evolution, they are modern survivors of the precursors of modern civilization. By studying their ways of life, one could learn how Europeans had progressed out of rude beginnings. Late-nineteenth-century anthropologists such as Tylor and Morgan developed the approach known as *unilineal evolutionism* to describe and account for the progress of humanity into civilization.

Diffusionists of the early twentieth century questioned that independent invention accounted for the wide geographic distribution of similar sociocultural "traits." They felt that diffusion generally accounted for sociocultural similarities among even widely scattered peoples. But the mechanism by which people such as the ancient Egyptians transmitted their "advanced" sociocultural traits to American Indians remains unclear, and many people feel there is an implicit prejudice or even racism to diffusionist ideas.

In the United States the historical particularist Boas noticed the inconsistencies and invalid assumptions in the work of the unilineal evolutionists. Notions such as "progress" and "complexity" involved value judgments and had little objective meaning or usefulness. A strong empiricist and inductivist, Boas believed that Tylor and Morgan engaged in too much speculative theorizing, and that only after more objective descriptions were available should anthropologists begin to talk about "laws of progress." His demands for more data had a lasting influence, leading to an emphasis on fieldwork as part of professional training and to the adoption of a relativistic outlook on members of other cultural traditions. On the other hand, Boas' view that each way of life is unique because it is the product of its own unique history led to an overemphasis on differences to the neglect of similarities, in the opinion of many.

In Great Britain the functional orientation was popular between about 1920 and 1950. Biopsychological functionalists, notably Malinowski, argued that the purpose of any sociocultural system is to meet the bodily, emotional, social, and cognitive needs of people. Structural functionalists such as Radcliffe-Brown assumed that sociocultural elements function to maintain a social structure in equilibrium and to maintain orderly relations between individuals and groups. Functionalists strengthened the holistic perspective of anthropology; but modern scholars feel that the approach cannot handle change well, neglects history, and gives an inadequate explanation for disputes, wars, feuds, and other conflicts.

In North America new evolutionary approaches gained popularity in the 1940s. White's general evolution proposed that sociocultural evolution is powered by technological changes. As new sources of energy are discovered, changes in economy, family life, and political organization occur; and these in turn lead to changes in values, norms, world views, and other elements of culture. White thus saw technological progress as the prime mover of change and technology as the prime determinant of everything else. Steward's specific evolution looked to adaptation to the natural environment as the major influence on the core elements of a lifeway. Both White and Steward felt that how and how well a people exploit nature are the most important influences on other aspects of their way of life.

Many contemporary theoretical orientations fall into one of two overall approaches: materialism and idealism. Materialists agree that the way a people acquire energy and materials from nature is the main determinant of their sociocultural system. Historical materialism goes back to Marx, who argued that the development of the forces of production lead to changes in the relations of production and to unequal access to the means of production. Societies become divided into classes—those who own the means of production and those who are forced to work for the owners. Class conflicts result from exploitation, revolutions follow and institute new relations of production, and so on in a dialectical process. Cultural materialists believe that the necessity to organize labor for production leads societies to develop certain kinds of groupings and power relations, which then are reinforced and justified by certain kinds of ideas.

Idealists believe that ideas affect as well as are affected by the material conditions of life; that humans seek meanings and social, emotional, and cognitive gratification as well as food; that resources themselves are culturally defined; that material forces impose only very broad constraints on a people's way of life; and that materialism is ethnocentric. Lévi-Strauss's structuralism argues that the universal properties of the human mind underlie culture and produce its many variants, so that much of the diversity in human lifeways is superficial. Interpretive anthropologists glory in the sociocultural diversity of humanity and largely give up attempts to explain this diversity in favor of gaining an understanding of particular ways of life.

Key Terms

uniformitarian theory

natural selection

unilineal evolution

diffusion

independent invention

diffusionists

historical particularism

functionalism

biopsychological
   functionalism

structural
   functionalism

general evolution

specific evolution

materialism

historical materialism

cultural materialism

idealism

structuralism

interpretive
   anthropology

Suggested Readings

A number of large volumes are available that provide detailed histories of the development of anthropological thought, including these:

■ Harris, Marvin. *The Rise of Anthropological Theory.* New York: Crowell, 1968.

■ Hatch, Elvin. *Theories of Man and Culture.* New York: Columbia, 1973.

■ Honigman, John J. *The Development of Anthropological Ideas.* Homewood, Ill.: Dorsey Press, 1976.

■ Voget, Fred. *A History of Ethnology.* New York: Holt, Rinehart and Winston, 1975.

A comprehensive reader in the history of anthropological theory, featuring original works by key figures, is:

■ Bohannon, Paul, and Mark Glazer. *High Points in Anthropology.* New York: Knopf, 1973.

Several works are helpful to those who want a fuller understanding of the contemporary split between materialists and idealists:

■ Geertz, Clifford. *The Interpretation of Cultures.* New York: Basic Books, 1973.
   Assorted works by an idealist and interpretivist. Good place to start to understand this approach.

■ _____. *Negara: The Theatre State in Nineteenth-Century Bali.* Princeton: Princeton University Press, 1980.
   Empirical, interpretive study.

■ Harris, Marvin. *Cannibals and Kings.* New York: Random, 1977.
   Intensification hypothesis of sociocultural evolution is explained and illustrated. Easy reading; excellent example of cultural materialist thought.

■ _____. *Cultural Materialism: The Struggle for a Science of Culture.* New York: Vintage, 1980.
   Title speaks for itself. Lays out theoretical principles of this approach and defends it from rival approaches, including dialectical materialism, structuralism, and idealism.

■ Kurzeil, Edith. *The Age of Structuralism: Lévi–Strauss to Foucault.* New York: Columbia University Press, 1980.
   An overview of French structural thought. Structuralism had its start in France and has been enormously influential in that country in many fields.

■ Lévi-Strauss, Claude. *Totemism.* Boston: Beacon, 1963a.

■ _____. *Structural Anthropology.* New York: Doubleday, 1963b.

■ _____. *The Savage Mind.* Chicago: University of Chicago Press, 1966.
   Three books considered to be the basic works of the most famous structuralist.

■ Sahlins, Marshall. *Culture and Practical Reason.* Chicago: University of Chicago Press, 1976.
   Essentially structuralist in orientation. Difficult going for beginners, but this book has become a bit of a manifesto for idealists in anthropology.

METHODS OF INVESTIGATION

(Above) *Anthropological field research emphasizes direct contact with the people being studied. Here Richard Lee converses with a group of San*

ny science has a set of methods that its practitioners use to explore the reality they investigate. In cultural anthropology, our primary interest is in human ways of life—particularly the sociocultural differences and similarities that exist among the world's peoples. Over the decades, anthropologists have developed certain methods of investigating human lifeways. These methods are described in this chapter.

Anthropological methods of investigation fall into two broad categories. The first is **ethnographic methods,** which involve the collection and analysis of descriptive data from a single society or several closely related societies. The end product of ethnographic research is either a case study describing the sociocultural system of some people (e.g., the way of life of the Cheyenne) or a descriptive account of some aspect of a people's sociocultural system (such as the Cheyenne religion). The second category is **ethnological methods,** which involve attempts to test hypotheses about relationships between certain aspects of sociocultural systems by using comparative ethnographic data from a number of different societies. The product of ethnological research is generally a monograph or article in a scholarly journal that tries to generalize about causal relationships between sociocultural phenomena. Although ethnographic and ethnological research have different objectives—the one descriptive, the other theoretical—most cultural anthropologists at one time or another are both ethnographers and ethnologists.

So anthropological research has two purposes: (1) the collecting and recording of new data about specific people (ethnography) and (2) the expansion of our theoretical understanding of human sociocultural systems in general through comparative analysis (ethnology). We first discuss the methods used to describe a single people, then summarize how ethnologists use descriptive accounts to test hypotheses.

Ethnographic Methods

The two main sources of information about a particular sociocultural system are the living members of the society and the existing written accounts or reports about that group of people. The collection of data by directly observing and interviewing living members of a society is called *ethnographic fieldwork,* whereas the study of a people's lifeway using earlier written accounts is termed *ethnohistoric research.*

Ethnographic studies—whether they use field research or ethnohistoric research—may be either synchronic or diachronic in focus. *Synchronic* studies describe the lifeway of a society at a particular point in time. For example, an ethnographer may conduct fieldwork on the contemporary lifeway of a people, describing their culture as of the 1980s. Today most ethnographic studies are synchronic studies of contemporary communities. Early American ethnographers usually wrote synchronic descriptions of prereservation Native American life by reconstructing earlier lifeways through interviews with older members of the tribe. Less commonly, anthropologists have written synchronic studies using ethnohistoric materials. Here the goal is generally to reconstruct how a particular group of people lived during the seventeenth, eighteenth, or nineteenth centuries, or sometimes for even earlier periods.

Diachronic studies examine the sociocultural changes among a people over time. In large part, the time frame being researched determines the method or methods used. For example, a study of recent changes, say over the past twenty-five to thirty years, can be accomplished largely through ethnographic fieldwork, relying on the memories of living people. In contrast, a study concerned with changes that occurred during the eighteenth or nineteenth century necessitates the use of archival and published literature from the period, and thus requires ethnohistoric research.

■ Historical Studies

As we have seen, anthropology is interested in the past as well as the present, partly because the history of any given people has shaped the way they are today. Our concern with the past also derives from our interest in documenting the full range of human sociocultural diversity. As we discuss in Chapter 17, sociocultural systems are constantly changing. Through historical research, anthropologists hope to recover enough information about peoples of the past so that their ways of life can be reconstructed, thus adding to our storehouse of knowledge about humanity. Historical studies generally use two methods: recall ethnography and ethnohistory.

Recall Ethnography   Late-nineteenth- and early-twentieth-century North American anthropologists commonly studied Native Americans, whose lifeways had been greatly changed through contact with whites. In fact, it can be said that American anthropology originated out of the desire to record and preserve information about the native peoples of the United States.

By the late nineteenth century, traditional Native American lifeways were rapidly changing as they adjusted to reservation life. The Native Americans were seen as the "vanishing Americans," and many scholars thought that they would soon disappear as distinct sociocultural communities. Accordingly, as discussed in chapter 5, early American anthropologists felt it was their duty to record as much about traditional Native American life as possible before the last knowledgeable individuals died.

Rather than study the contemporary lifestyle of the Native Americans, the anthropologists wanted to investigate and record the ways of life of native peoples before the reservations, before the diseases and the wars, and before the destruction of the native economic base. Although some sociocultural elements persisted, many had already disappeared or changed radically to meet the demands of reservation life. Ethnographers could study the Cheyenne language, hear folktales and myths recited, or watch some of the remaining ceremonies; but they could not witness a buffalo hunt, observe prereservation village life, see a raiding party organized, or watch how the chiefs and warrior societies settled disputes. The only way to collect data of this nature was by interviewing individuals and asking them to recall what the life of their people had been like when they were young adults or even children.

Recall ethnography, then, is the reconstruction of an earlier lifeway of a people based on the memories of individuals. It is accomplished by intensively interviewing the surviving members of a society. Early ethnographers usually conducted these interviews in the home of the person being interviewed or the residence of the researcher. In some cases, during the early part of this century, native informants were even brought to university campuses for interviews. Ishi, the last surviving Yahi Yana of California, actually lived the last years of his life in the Lowie Museum on the campus of the University of California at Berkeley. Regardless of where such interviews took place, most research was carried out in relative isolation from the everyday life of the community whose past lifeway was being studied. Field-research periods were usually limited to a few weeks or months.

A sense of urgency often accompanied the work of recall ethnographers. There were so many Native American peoples to be studied, yet so few anthropologists and so little time in which to accomplish the work. Sometimes research teams were organized to interview a few informants intensively. For example, in 1929 a research team of five students, supported by the Laboratory of Anthropology in Santa Fe and directed by Alfred Kroeber, descended on the Walapai Reservation in northwestern Arizona. Over an eight-week period nineteen elderly Walapai were interviewed at length, and the data were collected and compiled into a work called *Walapai Ethnography.*

Recall ethnography usually involved fieldwork, in the sense that the ethnographer visited the reservation and lived among the people for a time. Often, however, ethnographers spent only short periods of time in the field and had little contact with community members other than their informants. Often the researcher's knowledge was based solely on what he or she had been told by a handful of individuals, and in a few cases by a single individual. Further, human memories are always selective, and people everywhere distort and often romanticize their past. As a result, a highly idealized outline of the past lifeway of the people was often presented. Early recall ethnographers were usually particularistic (see chapter 5) in their theoretical orientation. Most tended to gather the information that was easiest to collect. As a result, we know considerably more about Native American folklore, mythology, and oral traditions than about economics, social organization, and political life.

Although recall ethnography as a research technique was far from ideal, it was well suited to the early needs of anthropology. Within a relatively short period of time this technique enabled the few available researchers to generate a tremendous data base, one that is now used in comparative studies. In addition, if it had not been for these early anthropologists, we would know little about the past lifeways of many peoples, particularly Native American societies in North America.

Although participant observation, which we discuss later in this chapter, has largely supplanted recall ethnography as the primary method, the recall-ethnography technique has not been totally abandoned. Anthropologists who want a better historical perspective on the people they are studying often attempt to reconstruct the lifeway of that people for a slightly earlier period by interviewing older individuals.

Ethnohistory   The study of past sociocultural systems through the use of written records is called **ethnohistory.** Since the late nineteenth century, anthropologists have used written materials in their studies, but the importance of this research has become widely recognized only during the past twenty years. The growing interest in ethnohistory has come with the realization that non-Western societies have changed far more dramatically over the past few hundred years than had been previously thought.

Like historians who study their society's past, ethnohistorians make use of records such as published books and articles, newspapers, archival documents, diaries, journals, maps, drawings, photographs, and other materials. Not surprisingly, many scholars treat history and

■ *Ethnohistorians try to reconstruct the history of non-literate peoples by studying and interpreting letters, reports, journals, and other written documents left by explorers, missionaries, traders, colonial officials, and other observers.*

ethnohistory as if they were synonymous. There are, however, critical—yet frequently overlooked—differences that distinguish ethnohistory from history.

- An ethnohistorian is primarily interested in reconstructing the sociocultural system of the people. The actual historical events themselves are of interest only because they cast light on the sociocultural system or changes in the system.
- Historical events have little significance outside the sociocultural context of the peoples involved. Ethnohistorians study nonliterate peoples. Thus, whereas historians can use accounts recorded by members of the society being studied, ethnohistorians have to use accounts recorded by members of other, literate, societies. As a result, the problem of interpreting accounts is usually more difficult for the ethnohistorian than the historian.

The varying interpretations of historical events are most evident in events that involved the members of two or more distinct sociocultural groups. In his 1981 study, *Historical Metaphors and Mythical Realities,* Marshall Sahlins illustrates how differently the Hawaiians and the English interpreted such an event. Captain James Cook was in command of the first European expedition to discover the Hawaiian Islands. Having never seen Europeans nor their technology before, the Hawaiians, not surprisingly, thought these British sailors in their large and powerful ships were somehow divine and that Captain Cook must have been a god—the question was, what god?

Lono was a mythical god-king whom the Hawaiians believed periodically returned to the islands and ruled in human form, usurping power from the earthly kings who were representatives of the rival god Ku. Several earlier Hawaiian kings had been identified as Lono ruling on earth. Every year, during a period called *Makahiki,* a series of rituals were dedicated to Lono. Lono symbolically returned to the islands at the beginning of Makahiki, at which time the priests of Lono took control of the temples from the priests of Ku. During the four lunar months that followed, the priests of Lono were in charge of rituals. Makahiki ended with Lono being symbolically sacrificed and returning to the sky. With Lono gone, control returned to the king and the priests of Ku, the earthly representatives of Ku.

As Cook sailed among the islands, the timing and direction of his movements coincidentally corresponded with the mythological movements of the god-king Lono. His arrival took place at the start of Makahiki, and he set sail from the islands at the end of Makahiki. The Hawaiians thus identified Cook as the personification of Lono, and the interpretation was further strengthened when Cook announced during his departure that he would return the following year.

Soon after departing, however, Cook had problems with his ship's mast and had to return to land for repairs. Cook's untimely return was ominously interpreted by the king and priests of Ku as Lono returning to claim earthly powers. Not surprisingly, the Hawaiian priests had him killed, and viewed the killing as the ritual sacrifice of the rival god-king Lono, which they symbolically reenacted every year. In contrast, the English felt that the Hawaiians viciously murdered Cook for no justifiable reason. Although an extreme case, this example illustrates the need for historical events to be interpreted within their proper sociocultural context. We could not understand the "murder" of Cook without being aware of how the Hawaiians interpreted his presence and his actions on the basis of their beliefs.

In ethnohistorical research the anthropologist has to use and analyze accounts of people who, not being members of the society, had at best only an imperfect understanding of the sociocultural context of the data they were recording. As a result, the ethnohistorian faces two major problems: (1) discerning whether the accounts are factually accurate, a problem that they share with historians, and (2) determining how the participants interpreted the events.

The problem of interpretation raises an additional question about the validity of particular reports. Not only do we have to ask about the accuracy of the account, but we also have to ask how knowledgeable the recorder was about the sociocultural context of the events. Ethnohistorians use certain criteria to evaluate the potential validity of an account. How long did the individual live among these people? Did the observer speak the language? What was the role of the individual? Soldiers, missionaries, traders, and government officials have different views, biases, and access to information.

The difficulty with ethnohistory is that no hard-and-fast rules can be used in evaluating these data. The longer an individual lived among members of a particular society and the better he or she spoke the language, the more reliable the account should be; however, this rule cannot be automatically assumed. In some cases, the writer may have had little interest in the people among whom he or she was living, perhaps because the contacts were only related to a job. This attitude is evident in the accounts of many traders and government officials. In other cases the account may be self-serving, with the individuals attempting to enhance their careers. Thus, soldiers and government officials sometimes falsified their official reports. Ethnocentrism is still another factor. Missionary accounts, in particular, often demonstrate overt bias against local customs and beliefs; one has to remember that an individual becomes a missionary because he or she is an avid believer. However, some of the most objective accounts of other societies were written by well-educated missionaries, who were often scholars themselves.

Thus, in ethnohistoric research there is no simple way to evaluate a particular document or account. At best, a single event may be recorded in several independent accounts that can each be used to verify the accuracy and interpretation of the others. However, multiple observations are the exception, not the rule.

A final limitation on the use of ethnohistoric materials is that rarely are all aspects of a particular society evenly reported. For example, data on economic activities may be the most abundant, whereas information on religious ceremonies and beliefs may be absent or limited. As a result, ethnographic studies based on ethnohistoric research tend to lack the depth and balance of those gleaned from research with living individuals. In spite of its problems and limitations, ethnohistoric research provides us with the only clues we have to the past of many societies, as well as the key to a vast store of sociocultural data hitherto virtually untapped.

■ Contemporary Studies (Fieldwork)

Today most ethnographic research, or **fieldwork,** consists of the collection of data from members of a particular society about their contemporary lifeway, using oral interviews and direct observations of their behavior. There are several reasons why fieldwork is still considered essential to cultural anthropology. For most non-Western societies, the available literature, both ethnographic and ethnohistoric, is at best fragmentary and often of questionable validity. Even the best written accounts rarely contain the depth or the specific data needed to answer adequately many important questions about a particular people. Also, all sociocultural systems are undergoing constant change. The behaviors and ideas of a people today may not have been present in the past, nor will they necessarily be continued into the future. The descriptive ethnographic data collected through fieldwork provide anthropology with its best source of data for comparative studies and analysis. In recent decades, most field research has shifted from being mainly the collection of as much descriptive data as possible to "problem-oriented research," which focuses on the collection of specific data that are used to investigate a particular research question.

As discussed, recall ethnography and the reconstruction of earlier lifeways characterized most research during the early decades of the twentieth century. By the 1930s the field-research methods and the research interests of anthropologists were rapidly changing, for several reasons:

■ In North American Indian studies there were few living people with any knowledge to "recall," for individuals born before the creation of reservations were dead, or close to death.
■ Anthropological researchers were increasingly turning their attention to the study of change and its causes and consequences. The interest in reconstructing *the* aboriginal customs of a people waned somewhat.
■ The goal of anthropology was changing from merely describing and recording the varieties of human lifeways to attempting to explain and understand sociocultural phenomena.

For these reasons, anthropologists increasingly turned to more intensive types of investigations through ethnographic fieldwork.

Ethnographic fieldwork involves four special kinds of observations:

■ *Firsthand observation:* Fieldworkers talk to others who are familiar with the people under study, and they read accounts of missionaries, travelers, officials, and so forth. But direct, firsthand experience with the people themselves is usually considered necessary for maximum understanding.
■ *Naturalistic observation:* Fieldworkers observe people as they go about their everyday lives, rather than setting up experimental situations under controlled conditions.
■ *Long-term observation:* Fieldworkers (and their teachers and peers) usually think that a few weeks or months in the field is not long enough to acquire sufficient information and understanding of a peo-

ple. A year is ordinarily considered minimal, and multiyear projects are not at all unusual.
■ *Participant observation:* Fieldworkers are not merely recorders of peoples' statements and actions. To a greater or lesser extent, they live in much the same ways as those they are studying. Residence in the community itself is the rule rather than the exception, although there are many "commuter fieldworkers." Many fieldworkers find they learn most about their subjects by living in the same houses, eating the same foods, speaking the same language, and adopting a lifestyle similar to that of the community they are studying.

The idea of studying the sociocultural system of a people through **participant observation** was popularized by Bronislaw Malinowski during the 1920s. The basic objective of participant observation differs from that of recall ethnography. To some extent, this strategy for field research became popular with the realization that in a few parts of the world (New Guinea, Amazonia, and the islands of southeast Asia) there were still people who had been only minimally affected by Western colonialism. More important, by researching a "living" lifeway, the ethnographer could understand how a sociocultural system actually operated and how its parts fit together, and thus study its dynamics.

Participant observation has often been misinterpreted, even by some anthropologists who have taken it too literally. It does not mean becoming a full

■ *Through participant observation, fieldworkers try to gain a deeper understanding of the lifeway of their hosts. Lila Abu-lughod interviews Bedouin women in Egypt's western desert.*

participant in the activities of the people — in other words, "going native." The emphasis of this technique is more on observation than participation. Participant observation usually does require that one live in the community, for only by doing so can one observe and record the behavior of individuals as they go about their daily work, visit their friends, interact with their relatives, participate in rituals, and so on. These observations of behavior serve to generate new questions concerning the people. Why does a man share food with some families but not with any others? Why do some men wear a particular type of hat or headdress? Does a particular color of clothing have any meaning? Some behaviors will have significance whereas other behaviors will not. For example, variations in types of headdress worn by individuals may be merely the result of personal preferences, or it may reflect status differences. The color of clothing may or may not have special significance. In American society black symbolizes mourning, but in other societies covering one's body with white clay symbolizes the same emotion. Obviously, participant observation allows the researcher to collect more detailed data than does recall ethnography, and thus it makes possible a deeper understanding of interrelationships between sociocultural phenomena.

Firsthand observations of the members of a society also allow the researcher to see how people diverge from the culturally defined, idealized model of behavior. An incident that occurred while Malinowski was working in the Trobriand Islands illustrates the divergence between cultural norms — the way people say they ought to behave — and the way they actually behave. One day Malinowski heard a commotion in the village and discovered that a young boy in a neighboring village had committed suicide by climbing a palm tree and flinging himself onto the beach. In his earlier questioning of the islanders, Malinowski had been told that sexual relations between a man and his mother's sister's daughters were prohibited. On inquiring into the suicide of the young boy, he found that the boy had been sexually involved with his mother's sister's daughter and that in fact such incestuous relationships were not rare. So long as such liaisons were not mentioned in public, they were ignored. In this particular case the girl's rejected boyfriend had become angry and publicly exposed the transgression. Although everyone in the village already knew of this incestuous relationship, by making it public the ex-boyfriend exposed his rival to ridicule, thus causing

him to commit suicide. It is doubtful that such behavior could have been discovered only by interviewing individuals.

■ Problems in Field Research

Every fieldwork experience is to some extent unique. Specific problems differ depending upon the individual characteristics of the researcher, the nature of the community, and the particular questions being studied. There are, however, several difficulties that to varying degrees affect virtually every field-research situation: (1) stereotyping, (2) defining the fieldworker's role in the community and developing rapport, and (3) identifying and interviewing consultants.

Stereotyping When we think of **stereotypes** — the preconceived generalizations concerning a particular group of people — we usually think only of their effects on the perceptions of one party to a relationship. Anthropologists ask themselves how they can overcome their own stereotypes and cultural biases about the people they study. Stereotyping, however, is a two-way street. Every society has stereotypes concerning members of other societies and of ethnic and racial groups. Thus, although the goal is for an anthropologist to put aside his or her personal stereotypes sufficiently to research the sociocultural system of another people with some degree of objectivity, those with whom the ethnographer will be living and working will not have shelved their stereotypes. Most anthropologists are of European ancestry, yet most subjects of anthropological research are non-European peoples. Even if a particular anthropologist is of Asian, African, or Native American ancestry, a similar problem exists, because anthropologists rarely belong to the local community they study, and thus are outsiders. As a result, an anthropologist entering another community must contend with local stereotypes about the ethnic group with which he or she is identified.

In the case of anthropologists of European ancestry, the local stereotyping about their ethnic group has most frequently been derived from contact with only a limited range of individuals, such as missionaries, soldiers, colonial officials, and government bureaucrats. Regardless of the nature and intensity of this contact, most non-Western peoples have a well-developed idea about the expected behavior of such individuals. The tendency of local people to fit the ethnographer into one of their stereotypical categories can prove at times a burden for fieldworkers. The behavior of anthropologists rarely conforms to the model that the local people have developed. Previous contacts with Europeans and Euro–Americans have often been structured in such a manner as to place the "native" in the position of social inferior. Thus, an anthropologist attempting to gain social acceptance in such a society is typically met with suspicion and not infrequently with hostility. The types of questions that anthropologists ask abut behavior and beliefs frequently arouse suspicions further and elicit guarded answers. Why does he or she want to know about our family structure, our political organization, our ritual secrets? What is this person going to do with this information? While the anthropologist is trying to understand the community, its members are attempting to understand what the anthropologist is doing. Depending upon the nature of previous contacts, certain types of questions may provoke more suspicion than others. For example, a minority or tribal group involved in some illegal or illicit activity—such as smuggling, poaching, or growing drugs—may wonder if the anthropologist will inform government authorities. Members of groups that have been more exposed to Western culture usually assume that the ethnographer's objective is to make money and that researchers become wealthy by publishing books.

In other cases, members of the community may be aware that Europeans and Euro–Americans do not approve of or believe in certain types of behavior, and few people will disclose information on topics that they think will be met with disapproval or scorn. This reticence is particularly evident in certain types of religious beliefs and practices. As a result of extensive activities of Christian missionaries, most non-Western peoples are well aware that Westerners usually deny the validity of witchcraft and the existence of wereanimals. Members of societies with these beliefs are usually hesitant about discussing such subjects with people who they perceive do not believe in them. They are understandably reluctant to talk openly about an uncle who they believe can turn himself into a deer or a snake with someone who will most likely view it as ridiculous. Likewise, they probably would not say that their father had been killed by a witch if they thought the outsider did not believe in witchcraft.

Developing a Role and Rapport   Often against a background of suspicion, distrust, and even in some cases fear, an anthropologist has to develop a status in the society that gives him or her rapport with local people. Rapport in this sense means acceptance to the degree that a working relationship is possible, although ethnographers are rarely, if ever, totally accepted by the people among whom they work. However, over a period of time most anthropologists succeed in gaining some degree of trust and friendship, at least with a few members of the group.

The particular role or roles that an anthropologist eventually defines for himself or herself within the society vary greatly with the circumstances of the particular situation. Depending upon the amount and nature of research funding, the anthropologist may be an important economic resource, paying wages to interpreters and assistants or distributing desirable goods as gifts. Anthropologists with a car or truck frequently find themselves providing needed transportation for members of the community. Ethnographers may also provide comic relief, by asking silly questions, behaving in a funny manner, making childlike errors in speaking the language, and generally being amusing to have around. They may be a source of information about the outside world, disclosing information to which local people would not otherwise have access. Community members are sometimes as curious about the anthropologist's society as he is about their society. Or the anthropologist may just be considered a harmless nuisance. During the course of research, the typical fieldworker at one time or another adopts all these roles plus many others.

Identifying and Interviewing Consultants   Ethnographers learn a good deal about a people simply by living among them and participating in many of their activities. This rather casual, informal participant observation provides a good feel for the general "tone" of life. For instance, it allows fieldworkers to report that village life seems "relaxed," that the people are "outwardly polite," that they "show respect for authority," and so on.

But for most purposes casual observation is insufficient. Kinship relationships tend to be more important in non-Western societies than in our own, so to make sense of social behavior fieldworkers usually need to know who is related to whom and how. The working out of kinship relationships necessitates the collection of genealogies, which requires specific questions and structured interviewing. Nearly all fieldworkers take a census of the community early in their work, for this is a good way to introduce themselves, find out about the composition of households, practice the language, and gain an idea about who is likely to be (and not to be) cooperative. A lot can be learned about what is important to a people by collecting quantitative data on how they spend their time and money. This objective requires intensive observations of a sample of households in the community. Ethnographers often collect life histories, for biographical data can shed light on the history of the whole community—besides, most people find it quite interesting to talk about themselves. For these and many other purposes, field-workers take surveys of various kinds and conduct many formal interviews.

An individual who supplies the ethnographer with information is called a **consultant** or **informant.** Field research involves the help of many consultants, who sometimes are paid for their services. Just as no one individual is equally well informed about every aspect of our own sociocultural system, so no one person in another society is equally knowledgeable about every aspect of his or her society's way of life. Women are more knowledgeable than men concerning certain things and vice versa. Shamans and priests know more about religious rituals than other people. The elderly members of the community are usually most knowl-edgeable about myths, stories, and histories. Thus, the anthropologist has to attempt to identify and interview those people who are the most knowledgeable about the particular subjects he or she is interested in. Individuals whom the local community considers to be expert in some particular area, and whom the ethnog-rapher spends much time with, are known as **key consultants** or **key informants.**

A number of factors affect the quality and accuracy of the data collected through interviewing. The people being studied rarely understand fully what the anthro-pologist is trying to accomplish. In some instances, especially among minority populations, there may be a deliberate attempt to deceive the researcher. For ex-ample, collecting livestock-ownership data on the Navajo Reservation can at times prove difficult. The total number of livestock on the reservation is con-trolled by the tribe, and each stockowner has a permit that allows him or her to keep a certain number of animals. Since some people keep more stock than their permit allows, they are reluctant to disclose the actual number in their herd. There is also the problem of humorous deception. The Osage men wear a deertail roach on their heads during dances. During a dance an Osage was once overheard telling an inquisitive visitor

that these roaches were made out of horse tails, and that a young Osage male proved his manhood by cutting the hair for his roach from the tail of the meanest horse he could find. In this case, the Osage was simply having fun at the expense of a visitor, but anthropologists also encounter this problem. To get around these and other difficulties, anthropologists try to interview a number of individuals separately about specific points in order to gain several independent verifications.

Some societies actually prohibit the relating of certain kinds of cultural knowledge to outsiders. The Pueblos of the Rio Grande Valley of New Mexico are extremely secretive about their non-Christian religious beliefs and rituals. Non-Indians are not allowed to witness these ceremonies, and members of these pueb-los are prohibited from talking about them to non-Indians.

Other kinds of cultural barriers also make it difficult to collect certain types of data. For example, collecting genealogies is not always as easy as it might seem, because in many societies it is customary not to speak the names of the dead. Among the Yąnomamö of Venezuela and Brazil, not only is it taboo to speak the names of the dead, but it is considered discourteous to speak the names of prominent living men, for whom kinship terms are used when possible. When ethnog-rapher Napoleon Chagnon persisted in his attempts to collect genealogies, the Yąnomamö responded by in-venting a series of fictitious names for individuals, living and dead, as well as creating fictitious genealog-ical relationships. Only after five months of intensive research did he discover the hoax. When he men-tioned some of the names he had collected during a visit to a neighboring village, the people responded with "uncontrollable laughter," because his informants had made up names such as "hairy rectum" and "eagle shit" to avoid speaking real names.

■ Fieldwork as a Rite of Passage

Fieldwork is important to cultural anthropology not just because it is the major source of our data on humanity but because it is a key aspect of the education of the anthropologist. It is one thing to read ethnog-raphies about other ways of life, but it is something quite different to live among and interact with indi-viduals from another cultural tradition every day for a year or more. As we have seen, the anthropologist generally lives in the native community, submerging himself or herself in the social life of the people, living in native dwellings, eating local foods, learning the language, and participating as fully as an outsider is allowed in daily activities. Living as social minorities, usually for the first time in their lives, anthropologists depend on the goodwill of people whose norms and values they neither totally understand nor accept. Under these conditions, the participant observer has to adjust his or her activities to fit the cultural ideas and behavior patterns of the people. This modification of the fieldworker's own behavior is one—necessary—part of the process of learning about the community. Fieldworkers usually work alone, and they are socially and physically vulnerable to members of the community. During the course of their research, anthropologists will violate, or at least be perceived as violating, some of the societal norms of behavior. Such incidents may destroy the rapport gained with some key consultants or result in the researcher being ostracized. In very serious cases, the fieldworker may find himself or herself the target of physical violence.

When in the field, except on very rare occasions, the anthropologist is there as the uninvited guest of the community. Regardless of how researchers may rationalize their work as being for the long-term good of the community or humanity, they are basically there to serve their own needs and interests, not those of the community. If a serious problem develops between the anthropologist and members of the community, the fieldworker must bear the primary responsibility and blame (see Box 6.1).

The fieldwork experience tests and taxes the attitude of cultural relativity that anthropologists teach in their classrooms. It is easy to dicuss the concept of relativity in a university setting, but it is more difficult to apply this concept to one's own situation. Regardless of which society it is, certain sociocultural aspects will offend one's own cultural norms and values. Fieldworkers are regularly exposed to certain attitudes and behaviors that are unacceptable in their own society. For example, according to the anthropologist's own cultural standards, some local people might "abuse" certain family members or certain powerful leaders might "exploit" lower-ranking members of the society. As the fieldworker develops friendships, this "abuse" or "exploitation" frequently becomes personalized. Under what circumstances, if ever, an anthropologist should attempt to intervene and impose his or her cultural standards on the members of another society poses a real and very personal dilemma. In theory such inter-

vention is never permissible, but in real-life situations the answer is not always so clear.

Many people experience a kind of psychological trauma when surrounded by people speaking a language they cannot fully understand and speak only imperfectly, eating foods that are strange, seeing architecture that is alien, and observing people using gestures and behaving in ways they either do not comprehend or do not approve. The strange sounds, smells, tastes, sights, and behaviors result in the disorientation of many fieldworkers. Out of their normal cultural context, they do not understand what is happening around them yet realize that their own actions are often being misunderstood. The symptoms of this **culture shock** are psychological and sometimes even physiological: paranoia, anxiety, a longing for the folks back home, nausea, hypochondria, and frequently diarrhea.

The attempts by ethnographers to maintain their relativistic perspective and objectivity in their daily interactions with members of the other society usually compound the normal trauma of culture shock. Socially isolated and unable to release their frustrations and anxieties through conversations with sympathetic others, they often have to cope with their psychological difficulties alone.

For many anthropologists much of their time in the field is extremely traumatic, and as a result most anthropologists view fieldwork as a rite of passage. More than any other aspect of their training, fieldwork transforms the individual from a student of anthropology into a real, professional anthropologist. Although many overemphasize the importance of fieldwork in the training of anthropologists, it is undeniably a significant educational experience. Most individuals return from their fieldwork with a different perspective on themselves and their own sociocultural system. Fieldwork thus often teaches us as much about ourselves as abut those we are supposed to be studying.

Ethnological Methods

So far we have discussed only how anthropologists collect sociocultural data on peoples, past and present, using fieldwork and historical materials. We currently have some sociocultural data available on over 1,200 different societies. As we will see in the following chapters, anthropologists have used these data to

ETHICS AND ANTHROPOLOGICAL RESEARCH

ost of the societies and communities that modern anthropologists work among are ethnic minority peoples within larger nation-states. Even when they are not social minorities, they can still be damaged individually or as groups by information collected by anthropologists. Thus it is ethically imperative that research findings not be "misused." In 1971 the Council of the American Anthropological Association adopted the "Principles of Professional Responsibility." This statement was amended in November 1976, and in 1989 additional revisions were proposed. The proposed revisions contain six parts; the following is only part I, the portion that addresses the question of fieldwork ethics.

I. **Responsibility to peoples whose lives and cultures anthropologists study.** Anthropologists' first responsibility is to those whose lives and cultures they study. Should conflicts of interest arise, the interests of these people take precedence over other considerations. Anthropologists must do everything in their power to protect the dignity and privacy of the people with whom they work, conduct research or perform other professional activities. Their physical, social and emotional safety and welfare are the professional concerns of the anthropologists who have worked among them.

A. *The rights, interests, safety, and sensitivities of those who entrust information to anthropologists must be safeguarded.*

1. The right of those providing information to anthropologists either to remain anonymous or to receive recognition is to be respected and defended. It is the responsibility of anthropologists to make every effort to determine the preferences of those providing information and to comply with their wishes.

   a. It should be made clear to anyone providing information that despite the anthropologist's best intentions and efforts anonymity may be compromised or recognition fail to materialize.

2. Anthropologists should not reveal the identity of groups or persons whose anonymity is protected through the use of pseudonyms.

3. The aims of all their professional activities should be clearly communicated by anthropologists to those among whom they work.

4. Anthropologists must not exploit individuals or groups for personal gain. They should give fair return for the help and services they receive. They must recognize their debt to the societies in which they work and their obligation to reciprocate in appropriate ways.

5. Anthropologists have an ongoing obligation to assess both the positive and negative consequences of their activities and the publications resulting from those activities. They should inform individuals and groups likely to be affected of any consequences relevant to them that they anticipate. In any case, however, their work must not violate these principles of professional responsibility. If they anticipate the possibility that such violations might occur they should take steps, including, if necessary, discontinuance of work, to avoid such outcomes.

6. Whether they are engaged in academic or nonacademic research, anthropologists must be candid about their professional identities. If the results of their activities are not to be made public, this should be made clear to all concerned from the outset.

7. Anthropologists must take into account and, where relevant, make explicit the extent to which their own personal and cultural values affect their professional activities. They must also recognize and deal candidly and judiciously with the effects that the often conflicting demands and values of employers, sponsors, host governments and research publications may have upon their work.

The principal point of this statement is that anthropologists must take all reasonable care to see that their research does no harm to the individuals and groups that provide them with information. ■

Source: Reproduced by permission of the American Anthropological Association from *Anthropological Newsletter,* 30:8, November 1989. Not for sale or further reproduction.

---

demonstrate a wide range of sociocultural variability among human populations. However, we are not merely interested in describing particular sociocultural systems and the range of variability in these systems. We are also interested in attempting to explain why these differences exist. In other words, anthropologists want to make generalizations concerning sociocultural systems, and thus explain why differences exist between peoples. Generalizations cannot be made based on the study of a single society; we need methods by which many societies can be compared in a systematic way. There are two major forms of multisystem comparisons: (1) cross-cultural comparisons and (2) controlled historical comparisons. The objective in both types of comparative studies is to test hypotheses.

■ Cross-Cultural Comparisons

The most frequently used comparative method is **cross cultural comparison.** In this method, hypotheses are tested by examining the statistical correlations between particular sociocultural variables, using synchronic data drawn from a number of different societies. Historical changes in the societies examined are ignored; the societies are compared at whatever time period they were studied. This research method involves three steps. First, the researcher must state the idea as a hypothesis—that is, state it in such a way that it can be supported or not supported ("tested") by data drawn from a large number of human populations. Second, the ethnologist chooses a sample of societies (usually randomly), and studies the ethnographies that describe their way of life. Third, the data collected from these ethnographies are then classified and grouped in such a manner that the correlations between variables may be shown statistically. What the ethnographer is attempting to find is the pattern of association: do two or more sociocultural variables consistently occur together or not? In most cases these tasks are far more difficult than they may sound.

To illustrate how the cross-cultural method is used to test an hypothesis, we shall examine the relationship between sorcery and legal systems within a group of societies. Sorcery will be discussed in some detail in chapter 15. Here it is sufficient for you to know that sorcery is the belief that certain people (sorcerers) have power, either supernatural or magical, to cause harm to others. Some anthropologists believe that sorcery serves as a means of social control in societies that lack a formalized legal apparatus—courts, police, and so forth—to punish wrongdoers. They argue that people will be reluctant to cause trouble if they believe that a victim of their trouble making has the ability to use supernatural power to retaliate against them. Overall, societies without a formal legal system should have a greater need for a mechanism such as sorcery to control

behavior. So if the hypothesis that sorcery is a mechanism for social control is correct, we ought to find that sorcery is more likely to be important in societies without formal means of punishment than in societies with a specialized legal system.

To see if this hypothesis is true across a variety of societies, we use the cross-cultural method. We determine for many societies (1) the relative degree of importance of sorcery, and (2) whether the society has a formal apparatus for punishing wrongdoing. We make a table in which all the possible combinations of the two sociocultural elements are recorded:

	SPECIALIZED LEGAL APPARATUS	
SORCERY	Absent	Present
Important	A	B
Unimportant	C	D

In the cells of the table we record the number of societies in which the four possible combinations are found. If the hypothesis is supported, we should find that cells A and D contain the greatest number of societies. If the hypothesis is not supported, we should find that the distribution of societies in the cells is random, or that cells B and C contain the greatest number of societies, or some other distribution.

In 1950, Beatrice Whiting actually conducted such a study by surveying the ethnographic literature for fifty societies. Her results were as follows (Whiting 1950, 87):

	SPECIALIZED LEGAL APPARATUS	
SORCERY	Absent	Present
Important	30	5
Unimportant	3	12

On the basis of this comparison, we might conclude that the hypothesis is supported, since most of the societies fall into the cells predicted by our hypothesis. We would not worry about the eight societies (the "exceptions") that appear in cells B and C. The hypothesis did not claim that social control was the *only* function of sorcery, so the importance of sorcery in the five societies in cell B might be explained by some other factor. Nor did we claim that sorcery was the *only* way that societies lacking a specialized legal apparatus had to control their members, so the three societies in cell C might have developed some alternative means of social control. (Although outside the scope of this text, statistical tests are available that show how confident a researcher can be that such associations did not occur by chance.)

Some confusions are caused by cross-cultural tabulations such as this. One of the most common is to mistake correlation for causation: simply because two sociocultural elements (X and Y) are usually found together does not mean that one (X) has caused the other (Y). Y could have caused X, or both X and Y could have been caused by some third element, W. In the preceding example, it was assumed that the absence of formal legal punishments "caused" many societies to need some other social control mechanism and that sorcery became important to meet this need. On the basis of the data in the table, we might also conclude that societies in which sorcery is important have little need for a formal legal apparatus, so they fail to develop one.

To acquire the data needed to test her hypothesis, Whiting read through ethnographic information on all fifty societies in her sample. This approach suffers from several disadvantages. It is so time-consuming that only a small number of societies can be included in the sample. There is also the problem of bias by the researcher, who must decide, for example, whether sorcery should be considered "important" or "unimportant" among some people. Borderline cases might tend to get lumped into the category that supports the researcher's hypothesis.

Thanks largely to a lifetime of work by George Murdock, another method is available to modern researchers that partially overcomes these two problems (although it has troubles of its own, to be discussed shortly). In the *Ethnographic Atlas*, Murdock and his associates have summarized information on over 1,200 societies in the form of coded tables. For each sociocultural system there are codes that show its form of kinship, marriage, economy, religion, political organization, division of labor, and so forth. Contemporary cross-cultural researchers no longer need to search through ethnographies for information relevant to their investigations; rather, they generally use the information already coded and analyze the results using a computer. This reduces the bias of the researcher, for whoever coded the information on a particular society had no knowledge of the hypothesis currently under investigation. It also allows a larger number of societies to be included in a sample, because the data can be retrieved far more quickly.

Using cross-cultural methods to see if some specific hypothesis applies to a large number of societies is thus easier today than ever before, but some difficulties still exist. One seems to be inherent in the method itself, which dissects sociocultural systems into parts ("variables" as we called them) and assigns a value (or "state") to each part. In the preceding example, the variables were sorcery, which had two states (important, unimportant), and specialized legal apparatus, which also had two states (present, absent). To test the hypothesis that the states of these two sociocultural elements are consistently related, we ignored everything else about them. We also ignored everything else about the societies in the sample, such as their family systems and their economies.

A more familiar example will make the point clearly. One element of sociocultural systems is the number of gods in which people believe. For purposes of some specific hypothesis the possible states of this variable might be monotheism (belief in one god), polytheism (belief in many gods), and no gods at all. Any researcher who included modern North America in the sample would probably consider our primary religion—Christianity—as monotheistic. Most of the Middle East also would be considered monotheistic. The problem is, Can North American monotheism be considered equivalent to the Middle Eastern monotheisms? If we consider them the same, we ignore the differences between the worship of the Christian God, the Jewish Yahweh, and the Islamic Allah. When we lump these three varieties of monotheism together into a single kind of religion, we certainly distort them to some degree.

Cross-cultural studies examine data ahistorically, or without reference to time. In other words, the sociocultural system of a particular society is treated as timeless or unchanging. Thus in cross-cultural studies and the *Ethnographic Atlas*, there is "a" sociocultural system coded for the Cheyenne: Cheyenne sociocultural system circa 1850. However, the sociocultural system of a society is never stable, but is constantly changing (in chapter 17 we discuss this process). For example, today the Cheyennes live in houses, drive cars and trucks, and participate in a wage-money economy. In 1850 the Cheyennes lived in hide-covered tipis, rode horses, and hunted buffalo. In 1650

■ *Christianity, Judaism and Islam all are monotheistic and have common historical roots. But Christians and Jews would not pray by prostrating themselves towards Mecca, as this Moslem man from New Delhi, India is doing. Should cross-cultural researchers consider them one kind of religion or not?*

the Cheyennes lived in permanent earth lodge villages, traveled by foot or canoe, and depended on farming and hunting for their subsistence. Although the Cheyenne sociocultural systems have continuity, all aspects of their lifeway changed to some degree over the period just described. Thus, in reality there is no stable Cheyenne sociocultural system, but an ever-changing system. The synchronic studies used in cross-cultural research create an artificial picture of the sociocultural system of a society.

■ *Controlled Historical Comparisons*

Only in the past decade or two have anthropologists attempted systematic diachronic analyses of sociocultural data. Such studies are called **controlled historical comparisons.** Unlike cross-cultural studies, controlled historical comparisons use changes in particular groupings of societies over time to define general sociocultural

patterning and test hypotheses. Controlled historical comparisons, like cross-cultural studies, are usually extremely complex. We illustrate this method by a simple example.

As we discuss in chapter 11, people organize their family lives in various ways. Two common ways are matrilineal descent and patrilineal descent. In matrilineal societies, family group membership is inherited through your mother; you belong to your mother's family. In patrilineal societies, group membership is inherited through your father; you belong to your father's family. Anthropologists have long attempted to explain why some societies are matrilineal and others patrilineal. Cross-cultural research has shown that a relationship exists between matrilineality and patrilineality and the relative economic importance of males and females in the society. However, cross-cultural studies can only show us correlations between descent and other synchronic aspects of their sociocultural system. For example, these studies can tell us what types of economic systems are most frequently found with matrilineal or patrilineal societies. Cross-cultural studies cannot measure the long-term effects of external changes on matrilineal or patrilineal societies. Is matrilineality or patrilineality more adaptive in some situations than others? If so, what types of situations favor matrilineal societies, and what types of situations favor patrilineal societies? To examine this question, we must turn to controlled historical comparisons.

Michael Allen (1984) has asserted that matrilineal societies in the Pacific appear to be more successful in adapting to European contact than are patrilineal societies. Is there a way to test Allen's assertion? First, we must restructure this statement as a testable hypothesis. What do we mean by success? The term *success* is rather subjective and cannot be directly measured. Thus we have to convert this term into some measurable quantity. One quantifiable measure of the success of a particular system is the relative ability of a society to maintain or expand its population over time. Thus our hypothesis would be that given the same degree of disruptive external pressures, matrilineal societies maintain their population levels better over time than patrilineal societies. Now we need to find a group of matrilineal societies and patrilineal societies that experienced a comparable intensity of external contact over a period of time, and compare their relative populations at the beginning and end of the period. If Allen is correct, the matrilineal societies should have a relatively higher population at the end of the period than the patrilineal societies.

The farming Native American tribes of the eastern United States present an almost ideal case for testing Allen's assertion. They had similar sociocultural systems, except that some were matrilineal and others were patrilineal. Their collective histories of contact with Europeans were also basically the same. During the historical period, all of these societies suffered the effects of epidemic diseases, warfare (with Europeans as well as intertribal), severe territorial dislocation, political domination, and social discrimination.

Now the problem is determining an appropriate time frame to examine and finding comparable population data. One problem with ethnohistoric research is that the researcher is forced to use the data available in the records. It is not until about 1775 that sufficient population data are available in missionary, military, and explorer accounts to estimate the populations of all these tribes with any accuracy. In 1910 the United States Bureau of the Census conducted a special Indian census, which was the first truly comprehensive census of Native American societies in the United States. Thus the time frame we will use is from 1775 to 1910. Using ethnographic data we can then classify particular societies as either matrilineal or patrilineal and determine their populations for beginning and end of this period:

	1775	1910	PERCENT
Matrilineal societies	88,590	82,714	93
Patrilineal societies	36,400	13,463	37
Totals	124,990	96,177	77

From this table we can see that during this 135-year period, the matrilineal societies declined by only about 7 percent of their total population, while patrilineal societies lost 63 percent of their population. Thus if maintenance of population is a measure of a society's success, then matrilineal societies in the eastern United States were more successful than patrilineal societies.

As is the case with all comparative studies, findings such as these raise more questions than they answer. Are these population figures and the historical experience of these societies truly comparable? If they are comparable, is the significant factor differences in descent form, or is it some other sociocultural factor we have not considered? We need to add at this point that not all matrilineal societies in this study were equally

successful in maintaining their population levels, and that a few patrilineal societies studied actually increased in population during this period. Thus there is room for argument. If in the final analysis, however, we decide that our findings are valid and that matrilineal societies are, under certain conditions, more adaptive than patrilineal societies, we still cannot directly say why.

It is important to note that cross-cultural comparisons and controlled historical comparisons give us distinctly different measures of sociocultural phenomena. They address different types of questions and test different types of hypotheses. Thus they are complimentary, not competitive, methodologies.

Some anthropologists (especially idealists—see chapter 5) believe that both kinds of comparative studies distort each sociocultural system in the sample so much that the whole method is invalid. They believe that human ways of life are too complex to be broken down into neat variables or elements that take on a small number of states or values. They also think that ripping each element out of the particular context in which it is embedded robs it of its significance, for each element acquires its meaning only in its local historical and sociocultural context. They therefore argue that comparisons of elements across sociocultural systems are at least misleading and possibly always invalid.

Despite these and other problems, comparative methods are the only practical means available for determining whether a hypothesis is valid among human sociocultural systems. Those who use these methods are aware of the difficulties, yet they believe that the advantage of being able to process information on large numbers of societies outweighs the problems.

Summary

Anthropological methods fall into two overall categories. Ethnographic methods involve the collection of information on a specific sociocultural system, whereas ethnological methods are used to test hypotheses or to investigate theoretical ideas by comparing information on numerous sociocultural systems. The basic aims of ethnographic methods are descriptive, whereas ethnological investigations aim to determine whether some hypothesis or theoretical idea is supported by the accumulated data on human lifeways.

The kinds of methods used by ethnographers depend on whether they are investigating a contemporary or a past way of life. Research into the past usually involves some combination of recall ethnography (interviewing living members of the society about past events and customs) and ethnohistory (perusal of written documents). These methods involve considerable interpretation by researchers. The elderly and others interviewed in recall ethnography often misremember events or romanticize the past of their people. Those who wrote the documents used in ethnohistoric reconstructions sometimes misinterpreted events because of their sociocultural backgrounds and ethnocentrism. Often the contents of documents are affected by the private interests of their authors.

Fieldwork is the primary method of acquiring data about living people. Fieldworkers usually live among those they study for a period of at least a year, conducting formal interviews and surveys and engaging in participant observation. Although the difficulties of conducting fieldwork vary with the personality and gender of the fieldworker and with the people and specific topic being studied, three problems are common. Fieldworkers must not only fight against their own ethnocentrism and tendencies to stereotype those they study, but they must also overcome the stereotypes local people have developed about foreigners. It is often difficult to establish a rapport with local people, for they may have had no previous experience with the kinds of questions fieldworkers ask. Identifying reliable informants and finding people willing to participate in intensive surveys may pose a serious problem. People sometimes deliberately deceive the anthropologist, for they mistrust his or her motives, do not want certain facts to become public, or are culturally forbidden to give away secrets of their religion. Today fieldwork is viewed as an essential part of the graduate education of anthropologists and is almost a prerequisite for professionalism. It is in some respects a rite of passage.

Ethnological methods involve ways of systematically and reliably comparing massive amounts of information collected by previous ethnographers. The use of comparative methods presents many difficulties, including stating the research hypothesis in such a way that it is testable, reliably defining and measuring the variables of interest for many societies, deciding whether similar sociocultural elements from two or more societies are the "same" or "different," and contending with unintentional researcher bias. The results of comparative studies can be difficult to interpret. Correlation is often confused with causation.

Many anthropologists (especially idealists) feel that all comparative methods are invalid, for they rip sociocultural elements out of the context that gives them meaning. They therefore inevitably distort the variables they claim to measure objectively, according to some. Despite such difficulties, comparative methods are the only way to test hypotheses and investigate theoretical ideas in a large sample of societies.

Key Terms

ethnographic methods	stereotyping
ethnological methods	consultant (informant)
recall ethnography	key consultant (key informant)
ethnohistory	
fieldwork	culture shock
participant observation	cross-cultural comparisons
	controlled historical comparisons

Suggested Readings

Works that deal with ethnographic methods include:

■ Agar, Michael. *The Professional Stranger: An Informal Introduction to Ethnography.* New York: Academic, 1980.
Quite good for the beginning student. Tells how ethnographers do their work, with lots of examples taken from the author's own field experiences.

■ Pelto, Perti J., and H. Gretal. *Anthropological Research: The Structure of Inquiry.* Cambridge: Cambridge University Press, 1978.
Emphasizes importance of quantification and measurement in fieldwork.

■ Spradley, James P. *The Ethnographic Interview.* New York: Holt, Rinehart and Winston, 1979.

■ _____. *Participant Observation.* New York: Holt, Rinehart and Winston, 1980.
Two books that complement one another, one focusing on structured interviewing of informants, the other on detailed observation.

A number of books deal with the actual experiences of ethnographers in the field. They are valuable for conveying the feeling of fieldwork, of problems ethnographers encounter, of relating to local people, and so forth.

■ Briggs, Jean. *Never in Anger: Portrait of an Eskimo Family*. Cambridge, Mass.: Harvard University Press, 1970.
A personal account of life with an Eskimo family.

■ Fernea, Elizabeth. *A Street in Marrakech*. New York: Doubleday/Anchor, 1969.
Journalist-author provides a lively account of her life among women in Morocco.

■ Freilich, Morris, ed. *Marginal Natives: Anthropologists at Work*. New York: Harper and Row, 1970.
Ten anthropologists discuss the problems of fieldwork.

■ Golde, Peggy, ed. *Women in the Field: Anthropological Experiences*. Chicago: Aldine, 1970.
Twelve female ethnographers discuss special difficulties they encountered because of their gender.

■ Maybury-Lewis, David. *The Savage and the Innocent*. Boston: Beacon, 1968.
A description of the author's fieldwork in the central Brazilian rain forest.

■ Powdermaker, Hortense. *Stranger and Friend: The Way of an Anthropologist*. New York: Norton, 1966.
Autobiographical work, with a description of the author's fieldwork experiences in four different sociocultural settings, including Hollywood.

■ Rabinow, Paul. *Reflections on Fieldwork in Morocco*. Berkeley: University of California Press, 1977.
An interesting discussion of the author's experiences in Morocco.

Part Three

DIVERSITY

erhaps the major contribution of cultural anthropology to the understanding of humanity is its documentation of the remarkable diversity of human ways of life. We have discovered how human populations vary in their adaptations to nature, their family and kinship systems, their relations between the sexes, their political organizations, their religions, and even their life cycles. In this part, we describe some of the most important ways in which sociocultural systems vary.

Although anthropologists know a great deal more about the facts of this diversity than they do about the causes of it, numerous ideas have been offered to explain why some elements of sociocultural systems take one form here, another form somewhere else. We also present and evaluate some of the major hypotheses that claim to account for this diversity.

■ (Facing page) *Anthropologists have documented the remarkable sociocultural diversity of humankind. Religions, for example, vary enormously, as this photo of Moslems prostrating themselves before Allah illustrates.*

ADAPTATION: FORAGING

■ *Contents*

■ (Above) *Adaptation refers to the ways organisms relate to their environment. Foragers are people who acquire their food from gathering wild plants and hunting wild animals. These San women and children are gathering wild plants.*

Like any other animal, humans must acquire resources from their natural environment if they are to survive and persist. Food getting is an essential part of this process of relating to nature, and various human populations have developed diverse ways of exploiting their environments for food. In this chapter, we first introduce some useful concepts that help us to understand the technical and organizational factors involved in acquiring food and other necessities of existence. We also describe the earliest and most enduring adaptation of humanity—foraging, or the exploitation of wild plants and animals. In chapter 8, we describe the adaptation that has nourished most of humankind for the last several thousand years—domestication, or the intentional breeding and care of plants and animals that have been selected for their usefulness to people.

Adaptation

The process by which an organism develops physiological and behavioral characteristics that allow it to survive and reproduce is called **adaptation.** A useful way to think about adaptation is that the environment (or *habitat,* the place where an organism lives) poses certain problems that living things must solve if they are to survive and reproduce; adaptation is coping with these problems. Because environments are constantly changing, organisms are constantly adapting; adaptation is then an ongoing process, not a steady state.

Natural selection is the most important mechanism by which nonhuman organisms adapt. Ordinarily, natural selection favors the survival and reproduction of those individual organisms who have inherited traits that allow them to cope most effectively with conditions of their local environment. Human populations likewise adapt to the environment through genetic/biological changes. For instance, diseases spare those who are most resistant, so over many generations populations who suffer from some disease will become more resistant to it. As in other living things, natural

selection works on our bodies to fashion physiological adaptations to viruses, bacteria, and other pathogenic organisms; to local climate; and to other environmental factors.

However, humankind differs from other animals in an important way: we adapt to environmental conditions primarily by means of technologies, behavioral patterns, and cultural knowledge, not mainly by alterations in our anatomy or physiology. If the climate grows colder, or if a people migrate into a colder area, they cope mainly by lighting fires, constructing shelters, and making clothing, not mainly by evolving physiological adaptations to cold. Humans hunt animals by making weapons and learning techniques of cooperative stalking and killing, not mainly by evolving the ability to run faster than our game. Technology (including both the material tools themselves and the socially learned skills of making and using them) and social organization allow us to adapt to a wide range of habitats without undergoing major alterations in our genetic endowment.

Any human population must adjust to three categories of forces in the environment. The first is the nonliving—or *abiotic*—environment, which includes temperature, precipitation, terrain, water, and so forth. The second is the living—or *biotic*—environment, including the nature, distribution, and abundance of plants and nonhuman animals that people eat, or that affect them in other ways. The third is the human environment, or the presence of other human populations with whom a population competes, fights, trades, or has other kinds of relations. Humans adapt their sociocultural systems (intentionally or unintentionally) to any and all of these external forces. But as we shall discuss, most populations do not simply respond to their environment; they also interact with it, modifying it to suit their needs and desires.

Biomes

The ways people adapt to their habitat are limited by its biotic and abiotic characteristics. In understanding human adaptations, it therefore is useful to have a broad knowledge of the types of terrestrial environments that occur on the earth. Ecologists divide the earth into several biological regions, or **biomes.** A biome is a large geographic region with similar climatic, edaphic (soil), and vegetational characteristics.

Generally speaking, annual precipitation, temperature, and incident solar radiation determine the kind of soil and vegetation found in a biome. In turn, these climatic and vegetational features broadly determine the kinds and abundance of fauna (animals) that will occur.

The map in Figure 7.1 shows the global distribution of biomes. (We discuss the characteristics of each biome that are most relevant for human adaptation to it as we go along in this chapter and the next.) Ecological conditions within each biome are not perfectly uniform, of course, and the boundaries between biomes are not as sharp as they appear in Figure 7.1. Biomes nonetheless provide a convenient classification of the earth's plant and animal communities for purposes of this text.

Some of the ways the ecological characteristics of a biome limit the methods a human population can use to exploit it are obvious: it is hard to farm deserts unless you irrigate, and it is tougher to raise cattle or sheep in a tropical forest than in a grassland or savannah. Other limitations on human adaptation imposed by a habitat are more subtle. For example, there are places where it is possible to farm, but low and unreliable rainfall make

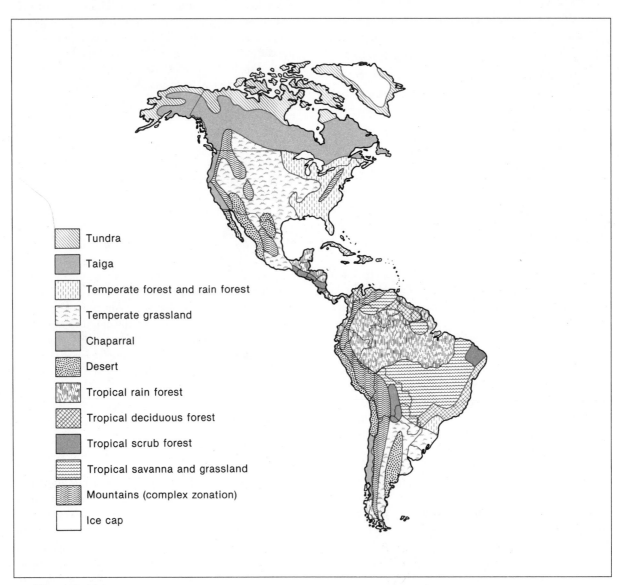

Legend:
- Tundra
- Taiga
- Temperate forest and rain forest
- Temperate grassland
- Chaparral
- Desert
- Tropical rain forest
- Tropical deciduous forest
- Tropical scrub forest
- Tropical savanna and grassland
- Mountains (complex zonation)
- Ice cap

■ *Figure 7.1A*
Distribution of Major Biomes (Western Hemisphere)

it risky; so people combine farming with keeping domestic animals.

Production

The acquisition of energy and materials from an environment is one of the most important ways in which people interact with nature. The activities in which the energy and raw materials available in a local habitat are exploited by people are called **production.** Production transforms nature's raw materials into things that satisfy people's material wants. Production thus takes something that is in the environment (a resource) and makes it into something that people can use (a good or product). Productive activities are obviously essential to the persistence of any individual human being and of any population. Indeed, some anthropologists—those who follow the materialist (see chapter 5) theoretical orientation— think that production is so essential that many other features of a population's sociocultural system are determined by it.

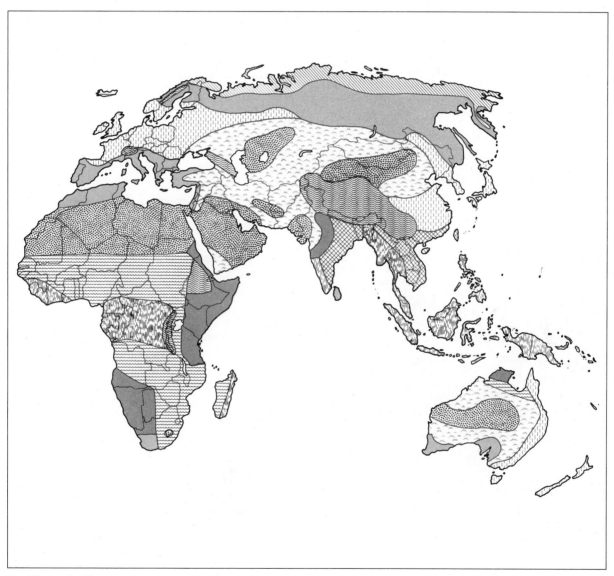

■ *Figure 7.1B*
Distribution of Major Biomes (Eastern Hemisphere)

The Factors of Production

Productive activities ordinarily bring together three components. In producing a good, people apply (1) their own time and energy and (2) available technology to (3) the resources available in their habitat. These three **factors of production** may be brought together in various ways to produce a good humans can use to satisfy their material needs and wants.

Another word for the human time and energy required to produce something is, of course, *labor* or *work*. As individuals working alone, or in cooperative groups, people must expend the energy of their muscles to produce a consumable product.

Technology, the second factor of production, has two components. The first is the physical objects themselves, the tools. Some tools reduce the amount of human time and energy needed to produce goods, and thus save labor (e.g., hoes). Others allow more goods, or a greater variety of goods, to be produced from a given area of land (e.g., fertilizer). Still other tools allow people to produce goods that human labor alone could not provide (e.g., an axe used to chop and split large trees). The second component of technology is that part of cultural knowledge that people bring to bear in exploiting their environments: how to make and use tools, how to define and recognize resources, the places and seasons where plants and animals are to be found, how to manage resources for long-term conservation, and so forth. This kind of cultural knowledge is often incredibly complex and detailed, among preindustrial peoples as well as ourselves.

Labor and technology work on or with *resources*, the third factor of production. A peoples' habitat influences the kinds of resources that are available, their abundance, their distribution in time and space, and so forth. Different biomes, for instance, offer different resources. However, the resources available to a human population do not depend *solely* on their environment. The raw materials present in a habitat are not always recognized and defined as resources. Coal, oil, wind, and geothermal energy were not resources until the technology became available to use them. Likewise, resources, as well as permissible uses of them, are influenced by cultural ideas people have inherited from previous generations (Box 7.1 discusses an example of the cultural definition of resource use). Thus, habitat, material technology, and cultural ideas all interact in determining the resources available to a people.

The Organization of Production

In satisfying their material wants and needs, people expend their own labor, use tools and skills, and exploit resources in ways that are allowed in their sociocultural system. In theory, nothing more is required to obtain life-sustaining and want-satisfying

■ *Technology reduces the amount of labor needed to perform some task and allows humans to produce goods that they otherwise could not obtain. This Efe pygmy is using an axe to cut down a tree to harvest the honey inside.*

■ *The resources available to a people can change as technology changes. Wind has long served to move ships, grind grain, and pump water. These windmills illustrate its newest use in generating electricity.*

energy and materials from an environment. Stranded on his island, Robinson Crusoe survived. But real individuals and real societies do not live in social isolation: they may have to worry about whether the products of their labor can be exchanged for the products of someone else's labor, or about other individuals or groups who would like to have access to the resources they are using, or about who is to perform what kinds of tasks. Production, in other words, is universally an *organized social activity*: individuals know what to do and what to expect others to do; they know who to work with and how; they know when and where to work so that they do not violate the rights of others. The organization of production has three important components: the **division of labor, patterns of cooperation,** and **rights of access.**

Division of Labor   To say that labor is divided is to say simply that different kinds of tasks (specific productive activities) are assigned to different categories or groups of people. Gender and age are universal bases for the division of labor, and in most societies differences in skill and knowledge also are an important basis for assigning tasks to individuals. One advantage the division of labor offers humanity is that, in theory, productive activities can be assigned to those individuals best suited, or at least well suited, to perform them.

Patterns of Cooperation   Accompanying the division of labor, and closely related to it, are patterns of cooperation in production. Most kinds of productive activity involve some kind of cooperation: people combine their labor with that of other people because this allows them to produce more goods with a given amount of labor.

Rights of Access   Another aspect of the organization of production is assigning (to individuals and groups) rights of access to resources. This is roughly what we call *property rights*. Generally, a given area of land or territory, or a specific resource of a territory, is allocated to some group. Members of this group are allowed to exploit the territory's resources; others are prohibited from doing so, or may do so only with permission.

There is great cross-cultural variability in the way sociocultural systems assign rights of access to resources. Anthropologists generally distinguish *ownership rights* from *use rights*, and *group rights* from *individual*

rights. In preindustrial populations ownership of territory and resources is frequently vested in a group—most often a kinship (e.g., family) or residential (e.g., village) group. Individual members of the group have the right (*use right*) to exploit the resources of the area, but they must do so without violating the other members' culturally legitimate rights over the territory's resources. The rights of individuals are always limited by the rights of others in the group. This is true even in our own private-property system. No individual is free to do anything he or she wishes to with his or her land, house, auto, or lawn mower, for some actions taken with these possessions would violate our cultural conceptions of the legitimate rights of others.

In sum, production organization includes who will do what and when, who will cooperate with (or take orders from) whom and how, and who has rights of access over which areas and resources. We can see that production requires the three factors of production—labor, technology, and land—plus organization. We can see also that organization is essential; without it, labor and technology would be less efficient, and competition and conflict over access to resources would disrupt the process of production.

We now have a good conceptual background with which to discuss the major ways that the human species has developed to wrest a living from the environment. In the remainder of this chapter we discuss the foraging

■ *Foreign observers who see cattle roaming around unharmed in the towns and countryside of India, while beggars and many famers are malnourished, conclude that the Hindu religion makes these animals economically useless. Such conclusions are erroneous (see Box 7.1).*

Box 7.1

WHO IS WORSHIPPING THE SACRED COW?

In traditional India the slaughter of cattle for eating is forbidden by teachings of the Hindu religion. To Westerners, this religious prohibition on the consumption of beef appears to be an example of inefficient or even irrational resource use: Indians allegedly "would starve rather than eat their sacred cows." This opinion arises partly from the observations of visitors, who see cattle roaming around unharmed in towns and countrysides even while beggars and many farmers are malnourished. It certainly looks like India has too many cattle!

The Hindu prohibition does not mean, however, that cattle are economically useless, that not eating them is irrational, or even that the country is overrun with nonproducing cattle. In India, cattle serve as resources in ways other than as a source of animal flesh. Harnessed to the plow, they help farmers prepare their fields for planting. Their excrement, spread over the farmer's fields, serves as useful fertilizer.

When allowed to dry and taken to the family hearth to burn, cattle dung also serves as cooking fuel. Although their yield is low compared to cattle bred especially for their milk, Indian cattle also provide dairy products. Cattle thus provide traction, fertilizer, fuel, and dairy products. It is easy for Westerners to overlook some of these other uses, for we use fuel-powered tractors for plowing, manufactured chemicals for fertilizing, and natural gas and electricity for cooking. Because of their religious beliefs, Hindus do not use cattle primarily as a food resource in the same way as do North Americans, but this does not mean that their uses are irrational.

At any rate, before North Americans condemn Hindus for not making efficient use of their sacred animal, we should examine the way we raise and feed our own cattle and other livestock. As discussed in the next chapter, domesticated animals are used most efficiently as human food when they convert vegetation that humans cannot eat into meat, milk, and other high-quality proteins that humans can digest. It is not efficient to feed livestock vegetable foods that people can consume, for most of the vegetables' food value is lost to the animals' metabolism.

Yet our North American economic system encourages farmers to devote much of their land to the production of animal feed. In the United States in 1975, over 90 percent of the vegetable

protein suitable for human consumption was fed to livestock. For every five pounds of vegetable protein consumed by livestock, only one pound of animal products (meat, milk, and eggs) was returned to humans. Stated differently, Americans could have eaten about the same amount of protein using only roughly one-fifth the amount of land simply by consuming the food directly rather than converting it into animal products. Food specialist Frances Moore Lappé emphasizes the point:

> Of the 145 million tons of grain and soy fed to our beef cattle, poultry, and hogs in 1979, only 21 tons were returned to us in meat, poultry, and eggs. *The rest, about 124 million tons of grain and soybeans, became inaccessible to human consumption. . . .* To put this enormous quantity in some perspective, consider that 120 million tons is worth over $20 billion. If cooked, it is the equivalent of 1 cup of grain for every single human being on earth every day for a year. (Lappé 1982, 69, 71)

Using agricultural land to grow grains or other crops to feed to cattle, poultry, or hogs is thus a poor use of our continent's agricultural resources. You don't have to go all the way to India to see food resources used inefficiently; you need look no farther than your own dinner plate. ■

Sources: Harris (1977, 1985), Lappé (1982), Pimentel, et al. (1975).

---

adaptation and its influence on the sociocultural systems of foraging peoples. In the next chapter we consider domestication and its effects on human ways of life.

Foragers

Foragers, also called **hunter-gatherers,** are populations who make little or no effort to control the natural resources that provide their subsistence. For the most part, they live by collecting (gathering) the wild plants and hunting (and sometimes fishing) for the wild animals that occur naturally in their habitats. Hunter-gatherers have great interest to scientist and layperson alike. For one thing, *Homo sapiens*—modern humanity—has existed as a species for between two and three hundred thousand years. Recent evidence indicates that our ancestors diverged from the evolutionary line leading to modern African apes at least five million years ago. Yet there is no evidence of any cultivation or animal domestication anywhere on the earth until around 10,000 years ago. Humanity thus has spent only a tiny proportion of its entire history cultivating foodstuffs and keeping domestic animals; for the rest of the past, humans lived by foraging. Presumably, then, what ethnographers have learned about hunter-gatherers who survived into the twentieth century will tell us something important about how our prehistoric ancestors lived. Another reason for studying foragers is that they provide a good opportunity to investigate how the lifeways of humans who live especially close to nature are influenced by their habitat. Further, as we shall see, recent fieldworkers have uncovered some surprising facts about many hunter-gatherers—how adequately they are nourished, how long and hard they work, and so forth. This information allows us to judge what the human species might have gained and lost as a result of agriculture, civilization, and—most recently—industrialization.

Until around 10,000 years ago, all human populations lived by hunting and gathering. As methods of cultivating plants and herding animals developed in a few regions, agricultural and herding peoples began to increase in numbers and expand geographically. Over the millenia, this increase and expansion pushed foragers into habitats that cultivators and herders found relatively useless or were unable to exploit effectively. As a result, when Europeans began to encounter non-Western peoples in the sixteenth and seventeenth centuries, most foragers were located in environments that are too cold or arid to support cultivation with preindustrial technologies (see Figure 7.2). By the twentieth century, foragers were found in only a few tropical rain forests, deserts or dry savannas, tundras, and boreal forest biomes.

How does their adaptation affect other elements of the way of life of hunter-gatherers? In particular, how is production organized, and how does this organization affect the sociocultural systems of foragers?

■ *Foraging and Sociocultural Systems*

We must always be careful in generalizing about foragers. They are surprisingly diverse, not only in the wild foods

■ *Figure 7.2*
Principal Regions of Foragers at Time of First Contact with Europeans

they exploit but also in other realms of their sociocultural lives. There is an enormous difference between the Indians of the northwest coast of North America, who lived quite a sedentary existence in sizable settlements, and the Shoshone, who roamed the Great Basin in tiny bands or even individual families. Despite the dangers of overgeneralization, we can identify sociocultural features that are widespread—but by no means universal—among foraging populations. Many of these characteristics are related to how hunter-gatherers organize themselves to exploit their habitats efficiently.

Division of Labor by Age and Gender   The division of labor among foragers is largely organized along the lines of age and gender, although special knowledge and unusual skill also serve as a basis for assigning tasks. Among the great majority of foraging peoples, men do the bulk of the hunting of animals and women most of the gathering of plants. It is not unusual for either sex to lend a hand with the activities of the other. For example, among the BaMbuti of the tropical forest of Zaire, the women and children help the men with hunting by driving the game into nets. But in general, hunting is men's work.

Seasonal Mobility   Most foragers are seasonally mobile. None of the earth's biomes offer the same kinds and quantities of resources year round. At the least,

there are seasonal differences in precipitation; outside the tropics there are usually marked seasonal variations in temperature as well. Ordinarily, game animals are available in some places and not others at different seasons, and nuts and fruits tend to be available only at certain times of the year.

Foragers generally migrate to where food or water is most plentiful, or easiest to acquire, during a given season. For example, the Hadza people of Tanzania lived in an arid region with a marked distinction between wet and dry seasons. In rainy months the Hadza dispersed around the many temporary water holes that formed, living from the wild plants and animals in the immediate vicinity. At another time of the year, when these ponds evaporated, they congregated into camps clustered around the few relatively permanent water sources.

Congregation and Dispersal   Among most foragers, seasonal mobility is accompanied by concentration and dispersal of groups. Not only do people move around, but they sometimes aggregate into relatively large settlements, only to split up again into small camps at another time of the year. This concentration/dispersal pattern generally follows the availability of wild animal and plant foods.

A good example of this pattern is provided by the Cheyenne, an American Great Plains tribe. After the

■ *In the division of labor among most foragers, men hunted and women did most of the gathering of wild plant foods. Here San women gather plants (left), while men provide meat with their hunting (right).*

horse diffused into the Great Plains, the Cheyenne lived mainly from hunting the gigantic herds of bison that once grazed the grasses of central North America. Spring and early summer are the times of greatest precipitation on the plains. During this time of the year, the native grasses grew luxuriant, and the bison congregated in herds of thousands to graze it. As the summer wore on, the land became drier and the grass patchier. As their forage declined, the bison broke into smaller herds, which persisted until the next spring. The Cheyenne followed the seasonal congregation and dispersal of their principal game animal. From June until late summer the Cheyenne lived as a single tribe in an enormous camp, from which mounted men hunted the bison herds cooperatively. But as the bison split up, so did the Cheyenne, for it was too difficult for the whole tribe to camp together when their major food was dispersed over a large area. So from roughly late summer until the following June, the Cheyenne split up into many small camps. This was not only a more efficient organization for hunting bison, but the dispersal of camps over a wide area also provided the Cheyenne horses with more abundant winter pasture. This also provided the people with heat to withstand the harsh winters, for in this nearly treeless biome dried dung was the major source of fuel for fires.

The Netsilik Eskimo, who lived mainly by hunting caribou and sea mammals and fishing in the tundra of north Hudson Bay in Canada, exemplify the same pattern of seasonal aggregation and dispersal. It is a testament to their technological ingenuity that the Netsilik were able to survive in this environment, one of the harshest on earth for human habitation. The tundra is nearly treeless, for no roots can penetrate the permafrost layer, and all water is locked up in ice for about nine months of the year. The Netsilik adapted to the shortage of wood by constructing their houses from snow and ice in the winter and their tents from sealskin in the summer. In the winter igloos, carved soapstone lamps were filled with liquified seal blubber and lit; as the blubber burned, it provided all the heat and light the occupants required. Wet feet would be deadly, but the Netsilik discovered that sealskin is waterproof and makes warm and dry boots. Sealskin also could be made into a cover for the frame of the kayak used for hunting caribou as they crossed inland waters in the summer. Clothing was sewn by women from the prepared skin of the caribou. Needles and thread for the job came from the wing bones of certain birds and the sinew of caribou. Harpoons and other weapons for the hunt were made from bone or, preferably, the

■ *The Inuit (popularly known as Eskimo) inhabited one of the earth's harshest environments. Marine mammals were an important source of food. Here a whale is butchered.*

harder antler of a caribou. Skins, bones and antlers, soapstone, and snow and ice—these were the main raw materials with which the people manufactured the complex technology that allowed them to survive in the tundra.

Like other Eskimo groups across North America and Greenland, the Netsilik are unusual among foragers because they depended almost totally on animals for their food. Other than the berries that ripened in late summer, animal flesh provided practically all their diet. Their principal summer game were caribou, musk oxen, and salmon; they relied on stored meat and sea mammals the rest of the year. The way these animals were distributed seasonally influenced the way the Netsilik organized themselves to hunt them.

To go after seals and other marine mammals effectively, the Netsilik grouped together in large camps from about January to May. After the ocean bays iced over in the fall, the people moved onto the ice to cooperate in seal hunting. The minimum size of the midwinter camp was set by the seals' habit of living under the ice. Being mammals, seals must breathe air, and to do so they keep open several breathing holes through the ice. The hunters took advantage of this fact during winter sealing. Once their dogs had sniffed out the breathing holes, a man was stationed at each. It was necessary for him to remain still, for significant motion would alert the seal. Another of the Netsiliks' many ingenious devices detected the presence of a seal at the hole. A bit of down was glued with frozen saliva to a tiny piece of antler and placed over the hole. When the down fluttered from the seal's breath, the hunter struck with his barbed harpoon and pulled the animal onto the ice, where its carcass was split up among the camp's families. To maximize the chances of a capture, it was necessary to have enough men in the camp to cover all of a seal's breathing holes. This required about fifteen hunters, together with their wives and children; hence, a winter settlement typically contained fifty or sixty people camped on the ice.

When summer (and the migrating waterfowl, salmon, and caribou) arrived, the winter camps gradually split up into smaller groups containing only a few families. By July most of the ice and snow were gone, and salmon began their annual run; the Netsilik trapped them in stone dams and speared them with multipronged spears. In late August and September the caribou gather in huge herds for their annual migration south. The Netsilik dug knife-lined pits along caribou routes; shot them using bows and arrows; or stampeded them into traps or into rivers, where they were speared from kayaks. In the fall the men fished through the thin ice of rivers, or in some areas they hunted musk oxen. Mostly, however, the people lived off stored meat acquired during the caribou hunt, while the women prepared the winter clothing from their hides. By December it was time to begin the movement onto the iced-over bays for seal hunting, for which a larger group again became the most efficient cooperative unit.

Bands   Another common characteristic of foragers is the relatively small size of the group that lives in and exploits a territory. Most hunter-gatherers live in groups of less than fifty individuals. As we have seen, these groups, which anthropologists usually call **bands,** typically fluctuate in size according to the seasonal distribution and abundance of critical resources such as food or water.

The Western Shoshone, for instance, lived in the arid habitat of the American Great Basin, which is now Nevada, western Utah, and eastern Oregon. Until the nineteenth century (when most of their territory was taken by white ranchers), the Shoshone got their meat from deer, antelope, and small mammals such as rabbits. Plant foods included roots and seasonally available seeds, berries, pine nuts, and other wild products. For most of the year, the Shoshone roamed the dry valleys and slopes of the Great Basin in tiny bands consisting of a few nuclear families, or even single families. Occasionally, bands would gather for cooperative hunting of antelopes and rabbits, which

they would drive into corrals and nets. But a more permanent aggregation of families was difficult, for a local environment did not have enough resources to support large numbers of people for more than a few days.

However, the Shoshone discovered one critical plant food, which became available in the fall and in most years was capable of supporting many families throughout the winter. Each year, around October, the cones of the piñon trees on the high mountains would ripen and produce large, nourishing pine nuts. During their wanderings in late summer, Shoshone families noticed which specific mountain areas seemed to have the most promising pine nut harvest. They would arrange their travels to arrive at these productive areas in the fall. Ten to twenty families would camp in the same region, harvesting and storing pine nuts. During favorable (i.e., rainy) years, the pine nut harvest would support these large camps throughout most of the winter. Spring would find the families splitting up again, to renew the pattern of dispersal into tiny bands until the next fall. No family or band had exclusive access to any particular territory in any season. Rights of access to resources were essentially on the basis of "first come, first served," here meaning that whichever group arrived at an area first would be free to harvest its plants and animals.

The small band size is best seen as an organizational adaptation to foraging. Over a period of days or weeks (depending mainly on the environment and its resources), bands exhaust the wild resources of a given area and must move into a fresh (actually a "recovered") environment. All else equal, the larger the band, the faster it uses up the wild plants and animals of an area, and hence the more frequently it must relocate. One reason for the small size of bands, then, is that smaller groups do not need to move as often as larger groups.

So most hunting and gathering bands are small, although their number typically varies seasonally according to resource availability. Among most foragers, the composition of bands is also flexible—individuals or families are not attached permanently to any band or to any territory, but have many options about where to live and whom to live with.

The !Kung San of southern Africa offer a good illustration of the band organization and its flexibility. The San people (formerly known as the "Bushmen") are an ethnic population with a similar foraging economy, customs, and language. The term *!Kung* refers to those San who live in what is now southeast Angola, northeast Namibia, and northwest Botswana. With respect to their diet, health, labor, productivity, and population, the !Kung San are certainly the most thoroughly studied of all surviving foraging populations.

The environment of the !Kung San is an arid tropical savanna, which in the south grades into the Kalahari desert. In aboriginal times, the !Kung exploited this habitat entirely by foraging. They gathered over 100 species of plants and hunted over 50 animal species, including mammals, birds, reptiles, and insects. Wild plant foods consisted of nuts, fruits, berries, melons, roots, and greenery. The main source of plant food was the mongongo nut, which ripens around April (autumn in the Southern Hemisphere) and provided roughly half of the food calories consumed. As among most foragers, women did most of the gathering and men most of the hunting.

Because their habitat received so little rainfall, and then only seasonally, the availability of water greatly influenced the rhythm of !Kung life. From about April to October there was very little precipitation, and practically no rain fell between June and September. During this dry season, water for people and animals was available only at a few permanent waterholes, around which San bands congregated into relatively large settlements of between twenty and fifty individuals. Between November and March—the summer months and wet season—temporary waterholes formed, and the bands split up to exploit the wild resources around them. But rainfall in this part of the world is not reliable, neither from year to year nor from place to place. In some years up to forty inches of rain falls during the wet season; in other years as little as six inches. Drought occurred in about two out of every five years. Precipitation also was erratic and unpredictable geographically; one area frequently received severe thunderstorms, while twenty miles away no rain fell at all.

These characteristics of their abiotic environment—its aridity, seasonality, and marked temporal and geographic variability in precipitation—influenced the band organization of the !Kung. Because the distribution of wild foods and water was determined by rainfall, the annual cycle of congregation and dispersal of !Kung bands followed the seasonal distinction between wet and dry. During the wet months, the bands were spread out among the temporary waterholes in camps numbering about ten to thirty. When the bands first moved to a "fresh" waterhole, wild resources were relatively plentiful; game was abundant, and nuts, melons, roots,

■ *!Kung San camps were temporary settlements. Their bands moved to a new foraging area once the time and energy needed to gather edible plants and hunt game became excessive.*

greens, and other plant foods were plentiful. But the longer a band remained around a waterhole, the more the surrounding resources became exhausted. The men had to roam farther afield in their hunting, and the women had to travel longer distances in their plant collecting. After several weeks a camp reached the point at which its members judged that the costs of continuing to forage in the area were not bringing adequate returns in food. They then moved to a new wet-season camp. One ethnographer, Richard Lee, succinctly notes that the !Kung "typically occupy a camp for a period of weeks or months and eat their way out of it" (Lee 1969, 60).

As the dry season approached, !Kung bands made their way back to the area around one of the permanent water holes. These settlements, obviously larger than the wet-season camps, commonly numbered between twenty and fifty, and often even more. By the end of the dry season, the supply of mongongo nuts and other preferred plant foods was exhausted, and the people ate the less-tasty bitter melons, roots, and gum. This was considered a relatively hard time of the year, and the !Kung waited in anticipation of the November rains, when they could again disperse into the smaller wet-season camps.

Another feature of !Kung bands also is affected by the geographic and annual variation in precipitation. Foraging bands typically do not comprise tightly knit, closed, and territorial social groups. The !Kung are no exception. In such an arid environment it might be thought that each band would jealously defend its rights of access to its scarce wild resources. In fact, the

!Kung had only a comparatively loose and vague notion of "ownership" of a water hole and its associated land and wild resources: a few people tended to return to the same territory year after year, and so others came to think of them as the owners of the area. But this does not mean that only these "owners" had rights of access to it. By merely asking permission, anyone with a kinship relation to one of the owners had the right to live in and exploit the water and food resources of an area. Because the !Kung trace their kinship ties bilaterally—that is, through both sides of their family (see chapter 11)—each !Kung family had a multitude of options about where and with whom they would live. And the composition of a !Kung band fluctuated radically, because each band received visiting relatives many times a year.

This social pattern again makes sense as an adaptation. The territory to which I share rights of "ownership" may have lush resources this year, but precipitation varies so much from year to year and place to place that I may be forced to abandon it temporarily in the future. By accepting my relatives this year, I help to ensure myself of being accepted by them in possible later hard times. The flexibility in the composition of camps thus allows the resident population of a territory to adjust its size to the resources available in the area in any given year.

To sum up, foraging peoples usually exhibit certain sociocultural features that organize their exploitation of whatever habitat they exploit:

■ a high degree of mobility, especially from season to season;
■ congregation and dispersal of groups, at least on a seasonal basis; and
■ settlements consisting of small bands with varying size and flexible composition.

The foragers whose adaptation we have described could have developed other forms of organization to exploit their environments. For instance the !Kung could, perhaps, have spent the entire year camped around the permanent water holes and still have *survived* in their habitat; but this would have meant additional travel time to the seasonally lush resources around the wet-season water holes. It would have meant additional time and energy spent in the food quest. It would, in other words, have been a less efficient way to adapt to their habitat—given, of course, the technology available to them.

As we mentioned earlier, the foraging adaptation is diverse. Not all hunter-gatherers fit the generalized description just presented, for not all were highly

mobile and lived in small bands that fluctuated in size. In some parts of the earth, habitats were sufficiently rich and constant in resources that foragers lived in large, sedentary villages. This was especially true if a people had the knowledge of food-preservation technology. By preserving and storing food when it is most abundant, a population can artificially even out natural fluctuations in resources, and this sometimes allows them to adopt a sedentary existence.

The Indians of the Northwest Coast of North America (from roughly northern California into the Alaskan panhandle) lived in such a resource-rich habitat. Settled mainly on offshore islands and along riverbanks, tribes such as the Kwakiutl, Tlingit, Bella Coola, Haida, Coast Salish, and Tsimshian exploited a wide variety of wild but fairly reliable plant and animal foods. Chief among the latter were fish (notably salmon), whose annual fall spawning migrations through the estuaries and up the rivers provided the Indians with an abundant source of food. Each fall the Northwest Coast peoples captured the fish in fish dams and nets and by other methods and smoked, dried, and preserved them for the rest of the year.

The abundance of fish and other resources, together with the knowledge of methods of preserving them, produced some sociocultural features that are somewhat unusual among foraging peoples. Northwest Coast tribes were settled in fairly well defined territories, which they defended against intruders who attempted to violate their exclusive access. Their elaborately decorated plank houses were built to last a long time—although some villages moved to a different location for part of the year to exploit seasonally available resources. Unlike most foragers, the tribes along the Northwest Coast developed significant differences between social ranks. In some tribes, certain members held formal, hereditary titles that gave them high esteem and authority over others. Rank differences were validated (and to some extent created) by the famous potlatch, a large-scale competitive exchange of blankets, large copper sheets, canoes, carved wooden boxes, and other wealth objects between kin groups. Whereas most foragers are unspecialized (meaning that gender and age are the main basis for the division of labor), Northwest Coast tribes featured some degree of specialization—artists, craftspeople, and weavers produced the stylized carvings, totem poles, wooden boxes, blankets, and other objects of beauty that adorn our modern museums.

The tribes of the Northwest Coast remind us to beware of facile generalizations about foragers—or, for that matter, about any other dimension of human life. The unusual productivity of their habitat allowed the original inhabitants of this region to develop a lifeway that in many respects—settlement permanence and size, vigorous defense of territorial resources, elaborate social ranking, semispecialization, and so forth—is more characteristic of cultivators than of foragers. The reasons that the Northwest Coast tribes were different are complex and controversial. Many scholars believe that the reliability and abundance of natural resources led to the possibility of producing and accumulating sizable surpluses over immediate needs and to different patterns of organized cooperation and intergroup conflict. In turn, these resulted in the previously described sociocultural features usually found among cultivators.

■ *The Original Affluent Society?*

In most of this discussion we have used the past tense to reflect that only a handful of populations still acquire much of their food from foraging. In the last several centuries, but especially since the expansion of Western peoples and their way of life in the last two or three centuries, foragers have been forced out of regions that cultivators, herders, and industrialized peoples find easily exploitable. In some cases they have been killed off intentionally. In others, introduced diseases have so decimated their numbers that foragers are now assimilated into other ways of life. We should not conclude from these facts that foraging is an inferior mode of adaptation (although it does not seem to be able to support a military force as effective as those of other peoples).

In fact, their tools and technical skills, together with the effective ways in which they organized themselves to acquire food and other resources available in their environments, appear to have served foragers well until they were forced to compete militarily with other systems of adaptation. Ethnographic work carried out since the 1960s among the few remaining hunter-gatherers generally indicates that their lives are easier than industrial peoples might expect.

We in industrialized countries believe ourselves to be relatively affluent. We eat and drink well (sometimes *too* well!). We think of ourselves as healthy and long-lived. Almost all of us believe that modern technology has reduced the amount of time we must work to "make our living," and thus has provided us with more "leisure time." We all know about the many pockets of poverty that exist in all modern nations. But we think that even the poor of today have it better

than Average Joe of the "stone age." Indeed, we think that human history reveals fairly steady progress, as our technological ingenuity has largely freed us from nature's constraints.

Anthropologists have no simple answer as to whether our notions of progress and development are entirely cultural or represent a genuine improvement in the objective quality of our lives. (It is likely that many of our ideas about historical "progress" are created to justify the way we live and the way our political and economic systems work.) Certainly, terms like *progress* and *development* imply "better," and the relativistic mind of most anthropologists wishes to know "better with respect to what?" If we mean "with respect to the quantity and variety of goods consumed per individual," then progress is real, but then are we not making a cultural judgment that high levels of material consumption are inherently valuable? If we mean "with respect to the satisfaction of human biological, psychological, and sociocultural needs," we have perhaps a more objective criterion. But in this respect it is not at all clear that we have progressed over some of our preindustrial ancestors. For what we learn from foragers—especially from the quantitative data on their working hours and diet collected by ethnographers since the 1960s—is that "development" is a mixed blessing.

You might think (as practically all experts thought until the 1960s) that hunting and gathering is a hard life. After all, foragers are at the mercy of natural forces over which they exercise no control, as we have seen with the Cheyenne, Netsilik, Shoshone, and !Kung San. With no human control over the distribution and abundance of life-sustaining resources, most foragers are unable to stay in one place, live in large settlements, accumulate many possessions, produce much of a surplus over their immediate needs, and have the leisure time needed to engage in artistic endeavors. But when some imaginary prehistoric genius figured out that plants grow from seeds, which could be planted to produce a crop in a few months, all these natural constraints on humanity were reduced. When some ancient Einstein realized that wild animals—as well as plants—could be domesticated, people no longer were at the mercy of uncontrolled movements of their meat supply or of the natural fluctuations in numbers of game. For the first time (this story goes) the supply of both plant and animal foods became controllable and, hence, greater, more reliable, and less labor intensive to harvest. After this agricultural revolution, populations could settle down in large permanent villages, begin to accumulate wealth, produce a surplus that allowed the development of specialists, and at last have the free time needed to develop their culture. Almost certainly, if you have learned or thought about this subject of agricultural origins at all, something like the preceding story is what you learned or figured out on your own.

Our best present evidence is that this story is a fairy tale. Ethnographic studies of foragers who survived into modern times—generally in marginal, unproductive biomes—indicate that in many respects the overall quality of their lives is at least equal to that of farming peoples. It is unfortunate that the studies are so few. By the time ethnographers began questioning the preceding tale, peoples still practicing foraging were rare. Even they were affected by Western technology, such as steel tools. So the conclusions will forever remain tentative. What we present here is some of the evidence that foragers have much better lives than most people think.

By far the best evidence comes from multidisciplinary studies conducted of the !Kung San. Thanks to the work of Nancy Howell, Richard Lee, Marjorie Shostak, John Yellen, Melvin Konner, and others, we have a fairly detailed knowledge of !Kung working hours, nutrition, reproduction, health, and longevity.

Taking working hours first, in 1964 Richard Lee kept records for four weeks during the dry season for the !Kung who lived around the permanent water hole called Dobe. From his data he estimated that each !Kung adult spent an average of only 2.4 days (or about seventeen hours) per week in foraging activities. Women, it turned out, spent less time gathering wild plants than men did hunting (actually, men did much plant collecting as well). Women spent around thirteen hours weekly in gathering, men about twenty-two hours per week in foraging. Further, the elderly (over sixty) and young people, who constituted 40 percent of the population, did practically no subsistence work at all. This means that the 60 percent of the Dobe people who foraged supported themselves and their dependents with an average subsistence effort of only seventeen hours per week. Obviously, the !Kung were not out grubbing for food all the time.

Still, there is more to work and survival than food-getting activities. The products have to be prepared, huts built, tools and clothing made and repaired, and so forth. Lee studied the time devoted to these activities as well. Dividing "work" into the categories of "subsistence work" (time actually spent foraging), "tool making and fixing," and "housework,"

he found that the "total work week" of an average !Kung was forty-two hours, or about six hours a day. Men worked slightly longer than women. The !Kung spend the rest of their ("spare") time visiting other camps, entertaining guests, or organizing dances—that is, socializing.

These figures compare favorably with most people who live in industrialized societies. According to recent studies of labor time in twelve European countries and in the contemporary United States, employed women spend between 10.5 and 12.6 hours daily in their jobs and housework combined, and nonemployed women average between 5.9 and 9.5 hours per day in work inside their homes. Men spend between about 7 and 8 hours daily at their jobs and working around the house. All these figures, incidentally, include "weekends off"; that is, they are averaged over a seven-day period, so the figures can legitimately be compared to the !Kung. The worries of some people about how people in modern societies will spend the "new leisure" made possible by industrialization are somewhat misplaced.

But how productive is the subsistence labor of the !Kung? Perhaps they are living at the edge of survival and do not spend more time foraging because wild foods are so scarce that it would be a waste of energy that they could ill afford. Lee's figures do not support this view. For the same four-week period Lee weighed everything foragers brought back into camp. The major foods—mongongo nuts, assorted fruits, berries, roots, and melons—were analyzed in the laboratory for their nutritive composition. In the end, Lee estimated that the !Kung consumed an average of 2,355 calories per person per day, an average of 96 grams of protein per person per day, and received an adequate supply of vitamins and minerals from their diet. These figures were well above the estimated requirements established by nutritionists for people of the !Kung weight and activity level.

The !Kung are not the only foraging population for whom these conditions are reported. Comparable low working hours have been estimated for some hunter-gatherers in Australia, for the Hadza of Tanzania, and for the BaMbuti pygmies of Zaire. Studies such as these have led some anthropologists to conclude that foragers are "the original affluent society," because they seem to acquire their food with minimal expenditure of time and energy. As always, we need to be careful with such sweeping generalizations about some segment of humanity: the Arctic Eskimo, the Western Shoshone, and some other foragers living in harsher biomes undoubtedly had a much harder time acquiring food than the tribes of California and the Northwest Coast. Nonetheless, we have many reasons to believe that in general the hunting and gathering way of life followed by humanity for most of its existence was efficient and satisfying.

If this is true, we might well wonder why people ever abandoned foraging for the cultivation of domesticated plants. The answer is probably that cultivation does offer certain advantages over hunting and gathering. In the next chapter we consider adaptations based on domestication of plants and animals and some of the implications of domestication for human lifeways.

Summary

Adaptation is the process by which organisms acquire characteristics that allow them to survive and reproduce in their habitats. Humans adapt to changes in their environments primarily by sociocultural changes, not by biological changes. This chapter discusses various components of adaptation, and one major variety of human adaptation—foraging.

Part of a population's adaptation is production—activities by which people exploit the raw materials and energy available in their environments. By expending their labor and applying technology to the raw materials they culturally define as resources, people transform resources into goods that satisfy their wants and needs. Because production is nearly everywhere a social activity, production must be organized: labor must be divided up, patterns of cooperation must be decided on and regulated, and rights of access to natural resources must be assigned. Production thus requires organization as well as labor, technology, and resources.

Foragers, or hunter-gatherers, adapt to their habitats not by controlling the distribution and abundance of resources but by exploiting resources when and where they are naturally available. Until about 10,000 years ago, all humans were foragers, but cultivators, pastoralists, and industrial peoples have spread into the biomes suitable for their mode of adaptation, and today only a handful of foragers survive.

There is great diversity in the foraging adaptation; yet certain patterns predominate, and a foraging existence has certain widespread effects on the sociocultural systems of those people who live(d) by it. The most common elements of the foraging way of life include high rates of mobility; regular and usually seasonally based congregation and dispersal of groups; and small, flexible units called *bands* as the major enduring territorial-based association. Not all foragers exhibited these characteristics. Where resources were very abundant and reliable, as on the North American Northwest Coast, people settled in fairly permanent villages and differences in rank developed.

Life among foragers was not as nasty, brutish, and short as it is sometimes made out to be. The few quantitative ethnographic studies made of those foragers who survived into the mid-twentieth century suggest that they did not have to work long and hard in the food quest, nor in other kinds of work, and that their diets were generally adequate. If anything, most foragers studied worked fewer hours than many cultivators. They appear to have had more leisure than most citizens of modern industrialized nations.

Key Terms

adaptation	patterns of cooperation
biome	rights of access
production	foragers
factors of production	(hunter-gatherers)
division of labor	bands

Suggested Readings

■ Bicchieri, M. G., ed. *Hunters and Gatherers Today.* New York: Holt, Rinehart and Winston, 1972.
A collection of original short ethnographies covering eleven twentieth-century foraging societies scattered throughout the world.

■ Cohen, Yehudi. *Man in Adaptation: The Cultural Present.* Chicago: Aldine, 1974.
A collection of important essays on human adaptation, many of which examine foraging societies.

■ Jochim, Michael A. *Strategies for Survival.* New York: Academic Press, 1981.
An advanced, theoretically oriented textbook with a novel approach.

■ Lee, Richard B., and Irven DeVore, eds. *Man the Hunter.* Chicago: Aldine, 1968.
Contains thirty-six articles on foragers from around the world.

■ Netting, Robert. *Cultural Ecology.* Menlo Park, Calif.: Cummings, 1977.

Brief introduction to human ecology, organized according to type of adaptation. Excellent place to start for an understanding of human-environment relations.

■ Schrire, Carmel, ed. *Past and Present in Hunter-Gatherer Studies*. Orlando, Fla.: Academic Press, 1984.
A collection of essays that attack many of the more popular ideas about foraging societies.

■ Service, Elman. *The Hunters*. 2d ed. Englewood Cliffs, N.J.: Prentice-Hall, 1979.
A general examination of hunting societies.

The following ethnographies are excellent descriptions of particular foraging societies or groups of related societies.

■ Balikci, Asen. *The Netsilik Eskimo*. Garden City, N.Y.: Natural History Press, 1970.
A study of Netsilik adaption, technology, kinship, marriage, and religion.

■ Hoebel, E. Adamson. *The Cheyenne*. New York: Holt, Rinehart and Winston, 1978.
A reconstruction of Cheyenne life during the mid-nineteenth century.

■ Jenness, Diamond. *The People of the Twilight*. Chicago: University of Chicago Press, 1959.
A highly readable, classic account of Eskimo life in the Canadian arctic based on field research conducted between 1913 and 1918.

■ Holmberg, Allan R. *Nomads of the Long Bow*. Garden City, N.Y.: American Museum of Natural History, 1969.

A very readable and interesting account of Siriono, a foraging society living in the tropical forest of eastern Bolivia.

■ Lee, Richard. *The Dobe !Kung: Foragers in a Changing World*. New York: Holt, Rinehart and Winston, 1984.
A study of the lifeway of the !Kung San (Bushmen) of the Kalahari desert of southern Africa.

■ Steward, Julian. *Basin-Plateau Aboriginal Sociopolitical Groups*. Smithsonian Institution, Bureau of American Ethnography, Bulletin no. 120. Washington: U.S. Government Printing Office, 1938.
A classic study of the economy and lifeway of the native American groups who lived in the Great Basin and Plateau region of the western United States.

■ Thomas, Elizabeth Marshall. *The Harmless People*. New York: Vintage, 1959.
A readable account of the !Kung San written from a personal perspective.

■ Turnbull, Colin. *The Forest People*. New York: Simon and Schuster, 1962.
An ethnography of the BaMbuti (pygmies) of Zaire. Good description of their hunting and organization.

■ Van Stone, James. *Athapaskan Adaptations: Hunters and Fishermen of the Subarctic Forest*. Chicago: Aldine, 1974.
A study examining the lifeways of the Indian groups of interior Alaska and northwestern Canada.

ADAPTATION: DOMESTICATION

■ (Above) *Domestication of plants and animals resulted in profound transformations in human ways of life. These pastoral nomads from Afghanistan live mainly from the products of their herds.*

omestication—the "taming" of certain species of plants and animals to increase their value to humans—was perhaps the major technological development in the history of humanity. Once vegetable foods began to be intentionally planted in controlled areas and protected against other creatures who also wished to eat them, a host of other changes in sociocultural systems followed. In this chapter, we discuss adaptations to habitats by means of domestication. We also consider some of the changes in sociocultural systems that result from farming and herding.

The Advantages of Domestication

For tens of thousands of years, foraging nourished humanity well enough to allow our species to spread over most of the land surface of the earth. Despite the evolutionary success it gave to *Homo sapiens,* hunting and gathering suffers from one major disadvantage compared to other adaptations: the number of people that can be supported per unit of land by foraging is relatively small. Only rarely does the population density of foragers rise above one or two per square mile; in many regions, several square miles of foraging area are needed to support a single individual.

The reason that foraging can support only low population densities seems clear: uncontrolled nature is indifferent to human desires, so the plants and animals that foragers use do not always occur in the abundance they would like, and are not always found when and where people would like them to be. Until people began to exert some control (which is never total) over the distribution and abundance of their food supply, the number of people that an area could support could not rise above a fixed limit. If an area's population rose above its long-term **carrying capacity,** either the environment degraded because natural food resources were harvested at a rate greater than their rate of recovery, or part of the population left the region. In fact, this budding off and subsequent dispersal of people due to local population pressure may be the principal reason for humanity's geographic expansion across the globe in prehistoric times.

Planting (cultivating) crops and keeping domesticated animals offers one major advantage over foraging: a great many more people can be fed from a given area of land. In effect, cultivation (and to a lesser degree herding animals) raises the carrying capacity of the available territory, supporting greater population densities.

Cultivation supports higher population densities for several reasons. The main one is that virtually all the plants growing in a cultivated area (a garden plot or field) are edible by humans. In essence, cultivators select areas of their habitat and attempt to control the kinds and numbers of plants that grow there. So the domesticated plants (or *cultigens*) grow more densely in plots or fields than do the wild plants gathered by foragers. Most modern scholars believe that this benefit—supporting larger numbers of people on a given area of land—is the chief (and perhaps the only) advantage of cultivation over hunting and gathering. (As we shall see, this benefit is far from cost-free.)

In the Old World, plant domestication was accompanied by the taming of several species of herd animals, including sheep, goats, horses, and cattle. These animals were kept for their hides, wool, meat, and milk, as well as for their ability to carry heavy loads. Animal domestication reduced, and eventually nearly eliminated in some areas, the time men devoted to hunting. When harnessed to the plow, cattle, horses, and water buffalo also supplemented human labor in farming.

The prehistoric origins of domestication are outside the scope of this text. Suffice it to say that, in the Old World, domestication had occurred by about 10,000 years ago in the Middle East, and by about 9,000 years ago in southeast Asia. In the next few thousand years it spread to encompass most of the environments in southern Asia, Africa, and Europe that were well suited to it. In the New World, a different set of plant species were domesticated, in Mexico by 5,000 years ago, and in northern Peru by 4,000 years ago (see Box 8.1). Unlike the Old World, the Americas contained few herd animals suitable for domestication; only llamas, alpacas, guinea pigs, dogs, and turkeys were kept by people until after European colonization of the continents.

(What about the horse, on which some American Indians were so intimately dependent in historic times? It was domesticated about 5,000 years ago on the grasslands of Asia—possibly in the Ukraine—and brought to the New World by the Spanish. It did not

DOMESTICATES IN THE OLD AND NEW WORLDS

The domestication of plants and animals occurred independently in the Old World (Europe, Asia, Africa) and the New World (North and South America). Before the age of European colonization the crops grown in the two hemispheres were completely different. A description of the places of origin for some of the most familiar food crops follows.

Old World Crops

Apparently, the first domestication occurred in southwest Asia (including parts of modern Iran, Iraq, and Turkey). Wheat, barley, lentils, peas, carrots, figs, almonds, pistachios, dates, and grapes were first grown in this region. Oats, cabbages, lettuce, beets, and asparagus were first domesticated in the Mediterranean. In West Africa, sorghum, finger millet, watermelons, and African rice were domesticated; sorghum and millet still feed millions of people on the African continent. Oriental rice, eggplants, cucumbers, bananas, taro, and coconuts originated in southern Asia and Southeast Asia. Soybeans, citrus fruits, and tea were domesticated in China. We get our morning caffeine from coffee, first domesticated in Ethiopia.

New World Crops

Maize, red pepper, avocado, cacao, and the squash family (squash, pumpkins, and gourds) originated in Central America and Mexico. From Peru came numerous crops that are still important to the region, and indeed to the world, including potatoes, sweet potatoes, and lima beans. From elsewhere in South America came manioc, peanuts, pineapple, Brazil nuts, and cashews.

Some plants were domesticated not just once but several times in various parts of the world. Separate species of rice were domesticated in Africa and Asia, apparently independently (that is, Africans did not get the idea of planting rice from Asians). Cotton was domesticated independently in three different places: South America, Central America, and either in India or Africa. Three different yam species were grown in West Africa, Southeast Asia, and tropical South America.

In the two or three centuries after Spain, Portugal, France, Britain, and the Netherlands established political control over most of the preindustrial world, many of these crops were taken to other continents. As a result, most people in the modern world are not aware of the origins of the plant foods they consume every day. North American meals include roots, greens, grains, seeds, and fruits that were originally domesticated in various parts of the earth. We all owe much of our diet to the prehistoric peoples of the Middle East, Asia, Africa, Mexico, Peru, and elsewhere. ∎

Source: Fagan (1986).

---

reach North America until the 1600s. It was not until then that the Indians mounted horses to fight off white settlers and hunt bison.)

So the domestication of plants and animals occurred not just once, but several times in prehistory, and in different parts of the world. The main advantage of modes of adaptation based on domestication is that they can support many more people per unit of available territory. The remainder of this chapter will describe the various forms of domestication found among humanity today and analyze the profound impacts of domestication on human ways of life. To organize our discussion, we divide this chapter into (1) adaptations based mainly on domesticated plants, or **cultivation,** and (2) adaptations based on domesticated animals, or **pastoralism.**

Cultivation

Cultivators acquire their vegetable foods by creating and maintaining an artificial community of plants that have been intentionally selected for their usefulness to humans. These cultigens are the product of generations of human selection for their edibility, resistance to disease and drought, suitability for local soil and climate, and so forth. In the process of domesticating a plant species, people select (sometimes unintentionally) those individual plants with the characteristics they like. They cultivate (plant, care for, and harvest) those individual plants with the greatest usefulness and allow the less desirable varieties to go unpropagated. Modern cultivators thus enjoy the benefits of the efforts of hundreds of past generations, from whom they have inherited a store of cultigens with useful genetic qualities.

As mentioned, the chief advantage of cultivation over foraging is its ability to support more people per unit of land. To get this benefit, people must pay some costs. Cultivators create and maintain an artificial community of plants on their plots. This creation and maintenance requires labor, time, and energy. First the plot must be prepared for planting. The plants that occur naturally on the plot must be removed—they become defined as unwanted "weeds." In some kinds of cultivation the landscape itself must be modified by constructing furrows, dikes, ditches, terraces, or other artificial landforms. Second, the crops must be planted, requiring more labor. Third, natural processes tend to destroy the artificial plant community and landscape that people have created: weeds invade and compete for light and soil nutrients, animal pests are attracted to the densely growing cultigens, and rainfall and floods may wash away physical improvements. Cultivators therefore must "beat back nature" by periodically removing weeds, protecting against pests, rebuilding earthworks, and so forth. Fourth, the act of cultivation itself tends to reduce the suitability of a site for future harvests, by reducing soil fertility if nothing else. In future years the cultivators must somehow restore their plots to a usable condition, or their yields will fall. All these necessities require labor and other kinds of energy expenditures.

Numerous types of cultivation exist, depending on environmental conditions (such as soil, temperature, and rainfall), the types of crops grown, and the technology used in working the land. Two of the most important differences between cultivation systems are the frequency with which particular plots are cropped, and the tools and kinds of energy used to keep the system running.

Cropping frequency refers to how often a particular plot of land is planted and harvested (how frequently a plot is used for cultivation). In *extensive* land use systems, plots are planted, worked, and harvested for only a year or two. They then are left alone for several years or, in some cases, for two or three decades. During this resting (or *fallow*) period, as the natural vegetation regrows it restores fertility, shades out weed species, and reduces insect infestations. In *intensive* land use, the same plot is cultivated almost every year. In tropical areas where temperature, sunlight, and

available water allow, the same plot may even be planted and harvested two or even three times each year. Obviously, extensive and intensive are relative terms. We can compare cultivation systems to one another based on their degree of intensity: the more intensive a system, the more frequently plots are planted and harvested. The intensity of a system is directly related to the number of people who must be supported from the cultivation system: generally, the more intense the land use, the more people can be supported per acre of available land.

The *technology and energy sources* used are also major factors in distinguishing types of cultivation. Some tools—such as hoes, shovels, rakes, and digging sticks—require only the energy of human muscles to operate. Here human labor provides most of the energy needed to clear, plant, maintain, and harvest plots. Other systems add animal muscle energy to human labor. Animal power is used to pull plows, power irrigation works, and fertilize fields. Still other (modern, twentieth-century) systems largely dispense with both human and animal energy, and rely on inanimate power sources such as electricity and fossil fuels. As with land use, no sharp boundary exists between these technological and energetic systems.

We can use these two sets of differences to identify three basic types of cultivation:

■ *Intensive agriculture is characterized by the use of domesticated animals to supplement human muscles. Here some young Senegalese men in a United Nations Development Program are learning to use a plow drawn by oxen. No plows were used in sub-Saharan Africa in preindustrial times.*

- ■ **Horticulture.** Technology and energy sources include mainly hand tools powered by the cultivators' own muscles. Land use tends to be extensive, meaning that plots are cultivated for a year or two, then abandoned to fallow for several years to allow their renewal.
- ■ **Intensive agriculture.** People plant and harvest their crops semiannually, annually, or biannually, so land use is intensive. Old World intensive agriculturalists used the animal-powered plow to turn the soil over before planting. In regions of inadequate or seasonally variable rainfall, irrigation works were constructed to provide water. In the Americas, however, there were no domesticated animals suitable for harnessing to plows, and hence no plows until the settlement of the New World by Europeans. Other methods were adopted by New World intensive agriculturalists to keep plots under cultivation for many years.
- ■ **Mechanized agriculture.** Farmers also use land intensively. This type of cultivation is made possible by the energy and materials supplied by complex machinery, irrigation facilities, artificial fertilizers and pesticides, and other products of the modern agricultural supply industry. This "high-tech" agriculture allows a very high degree of control over ecological conditions in agricultural fields, and hence is enormously productive in yields. But it too has its costs, as we shall see in part 4.

Of course, human muscle power is used in all three kinds of cultivation, although in mechanized agriculture it is quite unimportant compared to other sources of energy.

In this chapter we concentrate on horticulture and intensive agriculture, systems that anthropologists have studied most. However, description of these two preindustrial methods will later allow us to answer in part 4 an important question about mechanized agriculture: How does its efficiency compare to that of horticulture and intensive agriculture?

Horticulture

Horticultural peoples break up the soil using only hand tools, such as hoes, spades, and sharpened sticks. They clear the land for planting with simple tools such as knives, adzes, and axes, although fire is also frequently used for removing unwanted trees and grasses. They generally do not fertilize the earth at all, nor do they increase the supply of water to their fields by irrigating. Although horticulture is usually regarded as the simplest form of raising crops, it is, nonetheless, true cultivation. That is, the crops are fully domesticated—and have been for millennia—and the people expend much time and energy creating and maintaining the artificial community of plants they raise.

Horticulturalists vary in the way they obtain meat. Some—such as those who live in the Amazon basin of South America—continue to rely largely on wild game and, therefore, are hunters and fishers as well as horticulturalists. Others keep a stock of domesticated animals, such as cattle, pigs, chickens, dogs, or goats, which supplement their primary reliance on cultivated foods. By definition, horticultural peoples do not keep domesticated animals for purposes of powering the plow.

Horticulture is a subsistence method that works in a variety of environments. Of the major biomes, it is largely absent only in the tundra and northern coniferous forests. It is most common in temperate and tropical forests, and in temperate and tropical grasslands and savannas (compare Figure 7.1 with Figure 8.1). Some people practice horticulture even in deserts and mountains, although in these biomes it usually is accompanied by herding (for reasons discussed later). Two abiotic factors seem to limit its overall distribution. One is low average temperature in high latitudes or altitudes, which reduces the length of the growing season. The other is insufficient water availability, which makes cultivation without irrigation impossible or too risky to be viable.

The ways of life of horticultural peoples differ from those of foragers in several respects. First, with a dense community of edible plants growing under partly controlled conditions in a small area, the size of horticultural settlements tends to increase. Rather than living in bands or camps of around twenty to fifty, horticulturalists generally aggregate into villages, typically numbering in the hundreds.

Second, these settlements are more permanent than foraging bands; villages tend to remain in the same location for a longer time, usually years, decades, or centuries rather than the weeks or months typical of foragers. This relative permanence is not simply because cultivation allows people to settle down, as is often thought. Although cultivation does, in fact,

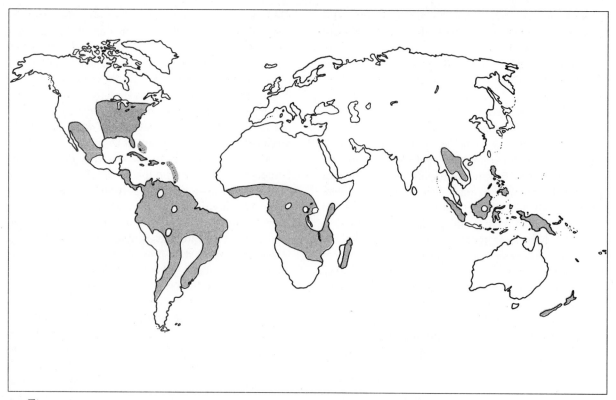

■ Figure 8.1
Principal Regions of Horticulture at Contact Period

allow a more sedentary existence, equally importantly it provides a positive incentive for increased sedentariness. The members of a horticultural village have invested considerable labor in creating their gardens; some of this labor would be wasted if they moved away before the gardens were fully harvested or before the plot was used to its full potential over many growing seasons. This labor input makes horticulturalists—and, in fact, all cultivators—reluctant to abandon an area that has been successfully cultivated. Thus, the labor investment encourages sedentariness by raising the costs of premature mobility.

In the last chapter we noted that exploitation of nature involves more than just applying technology and labor to raw materials to transform them into goods. It requires also that people develop an organization that allows them to produce food and other necessities efficiently, given their technology, local environmental conditions, and the resources they recognize and choose to exploit in their habitat. These organizational features of a population include the division of labor, the patterns of cooperation in pro-

duction, and the assignment of rights of access to resources. We already have seen some of the ways hunter-gatherers organize themselves to exploit their environments. Do horticultural peoples exhibit a similar set of widespread organizational patterns? To broaden the question, do they share many common sociocultural features?

Unfortunately for our desire for simplicity and consistency, the answer is no. Horticultural peoples are diverse in the ways they organize production activities and in their sociocultural systems generally. In some, the drudgery of day-in, day-out subsistence labor is allocated largely to women, and men spend much of their time politicking, hunting, guarding the settlement, or making wealth objects. In others, garden work is split up among the sexes in various ways: the men may take on the heavy work of clearing new land with axes or knives, whereas the women may do the planting, weeding, and harvesting.

Cooperative patterns and decision-making authority also vary. Among some peoples a whole village will clear and plant a common parcel of land as a single unit, with village elders or leaders deciding when and where the work will occur. Sometimes the members of a large kin group work together. In other populations individual families work alone in their gardens, and the family heads make most of the important cultivation decisions.

There is a similar degree of variation in how rights of access to land are assigned to individuals and groups. Sometimes any land not under cultivation at the moment is virtually free to all—whoever clears and plants an unused parcel first has full rights to cultivate it so long as he or she works that land; but once they have completed their last harvest, the plot again becomes freely available. Among other horticulturalists all land (in use or not) is held collectively by one or another kin group; the head of each group is responsible for granting use rights over specific plots of land to individual members. In other systems individuals or nuclear families have ownership rights to specific tracts of land, which they may pass along to their offspring or dispose of in any way they choose.

Thus, generalizing about horticulturalists can be even more misleading than doing so about foragers. We can, however, make one generalization that applies to the majority of these populations: in horticulture, families or other kinds of kinship groups invest their labor in improving a specific and relatively well defined territory. Each kin group lays a claim to a specific area of land by clearing, planting, and otherwise applying their labor to it. Their claim (that is, their rights over a specific area, minimally including the right to deny other people access to it) arises from their having worked upon the land, improving its usefulness to humans. Everyone with a claim to a specific parcel passes his or her rights along to his or her offspring. In any generation, any given individual or family group thus has ownership rights (recall here that these vary cross-culturally) over a specific territory. This territory includes, of course, the gardens they are presently cultivating. It also frequently includes abandoned plots that they or their ancestors cultivated in the past and to which they or their children may return in future years.

In studying how horticultural peoples allocate rights of access to resources, anthropologists usually find ownership rights by kin groups over specific parcels of land with relatively well defined boundaries. With foragers it is more common to find use rights over large territories that have vague boundaries. Further, kin groups in horticultural populations usually claim own-

ership over the land itself, for the earth may be made productive by planting crops on it. For foragers it is usually the wild resources of the territory over which any use rights are exercised, for the territory itself is valuable only because of the wild plants and animals that naturally occur on it.

Numerous subtypes of horticulture are practiced in the preindustrial world. Here we discuss only two of the most widespread: *dry land gardening* and *shifting cultivation*.

■ Dry Land Gardening

Dry land gardening is defined by the main ecological and climatic factor with which cultivators have to cope: low, erratic, and unpredictable rainfall. Like all horticulture, it uses no plow, and simple hand tools—hoes, spades, and so forth—powered by human muscles are the characteristic technology. Dry land gardening occurs in the American southwest, in parts of Mexico and Central America, in some of the Middle East, and in much of sub-Saharan Africa. In the more arid regions of Africa it is sometimes supplemented by cattle raising, for rainfall is too erratic and unpredictable for people to depend entirely on their crops. Generally, preindustrial dry land gardening is distributed in temperate grasslands, chaparral, and tropical savannas and grasslands.

In this type of horticulture, low and highly variable precipitation impedes the growth of crops. Cultivation in arid lands is risky: even if in most years rainfall and harvests are adequate, there is a good chance that in any given year not enough rain will fall. Therefore, people who cultivate in dry regions have developed a variety of gardening strategies to cope with the possibility of drought, which of course occurs unpredictably. One method is to combine gardening with the keeping of domesticated animals, which offers several advantages that we describe later. Another is to plant only along rivers and streams, where the roots can tap into the high water table.

The Western Pueblo of the North American Southwest exemplify another way to cope with aridity. In this desert region annual rainfall averages only ten inches, concentrated in the spring. Further, in this high country the growing season for corn—the Pueblo's major source of food—is only about four months long. The people are faced with extreme uncertainty: if they plant too early, a late spring frost may kill their crops; if they wait too long, they will lose some of the critical moisture from the spring rains. The Pueblo, then, must concentrate their efforts into a short spring-early summer period, and they must take measures to cope with potential frost and insufficient rainfall.

One way the Pueblo make the most of available water is to plant corn in those areas that are most likely to flood, for there soil moisture usually lasts until harvest time. Yet in some years—they do not know in advance which years, of course—the rains are so torrential that floods wash away the crops. The people therefore diversify both the place and time of their planting. They sow the seeds of corn, squash, beans, and other crops in several locations, so that no matter what weather occurs, some gardens produce a harvest. For example, gardens on the flood plains may be lost during an unusually wet year, but upland gardens still yield a crop. Staggering the time of planting likewise lowers the risk of cultivation; by planting crops weeks apart, the risk of losing all of a planting due to an untimely frost is reduced. Thus, by mixing up where and when they plant, the Western Pueblo reduce the risk of cultivation in an arid, highly seasonal environment.

■ Shifting Cultivation

Shifting cultivation involves cutting and burning an area of land to clear it of natural vegetation; planting crops on it for one to three years (rarely longer); then cutting, burning, and planting a new area for a new garden. The old garden is left alone (fallowed) for several years (often ten or more) to allow the natural vegetation to reestablish itself. A harvested garden is generally not abandoned all at once, but little by little, for often long-lived fruit trees are planted and people return for several years to pluck the fruits. After a fallowed plot has regrown, its soil fertility is partially or wholly restored, most weeds have been shaded out by regrown trees, and insect pests that invaded the garden when it was full of crops have gone elsewhere. The same parcel of land again may be cleared and burned for a new garden. Obviously, shifting cultivation is an extensive method of land use.

Also known as **slash-and-burn** and **swidden,** this method is practiced largely in heavily forested areas. Early cultivators in the temperate forests of Europe used it, and some white settlers of eastern North America borrowed the method from the Native Americans. Today, shifting cultivation is confined largely to

■ *Shifting cultivators use fire to clear the land of natural vegetation before planting crops. This man from the island of Tanna, Vanuatu, sets fire to his plot. The ashes from the burn are left to aid fertility.*

the tropical forests of South and Central America, Africa, and Southeast Asia.

The tools of most shifting cultivators are quite simple, yet remarkably efficient in labor requirements. Generally, when a new garden plot is to be cleared from the forest, the largest trees are felled with the adz or axe. The smaller trees and undergrowth are slashed down using a knife with a long blade. These tasks are done in the dry season (if there is one), for the woody material that has been cut down is not hauled off but is left to dry out for several weeks. When it is dry enough, and when the winds are right, the whole plot is set on fire. Thus, the clearing of land for new gardens usually requires only an adz or axe, a knife, and fire, which does much of the work.

Burning is more than a labor-saving method of clearing the land of vegetation; it also rids the plot of insects and provides nutrients for the crops. The usefulness of the burn arises partly from the ecological characteristics of tropical forests. Ecologists have clearly established that most of the nutrients in a tropical forest are found in the biomass (that is, in the living material, mainly the trees), not in the soil. The high heat and humidity of the tropics result in remarkably high rates of decay of dead organic matter. The decay process releases the nutrients into the soil, where they are quickly taken up by the shallow, splayed roots of the trees. The nutrients recycle as leaf litter, fallen branches, and dead animals (who have consumed the plants) accumulate on the ground, then decay, and are reused.

Tropical soils, then, are not the repository of nutrients familiar to most temperate folk. In spite of the luxuriant vegetation of the tropics, the soil is generally nutrient poor. In many areas it cannot support the permanent cultivation of crops, at least not without a heavy investment of fertilizers and other materials. Rather, the heavy precipitation tends to wash nutrients too deeply down into the soil for plant roots to penetrate (a process called *leaching*) or simply to carry them away with eroding topsoil into streams and rivers.

Thus, swiddeners have to overcome two problems of cultivating a tropical forest. First, most of the nutrients are locked up in the living vegetation and must be released before they can be used by the crops the swiddener hopes to grow. Burning is a labor-saving way to accomplish this release (it is not, however, very efficient at conserving some nutrients, for most of the nitrogen and sulfur in the dried vegetation goes up in smoke). After the burn the crops must be planted soon; otherwise, tropical downpours will wash the ash away, and the intense tropical sun will bake the soil.

Second, shifting cultivators frequently face the problem of nutrient loss by leaching or erosion. Underneath the natural forest the soil is protected by the treetop canopy of leaves that shields the ground from the worst force of rainstorms. Many swiddeners shield the soil of the garden plots they plant in the forest in a similar way. They leave some of the tallest trees standing when they originally clear the plot. They often are careful to spread the chopped and slashed plant matter evenly over the plot to protect the soil while the material is drying. Another way to cope with leaching and erosion in the tropics is to plant an enormous variety of crops in a single plot; some crops are taller than others and have leaves that spread horizontally, thus protecting the soil in much the same way that the canopy does in the natural forest.

A few examples will indicate the enormous variety of crops that many shifting cultivators plant in a single garden. The Hanunoó of the Philippines plant up to forty distinct crops in a plot, including rice, corn, sweet potatoes, yams, manioc, banana, and cacao. The gardens of the Maring, who live in the highlands of interior Papua, New Guinea (north of Australia),

regularly contain over thirty species of cultigens. The Yukpa, slash-and-burn cultivators of tropical Colombia and Venezuela, cultivate about fifty species, most of which are found in a single garden.

On the other hand, other swiddeners have less diverse crop inventories. The Iban of Sarawak (Malaysia) rely mainly on dry rice grown under slash-and-burn conditions, supplemented by a few other crops. And many shifting cultivators of Central America are heavily dependent on corn and beans, which grow symbiotically: the cornstalk provides the support needed by the beans, whereas the beans fix atmospheric nitrogen—a nutrient that corn requires in abundance—in their roots, where it becomes water soluble and available to the corn.

It was once common to condemn the slash-and-burn method as an extremely wasteful use of land. This judgment was based on the simple observation that many more acres of land are required to support a population than would be needed using intensive agriculture with shorter or no fallow periods. This observation is indeed correct: if a plot is cropped for two years and fallowed for twenty, then ten times the amount of land is needed per person than if there were no fallow, for example. For human populations the main implication of this extensive land use is that high densities of people cannot be supported by shifting cultivation. Densities of less than one hundred per square mile characterize most shifting cultivators. By contrast, intensive agriculture supports densities of several hundreds per square mile in many parts of the world. In some intensive agriculture areas—notably the island of Java (Indonesia) and parts of China under wet rice—densities per square mile reach into the thousands.

But it does not follow that shifting cultivation is a more wasteful method than its *viable alternatives*. Agricultural experts from temperate regions have frequently attempted to apply "advanced modern methods" to the tropics: clear-cutting wide swaths of the forest, planting a single crop in a plot (called *monoculture*), applying commercial fertilizers, tilling with plows, and so forth. They found that once enormous tracts of forest were clear-cut, there was nothing to protect the soil from the rains, so leaching and erosion occurred. They often discovered that monoculture is too susceptible to viruses, fungi, and insects to work without an enormous input of chemical agents, which were washed off by the rains. Because it is not the major storehouse of nutrients, the soil was too infertile to support more than a crop or two; attempts to improve its productivity with artificial fertilizers were often unsuccessful, because of the leaching and erosion of the unprotected soil. Plowing turned the earth over, greatly disturbing its structure and making it more susceptible to erosion and leaching. Prevention of the natural recolonization of the plot from the surrounding forest for several seasons led to the invasion of hardy tropical grasses, which became so well established on the impoverished earth that trees could not regain a foothold. As a result of such experiences, many of those who used to claim that swidden was primitive and wasteful now admit that the methods that work in the temperate latitudes often fail in the tropics.

As we have seen, the chief limitation of shifting cultivation and other extensive land use systems is that they can support only relatively low population densities. If we look broadly at the history of cultivation—if we take a bird's-eye view of the long-term evolution of farming methods on our entire planet—we find that methods have grown more intensive: plots have been planted more frequently and fallow periods have grown shorter or even disappeared. The reasons for this broad shift in land use and methods are complex and controversial, but there is little doubt that population growth was an important factor. As densities grew and regions became filled up with people, plots had to be kept under cultivation longer. In some parts of the world with very high densities, fallow periods eventually almost disappeared.

As cultivation periods grew longer and fallow lengths shorter, farming tasks changed. For example, less labor time was spent in reclearing fallowed plots; but more labor had to be devoted to maintaining plots already under cultivation, for natural fallow no longer was sufficient to restore soil conditions, reduce pest infestations, and shade out weeds. If not removed, weeds greatly reduce yields by competing with crops for water, nutrients, and light, so human labor had to be used to remove them. Turning over the soil between plantings became necessary, both to remove unwanted vegetation and to bring nutrients to the surface. For this task, a new tool, the plow, and a new source of energy, draft animals, proved useful, and harnessing domesticated animals to plows developed in several regions of the Old World. Oxen, horses, or water buffalo commonly serve as the power (energy) source for the plow. In some regions, animals were harnessed

■ *Intensive agriculturalists plant and harvest fields more frequently than horticultralists. Draft animals supplement the energy of human muscles and allow plows to be used in the cultivation process. Here a farmer in Laos plows land to be planted in rice.*

to mechanical pumps to bring water to fields, or harnessed to heavy stone wheels used to grind grain. Besides supplementing human muscle energy in these and other ways, the animals' manure was used to fertilize fields, a step made necessary by the practice of keeping fields under cultivation year after year.

Before the coming of Europeans, New World peoples had no domesticated animals suitable for pulling plows. In the valley of Mexico and in the Andes, as populations grew and land use intensified, human labor continued to be the main source of energy. In the valley of Mexico, for example, natural swamps were reclaimed by filling in earth and constructing raised fields that were planted with crops like tomatoes, squash, and corn. By continually adding new materials to these so-called floating gardens, the people could keep them under almost continuous cultivation. In the Andes, stepped terraces were constructed to reduce erosion and an incredible variety of sweet potatoes and other crops were grown during the summer.

These kinds of changes occurred over many centuries, the details varying with crop variety, climate, soil, local technology, and the like. But the end result was that in many regions extensive systems evolved into more intensive ones, culminating in the modern type of cultivation generally known as intensive agriculture.

Intensive Agriculture

Intensive agriculture differs from horticulture in several ways. Most important, the land is used more fully: over a period of years intensive agriculturalists plant and harvest plots more frequently. Many use the same field for many years with only a year or two of fallow. This more intensive use of the land is made possible mainly by fertilization and relatively thorough removal of weeds. Intensive agriculturalists usually apply some form of organic fertilizer to maintain the productivity of their soil. Often, domestic animals are turned loose after harvest or in fallowing fields to replace soil nutrients with their dung. Manure is gathered and spread over fields. In some areas, including modern China, human excrement ("night soil") is collected and used to recycle nutrients ·back into the soil. Frequent removal of invading weeds is practiced so that growing crops have less competition.

Most intensive agriculturalists establish some form of artificial irrigation works because rainfall occurs only seasonally where they live, or because yields would be limited by low or unreliable rainfall but can be increased by artificial watering. Therefore, to farm during the dry season, they store water in reservoirs or tanks. A variety of irrigation methods are employed around the world. Streams are sometimes dammed to conserve runoff, and ditches are dug to transport water to the fields. In Mexico's arid Oaxaca valley, farmers of the valley floor plant maize and other crops around shallow wells and water the crops with pots. In some Asian river valleys channels are dug to transport water (and fertile silt!) to fields during the annual monsoons, when the rivers overrun their banks. In many mountainous regions of Southeast Asia the level of water in hillside rice fields is controlled with an elaborate system of diked terraces.

Intensive agriculture can support much greater numbers of people on a given area of land—five, ten, and even twenty times the densities of horticultural methods. In essence, intensive agriculture further raises the carrying capacity of the habitat. Some scholars believe that this advantage is the main or even the only benefit intensive methods offer over horticulture.

Higher densities are possible mainly because plots yield their harvests more frequently, there being little fallow, but this is not the only reason an area of land supports more people. Preparing land more thoroughly,

tilling the soil more completely, controlling the supply of water, removing weeds, artificially adding nutrients—these activities give intensive agriculturalists greater control over the conditions under which their crops grow. This control also contributes to greater outputs per unit of land.

Of all forms of modern intensive agriculture, wet rice cultivation is the most widespread and feeds the greatest number of people. It serves as our example of intensive methods.

■ Wet Rice in Asia

The wet rice fields of Asia are the most productive of all preindustrial intensive agricultural systems. This method provides food for most of the rural population of the Far East, including China, South Korea, Taiwan, Vietnam, the lowlands of Thailand, the river valleys and coastal plains of India, and Indonesia (see the map in Figure 8.2)

As the term *wet rice* suggests, the method involves flooding the fields for most of the growing season. In some areas the water comes entirely from the natural rainfall of the monsoons, but often the water level is controlled by artificial irrigation. Most wet rice is therefore grown on the flood plains of rivers. In parts of Southeast Asia, southern China, and the Himalayan fringes, wet rice is grown on terraced hillsides originally constructed centuries ago.

Perhaps the most remarkable feature of wet rice cultivation is the capability of a plot to yield a harvest year in and year out, with little or no fallow. Indeed, where the seasonal availability of water is adequate, the same plot may yield two or even three harvests in a single year, being under almost continuous cultivation. According to agricultural economist D. B. Grigg, this capability is attributable to four factors: (1) the protection from erosion the water gives the soil, (2) the high water table of the rivers' flood plain that reduces leaching, (3) the replacement of soil nutrients by the silt carried in the rivers' flooding, and (4) nitrogen fixation from the blue-green algae that live in the floodwater. The chief benefit of wet rice—its ability to grow in the same field year after year—is then related to the practice of flooding the fields and allowing the water to remain throughout most of the maturation period.

Like horticultural peoples, wet rice growers have developed a diversity of patterns to organize agricul-

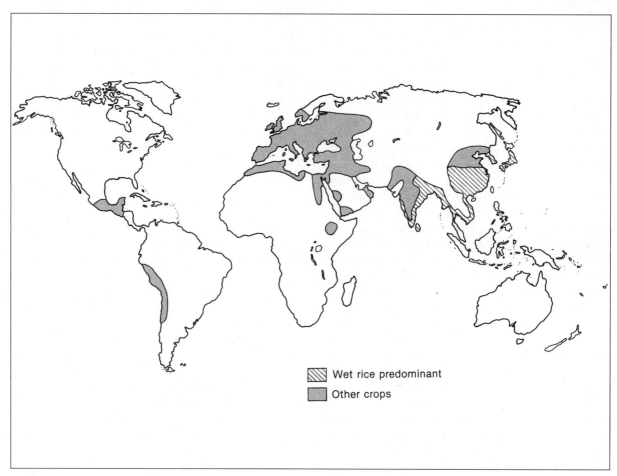

Wet rice predominant
Other crops

■ *Figure 8.2*
Principal Regions of Intensive Agriculture at Contact Period

tural tasks and access to land. Besides the difficulties faced by all cultivators, wet rice growers must solve other problems relating to the management of water, for the proper supply of water at the proper time is important for a good yield. In general, it is more efficient if storage ponds or tanks, canals or ditches, and other improvements are held and managed communally, for less labor is required to construct and maintain them than if each family owned their own. Water may be stored in small lakes or ponds, or captured and held in tanks until it is used to flood the fields. It is important that the water level is controlled fairly precisely while the rice is growing: if it rises too high, the plants will be unable to photosynthesize; and if it falls too low, the benefits of

having standing water in the fields will be reduced. Unless the land is naturally flat, the plots therefore must be leveled to keep the height of the water constant in different areas of the field. The water level must be controlled by low dikes, usually constructed of earth, which can be easily breached to drain the plot for the harvest.

Managing the supply of the water that is so critical in growing wet rice requires sophisticated organization, especially with respect to cooperative labor patterns and rights of access to both land and water. Each family may work its lands on its own, but who will construct and maintain public irrigation works? Who will decide when dikes, dams, ditches, and tanks need to be repaired, and how will the labor to repair them be

■ *Wet rice is an enormously productive form of preindustrial intensive agriculture. As seen in this photo of a rice paddy in Thailand, cultivators invest much labor in controlling the level of water in their fields.*

coordinated? The water used on the fields of one family is not available to other families. How shall the consumption of water be coordinated? Who will get how much water and when? How, in short, will use rights to water be determined? These are all, essentially, problems of organizing production in wet rice areas.

Here is how one population, the Sinhalese of the dry zone of Sri Lanka, traditionally solved the problem of organizing the allocation of water to fields. Each village subsists from wet rice cultivation, the water for which is drawn from a collectively owned rain-fed reservoir constructed from earth. Most villages have their own separate reservoirs, filled with water that their residents alone may use. The people of the village are responsible for maintaining the earthworks of the reservoir and for managing the allocation of water to each family plot. The capacity of the tank determines the maximum number of acres of land that the village may have in cultivation. This is because the supply of water is so critical to wet rice cultivation that land cannot be farmed without it (especially in this part of Sri Lanka, in which all the rain falls in one season, and water must be stored the rest of the year).

All the cultivated land of a village is in a single area, below the reservoir. The entire field is laid out into bounded, diked plots of equal size. Each plot receives a fixed amount of water from the communal reservoir. The number of owners of a single plot varies: poor families must share rights of access to one plot with other families, whereas other (richer) families have access to several plots with their accompanying ration of water. Thus, the ownership of plots within the entire village field carries with it rights to a certain proportion of the communal water supply. By allocating each plot (rather than each family) a fixed proportion of irrigation water, the chance that a given plot will receive insufficient moisture is reduced.

■ Intensive Agriculture and Sociocultural Systems

The development of intensive agricultural methods had profound sociocultural consequences. Some of these arose from the need to manage the supply of irrigation water, which gave rise to a variety of new social organizations. (The Sinhalese are only one of many variants.) Other consequences result from a potential that is greater in intensive agriculture than in either foraging or horticulture: the production of a food **surplus.** That is, a single worker using intensive agricultural methods can feed many more people than just him- or herself and his or her family.

As we have seen, intensive agriculture generally produces significantly more food per unit of available land than horticulture. As Box 8.2 shows, intensive agriculture also is more productive per unit of *labor*—and for many reasons. In the Old World, animal muscle supplemented human labor in preparing the land for planting. Milk and meat from cattle, sheep, horses, pigs, and other domesticated animals reduces the need to hunt, conserving male labor that can be put into cultivation. In both hemispheres, the labor needed to clear land and establish irrigation was put in long ago, so fields and irrigation works need only be maintained and extended occasionally. Even more so than horticulturalists, intensive agriculturalists live partly off the labor of past generations. For these and other reasons, it is clear that—at least after intensive agriculture is fully established in a region—a single worker or farm family can produce a significant surplus over their own immediate needs.

What happens to this surplus? To answer this question, we must realize that intensive agricultural peoples usually are not politically independent and economi-

Box 8.2

LABOR AND ENERGY INPUTS AND OUTPUTS

How do the food-production systems we have discussed so far compare in how hard people work to produce their food and how much each worker produces per unit of labor? Available data on this subject are very scanty, so only very rough comparisons can be given.

For a few populations we know about how much time producers actually spend in subsistence labor. We therefore can state the *labor input into subsistence;* but we must keep in mind that time spent in making tools, processing food, cooking food, and so forth is usually not recorded by fieldworkers. We also know how much food is produced per unit (e.g., hour) of labor input, measured in weight. If we can determine how much food value is locked up in the foods produced, we can state roughly how *productive* a system is in the amount produced per unit of subsistence labor. To do this, we need a common measure that will apply to all kinds of foods and that, therefore, can be used to compare them. (To see why, ask, How do we compare the food value of a pound of mongongo nuts eaten by the San with that of a pound of rice consumed by the Sinhalese?) The only common measure available is kilocalories (commonly called *calories*), which are a unit of energy. By determining in a laboratory the number of kilocalories contained in a gram of mongongo nuts and a gram of rice, we can compare the productivity of mongongo-nut gatherers with that of rice growers.

Table B.1 compares working hours and productivity of sample foragers, horticulturalists, and intensive agriculturalists. The figures in the column "Subsistence Working Hours" refer to the approximate number of hours a subsistence worker spends per week in food production. The figures under "Output/Input Ratio" show the approximate number of calories of food energy obtained per calorie of human-labor input. This column also might be headed "labor efficiency," since it shows how much food energy an average worker produces from each unit of muscle energy he or she expends in subsistence labor.

On the basis of these limited data it seems that foraging and horticulture are roughly comparable in the hours actually spent in producing food and in the amount of food a worker produces. Only intensive agriculture is notably more productive: agricultural workers produce about five times the amount of calories with their labor as do horticultural workers. We can see that an intensive agricultural village can potentially produce enough food to support many people who are not themselves engaged in food production.

In chapter 19 we compare the output/input ratio—or labor efficiency—of these preindustrial food-production systems with that of mechanized agriculture. As we discuss further, the latter is far more efficient in its output/input ratio; a single mechanized agricultural worker in the United States and Great Britain produces enough food to feed sixty or seventy people. But this labor efficiency is achieved only with an enormous input of energy in the form of fossil fuels and electricity. The "energetic efficiency"—the number of calories of energy needed to produce one calorie of food energy—of mechanized agriculture is far lower than that of any of the preindustrial systems discussed in this chapter. ∎

■ *Table B.1* **Working Hours/ Productivity Comparisons**

PRODUCTION SYSTEM	POPULATION	SUBSISTENCE WORKING HOURS	OUTPUT/INPUT RATIO
Foraging			
Horticulture	San	17	10
Hoe cultivation	Genieri (Gambia)	16	11
Grassland gardening	Enga (Papua New Guinea)	19	9
Swidden plus pigs	Maring (Papua New Guinea)	?	10
Intensive agriculture			
Wet rice	Luts'un village (China)	22	54

Sources: Lee (1979), Harris (1985), Waddell (1972), Leach (1976), Little and Morren (1976).

PEOPLES OF
ASIA

Asia as a sociocultural region and Asia as a geographical area are not the same. The peoples and sociocultural institutions in many regions geographically classified as Asian are actually European. Likewise, north Africa is more closely related socioculturally to Asia than to sub-Saharan Africa. Asia comprises four major sociocultural areas: East Asia, the Middle East, South Asia, and Southeast Asia.

EAST ASIA   East Asia includes the modern countries of China, Korea, Taiwan, and Japan. This region traditionally was characterized by intensive agriculture, small villages, hereditary rulers, and state level political systems. The arts, architecture, technology, writing system, and social and political institutions of the entire region are primarily derived from ancient China. Buddhism, Taoism, and Confucianism (a political philosophy), mixed with earlier belief systems such as Japanese Shinto, are the primary ideological influences in the region. East Asia has three main ethnic groups: Chinese, Korean, and Japanese. For its population size, East Asia is one of the most socioculturally homogeneous regions of the world.

THE MIDDLE EAST   The Middle East stretches from Morocco across north Africa, north into Turkey, and east to Afghanistan and the Arabian peninsula. It includes Arabic-, Turkic-, and Farsi-speaking peoples.

The Islamic religion gives this region its distinctive sociocultural character. As it spread, Islam carried with it distinctive art and architectural styles, a writing system, and social and political institutions derived from the Koran and Arabic society. Economically, the region was extremely diverse, including nomadic herders of camels, sheep, and goats; intensive farmers living in settled villages; and working in urban trade and manufacturing centers. Politically there was a mixture of tribal and state systems, with hereditary rulers and religious leaders. Scattered throughout the region were small but significant Christian and Jewish communities.

SOUTH ASIA   South Asia is bounded by the Indus Valley on the west, the Ganges Valley on the east, and the Himalaya Mountains on the north. It includes the modern countries of India, Pakistan, Bangladesh, Nepal, and Sri Lanka. Intensive agriculture, small villages, hereditary rulers, and multiethnic states traditionally characterized this extremely diverse region. The population was divided into several hundred ethnic groups with dozens of major languages, many with their own literature. Hinduism and its associated caste system has been a strong influence and is responsible for much of the region's unique character. However, Islam, Buddhism, and Sikhism have large, geographically localized followings. The result is a

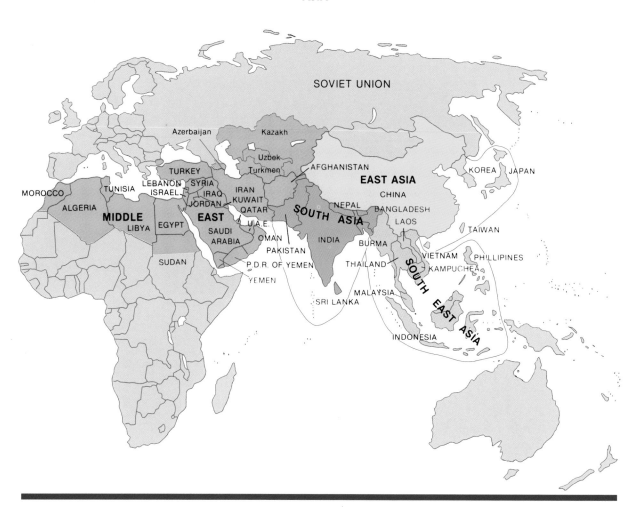

highly complex region with numerous localized differences in sociocultural institutions.

SOUTHEAST ASIA Southeast Asia includes modern Burma, Thailand, Laos, Cambodia, Vietnam, Malaysia, most of Indonesia, and the Philippines. This region, with several hundred distinct ethnic groups and languages, is characterized by small villages dependent on intensive agriculture, horticulture, fishing, or maritime trade. Multiethnic states with hereditary rulers formerly existed in Cambodia, Thailand, and other areas. The ancient maritime trade routes that linked East Asia, South Asia, and the Middle East passed along the coasts and through the islands of Southeast Asia. At different times, the peoples of Southeast Asia came under the influence of these three regions. Starting in the second century A.D., Hinduism and Buddhism, together with other South Asian sociocultural influences, spread into the region. In the thirteenth century Moslem traders introduced Islam, which quickly spread through the areas known today

as Indonesia and Malaysia. Throughout this period, trade with East Asia provided a steady source of sociocultural influences. These outside influences left their mark on the peoples of Southeast Asia, resulting in an extraordinarily complex array of distinct sociocultural systems.

OTHER PEOPLES On the periphery of these Asian sociocultural areas were numerous peoples who were never completely integrated, politically or socioculturally, into the dominant traditions. These peoples were organized into bands, tribes, or chiefdoms. Some were foragers; others were pastoralists or horticulturalists. These "marginal" peoples occupied the mountains, deserts, jungles, and northern forests of present-day Siberia, Mongolia, Taiwan, the Philippines, and Borneo (Kalimantan), among other areas. These peoples include the Dyak of Borneo, the Ainu of Japan, the Chukchi and Eskimo of Siberia, the aborigines of Formosa (Taiwan), and the tribal peoples of Luzon in the Philippines.

■ (Above, left) Today as in the past, a multitude of languages and traditions exist in South Asia, making it one of the most heterogenous regions of the world.

■ (Above right) The civilization of ancient China was unrivalled in riches, power, and size. As this photo of the Imperial Palace in the Forbidden City of modern Beijing suggests, at the height of their empire Chinese emperors were among the most powerful men in the world.

■ (Left) Although as modernized and industrialized as any Western country, Japan's traditions remain strong, especially in the countryside. This is a rice field after harvest.

■ (Top) Much of the Middle East is inhabited by nomadic peoples who live in tents and herd camels, sheep, and goats. These Bedouin women of the Egyptian desert are preparing tea.

■ (Above, left) Eighty percent of China's 1 billion people live in rural areas. These barges are being loaded with hay.

■ (Right) Many small states existed in Southeast Asia in Pre-European times. This Burmese water cart passes the ruins of one such state.

Sources for the creation of this insert: Robinson (1967), McVey (1967), Kolb (1971), and Eickelman (1989).

cally self-sufficient societies. Instead, they generally are incorporated into larger political units. By this we mean that the villages in which most of them live are part of an inclusive political system that dominates or rules them in some way. The surplus is used to support people who do not themselves perform agricultural labor, such as rulers and aristocracies, priests, armies, traders, and craft specialists of various kinds.

The association of intensive agriculture with large-scale political organization is an ancient one. In prehistoric times intensive agricultural peoples were incorporated into the four major civilizations of the ancient Old World: the valley formed by the Tigris and Euphrates rivers of Mesopotamia, the Nile valley of Egypt, the Indus River valley of Pakistan, and the Shang cities of China. The food supply of these civilizations was produced by intensive agriculturalists, who paid tribute or taxes to support the rulers, priests, armies, and officials who ran the government apparatus. In the New World, too, agricultural peoples were part of large-scale political units, such as the Mayans of the Yucatan peninsula, the Toltecs and Aztecs of Mexico, and the Incas of highland Peru (see the map in Figure 8.3).

In these parts of the world, within a few centuries or millennia after the development of intensive agricul-

ture, the socially and politically complex organization we call **civilization** (or "living in cities") emerged. All these ancient civilizations were supported by intensive agriculture, and all involved large-scale irrigation works and water control. In fact, some prehistorians have argued that civilization—and the despotic control of rulers and priests that everywhere accompanied it—developed out of control over the supply of irrigation water. (This theory, however, is very controversial, and numerous alternatives have been proposed.) Certainly, it appears from present evidence that intensive agriculture is virtually a prerequisite for civilization. No known civilization ever developed out of a horticultural cultivation system. (The Mayan civilization was once thought to have been an exception, but recent evidence shows that the Mayans too used intensive methods.)

In the modern world, of course, most people are incorporated into large-scale political units, namely, into nations. Even in some developed countries—notably in Europe, South Korea, and Taiwan—intensive agriculturalists survive. However, in most industrial nations intensive agriculture has been largely replaced by mechanized agriculture based on energy derived from electricity and fossil fuels rather than from humans and animals. Today, most intensive agriculture occurs in the less-developed countries of southern Asia and Southeast Asia, Latin America, and Africa. Intensive agriculturalists typically fit into these nations economically as peasants.

Peasants are rural people who are integrated into a larger society politically (i.e., they are subject to laws and governments imposed from outside their communities) and economically (i.e., they exchange products of their own labor for products produced elsewhere). In most Third World countries they make up the bulk of the population and produce much of the food consumed by town and city dwellers. Peasants typically subsist mainly from foods they grow themselves, although many also produce nonagricultural products for market sale. Peasant households produce goods that are sold for money, traded or bartered for goods produced by other people, paid to a landlord as rent, or rendered to a central government as taxes.

But subjection to external political authorities and exchange with a wider economy are not enough to define the term *peasant*. (Otherwise, California's small farmers—or the few left—would be classified as peasants.) Peasantries nearly always fit into their larger

■ *Intensive agriculture increased productivity so much that it became possible for a single cultivator to produce a large surplus. Early civilizations relied on the labor of peasants, who produced the food that fed administrators and specialists. Here Indian peasants transplant wet rice.*

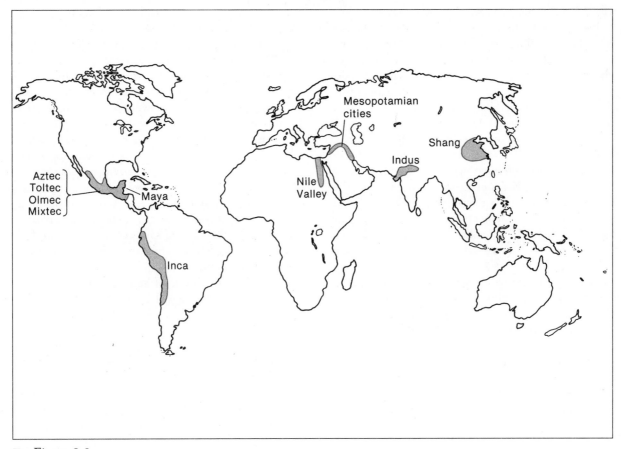

■ *Figure 8.3*
Ancient Civilizations

societies at or near the bottom of the social and economic pyramid. They have little prestige in the view of other categories of people in the society. Although the foods they produce often feed almost everyone else, their labor is not valued and their lifestyle is not envied. Also, they are among the poorest people in the society, for in one way or another they are dominated or exploited.

The peasantry first arose in the ancient civilizations just discussed. The agricultural labor of prehistoric peasants fed the craft workers; the merchants; the state-sponsored priesthoods; the political elite; the warriors; and the builders of transportation facilities, buildings, and cities themselves. The tribute (paid usually in food, labor, or both) rendered by peasants was extracted from them by armed force or threat of force. This rendering of goods and labor by peasants to

members of a more powerful social category continued into historic and modern times. The peasantry of medieval Europe, for example, eked out a meager living, paying a substantial portion of their annual harvest to their lords or working many days a year on their lord's estate.

Given this information, we might well wonder whether the development of intensive agriculture was a curse or a blessing for most of humanity. There is little doubt that it is a blessing to those who throughout history have received the surplus made possible by intensive methods. And most scholars agree that the productivity of intensive agriculture allowed the specialized division of labor that led to writing, metallurgy, monumental architecture, cities, and the great religious and artistic traditions we associate with civilization.

But how about the peasants, who actually produced the food that made such "progress" possible? For them, writing meant that more accurate accounts could be kept of their tribute payments or of the number of days they worked for overlords. Iron and other metals meant that peasants had better agricultural tools; yet generally they were not allowed to use them to ease their own labor, but only to produce more surplus for others to consume. Metal also meant that weapons became more effective, so that the citizens of one state could slaughter the citizens of another state more effectively. Most peasant families continued to live in hovels, even while great palaces, religious structures, and walled cities and towns were constructed and the workers were fed by the peasants' agricultural labor. Both prehistorically and historically, peasants around the world have been denied many of the benefits offered by technological progress, although their agricultural labor has made much of this progress possible.

Occasionally, peasants have organized themselves to resist these conditions. Peasant revolts have occurred in many areas. Peasants in Mexico, Russia, China, Vietnam, and Nicaragua played an important role in the revolutions of these countries. More recently, guerilla movements have been backed by many peasants in Guatemala, El Salvador, Peru, and the Philippines. Denied most of the benefits of whatever progress their nations have managed to achieve, modern peas-ants often join these movements in the hope of obtaining a greater share of the land and other resources that have been denied them.

Pastoralism

Except for some New World peoples in precolonial times, cultivators usually keep domesticated animals. For example, Southeast Asian and Pacific horticulturalists raise many pigs and chickens. Intensive agriculturalists raise horses, oxen, water buffalo, and cattle, which they use to pull their plows, fertilize their fields, and provide dairy products and meat. These domesticated animals should not be seen as supplementary to the horticultural or agricultural adaptation: because of the meat, eggs, milk, hides, wool, transportation, fertilizer, and horsepower they provide, they are usually critical to the survival and nutrition of assorted cultivators.

Cultivators, however, do not depend on their domesticated animals to the same extent as do peoples known as *pastoralists*, or herders. Herders acquire much of their food by raising, caring for, and subsisting on the products of domesticated animals. With a few exceptions, the livestock are gregarious (herd) animals, with cattle, camels, sheep, goats, reindeer, horses, llamas, alpacas, and yaks being the common animals kept in various parts of the world.

But the simple degree of dependence on domesticated animals is not all that distinguishes pastoralists from cultivators, for a great many pastoralists also cultivate; indeed, many acquire the bulk of their food calories from their crops rather than from their animals. More important, when we characterize a people as "pastoral," we mean that the needs of their animals for naturally occurring food and water profoundly influence the seasonal rhythms of their lives. The key phrase here is "naturally occurring." Most cultivators raise crops that they feed to their livestock or maintain fields in which their animals graze. In general, pastoralists do neither of these. Their herds subsist on natural forage and therefore must be moved to where the forage naturally occurs. This means that some or all of the people must accompany their livestock as they follow the seasonal distribution and abundance of grasses or other forage. This high degree of mobility, known as **nomadism,** characterizes most pastoralists. Most commonly, pastoralists are seasonally

■ *Peasants make up the majority population of many modern Third World nations, including India.*

nomadic—they do not wander aimlessly. Their migrations are often "vertical," meaning that animals are taken to highland areas to graze during the hottest season of the year.

Few pastoralists subsist entirely from the products of their livestock; animal products nearly always are supplemented by cultivated foods. Herders acquire these in one of four major ways.

- They practice some horticulture or agriculture themselves (often men and boys watch the herds and women cultivate).
- They trade animal products for vegetable foods and other goods with neighboring cultivators.
- They sell livestock, meat, hides, wool, milk, cheese, or other products of their animals for money, which they use to buy food and other supplies.
- They use their livestock partly as beasts of burden, which allows them to undertake long-distance trade from which they profit.

We briefly discuss some examples of these methods in upcoming sections. First, we need to discuss the distribution of the pastoral adaptation and the characteristics that make it advantageous in some kinds of environments.

■ *Distribution of Pastoralism*

Herders are scattered across the globe, but not in a random distribution. By comparing Figure 7.1 with Figure 8.4, you can see that the pastoral adaptation occurs largely in deserts, grasslands, savannas, and mountains. (A few peoples, such as the Lapps of northern Scandinavia and the Tungus and Chukchee of Siberia, were reindeer herders in the tundra biome.) These areas do have something in common: cultivation is impossible, extremely difficult, or highly risky because of low average annual precipitation, great fluctuations in rainfall from year to year, or short growing seasons. As always, there are exceptions to our generalizations, but pastoralists tend to be found in regions that are not well suited to cultivation using preindustrial technologies.

Some of these regions are too cold or have a very short growing season, such as the northern Scandinavian and Siberian tundra or the high mountains of the South American Andes and parts of Tibet. In the northern Scandinavian and Siberian tundras the high latitude makes cultivation impossible. The meat and milk of

reindeer and the trade in reindeer products allow the Lapps, Chukchee, and Tungus to exploit these areas. In the high mountains of the Andes, Tibet, and parts of Afghanistan, it is the high altitude that greatly restricts the length of the growing season. In parts of the Andes, people move their llamas and alpacas to highland pastures for the summer, making much of their living from selling wool and using the animals for transport. In Tibet the yak not only serves as a beast of burden for long-distance trade but also is harvested for its flesh, milk, and hide. In central Asia, north and west of the Himalayas, the horse herders known as the Kazakh roam the grassy plains. They subsist partly from mare's milk and periodically shear the wool from their herds of sheep to trade with neighboring peoples.

In other areas cultivation is possible and does occur, but precipitation is so low or unreliable from year to year that droughts frequently cause crop failure. This is the case in eastern and southern Africa, parts of Turkey and the eastern Mediterranean, and certain arid regions of modern Iran and Iraq. In the savannas of eastern and southern Africa, peoples such as the Karimojong, Dinka, Nuer, Swazi, and Tswana combine cattle raising with the cultivation of African grains such as millet. In the chaparral and grasslands of the eastern Mediterranean, herding is the dominant activity among several ethnic populations, including

■ *Pastoral people live primarily off their herds, eating their flesh and drinking their milk, trading animal products with thier neighbors, or—like this Egyptian—selling the animals themselves.*

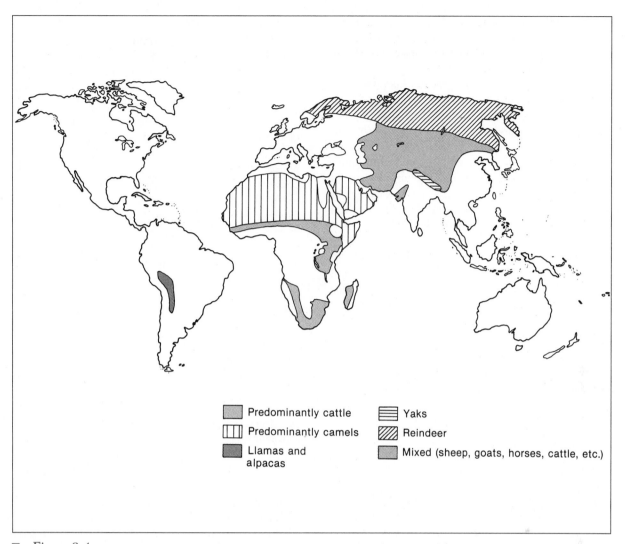

Predominantly cattle	Yaks
Predominantly camels	Reindeer
Llamas and alpacas	Mixed (sheep, goats, horses, cattle, etc.)

■ *Figure 8.4*
Principal Regions of Pastoralism at Contact Period

the Yörük and some local Bedouin groups. Adaptive patterns vary, but most of these peoples subsist only partly off the meat and milk—made into butter, cheese, and yogurt—of their sheep, camels, and goats. More important, they sell or trade the meat, dairy products, and wool to their cultivator neighbors and receive vegetable foods and other necessities in return. Sometimes the wool is dyed locally, woven on hand looms into beautiful rugs, and exported to neighboring townsmen—or nowadays, to the international market.

Still other regions in which the pastoral adaptation occurs are outright deserts, in which aridity makes cultivation difficult or impossible, such as the African Sahara and much of the Arabian peninsula. Here the dominant livestock is the camel. Both its milk and flesh are eaten, but the animal is equally significant as a resource because of its well-known ability to survive long periods with little water. The camel is used as a beast of burden on the long-distance caravans for which these regions are famous. Many indigenous peoples of the Sahara (such as the Tuareg) and Arabia (including some Bedouin and Kurds) make their living primarily through the trade made possible by their camels.

■ The Benefits and Costs of Herding

In such arid or cold environments the breeding and exploitation of domestic animals offer several advantages over the planting and harvesting of domesticated plants. First, most of the vegetation of grasslands and arid savannas (grasses and shrubs) and of tundras (lichens, willows, and sedges) is indigestible by humans. Livestock such as cattle, sheep, and reindeer are able to eat this vegetation and transform it into milk, blood, fat, and muscle, all of which are drunk or eaten by various pastoral peoples. Thus, in some areas livestock allow people to exploit indirectly certain wild resources not directly available to them.

Another advantage of herding may be called *subsistence risk reduction*. Under preindustrial conditions in areas of low and unreliable rainfall, crops often fail because of drought. Livestock provide an insurance against these periodic, unpredictable droughts and accompanying low yields. Not only do they store meat "on the hoof," but they also can be traded to neighboring peoples for cultivated foods.

Finally, a big advantage of keeping livestock is their mobility: herds can be moved to the areas of freshest or lushest pasture, to sources of water, away from neighbors who have grown too aggressive, or even out of easy range of tax-seeking governments who often want the nomads to settle down.

■ *One advantage of herding is that animals can be moved when the local environment is unfavorable, carrying people and possessions on their backs. These Chadians are relocating in face of a drought.*

With advantages like these, you may well wonder why pastoralism was not more widespread in the preindustrial world. Why did the herding adaptation not spread to areas where cultivators lived? Part of the reason is that environmental conditions are not always conducive. For example, until recently pastoralism was rarely found in tropical forests, largely because of lack of forage. (Today, however, enormous tracts of tropical forest in Central America and Brazil are cleared and replanted in grasses, which cattle graze and people convert into hamburgers, partly for North American fast-food chains.) Livestock diseases also limit the distribution of pastoralists. For example, much of eastern and southern Africa is occupied by cattle herders (most of whom also farm, however). Herders would presumably be even more widespread on the continent were it not for the limitations imposed by the presence of the tsetse fly, which transmits the debilitating disease, sleeping sickness, to cattle.

Perhaps the main factor limiting the distribution of pastoralism is that herding is not the most productive way of using the land of areas in which cultivation can be carried out reliably. The best way to understand why is to apply the ecologists' "10 percent rule." The food energy produced by photosynthetic plants lies at the base of any ecosystem except the deep oceans. In the presence of sufficient water, carbon dioxide, and minerals, plants convert the energy of sunlight into simple sugars, from which they derive the energy to grow and reproduce. Herbivores (plant-eating animals) consume the vegetation and use it to maintain their own bodies and produce offspring. Carnivores (animal-eating animals) in turn feed on herbivores. At each of these levels of the food chain, most of the energy is lost as it is carried to the next level. Thus, herbivores transform only about 10 percent of the plant energy they consume into their own flesh and blood (and hoofs and horns); and only around 10 percent of the energy carnivores acquire by eating herbivores is available to make more carnivore flesh (and teeth and claws). At each level, 90 percent of the energy consumed is lost to respiration, waste production, and other processes. The 10 percent rule says that only 10 percent of the energy locked up in living matter at one level is available to the next level.

Now we can see why herding is generally not as efficient a way of exploiting an environment as cultivation: overall, pastoralists eat higher on the food chain. Local abiotic and biotic conditions permitting, more total energy can be obtained from an environment by cultivation, for much more energy can be gained from (cultivated) plants than from (domesticated) animals. People are not directly concerned with how much total energy they can extract from an environment, of course; populations did not figure out that they could most productively exploit an environment by growing crops rather than raising animals, and then opt for cultivation. More likely, cultivation won out over herding—in areas that are suitable for both—because of its greater labor productivity. If several times the food energy can be gained from an area of land by cultivating it rather than by grazing livestock on it, then 100 herders would have to range over a much larger area to support themselves than would 100 cultivators, and these movements would consume time and energy. Further, the 10 percent rule also would translate into higher potential (and actual) population densities for cultivators, who in the past may have outcompeted pastoralists for those territories that both could exploit.

For reasons such as these, cultivation rather than pastoralism tends to occur in areas well suited for growing crops, although people frequently also could live in these areas by herding. The pastoral adaptation tends to occur in regions where cultivation alone is unreliable, usually because of short growing seasons or inadequate precipitation.

Aridity, temperature, short growing seasons, and other ecological and climatic factors do not totally explain the distribution of the pastoral adaptation, however. Some pastoralists live in areas where crops could be grown, and they certainly know how to cultivate, but they consciously choose not to grow crops. The cattle-herding Masai of Kenya and Tanzania are an example. In some parts of the Masai territory, cultivation is possible, and in fact most neighboring tribes combine cattle herding with cultivation of sorghum and other crops. The proud Masai, however, look down on cultivation, for their herds represent wealth and are the main symbol of their sociocultural identity relative to their neighbors. Masai therefore live largely off the products of their cattle—blood, milk, meat, curds—and trade with their neighbors for the cultivated foods they do eat. The reasons they continue their pastoral adaptation are therefore as much "cultural" as "ecological."

■ Herding and Social Organization

When a population acquires much of its foods and other necessities from livestock, this adaptation inev-

itably affects other aspects of its way of life. As we define *pastoralism* in this text, the herds subsist largely or entirely from natural forage. Because the location of water and the best forage for livestock typically varies from season to season, the herds—and at least some of the herders—must also be seasonally mobile. Herds must also be managed, which requires some minimum number of people of the appropriate sex and age in a settlement at any given time. Finally, herders must have some ways of deciding whose animals have access to which areas of forage—the rights of access of people's livestock to land. We now look at two specific pastoral populations to see how their lives are affected by their adaptation.

Basseri   The Basseri are one of several nomadic pastoralists of the desert and arid grasslands of southern Iran. When studied by Norwegian anthropologist Fredrik Barth in the late 1950s, the 16,000 Basseri made their living by herding. Sheep and goats provided much of their food in the form of milk, cheese, and meat. Donkeys, camels, and horses provided transportation for people and possessions. The Basseri traded products made from the fur and hides of sheep, goats, and camels with their cultivator neighbors. In return, they received cereals and other foods produced by irrigated agriculture. Although much of their diet thus came from exchange with surrounding peoples, the Basseri culturally looked down on agriculture and did very little of it themselves. Basseri and their agricultural neighbors also benefited from one another's activities in another way: in their seasonal migrations the Basseri flocks grazed on the stubble in the harvested fields of the cultivators. For their part, the farmers generally were glad to have the Basseri livestock fertilize their just-harvested and fallow fields with their manure.

The Basseri had traditional rights to exploit pasture lands on which their livestock relied. The grazing rights were complex, but in essence Basseri could pasture their animals on a strip of land (their "tribal road") that ran from the mountains in the north through some central grasslands to the hot, arid desert of the south. On this strip, about 300 miles long and 20 to 50 miles wide, different areas contained good pasture at different times of the year. In the winter, snow covered the northern mountains, but pasture was available in the south. In the spring people and livestock began moving northward, arriving in the highlands in time to take advantage of the summer pasture. In autumn they made their way south again, the livestock grazing largely on the cereal stubble of the harvested fields of the cultivators who lived along the central portion of the tribal road.

Because of their frequent moves, the Basseri lived in portable tents woven by women from goat hair. Each tent ordinarily was occupied by a single family. Each family owned its tents, textiles, and other household equipment and, on the average, about 100 sheep and goats. If a family was to manage its flocks and run its other activities independently, it would need at least three members: a man, a woman, and a shepherd (usually a boy). But many young couples were childless, so they either had to acquire a shepherd through a contract (of which there were several kinds) or make an arrangement with another family to intermingle their flocks. In fact, since a single shepherd could look after a flock of around 400, it was common for several tents to use a single shepherd, for this required less labor. So two to five tents typically formed a "herding unit," the members of which cooperated by using a single young shepherd. Ownership of the livestock always remained separate, however, and tent families frequently pulled their livestock from one herding unit and associated with another.

The number of tents that camped together and jointly used an area of pasture varied seasonally. In the winter, when most Basseri lived in the arid southern lowlands, grass for the flocks was so sparse that the animals had to range widely to acquire sufficient food. Accordingly, the typical winter settlement group was the herding units of two to five families, which lived scattered throughout the territory, separated by a mile or more from other herding units. At other times of the year, grass was more abundant, and the number of tents that associated together in a single area increased to as many as forty. These larger "camps" migrated as a single group under the limited authority of a headman, who consulted with the heads of the various tents in deciding when to move, where to move to, what route to take, and where to pitch the tents.

Tents, herding units, and camps were not the only groups formed by the Basseri. Camps were in turn associated into an overarching group called the *oulad* (a term that has no suitable English translation). The *oulad* was an important group, for the camps that it comprised had joint rights to exploit certain areas of pasture along the tribal road. These grazing rights to specific areas were use rights, not ownership rights. No

oulad, much less any lower-level group, could permanently claim an area of pasture as its own, for the various *oulad* were subgroups of yet a higher level of organization.

The entire Basseri "tribe" of 16,000 was subject to the authority of a single chief, who inherited his office from his father. The chief exacted small, irregular taxes from the general population. He represented the tribe as a whole to surrounding sedentary cultivators and often settled disputes between tribal members. The tribal chief also periodically reallocated use rights to pasture lands between the *oulad,* so the various camps that made up a single *oulad* shared grazing rights to pastures allocated to them by the tribal chief. As the size of an *oulad* increased or decreased, the chief allocated it more pasture or reduced the area of pasture to which it had grazing rights. Through this organizational mechanism, the members of each *oulad* knew to which areas they enjoyed grazing rights at any given time. Presumably, this reduced disputes over pasture between members of different *oulad.*

We see that the Basseri developed a fairly complex organization. Livestock were owned by families; families formed herding units to save labor; herding units aggregated into camps most of the year, which migrated as a single group; several camps composed an *oulad,* whose constituent camps had joint grazing rights over specific pasture lands; in turn, *oulad* formed a tribe, which was subject to the authority of a single chief, who periodically reallocated use rights to pasture among the *oulad.* Through the complexity, you can see how the various levels of organization helped relate the Basseri and their livestock to their habitat, organized their migrations, and regulated access to pasture lands without much internal dispute and conflict.

Karimojong   The Karimojong are an East African people of Uganda. Living on an arid savanna with marked seasonal differences in rainfall, they subsist by a combination of horticulture and cattle pastoralism. The 60,000 Karimojong are a fairly representative example of a sociocultural type known to anthropologists as the "East African cattle complex." In this complex, found throughout the East African savannas, cattle are more than an ordinary source of food. The East African man loves his cattle like some North Americans love their cars. Cattle represent wealth and manliness. They are the source of prestige, influence in tribal affairs, and wives (for an East African man must transfer cattle to his wife's relatives in order to marry her, a practice we discuss in chapter 10). When sacrificed ritually, cattle are religious symbols and are the source of benefits from the supernatural. Underlying these other sociocultural elements of the cattle complex, according to Rada and Neville Dyson-Hudson, who studied the Karimojong, is the important role of cattle in subsistence: "First, last and always the role of cattle in Karimojong life is to transform the energy stored in the grasses, herbs and shrubs of the tribal area into a form easily available to the people" (Dyson-Hudson and Dyson-Hudson 1969, 4).

This transformation is not mainly achieved by eating the animals' flesh, as we Westerners might expect. Rather, the Karimojong—and most other East Africans—consume the products of living cattle: milk and blood. Lactating cows are milked twice daily. Every three to five months, several pints of blood are taken from the jugular of some animals and drunk, usually immediately. Cattle meat is consumed, of course, but ordinarily only on religious occasions; the meat is shared among all participants.

There is a marked sexual division of labor in Karimojong subsistence activities. The central portion of the tribal territory is crossed by several rivers, and hence is relatively well watered during the rainy season. Here the women live in permanent settlements, where they cultivate sorghum (an African grain) and a few other crops. The central area, however, produces good grasses only during the rainy season, so for most of the year the cattle must be taken to greener pastures, often miles away from the settlements. The Karimojong thus also have another kind of

settlement, the mobile "cattle camps" that are manned by males, especially by young men. Rainfall is quite unpredictable, especially during the driest half of the year. But localized storms do occur, and for many days afterwards grass grows well in restricted areas. The men of the cattle camps—accompanied, of course, by the cattle—therefore move frequently in search of pasture. While living in the cattle camps, men live largely from the milk and blood of their animals, supplemented by the beer made from sorghum that the women sometimes bring when they visit.

Both cultivated crops and livestock are necessary foods for the Karimojong. Even a short three-week drought during the sorghum-growing season will seriously reduce the harvest, but the mobility of the livestock allows them to be taken to places where there is sufficient forage. Cattle thus provide an insurance against climatic and other forces that make cultivation too risky to rely on. They also allow the Karimojong to make use of those parts of their territory that are too dry to support cultivation. The cattle transform vegetation indigestible to humans into milk, blood, and meat, which are eventually eaten by the people.

Summary

Adaptations based on domestication change and control plants and animals so as to increase their use value to humans. Domestication's major advantage is that it increases the carrying capacity of a habitat over adaptations based on foraging.

Cultivation refers to adaptations based mainly on domesticated plants. The three basic varieties of cultivation—horticulture, intensive agriculture, and mechanized agriculture—differ mainly in the degree of nonhuman energy they use in the production of foods. They also have certain generalized impacts on other elements of the way of life of people who live by them.

Whether they practice dry land gardening or shifting cultivation, horticulturalists live in larger and more permanent settlements than foragers, partly to recover and protect their labor investments in their plots. Horticultural people are quite diverse in the way they organize production and establish access rights to resources. Commonly, a group of relatives establish a claim to an area of land by clearing and investing their labor in it, then passing their ownership rights along to future generations.

■ *East African pastoralists live mainly from the products of living cattle. This ox is about to yield blood.*

Over long spans of time, cultivation methods became more intensive—plots were kept under cultivation for longer periods. Increasing intensity led to changes in production methods—more labor was devoted to maintaining the plots by weeding, adding animal dung, turning over the soil, and so forth. For such tasks, new tools (plows) and a new source of energy (draft animals) became useful, and intensive agriculture developed. Intensive agriculture greatly increases an area's carrying capacity, which is its major advantage over horticulture. It can also raise the amount of food an average farmer is able to produce and thus allow the production of a large surplus.

The surplus potential of intensive agriculture made possible the development of civilization in several regions of both the Old and New worlds. Peasants produced the food supply for the government officials, priests, craftsmen, miners, warriors, and other specialists of the ancient civilizations. The peasantry is a consequence of the emergence of civilization; and modern peasants in Asia, Latin America, Africa, and Europe retain many of the economic and political characteristics of their prehistoric forbears.

Pastoralists acquire many of their material needs and wants from their herds of domesticated animals, either directly or indirectly. Because by definition the herds of pastoral people depend on naturally occurring water and forage, most pastoralists lead a seasonally nomadic life. Herders acquire food and other products they do not take from their herds by engaging in cultivation, trading with neighboring cultivators, selling the products of their herds, or using their livestock as beasts of burden on long-distance trade.

Pastoralists are generally found in regions that are not well suited to reliable cultivation, typically because of rainfall or temperature. In these arid or cold environments herding allows people to transform plant matter that is indigestible to humans into edible animal products. It also reduces the risk of living in certain environments, both because livestock are a way of storing food and because the herds can be taken to a more favorable location in times of drought. Despite these advantages, herders are able to acquire less food from an area of land than cultivators, because most of the energy locked up in the plant matter eaten by livestock is lost to the animals' waste and respiration. The pastoral adaptation affects sociocultural systems in many ways, two of which are exemplified by the Basseri of southern Iran and the Karimojong of East Africa.

Key Terms

domestication

carrying capacity

cultivation

pastoralism

horticulture

intensive agriculture

mechanized agriculture

dry land gardening

shifting cultivation (slash-and-burn, swidden)

surplus

civilization

peasants

nomadism

Suggested Readings

■ Cohen, Yehudi, ed. *Man in Adaptation: The Cultural Present.* Chicago: Aldine, 1974.
    A well-edited collection of important essays, many of which discuss adaptation among pastoral and farming societies.

■ Little, Michael A., and George E. B. Morren, Jr. *Ecology, Energetics, and Human Variability.* Dubuque, Iowa: William C. Brown, 1976.
    A slim volume introducing the energetic approach to adaptation.

■ Potter, Jack M., May N. Dias, and George M. Foster, eds. *Peasant Society, A Reader.* Boston: Little, Brown, 1967.
    An edited volume that reprints many classic articles on peasants.

■ Wolf, Eric. *Peasants.* Englewood Cliffs, N.J.: Prentice-Hall, 1966.
    A relatively brief theoretical treatment of peasants, which serves as a good introduction to the subject.

The following ethnographies provide excellent descriptions of particular pastoral and farming peoples around the world.

■ Barth, Fredrik. *Nomads of South Persia.* New York: Humanities Press, 1961.
    A study examining the lifeway of the Basseri, a pastoral, sheep- and goat-herding society of southern Iran.

■ Evans-Prichard, E. E. *The Nuer.* Oxford: Clarendon Press, 1940.
    A beautifully written ethnography of the Nuer, a cattle-herding people of the Sudan.

■ Geertz, Clifford. *Agricultural Involution.* Berkeley, Calif.: University of California Press, 1963.
    A case study of agricultural intensification of wet rice in Indone sia caused by population growth and Dutch colonial policy.

■ Harner, Michael J. *The Jívaro: People of the Sacred Waterfall*. New York: Natural History Press, 1972.

A very readable and interesting ethnography about a horticultural society of the Ecuadorian Amazon.

■ Hanks, Lucien M. *Rice and Man: Agricultural Ecology in Southeast Asia*. Chicago: Aldine, 1972.

A discussion of historical changes in methods of rice cultivation in Southeast Asia and the effects of various modes of production on the lifeways of the people.

■ Rappaport, Roy. *Pigs for the Ancestors: Ritual in the Ecology of a New Guinea People*. New Haven: Yale University Press, 1968.

A detailed account of the interplay between ecology and ritual in a horticultural society of highland New Guinea.

■ Redfield, Robert, and Alfonso Villa Rojas. *Chan Kom: A Maya Village*. Chicago: University of Chicago Press, 1962.

An account of life in a small Maya farming community in the Yucatan region of Mexico during the 1930s.

■ Wagley, Charles. *Welcome of Tears: The Tapirapé Indians of Central Brazil*. New York: Oxford, 1977.

A well-researched study of a horticultural society of the Brazilian Amazon.

Chapter 9

EXCHANGE AND CONTROL IN ECONOMIC SYSTEMS

■ *Contents*

■ (Above) *Exchange is part of the economic system. This Guatemalan scene illustrates one form of exchange known as market exchange.*

ood production, the main topic of the previous two chapters, is part of a peoples' adaptation to their habitat, for it is through production that humans acquire the energy and materials locked up in the natural environment. Food production also is part of the **economic system,** defined as the patterned activities by means of which people procure and distribute the material goods they consume. We considered some of the variations in the organization of food production in the previous two chapters. In this chapter we discuss two other dimensions of economic systems: (1) the ways in which material goods are exchanged among groups and individuals, and (2) the ways in which control over natural resources, over labor, and over the distribution of wealth are organized.

Exchange

Production may be only the first step toward the final use (consumption) of goods. Once they are produced, many goods change hands before they are consumed; that is, those who produce the goods transfer them to someone else, who may in turn transfer them to yet another person, until the goods finally are consumed. The transfer of goods between individuals or groups is **exchange.** Different human populations organize the exchange of goods in different ways, some of which we consider in this section.

Anthropologists usually classify exchanges into three modes or types:

■ **Reciprocity,** in which two individuals or groups pass goods back and forth, with the aim of (1) helping someone in need by sharing goods with him or her; (2) creating, maintaining, or strengthening social relationships; or (3) obtaining goods for oneself.
■ **Redistribution,** in which the members of an organized group contribute goods or money into a common pool or fund; usually a central authority has the privilege and responsibility to make decisions about how the goods or money later will be reallocated among the group as a whole.

■ **Market,** in which goods are sold for money, which in turn is used to purchase other goods, with the ultimate goal of acquiring more money and accumulating more goods.

Although most goods change hands through the market mode in capitalistic, industrial economies, enormous quantities of goods also are transacted through reciprocity and redistribution. Examples of reciprocity are various gifts we give and receive on holidays, birthdays, weddings, baby showers, and on other culturally special occasions. If you are employed, every pay period you participate in redistribution, for the federal and state governments collect a portion of your wage or salary as taxes, which they expend on public purposes or transfer to other members of society.

Although all these exchange forms exist in modern societies, not all preindustrial societies have all three. Some kind of reciprocity occurs in all human populations. But redistribution implies the existence of a central authority to organize the collection of goods from the group and to make decisions about how the goods will be reallocated. Redistribution, therefore, is an insignificant exchange mode in societies that lack strong leaders who make decisions on behalf of the group. The market mode of exchange requires the existence of money, private property, and certain other features that are absent in many preindustrial populations.

■ *Reciprocity*

Reciprocity refers to the giving and taking of objects without the use of money or other media of exchange. It can take the form of sharing, hospitality, gift giving, barter, or theft (although with the last the thief hopes the "transfer" will be one-way). Obviously, the term *reciprocity* covers a wide variety of exchanges: there is a big difference between a Plains Indian sharing the meat of a bison with other members of his camp and the same man participating in a raid against neighboring tribes to steal their horses. To cover these differences, anthropologists usually identify three forms of reciprocity.

Generalized Reciprocity The defining feature of **generalized reciprocity** is that those who give goods do not expect the recipient to make a return of goods at any definite time in the future. Generalized reciprocity occurs between individuals who are (or are culturally expected to be) emotionally attached to one another and therefore have an obligation to help each other on the basis of relative need. In North America parents who provide their children with shelter, food, vehicles, college educations, and interest-free loans are practicing generalized reciprocity. Giving without expectation of quick return also should occur between parties to certain other kinds of social relations, such as wives and husbands, siblings, and sometimes close friends.

This exchange mode occurs in all human populations. However, among some peoples it is the dominant form of exchange, meaning that more goods are passed around using this form than any other. For example, most foragers expect band mates to share food and be generous with their possessions. (This fits with the kinship relations between most members of a small hunting and gathering band.) Among the San (see chapter 7), only some band members search for food on any given day. But the products of men's hunting and women's gathering are passed around within the band, so that even those families who did not participate in foraging that day receive an equitable share. The band or camp itself is a social group

■ *When the Efe, foraging pygmies of Zaire, kill a large animal, the meat is widely shared on the principle of generalized reciprocity. Here Efe and their Lese neighbors carve up an elephant to distribute the meat.*

within which food sharing is culturally expected, and those who are stingy with possessions or who fail to share food with band mates are subjected to ridicule (or worse).

Balanced Reciprocity   In **balanced reciprocity,** goods are transferred to someone, and the donor expects a return in goods of roughly equal value (i.e., the exchanges ideally should "balance"). The return may be expected immediately, or whenever the donor demands it, or by some specified time in the future. With generalized reciprocity the giver continues to provide material assistance even though the receiver is unable to return anything for a long time. With balanced reciprocity the giver refuses to continue to transfer goods to the receiver if the latter does not reciprocate within the appropriate time period. Donors may merely be angry if the receivers fail to reciprocate, may complain or gossip to others, may try to force reciprocation, or may end all further relations until goods of equal value are returned.

Although the cultural value of the goods transacted is supposed to be equal (at least roughly), balanced reciprocity is characterized by the absence of bargaining between the parties. In some preindustrial economies the exchange of goods without having to negotiate for each transaction (How much of A will you give me for my B?) is frequently organized by a special relationship between two individuals known as a *trade partnership.* Individuals of one tribe or village pair off with specific individuals (their "partners") from other regions with whom they establish long-lasting trade relationships.

For instance, in the Trobriand Islands, off the eastern tip of the island of New Guinea, there was a form of balanced reciprocity called *wasi.* Residents of coastal villages traded fish for yams and other garden crops produced in the mountainous interior. The *wasi* exchange was formalized: a coastal village paired off with an interior village, and within each village individuals formed trade partnerships. The rates at which produce exchanged for fish were established by custom, so there was no haggling at any particular transaction.

In *wasi* each trade partner received foods not readily available locally, so parties to the transaction gained a material benefit. In many other cases balanced reciprocity takes the form of mutual exchanges of gifts or invitations for social and political purposes. That is, the exchange is not motivated primarily by the desire of the parties for the objects (unlike *wasi*) but by their desire to establish and maintain good relations with one another. (On your friend's birthday, instead of giving her a gift in exchange for a gift of about equal value on your own birthday, you both could save the cost of wrapping paper and cards by buying the objects for yourselves. But then the social goal of the gift—expressing and strengthening your friendly relationship—would not be attained.)

We all are familiar with the anger or disappointment of not having our gifts or dinner invitations reciprocated. Many of us also know the embarrassment of being unable to return a gift of equal value to one we have received. We also are familiar with the use of gift giving for social and political goals. We know that friends make gifts to one another because giving a gift to someone re-creates and strengthens feelings of goodwill. Gifts are a material symbol of good relations. They sustain relations of solidarity and mutual aid between individuals and groups. This is why, cross-culturally, gift-giving ceremonies frequently are part of peacemaking between formerly hostile groups; the gifts symbolize the beginning of a new period of peaceful coexistence.

In our personal lives, too, the back-and-forth flow of tangible objects often symbolizes warm personal feelings about a relationship as well as words—or perhaps better than words, since "talk is cheap." The failure to present objects of appropriate value on certain occasions also symbolizes one's personal feelings, although in a less "warm" way.

But gifts not only express existing social relations with material symbols; they can also be used to create social bonds that are useful to the giver and to obligate people from whom the giver wants something. Gift giving makes someone indebted to you, and therefore can be used to create an obligation to return a favor. Lobbyists and sales representatives know this use of balanced reciprocity.

For a preindustrial example of how balanced reciprocity helps to create and sustain political alliances, we turn to the Maring of highland Papua New Guinea. These people live by a combination of shifting cultivation, pig keeping, and hunting. The Maring live in settlements composed of clusters of kin groups. Each settlement is engaged in periodic warfare with some of its neighbors. Unless a settlement is unusually large, its members form a political alliance with one or more nearby settlements. When warfare occurs, the warriors of each settlement rely on their allies for military

■ *In many preindustrial societies, balanced reciprocity helps establish and maintain political alliances. This pig about to be slaughtered on Tanna, Vanuata will be given as a gift to someone, who is obliged to return a pig to the donor. The goal is sustaining political relationships between the island's communities.*

support and, should defeat occur, for refuge. Most Maring settlements must establish and sustain military alliances if they are not to be defeated in warfare.

An important expression of continued goodwill between allied groups is periodic invitations to feasts and exchanges of wealth objects and other goods between the friendly settlements. Every few years, whenever they accumulate sufficient pigs, the members of a settlement invite their allies to an enormous feast, appropriately called a *pig feast*. At the pig feast, which is attended by hundreds of people, allies bring large quantities of wealth objects to exchange and pay off debts; they consume enormous quantities of pork provided by their hosts; they are on the lookout for potential spouses and sexual partners; and they aid the host settlement in the ceremonial dancing that the Maring believe is ritually necessary for success in the fighting that will soon occur. The host group uses the occasion of their pig feast to gauge the amount of military support they can expect from their allies: the more people who attend the feast, the more warriors the host settlement will be able to put on the battleground. Later, the guests will have accumulated enough pigs to sponsor their own pig feast. They will reciprocate by hosting a pig feast for their allies, who come with wealth objects and pledge their military support by helping the host group in their ceremonial dancing.

The Maring pig feast, and the reciprocal exchanges between the hosts and guests from various allied groups that occur during it, is an important event in maintaining good relations between allies. A group sponsors a pig feast to compensate their allies for their previous military aid, as well as to reciprocate previous pig feasts they have attended. The failure to organize a pig feast large enough to compensate one's allies can result in the weakening and sometimes even termination of an alliance. Thus, mutual invitations to feasts are critical to the military success and continued survival of a Maring settlement.

Negative Reciprocity The distinguishing characteristics of the third kind of reciprocity—generally known as **negative reciprocity**— is that both parties attempt to gain all they can from the exchange while giving up as little as possible. It usually serves economic purposes, meaning that it is motivated largely by the desire to obtain material goods at minimal cost.

Insofar as it is motivated by the desire for material goods, negative reciprocity is like market exchange; it is different mainly because no money changes hands between the participants. In populations that use money to purchase goods and services, market exchange partly or largely replaces negative reciprocity. Thus, in industrial economies negative reciprocity has largely been replaced by markets in which goods are exchanged for money.

But in economies with no money negative reciprocity is an important way for individuals and groups to acquire goods that they do not produce themselves. Few populations are entirely self-sufficient: some foods they like to eat do not occur in their habitats, some materials they need to make tools are not found locally, or they lack the skill to produce some of the objects they use. To acquire these goods, people produce other goods to exchange for "imports."

Negative reciprocity in the preindustrial world often takes the form of barter. In the interior highlands of Papua New Guinea, many indigenous peoples manufactured money or wealth objects by stringing shells together into long chains or belts. Since these shells did not occur naturally in the interior, they were traded from people to people until they reached their final destination. Salt also was a trade object, for it occurred in only a few areas.

In western North America, the obsidian (volcanic glass) used to make stone tools occurred in only a few areas; other peoples acquired it through trade. In some cases these trade routes stretched for hundreds of miles, with the obsidian passing through the hands of numerous middlemen before finally being made into a tool.

■ Reciprocity and Social Distance

Can we do anything more with this typology of reciprocity other than merely noting its existence and providing an example or two of each type? Indeed, we can. As Marshall Sahlins, who first distinguished the three varieties, noted, the kind of reciprocity that occurs between two individuals or groups depends on the **social distance** between them. By *social distance* is meant the degree to which cultural norms specify they should be intimate with or emotionally attached to one another. In other words, a given mode of reciprocal exchange is culturally appropriate with only certain kinds of social relationships.

This is seen clearly in North American cultural norms. We expect an individual to practice generalized reciprocity with his or her children, and perhaps with siblings and elderly parents; in fact, we are likely to judge them as uncaring or selfish if they do not. But if a middle-income person repeatedly lends money to a cousin or puts a niece through college, we are likely to regard him or her as either unusually generous or a bit foolish. He or she has extended generalized reciprocity beyond the range of relatives to whom we culturally consider it appropriate.

A cultural association of exchange form with kinds of relationships applies to market transactions, which, as we have seen, have largely replaced negative reciprocity in modern societies. In market exchange, individuals are supposed to be "looking out for their own private interests," "trying to get the most for their money," and so forth. We regard this as fine—in fact, as smart shopping—with transactions between strangers in a department store or car lot. But when the seller and buyer are friends or relatives, it is difficult for them to disentangle their economic transaction from their personal feelings for one another. Most of us believe kinship and friendship bonds cannot easily be mixed with market exchange, for kinship and friendship are supposed to have an element of selflessness, whereas buying and selling are assumed to have selfish motives. Therefore, although I may buy my friend's used car, I feel uneasy about the transaction: Is he screwing me? What will I do if the car's a lemon?

Further, as our social relations with other people change, so does the kind of reciprocity we practice with them. Most adults have experienced one way in which this occurs: as we grow up, our increasing independence from our parents is manifested by a change in the way we exchange goods with them. We go from being the recipients of generalized reciprocity to more of a balanced reciprocity as we become more independent and finally—at least until the advent of social security—to being the provider of generalized reciprocity.

Finally, changing one form of reciprocity into another can be used as a way of changing the nature of a social relationship. Because the form of reciprocity practiced between two individuals is related to the degree of social distance between them, the social distance can be decreased or increased by one party beginning to initiate a new form of exchange. Or someone can signal his or her wish to draw another person closer (reduce the social distance between them) by tentatively initiating a relationship of balanced reciprocity. In other words, reciprocity has social uses in our sociocultural system, just as it has among preindustrial peoples. It also probably has significant consequences for our market economy (see Box 9.1).

Thus, I can let you know of my desire to become your friend by giving you an unexpected gift or invitation to dinner. In turn, you tell me whether you share my feelings by whether you return my gift on an appropriate occasion, or repeatedly find reasons to refuse my dinner invitation, or come to dinner several times at my place without reciprocating. If we both use this "strategy of reciprocity," neither of us needs to be put in an embarrassing position of verbalizing our feelings. I signal my wish by my initial gift or invitation, and you decline or accept my offer of friendship by your response.

In sum, forms of reciprocity are culturally associated with types of social relations, so the reciprocity practiced between people changes as their relationship changes. And we can use reciprocity to achieve social goals: reciprocating or refusing to reciprocate gifts or invitations sends messages that are too embarrassing to say outright. Finally, reciprocity can serve as a social strategy, a way to shorten or lengthen social distance.

▪ Redistribution

The major difference between reciprocity and redistribution—the second major mode of exchange— is the way the transfer of goods is organized. With reciprocity, goods pass back and forth between two participants, with no third party to act as intermediary. With redistribution, goods or money collected from many individuals or groups is taken to a central place or put into a common pool or fund. Some overarching authority (who is empowered to make decisions on behalf of those who contributed) later draws from this pool or fund in returning public goods and services that allegedly benefit the group as a whole.

In modern nations redistribution takes the form of taxes on wages, profits, retail sales, property, and other income and assets. To understand redistribution, it is instructive to review how our tax system is supposed to operate. Federal tax revenues, for example, are used for two main purposes. First, they are expended in such a way as to benefit the whole country. The citizens receive police protection, law enforcement, national defense, infrastructure (e.g., dams, roads, airports), regulation of polluting industries, and so forth. Resources collected from the citizenry are expended on public goods and services. Second, taxes are used to provide assistance for individuals in need. These are "transfer payments" in the form of Aid to Families with Dependent Children, social security, Medicare, disaster relief, and so forth. Such public expenditures are based on moral norms and cultural values about social justice and equal opportunity. Redistribution systems around the world generally are used for similar purposes: to provide public goods and services, and to provide assistance to individuals and groups in need.

But there is another side to most systems of redistribution, a side with which we also are familiar. First, there is often conflict over who should provide the public resources, how the resources should be expended, and how much of a share of them should be given to those who collect and distribute them. One common social and political problem with redistribution is disagreement: where many individuals have contributed to the public pool or fund, not everyone is likely to agree on how the "public resources" should be spent for the "public good."

Second, those who control the redistribution frequently apply the public resources toward their own pleasure or ambitions rather than to benefit the entire population. In modern nations officeholders frequently use redistribution for political purposes. For instance, taxpayers finance dams, allegedly for flood control, hydroelectric power, irrigation, or recreation. Actually, the purpose is to get "federal money" (i.e., tax dollars from elsewhere in the country) into some elected official's district to provide jobs or serve special-

Box 9.1

RECIPROCITY AND THE AMERICAN ECONOMY

In many preindustrial economies most exchanges are organized by the principles of reciprocity and redistribution rather than by the market principle. As we have seen, reciprocal and redistributive exchanges are by no means absent in modern market economies. In fact, many economists spend most of their time analyzing the impacts of different redistributive policies (taxation rates, transfer payments, and so forth) on the market. What is less well studied is the impact of reciprocity on the American economy.

The basic difference between reciprocity and market exchange is the essentially social nature of the former. When you give a record album as a gift, you have in mind social goals: creating a new relationship, maintaining an old one, reciprocating something that was given to you, and so forth. Further, when you give a gift to a friend or to many relatives, something usually comes back to you in the future, for most gift giving is based on balanced reciprocity. This means that gift giving tends to reproduce itself: one gift breeds another on some future occasion in a cycle that need never end as long as the relationship continues.

So we, too, have a gift economy. Certain kinds of relationships practically require gifts on certain culturally defined occasions, such as Christmas or Hannukah, birthdays, parents' days, valentine's days, and so forth. Gift giving is necessary to maintain and improve relationships that individuals value in their own right. One gift is usually paid back with another, so the gift economy tends to be self-perpetuating, although it does, of course, respond to changes in relationships.

This gift economy probably has important effects on the "real" economy. Because we feel socially obliged to give gifts, we buy goods on the market that we would not otherwise need or want. For example, we buy perfumes and flowers for our wives and girlfriends, tools and belt buckles for our husbands and boyfriends, toys and games for our children, and clothing and recreation equipment for everybody. Whole industries are supported almost entirely by the gift economy, such as floral, greeting-card, and gift-shop businesses. Other industries—such as businesses involving tools, toys and games, clothing, jewelry, records, cosmetics, publishing, and many other products—enjoy a dramatic increase in the sales of their products because of the gift economy.

To our knowledge, no quantitative studies exist of the magnitude of the gift economy, its impact on consumer-spending habits, or its aggregate effects on the economy as a whole. If you want to gain some idea of how important gift giving might be, try keeping a record over several months of how you spend your discretionary income (the money you have left after essential bills are paid). How much of it is spent on some form of gift—including taking someone out to dinner? Or make an inventory of your possessions, recalling where you got each item and roughly estimating its dollar value. We think you might be surprised at how much you've received as gifts over the years.

From a strictly utilitarian perspective, all this gift giving is quite unnecessary. Much of it is even wasteful, because much of what we receive as gifts we never would have bought for ourselves. (If you make an inventory, ask yourself whether you would have bought all those shirts or blouses or sweaters for yourself. Better yet, ask yourself if you ever wear them!) But usually the purpose of gifts is not to supply the receiver with some object he or she needs or wants; it is rather to supply the giver with the continued goodwill of the receiver by offering an object that symbolically expresses the character of their relationship. Florists, jewelry dealers, and perfume manufacturers depend on these symbolic expressions for most of their living. In the gift economy we glimpse the impact of cultural norms and symbolic expressions of social relationships on material life. ■

---

interest groups. (We even have a term that describes this political use of redistribution: *pork barrel.*) So, like reciprocity, redistribution can be manipulated.

A common form of redistribution in the preindustrial world is usually known as **tribute.** The subjects of a chief or other officeholder contribute goods (usually including food) into a common pool. Some of the accumulated products are consumed by public officials and other specialists, and some are redistributed to the whole population. We examine these systems more thoroughly later.

Good examples of redistribution systems using tribute payments have been found on many of the islands of Micronesia and Polynesia. The entire population was divided into at least two classes. Members of the noble class did little agricultural work but instead ran the political system and sponsored religious ceremonies. The commoner class produced the food and other material goods that supported the nobility. Periodically, each commoner household or settlement was obliged to render tribute to the chief who had authority over them. The chiefs used part of these payments to support—and sometimes to enrich—themselves and their families, as well as their servants, attendants, and officials. The rest of the tribute was redistributed among the population in various ways. It fed the commoners who worked on public buildings or trails; it was sometimes used for famine relief; and it was consumed on various enormous public feasts and celebrations.

■ Market Exchange

To say that goods are exchanged "on the market" means that they are bought and sold at a price measured in money. Person A possesses goods that person B wishes to acquire; B acquires the goods by giving A some quantity of money that both A and B agree on; A then uses the money to acquire goods from other persons. Market exchange thus requires (1) some objects used as a medium of exchange, that is, money; (2) a rate at which goods exchange for money, that is, prices; and (3) parties to exchanges who have alternative buyers or sellers and are free to make the best deal they can, that is, prices determined by supply and demand. On the third point, markets imply the absence of physical coercion: if prices are set by supply and demand, neither party to a transaction can be forced to buy or sell from the other party. This is what we mean by a "free" market—no third party (a government, for example) sets prices or forces anyone to buy or sell from anyone else, and no single supplier of a good controls enough of the market to force people to buy from him, her, or it (in the case of firms).

Since markets (as we define them in this text) require the presence of money, we begin by discussing some of the diversity in money objects and money uses.

Money   Money consists of objects that serve as a medium of exchange in a wide range of transactions of goods, services, or both. This facilitation of exchange is the main function of money, in most cases. If an economy uses money, individual A can acquire something from individual B without having to return an object desired by B; money can be given instead, and

B can then use the money to buy an object or service of her or his choice.

Some other characteristics of money are derived from its function as a medium of exchange. For example, money serves as a standard of value: the value of the goods and services that can be exchanged for money can be compared with one another, for money serves as a common measure of "how much things are worth." Money also is a store of value: because it can be used to purchase a variety of goods, it represents wealth in a portable form.

These characteristics mean that not just any object is suitable to be used as money. Money objects must be durable, or the value they store deteriorates over time. The supply of the money object must be controllable, for if people can get all they want of it, its value inflates and it becomes worthless as an exchange medium. The monetary supply can be controlled by a government, which manufactures the only "legal tender" in the society; or the supply can be controlled by using only imported or rare objects as money. Imported shells are especially common, partly because of their durability. The supply also can be controlled by having the money stuff require a lot of labor to manufacture: money remains scarce because it takes much time to make it.

An enormous variety of objects serve as money in one or another region of the world. We already are familiar with currencies of modern nations, issued by governments that control the money supply. In preindustrial economies the kinds of objects that take on the characteristics of money are surprisingly diverse. In Africa, for example, the following objects served as money in one or another part of the continent: iron, salt, beads, cowry shells, cloth, slaves, gin, gold dust, metal rods, brass bracelets, and livestock. In Melanesia the list of money objects is also diverse: assorted shells (often modified in some way and sewn into fibers to form long belts), salt, the red feathers of a certain bird (also woven into belts), and pigs. Livestock, such as Melanesian pigs and African cattle, often are exchange media. Although they are not especially "durable," they have the advantage of multiplying themselves.

There are, of course, nonmonetary economies, in which all exchanges are based on one of the three forms of reciprocity. But even in economies that do have an exchange medium, the range of goods that can be acquired with money varies greatly. In some, the range is broad: many different kinds of resources and goods can be bought and sold, including labor, land, tools, and sometimes even people (slaves). In these systems money serves as a *generalized* medium of exchange; that is, it can be used to acquire many different kinds of goods and services, including land and labor. Anthropologists sometimes call this **multipurpose money.**

Money is multipurpose in modern North America. In principle, privately owned natural resources, labor, goods, and money itself can be sold for money. Some preindustrial peoples also have multipurpose money. For example, the Kapauku people of Irian Jaya, which is now part of Indonesia, used imported cowrie shells and two types of necklaces as currency. Kapauku money could be used to purchase almost anything, including land, labor, crops, pigs, tools, and medical services. In fact, Kapauku money can be said to be even more multipurpose than our own. Leopold Pospisil (1963), the ethnographer, writes:

> Among the Kapauku an overwhelming amount of goods is exchanged through sales. . . . In their selling and buying most of the Kapauku are strictly profit motivated. Often they invest money in pigs, chickens, large *woti* (bailer shell), inner bark, or animal teeth, for the purpose of breeding the animals for profit, speculating on sales of the bailer shell, or for making artifacts for sale. . . . Besides the necessity of having to buy with money such commodities as land, manufactured products, labor, and services such as surgery, curing, and midwifery, the Kapauku have to pay for favors and acts for which even in our capitalistic society there is no charge. For example, one pays a bride price for a wife, the services of a foster father have to be paid for by the grown boy, a grief expressed by strangers or distantly related people over the death of a close relative has to be recompensed in money, and almost all crimes can be settled through a proper transfer of shell currency. (21–22)

Kapauku sales occurred on a daily basis, much as we make purchases of one or another item regularly. Periodically, however, Kapauku political leaders (called *big men*) organized enormous ceremonies often attended by hundreds of people who came to sell and buy and to make and pay off loans.

We should add that the Kapauku represent an extreme in the range of uses to which money could be put, as well as in their intense desire to accumulate wealth. More often, we find the range of money uses in preindustrial economies to be narrow: only a few categories of goods are purchased with money. For example, it may be possible to buy food, clothing, and a few other goods, but land is not available for sale at any price and labor is almost never sold. Here money is called **limited-purpose** (or **special-purpose**) **money.**

A famous example of limited-purpose money comes from among the Tiv of Nigeria, studied by Paul Bohannon. Tiv money consisted of metal rods, but the rods could not be used as an exchange medium for all other goods. For one thing, land could not be sold at all, and labor was exchanged among relatives on the principle of generalized reciprocity. For another, among these people goods circulated in different *exchange spheres.* Certain kinds of goods could only be transacted for certain other kinds of goods. Goods were culturally classified into categories, within which they were freely exchangeable, but between which exchange was difficult.

The "subsistence sphere" category included cultivated crops, chickens and goats, and some tools and household goods. Goods within this sphere were exchangeable for one another by means of barter. The "prestige sphere" included slaves, cattle, a special kind of white cloth, and metal rods. Within the prestige sphere metal rods functioned as an exchange medium: one could sell cattle for metal rods and then use the rods to acquire white cloth or slaves, for example, but the monetary function of metal rods was normally limited to the prestige sphere.

However, it was *possible* to acquire subsistence goods in exchange for metal rods; but these transactions were rare, for two reasons. First, few people were willing to trade their metal rods for subsistence goods. This is because goods that circulated in the prestige sphere had much greater cultural value to Tiv than subsistence goods. Second, metal rods were worth an enormous amount of subsistence goods. Yet the metal rods had no denominations—that is, unlike our dollars and cents, they were not divisible into fractions. So for a Tiv to try to exchange one metal rod for subsistence goods would be like an American taking a thousand-dollar bill into a grocery store to buy food, with the clerk unable to make change. As a result of these two factors, Tiv metal rods were largely limited-purpose money.

The Tiv case serves to remind us that just because we find it convenient to call some object "money" does not mean that it has all the characteristics of our own currency. Indeed, some anthropologists believe that money objects are lacking in preindustrial economies and that money is a Western concept that we should not attempt to apply to other peoples. This problem is mainly semantic, however: if we define money simply as a medium of exchange, it is found in many other economies. To avoid confusion and false impressions, we do need always to specify its uses and its cultural meaning to the local people.

As we discuss next, we also need to be careful with the use of the term *market*, for many non-Western markets do not work exactly the same way as ours.

Market Economies and Marketplaces   Two uses of the term *market* can be distinguished. The first refers to the **market principle.** The market principle exists when goods and services are mutually exchangeable at a price determined by supply and demand. In some economies—such as those of the capitalist nations of today—a wide range of goods and services are exchanged according to the market principle. In this case, we speak of a market economy, which has four characteristics:

- Practically all goods and services have a monetary price: the value of one good (e.g., a piece of land) can be compared to the value of something else (e.g., an auto, or so many hours of someone's labor) using a common measure (money).
- Most people make their living by selling something—goods, services, or their own labor—on the market. For most people this means selling their labor to someone else, either to another individual or more often to a group (firm or public agency) in return for a wage. Workers sell their labor because they themselves do not own the natural resources and capital with which to produce goods.
- The factors of production are allocated by the market: natural resources, capital, and labor are bought and sold on the market, which implies that the supply of and demand for these factors of production determine the uses to which they will be put. The market allocates them in such a way that they flow into those uses in which they receive the highest return (profit).
- The economy is self-regulating. This means that the interaction of impersonal forces such as supply and demand—rather than a government or particular individuals—regulates the kinds of economic activities that occur. For example, if the worldwide supply of oil dwindles, people get upset about an "energy crisis." But the market for energy is self-regulating: energy prices rise, which encourages new exploration, increased production, and a switch to alternative sources of power. In the end, the "energy crisis" becomes an "oil glut," during which prices fall because of the market's "invisible hand." (This last point is a somewhat idealized view of market systems: it represents the way the market is supposed to work.)

These four features characterize market economies. But it is possible for the market *principle* to operate without having a market *economy.* For example, only a few goods may sell for money; only a few individuals make their living by selling something on the market; land, technology, and labor are seldom or never sold; and the economy is regulated by the quite "visible hand" of centralized leadership. In these cases, the market principle still exists; but it operates only for certain categories of goods, for only some kinds of things are bought and sold. This leads us to the second meaning of *market.*

In its second meaning, *market* refers to the location—the **marketplace**—where buyers and sellers meet for purposes of acquiring goods and making money. For example, peasant marketplaces are common in West Africa, southern and Southeast Asia, the Caribbean, and Central and South America. Peasant vendors sell food, cloth and clothing, leather products, livestock, and other goods produced by their families. Traveling merchants (middlemen) bring commodities imported from the developed world or from elsewhere in the region to sell to local people at the marketplace.

Peripheral markets is the phrase often used to emphasize several characteristics of these marketplaces and of the regions in which they occur. First, the categories of goods sold at the marketplace are limited, and, in fact, most people produce most of their own subsistence using family labor. Most people do not acquire their livelihood from selling their labor for a wage. Rather,

■ *Peasants visit peripheral markets to purchase goods they cannot easily make for themselves.*

they rely on the marketplace for only certain categories of goods that they cannot produce for themselves efficiently. The existence of marketplaces thus does not imply a market economy, for most people are not making their living by selling something (goods, labor) on the market.

Second, producing and marketing goods for monetary profit are part-time activities for many vendors. Often, marketplaces are staffed mainly by peasants, who market small quantities of food, pottery, furniture, fibers, or other goods they have produced with family labor. Indeed, marketplaces are frequently periodic, meaning that they do not open every day, but only a day or two a week. Peasant vendors sell their products on whatever days the market is open in their region. Traveling merchants typically visit several markets in different regions in a single week, often buying products for sale at one market and reselling them at a distant market a day or two later.

Third, peasant vendors usually sell products that they or their family members, rather than hired laborers, produce. This means that the kinds and quantities of goods offered for sale by any single vendor are usually small. However, most marketplaces also feature goods sold by people who specialize in buying goods wholesale and selling them retail. Such people are dependent on the market—with all its insecurities and risks—for their livelihood. They therefore have developed a variety of marketing strategies to reduce the risks they face. We conclude this section by considering some of these strategies.

When we who live in a market system visit a marketplace—a store or car lot, for instance—we normally buy goods from strangers. We do not expect any special treatment. We pay the same price as everyone else. If we need credit, we expect to pay the market rate of interest. We expect sellers to be looking out for themselves, just as sellers expect us to be trying to get the most for our money. This characteristic of our market exchanges is sometimes referred to as the "impersonality of the marketplace." This impersonality is expressed nicely by the saying that "one person's money is as green as anyone else's."

Marketplace vendors in much of the preindustrial world frequently develop more intimate and personal relations with their customers. In the Caribbean nation of Haiti, for example, the parties to a market exchange frequently establish long-lasting special relationships with one another. The market intermediary (whom we know as a middleman, although most of them are women in Haiti) purchases food and other goods wholesale from several farmers for transport and retail sale at a marketplace. She establishes a special relation, known as *pratik*, with many of her suppliers and customers. *Pratik* involves certain concessions an intermediary makes to many of her suppliers and customers. For instance, when she buys produce from a farmer, she may pay a little more than the market rate or give the producer a loan against a future crop. Market vendors give special treatment to some of their best customers as well. When a *pratik* partner approaches her stall, she quotes the going price for the good on that particular day; but when the transaction is consummated, the seller throws in a few extra items of produce.

According to Sidney Mintz, who studied Haitian marketplace relations, *pratik* are not "economically irrational." Because they themselves are usually poor, and because competition between them is severe, Haitian market intermediaries seek long-term security in their relations. They therefore are willing to grant concessions by giving better deals to their *pratik* than the market rate, for this increases the chances of maintaining their suppliers and customers.

The same personalistic relations are reported for a marketplace in a Philippine town studied by William Davis. Here, also, sellers attempt to reduce their risks by gradually building up a steady, large clientele of customers rather than by squeezing all the money they can from a single transaction. Each vendor maintains "special customer" relationships (called *suki*) with numerous people who regularly buy his wares. The customers receive credit, favorable prices, extra quantities of goods at a given price, the best-quality goods his *suki* partner has to offer on a particular day, and certain services. Of course, the vendors benefit as well: their *suki* customers are expected not to patronize any other suppliers of goods they carry. This is a great advantage in calculating the minimum quantities of goods they will be able to sell and, hence, helps keep them from unintentionally stocking more of some categories of goods than they can sell.

In both Haiti and the Philippines the impersonality of the marketplace is modified by the formation of personal ties between sellers and buyers. Both *pratik* and *suki* increase the security of marketplace trade for vendors, their suppliers, and their customers.

As we have noted, in market economies the kinds of economic activities that occur are regulated by impersonal forces. Supply and demand are impersonal because— assuming a free market—no small number of individuals or groups controls them, prices, or the overall allocation of the factors of production. The market regulates what and how much is produced, the activities to which labor is allocated, the uses made of capital, how wealth is distributed, and so on.

In nonmarket economies, in contrast, the complex of activities we call an economic system is more under the control of particular persons who hold certain statuses and belong to certain groups. We now consider these mechanisms of control.

Control in Economic Systems

As we discussed in chapters 7 and 8, production is the organized act of expending labor and applying technology to natural resources. Someone controls this process of production. By *control* we mean who decides how the factors of production are allocated to produce goods: who works and how hard, which natural resources are used and how, what is produced and when, and so forth. This control over the process of production is another component of the organization of production, along with the division of labor, patterns of cooperation, and assignment of rights of access to resources. In some systems control is diffuse; that is, those who actually carry out the production make most of the decisions. In others, control is centralized; that is, decision making is hierarchically organized, and producers do not control the allocation of much of their own labor.

But production is not the only activity that is subject to control in economic systems. As seen in the previous section, exchange also is universal, although the form it takes varies from people to people. Exchange moves goods or money around between individuals and groups. Because of exchange, those who consume goods may not be the same people who produced them. Potentially, by controlling exchange activities, a few people can transfer the products of other peoples' labor to themselves.

Here it is useful to distinguish exchange from *distribution*. *Exchange* refers simply to a transfer of any kind of good between parties, using one of the three forms already discussed. Economic activity goes on continually, but imagine that we could freeze all acts of production and exchange in an economy for a short period. During that period we would find that individ-

uals and groups have a certain quantity of goods in their possession, which they expect to consume or to continue to own. We also would find that individuals and groups have rights to exploit certain areas of land or other natural resources and rights to use certain technologies for future production. The way the use or possession of goods, resources, and technology is spread out among the members of a population is known as **distribution.** Distribution is the relative share of these valuable things (we shall now call them *wealth*) that different individuals and groups consume or possess.

The distribution of wealth can be relatively equal in a population: all families consume about the same quantities and kinds of goods, and they all enjoy about the same access of resources and tools. Or the distribution of wealth may be unequal: only a few people possess and consume a large share of the goods (including money) produced, and only a few people control the natural resources and technology used in production.

What major kinds of control over production and distribution do we find in preindustrial economic systems? If we wish to make fine distinctions, we could certainly identify dozens of types of control. For purposes of this text, we collapse this variety into only four forms: band, kin group, chiefly, and state control. In each, some individual or the members of some group decide how production will occur and how products will be distributed.

▪ *Band Control*

In chapter 7, we emphasized the small size, mobility, and flexibility of hunting and gathering bands, which are organizational features usually associated with the foraging mode of adaptation. Here we wish to discuss the organization of control over resources and distribution of products among most foragers.

The members of a band harvest the plants and animals of the region in which they live, but they generally do not deny access to other bands. Indeed, the composition of bands fluctuates greatly from season to season, as individual families of one band receive rights to harvest resources in the territories of other bands for long periods. Why doesn't a stronger association of a specific band with a well-defined area of land develop among most foragers?

Rada Dyson-Hudson and Eric A. Smith suggest that the reason bands do not maintain exclusive access to a territory is that wild resources usually are not "economically defendable." This hypothesis begins with a simple observation: the time and energy required to defend a territory against intruders increases as the area of territory increases (all else equal, of course). Further, the more sparsely resources occur in the territory, the less the reward (in food) of defending any territory of a given size. Finally, the rewards from maintaining exclusive access to a territory are less if the resources found in the territory are unreliable in their abundance; that is, if resources are abundant in one year or season, but scarce at other times. The economic defendability hypothesis states that exclusive access to territories will not be maintained if resources are sparsely distributed and unreliable in their abundance. Under these conditions it is "uneconomic" (i.e., the costs outweigh the benefits) to "defend" (i.e., maintain exclusive access to) a given territory.

This hypothesis seems to apply to numerous foraging populations, including the !Kung San, the Cheyenne, the Hadza, and the Western Shoshone. Among these peoples, low, erratic, seasonal, and unpredictable variations in rainfall—and hence in the distribution and abundance of resources—made it uneconomic for the members of a band to defend a specific area.

How is the production process controlled in foraging bands? Generally, the individual families or adult members of the band decide by consensus what individuals of the family or whole band are to do on a given day: who hunts or gathers and where. Many bands do

■ *San bands are not territorial, for each family has rights of access to several hunitng and gathering areas. San bands sometimes get together for social occasions. Here bands are gathered for a feast.*

have headmen, who are respected for their intimate knowledge of the environment or for their hunting prowess. But headmen do not generally "control" labor, in the usual sense of the word; rather, they give advice and make suggestions, and people often heed their advice because their opinion is so often correct. Control over production is therefore generally decentralized and individualized among foragers.

Finally, what about control over the distribution of food and wealth objects within bands? Generally, there is little inequality in food consumption or in possession of tools, jewelry, or other forms of wealth in band societies. There are many reasons for the social and economic equality typically found among foragers. First, the need to pack up and move every few weeks inhibits the accumulation of large quantities of possessions. Second, the value placed upon sharing of goods helps prevent any individual or family from becoming wealthier than their band mates. Third, as a rule control over distribution is acquired and maintained by restricting other peoples' access to resources, and the ability of any individual to limit access to resources is low or absent among most hunter-gatherers. (The Northwest Coast Indians are an exception to this generalization, as shown in chapter 7). This inability to maintain control over resources is, in large part, because of the seasonal and annual fluctuations in wild resources: would-be controllers of rights of access to territory sometimes need to hunt and gather in other territories, so they need to allow other individuals access to their own. For such reasons, there is little inequality in the distribution of food and wealth in most hunting and gathering populations.

■ Kin Group Control

Domestic group or *household* refers to a group that shares a common dwelling or domicile. In North America most domestic groups are made up of nuclear families. Further, our households/nuclear families are relatively independent units economically: wage earners spend most of their income "on their families," and bills are paid largely from the income earned by family members. (As usual, we are here speaking generally, and we mean "relative to other societies we are about to mention.")

In contrast, among most preindustrial peoples, related families are united into much larger associations of kinfolk known as *kin groups*. We consider some of the kinds and functions of these kin groups in later chapters. Here we concentrate on how kin groups control access to resources and how they make decisions about production and distribution.

In many horticultural societies land is not owned by individuals nor even by the members of a single nuclear family; rather, it is owned jointly by a kin group. The families that each kin group comprises are allocated temporary use rights to specific plots of land for their subsistence needs. This allocation may be done by consensus of the family heads of the kin group, by decree of the head of the entire kin group, or by simply being the first family to plant crops on a specific plot. But the rights allocated to a family do not include the authority to transfer the land they are using to members of other kin groups. Domestic groups thus exploit land to which they have use rights, but not disposal rights. If we look at overall control of land and resources in the whole society, we generally find that each kin group believes its members have the right to cultivate particular areas of land. Their rights, however, are frequently disputed, and each kin group may have to be prepared to defend them militarily. Warfare is widespread in kin group control systems, and changes in access to land occur mainly whenever larger and expanding kin groups defeat smaller and declining groups and take over a portion of their territory.

What about control over technology and labor? In general, all families have access to the same tools and knowledge. Each household (or its head) decides what crops it will produce, which of its members will work the plot, how hard they will work, and so forth. Further, by and large, the head or members of the household control what happens to the products of their labor. They themselves consume most of the food and other goods they produce.

But nowhere do households consume everything they produce. For one thing, they share food with other relatives, often on the principle of generalized reciprocity. For another, the kin group as a whole participates in exchanges with other kin groups, usually based on balanced reciprocity. The households contribute vegetable foods, domestic animals, wealth objects, or other goods to the exchanges organized by their common kin group. From time to time, each household thus contributes a portion of its products to the activities of a higher-level kin group.

There are several reasons for engaging in these exchanges. They are often customarily required between kin groups whose members have intermarried (see chapter 10). Or exchanges may be made between groups who need to maintain political alliances with one another for purposes of cooperative offense and defense, as we discussed for the Maring in the previous section. So people produce goods for social or even military purposes, not merely to satisfy the needs of their families for food, shelter, and other necessities.

To summarize economic systems using kin group control: The entire population making up a sociocultural system is divided into numerous large kin groups. Each group has rights of access to a given territory, and it allocates use rights to specific parcels among its constituent individual families. Within a single group, there is not much inequality in the distribution of life-sustaining resources, for kinship obligations lead to much generalized reciprocity. Kin groups may compete for or fight over land with other like groups, with larger groups often displacing smaller ones and appropriating all or part of the latter's territory. Everywhere kin groups engage in exchanges—usually of the type called *balanced reciprocity*—with other kin groups for purposes of cementing social, political, and military alliances.

Kin group control is found mainly among horticultural and pastoral peoples. Among horticulturalists, producing and sometimes fallowing lands are allocated among the many kin groups that make up the population. Among pastoralists, rights to pasture lands are sometimes split up on the basis of kinship. Among other herders, such as the Karimojong, grazing lands are allocated on a first come–first serve basis, and only the livestock themselves are owned by families or kin groups.

However, many horticulturalists and herders have political leaders whose authority extends beyond the members of their own kin group. Control over production and distribution among these peoples may be called *chiefly.*

■ Chiefly Control

A *chief* is not just any kind of leader in a "primitive society," although this is the way the term is used in everyday conversation. Rather, chiefs occupy formal offices or hold titles. Chiefs are usually formally installed into their office in a public ceremony. The right to occupy the office or hold the title is limited to only some people in the society, usually to the members of a special kin group or to a special family within a kin group. Societies whose political leaders have these characteristics are called *chiefdoms* (discussed further in chapter 13).

Chiefly systems of control incorporate some elements of the kin group system. Each individual's use rights to resources are acquired from the kin group to which he or she belongs. But with kin group control, the rights of the kin group to territory cannot legitimately be taken away from the group by any overarching, higher-level authority. Indeed, such higher-level leaders are often absent altogether in kin group control; even if they are present, they have no rights to strip kin groups of their land, nor to reallocate lands among kin groups. In chiefdoms, however, a group's use-rights to resources can be taken away and reallocated to another group by the chief, who is an overarching political leader with the authority to reallocate rights to resources within his political domain. (In some chiefdoms the chief's power to do this may only be nominal; that is, serious resentment and perhaps bloodshed results if a chief actually tries to seize the land used by a kin group.)

Further, some labor and a portion of its products are under the control of chiefs, rather than being largely controlled by households and kin groups. Sometimes the chief has the right to call out people to work on public projects, such as making trails, clearing land, building canoes or storehouses, or going on cooperative trading expeditions. Here people are obliged to contribute their work for some public purpose, under the direction of the chief. In other systems the population's labor obligations to their chiefs are only partly for public purposes. A chief periodically demands that his subjects contribute labor for his personal benefit: to cook food for himself and his family, build his dwelling, paddle his canoe, make his clothing, and so forth.

Chiefs often collect tribute as well. Members of various kin groups under the control of a single chief render a portion of their harvest or present some of their animals to the chief. This is another way in which chiefly systems differ from kin group systems of control: domestic groups still produce most of their own subsistence, but they also must produce an excess that is rendered to a holder of a political office who has traditional rights to receive some share of the products. The amount of tribute taken by chiefs varies. In some systems, only a token is offered—an animal or two a year, or the first fruit harvested from a family's garden. In others, the demands of chiefs for tribute are quite onerous; people may spend as much or more time laboring to fulfill their tribute obligations as they do working to produce food for themselves and their families.

Through their collection of tribute, chiefs then sometimes control a sizable proportion of the products of the labor of ordinary people. This means that they also have a great deal of control over the overall distribution of wealth in the society. Again, how chiefs use this control varies. In some chiefdoms most of the food and other goods collected by chiefs are redistributed to the population at large. In such systems chiefs are obliged to give away most of the tribute they receive in large public feasts, provide hospitality, or feed those who contributed their labor for public projects. The rewards of chiefly office in these cases are largely nonmaterial. Chiefs sometimes are allowed to have more wives than other men, but in many cases they merely receive the respect and love of their people in rough proportion to their generosity.

On the other hand, chiefs can potentially use the products they collect for political and selfish purposes. A chief expands or consolidates his political control by means of his control over the resources he collects from his subjects. In one way or another he rewards other, lesser chiefs or those of his subjects who support him. They receive additional land, food, wealth objects, titles, spouses, or whatever rewards are locally valuable. A chief and his relatives (who sometimes make up a "nobility") also appropriate part of the tribute rendered by their subjects for their own private use, thus enriching themselves and their families. By these processes we see in many chiefdoms the beginnings of marked inequalities in the distribution of wealth, discussed further in chapter 14.

Chiefly control may be summarized as follows. To varying degrees, rights to land and resources are subject to chiefly consent or reallocation. Chiefs have traditional rights (which sometimes need to be backed up by armed force) to receive tribute from their subjects and to call out labor for public purposes. The degree to which chiefs use this control over tribute and labor to enrich themselves varies: sometimes most of the tribute they receive is redistributed; sometimes most of it is consumed by chiefs and their families or converted into wealth for the chief's noble relatives. Ordinary people, then, work both to support themselves and to support or enrich the chief who has control over the resources they exploit and much of their labor.

■ State Control

No sharp line separates chiefly from state systems of control. In both, natural resources are allocated by a formal authority. But in state control the central authority is stronger, and the government is run by a bureaucracy staffed by officials who specialize in administration.

The geographic area and population subject to overarching control also are larger in state systems. The residents of a large region (hundreds or thousands of square miles) are subject to governmental commands for their labor and its products. In a chiefdom hundreds or occasionally thousands of people are subject to the tribute and labor demands of a chief. In states tens or hundreds of thousands (and sometimes millions) of people are united under a single ruler and government. Taxes paid to the government pass through several levels of bureaucracy, and each level intercepts some share of the total.

State systems also generally have more levels than do chiefdoms. For example, households may be grouped into villages, villages into districts, districts into provinces, and provinces into the whole state. At each level control is hierarchically organized: kings or other rulers pass commands to provincial governors, who give orders to district officials, who pass them along to village headmen, who organize the households of the village to carry them out.

States also tend to have a greater number and variety of occupational specialists—including priests, merchants, craftsmen, and often standing armies—than do chiefdoms. These specialists, of course, must be fed if they are to devote full time to their crafts. States often include large central places that serve as governmental, religious, and commercial centers.

The ancient civilizations mentioned in the last chapter are examples of state systems of control over production and distribution. In these civilizations peasants produced the food that fed the elite classes of rules and priests, as well as craftsmen, artists, warriors, merchants, and other specialists. Peasants were often ordered to participate in large-scale public-works projects under a forced-labor arrangement. We can best see how state control works with an example.

In the civilization of prehistoric Peru, the ruling dynasty, known as the *Inca,* had great power to allocate natural resources and to control the distribution of wealth within the empire. The empire was divided into provinces, each governed by a member of the aristocratic class. In turn, the provinces were divided into many village communities, each administered by an official we call an *overseer.* Under this hierarchical power structure the Inca ruler was able to exert control

■ *The emperor of the Inca state, shown here, ruled over a vast and complex empire.*

over several million people, who lived scattered over thousands of square miles, in one of the most mountainous regions of the planet.

At the community level, village males held and worked some land in common, subject to the orders of the overseer. Use rights to other land were allocated to the kin groups that made up the village. Peasant men of a single village apparently maintained at least four sets of fields: one they farmed for the subsistence of their families, one for the subsistence of their overseer, one for the Inca, and one for the Sun (the Inca god). The community's men were obliged to work the fields of the overseer, the Inca, and the Sun as a tax. They also kept the llamas and alpacas of the Inca, for the village's women wove fine textiles from the wool of these animals to pay their tax.

How were these products distributed? Part of the food grown as tax labor for the Inca maintained the courts of the provincial governors, the ruler himself, and other members of the Inca aristocracy. Part fed the many servants and crafts specialists (miners, goldsmiths and silversmiths, weavers, potters, stoneworkers, and so forth) who produced the wealth of the empire that so attracted the Spanish conqueror Pizarro. Part was used to provide subsistence to the peasants, who were called on periodically to construct and maintain public works. Finally, the food that peasants grew on the lands of the Sun supported the large religious bureaucracy and financed temples and sacrifices.

Growing food under the labor-tax laws was not the only obligation of the peasants. Peasants cleared and terraced new lands for intensive agriculture under the labor-tax laws. But because the Inca considered this land to be state property, the peasants received few rewards for extending the area under cultivation. When the central government needed labor for some construction project, villagers were recruited and their labor was directed by engineers. The workers constructed huge ceremonial centers, fortresses, irrigation canals, bridges, and an extensive network of roads (complete with resthouses) that linked the empire together for purposes of communication and trade.

Knowing all this, it is not surprising that the Inca aristocracy controlled the overall distribution of productive resources and wealth objects in the empire. Censuses were made periodically and the land was reallocated among the communities to adjust their landholdings to their population size. Aside from these lands held and worked communally by peasants, the Inca ruler sometimes made a private "land grant" to individuals who gave him unusual service as warriors or engineers.

The empire had *sumptuary laws*, that is, laws regulating the possession of wealth objects, such as certain kinds of cloth and jewelry. Overseers and provincial governors taxed the peasantry for food, which was used partly to feed the craftsmen who produced fine cloth and objects made from precious metals. Yet under the sumptuary laws, overseers themselves could not possess this kind of wealth unless it had been given to them by the Inca, so they presented such items to the Inca as gifts and relied on Inca generosity toward them for their wealth objects.

The Inca example reveals the main elements of state control. A centralized government allocates most or much of the productive resources among the population. The organization of this control is hierarchical: there are administrative levels between the ordinary person and the top echelons of the state. Commands and some services and public goods flow "down" the hierarchy under the principle of redistribution, but the flow of goods is mostly "up": unspecialized peasants produce food and other products for their tribute or tax obligations as well as for their own subsistence. Part of the products of their labor support craftspeople, warriors, priests, and other specialists. Another part supports others of their class who work on public projects under the direction of the state. But much of their tax or tribute supports an aristocracy in grand style. By controlling the distribution of wealth in the empire, rulers and other officials reward their supporters and punish their detractors. They thus use their control over the tax and tribute system to reinforce their political power.

■ An Evolutionary View

We conclude by stepping back and taking a bird's-eye view of these four systems of economic control over production and distribution. First, the order in which we discussed these systems is the evolutionary order in which they developed among humanity. There was a time in the prehistoric past when all humans lived in foraging bands; generally, all adult members of a band had a say in decisions about work, access to resources was relatively equitable, and little inequality existed between families in possessions or wealth. Some time after the evolution of domestication, kin group control developed among most cultivators and pastoralists as a way of assigning rights of access to particular areas of land to definite kin groups—although a group's rights often had to be defended militarily. Still, economic and political inequality generally remained relatively undeveloped, for within a kin group generalized reciprocity tended to equalize access to life-sustaining food and other resources. In some parts of the earth, kin group control persists even today, but in other areas chiefly control developed out of the kin group system. (Just how and why this happened is the subject of considerable controversy.) In some chiefdoms the chiefs' control is only nominal and their rewards are mainly honorific, for custom obliges them to redistribute most of the tribute they collect from their subjects. But in others, chiefs use their authority to exact onerous tribute and to command labor, which they use to increase their own wealth and power. Finally, in a few parts of the earth, state control developed out of the chiefly system. Again, the "hows" and "whys" of this transformation are controversial, but it is likely that one chiefdom conquered surrounding peoples by means of superior military power and established a ruling dynasty. It forced subject peoples to pay tribute or tax and to contribute labor. Over time, a complex social machinery evolved to administer the region, and out of this developed the complex administrative hierarchy, specialization, economic and political inequality, intricate tax and tribute systems, and other features by which we define the state system of control.

Second, notice that a major difference between the four systems is their *scale:* control of natural resources, of labor, and of the distribution of food and wealth is exerted over ever-larger territories and over ever-increasing numbers of people. Foraging bands typically number around twenty to fifty members; kin groups a hundred to several hundred; chiefdoms several hundred to several thousand; and states tens of thousands, or even millions. Accompanying this increased scale of control is, of course, ever-increasing concentration of wealth and power. Such things are difficult to measure, but it is likely that the peasants of the ancient civilizations (as well as many of those of modern nations) lived no better than prehistoric foragers. Almost certainly they had to work harder and longer, for they were no longer working mainly for themselves and their families. Rather, they worked partly to feed specialists whose crafts they rarely were able to own and partly to support an aristocracy whose wealth they could enjoy only vicariously.

Summary

Economic activities encompass the patterned ways people acquire and distribute material goods. This chapter covers two aspects of economic systems: exchange, or the ways goods are acquired by means of transfer from one individual or group to another, and control, or the diverse ways in which ownership or use rights to resources, power to allocate labor, and ability to acquire wealth are organized.

One form of exchange is reciprocity, or the giving and receiving of objects without the transfer of money. Generalized reciprocity usually occurs between parties who are culturally obliged to assist one another in times of need, as among relatives and sometimes close friends. With balanced reciprocity, a return of an object of equivalent value is expected. The goal of balanced reciprocity may be the acquisition of goods for their utility, as in the Trobriand *wasi*. More often it is motivated by the desire to create or sustain good relations between individuals (as in gift giving) or political alliances between groups (as with the Maring

pig feast). Negative reciprocity is characterized by the desire of both parties to acquire as many goods as possible while giving up as few as possible, as in barter.

The variety of reciprocity that is likely to characterize transactions between individuals and groups depends on the normative degree of social distance between them, so exchange relations alter if social relationships change. Conversely, one party can initiate an attempt to alter a relationship by an offer of a good, and the other party can signal acceptance or rejection by his or her response. Therefore, varying the type of reciprocity is part of a social strategy.

Another form of exchange is redistribution, in which the members of a group contribute goods or money into a pool or fund, and a central authority reallocates or uses them for public purposes. Taxes in modern nations and tribute in chiefdoms are examples. Normatively, redistribution is supposed to provide resources to increase public welfare, either to provide public goods or to support those in need. In fact there is much conflict over the collection and allocation, and frequently those officials who do the collecting and allocating use their authority for private rather than public interest.

Market exchange involves the buying and selling of goods; it therefore requires money and prices determined by supply and demand. Money functions as a medium of exchange, a standard of value, and a store of value. These functions mean that money objects must be durable, and their supply must be limited or controlled in some way. The range of goods and services that can be bought with money varies between economies. Money types can be characterized as multipurpose (like modern currencies) or limited-purpose (like Tiv metal rods).

It is important to distinguish between the market principle, or the principle by which modern market economies operate, and the marketplace, or the physical location at which buyers and sellers exchange money for goods. In many peasant and other preindustrial economies, the market principle exists, but it allocates only a limited range of resources, for most people do not make their living by selling goods or their labor on the market. Market venders in peasant economies frequently seek to reduce their risks by developing special relationships with some of their customers, as illustrated by the Haitian *pratik* and the Philippine *suki*.

Systems of control over production and the distribution of wealth may be classified into four overall forms. In the bands that characterize most foragers, ownership over productive resources is rather loose and flexible, partly because wild resources are usually not economically defendable. There is little inequality in access to resources even within a band, for families generally make production decisions for themselves or by consensus, and it is difficult for any individual or family to maintain exclusive control over territory or technology.

In the kin group control characteristics of many horticulturalists and pastoralists, kin groups control access to land, allocating use rights to specific parcels to particular domestic groups. Although domestic groups are potentially largely self-sufficient, in actuality they engage in reciprocal exchanges with related domestic groups, which fosters the persistence of a relatively even distribution of wealth. Entire kin groups participate in balanced reciprocal exchanges with other groups into which their members have married to form or strengthen military alliances or to acquire political influence. Generally, each kin group must be prepared to defend its access to territorial resources from other groups.

Chiefly control exists when there are formal offices or titles which only members of certain kin groups or families are eligible to acquire. Chiefs have the formal authority to reallocate land or resources among the kin groups subject to their control. Some labor or tribute is rendered to chiefs, who use it for public projects and sometimes to support themselves and their family and retainers. In some systems chiefs have extensive control over the distribution of wealth, which leads to marked inequalities. But in others, chiefly control is only nominal and the rewards of office are mainly honorific, for chiefs are obliged to give away most of what they receive.

As compared to chiefly systems, in state control extralocal political authority is stronger, the geographic area and population subject to state control are much larger, more administrative levels exist, and a greater number and variety of occupational specialists exists. The central government, usually in the person of a single ruler, has the authority to allocate productive resources among the citizenry. Control is hierarchically organized, with commands flowing "down" to peasants and workers. Food and other goods move "up" administrative levels, with each level intercepting some portion of the total for their own consumption and riches. Enormous inequalities in wealth, power, and honor exist, for states always include a rich aristocracy and a poor peasantry. The Inca empire of ancient Peru illustrates all these features.

These systems of control emerged in the history of humanity in the order discussed. Taking a bird's-eye view, the scale of control has increased in economic evolution: control has been achieved over ever-larger territories and over increasing numbers of people. The trend has been toward increased concentration of control and more unequal distribution of wealth.

Key Terms

economic system	multipurpose money
exchange	limited-purpose money
reciprocity	(special-purpose money)
redistribution	
market	market principle
generalized reciprocity	marketplace
balanced reciprocity	distribution .
negative reciprocity	kin group control
social distance	chiefly control
tribute	state control

Suggested Readings

◼ Belshaw, Cyril S. *Traditional Exchange and Modern Markets*. Englewood Cliffs, N.J.: Prentice-Hall, 1965.
   A good, short introduction to exchange systems.

◼ Bohannon, Paul, and George Dalton, eds. *Markets in Africa*. Evanston, Ill.: Northwestern University Press, 1962.
   A collection of essays that address both the economic and noneconomic functions of markets in the life of African peoples.

◼ Dalton, George. *Tribal and Peasant Economies*. Garden City, N.Y.: Natural History Press, 1967.
   A collection of important and classical essays on economic anthropology that uses data from around the world.

◼ Davis, William G. *Social Relations in a Philippine Market*. Berkeley, Calif.: University of California Press, 1973.
   An empirical study of a marketplace in a Philippine town, emphasizing market relationships.

◼ Douglas, Mary, and Baron Isherwood. *The World of Goods: Toward an Anthropology of Consumption*. New York: W. W. Norton, 1979.
   An examination of cultural theories of consumption.

◼ Leclair, Edward E., Jr., and Harold Schneider. *Economic Anthropology: Readings in Theory and Analysis*. New York: Holt, Rinehart and Winston, 1968.

A collection of important articles in economic anthropology that includes both theoretical and descriptive case studies.

■ Nash, Manning. *Primitive and Peasant Economic Systems.* San Francisco: Chandler, 1966.

Primarily a theoretical book focusing on social and economic change.

■ Neale, Walter C. *Monies in Societies.* San Francisco: Chandler and Sharp, 1976.

A good, brief book about the uses, forms, and functions of money in a variety of economies.

■ Rubel, Paula G., and Abraham Rosman. *Your Own Pigs You May Not Eat.* Chicago: University of Chicago Press, 1978.

Based on existing ethnographic accounts of numerous societies in Papua New Guinea, this comparative study analyzes the symbolic nature of exchange relations.

■ Sahlins, Marshall. *Stone Age Economics.* New York: Aldine, 1972.

Deals with the organization of production and modes of exchange in preindustrial economies.

■ Schneider, Harold. *Economic Man.* New York: The Free Press, 1974.

A study of social exchange theory and economic life with a strongly formal economic orientation.

■ Service, Elman R. *Origins of the State and Civilization.* New York: W. W. Norton, 1975.

A description and functionalist analysis of the evolution of states and civilizations and the control over production and distribution that accompanied their emergence.

Chapter 10

THE DOMESTIC SPHERE: MARRIAGE, FAMILY, AND RESIDENCE

■ Contents

■ (Above) *Human societies vary in their marriage patterns, family forms, and domestic organizations. This Bedouin man is polygamous, which is permitted in his society.*

Domestic life refers to relations between family members who live in a common household. Among most human populations, new families are created by marriage. Therefore we cannot understand domestic life in a sociocultural system without also understanding its marriage patterns—the ties marriage creates between individuals and groups, who marries whom, and how wives and husbands typically relate to one another. The forms of households and families established by a new marriage are influenced by *postmarital residence patterns*—that is, by where newly married couples set up their domestic unit after they marry. The variation among humanity in these subsystems—marriage, family and household, and postmarital residence—is the subject of this chapter.

Definitions

Before describing this variation in domestic life, we must first define some terms. **Kin group** refers to a group of people who conceive of themselves as relatives, who share common interests and a sense of common identity because they are relatives, and who cooperate in certain kinds of activities. **Domestic group** refers to those individuals who live together in a single household, or domicile. Because the residents of a household are usually also relatives, a domestic group is one type (but only one type) of kin group. Other kinds of kin groups (much larger than domestic groups) also exist, as we shall see in chapter 11.

Anthropologists find it convenient to use the term **consanguines** to refer to "blood" relatives—people related by birth. We use the term **affines** to refer to "in-laws"—people related by marriage. So a *consanguine* is any blood relative, and a person's *consanguineal relatives* are all of her or his blood relatives, while an *affine* is any relative by marriage and one's *affinal relatives* are all of one's relatives by marriage. Your parents, siblings, grandparents, parents' siblings, and all cousins are examples of your consanguines. Your sister's husband, wife's mother, and father's sister's husband are some of your affines. Note that affinal

relationships are always created by marriage: for instance, a woman is an affine to you because one of your consanguines married her or one of her blood relatives.

Societies everywhere have domestic groups and kin groups, and all peoples distinguish between consanguineal and affinal relatives. But the nature of these groups and relations between kin are highly variable cross-culturally. In North America and most other highly industrialized, urbanized societies, the most important domestic unit is made up of a married couple and any unmarried children they may have. We call this the **nuclear family,** and this kind of group is what we ordinarily mean when we say "my family." In many other societies, the nuclear family is not the main kind of domestic or kin group. Rather, nuclear families are embedded in and merged into much larger kinds of groups. Some of these are enormously large, consisting of hundreds of members. We discuss these larger kin groups in the next chapter; here we deal only with domestic groups, showing some of the ways they are formed and the major types of groups that exist in the human species. The best place to start is marriage, for this relation is the basis of all kinds of kinship groupings and relationships.

■ *Nuclear families, such as this one from Java (Indonesia), consist of a married couple and their offspring.*

Marriage: Definitions and Functions

If someone were to ask you for a definition of marriage, you might well offer something like the following:

> Marriage is a personal relationship between a woman and a man involving love, exclusive sex, cohabitation, reproduction and childrearing, and sharing the joys and burdens of life.

If you are trained in law, you might also note that marriage has legal aspects, such as joint property rights. If you are familiar with the writings of some economists, you might add that the marriage tie creates new households, which are important consumption units in a society. And if you are a religious person, you will want to include your belief that marriage is a relationship sanctioned by God, a relationship that should last until the parties are separated by death.

This definition is fairly serviceable in North America, but it is not broad enough to include all the diversity in the marital relationship that anthropologists have uncovered in the last hundred years. In many preindustrial populations one or more of these aspects of marriage are absent. For example, we tend to think of marriage as a private matter between a man and a woman, although we usually seek the "blessing" of our parents and other relatives before the wedding. Among preindustrial peoples marriage is much more likely to be a public matter that concerns a broad range of kinfolk of the bride and groom, who must consent to—and quite often even arrange—the marriage of a couple. Also, cohabitation in the same house is by no means universal: in many villages in Melanesia, Southeast Asia, and Africa, the men sleep and spend much of their time in a communal house (called, appropriately, the *men's house*), whereas their wives and young children live and sleep in a separate dwelling.

Similarly, more often than not romantic love between a man and woman is not considered necessary for marriage, and indeed is usually not very relevant to the relationship. Couples do not marry because they "fall in love." For example, in traditional China and Japan, a man and woman had no chance to fall in love before they were married, because they usually hardly knew one another and quite often had not even met. Sometimes boys and girls were betrothed at birth. In China it was not uncommon for a couple with a young son to adopt an infant girl. They raised her much like a daughter, except that she was adopted with the express purpose of marrying their son when they both came of age. In both Japan and China, even when couples were married as adults, the marriage was arranged by their parents with the aid of a matchmaker, usually a female relative of the groom's family or a woman hired by them. She tried to find a woman of suitable age, wealth, status, and disposition who would become a wife for the young man. The matchmaker would "match" not only the couple to one another, but also the woman to the husband's parents. Once she married the son, the wife would be fully incorporated into her husband's family; her labor would be very much under the control of her husband's parents, especially her mother-in-law; she would worship the ancestors of her husband's family, not those of her own parents; her behavior would be watched closely lest she disgrace her in-laws; and her children would become members of her husband's kin group, not her own. The incorporation of a wife into the family of her husband was one reason why Chinese parents often adopted an infant girl to marry their son: they would be able to train the girl themselves, so that she would be more pliable to them and compatible with other family members.

The same ideas apply to most other Western cultural notions of and customs about marriage: things we consider normal are not practiced among other peoples. Sex is not always confined to the marriage bed (or mat). The marital tie may be fragile or temporary, with individuals expecting to have several spouses during the course of their lives. Or the tie may be so strong that even death does not end it. In traditional India there were strict rules against the remarriage of a high-caste widow, and a high-caste widow often would follow her husband to the grave by throwing herself onto his cremation fire. There are even a few cases—notably the Nayar of southern India—in which marriage is not the normal relationship that conceives children, and husband-fathers and wife-mothers are not the primary statuses responsible for enculturation. Perhaps most surprising of all to Westerners, there are culturally legitimate marital relationships that are not between a man and a woman: among the Nuer of the southern Sudan, an old, well-off woman sometimes pays the bridewealth needed to marry a girl; the girl takes male lovers and bears children, who are incorporated into the kin group of the old woman.

Formulating a definition of marriage that encompasses all the cross-cultural variations in the relationship is, then, a difficult task, for somewhere there will be a population that does not fit the definition. As you can imagine, numerous definitions have been offered, but still there is no agreement on the "best" or "most encompassing" one. However, most anthropologists will agree that marriage ordinarily involves

- a culturally defined special relationship between a man and woman from different families, which regulates sexual intercourse and provides for reproduction;
- a set of rights the couple and their families obtain over one another, including rights over the couple's children;
- an assignment of responsibility for enculturation to the spouses or to one or both sets of their relatives; and
- a division of labor in the domestic sphere of the sociocultural system.

This conception of marriage has the virtue of defining the term by its most common and distinctive features, although doubtless it is possible to roust out human populations whose "marriage" does not share all these features.

It is important to notice here that in most sociocultural systems (an exception will be presented shortly), marriage is the relationship that normatively gives rise to new nuclear families. Sociologists often distinguish between an individual's family of orientation and his or her family of procreation. The *family of orientation* is the one a person is born into (i.e., the family formed by the marriage of one's parents). The *family of procreation* is the new one a person forms upon his or her marriage (i.e., the family one forms with her or his spouse and children). Marriage is usually the relationship through which new families of procreation are formed in a population.

This way of defining marriage also is useful because it points to the major, nearly universal functions and social benefits of marriage:

- a reduction (but not elimination) of conflict over sexual access;
- a formation of social bonds that provide for the material needs, social support, and enculturation of children;
- an establishment of relations between intermarrying families or other kinds of kin groups;
- a provision for the exchange of domestic services between the sexes; and
- the formation of new families of procreation in a population.

Marriage creates new families of procreation and new relations between individuals and groups, creations which are usually symbolized by a special ceremony, a wedding. The relatives of the couple have gathered for this French wedding.

Some kinds of relationships—usually but not always a marital relationship—must perform these functions in a human society because of several universal characteristics of humanity. These characteristics include (1) the human female's ability to receive sexual partners continuously, regardless of her ovulatory cycle; (2) the prolonged infancy and childhood dependency of human children; (3) the sexual division of labor found to varying degrees in all sociocultural systems; and (4) the definition of sexual intercourse within the nuclear family as incestuous. We now look at how each of these characteristics gives rise to needs that are usually satisfied by the marital bond and the families it creates.

Unlike females of other primates, human females are continuously receptive sexually, and most human males are able and willing to have intercourse with a female regardless of the chances of impregnating her. Marriage establishes special relationships that constrain people's sexual behavior by defining and limiting most people's sexual access to certain individuals. (It does not, however, always limit everyone's sexual partners to their spouses alone, the way our own cultural norms prescribe.) This undoubtedly reduces the amount of conflict over sexual access. Do not conclude, however, that it eliminates the conflict, for people still quarrel over who will marry whom and over who has the right to have intercourse with whom.

Human children also have special requirements. Until they reach ten or more years of age, they are totally or largely dependent on adults for food, shelter, protection, and other bodily needs. Equally important, they require the presence of adults for the social learning crucial to complete psychological and cultural development. It is theoretically possible that only one adult, the mother, is required; but almost everywhere marriage helps to create and expand the relationships through which children receive the material support and enculturation necessary for their immediate survival, future maturity, and eventual reproduction.

Humanity also differs from other mammals in the degree to which economic tasks are assigned to sexes. For reasons discussed in chapter 12, a sexual division of labor exists worldwide: men do some kinds of activities, women other kinds. Ordinarily the tasks overlap, but there is enough differentiation that the goods and services produced by women somehow must be made available to men, and vice versa. Marriage usually establishes domestic relationships between men and women in which these goods and services pass back and forth. It also defines the duties each partner is normatively obliged to render to the other and to their offspring. Indeed, the failure to meet one's domestic obligations is often a major reason for divorce.

Finally, in some human populations nuclear families are able to *survive* independently, but in no known population do nuclear families *reproduce* themselves without establishing relations with other families. Everywhere there is a cultural prohibition on mating within the nuclear family. The question of whether this incest taboo has an innate biological basis is addressed in the next section. Whether biologically based or not, the nuclear family incest taboo means that people must seek their mates from other families. They must leave their families of orientation if they are to form families of procreation. This, of course, has the effect of bringing intermarrying families or other kinds of kinship groups into affinal relationships with one another. In most sociocultural systems these affinal ties are the basis for establishing relationships of other kinds, such as trade or political alliances.

These universal characteristics of humankind—continuous sexuality, prolonged infant dependency, sexual division of labor, and the incest taboo—make a relationship like marriage and a group like the family nearly universal. However, they do not make any particular *form* of marriage or the family universal. Sexual access must be defined, children must be cared for, the products of the sexes must be exchanged, and people must leave their families of orientation to seek their mates—these universal needs do not impose any specific form of marriage or family on a population. Indeed, human populations have evolved diverse solutions to these problems. Some of these solutions are considered in the remainder of this chapter. For now, to show how very different from our own marriage and family system other populations can be, we consider one of the most unusual systems recorded by anthropologists, the Nayar of southern India.

Before Great Britain assumed colonial control over part of India in 1792, the Nayar were a caste (see chapter 14) whose men specialized in warfare. A great many Nayar men were away from their villages much of the time, for as a warrior caste they served as soldiers for several surrounding kingdoms and in other parts of India. Nayar women, however, were required to confine their sexual activity to men of their own or of a higher subcaste. They suffered severe penalties—death or ostracism—if they transgressed this norm. The fascinating thing about the Nayar is that they almost certainly lacked nuclear families, and—by the conception of marriage just described—lacked marriage as well. Yet they perpetuated themselves until the time of British rule. What alternative system did they use?

Nayar villages were composed of a number of kin groups. Each child joined the kin group of his or her mother. Each kin group was linked for certain ceremonial purposes to several other kin groups: some from its own village, others from neighboring villages. Any Nayar caught having sexual relations with anyone in his or her own kin group was put to death, for intragroup intercourse was regarded as incestuous. Every few years, all the girls of a kin group who had not yet attained puberty gathered for a large ceremony. This ceremony was attended also by people from the linked kin groups, for the purpose of the event was to ceremonially "marry" these young girls to selected men from the linked kin groups (whether these really deserve to be called "marriages" depends, as you will see, on how we define the term). At the ceremony each "groom" tied a gold ornament around the neck of his "bride," and each couple retired to a secluded place for three days, where they may have had sexual relations if the girl was nearing puberty. After this period the "grooms" left the village, and each had no further responsibilities to his "bride"; indeed, he might never even see her again. For her part, the "bride" and the children she would later bear had only to perform a certain ritual for her "husband" when he died. The ritual tying of the ornament by a man of a linked kin group did, however, establish a girl as an adult, able to have sexual liaisons with other men when she reached sexual maturity.

After her "marriage," each girl remained with her own kin group. When she reached sexual maturity, she began to receive nocturnal male visitors from other kin groups. She established long-lasting sexual relations with some of her partners, who were expected to give her small luxury gifts periodically. Her other, more casual, partners had no obligations toward her at all, and any of her sexual relationships were easily terminated. None of her partners supported her or her children in any way other than these occasional gifts; indeed, they also visited other women and sired other children. The food and clothing of a woman and her children were supplied by her brothers and other members of her kin group, who were also responsible for disciplining and providing an inheritance for her children. A woman's early "marriage," then, did not establish a nuclear family, nor did her later sexual partners ever live with her or support her children. There was only one other thing a Nayar woman required from her partners: when she became pregnant, one of them had to admit that he could have been the father of her child by paying the fees for the midwife who helped deliver the baby. If none of her partners did so, it was assumed that she had had sexual intercourse with someone of a lower caste, and she, and sometimes her child, would be expelled from her kin group or killed.

We see that a Nayar girl's early, prepuberty "marriage" ceremonially marked her entry into adulthood; only after she had been "married" to someone of a linked kin group should she begin (legitimately) to receive male visitors. Later, when she bore a child, the infant was believed to be the product of a legitimate union if one of its mother's partners paid the birth fees. Her child then became a member of the kin group of herself, her sisters, and her brothers, who gave the child material and social support. No nuclear families—or any other kind of family of procreation—existed, and the Nayar had no marriage as the term is used in this book.

Although the Nayar might strike us as promiscuous, their sexual behavior was in fact governed by strict cultural rules. A woman could not legitimately engage in sex with certain of her relatives nor with anyone of a lower subcaste. As we discuss in the next section, prohibitions of one particular kind are found in all human populations.

Incest Prohibitions

Some anthropologists in the nineteenth century believed that in its primeval condition—in the stage of "lower savagery," for example—humanity possessed an intrafamily mating pattern: sisters married their own brothers. It was thought that these "savages" were so ignorant that they had no conception of incest, much less of its deleterious consequences for the children of such unions. But an important finding of twentieth-century ethnographers is that not a single population has been discovered that lacks incest prohibitions between certain categories of biological relatives.

The rules against sexual intercourse between relatives are called **incest taboos.** Practically all known human populations prohibit mating between members of the nuclear family. There are only three well-documented cases in which sexual intercourse was permitted between nuclear family members: among the aboriginal Hawaiians, the prehistoric Inca, and the ancient Egyptians. Even among the Hawaiians and Incas, incest was allowed only to members of the royal family and existed to preserve the "spiritual purity" of the royal bloodline. Everywhere else in the known world, mating between siblings and between parents and children is culturally forbidden (which is not the same as saying it does not occur).

Sexual acts between brothers and sisters and between parents and children are not, of course, the only kind of erotic relations forbidden by incest taboos. In most populations the incest taboo is extended outward beyond the nuclear family to prohibit liaisons between uncles and nieces, aunts and nephews, and some kinds of cousins. Other than the widespread extension to these relatives, sociocultural systems vary in the categories of kinfolk with whom sex is tabooed.

Anthropologists have wondered a lot about why nuclear family incest is almost universally tabooed. This wonder sometimes surprises people who are not anthropologists, who usually think that intercourse within the family is universally prohibited because inbreeding "is potentially harmful to the children." Indeed, in modern Euro-American societies we say we prohibit incest because scientific genetics has demonstrated that the offspring of incestuous matings have a significantly higher chance of exhibiting harmful recessive genes. But humans had laws against incest long before genetic science even existed, so our "medical" reasons for the taboo may be our cultural rationalization for a prohibition that has other causes. Further, if concern for the children of incestuous matings is the only reason we legally and morally prohibit incest, then we ought to prohibit it only if the partners do not use contraception, and we ought not to prohibit it between sons and their postmenopausal mothers. At any rate, conscious knowledge of the medical reasons for the taboo certainly cannot explain why it is nearly universal amongst humanity, for many populations have no knowledge of such reasons yet still forbid nuclear family incest.

What reasons have been suggested for the near universality of the nuclear family incest taboo? The hypotheses fall into two overall types. The first assumes that people have a sexual desire for their relatives; but the fulfilling of this desire would be harmful somehow to others in their group, and the incest taboo serves to keep their lust in check. The second type of hypothesis assumes that most people have little desire to mate with their relatives; the incest taboo merely expresses and institutionalizes this lack of lust. Let's look at the variants of each type.

■ Type I Hypotheses

Type I hypotheses begin with the assumption that close relatives would frequently mate with one another were it not for the incest prohibition. They argue that most of us want to have sex with our kinfolk; but generally children are taught that incest is one of the most reprehensible crimes, and this culturally imposed prohibition leads us to repress our desire. (For later purposes, notice that if you are not aware of your desire for your sibling, parent, or child, it can be either because your culture has led you to repress your urge, or because you never have had the urge.) Several specific hypotheses make these assumptions. They differ primarily in what they see as the benefits that the incest taboo provides for a group. We discuss only two of the most popular.

"Marry Out or Die Out"   This idea was first proposed by E. B. Tylor, one of anthropology's founding fathers, whom we introduced in chapter 5. He noticed that a rule prohibiting marriage between close relatives would force people to seek their mates outside their domestic groups. These marriages would serve to es-

tablish relations between groups: relations that would widen the scale of economic and political cooperation. Groups that practiced outmarriage would then have an advantage over those that did not, all else equal. Inmarrying groups would subsequently have died out, leaving only outmarrying populations to be recorded by anthropology.

As we note later in this chapter, Tylor's hypothesis contains an important insight: outmarriage does indeed offer significant advantages to those domestic groups that practice it. Unfortunately, this insight does not pertain to the incest taboo. There is no necessary reason why a successful group could not allow sexual relations between its members but forbid them to marry one another. This hypothesis thus confuses the incest taboo ("thou shalt not have sexual intercourse within thine own domestic group") with outmarriage rules ("thou shalt not marry within thine own domestic group").

"Peace in the Family"   This hypothesis, also called the *family disruption hypothesis*, argues that nuclear family incest would lead to intrafamilial sexual rivalry and competition. It would interfere with the normal and essential functions of the family, such as economic cooperation and enculturation. It also might usurp the authority of the male head of the family, who would be constantly challenged by his sons. Brothers would be brought to blows over their sisters. And imagine the status and role confusions: for example, if a man had children by his daughter, the daughter's children would also be her half-siblings, and the father's children would simultaneously be his grandchildren.

What should we make of this idea? For one thing, we do not know whether sex in the family would threaten peace in the family, since the nuclear family incest taboo is well-nigh universal. Would brothers and sisters peacefully wait their turns for one another? Probably, they would not, but we have no way of testing the hypothesis. At any rate, the incest taboo is sometimes extended to very distant relatives who hardly know one another, and family disruption cannot explain these extensions.

■ Type II Hypotheses

Type II hypotheses, of which there are only two, are closely related—indeed, one may be necessary if the other is to work. They are similar in assuming that, in general, people have little sexual desire for their close relatives. Also, the same objection applies to both: If there is so little lust between close relatives, then why is a taboo needed at all?

Inbreeding Avoidance This is our own cultural rationale for the taboo, as mentioned. It also is supported by the great majority of geneticists. Both genetic theory and experimentation have firmly established that the offspring of sexual unions between close relatives have a significantly higher probability of inheriting homozygously recessive harmful alleles that show up phenotypically, that is, "it's bad for the children." Most anthropologists admit that it would be beneficial to a population if its members were to avoid intercourse with their close relatives. (Some sociocultural anthropologists stubbornly refuse to admit this, mistakenly thinking its smacks of biological determinism.) The inbreeding-avoidance hypothesis simply states that the incest taboo exists to reduce the incidence of mating between close relatives.

Why, then, do anthropologists not embrace the notion that avoiding intercourse with one's close relatives has the biological function of preventing the deleterious genetic effects of inbreeding? One reason has already been mentioned: Many preindustrial peoples are unaware of these harmful genetic effects, and these effects therefore cannot *consciously* be the reason for the taboo. This objection, however, is not fatal to the inbreeding-avoidance hypothesis, for it does not require people to be aware that "it's bad for the children." Nonhuman primates do not "know" that inbreeding increases the expression of deleterious alleles, but they act as though they know—that is, they generally do not mate with close genetic relatives. We need only postulate that throughout humanity's evolutionary history, those individuals who mated with their close relatives left fewer surviving and reproducing offspring than those who did not. The genes of those who did not interbreed with their close relatives would have spread within the population. Evolution then "built in" a lack of sexual desire for close relatives over a long time span; our knowledge is instinctive, not conscious. (Notice that evolution would also have had to build in a knowledge of who one's close relatives are, or who they are most likely to be.)

Another objection is more serious: Many peoples do not apply the taboo to the kinds of relatives that the inbreeding-avoidance hypothesis predicts they should. For example, some peoples allow or encourage marriage (which normally involves reproduction) between one set of cousins but prohibit both marriage and sexual intercourse with another set of cousins who are equally closely related genetically. Among certain populations it is indeed quite common for a man to marry his mother's brother's daughter, but for his father's brother's daughter to be prohibited as both a sexual and marriage partner. Among other peoples, a man is encouraged to marry his father's brother's daughter. Now why should some populations prohibit sex with one kind of cousin and others encourage it, if the inbreeding-avoidance theory is correct? The second objection, then, is that inbreeding-avoidance theory does not explain the cross-cultural variability in the kinds of relatives to whom the taboo applies. It predicts (or seems to predict) that all peoples ought to prohibit the same relatives.

The inbreeding-avoidance hypothesis has other arguments against it, which are best discussed after we have presented the other Type II hypothesis, since they apply to it as well.

"Familiarity Breeds Disinterest" This hypothesis holds that males and females who are closely associated during childhood have little sexual desire for one another when they grow up. Also called the *childhood-familiarity hypothesis*, this hypothesis was first proposed by a nineteenth-century scholar named Edward Westermarck. It was rejected for decades but has recently become a popular hypothesis because of some ethnographic studies that seem to support it.

One study is from the Israeli *kibbutzim*, a kind of agricultural collective established by the Israelis after the country was granted its present territory by Great Britain. On a *kibbutz* (*kibbutzim* is plural), children are

■ *The childhood familiarity hypothesis holds that people who were intimately associated as children have little sexual interest in one another when they reach sexual maturity. These Hopi children seem sufficiently intimate.*

raised not in families by their parents but in communal peer groups by specialists in child care. Several infants of similar age are placed into a nursery soon after birth; they subsequently move through the various stages of enculturation as a group, with more children joining them later around our kindergarten age. A peer group of around ten to twenty children is raised together until adolescence, more or less as if they were siblings.

Boys and girls raised in the same peer group are not forbidden to marry—indeed, such marriages are often encouraged. But if the childhood-familiarity hypothesis is correct, then *kibbutz* children of the same peer group should show little sexual interest in one another, and this disinterest should be revealed in marriage patterns. In fact, the evidence on marriage supports the hypothesis: males and females reared in the same peer group almost never get married, although, of course, they have plenty of opportunity to get to know one another.

Further data supporting the hypothesis that childhood familiarity leads to sexual aversion is supplied by Arthur Wolf's study of marriage in Taiwan. Some Taiwanese couples with male children will "adopt" a girl with poor parents to be reared and trained in their households as a future wife for their son. The boy and girl grow up together in the same household, in most respects just like brother and sister, and marry as adults. If Westermarck's hypothesis is correct, we should expect to find evidence of less sexual activity and greater marital difficulties for these couples than in other Taiwanese marriages. Wolf found that in fact these couples had fewer children, higher rates of divorce, and more extramarital sexual activity than other couples.

Finally, evidence from an Arab village in Lebanon studied by Justin McCabe supports Westermarck's hypothesis. For a variety of reasons it is fairly common in the Middle East for a man to marry one of his father's brother's daughters. In fact, in the village studied, about 20 percent of all marriages were between men and women whose fathers were brothers. These cousins were in constant childhood association with one another because of the close personal relationship between their fathers. If childhood familiarity does indeed produce adult sexual disinterest, then it should be revealed in these marriages. In fact, it is: These cousin marriages had three times the divorce rate and produced fewer children than other kinds of marriage.

Some evidence therefore suggests sexual disinterest between individuals who have intimate childhood associations. This lack of desire cannot be universal, or

there would never be any nuclear family incest. And the disinterest is not absolute, or the unusual marriages in Taiwan and Lebanon just described would have produced no children at all. However, the childhood-familiarity hypothesis does explain why most people do not commit incest within the nuclear family—they have no great desire to do so.

Further, if childhood familiarity does lead to erotic disinterest as adults, then the inbreeding-avoidance hypothesis might also be supported. To avoid inbreeding, people must have some way of recognizing their close relatives. In general, my close relatives are likely to be those with whom I was raised, so if I avoid mating with my childhood associates, I generally will not be inbreeding. So both these hypotheses together are capable of explaining why nuclear family incest is uncommon.

Notice, though, that neither the inbreeding-avoidance nor the childhood-familiarity hypothesis explains why nuclear family incest is usually punished whenever it does occur. The taboo is a *culturally imposed constraint* (as this term is defined in chapter 2) on the behavior of individuals. It is easy to see why, for example, a sister would rather reproduce with a non-relative than with her brother (at least it is easy to see if we think she lacks desire for her brother!). But how does the lack of desire by individuals become a culturally imposed constraint? Why should anyone else care? One objection to both Type II hypotheses, then, is that they explain only the lack of desire but not the reasons for other people caring enough to make incest among the most abhorrent of crimes, punishable by death in many populations.

Some scholars have used the very existence of a taboo on incest to argue against Type II hypotheses. The argument here is that if in general we lack erotic feelings toward our close relatives, then we do not need a taboo. The fact that there is a taboo shows that people do lust after their close kin, for why prohibit an action that people have no desire to commit? But this objection is unfair, for neither Type II hypothesis denies that some people have sexual desire for their relatives; there is merely evidence suggesting that most people do not. We can best see why this objection is unfair with an analogous legal prohibition: No one argues that a legal prohibition on murder, rape, or theft proves that most people want to commit these acts.

Another related objection to both Type II hypotheses is that nuclear family incest does in fact occur and is more widespread than most people realize. If there is an inborn aversion to mating with childhood associates, there should be no incest. This objection, too, is unfair, for neither the inbreeding-avoidance nor the childhood-familiarity hypothesis purports to explain why incest *does* occur. Both try to explain only why most people do not mate within their nuclear families; neither says anything about why some people do commit incest.

To return to our overall discussion, notice that three of the four hypotheses account mainly for incest prohibitions within the nuclear family. They therefore cannot explain everything about incest taboos, for in most human populations the prohibition is extended to more-distant relations. Only the "marry-out-or-die-out" hypothesis explains the extension of the incest taboo beyond the nuclear family. But as we saw earlier, this hypothesis explains only why people marry outside the domestic group, not why cultures prohibit incest within domestic groups. This point leads us into our discussion of marriage.

Marriage: A Cross-Cultural Perspective

The universal prohibition on sexual activity within the nuclear family means that ordinarily people leave their families of orientation to establish new families of procreation. When they do so, they enter into a relationship—known as *marriage*—with one or more persons of the opposite sex, but the nature of this relationship varies enormously cross-culturally. For one thing, the majority of preindustrial peoples allow multiple spouses. For another, the nature of the marital relationship—living arrangements, what wives and husbands expect from one another, who decides who marries whom, authority patterns, how the kinfolk of the couple relate to one another, and so forth—differs from people to people. We can only provide a brief glimpse of this diversity.

■ Marriage Rules

Everywhere, the choice of a spouse is governed by cultural norms that identify members of some social groups or categories as potential spouses and specify members of other groups or categories as not eligible for marriage. One set of rules is called **exogamous rules.** Exogamy ("outmarriage") means that an individual is prohibited from marrying within her or his own family or other kin group, or—less often—village or settlement. Since the incest taboo applies to those people whom the local culture defines as close relatives, members of one's own nuclear family and other close kin are almost everywhere prohibited as spouses. Exogamous restrictions often extend to large kin groups with hundreds of members—no one in the kin group may marry any other member, although many of these individuals are not closely related biologically.

Other kinds of marriage rules are known as **endogamous rules.** Endogamy ("inmarriage") means that an individual must marry someone in his or her own social group. The classic example of endogamous groups is the castes in traditional Hindu India (see chapter 14). Other kinds of endogamous categories are orthodox Jews, races in the American south during the slave days, and—more recently—in South Africa, and noble classes in many ancient civilizations and states.

The purpose of endogamous rules is most often to maintain social barriers between groups of people of different social rank. Rules of endogamy maintain the exclusiveness of the endogamous group in two ways. First, they reduce the social contacts and interactions between individuals of different ranks. Intermarriage creates new relationships between the families of the wife and husband, and potentially is a means of raising the rank of oneself or one's offspring. Endogamy has the effect of keeping affinal relationships within the caste, class, ethnic group, race, or whatever; this reinforces ties within the endogamous groups and weakens those between the groups. Second, endogamy symbolically expresses and strengthens the exclusiveness of the endogamous group by preventing its contamination by outsiders. This is most apparent with Indian castes, for the cultural rationale for caste endogamy was to avoid ritual pollution: the Hindu religion held that physical contact with members of lower castes put high-caste individuals in a state of spiritual danger, precluding the possibility of marriage between them.

Technically, the term *endogamy* applies only to rules or laws about confining marriage to those within one's own group. But it is important to note the existence of *de facto* endogamy, meaning that although no formal rules or laws prohibit outmarriage, most people marry those whom they consider to be like themselves. De facto racial and class (here in the sense of "social status" or "rank") endogamy exists in most modern nations, including North America. This is partly because opportunities for members of different classes to get to know one another often are limited. For instance, members of different classes tend to go to different kinds of schools and often hang out with different sets of friends. Such practices decrease social interactions and, hence, the possibilities for people of different classes to meet and fall in love. De facto endogamy also exists because of powerful norms against marrying outside of one's own "kind." Members of elite classes (and parents and other relatives of young people) may worry that would-be spouses of lower-class standing would not fit in with their social circle (to put their objection politely). Likewise, interracial couples are warned about the social stigma attached to their relationship and about the "problems" they and their children will encounter.

(Incidentally, notice how the norm against interracial marriage and even dating is self-reinforcing. The norm exists partly because of racial prejudice and partly because of the cultural fact that so many people think interracial couples and their children will face special difficulties. So interracial marriages are uncommon, mainly because of the norm. In turn, the rarity of interracial marriage reinforces the widespread opinion that society is not yet "ready" for them; if it were, there would surely be more interracial couples!)

■ *How Many Spouses?*

One clear way in which sociocultural systems vary in marriage practices is in the number of spouses an individual is normatively allowed at a time. There are four logical possibilities:

- **monogamy,** in which every individual is allowed only one spouse
- **polygyny,** in which one man is allowed multiple wives
- **polyandry,** in which one woman is allowed multiple husbands
- **group marriage,** in which several women and men are allowed to be married simultaneously to one another

The last three possibilities are all varieties of **polygamy**—meaning "plural spouses." Notice that the three types of polygamy refer to the number of spouses allowed to a person, not necessarily to how many spouses most people have. For example, in sociocultural systems that we characterize as polygynous, men are permitted more than one wife, but only a minority of men actually have more than one.

It may surprise members of monogamous societies to learn that the majority of the world's societies allow polygamy. The most common form of plural marriage is polygyny, which is allowed in about 75 percent of the societies of the world. Polyandry, on the other hand, is rare. There are less than a dozen societies in which it is well documented—less than 1 percent of the world's people. Group marriage, so far as we know, has never been a characteristic form of marriage of a whole human society. Indeed most anthropologists believe that group marriage, where it has occurred, has been a short-lived phenomena brought about by highly unusual circumstances, such as in utopian or communitarian groups (see Box 10.1).

Comparisons of frequencies such as those just mentioned face difficulties in assigning a particular people unambiguously to one of these four categories. (To appreciate this problem, answer the following question: Did the Nayar have polyandry, group marriage, or no marriage at all?) But they do give an accurate impression of how common or rare each form of marriage is in the human species.

Monogamous peoples often misunderstand the nature of polygamous marriages, seeing them mainly as attempts, usually by men, to get access to more sexual partners. We fail to recognize the social and economic conditions that make these forms of marriage advantageous. We now look at these conditions for polygynous and polyandrous societies.

Polygyny Even though most peoples allow polygynous marriage, usually only a minority of men in these societies actually have more than one wife. Thus polygyny exists as an alternative form of marriage in these societies, rather than as the predominant (most common) form. However, in those societies that allow it, polygyny is ordinarily the preferred form of marriage for men, and often for women. Men, in particular, desire to have multiple spouses, although most men are unable to achieve their goal.

Even with only a minority of men married polygynously, an obvious problem exists for some other men—namely, if some men have plural wives, this reduces the number of marriageable females so that some men cannot marry at all. This is, in fact, often the case. But in other cases, this problem is not as acute as one might think, for in many societies there are more marriageable women than men at any one time, for several reasons.

First, females mature socially and sexually at a younger age than males. A fifteen-year-old female in

Box 10.1

GROUP MARRIAGE IN THE UNITED STATES

Most Americans know about the communes popular with many young people in the 1960s and 1970s, which practiced free love and renounced personal property. Whether these communes represent cases of group marriage is debatable, for there are questions about whether "love" was quite as "free" in them as usually depicted. At any rate, most lasted only a few years. No doubt many of their former members are now monogamous stock brokers and attorneys.

So "hippie" communes may or may not represent group marriage, depending on how strictly we wish to define the term. But there is at least one well-documented case of group marriage in the United States. It occurred in an unexpected time—the nineteenth century—and among an unexpected subculture—conservative Christians.

Of course, mainstream Christians of this time stressed premarital chastity and marital fidelity. Ever since the Reformation, however, Christian sects that draw important elements of their doctrine from small passages of scripture have sprung up. One such passage is from Acts 4:

[32]The host of believers were one in heart and soul; no one claimed his belongings just for himself, but everything was theirs in common. . . .[34] Not one among them suffered need; for those who owned fields or houses sold them, brought the proceeds of the sale[35] and deposited the money at the feet of the apostles. Then it was distributed to each according to his need.

This passage served as the basis of a radical utopian experiment in Oneida, New York, initiated in 1847 by a theologian named John Humphrey Noyes. Noyes believed—not unreasonably—that the preceding scripture exhorted believers to hold property in common. He attracted some converts and founded a community based on his beliefs.

But he took the exhortation one step further. Not only were Noyes's followers required to sign over their wordly goods to the community, to eat together, to live in a single enormous house (still standing), and to work together like a giant family; "private property" in marriage and sexual matters was also forbidden. All men and women were to consider themselves husbands and wives and were allowed sexual access to one another. The tricky part was that during the first twenty years of the community the men were not supposed to ejaculate, for no children were allowed to be born, and Noyes believed that the spilling of semen was debilitating to male strength. But Noyes did make one concession to human frailty: he required young men to sleep only with postmenopausal women until they learned to control themselves. Astoundingly, in a community of around 500, only two children were born between 1848 and 1868!

The sexual aspects of group marriage in the Oneida community apparently worked as follows. A committee (no doubt under the control of Noyes, who was something of an autocrat) had the final word over who spent the night with whom. A man who wished to sleep with a particular woman submitted a written request to the committee, who sought the consent of the woman. The woman could refuse permission, or the committee itself could deny the request on the grounds that this man and woman were showing too much "special love" for one another rather than loving all community members equally. This rather unusual arrangement was a bit titillating to outsiders, and the community supplemented the income that it got mainly through the manufacture of steel traps by selling lunches to thrill-seekers who came up from New York City to see the community.

After 1868, children were allowed, but not just anyone could have them. Noyes thought that only the worthiest and most mentally and physically fit members should be allowed to reproduce. He set up another committee to which members could apply for a child-bearing permit. Thirty-eight men and fifty-three women were selected as parents, and they had about sixty children. Children knew their parents and had some special contact with them, but they were raised in a communal nursery; and all adults were supposed to love and nurture the children as if they were their own.

The Oneida community disbanded as such in 1879, largely because of internal discord and resentment caused by the elderly Noyes's attempt to monopolize the young women. But many former members continued to live nearby and formed a very successful company, also known as Oneida. Perhaps you have some of their silverware.

Sources: Van den Berghe (1979), Whitworth (1975).

most societies is socially and physically capable of being both a wife and mother. A boy of the same age may be physically able to father a child, but rarely is he capable of living up to the social responsibility of being a husband and father. Males do not attain their full physical strength and stature until their late teens or early twenties and usually it is not until at least then that they begin to fully participate in male economic and social activities. Thus women are usually considered ready for marriage at an earlier age than men, and in most polygynous societies women marry relatively young. Many or most females marry as teenagers, soon after puberty (in many cases, they are betrothed even earlier—often at birth!), whereas men often must wait until they are well into their twenties or even thirties before taking a wife. This has the effect of raising the ratio of marriageable-age women to men, and thus increases the number of men who can be married.

Second, women usually live longer than men. In large part this is due to a higher frequency of deaths among young men. They are normally engaged in more hazardous activities, such as hunting and—especially—warfare, which take a larger toll on men than women.

So polygyny does not necessarily mean that many men cannot marry because some men are monopolizing the women. Indeed, looked at from the female perspective, polygyny may have the beneficial effect of assuring that virtually all women find husbands. This is important for a woman because marriage legitimizes children, and children are generally her main or only source of social security—they are the people she depends on to support her in old age. There is another reason why it is important for a woman to marry in polygynous societies: to ensure that her children are well provided for. In the vast majority of polygynous societies, inheritance of land, livestock, and other wealth and productive property is from fathers to sons. A woman need not marry to bear children, of course, but she often does want a husband to assure her sons of having rights to an adequate inheritance; her married daughters usually acquire their rights of access to resources from their husbands. Thus, in societies in which for some reason there are more adult women than men, polygyny provides a means for almost all women to gain the benefits of a husband for both herself and her children.

As mentioned, in societies that permit it, polygyny is generally the preferred form of marriage, for it offers many social and economic benefits to both men and women. Men, in particular, generally want multiple wives. A man has both social and economic incentives for marrying several women. Socially, in many of these societies a man's status is directly related to the size (number of wives and children) of his family. Economically, there are short-term and long-term benefits, especially where woman's labor is important in providing food and wealth to her family. The more wives and children a man has, the larger the work force available. In pastoral societies in Africa and elsewhere, polygyny enables a man to increase the size of his herds, since he has more herders (wives and children) to tend livestock. Similarly, in those farming societies in which female labor is important, a polygynous man has more workers to tend fields and harvest crops. As he grows older he will have more children and grandchildren to look after his herds or work his fields and care for him. Thus as long as he has the resources to support them, a man usually tries to acquire additional wives.

What determines whether a particular man is *able* to acquire more than one wife? Usually, the answer is wealth: only well-to-do men are able to afford more than one wife. "Afford," however, does not mean what North Americans might think; it is more often a matter of being able to acquire additional wives than of being able to support them. Most polygynous peoples have the custom of bridewealth (discussed later), which requires a prospective groom and his relatives to give livestock, money, or other wealth objects to the kin of the bride. Although fathers and other relatives typically are obliged to help a young man to raise bridewealth for one wife, only a minority of men can get together sufficient resources to provide bridewealth for additional wives.

Thus far, we have emphasized the benefits to the husbands of polygynous marriages. There are also social and economic advantages for the wives. We might think a woman would not want to be part of a "harem." But generally the most prestigious marriages for a woman are to husbands of wealth and status—the very men who are most likely to have married other women. Not only are these women economically better provided for by their husbands, but polygynous marriages frequently lighten their workloads. Co-wives usually work together and cooperate on chores such as producing, processing, and preparing food, tending livestock, and caring for children. Thus it is not unusual for a wife to encourage her husband to take additional wives to assist her in her chores.

Although they have advantages for both men and women, polygynous marriages also have inherent problems. A frequent problem is rivalry between co-wives and favoritism by husbands. Several different strategies are used in polygynous societies to minimize friction within these families. One strategy is for a man to marry women who are sisters, a practice called *sororal polygyny*. Among groups who practice sororal polygyny, sometimes the husband of the oldest daughter of a family will have a marriage claim on her sisters as they come of age. The reasoning is that sisters are raised together, have sentimental ties, enjoy working together, are less jealous of each other, and are thus more compatible. An advantage of sororal polygyny is that the family can frequently occupy a single dwelling in harmony. In cases where a man marries a number of unrelated women, each wife usually has her own separate dwelling to minimize potential conflict with other wives. In these cases, the husband lives or spends time with each of his wives alternatingly. Regardless of whether the wives live in one dwelling or several, or whether they are sisters or unrelated, these societies generally emphasize that the husband should show no overt signs of favoritism.

Polyandry   Polyandry, the marriage of one woman to two or more men, is documented in less than a dozen societies. Although much has been written about the practice, anthropologists disagree on the factors that lead men to share a common wife and a woman to take more than one husband. Here we can discuss only two such factors: (1) female infanticide, which results in fewer marriageable females than males, and (2) resource scarcity, in which polyandry has the effect of limiting family size.

The Inuit foragers of Canada occasionally practiced polyandry up to the nineteenth century. Life in the Canadian arctic was seasonally difficult and starvation was always a possibility. Recognizing such potential problems, the Inuits tried to limit family size. One common form of population control was infanticide; unwanted babies were taken at birth and killed. Both boys and girls were killed, but male children were considered more desirable than females, and thus a disproportionately higher number of female babies fell victim to infanticide. The higher accident rate among Inuit males while hunting partly compensated for the difference in the infanticide rates, so usually the sex ratio was fairly balanced in a region. However, the Inuits were so widely scattered that social contact was frequently limited to only a few hundred people from among whom potential spouses would be obtained. Not surprisingly, occasionally shortages of marriageable females occurred within some Inuit groups.

Among the Inuits, a husband and wife working as a team was more necessary to ensure survival than among most other peoples. For example, during winter months game was frequently scarce, and the Inuits lived in small family units, moving regularly in search of game. Because an individual cannot survive long in the open during the winter, every move in search of food required the building of an igloo—a dome-shaped structure made of snow blocks. Only about an hour was spent in igloo construction, but the task required the labor of two people. Neither a man nor a woman alone could travel or secure food. For these and other reasons, a man whose wife died or left him had to quickly find another wife, so he sometimes joined the family of and became a co-husband with a brother or close friend. This arrangement was usually considered neither desirable nor necessarily permanent. The "second" husband usually moved out and married the first eligible woman who became available. Conversely, an Inuit woman whose husband was killed or died had also to find a new husband immediately. As a result, polyandry, polygyny, and monogamy were practiced by the Canadian Inuits, according to circumstances.

Resource scarcity has also led some people to practice polyandry. The problem of too many heirs for available resources has confronted many farming peoples. The family farm would support only a single couple, yet the family sometimes had three or four sons. Many European groups faced this problem during the Middle Ages and even up to the nineteenth century. In Ireland and some other parts of Europe, the problem was solved by the rule of primogeniture, under which the oldest son inherited the land and the younger sons had to make their own ways in the world. Fortunately there was usually a war somewhere so that some could serve in the army. Others might join the church as a priest, a monk, or in some other capacity. Daughters who could not find husbands usually either remained at home or joined a nunnery.

Some Tibetan peoples found another solution—polyandry. Tibet is an extremely mountainous region, whose rugged topography and high altitude sharply limited farm land. Traditionally, all sons, regardless of age, have an equal claim on Tibetan family property. Frequently a farm is adequate to support only a single family, but a couple may have three or more sons. If the sons divided their inheritance, none would have enough land to support a family. To solve this problem, all of the sons sometimes marry one woman. This form of polyandry, called *fraternal polyandry*, helps keep the farm and family intact and limits the number of children in the family. Though the oldest son assumes primary responsibility for the wife and children, he is not supposed to be shown sexual favoritism by the wife, who has sexual relations with all of her husbands. When children are born, each brother treats them as if they were his own, even if he knows that a particular child was fathered by one of his brothers. To the brothers, the advantage is that polyandry preserves the family property, keeping the land, the livestock, the house, and other wealth together. Also, one brother can stay behind and work the family land during the summer, while another brother takes the livestock to high mountain pastures and a third brother (if present) visits the lowland for purposes of market trade. This system also has advantages for the wife, who has multiple husbands to work for, and help support, her and her children. Her life is usually less physically strenuous and she usually has a higher standard of living than a woman married to only one man.

Although polyandry has its economic advantages, problems sometimes arise. A younger brother can at any time decide to end the arrangement, claim his portion of the family property, marry another woman, and establish his own family. The oldest brother does not have this option, because as head of the family he bears primary responsibility for supporting their wife and children.

■ Marriage Alliances

In a few sociocultural systems, getting married and being married are treated rather casually. Among the Navajo of the American Southwest, for instance, getting married usually consists of simple cohabitation, and the spouses retain their own separate personal property.

In fact, considering our own marriage practices—as opposed to our marriage norms—from a comparative perspective, many North Americans treat their marital duties rather lightly. In two studies conducted in the 1940s, Alfred Kinsey found that half of American husbands and a quarter of American wives had had extramarital affairs. (The nation was shocked, but apparently much of the surprise was faked!) Marriages also are quite liable to be terminated in the contem-

porary United States: the chances that a 1990s marriage will ultimately end in divorce approach 50 percent. We call ourselves monogamous, which we are, but divorce is sufficiently common that some sociologists have suggested that the phrase *serial monogamy* (meaning "only one legal spouse at a time") is more appropriate. Obviously, there is a large gap between our actual behavior and our norms of marital fidelity and lifelong commitment.

Most populations treat marriages as a far more serious business—so serious, in fact, that it cannot be left entirely to the free choice of the partners. Marriage frequently establishes a bond not just between the couple itself but also between their relatives. The affinal ties between kin groups created by the fact that one or more of their members are married to one another frequently are important not just socially but also economically and politically, and often ritually. Marriage establishes an *alliance* between the members of two kin groups, and **marriage alliances** are sometimes critical for the well-being and even survival of the intermarried groups. This appears to have been the case, for example, among the ancient Israelites, for Moses wrote in Genesis (34:16): "Then we will give our daughters unto you, and we will take your daughters to us, and we will dwell with you, and we will become one people." In many preindustrial populations, E. B. Tylor's hypothesis that "primitive man" was faced with the choice of "marry out or be killed out" contains an important truth.

A good example of how intermarriage is used to create and maintain ties between kin groups comes from among the Yąnomamö, a horticultural and hunting tribe of the Amazon region of South America. Every Yąnomamö village had numerous enemies with whom it was engaged in warfare. Each village was constantly under threat of attack, so each had to be prepared to defend itself; likewise, the males of each village periodically went on raids intended to capture the women and other resources of its enemies. It was therefore advantageous for a village to establish and maintain alliances for mutual defense and offense with other villages, for the more men a village could mobilize as warriers, the more likely it was to be successful in conflicts. The smaller villages were, in fact, obliged to enter into alliances, or they were soon victimized by their more numerous enemies. Another advantage of alliance formation was realized in the case of military defeat: a defeated group could take refuge with an allied village, whose members would feed and protect the refugees until they could establish producing gardens in a new location.

Marriage was a key strategy in creating and maintaining these alliances. When the men of a Yąnomamö village wished to make an alliance with another village, they began by trading. For instance, one village might tell the other it needed clay pots and would be willing to trade its bows for them; or it might say it needed hallucinogenic drugs and would trade its hammocks for them. The people of each village were capable of making all these products for themselves, but no matter: trade provided the excuse that villages used to visit one another to begin alliance formation. If no trouble broke out during the trading—for a Yąnomamö village did not even trust its long-time allies, much less its prospective allies—the relation might extend to mutual invitations to feasts. If the feasts did not turn violent, the men of the two villages would agree to give some of their "sisters" (female consanguines) to one another. This was considered the final stage of alliance formation; once the villages had exchanged women, the alliance was—by Yąnomamö standards—secure.

For the Yąnomamö, however, the "security" of an alliance was in fact uneasy. The men of one kin group (each village had at least two kin groups) would exchange their women for the women of another kin group in an allied village. These sister exchanges were supposed to continue throughout the generations: the two kin groups were obliged to continue to intermarry with one another, for each woman given required a woman to be returned. But each village, and each kin group within the village, had alliances with several other villages. The men of every kin group then had to decide to which of their several allies they would grant each of their sisters. Every time a group gave a sister to another group, they were withholding her from the other groups to whom they also owed women. Politically smart groups granted their women to those allies they needed most and withheld women from their weaker allies, who could not afford to retaliate or end the alliance. Marriage, then, was part of the political strategy of a Yąnomamö village; successful villages manipulated their sister exchanges so as to improve their odds in warfare and increase the number of wives they extracted from their weaker allies.

The importance of the ties between kin groups created by intermarriage is also revealed by two more widespread customs. In one, called the **levirate,** if a woman's husband dies, she marries one of his close kinsmen (usually a brother). The relations between the intermarried kin groups are too valuable for a woman to be returned to her own family of orientation, for then she might marry into another kin group. Therefore, a male relative of her deceased husband takes his place; and since both her dead and her new husband belong to the same kin group, the affinal relationship remains intact. The converse custom, the **sororate,** also preserves the affinal ties between kin groups even beyond the death of a spouse. With the sororate, if a woman dies, her kin group is obliged to replace her with another woman, for which no additional bridewealth need be transferred. The Zulu of southern Africa, as well as many other African peoples, practiced both the levirate and sororate. In societies with these customs, marriages—and the affinal ties they create—endure even beyond death.

■ Marital Exchanges

In most sociocultural systems the marriage of a man and a woman is accompanied by some kind of a transfer of goods or services. These transfers—called *marital exchanges*—take numerous forms. Our own custom of wedding showers and wedding gifts is only one variety. In these, the presents given by the kin and friends supposedly help the newlyweds establish an independent household. Part of our cultural knowledge is knowing the kinds of gifts that are appropriate for someone's wedding. We tend to give things that are useful to the couple jointly, with food-preparation and eating utensils easily the most common type of gift. From a cross-cultural perspective, the most unusual feature of North American marital exchanges is that nothing is transferred between the relatives of the groom and bride: the couple treats the gifts as their private property. Like most of our other customs, this seems natural to us. Of course the goods go to the couple—what else could happen to them?

Plenty else, as we shall see in a moment. For now, notice that the fact that the goods go to the couple fits with several other features of Euro-American marriage. First, it usually is the bond through which new independent households are started, so the husband and wife "need their own stuff." If, in contrast, the newlyweds moved in with one of their relatives, they would not have as great a need for their own stuff. Second, our marriage-gift customs fit with the importance our culture gives to the privacy of the marital relationship: it is a personal matter between the husband and wife, and in general their relatives should keep their noses out. If the in-laws like one another and socialize together, well and good, but our marriages do not generally create strong bonds between the families of the bride and groom. (In fact, the two families often compete for the visits and attention of the couple and their offspring.) As we saw in chapter 9, gifts make friends and vice versa; the fact that the affines do not exchange goods with one another is a manifestation of the absence of a necessary relation between them after the wedding. If, in contrast, the marriage created an alliance between the two sets of relatives, some kind of an exchange would most likely occur between them to symbolize and cement their new relations. Third, the gifts are presented to the couple, not to the husband or wife as individuals, and are generally considered to belong equally and jointly to both partners. But there are marriage systems in which the property of the wife is separate from that of her husband; should divorce occur, there is no squabbling over who gets what.

With this background in mind, what other kinds of marital exchanges occur in other sociocultural systems?

Bridewealth   Bridewealth (also known as *brideprice*) is the widespread custom that requires a man and his relatives to transfer goods to the relatives of his bride. It is easily the most common of all marital exchanges, found in over half the world's sociocultural systems. The term *bridewealth* is well chosen, for usually the goods transferred are among the most valuable symbols of wealth in the local culture. In sub-Saharan Africa, cattle and sometimes other livestock are the most common goods used for bridewealth. Peoples of the Pacific Islands and Southeast Asia usually pay their bridewealth in pigs or shell money and ornaments. Many Native Americans of the Great Plains used horses after the Spanish reintroduced them into the continent, although not all Great Plains tribes had the custom of bridewealth.

Much anthropological ink has been devoted to answering the question of whether peoples with the custom of bridewealth are "buying" their wives. Is bridewealth to be equated with *brideprice?* Bridewealth does indeed often have some elements of a commercial transaction: the "price" of the bride often is negotiated; the rights over the woman are not given to her husband until the "deal" is sealed by the handing over of the appropriate quantity of goods; the goods often must be "refunded" to the husband's relatives if the

woman proves barren or troublesome; and the goods used in the transfer commonly serve as media of exchange in other contexts.

Despite these similarities to our own commercial transactions, most anthropologists do not think it useful to consider the bridewealth transaction as equivalent to our own "buying and selling." For one thing, the object of the transaction—the woman herself—usually has at least some voice in who her husband will be. For another, unlike commodities, she has rights of her own in her marital relationship, and she and her kinfolk usually can end the marriage if she is sufficiently mistreated or if her husband does not meet his obligations to her and her children. And finally, our buying and selling of most commodities are one-time events: we pay our money and get our goods, and our relationship with the seller usually terminates and has no other aspects to it. In contrast, bridewealth nearly always establishes an enduring bundle of reciprocal rights and obligations between the relatives of the couple, rights and obligations that will last at least as long as the marriage itself (and sometimes longer).

One of the most common rights a man and his relatives acquire when they transfer bridewealth to his wife's family is rights over the woman's children. Reciprocally, one of a wife's most important obligations is to bear children for her husband. This is well exemplified by the Swazi, a traditional kingdom of southern Africa. A Swazi marriage is a union between two families as well as between the bride and groom. The payment of bridewealth—in cattle and other valuables—to a woman's relatives establishes the husband's rights over his wife. A woman's main duty to her husband is to provide him with children. Should she be unable to do so, her relatives must either return the bridewealth they received for her or provide a second wife to the husband, for which he need pay no extra bridewealth. Reciprocally, a man must pay bridewealth to gain rights of fatherhood over the child of a woman, even though everyone knows he is the child's biological father. If he does not do so, the woman's relatives will keep the child; if the woman herself is later married to another man, her new husband will not receive rights over the child unless he pays bridewealth.

Brideservice   As the term implies, **brideservice** is the custom whereby a husband is required to spend a period of time working for the family of his bride. A Yąnomamö son-in-law is expected to live with his wife's parents, hunting and gardening for them until they finally release control over their daughter. Among some San bands, a man proves his ability as a provider by living with and hunting for his wife's parents for a period of three to ten years, after which he is free to camp elsewhere.

Brideservice is the second most common form of marital exchange; it is the usual compensation given to the family of a bride in roughly one-eighth of the world's peoples. However, it sometimes occurs alongside other forms of marital exchange and occasionally can be used to reduce the amount of bridewealth owed.

Exchanges of Gifts   Rarer than bridewealth or brideservice are customs in which the relatives of both the bride and groom exchange gifts of approximately equal value with one another. Such a **gift exchange** is the custom of the inhabitants of Kosrae, an island in the Federated States of Micronesia in the western Pacific. The fathers of the couple organize the exchanges. Each father asks his relatives to provide store-bought goods for a presentation he will make to his counterpart. What kinds of goods a relative gives depends on whether he is kin to the bride or to the groom. The father of the bride asks his relatives to contribute "men's things," that is, things that a man uses (mainly clothing articles). The father of the groom asks his kin to give "women's things," mainly clothing worn by females. On the day of the wedding each father presents the goods contributed by his "side"

to his counterpart. The groom's father, upon receiving the men's things, redistributes them—either at the ceremony or later—among his own relatives. So contributors to the groom's side give women's things but receive men's things in return, either at this wedding or at a later one.

Although the couple does receive a share of the gifts, most of them are redistributed among the contributors. Indeed, the clothing items that appear on the wedding day are of assorted sizes, frequently including children's sizes. This is because in Kosrae the purpose of these exchanges is not mainly to provide the newlyweds with a stock of household goods but to provide a material symbol of the relations between the new affines. It is the initial act of balanced reciprocity that begins a life-long relation of mutual help between the relatives of the bride and groom. Again we see how exchanges of marriage gifts help to create and cement culturally appropriate relations between affines.

Dowry   A population is said to have a **dowry** when the families of a woman transfer a portion of their own wealth or other property to their daughter and her husband. The main thing to understand about dowry is that it is *not* simply the opposite of bridewealth; that is, it is not "groomwealth." It is, rather, the share of a woman's inheritance that she is allowed to take into her marriage for the use of her new family, although her parents are still alive. The woman and her family do not acquire marital rights over her husband when they provide a dowry, as they would if dowry were the opposite of bridewealth; rather, the bride and her husband receive property when they marry rather than when the bride's parents die. By doing so, parents give their female children extra years of use of the property and also publicly demonstrate their wealth.

Dowry transfers are largely confined to Europe and southern Asia. Practically all peoples that have it are intensive agriculturalists and have significant inequalities in wealth. It is a relatively rare form of marital exchange, occurring in only about 5 percent of the peoples recorded by anthropology.

Dowry is well documented for parts of India, where it includes jewelry, household utensils, women's clothing, and money. Much of the dowry is presented to the bride on her wedding day, but often her parents and maternal uncle provide gifts periodically throughout her marriage. Dowry, then, is not always a one-time expense for a family but may represent a continual drain on their resources.

■ In Fiji, the relatives of the couple gather to exhange gifts and food at a marriage. The bride's kin are on the left, the groom's on the right.

Kinship Diagrams

Before going further, we need to introduce a set of notational symbols that will be useful in the remainder of this chapter and the next. This notation allows us to express diagrammatically how any two people are (or believe themselves to be) related by bonds of kinship. The symbols appear in Figure 10.1, along with an example of how they would be used to show a married couple with five children. By stringing a number of symbols together, it is possible to make a complete chart—called a *genealogy*—that shows all the relatives of a given individual and how they are related to that individual. In these charts, or kinship diagrams, it is useful to have a reference individual, or a person to whom everyone on the chart is related. It is customary to call this reference individual "ego." In Figure 10.1, ego is symbolized by a square, to show that his or her gender is irrelevant for the purposes of the genealogy. (If ego's gender mattered, we would symbolize him or her with either a triangle or a circle.)

Postmarital Residence Patterns

A newly married woman and man establish a new family of procreation. In modern Euro-American societies they also establish a new domestic group (household)—most newlyweds get their own apartment, condo, or house. Couples do not always set up a new household in human populations; in fact, usually they move into an existing household, either that of the husband or that of the wife. In a given society, where most new couples establish their residence is known as the society's **postmarital residence pattern.** Cross-cultural research shows that our own pattern, in which couples form new households separate from their parents, is uncommon; in fact, it occurs in only about 5 percent of the world's sociocultural systems.

What are the other common patterns? By splitting enough hairs, it is possible to identify about ten different patterns, but here we present only five. In order of most frequent to least frequent, they are

Patrilocal: Couples go to live with or near the parents of the husband.

Matrilocal: Couples live with or near the wife's parents.

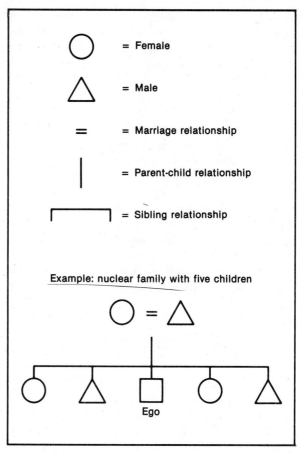

■ *Figure 10.1*
Symbols Used on Kinship Diagrams

Bilocal: Postmarital residence is optional between either the wife's or husband's kin; roughly half of all couples choose each.

Neolocal: Couples live apart from both parents, establishing a separate dwelling and independent household.

Avunculocal: Couples live with the maternal uncle of the husband.

Roughly 70 percent of all societies have patrilocal residence as the predominant pattern. Thirteen percent have matrilocal residence. The preceding two are easily the most widespread, accounting for about 83 percent of all societies. Bilocality is characteristic of 8 percent, neolocality of 5 percent, and avunculocality of only 4 percent.

What kinds of factors affect postmarital residence patterns? What determines whether newly married couples live separately or move in with some kind of relative? There is no simple answer, but property rights and inheritance forms are important influences on postmarital residence patterns. In societies in which the most important productive property is held by men, and in which inheritance passes from fathers to sons, brothers will have good reasons to join their fathers (and each other) in a common household to cooperate and protect their interest in land, livestock, or other wealth. And when the sons of most families in a society bring their wives and children into their father's existing household, this results in the residence pattern anthropologists call patrilocal. (The people themselves do not know they are practicing "patrilocal residence," of course—this is a term anthropologists use to describe and compare systems to one another.) Where important subsistence resources are controlled or owned by women, and especially if female labor is also important in supplying food for their families, then sisters will tend to live and work together, and matrilocal residence is most likely to develop.

Neolocal or bilocal patterns tend to be found in societies in which inheritance of life-sustaining resources passes through both sexes, or in which rights of access to resources are ill defined, or in which most people rely on wage labor for their livelihood. This may be why both foragers and modern industrialized countries tend to be neolocal or bilocal. Among foragers, people need to maintain access to several territories, so rights to critical resources are loose and flexible (as explained in chapters 7 and 9). Nuclear families may live off and on with the husband's and wife's bands, according to sentimental ties, short- or long-term availability of resources, or idiosyncratic considerations.

Modern industrialized peoples are generally neolocal, for two major reasons. First, job availability forces many couples to move away from their home town. This is especially true for "upwardly mobile" couples seeking increased income, better opportunities, and the more personally and materially rewarding lifestyle valued by many in the late twentieth century. Second, in industrial countries most workers do not rely on their family connections for access to their livelihood, but sell their labor on an impersonal market for labor to an employer they have never met. In other words, most ordinary citizens do not inherit productive property (capital) from their parents and do not rely on their parents for their livelihood, so they establish independent domiciles free from parental control and interfer-

ence. The result is neolocal residence and an emphasis on nuclear family ties.

It is important to add that there is no single factor that "determines" postmarital residence everywhere. Patterns of control over resources and inheritance form are important overall influences. They operate as major constraints (see chapter 2) on the choices couples make about where to live. For instance, if most couples rely on the wife's family for access to the resources they need to survive and raise children, then most couples will live with the wife's family and matrilocal residence will be predominant in the society. But a multitude of other factors also affect residence choices. Consequently, in some societies women have much control over land, yet residence is not matrilocal because these other factors are locally more important than keeping sisters together in a common household. The same complexities apply to the other residence patterns.

Family and Household Forms

At first thought, the subject of postmarital residence seems trivial (almost like a topic anthropology professors thought up to befuddle their students!). What differences does it make where newly married couples go to live? In fact, there is a good reason why residence patterns are worth studying. A moment's thought shows that the prevalent pattern of postmarital residence in a population will spatially associate a new family of procreation with one set of relatives and isolate it from other sets. This spatial association influences which sets of relatives a newly married couple cooperates with. If the postmarital residence pattern is patrilocal, for instance, the husband works with his own consanguines (father and brothers), and the wife cooperates in household chores or gardening with her affines. Postmarital residence affects the relatives with whom their children are most likely to develop strong sentimental attachments. If the residence pattern is matrilocal, for example, the children of sisters live together in a single household much like brothers and sisters and are likely to conceive of their relation as being like "real" siblings. The residence pattern influences who has main authority over the couple and their offspring. If it is avunculocal, for instance, the mother's brother of the husband is the head of the household and manages its activities. So residence patterns affect all kinds of kinship relationships in a society.

Perhaps most important, the prevailing form of residence affects the kinds of household and family units that exist among a people. Consider neolocal residence, for example. If all or most newlyweds set up their own household, separate from and independent of that of either of their parents, then a new household and family unit is established with each new marriage. This tends to emphasize the social and economic importance and independence of nuclear families, for mothers and fathers—and not more distant relatives—are most likely to be the main teachers of children and "breadwinners" for the household. The couple maintains relations with their parents, siblings, and other relatives, of course, but neolocal residence tends to lead to an emphasis on nuclear families as the most culturally important and stable family unit.

(You can see this phenomenon in modern North America: when sociologists, psychologists, and politicians worry about the decline or breakup of the American family, they are talking about the nuclear family, which they think is threatened by high divorce rates, unmarried couples living together, absent fathers, high illegitimacy rates, homosexuality, and so forth. In recent years, so many "families" have "split up" that family stability has become a major "social problem." But no one worries much about the "decline" or "breakup" of relations between married children and their parents, nor about how many married siblings do not speak to one another or have not seen one another for years. We consider it normal—which is to say, we do not consider it to be a "social problem"—when married children move out on their parents and away from their siblings. Indeed, it is generally regarded as unfortunate if newlyweds live with either set of parents, for we think that only economic necessity could force them to do so. Many of us believe that young marrieds who visit or seek advice from their parents too often are a little strange for not making their own choices and establishing their own friendships.)

But other kinds of households and family groupings exist among the world's peoples. These units—known as **extended families**—are generally made up of related nuclear families. For example, the married sons of an elderly couple may live together, and after the parents die the brothers and their wives and children may continue to live together. Because usually the related nuclear families live in a single household, here we use *extended family* and *extended household* as synonyms. Extended households usually include three and often four generations of family members.

Many anthropologists think that the form of family (household) that is prevalent in a society depends on its postmarital residence pattern. For example, with patrilocal residence, the married sons of an older couple remain in the household of their parents (or, often, each son builds his own house on his parents' land, near their dwelling). As they grow up and marry, the daughters go to live with their husbands' parents. If all the sons and daughters of a couple do this, the resulting household is of a type called *patrilocally extended*—brothers live in a single household with their own nuclear families and parents (see Figure 10.2a). If all families in the village, town, or other settlement follow this pattern, then the settlement consists of patrilocally extended households. Notice that the residents of each household are related to one another through males. The married women of the community will live scattered in the households of their husbands, or perhaps many of them will have married out of the community altogether.

The converse occurs with matrilocal residence. The mature sons leave as they marry, and the daughters bring their husbands to live with them in or near their parents' households. The household type formed by the co-residence of daughters and sisters with their parents is called the *matrilocally extended household* (see Figure 10.2b). The sons of an elderly couple will be scattered in the households of the women they have married, either in their own home community or in another community into which they have married. If most people follow this residence pattern, then the

■ *In many societies, including most of rural India, relatives live in extended households.*

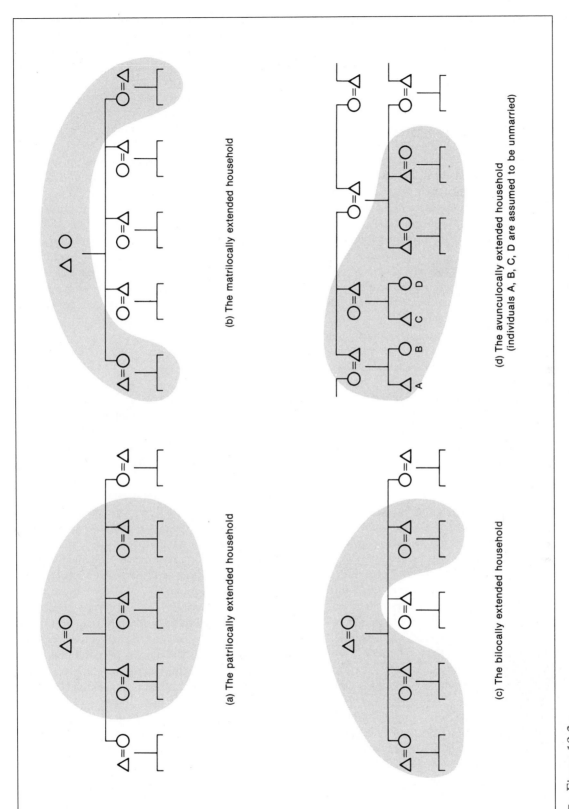

(a) The patrilocally extended household

(b) The matrilocally extended household

(c) The bilocally extended household

(d) The avunculocally extended household
(individuals A, B, C, D are assumed to be unmarried)

■ *Figure 10.2*
Household Forms

community consists of numerous households, each of which is lived in by women related through females plus their husbands and children.

The same relationship between residence and prevalent household form applies to the other residence patterns. With bilocal residence, there is no consistency in whether households are made up of people related through males or females: some couples live with the husband's family, others with that of the wife. The household type is *bilocally* (or *bilaterally*) *extended* (see Figure 10.2c). The community's households are a mixture of people related through both sexes, in roughly equal frequency. With neolocal residence, the settlement—be it village or modern suburb—consists of relatively small domestic units made up of nuclear families.

The avunculocal residence pattern associates nuclear families with the husband's mother's brother; if everyone in the community adopted this practice (which they usually do not), then the community would consist of households composed of older men (the household heads) and the families of their sister's sons. This is called the *avunculocally extended household* (see Figure 10.2d)—it includes men (and their wives and children) who are related to one another through women (their mothers)! (Confused by this one? We shall see in the next chapter that avunculocal residence makes good sense in many societies that trace their main kinship relationships through women.)

We can now see one reason why postmarital residence patterns are important: they give rise to various household and family forms. The kinds of family and domestic groups found among a people result from where newly formed families of procreation go to live. Stated differently, the prevalent household type in a human community represents the crystallization of the pattern of postmarital residence. And who lives with whom—the household type—is obviously important, since households so often hold property in common, cooperate in production and other economic activities, enculturate children together, and sometimes even worship the same ancestral spirits.

Because the prevalent household form varies with postmarital residence, the same things that influence residence also affect household form—notably ecological and economic factors like the sexual division of labor, property rights, and inheritance patterns. For instance, in most pastoral societies men are most responsible for maintaining the herds, men own the animals (either as individuals or as groups of brothers), and

men inherit their livestock from their fathers. Patrilocally extended families are therefore characteristic of most pastoral people. Again, though, we need to be careful with such generalizations. Adaptation to environment and economics are important, but their effects may be overridden by social and political factors.

In this chapter we have given an overview of some variations in the "domestic sphere" of sociocultural systems. If we were writing a book about industrial societies, we might stop our discussion of groupings formed on the basis of kinship relations at this point. This is because, among the industrialized portion of humanity, other kinds of relations and groupings—economic, educational, political, religious, and so on are organized by relationships other than kinship—by specialized firms, schools, parties, governments, churches, and so on. But, as we discuss in the next chapter, in preindustrial populations kinship principles are used to form much larger kin groups that organize and perform a range of other activities.

Summary

Domestic relations are those that exist among close relatives who live together in a common household, or domestic group. New nuclear families are formed by marriage, which reduces conflict over sexuality, forms social bonds that provide for children, establishes new relations between intermarrying families, and involves the exchange of goods and services between husbands and wives. Human biological characteristics make a relationship like marriage universal in human societies, although the form of marriage, the kinds of rights and duties it establishes, and many other aspects of the marital relationship vary. The Nayar illustrate an unusual form of marriage, if it is marriage at all.

Sexual and marital relationships are everywhere constrained by incest taboos. Sexual activity between members of the nuclear family is prohibited nearly everywhere, but societies vary greatly in the kinds of other relatives to whom the taboo is extended. Explanations proposed for the incest taboo may be divided into two types. One set assumes that family members have sexual desire for one another, so the taboo serves to ensure that these desires do not lead to actual intercourse. The other set assumes that most people have little sexual desire for their close relatives, and the taboo expresses and institutionalizes this fact.

Marriage is everywhere governed by rules, including exogamy and endogamy. Marriage systems are often classified by the number of spouses an individual is allowed: polygyny, monogamy, polyandry, and group marriage, in order of relative frequency in human societies. In preindustrial societies marriage is likely to be the cornerstone of an alliance relationship between affinal families or kin groups. The Yąnomamö illustrate the use of strategic marriages to create and sustain military alliances, a practice quite common in the preindustrial world. The levirate and sororate are customs that preserve affinal relationships even after the death of a spouse.

Ordinarily, new marriages are accompanied by the exchange of goods or services between the spouses and the families of the bride and groom. The most common forms of marital exchange are bridewealth, brideservice, gift exchange, and dowry. Generally, these exchanges are used to create affinal relationships, compensate a family or larger kin group for the loss of one of its members, provide for the new couple's support, or provide a daughter with an inheritance that attracts a husband.

Postmarital residence patterns refers to where newly married couples establish their residence. In order of most common to least common, the patterns are patrilocal, matrilocal, bilocal, neolocal, and avunculocal. There are many influences on which of these forms will be most prevalent in a given community, including economic forces and inheritance patterns. No single factor is adequate to explain the cross-cultural variation in residence patterns, however.

Anthropologists are interested in postmarital residence patterns mainly because where a newly married couple go to live influences which kinship relationships will be most emphasized in a society. In particular, the prevalent forms of family and domestic groups in a community arise out of many couples living with one or another set of relatives. The common household and family forms are extended families of some kind, including patrilocally, matrilocally, bilocally, and avunculocally extended families.

Key Terms

kin group
domestic group
consanguines

affines
nuclear family
incest taboo

exogamous rules
endogamous rules
monogamy
polygyny
polyandry
group marriage
polygamy
marriage alliances
levirate
sororate
bridewealth
brideservice

gift exchange
dowry
postmarital residence pattern
patrilocal residence
matrilocal residence
bilocal residence
neolocal residence
avunculocal residence
extended family (household)

Suggested Readings

■ Bohannon, Paul, and John Middleton, eds. *Marriage, Family, and Residence.* New York: Natural History Press, 1968.
   A collection of studies with descriptions of marriage, family, and residence from societies around the world.

■ Goody, Jack, and S. J. Tambiah, eds. *Bridewealth and Dowry.* Cambridge: Cambridge University Press, 1973.
   A collection of papers examining the causes and consequences of bridewealth and dowry.

■ Murdock, George P. *Social Structure.* New York: The Free Press, 1965.
   A study originally published in 1949 and thus now somewhat dated. Chapters on family, incest, and sex still serve as a good basic introduction.

■ Needham, Rodney, ed. *Rethinking Kinship and Marriage.* London: Tavistock, 1971.
   A collection of papers that examine cross-culturally a range of theoretical questions concerning marriage and kinship.

Most ethnographies contain a description of the domestic life of the people studied. The following are a few ethnographies specifically focused on domestic life.

■ Blesdoe, Caroline. *Women and Marriage in Kpelle Society.* Stanford: Stanford University Press, 1980.
   A description of an African society.

■ Goodale, Jane C. *Tiwi Wives: A Study of the Women of Melville Island, North Australia.* Seattle: University of Washington Press, 1971.
   Detailed account of social organization and experiences of aboriginal women.

■ Malinowski, Bronislaw. *The Sexual Life of Savages.* New York: Harcourt, Brace, Jovanovich, 1929.

Not what you may think from its title. An ethnography that describes courtship, sexual norms, marriage, domestic relations, and love magic in the Trobriand Islands.

■ Stack, Carol B. *All Our Kin: Strategies for Survival in a Black Community.* New York: Harper and Row, 1974.
An outstanding ethnography that shows how blacks in a midwestern city use family ties to cope with poverty.

■ Turnbull, Colin M. *The Mountain People* New York: Simon and Schuster, 1972.

A very well written and readable account of the Ik of east Africa. The study is disturbing because it shows the deterioration of the family under extreme economic pressures.

■ Wolf, Margery. *The House of Lim.* Englewood Cliffs, N.J.: Prentice-Hall, 1968.
A very readable study of family life in a Taiwanese Chinese farm family.

TRACING AND CLASSIFYING RELATIVES

■ *Contents*

■ (Above) *In preindustrial communities, kinship relationships organize a variety of common activities. Here a San family relaxes around the family fire.*

Those of us who live in industrialized societies find it hard to appreciate the significance and complexity of kinship relationships in most preindustrial societies. In the latter, kinship is a far more pervasive influence on the daily economic and social lives of people. It also profoundly affects how they think about themselves and conceptualize the organization of their society.

This chapter introduces the diversity of human kinship systems. As we shall see, in most societies the social bonds and groupings based on kinship relationships organize a great many kinds of activities, from production to religious rituals. We shall show how a few simple principles of kinship are used by various human populations to create groups of all sizes and to organize cooperative relationships between individuals. We also cover some of the mystifying ways in which different populations culturally classify their kinfolk into labeled categories.

Kinship

In every sociocultural system people have ideas about how they are biologically related to one another. These ideas are in part cultural, for they vary from people to people. Nonetheless, how any given people trace their ties to their many relatives seems quite natural to them. In the United States, for example, the children of one's parents' siblings all are considered to be the same kind of relative: first cousin. *Cousin* seems like a natural (i.e., biologically given) category of kinship. In actuality, the people you call *first cousin* are related to you differently. Some are your mother's sisters' children, some your mother's brothers' children, some your father's brothers' children, and the rest are your father's sisters' children. If you reply, "Yes, but what they all have in common is that they are the children of my aunts and uncles," then we have to ask, "But what makes you think that both your father's sister and your mother's sister are the same kind of relative (aunt)?

After all, you call your mother and your father by different terms because of their gender; why then should you ignore the gender of your parent when you call the sisters of both your parents *aunt?*" You might ask in disgust, "How else would you do it?"

In fact, there are several other ways to do it. There are human kinship systems in which the brothers of your father are not culturally categorized as the same kind of male relative as the brothers of your mother. In some of these, the brothers of your father are called *father* (like your biological father), whereas the brothers of your mother are called by a kinship term that translates roughly as *male mother*. There are kinship systems in which all your relatives through your mother are considered to be different kinds of kin to you than all your relatives through your father. In its kinship systems humanity is surprisingly diverse: various populations view the biological connections between relatives differently and make use of them differently in forming groups, allocating roles to people, culturally classifying kin, and establishing norms of proper behavior between relatives.

However, humanity is not endlessly diverse in its ways of reckoning and classifying kin. Most kinship systems can be collapsed into a few types, although any such typology necessarily ignores many unique features of any single system.

Before proceeding further, we should note why kinship is a topic to which anthropologists have devoted much attention.

■ *The Significance of Kinship*

In industrialized nations there are thousands of kinds of groups that organize different aspects of our lives—some economic, others social, political, and religious. Each individual participates in the common activities of a number of formal and informal groups. For example, we might belong to formal groups such as a labor union, the Audubon Society, the Republican party, and the Methodist church. At the same time, we are active in many informal gatherings made up of our co-workers, neighbors, and friends, with whom we socialize or share common interests.

Notice two important characteristics of these groups. First, they are *voluntary*: if individuals' interests change, or they find some other group of people who better meet their goals, they are free to change jobs, churches, neighborhoods, friends, and so forth. Second, they have *nonoverlapping membership*: each group generally consists of a different collection of people; we therefore cooperate and interact with different individuals in the various groups to which we belong. Socially, we are compartmentalized and fragmented: one fragment of our total self is manifested when we go to work, another aspect of our self appears when we interact with our families, and yet another appears when we worship at church. Members of each of these groups have varying and sometimes contradictory expectations about how we should behave, for we perform different roles in each of the groups. Our fellow church members might be surprised if they could see how we act on the job, but—probably fortunately—they ordinarily don't.

In contrast, among most preindustrial peoples, one lives with, works with, socializes with, and often worships with one's kinfolk. Kin groups and relationships are *multifunctional,* meaning that they organize many kinds of activities. It is as if most of the activities organized by the firms, schools, governments, churches, and other specialized groups in our own society were organized by one or another kind of kin group. Thus kinship relations are far more important to the organization of these preindustrial societies than they are to our own. In fact, when we study their organization, we generally find that it is based on the bonds created by kinship. We can no more understand these societies without studying their kinship systems than we could understand the modern world without knowing about nations.

■ *How Sociocultural Systems Vary in Kinship*

Before describing some of the cross-cultural diversity in kinship, we present a brief overview of the major ways that different sociocultural systems vary in kinship.

Range One way that kinship systems differ is in the range of people who are considered relatives. Most people have many hundreds of actual biological relatives. All populations reduce this number by (1) forgetting or ignoring some of the more remote (distant) kinship connections, and (2) emphasizing some connections and playing down others. In our own system, for example, relations beyond the range of second cousin are usually forgotten. Indeed, most North Americans do not know many of their second cousins, even by name; many of us are even confused

about the meaning of the term *second cousin,* which we cannot distinguish from *first cousin once removed.* In contrast, a great many preindustrial peoples can state precisely how they are related to very distant relatives. This is, of course, partly because kinship groups and relations are so important in the organization of common activities.

Kinds of Kin Groups A **kin group** is a group that recruits its members using some kind of kinship principle; an individual is a member of the group because a relative (usually one's mother or father, or both) is or was in it. Populations vary in how they use kinship recruitment principles to form kin groups. For example, if the recruitment principle states "everyone joins the kin group of his or her mother," the kinds of relatives in the group are different than if the principle states "everyone joins the kin groups of both parents." In the American kinship system individuals think they are equally related to the relatives of both their mother and their father (although most of us use the family names of our fathers). But some other systems largely ignore one of the parents for purposes of allocating individuals into a kin group: a person becomes a member of the group either of his or her mother *or* father, but not of both.

Normative Expectations of Kin Statuses The kinds of social relations a people believe they should have with individuals related to them in a certain way are part of the norms of a kinship system. Cross-culturally, these norms are surprisingly variable. There are systems in which husbands and wives do not sleep and eat in the same dwelling; in which brothers must rigidly avoid their sisters after puberty; in which sons-in-law are not supposed to speak directly to their mothers-in-law; in which a boy is allowed to appropriate the property of his maternal uncle but must show utmost restraint and respect toward his paternal uncle; and in which people are expected to marry one kind of cousin but are absolutely forbidden to marry another kind of cousin. In sum, many of the ways of acting toward relatives that members of one culture regard as normal are absent from other ways of life.

Cultural Classifications of Relatives Kinship seems to be a biological fact—each category of relative (aunt, cousin, or whatever) is related to you in a certain biological way, through one of your parents. Even the proportion of genes that a given kind of relative shares with you can be estimated with some precision. In spite of this, anthropologists generally claim that kinship is a sociocultural, rather than a biologically determined, phenomenon. We make this claim mainly because societies differ in the way they use the biological facts of kinship to create groups, allocate roles, form networks, and carve up the domain of relatives into various kinds of relatives. They vary in how they perceive and categorize their biological relationships. They also vary in the criteria they use to place a specific relative into a certain category. In our own kinship system, for example, whether a woman is our maternal or paternal aunt makes no difference: we still call her *aunt* and think of both our maternal and paternal aunt as the same kind of relative. But side of the family makes a difference in some other kinship systems: father's sisters and mother's sisters are completely different kinds of relatives and are called by different terms.

Keeping this overview of kinship diversity in mind, let's look at kinship in more detail.

Descent

You probably do not think about it, but you have an enormous number of living relatives. In fact, every individual has so many relatives that to be biologically related to another person in itself has little social significance. For example, if you could actually trace the genealogies of all families in any society, you would find that virtually every individual would be to some degree biologically related to every other individual. A statistician once determined that no person of English ancestry could be any more distantly related than thirteenth cousin to any other person of English ancestry. In other words, all native English people—from the Queen to a street sweeper—are related.

If this statement seems farfetched, approach the issue statistically. You have two parents, four grandparents, and eight great-grandparents. Going back in time, with every preceding generation, the number of your ancestors doubles. Assuming 25 years between generations, in A.D. 1500 (about 20 generations ago), you had over 1,000,000 ancestors. Going back four more generations to around A.D. 1400, the number jumps to over 16,000,000. Given these numbers, it is not surprising that all peoples reduce their biological

relatives to a manageable number by (1) forgetting or ignoring some of their remote kinship connections and (2) emphasizing some kinds of kin connections and playing down others.

To understand how people systematically define some *potential* biological (consanguineal) relatives as kin and others as not kin, we need to consider what makes someone a relative of someone else. A *relative* is any person with whom one shares a common ancestor. For instance, your first cousins are not your relatives because they are the children of your aunts and uncles, but rather because both they and you are descended from one of your grandparents. The relevant connection is in your grandparental generation, not your parental generation. This is because the only reason your parents are related to your aunts and uncles is because they have common parents—your grandparents. In the same way, you and your second cousins share a common set of great-grandparents.

Thus the basis for defining kinship connections is **descent** from a common ancestor, some number of generations back. The degree of "closeness" depends on how many generations back the parties must count to find their common ancestor—one for siblings, two for first cousins, three for second cousins, and so on. One way of reducing the number of kin, then, is not to recognize remote biological relatives as kin.

Another way—not used much by ourselves but quite important to other peoples—is to use the gender of connecting relatives as the basis for defining kin. A people may recognize that kin relations between mainly or only males or females (but not both) are important. If relations through males are most significant, any individual considers that people related to him or her through the father are close kin, and relatives on the mother's side of the family will be deemphasized and perhaps forgotten in two or three generations.

■ Forms of Descent

We have seen how kinship relationships are defined by how people trace their descent from previous generations. How the members of a society trace their descent, using gender and generational distance as criteria, is called the **form** (or **rule**) **of descent.** Cross-culturally, we find five widespread ways of tracing descent.

We shall consider each of these descent forms from the point of view of an individual commonly known as the *ego*, who is keeping track of and interacting with his or her relatives. To illustrate why the descent form is important, for each of the following forms we will state from whom ego will receive rights to property in the form of land, wealth, or whatever. The five forms of descent fall into two broad categories, **unilineal** ("one line") **descent** and **nonunilineal descent.**

Unilineal Descent   Unilineal systems place primary importance on the gender of connecting relatives. Descent is traced through either the male or female line.

■ **Patrilineal descent.** In this form, ego traces his or her primary kinship connections to the ancestors and living relatives of his or her father. In patrilineal ("father's line") descent systems, ego's father's kin are of primary importance, and ego is likely to inherit property from his or her father, father's

father, father's brother, and other people related to him or her through the father (see Figure 11.1).

■ **Matrilineal descent.** In this form, ego traces his or her most important kin connections to the ancestors and living relatives of his or her mother. In matrilineal ("mother's line") descent systems, ego's mother and her relatives are most important, and ego is most likely to inherit from his or her mother, or from some male relative of the mother, usually the mother's brother (see Figure 11.2).

■ **Double descent.** In this form, ego belongs to two distinct groups of kin, that of the mother and that of the father. Membership in both groups is not contradictory, since the groups operate at very different levels in the society. Certain categories of property are owned by patrilineal groups, and ego will inherit these from his or her father or father's father. Other categories of property are owned by matrilineal

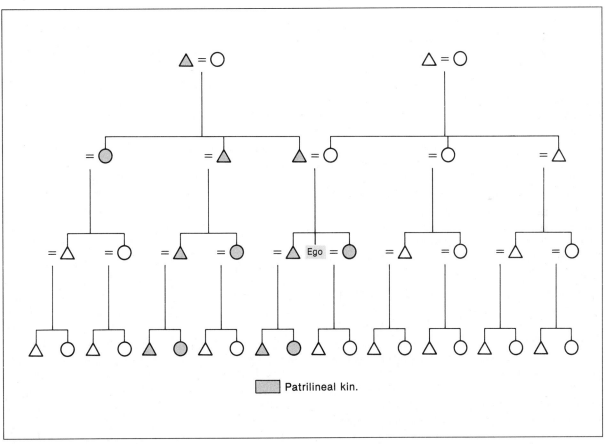

Patrilineal kin.

■ *Figure 11.1*
Patrilineal Descent

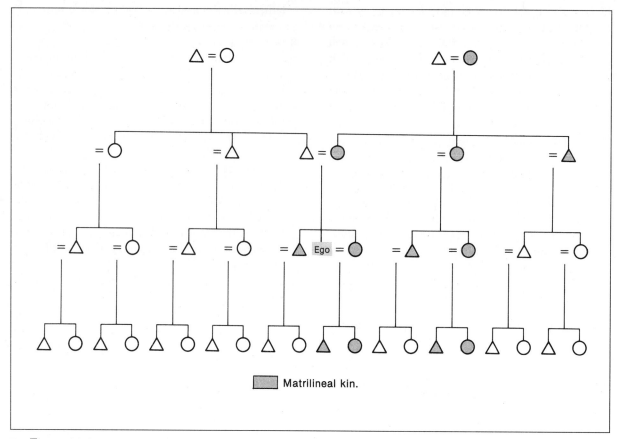

Figure 11.2
Matrilineal Descent

groups, and ego will inherit these from his or her mother's side—from his or her mother or mother's brother (see Figure 11.3).

Nonunilineal Descent Nonunilineal descent systems ignore the gender of connecting relatives in defining kinship relations.

■ **Bilateral descent.** In this form, ego sees his or her relatives on both the mother's and father's sides as being of equal closeness and relevance. In bilateral ("two-sided") systems, ego's kin through both parents have equal importance to him or her, and ego may inherit from either or both parents and from relatives of both parents. In bilateral systems, the degree of closeness between kin is based on the generational distance separating the individuals, as we know from our own bilateral system.

■ **Ambilineal descent.** In this form, ego can choose to identify with relatives of either parent, but contact with the relatives of the other parent gradually withers once the choice is made. Ego receives most of his or her inheritance from those relatives with whom strong relations are formed and gets little or nothing from the deemphasized side of the family.

Now that we have defined the five major ways of tracing descent, we shall see how they affect the behavior of individuals. Take patrilineal descent, for instance. Who are your patrilineal relatives? What individuals are related to you through males? Look at Figure 11.1. To help you identify patrilineal kin, we have shaded the individuals in the figure who are ego's patrilineal relatives. First there is your father and his father (your paternal grandfather). You can go further back in time to your father's father's father, or to your father's father's father's father, and so on. These are not, however, all of your patrilineal kin. The brothers and sons of these men are also included. Thus your father's brothers and their sons, your paternal grandfather's brothers and their sons (and their son's sons) are also your patrilineal kin. Your father's sister and the daughters of your other male kin are also your patrilineal kin. However, their children are not. Thus, although your father's sister is part of your patrilineal kin group, her children (your cousins through her) are not. Their patrilineal kin are their own father's relatives. (If you don't grasp this idea right away, think of your surname and your relatives, living and dead, who had that name. Surnames are transmitted patrilineally in our society. Thus if your last name is Brown, your patrilineal kin include all of your relatives who carry the name Brown, as well as married women who had Brown as their maiden name but did not pass the name Brown along to their children. People with the name Brown would all be related to one another patrilineally.)

How does patrilineal descent affect behavior toward different relatives? Probably the most widespread and noticeable effect is in the inheritance of property. In patrilineal societies property is passed down through the male line or, in other words, from fathers to sons. We can see the significance of this effect on inheritance by contrasting it with inheritance in our own bilateral society. You probably do not distinguish between your two grandfathers, but think of yourself as related in the same way to both. You may potentially inherit from both. But in a patrilineal society, your father's father would play a far more significant role in your life and it would be from him that you would expect to inherit wealth or receive land rights. Your mother's father would pass his property on to his sons and sons' sons—not to you, for you are related to him

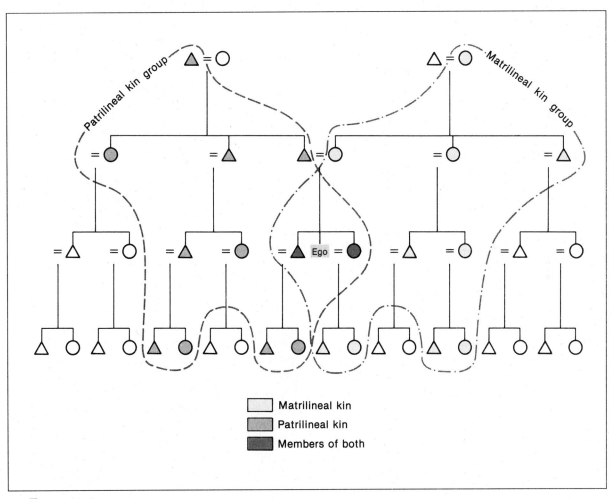

■ *Figure 11.3*
Double Descent

through your mother, not your father. A similar distinction exists between paternal and maternal uncles: paternal uncles are far more important. Finally, some of your four sets of cousins are more important than others—those related to you through males, or your father's brothers' children. It is these people who would be primarily responsible for your economic and social welfare, and it is with them and your own siblings that you would most likely cooperate and associate.

We can use the same logic to examine matrilineal descent. Your matrilineal kin are related to you through female links. They include, as core members, your mother, mother's mother, mother's mother's mother (if she is alive), plus the daughters of all these women and their children. The sons and brothers of these women are your matrilineal kin, but their children are not. On Figure 11.2, we have shaded the people who are ego's matrilineal relatives. Note that only one set of cousins—ego's mother's sisters' children—are shaded in the diagram. They are the individuals who are related to ego through female links, and therefore ego is likely to have closer relationships with them than with other cousins. Property is most likely to be inherited from one's mother and maternal grandmother and from the brothers of these women. In matrilineal societies, usually men leave most of their property not to their own children, but to their sister's children. As a result, maternal uncles (mother's brothers) are important figures in one's life, and in some respects they assume the role we usually associate with fathers, as we shall discuss later.

As we have seen, in unilineal descent systems relations such as aunt, uncle, and cousin differ from those we are accustomed to. Some cousins, in particular, will be more important relatives than other cousins: father's brothers' children in patrilineal systems, mother's sisters' children in matrilineal systems. The recognition of the fact that not all cousins are "alike" in unilineal societies has led anthropologists to distinguish between *parallel cousins* and *cross cousins*. Two sets of cousins are parallel cousins if their parents are of the same sex: so your parallel cousins are your mother's sisters' children and your father's brothers' children. People are cross cousins if their parents are siblings of the opposite sex: so your cross cousins are your father's sisters' children and your mother's brothers' children. The significance of this distinction is that in unilineal descent systems, one set of parallel cousins is always in the same kin group as ego, as you can see by contrasting the cousins shaded in Figures 11.1 and

11.2. On the other hand, no cross cousin is ever in ego's kin group in a society with a unilineal descent form.

Double descent is more complicated, for an individual belongs to a patrilineal group and a matrilineal group at the same time. In Figure 11.3, we have identified and drawn lines around people related to ego through males and females, respectively. Ego has important relations with both his or her matrilineal and patrilineal kin, but these relations are not conflicting because each set of kin performs distinct functions in ego's life. To understand this descent form, a specific case is useful.

The Ashanti of Ghana in west Africa have frequently been classified as having double descent. According to Ashanti beliefs, people receive their body from their mother and their spirit from their father. Ashanti believe that the mother's family is responsible for the nourishment of one's body, and that the father's family must provide for the nourishment of one's soul. The Ashanti are a farming people, and most land is owned collectively by groups of matrilineal kin. Rights to use this land are inherited matrilineally, through one's mother. Individuals have no rights of inheritance to land owned jointly by their father's family. (However, a man can leave property that he individually owns to his children.) Through their father's patrilineal line, children inherit their "spirit," or "soul"; and with this come ritual obligations. Individuals and their patrilineal kin observe certain religious taboos and collectively carry out religious rituals associated with their patrilineal group. The Ashanti also believe that an individual inherits his or her personality traits from the father, and thus patrilineal kin allegedly share a common personality.

In the patrilineal and matrilineal forms of unilineal descent, an individual traces his or her primary kinship relationships through either males or females, respectively. In double descent, an individual acquires different resources or rights through his mother's and father's line of descent. In nonunilineal descent forms, by contrast, people recognize relationships through both males and females: both the mother's and father's relatives are or may be important to an individual, depending on circumstances. What is the difference between the bilateral and ambilineal forms of descent?

In bilateral systems, kin ties are extended through both males and females, more or less equally. An individual considers relatives through both parents to be the same kind of relative, and may receive economic assistance or emotional support from both the mother's and father's side of the family. This means that individuals have many choices about who to associate with, cooperate with, give assistance to, pass wealth along to, and so forth. Relative to unilineal systems, bilateral kinship has the effect of widening the range of an individual's relatives and, hence, the number of people whom one can turn to for help or cooperation. Recognition of this advantage is important for understanding the conditions under which bilateral kinship is most likely to occur, as we shall discuss later.

In ambilineal descent, kinship ties are extended equally through males and females, as in bilateral descent. However, in ambilineal societies you do not become an equal participant in both your father's and mother's kin group. At some point you will join either your father's or mother's kin group. Relations with your other parent's relatives will gradually wither and you (or your children) will lose your property and inheritance rights in that kin group. In effect, although you are equally related to both groups of kin, you will become a member of one or the other. Systematically and formally including and excluding individuals from participation and rights within the kin group has the effect of limiting the size of the group and creating discrete groupings of kin that do not overlap with any other kin grouping.

It is not always easy to determine a society's descent form. Among many peoples, for instance, kin relations through males have primary importance in spheres such as control and inheritance of land, ancestor worship, economic cooperation, and succession to political office. Yet an individual may have quite close emotional ties to his or her mother's kinfolk, may expect to inherit some of their possessions, may have ritual responsibilities to them, and so forth. In most sociocultural systems, the so-called descent rule is really a descent emphasis, meaning that most people take their main relations according to the rule but many make exceptions because of special circumstances. Here again, the diversity of humanity—and indeed the complexity of actual behavior in any particular sociocultural system—makes it difficult to classify kinship systems without a good deal of ambiguity and indecision.

Despite this difficulty, we do know roughly how common each of the descent forms is among the several hundred kinship systems for which information is available. Almost half the kinship systems emphasize relationships through males, making patrilineal descent the most common form. Almost a third feature bilateral descent. About one-seventh are matrilineal, and less than one-tenth have ambilineal or double descent.

■ *Unilineal Descent Groups*

We are familiar with one way that kin relations are used to form groups, for our nuclear families are one such kin group. But much larger groupings of people can be established on the basis of kin ties. Now that we know the major ways in which descent from previous generations is traced, it is easy to see how larger kin groups—also called **descent groups**—develop.

Take matrilineal descent, for example. A matrilineal descent group exists when people descended from the same woman through females recognize their group identity and cooperate for some purposes. When a matrilineal rule of descent forms a group of people all related to one another through females, we say that the group is created using the *matrilineal principle*. We can state the matrilineal principle as "everyone joins the descent group of his or her mother." Alternatively, we can say "only the children of the female members of a group become members," or "only the group's women transmit membership rights and duties in the group to their offspring." Looking back to Figure 11.2, all the shaded individuals on the diagram are members of a single descent group. Check for yourself that only the female members pass their membership in the group along to their offspring. (What happens to the children of the group's men? They join the descent groups of their mothers, which usually will be a different group, because incest and exogamy rules typically prohibit sex and marriage between any of the group's members.)

Groups also can develop by repeated application of the *patrilineal principle*. In any given generation, only males transmit their membership rights and duties in the group to their offspring. The result of applying this principle for several generations is a group of people related to one another through males. Check this on Figure 11.1: All the shaded individuals are in the same descent group, and everyone joined the groups of their fathers. Assuming the patrilineal kin group is exogamous, the children of the group's women become members of their father's patrilineal group.

A **unilineal descent group** is a grouping of relatives all of whom are related through only one sex. A *matrilineal descent group* is a group whose members are (or believe themselves to be) related through females, or who trace their descent through female links from a common ancestress. A *patrilineal descent group* comprises people who trace their descent through males from a common male ancestor.

Using either of the unilineal descent principles, groups of various sizes can be formed in such a way that smaller groups are nested inside larger groups. A nuclear family can be made a part—or "segment"—of a unilineally extended family. The unilineally extended family is a segment of a somewhat larger group, which in turn is a segment of a still larger unilineal group. This segmentation of unilineal groups can continue until groups with thousands of members are formed. It is not even necessary that two members of the larger and more inclusive groups know exactly how they are related. If the descent principle is patrilineal, for example, everyone only need remember to which group their fathers belong. So long as only the males of the group transmit this membership to their offspring, everyone whose fathers were members will know that they too are members of the same patrilineal descent group and therefore are somehow related through males.

Unilineal descent groups therefore can be small or enormous, depending on the fertility of members of previous generations and on the genealogical depth of the group—that is, on how far back in time any two members of the group must go to trace their relationship to one another. Genealogical depth provides a convenient way to classify the kinds of unilineal

Patrilineal descent groups consist of people who are related through males. Such groups often own common property, regulate access to land, engage in cooperative activities, and share a sense of strong identity as kinfolk. These Fijian men enjoy a meal together.

descent groups that are most common cross-culturally. From "shallowest" to "deepest," they are unilineally extended families (chapter 10), lineages, clans, phratries, and moieties (see Figure 11.4).

Lineages   A **lineage** is a unilineal group composed of several unilineally extended families whose members are able to trace their descent through males or females from a common ancestor or ancestress. By the conven-

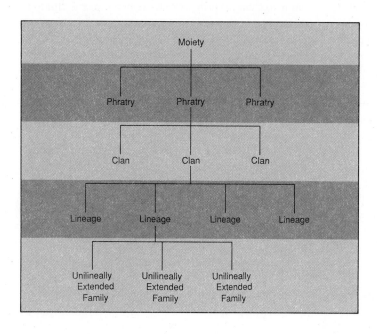

■ *Figure 11.4*
Typology of Kinship Groups

tional definition, the extended families that make up the group must actually be able to state how they are related to one another in order for anthropologists to call the group a lineage. Lineages may be either patrilineal (patrilineages) or matrilineal (matrilineages), depending on the form of descent prevalent among a people.

In many populations small lineages are in turn aggregated into larger ones. This happens because the size of lineages tends to grow through several generations. Consider a small patrilineage, for example. The group will increase its numbers as long as its male members on the average have more than one son who lives to reproduce. After several generations each member can trace his or her relations to some other members by counting back three generations (for example) to their common great-grandfather. But for other members, ego must go back five generations, to their common great-great-great-grandfather. So the largest patrilineage is segmented into smaller patrilineages; or, stated conversely, small lineages are "nested inside" larger ones.

Clans   **Clans** are unilineal descent groups whose members are descended from either a common ancestor through the male line (patriclans) or a common ancestress through the female line (matriclans). The major difference between a clan and a lineage is generational depth. The common ancestor or ancestress lived so far in the past that not all the members of the clan are able to state precisely how they are related to one another. Common descent is assumed solely on the basis of shared clan membership. Like lineages, clans are usually exogamous. Members of the clan think of themselves as relatives, and frequently refer to each other as "clan brother" or "clan sister." Clans are also named and usually corporate groups that may own or control land, religious rituals, political offices, and other forms of tangible and intangible property. Clans are often totemic, meaning that their members are symbolically identified with certain supernatural powers associated with particular animals, plants, and other natural forces such as lightning, the sun and the moon. Clans usually take the name of their primary totemic symbol, and thus have names such as the bear clan, the sun clan, the eagle clan, and so forth. It is the association with particular supernatural powers that gives specific clans control over particular religious rituals. Although the function of clans varies from one society to another, they are usually among the most significant economic, social, and religious or political units in the society.

Whereas lineages may exist without being aggregated into clans, clans are almost always subdivided into lineages. Clans themselves are also frequently aggregated into larger groupings called *phratries* and *moieties.*

Phratries and Moieties   Phratries and moieties are not technically descent groups, for their members are not thought of as being descended from a common ancestor or ancestress. *Phratries* and *moieties* are simply loose associations of clans, based on historical or religious factors. Some societies have only phratries, others have only moieties, and still others have both.

A society has phratries if its clans are grouped into three or more, usually named, associations. Frequently, a myth exists telling why a particular association of clans forms a phratry. Sometimes the myth tells of the clans living together in the distant past, and later joining with the other clans to form the existing society. The functions of phratries vary greatly. In some societies phratries are exogamous. In other societies, the clans of a phratry may collectively have the responsibility for a particular religious ceremony. In still other societies phratries are of only symbolic or historical significance.

A moiety (from the French word for "half") is any grouping of clans or phratries into two associations. Moieties are named, formally organized groups. Membership in a moiety is based on membership in a particular clan. There is usually a myth telling why particular clans or phratries belong to a particular moiety. The reasons given in the myth may be either historical or religious in emphasis. Moieties play a variety of roles in the societies where they occur. They are usually exogamous: the members of the two moieties intermarry. Villages are often divided into two halves, one for the dwellings of each moiety. Moieties may also be political units, with each moiety having its own political head. Moieties also frequently play a significant role in religious rituals. The moieties may be symbolized by contrasting elements in the universe: earth-sky, war-peace, night-day, summer-winter, or land-water. The name of the moiety is usually taken from this symbolic association, such as earth people, land people, and summer people.

Thus far, we have described the major rules of descent and the kinds of groups formed by the application of these rules over a long period of time. We have seen that groups of varying sizes and compositions can be created by using one of the descent rules as a recruitment principle. All this is abstract and somewhat technical, and you may wonder why anthropologists bother so much with kinship.

We bother because descent groups are made up of living people who work in gardens, quarrel, conduct rituals, go to war, teach their children, construct their dwellings, and carry out innumerable other activities together. If people are to work together for common purposes, they must have ways of creating groups and ensuring their continuity over time; they must have ways of assigning group members to statuses, with roles to perform; they must have ways of making decisions that affect the members. In short, they must be organized. More often than not, descent groups and kinship relations provide the organizational basis on which a variety of cooperative activities are carried out.

■ Kinship in Action

Two examples illustrate how unilineal descent principles organize cooperative activities. One is a patrilineal people of a Pacific island who call themselves the *Tikopia.* The second is the *Hopi,* a matrilineal Native American people of the Southwest.

Tikopia: A Patrilineal Society   Tikopia is a western Pacific island covering about three square miles. In the 1920s, when it was studied by Raymond Firth, Tikopia had a population of about 1,200. Tikopians traced their descent patrilineally and used this principle to establish groupings of people related through males. They viewed their society as composed of four patriclans, each with a name that passed from fathers to sons. Each patriclan was subdivided into several patrilineages, averaging about thirty members. The members of each patrilineage traced their descent in the male line back to a common ancestor—the founder of the patrilineage—who lived four to six generations ago. Each patrilineage ordinarily considered the oldest male descendant of this founder to be its head. Patrilineages were exogamous: the women of a lineage had to marry men of other lineages, so the children of the lineage's women usually did not become members of it.

What were the functions of Tikopian lineages and clans? To consider the lineage first, it controlled rights over land and certain other kinds of property. Each lineage owned several parcels of land that were planted in crops, including yams, taro, coconut, and bread-fruit. The families that made up the lineage had the right to plant and harvest crops on lineage land; once they had planted a parcel they had the right to continue to use it. They could not, however, sell, trade, or give it away to members of other lineages. The same rights applied to the parcels of land on which a family established their dwellings: they could live on one of the lineage's house sites but could not dispose of it to outsiders. The patrilineage then owned land and allocated use rights to parcels amongst its members, and each family acquired most of its subsistence through its members' access to the land of their lineage.

Ordinarily, each nuclear family cultivated primarily the lineage land of its husband-father. In Tikopia, unlike in most other patrilineal societies, the female members of a patrilineage retained their use rights to lineage land even after they married. When a woman married, a parcel of the land of her lineage was divided off for her own and her husband's and children's use. A woman could not, however, pass any of her rights to this land along to her children; when she died, the use of the parcel reverted to the patrilineage she was born into, and her children had no more use rights to it. Thus, each patrilineage allowed its female members who had married out of it to use a plot of land for subsistence during their lifetimes but not to transmit rights in the land to their offspring. (The children of the women of the patrilineage, of course, received use rights to land from their own father's lineage.)

Land was not the only property controlled by Tikopian patrilineages. Much of the food supply came from the surrounding ocean. Effective harvesting of the sea required various kinds of fishing equipment and canoes. Many, but not all, canoes were owned jointly by the members of a patrilineage, whose males members used them on cooperative fishing expeditions. A lineage thus counted ownership of another factor of production—the canoe—among its functions and organized some kinds of labor—fishing expeditions.

The social rank of individuals also was determined largely by which kin group they belonged to and their status within it. As we have discussed, the various lineages were aggregated into four patriclans. One lineage of each clan was considered the noble lineage; its living members were believed to be directly descended (through males) from the founder of the clan. They received certain kinds of respect from their clanmates. The noble lineage of each clan also had the right to select one of its male members to serve as the clan chief. Just as the lineages were ranked relative to one another on the basis of genealogical closeness to the noble lineage, so families within a single lineage were ranked by their closeness to the head of the lineage. Tikopian kinship thus had a political aspect, since authority over others was granted or refused to an individual or group largely through their descent-group membership and status.

Tikopians did not live by breadfruit alone. Like other systems of cultural knowledge, the Tikopian world view included a belief in certain supernatural powers. These beliefs also were tied into the descent system, for each descent group was allocated ritual duties to perform. Each of the four clan chiefs served as the religious leader and organizer of certain religious ceremonies. Each clan had its own ancestral spirits, which were the deceased former chiefs of the clan. Each clan also had its own gods, with whom its chief acted as intermediary.

One religious function of a clan was to carry out rituals that ensured the availability of food. Each of the four major subsistence crops was spiritually associated with one of the clans. The gods of this clan were believed to control the crop. The chief of the clan performed important rituals that ensured the continued supply and fertility of whichever crop "listened to" (as the Tikopia phrased it) the gods of his clan. Thus, each clan—in the person of its chief—had ritual responsibilities toward the other three clans.

Like clans, Tikopian patrilineages cooperated in religious contexts. Patrilineages were not residence units; rather, the members of a single patrilineage usually lived scattered along several settlements. Each patrilineage did, however, have a house that its scattered members regarded as sacred, for it was believed to be the ancestral home of the entire lineage. Periodically, the members of a lineage held religious ceremonies at this place to honor the deceased ancestors of their kin group.

The Tikopian example shows the diverse kinds of functions that often are assigned to kin groups in preindustrial populations. Patrilineages controlled use rights to land and some other kinds of property, influenced an individual's social rank, and performed joint rituals. Patriclans also had political functions, and their chiefs carried out rituals that Tikopians believed were essential for the well-being of all islanders.

Hopi: A Matrilineal Society In northeastern Arizona live a matrilineal people known as the Hopi. The Hopi divide themselves into about fifty exogamous matriclans (some of which are now extinct). Clans are not residential groups, for most have members who live in more than one of the Hopi's nine *pueblos*. A Hopi pueblo, or village, is often a single large apartmentlike building divided into many rooms, in which families reside. Each clan is subdivided into several matrilineages. The female members of a Hopi matrilineage usually live in adjoining rooms within a single pueblo.

The Hopi postmarital residence pattern is matrilocal, so after marriage a man joins his wife, her sisters, and her other matrilineal relatives to form a matrilocally extended household. Most Hopi extended families consist of one or more older women, their daughters together with their husbands, and sometimes even their granddaughters and their husbands. Because of lineage and clan exogamy and matrilocal residence, husbands are outsiders and—as the Hopi say—their real home is with their mother's extended family. The residential core of a matrilineage thus consists of its women, who live close to one another throughout most of their lives. The married men of the lineage are scattered among the households of their wives, although they frequently return to their matrilineal home for rituals and other responsibilities, or in case of divorce.

Most property, both secular and ceremonial, is inherited matrilineally. Living space, for instance, is passed from mother to daughter. Farmland, on which the Hopi formerly depended for most of their subsistence, is owned by a clan, with each lineage having use rights over particular parcels at any one time. The

In Hopi pueblos like this one, related women usually live in adjoining apartments. Although the women traditionally owned the land, their husbands did most of the gardening that supported their family.

husbands of the lineage's women, however, do most of the farming to support their families, although they themselves do not own the land.

Membership in a matriclan not only defines one's primary social relationships but also establishes one's relationships with the supernatural world. Each clan is mystically associated with a number of supernatural powers called *wuya*. Clans usually take their name after their principal wuya, such as bear, rabbit, corn, snake, cloud, sun, reed, and so forth. The members of a matriclan pray to their wuya, asking them for protection and for bountiful harvests.

Hopi religion features a ritual calendar that includes a large number of annually required ceremonies. In most cases, each ceremony is "owned" by the members of a certain clan, meaning in Hopi culture that this clan has primary responsibility to see that the ceremony is performed on time and in the proper manner. Every clan represented in a village has a clanhouse, in which the masks, fetishes, and other sacred items used in the ceremonies it owns are kept when not in use. The clanhouse usually consists of a room adjoining the dwelling of the senior female member of the clan. This woman, known as the *clan mother*, is in charge of storing ritual paraphernalia and of seeing to it that they are treated with the proper respect. The position of clan mother is passed down from a woman to either her younger sister or daughter, depending on age and personal qualities. There is also a male head of each clan whose duties likewise are partly religious, for he is in charge of the performance of ceremonies owned by his clan. A male clan head passes his position, together with the ritual knowledge required to hold it, down to either his younger brother or sister's son. In this way, the inheritance of important statuses as well as ritual knowledge is kept within the clan.

Among the Hopi, as with most other matrilineal systems, the role of father and husband differs from that in most patrilineal and nonunilineal systems. As we have seen, husbands move in with their wives and her relatives after marriage, usually occupying rooms adjoining those of the wives' sisters. A man brings little property into the marriage other than his clothing and a few personal items. Nor does he accumulate much property as a result of his marriage, for the house, its furnishings, the food stored there, and other goods remain the property of his wife's family. Although a man provides food for himself and his family by working in the fields of his wife, the products of his garden labor belong to his wife. The children similarly are viewed primarily as members of their mother's lineage and clan, and indeed they have no rights to use land, nor any claim to ritual knowledge or property, of their father's kin group.

All these factors mean that a Hopi husband has a rather anomalous position in his wife's household, for each spouse owes his or her main loyalty to his or her own matrilineal relatives, and there is little common property in which they share an interest. This feature of the kinship system seems to put stress and strain on marriages, for divorce rates are comparatively high. After separation or divorce, a man retires to the residence of his own mother and sisters until he remarries.

The combination of matrilineal descent and matrilocal residence profoundly affects relationships between fathers and their children. A child's relationship with his or her father is generally close and tolerant. A man rarely punishes his own children. Culturally this is not considered his appropriate role, for—after all—children and fathers belong to different descent groups. The father's sisters and brothers likewise exhibit warm feelings for their nieces and nephews, often spoiling them with gifts and affection. The main disciplinarians of children are their mother's brother and other members of their mother's kin group. This is partly because a child's behavior reflects well or poorly on the kin group of the mother, so members of this group have the primary duty of monitoring and correcting children.

The Hopi illustrate how the matrilineal principle recruits individuals into kin groups, in which they perform a variety of economic, religious, and social roles. They also show how the form of descent found among a people influences interpersonal relationships between relatives, such as between husbands and wives and between fathers and children.

It is important to note that neither the Tikopia nor the Hopi "typifies" patrilineal and matrilineal kinship. A wide range of diversity occurs in patrilineal and matrilineal systems: sometimes men and women have important ritual responsibilities toward their maternal relatives even in patrilineal systems; often even in matrilineal systems men have rights over land in their father's kin group or are able to extract favors from their father and his brothers; and so on. However, the Tikopia and Hopi do illustrate some of the differences between patrilineal and matrilineal peoples with respect to recruitment into groups, the allocation of roles, the nature of sentimental attachment, and the organization of common activities. They also exemplify a fundamental organizational feature of many preindustrial societies, namely that kin groups carry out most of the cooperative activities that more specialized groups perform in industrialized nations. If we compare ourselves to many preindustrial peoples for whom kinship ties are the organizational basis for most activities, we see that family relations are not the backbone of our nation, contrary to the statements of some politicians (see Box 11.1).

■ Avunculocality Revisited

Comparatively speaking, Hopi women have a great deal of influence on domestic life and control over property—land in particular. (As we discuss in chapter 12, Hopi women owe their relatively high status partly to their control over land and partly to matrilineality and matrilocality.) Because they are a matrilocal people, sisters live together and their husbands live apart from their matrilineal relatives for as long as the marriage lasts.

But not all matrilineal people are matrilocal. The most common pattern of postmarital residence among matrilineal peoples is avunculocality, in which married couples live with or near the husband's mother's brother (chapter 10). Over one-third of all matrilineal societies have avunculocal residence as the predominant pattern. Most of the others are matrilocal or patrilocal. Now that we are aware of matrilineal descent groups and know that they often control property, we can understand this seemingly bizarre residence pattern.

First, the fact that a people are matrilineal does not mean that women control property and politics. That is, *matrilineality*—descent through females—should not be confused with *matriarchy*—rule by women. Generally, even in matrilineal societies men control and make decisions about the use and allocation of land and other forms of wealth, and have more of a say than women do in public affairs. Usually the oldest competent man of a lineage has the greatest control over life-sustaining or culturally valuable property in a matrilineal society. Unlike patrilineal peoples, in a matrilineal society a lineage elder has authority over his sister's children rather than his own children, for the latter are not members of his own descent group and supposedly have their property and loyalties with the group of their mothers.

How can a lineage elder have his sisters' sons living with or near him, where he can keep an eye on them, and where they can look after their own interest in land and common property? The answer is avunculocal residence. If a man's sisters' sons bring their wives to live with them in a common residence, then the elder and young male members of a single matrilineage are localized in a single place. The married women of the matrilineage are scattered among the households of their husbands' mothers' brothers. The children of the matrilineage's women are likewise scattered among the households of their fathers, so long as they are unmarried. But as they marry, they return to their own mothers' brother's households—the place of their own lineage. In short, avunculocal residence has the effect of localizing male matrilineal relatives who have a common interest in land, wealth, or other property. It therefore is explicable once we understand how the matrilineal principle forms kin groups that hold common property, and once we realize that men usually have most control over wealth and public affairs even among matrilineal peoples.

■ Nonunilineal Descent Groups

As in unilineal descent, nonunilineal principles can establish groups of relatives who identify with one another and who are involved in common activities. They also establish many of the most important social relations people have with others. We now look briefly at the two varieties of nonunilineal descent.

Ambilineal Descent Groups The ambilineal principle establishes groups much like unilineal descent groups, except that the members are not all related through only one sex. Usually individuals themselves choose whether to affiliate with their mother's or their father's groups. In some systems people can change their minds later; in others, a choice to affiliate is difficult to alter once it is made. Like lineages and clans, **ambilineal descent groups** can hold property in common or have rights to political offices.

An excellent example of ambilineal descent is found among the Iban, a people of the tropical island of Sarawak (Borneo) in Malaysia. Traditionally, the Iban were slash-and-burn horticulturalists who lived in longhouses that were subdivided into numerous apartments. Each apartment was occupied by an independent bilocally extended family called a *bilek*. The bilek usually included three generations: an elderly couple, one of their married children and his or her spouse, and their grandchildren. The bilek owned the section of

BACKBONE OF THE NATION?

How often have you heard it said that "the family is the backbone of our nation"? From a comparative perspective, our nuclear family is a rather weak and insignificant kind of group for society as a whole. You can see this in several ways now that you have some feeling for the cross-cultural diversity in marriage, family, and kinship.

First, what do we typically want to know about people as individuals? When we meet someone for the first time, do we ask "Who is your father?" or "Who is your mother?" No, we ordinarily do not. Who a stranger's kinfolk are is of no special interest to us. We are much more likely to ask "Where do you work?" or "What do you do?"—the latter being a question that could mean lots of things but (significantly) usually is a question about occupation. College-age students may instead ask "What's your major?" This last question usually means "What occupation will you perform when you've finished school?" (You can see this by answering "anthropology" and waiting for the question that often follows: "And what are you going to do with *that?*") Culturally, we tend to identify an individual by his or her occupation; the occupational status of a person is his or her *master status*, as the sociologists call it.

Second, how do you think about and culturally categorize the organization of your society? Certainly, you do not think of it as a kinship group. You do not think of small domestic groups fitting into larger kin groups, which in turn fit into still larger kin groups, and so on. More likely, you think of it as one political and territorial unit fitting into others: cities into states, and states into the nation as a whole.

Third, what are the functions of the nuclear family—our most important kin group—in North American society, and how do they compare to the functions of kin groups in other human populations? The kinds of activities organized by the family are fewer in number than in most preindustrial societies. Even these functions are increasingly becoming alienated from the family in our society. For example, enculturation and child care, which are among the most important "traditional functions" of a husband-father and wife-mother, increasingly are being handled by babysitters and professionals in day-care centers. Domestic chores are being farmed out to housekeepers, gardeners, and others, and not just among the elite. Restaurants cook much of our food and wash the dishes afterward. The elderly typically live by themselves or in retirement communities and rest homes rather than with their adult children. Television shows and commercials entertain and— whether we know and like it or not— enculturate our children.

You may think that all this is for the better. But the next time you hear a politician using the cultural theme of "traditional family values" to win your vote, you might pause to consider what he or she means by the phrase. In particular, if you are a woman, you might wonder how this politician plans to arrange things so that you can enjoy these "family values" by staying at home with chores and children, and still achieve the standard of living you would like. ■

the longhouse in which its approximately six or seven members resided. It formed an economically independent unit, with its members cooperating in the growing of dry rice. It owned its own land, which it had inherited from previous generations in the bilek.

How was a bilek perpetuated through the generations? If the Iban had been patrilineal, each member would have belonged to the bilek of his or her father, and perpetuation would have been achieved through the reproduction of the males of the bilek. The bilek, however, was an ambilineal group: it recruited new members sometimes through its males, sometimes through its females. It worked like this: When a couple married, they moved either into the apartment of the husband's family or of the wife's family. (Although the Iban did not plan it this way, the newly married couples lived with the husbands' and wives' families with almost equal frequency.) Once they had moved in with either set of parents, the couple lost the right to use or inherit the land of the other set of parents. So if the couple lived with the wife's parents, they gave up the husband's rights to the property of his parents, for no Iban could have rights to the land of more than one bilek at a time. When, in the course of time, this couple matured and had children of their own, they assumed control over the bilek's land and heirlooms. When their children grew up and married, they in turn would have to choose between their bilek and the bilek of their spouses. And once they chose, their children had no more rights in the land of the bilek that they abandoned.

Bilateral Descent Groups and Networks With unilineal descent, individuals acquire membership in the group of only one of their parents. With ambilineal descent, although there is no consistent pattern of affiliation with either parent, individuals likewise end up as effective members of only one group.

What about groupings of relatives formed using the bilateral principle? It might seem that the bilateral principle works much like the others, except that everyone becomes a member of the groups of both their parents, so that everyone belongs simultaneously to two groups rather than one. In fact, however, everyone would belong to several groups, for everyone would belong to all the groups to which their parents belonged. This would be four groups, at least, since both parents belong to two groups (from each of their parents) and perhaps people would belong to eight or even sixteen groups (if their parents kept membership in all the groups to which they belonged).

This means that bilateral kinship relations are usually not the basis for forming large groupings of kin who own common property, worship common ancestors, or perform the other functions discussed for unilineal and ambilineal descent groups. This is because such large groups would have greatly overlapping membership: if everyone belongs to all the kin groups to which their parents belong, then over the course of two or three generations everyone could trace a kinship connection to practically every group in the community. So practically everyone would have a "right" to use the land, to inherit or benefit from the wealth, and to worship the ancestor of every group. The rights would be so diffused, the membership would overlap so much, and the group would be so ill defined that the terms *rights, membership,* and *group* would have little meaning. Consequently, societies that trace their kinship ties bilaterally rarely have kin groups much larger than bilocally extended families.

Yet in many bilateral societies distant relatives are still important in the lives of individuals. For instance, people may want to call out their kinfolk to help them clear land or construct dwellings; to help them in a dispute or feud; to offer hospitality when they are away from their communities; to attend and provide economic and emotional support at their weddings; or to pay respects at their funerals. In bilateral systems, individuals mobilize their bilateral kinfolk for these and other specific purposes.

The people whom an individual mobilizes on such occasions are called the individual's **kindred.** A kindred consists of all the relatives that a specific person traces "outward" from himself or herself. If we imagine a woman named Sarah, all the relatives she recognizes make up her kindred. (In the United States, the kindred would be the people who attend weddings and who get together for what we call family reunions.) When she wants help or cooperation or support, Sarah calls upon ("mobilizes") certain members of her kindred. Although these people may not be relatives to each other, and certainly do not own any property in common, they get together on Sarah's behalf whenever she asks them for help, or whenever local cultural norms require them to gather for a special occasion in Sarah's life.

The inhabitants of Kosrae Island in Micronesia, whom we introduced in the last chapter, exemplify some of the ways kindreds are formed out of bilateral relations. Kosraens keep fairly close track of their bilateral kin connections with other people. Members of an individual's kindred have rights and obligations toward him or her. At weddings many bilateral kin attend the ceremony and present the appropriate kind of gift. A man also is likely to call upon members of his kindred to supply labor when he wishes to build a new house; scores of relatives and friends gather on the house site and devote a day of work to their kinsman. He later reciprocates when one of his relatives needs labor for a similar purpose. Funerals also are occasions on which bilateral kindreds are activated. The relatives of the deceased gather at one of the dwellings of his or her sons for an enormous feast. They bring massive quantities of food, in olden times enough to feed themselves and other guests for several days. They mourn, sing religious songs, and generally try to comfort the closest relatives of the dead person.

Kosrae exemplifies how people mobilize their kindreds for specific purposes. Although there are no kin groups larger than extended households, there are rights and duties that accompany distant kinship statuses, and people rely on their bilateral relatives for aid on culturally defined occasions.

■ Influences on the Form of Descent

As we have seen, descent principles can be used in several ways to establish groups and networks of kinfolk. Why does a given population develop one form of descent rather than another? More broadly, are there any general explanations for patrilineal, matrilineal, ambilineal, and bilateral descent? In spite of decades of searching for answers to such questions, we have not yet identified a single influence or small number of influences that account for all or even most cases. Anthropologists agree that descent systems are strongly affected by other aspects of the way of life of a people, but do not agree on what these "other aspects" are. We present only a few of the popular hypotheses.

One proposed influence is the primary mode of adaptation of a population. For instance, one might argue that foraging bands trace their descent bilaterally, for the following reasons. Because most foragers are subject to seasonal, annual, and spatial fluctuations in their natural food supply, they find it advantageous to maintain kin ties with a large number of other bands (see chapters 7 and 9). Tracing descent unilineally in effect reduces the number of potential bands with which a family can affiliate when the need arises. Therefore, bilateral descent emerges as a way to increase the number of social contacts and the number of territories to which a family has access when times are hard in their usual foraging areas. This hypothesis is supported by some cross-cultural studies. In one comparative study, 61 of 101 hunting-gathering populations were found to be bilateral, only 19 patrilineal, and only 13 matrilineal.

A similar adaptive argument might apply to pastoralists. One hypothesis begins with the observation that herds most often are managed and owned by men.

■ *Most nomadic pastoralists are patrilineal, because, according to one hypothesis, men usually own and manage the livestock. These Bedouins are taking their sheep to market.*

To conserve labor in herding, owners often combine their animals into a single herd, usually owned and managed by a group of brothers. Descent therefore develops through males, because brothers will want to stay together for cooperative herd management after their marriages. Comparative data support this hypothesis: fifty-one of sixty-six pastoral populations in the study just mentioned traced their descent patrilineally.

Patrilineal descent also has been interpreted as a way to improve success in intergroup warfare. It keeps a group of related males together and thereby increases their willingness to cooperate, as well as decreases the chances of male relatives becoming antagonists in battles. Several cross-cultural studies have found a strong association between patrilineal descent and intergroup warfare. But exactly why this correlation exists is a subject of much dispute.

What are some hypotheses about the causes of matrilineal descent? It was once thought that the tracing of kinship ties through the maternal line was a primeval characteristic of early humans. That is, in the early stages of sociocultural evolution, descent must have been matrilineal. The logic was that in "primitive hordes"—as these imaginary early populations were often called—people would have been ignorant that the sexual act is responsible for children, so they could have had no concept of paternity. But such a concept seems to be required to develop descent through males. At any rate, it was argued that mating was so promiscuous that people could not have known which of their mother's many sexual partners was their father. If these "savages" were ignorant of the biological basis of reproduction, and promiscuous besides, then descent had to have been reckoned through one's mother. The matrilineal peoples of today were explained as holdovers from this primitive condition, which once characterized all of humankind.

Thanks to the ethnographic research of the twentieth century, we now know that few, if any, "savages" fail to realize the connection between sexual relations and children. We also know that, if anything, mating and marriage are everywhere governed by cultural norms of incest and exogamy and nowhere are totally promiscuous. Matrilineality must have another explanation.

Unfortunately, there is no agreement on this explanation. As with nonunilineal and patrilineal rules, some ethnologists think matrilineal descent is somehow connected to the way matrilineal peoples make their living. In 1961, David Aberle published a cross-cultural tabulation of the relationships between descent form and subsistence types. He found that 56 percent of all matrilineal peoples derive most of their food from horticulture, only 16 percent are foragers, 11 percent practice plow agriculture, and a mere 4 percent are predominantly pastoral. The remaining 13 percent of matrilineal peoples practice some combination of these types of subsistence. So matrilineality is more likely to be found among horticultural populations than among those with any other system of food production.

Yet the reverse is not true: the majority of horticultural peoples are not matrilineal, but patrilineal or nonunilineal. That is, if a people are matrilineal, the odds are better than 50–50 that they practice horticulture; but the fact that they practice horticulture does not by itself cause them to develop matrilineal descent. Apparently, then, matrilineality is most likely to be found among horticulturalists, who also have some other characteristics.

A study by Melvin and Carol Ember suggests that horticulture plus long-distance warfare or trade is likely to lead to the development of matrilineal descent. The reasoning is that if the menfolk are far away fighting or trading much of the time, they cannot at the same time be gardening to feed their relatives; so women will have to take over most of the subsistence labor. They are unlikely to do this effectively if postmarital residence is patrilocal, for then they would be working for their husbands' kinfolk rather than for their own. At any rate, a middle-aged or elderly couple will want to keep their daughters around after they marry, to work their land. So postmarital residence is most often matrilocal. Matrilocality has the effect of localizing a group of sisters and other women related through females in a single area; their brothers and male relatives disperse as they move away after their marriage. This ultimately leads to the tracing of descent through the mother, since most people will have closer relations to their mother's kin than to their father's kin.

It is important to note that this hypothesis is not accepted by all anthropologists, many of whom believe that there is no universal explanation. It does seem to work reasonably well for some matrilineal peoples, such as the Iroquois and Huron of North America and the Nayar of south India. Almost certainly, no single or small number of determinants suffice to explain all cases of matrilineality, or, for that matter, the other forms of descent. Thus, there is no agreement among anthropologists on how best to explain the cross-cultural variations in forms of descent. It may be that the form of descent a people develops is influenced by so many kinds of complex factors that no generalized explanation is possible.

Systems of Classifying Relatives

So far, we have dealt primarily with the *social* dimensions of human kinship systems: kinship groups, roles, relationships, networks, and the like. There is, of course, also a *cultural* dimension to any kinship system: there are a peoples' classifications of kinds of relatives, norms about how specific relatives ought to act toward one another, feelings toward kin and symbolic expressions of those feelings, and other kinds of shared knowledge about kinship.

Here we discuss only one aspect of the culture of kinship, namely, the ways in which various populations classify their kinfolk into kinds, or labeled categories. The labeled categories are called **kin terms,** and the way in which a people classify their relatives into these categories is called their **kinship terminology.**

We generally think of kin terms as reflections of biological (genetic) relationships between individuals: we think the persons we call *cousin* are related to us through certain biological connections, for instance. This is true for some English kin terms: the terms *mother, father, son, daughter, sister,* and *brother* define individuals related to us in distinct genetic ways. However, this is not true for all our kin terms. Consider the term *uncle.* It actually classifies together into a single term men who are related to you in four different ways: your father's brother, mother's brother, father's sister's husband, and mother's sister's husband. Note that both consanguineal and affinal kin are included in the term *uncle.* The same idea applies to some other English terms; a particular term will group together several individuals related to you in different ways. Thus, *grandfather* includes both mother's father and father's father; *grandmother* is used for both mother's mother and father's mother; and *aunt* is applied to all female siblings of parents as well as to the wives of all male siblings of one's parents. The term *cousin* likewise applies to a wide range of relationships.

Generally speaking, a peoples' kinship terminology only partly reflects the biological relationships between individuals. More fundamentally, it reflects the various social norms, rights and duties, and behavioral patterns that characterize relationships between kinfolk. Collapsing relatives of different kinds into a single term reflects the social and cultural fact that people think of them as the same kind of relative; in turn, people conceive of them as the same kind of relative because they have similar kinds of relations with them. Thus the men we call *uncle* have the same general kinds of social relationship with us regardless of whether they are our mother's or father's brothers. Under most conditions, people in American society would not expect to inherit much from their uncle (unless he was childless or very rich), but if a parent or grandparent left you out of their will you would probably be hurt. Similarly, we think that a child should be disciplined mainly by mothers and fathers and only secondarily by uncles and aunts.

Before we can discuss particular kinship terminologies, we need to understand the logical principles by which they are constructed. No matter how strange some systems may appear to us (and some seem strange indeed), all are logically constructed. For one thing, every term has a reciprocal term. For example, the reciprocal of *grandfather* is either *granddaughter* or *grandson*. If you call a woman *mother*, she will call you *son* or *daughter*.

Kinship terminologies are constructed using several criteria. Three of the most important are type of relative, gender, and generation. In the following discussion, "ego" refers to the person using the given kin term.

Everyone has two types of relatives, consanguines and affines (see chapter 10). Some kinship terminologies make a distinction between these two types of relatives and some do not. In English we are not consistent. The terms *uncle* and *aunt*, for example, are applied to both consanguines and affines. However, we also use terms like *mother-in-law* and *son-in-law*, which allow us to differentiate between whether an individual is a blood relative or an affine.

The gender of the individual being referred to is usually a relevant criteria for the kin term used. In English, gender matters for terms like *brother* and *sister*, *uncle* and *aunt*, and *grandfather* and *grandmother*. Indeed, gender is the only criteria that distinguishes the relatives just mentioned from one another. However, gender is irrelevant for another of our kin terms, *cousin*.

Kinship terms usually, but not always, reflect whether the individual referred to is of the same or a different generation than ego's. Thus specific terms are used for relatives in ego's own generation, in ego's parents' generation, and in ego's childrens' generation. In describing kinship terminologies, we call ego's parents' generation the *first ascending generation* and ego's children's generation the *first descending genera-*

tion. Although the terms used in most kinship terminologies reflect generations, two systems of terminology use terms that transcend generations. In one of these, the Omaha, ego calls a certain newborn infant by the same kin term she uses for her mother's brother!

■ *Varieties of Kinship Terminology*

We shall discuss only the six most common types of kinship terminology: Eskimo, Hawaiian, Iroquois, Omaha, Crow, and Sudanese. Do not be misled by the names of these systems. Lewis Henry Morgan, the American anthropologist who we mentioned in chapter 5, developed the basic classification system for kinship terminology in 1871. He named each system after the first people among whom he discovered it. Most systems are named after Native American groups, but all these systems are found scattered around the world. To simplify our discussion, we consider only terms used for consanguineal relatives in ego's generation and in ego's first ascending (parental) generation. To make these systems easier to understand, we translate the terms into what would be their closest English equivalents. Keep in mind that these translations are only rough approximations, and that some terms have no English equivalents.

Eskimo   Eskimo kinship terms are the easiest for English speakers to understand because this is the system we use (see Figure 11.5). In this system, ego's biological mother is called *mother* and ego's biological father is called *father*. These are the only two people to whom these terms apply. The term *aunt* is used for both ego's father's sister and mother's sister, and the term *uncle* is used for father's brother and mother's brother. The terms *brother* and *sister* are used only for the children of ego's biological mother and father. The term *cousin* is used for all children of ego's uncles and aunts. Whereas in English we do not distinguish gender in our cousin terms, in Spanish the term *primo* is used for a male cousin and the term *prima* for a female cousin. It does not matter if a particular terminology distinguishes the gender of ego's cousins; it would still be classified as an Eskimo system as long as unique terms are applied to members of ego's nuclear family.

Hawaiian   Hawaiian kinship terminology is the simplest because it uses the fewest terms. It is sometimes referred to as a *generational system* (see Figure 11.6). All relatives in ego's first ascending generation are called

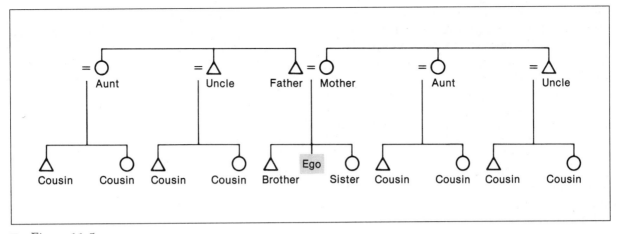

■ *Figure 11.5*
Eskimo Kinship Terminology

either *mother* or *father*: the term *mother* is extended to include ego's mother's sister and father's sister, and *father* is extended to include father's brother and mother's brother. In ego's own generation, everyone is called either *brother* or *sister*. Thus Hawaiian terminology includes no terms equivalent to the English terms *uncle*, *aunt*, or *cousin*. Although the Hawaiian system extends the terms *mother* and *father*, this does not mean that individuals do not know or are unable to distinguish their biological parents from their other relatives of the parental generation.

Iroquois   Iroquois kinship terminology categorizes relatives very differently than do either the Hawaiian

or Eskimo systems (Figure 11.7). The term *father* includes father's brother, but not mother's brother. *Mother* includes mother's sister, but not father's sister. The term *uncle* is used only for mother's brother; *aunt* is used only for father's sister. If we look at ego's generation, we also see a difference. The children of father's brother and mother's sister are called *brother* and *sister*. The term *cousin* is used only for the children of mother's brother and father's sister. Thus in the Iroquois system, ego differentiates cousins. Although this distinction may seem unusual to us, it also exists in the Omaha, Crow, and Sudanese systems, so we need to understand the reasoning behind it.

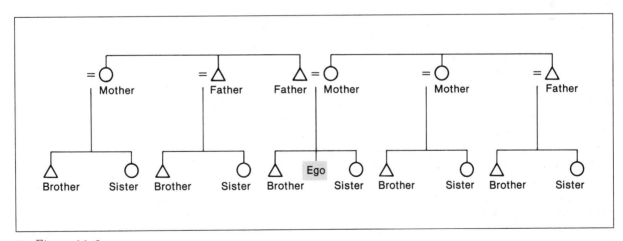

■ *Figure 11.6*
Hawaiian Kinship Terminology

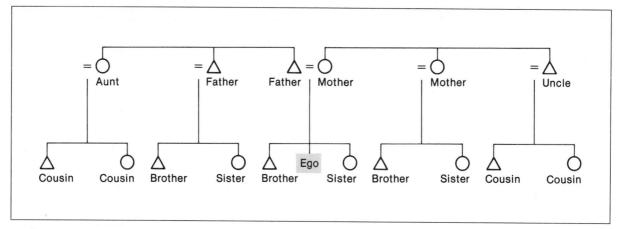

■ *Figure 11.7*
Iroquois Kinship Terminology

The Iroquois system distinguishes between parallel and cross cousins. Parallel cousins are terminologically classified with ego's own brothers and sisters. Cross cousins are distinguished from parallel cousins and called by a term that we would probably translate as *cousin*. To understand the logic behind calling parallel cousins *brother* and *sister* and cross cousins *cousin*, we have to go back to the terms used for ego's parents' siblings. Ego's father's brother and mother's sister, who are parents of ego's parallel cousins, are called *father* and *mother*, respectively. Thus it is logical to call their children *brother* and *sister* (what do you call the children of the people you call *mother* and *father?*). Ego calls his father's sister *aunt* and his mother's brother *uncle*, so it is logical to call their children (ego's cross cousins) by a term we would translate as *cousin*.

Omaha Omaha is the most difficult kinship terminology for English speakers to understand (see Figure 11.8). The terms used in the first ascending generation are identical to the Iroquois system. Also, as with the Iroquois system, parallel cousins are called *brother* and *sister*. The only difference between Iroquois and Omaha is how cross cousins are treated. Omaha terminology has no equivalent to the English term *cousin*. In addition, in Omaha terminology a distinction is made between cross cousins on the mother's side (the children of mother's brother) and cross cousins on the father's side (the children of father's sister). Mother's brothers' daughters are called *mother*, and mother's brothers' sons are called *mother's brother* (or *uncle*).

Thus ego's maternal cross cousins are grouped with individuals in ego's parents' generation. The situation appears even more confused for ego's paternal cross cousins, since the terms used depend on ego's sex. If ego is a male, he calls his father's sisters' children *niece* and *nephew*. If ego is a female, she calls her father's sisters' children *son* and *daughter*.

Why are there two separate terms for father's sisters' children, depending on the sex of ego? Actually this distinction is perfectly logical. Remember that kinship terms are reciprocal and that we have only indicated the terms used by ego. To understand why the sex of ego is important in this relationship, we must ask: What would father's sisters' children call ego? In Figure 11.8 you can see that ego is their mother's brothers' child. Thus if ego is female, they would call her *mother*, and she would reciprocate by calling them *son* or *daughter*. If ego is male, they would call him *uncle* and therefore he would call them *niece* or *nephew*.

Crow Crow terminology is sometimes said to be the mirror image or reverse of Omaha (see Figure 11.9). First ascending generation terms are the same as in the Omaha and Iroquois systems. As in the Omaha and Iroquois systems, parallel cousins are called *brother* and *sister*. Once again the difference is in the terms used for cross cousins. In the Crow system, father's sisters' children are called *father* and *father's sister* or *aunt*. Using the same logic discussed for Omaha systems, in Crow systems mother's brothers' children are called *son* or *daughter* if ego is male and *niece* or *nephew* if ego is female.

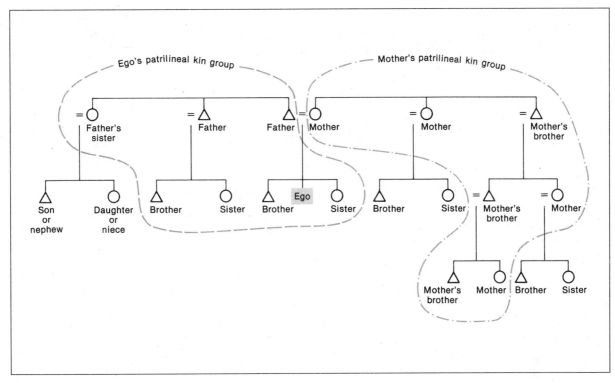

■ *Figure 11.8*
Omaha Kinship Terminology

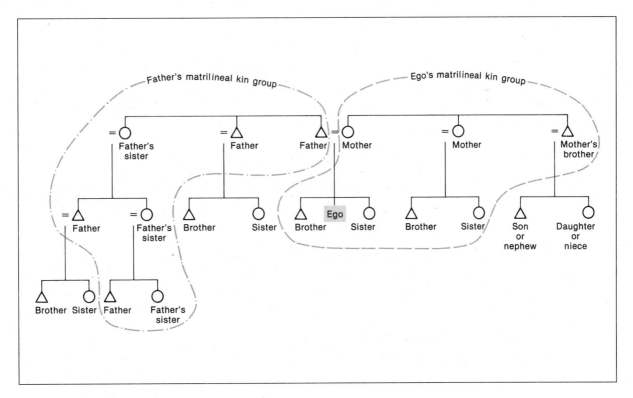

■ *Figure 11.9*
Crow Kinship Terminology

Sudanese Sudanese terminology maximizes the number of distinctions made, and hence the number of terms (see Figure 11.10). The terms *father* and *mother* are used only for one's biological parents. Our general term for *uncle* has no equivalent. Instead, distinct terms are used for father's brother and for mother's brother. Similarly, there is no equivalent to our term *aunt*; rather, separate terms exist for father's sister and mother's sister. In Sudanese, as in Eskimo terminology, the terms *brother* and *sister* are applied only to ego's siblings. There is no equivalent to the English *cousin*. Parallel cousins are distinguished from cross cousins, and separate terms are used for each.

There are a few other systems, but these six are the most widespread. This diversity is surprising, and some of the ways of classifying relatives are puzzling. Can we account for them?

■ *Determinants of Kinship Terminology*

In previous chapters, we have emphasized that sociocultural systems are integrated: one aspect "fits" with others and sometimes makes sense only when understood in context. In kin terminology systems we have a prime example of this integration, so it is worthwhile to see how we can make sense of them.

A good way to begin is by noting that the six terminologies described can be separated into two types. In the Eskimo, Hawaiian, and Sudanese, the side of the family does not matter in classifying relatives; in the Iroquois, Omaha, and Crow, it does.

Stated another way, among the diverse peoples who use the Eskimo, Hawaiian, or Sudanese system, the logical principle of distinguishing relatives according to side of ego's family is irrelevant; they *could* recognize the distinction between mother's and father's kin, but (like ourselves) they do not. Among the many peoples who use the Iroquois, Crow, or Omaha system, the logical principle of distinguishing relatives according to family side is relevant. Why should the side of the family matter in some terminological systems, but not in others?

You might already have guessed the answer. The side of the family matters in some systems because some people trace their descent through only one of their parents. The side of the family makes no difference in other systems because these populations trace their descent through both parents. The prevalent rule of descent and the relationships between kin are the most important "other aspects" of a peoples' sociocultural system that influence the way they culturally categorize their relatives. *In general* the way a people trace their descent affects the relationships between kinfolk, which affects how relatives are placed into cultural categories, which affects the terms that are used to refer to various kin.

Why say "in general"? Because the correlations between types of kinship terminologies and forms of descent are far from perfect. In a moment, for example, we shall show that the logical principles underlying the Omaha classification make sense for systems in which patrilineal descent is predominant; unfortunately, not

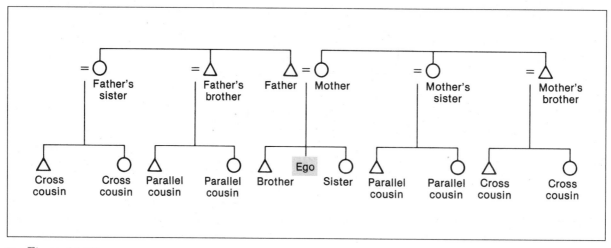

■ *Figure 11.10*
Sudanese Kinship Terminology

all patrilineal systems also have Omaha terminologies, and not all Omaha terminologies occur in patrilineal systems. Here again, humankind's complexity defies our attempts to explain something totally, and we must be satisfied with general correlations that have many exceptions.

Since the Eskimo classification is most familiar, we begin with it. If we compare it with the other systems, it differs in two main ways: (1) it makes no distinctions between ego's father's and mother's relatives, and (2) no other relatives of any kind are lumped together with nuclear family relatives. Assume that these two features reflect our ideas about how various kin are related. We might conclude that people think (1) that both sides of the family are of equal importance to an individual (or, rather, there is no systematic *pattern* of importance through one side over the other), and (2) that nuclear family relatives are somehow special and are thought of differently than are other kinds of relatives. In the case of the contemporary United States, we happen to be right. Our surnames are inherited through males, but other than this, we are no more likely to have special relationships with our kin through our fathers than through our mothers. And, generally, the members of our nuclear families *are* special: we do not expect to inherit much, if anything, from other relatives; we usually do not live in extended households; we do not have any ancestors to worship as a large kin group; kin groups larger than the nuclear family do not usually own property in common; and so on. The hypothesis that the prevalent forms of descent, groupings, and relationships are reflected in kin terminology seems to account nicely for why the Eskimo system developed among ourselves.

More generally, we ought to expect the Eskimo classification of relatives to be associated with nonunilineal descent systems. And, usually, it is: about 80 percent of all societies that use the Eskimo terminological system have either bilateral or ambilineal descent. This is because, in nonunilineal systems, neither side of any given ego's family is consistently emphasized, nor does any ego consistently join the kin group of her or his mother or father. Ego therefore does not have different relations with his parents' relatives, and therefore does not think of his or her mother's or father's relatives as being any different. This view is reflected in the terminological system.

What about the Hawaiian system? Like the Eskimo, family side is irrelevant. Logically, it ought, then, to be associated consistently with nonunilineal descent. The fact that it lumps other relatives with nuclear family members seems to indicate that the nuclear family is submerged or embedded in larger extended households or some other kind of nonunilineal group or category. Ego should have important relations with the siblings of his or her parents and with their children. In spite of this logic, the Hawaiian terminology is not as consistently associated with nonunilineal descent as is the Eskimo terminology: only about 60 percent of societies that use the Hawaiian classification are nonunilineal. Apparently the Hawaiian system is also compatible with unilineal descent.

And the Iroquois? Ego's father and father's brother are assigned a single term, which is different from mother's brother. Mother and mother's sister are given the same term, which is not the same term as ego uses for father's sister. Thus ego distinguishes between maternal and paternal aunts and uncles in the first ascending generation. The fact that the side of the family matters in this generation seems to imply unilineal descent. And in fact the Iroquois system is usually found among peoples who trace their descent unilineally: around 80 percent of all Iroquois terminologies occur in unilineal descent forms. If you look back to Figure 11.7, you will see that ego classes with his own brother and sister the children of relatives he classes with mother and father. This certainly makes logical sense—if you call someone *mother*, it is sensible to call her son *brother*. The cross cousins have a separate term because their parents are not classed with ego's own biological parents, which again is logically consistent.

The Omaha system also distinguishes between sides of the family, like the Iroquois. In fact, it carries the distinctions between the mother's and father's side "down" into ego's own generation. If you look back to Figure 11.8, you will see that the Omaha differs from the Iroquois by its splitting of cross cousins according to whether they are related to ego through ego's mother or father. Mother, mother's sister, and mother's brother's daughter are lumped, although they are members of different generations. Mother's brother and mother's brother's son likewise are lumped together under a single term.

What can explain this way of classifying relatives? The fact that these relatives are all related to ego through ego's mother must mean something; and the fact that they are classified ("lumped") together and distinguished only by their gender must be significant. Indeed, both these features are clues to the logic behind the Omaha terminology. It tends to be found among peoples who use the patrilineal principle to form kin groups.

How does patrilineal descent make sense of the Omaha system? In Figure 11.8, we have drawn a line around all those relatives on the chart who belong to ego's own patrilineal group. Notice that the cousins in ego's group are called *brother* and *sister,* to reflect the fact that they are in ego's own lineage or other kin group. We have drawn another line around those relatives who are members of ego's mother's patrilineal group. Notice that all the members of this latter group are assigned only two terms—one for the male members of the group, one for the female members of the group. We might translate the two kin terms that apply to them as "female member of my mother's group" and "male member of my mother's group." Their common characteristic as members of ego's mother's kin group overrides the fact that they are members of three different generations. If you have followed the argument, you will agree that the Omaha system makes perfect sense, provided it is associated with patrilineal descent forms. And, indeed, over 90 percent of all societies who use the Omaha terminological system are patrilineal.

Because the Crow system is the mirror image of the Omaha, we can make sense of it by showing how it reflects kinship relationships among matrilineal peoples. Go back to Figure 11.9 and look at the lines drawn around ego's own matrilineal descent group and around the matrilineal group of ego's father. You will see that all the male members of ego's father's group are called by the same term, as are all the female members of the same group. The underlying logic of the Crow terms is apparent, given matrilineal descent: ego lumps together relatives who belong to the same descent group as his or her father. Over 70 percent of all people who use the Crow terms are also matrilineal.

The Sudanese terminological system is the most mysterious. It seems to suggest nonunilineal descent, since there are no terminological differences in relatives through the mother and father. Yet over 80 percent of the societies who have the Sudanese-style terminology have patrilineal descent. Why this is so is not well understood.

Hopefully, the preceding discussion shows how the strange-looking Hawaiian, Iroquois, Omaha, and Crow terminological systems make sense once we understand that they reflect the prevalent relationships and groupings of kin produced by various ways of tracing descent. The ways in which various people

classify and label their relatives looks mysterious indeed, until we put these classifications and labels in the context of the kinship systems that give rise to them. The Eskimo system used by ourselves would probably look rather exotic to people who use, say, the Crow or Omaha terminology. To them, our failure to distinguish between relatives through one's mother and father would be strange, for these relatives would be clearly differentiated given the way their descent forms place people into different kin groups.

Along these same lines, it is important to stress that the various peoples who use one or another of these kinship classification systems cannot state the logic of their classifications in the same way as we just did. For instance, people who use the Omaha terminology cannot tell you why they label their relatives as they do, for they lack a comparative perspective on their own kinship system. To them, their mother, mother's sister, and mother's brother's daughter are called by the same term because all these women are the same kind of relative, just as aunts are all the same kind of relative to us. They do not realize that in Eskimo systems these females all have separate terms; nor are they aware that their terminology reflects the groupings and relationships of their kinship system. But then again, people who use the Eskimo system cannot account for their own classification system either, unless they are aware of the diversity in human kinship systems discovered in the last century by anthropologists. As is so often the case, the way a people classify their kinfolk seems quite natural or obvious to them, until they become aware that other people do it differently.

Summary

Relationships and groups based on kinship are an especially important component of the social organization of preindustrial peoples. Although kinship is everywhere based on biological relatedness, societies vary in their kinship systems. There is diversity in the range of relatives that are recognized, in the kinds and sizes of groups formed using kinship principles, in the norms attached to kin roles, and in the way people culturally categorize their relatives.

One way kinship systems vary is in how people trace their relationships back to previous generations. The most common forms of descent are patrilineal, matrilineal, double, bilateral, and ambilineal. The first three are varieties of unilineal descent, whereas the last two are types of nonunilineal descent. It is usually possible to classify a people as "having" one of these forms, but often descent is more an emphasis than a rule.

Descent principles are used as a basis for recruitment into groups and roles. Unilineal descent groups may be formed using the matrilineal or patrilineal principle, yielding kin groups composed of people related through females and males, respectively. In order of increasing inclusiveness and genealogical depth, the main kinds of descent groups are extended families, lineages, clans, phratries, and moieties. All may be based on either the matrilineal or patrilineal principle. The multifunctional nature of descent groups and the diverse kinds of activities organized by such groups are illustrated by the patrilineal Tikopia and the matrilineal Hopi.

Nonunilineal principles also can establish important groups and relationships. Ambilineal groups, such as the Iban *bilek*, can organize the same general kinds of activities as unilineal groups, although their members are not all related through one sex. In bilateral systems each individual potentially belongs simultaneously to several descent groups, but in practice this overlap is reduced by the choice to associate with only some kinfolk. In bilateral systems such as that of Kosrae, people mobilize their kindreds for specific activities and purposes.

Bilateral descent is common among foragers, where it maximizes social contacts and access to diverse territories. Nomadic pastoralists are usually patrilineal, which is probably related to the tendency for males to own and manage herds. Patrilineal descent also is likely to be found among peoples who are heavily engaged in warfare with close neighbors. Matrilineality is most likely to occur among populations who are horticultural and whose men are absent for prolonged periods when engaged in long-distance trade, warfare, or both. These very general associations have been supported by cross-cultural studies, but so many forces influence descent forms that no single explanation suffices to account for their occurrence.

People culturally classify their relatives into labeled categories by recognizing some differences between relatives and ignoring others. This classification gives rise to systems of kin terminology. Six systems are most widespread: Eskimo, Hawaiian, Iroquois, Omaha, Crow, and Sudanese. With the exception of the Iroquois, each terminological system tends to be associated with one form of descent. This is because the ideas people have about how they are related to one another are strongly influenced by how the descent form of their society sorts people into groups and establishes relations of one or another kind between kinfolk.

Key Terms

kin group	descent group
descent	unilineal descent
form of descent (rule	group
of descent)	lineage
unilineal descent	clan
nonunilineal descent	ambilineal descent
patrilineal descent	group
matrilineal descent	kindred
double descent	kin terms
bilateral descent	kinship terminology
ambilineal descent	

Suggested Readings

There are a number of excellent texts and collections of readings on kinship, descent groups, and the classification of relatives. The following is a list of such books.

■ Fox, Robin. *Kinship and Marriage: An Anthropological Perspective.* Baltimore: Penguin, 1968.
   An excellent introduction to the topics covered in this chapter.

■ Keesing, Roger M. *Kin Groups and Social Structure.* New York: Holt, Rinehart and Winston, 1971.
   An introduction to the theory of kinship, but can be difficult reading for undergraduate students.

■ Pasternak, Burton. Introduction to Kinship and Social Organization. Englewood Cliffs, N.J.: Prentice-Hall, 1976.
   A short introductory text with a cross-cultural orientation.

■ Radcliffe-Brown, A. R., and Daryll Forde, eds. *African Systems of Kinship and Marriage.* London: Oxford University Press, 1950.
   A collection of still-valuable essays by British anthropologists on kinship among nine African peoples. Radcliffe-Brown's introduction is regarded as a seminal paper.

■ Schusky, Ernest L. *Manual for Kinship Analysis.* 2d ed. New York: Holt, Rinehart and Winston, 1972.
   A short text designed to teach students how to diagram kinship ties and analyze kinship systems.

■ Schneider, David M. *American Kinship: A Cultural Account.* 2nd ed. Chicago: University of Chicago Press, 1980.

A symbolic account of American kinship written by a leading idealist.

■ Schneider, David M., and Kathleen Gough, eds. *Matrilineal Kinship*. Berkeley, Calif.: University of California Press, 1961.

Contains a description of nine matrilineal systems and an analysis of some dimensions of variation in matrilineal societies. Introductory essay by Schneider is a good overview.

The following ethnographies include excellent descriptions of specific kinship systems.

■ Chagnon, Napoleon A. *Yąnomamö: The Fierce People*. 3d ed. New York: Holt, Rinehart and Winston, 1983.

A well-written and interesting account of a South American tropical forest people.

■ Colson, Elizabeth. *The Plateau Tonga of Northern Rhodesia*. Manchester: University of Manchester, 1962.

An ethnographic account of a southern African people.

■ Eggan, Fred. *Social Organization of the Western Pueblos*. Chicago: University of Chicago Press, 1950.

A study in which the author describes and compares the social organization of the Hopi, Hano, Zuni, Acoma, and Laguna pueblos.

■ Evans-Pritchard, E. E. *The Nuer*. Oxford: Clarendon, 1940.

An ethnography of an African society, long considered one of the classic studies in social organization.

■ Firth, Raymond. *We, The Tikopia*. Boston: Beacon, 1936.

An ethnographic study of domestic life, kin relationships, descent groups, and marriage on a tiny Polynesian island.

■ Hart, C. W. M., and Arnold R. Pilling. *The Tiwi of North Australia*. New York: Holt, Rinehart and Winston, 1979.

A short ethnographic account of an Australian people with an unusual marriage system.

GENDER IN COMPARATIVE PERSPECTIVE

■ (Above) *Ethnographers have documented the diversity in roles allocated to women and men in human societies. These South Asian women are selling bananas at a market.*

cholars do not work in a sociocultural vacuum. Our research and teaching is influenced by what is going on in the societies in which we ourselves live. This sociocultural context affects the interests and theoretical orientations of anthropologists just as it does scholars in other disciplines. So it is not surprising that the feminist movement—one of the major social and political forces of the late twentieth century—has given rise to increased interests in and research about gender relationships. Before 1970 only a handful of anthropologists concerned themselves with gender; today there are many hundreds. Our understanding of humanity already has been enriched by their contributions. We now better see how relationships between women and men vary cross-culturally, and we are beginning to gain some understanding of the forces that affect these variations.

In this chapter, we make no effort to cover all elements of relationships between the sexes. Instead we concentrate on two areas in which much research has focused: (1) the cross-cultural variations in the sexual division of labor and (2) the differences in the status of women.

In the previous chapter, we saw the ways in which biological connections between kinspeople serve as the basis for defining social relationships between individuals and for assigning people to (kin) groups that serve a variety of functions. Such kin connections are relevant in all societies for role allocation and group recruitment. But we also showed how the biological facts of genealogical (genetic) relatedness are used in many different ways by various human populations. Biological kinship provides the basis for assigning roles and for establishing organized groups everywhere, but different peoples make use of kinship principles in a multitude of ways. The same generalization applies to gender: the biological differences between males and females matter in all societies, but they matter in different ways and to varying degrees.

The Sexual Division of Labor

The **sexual division of labor** in a sociocultural system refers to the patterned ways in which productive and other economic activities are divided between men and women. The sexual division of labor is one of the most important elements of social organization that distinguishes humanity from primates and other mammals. In other mammals there are few systematic year-round differences between the foraging activities of males and females. In humans, however, a sexual division of labor is universal. It implies, necessarily, that males and females share or pool some of the products of their labor. Each sex has access to the goods produced by the other, so that the tasks of males and females are to some extent complementary.

In modern North America, the sexual division of labor, and indeed the overall social roles of males and females in general, is rapidly changing: males are carrying out activities and performing roles that twenty or thirty years ago were associated with females, and vice versa. In many other societies, however, the roles of females and males are more sharply divided and the sexual division of labor is quite clearly defined. Among the Plains Indians, for instance, men and women ordinarily engaged in different, but complementary, economic activities. Yet sex role "options" or "deviations" existed for individuals: there were culturally allowable and even socially rewarded ways in which males could assume the normal roles of females, and vice versa (see Box 12.1).

The past hundred years of ethnographic fieldwork provide all the information needed to demolish one popular idea on this topic: that it is only natural for men to be the breadwinners for and women the caretakers of the family. Breadwinning—that is, producing the supply of food and other material needs and wants of domestic groups—is definitely not an activity of men exclusively, or even largely. As we shall discuss, in many populations men produce most of the food; but in almost as many populations women's contribution to daily subsistence equals or exceeds that of men; and it is the rule, rather than the exception, for women to produce a significant proportion of the food supply for the camp, household, or domestic group.

This finding of ethnographic research contradicts the opinion of those who think that the domination of men over women is rooted in the "fact" that men's labor is more important to physical survival and

■ *Many of our stereotypes about the kinds of tasks that are appropriate for males and females are ethnocentric. The Hopi man on the left is spinning yarn, whereas the Sudanese woman on the right is harvesting cotton.*

material well-being than women's labor. Those who hold this view argue that women are everywhere dependent on men, which in turn makes women everywhere subordinate to men. But where females are subordinate to males, it is not because the things men do are somehow more important to family and group survival than the things women do. This ethnocentric idea probably comes from the way most modern industrial economies worked until the mid-twentieth century: By and large, men earned the money that allowed their families to purchase the goods they needed to survive. It is falsely concluded that the same economic dependence of wives upon husbands characterized other peoples.

This is our usual warning about confusing the practices and ideas of one's own society with those of humanity in general: our own cultural ideas about what is and is not natural for people to do and think are usually wrong. They are wrong because those who espouse them have little knowledge of the sociocultural diversity of humanity, so they regularly—and mistakenly—conclude that the ideas and practices of their own society are only natural and universal.

We now look at some of the patterns anthropologists have discovered in the sexual division of labor and at some of the hypotheses they have offered to explain these patterns.

■ Patterns and Hypotheses

Table 12.1 summarizes the cross-cultural similarities and differences in some specific tasks. Those activities toward the left of the table are more likely to be male; those to the right more likely to be female. The nearer an activity is to the right, the more likely it is to be done by females, and vice versa for males. Notice both the patterning of differences and the range of overlap. A few tasks, such as hunting and smelting, are almost exclusively male activities in those populations in which they are carried out; some, such as clearing land and tending large animals, are predominantly the work of men almost everywhere; others, such as planting crops, are done by both sexes with approximately equal frequency; still others are done by women in most societies.

Note that Table 12.1 includes *only* those activities in which some kind of material good is produced. Other activities that are predominantly or exclusively male, such as managing households, holding political offices, and fighting wars, will be discussed later. Also not

Box 12.1

ALTERNATIVE SEX ROLES AMONG THE PLAINS INDIANS

The Plains Indians of the nineteenth century made a sharp distinction between male and female social roles and behavior. As hunters and warriors, men were aggressive and independent in their social behavior. In contrast, women were mainly involved in the domestic sphere—with activities such as cooking, working hides, making clothing, and decorating items with quill and beadwork. Women were supposed to be passive and reserved in their public behavior.

However, even among Plains tribes not all individuals adhered to the normatively appropriate role and behavior of their gender. There was *gender mixing* (sometimes called *gender crossing*), here meaning that some men or women adopted some of the attributes usually accorded the other gender. Particular types of gender mixing were culturally defined alternatives to normatively prescribed gender roles and behaviors. Among the Plains Indians gender crossing took three main forms: (1) berdaches, in which men took on some aspects of feminine roles, (2) manly-hearted women, in which a female acted like a male normally acted, and (3) women chiefs, in which a woman assumed a role usually occupied by only men.

Berdaches

A berdache was a man who dressed in women's clothes, performed women's work, and in general assumed the social behavior normatively appropriate for women. Among the tribes of the plains, the Arapaho, Arikara, Assiniboine, Blackfoot, Cheyenne, Crow, Gros Ventre, Hidatsa, Iowa, Kansa, Mandan, Omaha, Osage, Oto, Pawnee, Plains Cree, Ponca, and Sioux are known to have recognized berdaches as alternatives to the normal male role. There is little specific information about the frequency of berdaches among these tribes, but early traders and explorers commonly remarked that they were "numerous" among some tribes.

Variation did exist in the particular characteristics of berdaches from one plains society to the next. Sioux berdaches are the best reported in the literature. The Sioux called berdache *winkte*. Winkte dressed like women and lived in their own separate tipis at the edge of camp. They performed women's tasks such as tanning hides and working with quills and beads. In these activities winkte were said to excell. Ceremonial and ritual items made by a winkte were especially sought after because of their fine quality. To say that a woman had "fine possessions like a winkte's" was the highest compliment to her skill.

It is not clear when a man began to exhibit the characteristics of a winkte. Some began dressing as girls while quite young; others not until after they reached puberty. Generally, it was not thought that a man chose to become a winkte, but became one by dreaming about female supernatural forces. Through their visions, winkte had supernatural powers, such as the ability to cure the sick. They appear to have had the right or supernatural authority to grant children special secret names, which protected the children from illness and prolonged their lives.

Although most of their activities were those normally associated with women, winkte did take part in male activities. Many were outstanding hunters. This, together with their great skills as craftspeople, made many of them wealthy. Some winkte also participated in war parties and thus engaged in the male role of warrior.

Many questions remain unanswered concerning the winkte in traditional Sioux society, such as whether they were homosexuals. The degree to which they were accepted by other members of the community is also uncertain. Some say that they were well accepted and respected in the community for their skill, hard work, and supernatural powers; and that they were intelligent and compassionate individuals who frequently cared for the aged and infirm. Others say that the winkte were disliked and discriminated against. Most likely, different Sioux individuals had different opinions about the winkte.

Manly-Hearted Women

In the northern Plains tribes, certain women adopted elements of male social behavior, acting aggressive and domineering. The Blackfoot called them *ninauposkitzipxe*, which means literally "the manly-hearted women." Ordinarily, women were passive and docile, but manly-hearted women were aggressive and outspoken in public affairs. However, at the same time they were wives and mothers and were involved in female tasks.

Manly-hearted women were invariably wealthy women. In large part, their greater wealth came from their own industry. They worked harder and longer at their tasks. They could tan more buffalo robes and produce better quality and greater amounts of quill and beadwork than other women. Many were also medicine women, which not only enhanced their status but also brought them additional wealth. Their wealth was a key factor in their relations with men, for among the Blackfoot wealth and generosity were more highly regarded than bravery and war deeds in determining social status.

Because of their wealth and industry, manly-hearted women were major economic assets to their husbands, and thus desirable wives. However, these same characteristics also made them independent. Within the family a manly-hearted woman had an equal say, if not the dominant voice. As a Blackfoot once commented to Oscar Lewis (1941:181) "It's easy to spot a manly-hearted woman; the husband simply has nothing to say." Not only did they retain control of their own wealth, but they frequently controlled the property of their husband as well. Because they were economically more self-sufficient than other women, many manly-hearted women chose to divorce their husbands and support their children by their own industry.

Their public behavior also distinguished them from other women. Their wealth made it possible for them always to dress in the finest clothes. While other women modestly covered themselves with shawls and blankets, manly-hearted women usually did not. While most women were retiring and quiet in public discussions, manly-hearted women joined in and even argued with others, "just as though they were men." While other women were shy at dances, manly-hearted women aggressively chose their own partners. They were known for their sharp and cutting remarks, and it was said that a manly-hearted woman would "take no lip" from either a man or another woman. Not surprisingly, they were believed to be sexually aggressive and passionate.

Women Chiefs

Among many Plains tribes, women sometimes assumed the role of chiefs. Detailed information is lacking; but fortunately an early trader (Edwin Denig) wrote a biographical account of a Crow woman, called "Woman Chief," who lived in the early nineteenth century.

Woman Chief was born into the Gros Ventre tribe. At the age of ten, she was captured by the Crows and adopted by a Crow family. As a girl she showed a fondness for such typically male activities as riding horses, hunting, using bows and arrows, and shooting guns. She was indulged by her foster father, who made her guard of the family's horses—a responsibility usually assumed by a son. She became an excellent rider and markswoman and spent most of her time hunting deer and bighorn sheep as she grew older. She was said to be able to kill four or five bison in a single chase, to butcher the animals, and to pack the meat and hides back to camp with no assistance. When her foster father died, she assumed the role of family head, hunting to feed her mother and siblings.

While Woman Chief was still a young woman, her camp was attacked by the Blackfoot. Several Crow men were killed, and the survivors took refuge in a fortified trading post nearby. After surrounding the post, the Black-foot asked for a parley; but, fearing a trap, the Crow men refused. Finally Woman Chief ventured out alone and was attacked by the Blackfoot. She killed one and wounded two before running back to the post. Accorded the honors of a warrior for her acts of bravery, the next year Woman Chief led a raid on the·Blackfoot. Her party captured seventy horses, and she herself killed one Blackfoot and took the gun of another. In the following years, she organized numerous raiding parties against the enemies of the Crow.

Accepted as a family head and warrior, Woman Chief was admitted to full participation in the council deliberations of the men. She eventually came to be ranked third out of the 160 family heads in her band. Because of her role as a frequent leader of raiding parties, she became wealthy in horses. Disdaining traditional women's tasks such as tanning, sewing, quilling, and beading, she paid the brideprice for and married four women to do these jobs for her.

Although Woman Chief was unusual, she was not unique. Women chiefs and women warriors were reported among other plains tribes. The cases of the berdache, manly-hearted women, and Woman Chief show us how individuals are not forced to conform rigidly to the normal social roles and activities of their gender in many societies. Alternatives are frequently available to both sexes, even in those preindustrial societies in which sex role "deviance" is—according to our stereotypes—supposedly not allowed. ∎

Sources: Benedict (1934), Callender and Kochems (1983), Demallie (1983), Denig (1961), Hassrick (1964), Lewis (1941), Medicine (1983).

■ **Table 12.1 Patterns in the Sexual Division of Labor**

	TASKS PERFORMED BY GENDER				
	Exclusively Males	Predominantly Males	Either or Both Sexes	Predominantly Females	
Extracting Food and Other Products	Hunting Trapping Woodworking Mining Lumbering	Fishing Clearing land Preparing soil Tending large animals	Gathering small land animals Planting crops Tending crops Harvesting crops Milking animals	Gathering shellfish, mollusks Tending small animals Gathering fuel	Gathering wild plant foods Fetching water
Manufacturing, Processing, and Preparing Goods for Consumption	Butchering Boat building Working with stone, horn, bone, shell Smelting ore Metalworking	House building Making rope, cordage, nets	Preparing skins Making leather products	Making clothing Matmaking Loom weaving Making pottery	Processing, preparing plant foods Cooking

Source: Adapted from Murdock and Provost (1973).

included is one activity—nursing infants—that is universally allocated to women. There is another—caring for young children—that is predominantly women's work. Of course, there is a sense in which all activities are "productive" (of social order or offspring, for example), but for convenience our present discussion is restricted to activities popularly known as "economic tasks."

We want to account for two things revealed by Table 12.1. First, we would like to know why there are widespread similarities between societies in how productive labor is divided up. For instance, hunting, land clearing, working with hard materials (bone, etc.), and cutting wood are predominantly men's work everywhere. Gathering wild plants and processing plant foods are mainly female work everywhere. Table 12.1 also reveals that many tasks are not sex-specific (i.e., allocated either to male or females, depending on the society). The second thing we would like to account for is these cross-cultural variations in the sexual division of labor.

This section deals with hypotheses that try to account for the first pattern: the widespread similarities between societies shown in Table 12.1. In the next section we discuss hypotheses about the second pattern: the variation among societies in sexual division of labor.

First, what can explain the similarities? The physical differences between males and females provide one possible explanation. Perhaps men are biologically well equipped to handle certain kinds of tasks, and women to perform other tasks. Societies divide these activities in such a way that each sex does what it is biologically or physically able to do best. Since men and women differ in the same biological ways everywhere, of course these differences are reflected in widespread similarities in the sexual division of labor.

This idea is not simple, outdated, and sexist biological determinism. Most of those who believe that physical differences between the sexes play a part in explaining the sexual division of labor say only that these differences are *relevant* in accounting for why societies allocate different tasks to the two sexes. They do not claim that biological differences alone explain the sexual division of labor. This would be an absurd claim, because only hunting, lumbering, smelting, and metal working are nearly everywhere exclusively male tasks.

What, then, are the claims of those who believe the biology and physiology of males and females are important influences on the sexual division of labor?

Because of biological factors, they contend, men are better equipped to handle some tasks than women and vice versa, and these physical differences are reflected in how labor is divided in human populations.

For example, anthropologists used to say that there was at least one task that was everywhere done by men: hunting. Hunting seems to require certain biological capabilities—such as speed, strength, and endurance—that men have "more of" than women. It also was thought to be incompatible with certain responsibilities universally borne by women for biological reasons: pregnancy, lactation (breast-feeding), and child care. Pregnant women would have a hard time chasing game; lactating mothers would have to quit the hunt several times a day to nurse their infants; and the risk of injury to both mother and child would be high. Since men could hunt more effectively than women, foraging populations allocated hunting to men. Gathering, in contrast, required less strength and ability to run fast and long, so societies allocated gathering largely to women.

These arguments are probably correct, but we need to be aware that female and male biological differences do not dictate that males are the hunters and females are the gatherers in foraging populations. For one thing, not all kinds of hunting and not all tasks connected to hunting require strength, speed, and endurance. For another, there are questions about whether males have more endurance than females for biological reasons. Finally, there is no necessary *biological* reason why a woman could not give up hunting only during her pregnancy and lactation and leave her older children in camp under the care of someone else.

In fact, it is just not true that hunting is *universally* an exclusively male activity. When the BaMbuti pygmies of the Zaire rain forest hunt animals with nets, the women help with hunting by driving game into the nets manned by men. In another example, Agnes Estioko-Griffin has reported on hunting by women among the Agta, a mountain tribe of the Philippines who live on the island of Luzon. Agta men do most of the hunting, but women often accompany them in teamwork efforts, and women frequently hunt together without the company of men. Interestingly, women sometimes take their infants with them on the hunt, carrying the children on their backs. There are some differences between the methods used and types of game hunted by women versus men. Still, cases such as the Agta and BaMbuti show that the "man the hunter" image is over-simplified.

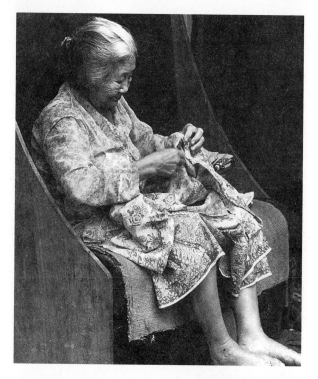

■ Here are four tasks that are predominantly performed by women. Clockwise from upper left: gathering wild plants (San); making clothing (Indonesia); weaving (Micronesia); gathering fuel (Yanomamö).

It is not, however, wrong. The great majority of populations in which hunting is a significant means of acquiring food are foragers or horticulturalists. There is no question that in most of these populations women do most of the gathering of wild plants or the planting, weeding, and harvesting of cultivated plants, whereas men hunt to provide meat. The male hunting/female gathering pattern is not universal, as we have just seen, but it is clearly the predominant pattern. The images of

"woman the gatherer" (or gardener) and "man the hunter" do not apply to all people everywhere, but they are common enough that many anthropologists believe there must be some physical differences between men and women that contribute to this particular division of labor.

What kinds of differences between the sexes seem to matter most? The simplest idea—which we call the **strength hypothesis**—is that men are generally stron-

■ *The strength hypothesis holds that women cannot perform tasks that require great strength. Superior male strength does affect the sexual division of labor, but women are not always assigned "light work," as this Nigerian woman can testify.*

ger than women, so that work requiring great strength is allocated to males. Male strength probably does play a role in explaining why some tasks are nearly universally allocated to males, such as working with hard materials, cutting wood, mining, and perhaps hunting. It also might explain why males predominate in two important cultivation tasks—clearing land and preparing soil for planting. But male strength has no obvious relation to other predominantly male tasks, such as trapping, butchering, and working with fibers. Also, women often do tasks that require significant strength, such as gathering fuel and fetching water.

Women have another physical characteristic that might explain why some activities are generally allocated to males. Modern female athletes—especially long-distance runners—know that they often do not menstruate and ovulate monthly. Apparently, this is because of a low ratio of body fat and complex hormonal changes in women who engage in prolonged physical exercise. It has been suggested that productive activities requiring comparable exertion—notably hunting—would depress a woman's fertility, and thus help explain why most hunting is done by men. We might call this the **fertility maintenance hypothesis,** for it suggests that female reproduction would be so decreased by the strenuous exercise involved in activities such as hunting that the population might not be able to maintain its numbers over the course of many generations. It is difficult to know whether this hypothesis adequately accounts for why women so rarely hunt or go to war. For

instance, we do not know how much (or even if), the exertion involved in hunting would lower women's ability to bear children. This is because we must find and study several cases of women hunting in the same way as men before we can measure hunting's effects on female fertility. How much would the exercise of hunting depress a woman's fertility? We do not know.

A third idea is the **child-care-compatibility hypothesis.** First proposed in 1970 by Judith Brown, this hypothesis holds that women tend to perform those tasks that they are able to combine effectively with nursing and other child-care duties that they have almost everywhere. Brown argued that such tasks have several characteristics:

■ They are fairly routine and repetitive, so they do not require much concentration.
■ They can be interrupted and resumed without harming their efficient performance.
■ They do not place the children who accompany their mothers to the site of the task in potential danger.
■ They do not require women to travel very far away from home.

The gathering of various products and the domestic work listed in Table 12.1 are highly compatible with child care. In addition, in horticultural populations, garden tasks such as planting, weeding and tending crops, and harvesting are in fact usually done by women; these activities too seem to be highly compatible with caring for children.

Notice that none of the three hypotheses can explain the variability in the allocation of tasks. In fact, no biological difference between the sexes can explain the cross-cultural *diversity* in the sexual division of labor. The biological differences between males and females are about the same everywhere. A condition that is constant across all societies cannot, by itself, account for conditions that vary across these societies. We need another explanation for the variations shown in Table 12.1. Such an explanation would take the physical differences between the sexes into account but would see these differences as manifesting themselves in various ways because of variations in local conditions.

■ Intensive Agriculture and Women's Labor

Anthropologists have given considerable attention to one cross-cultural variation in the sexual division of labor: that between women's relative importance to

■ *The childcare compatibility hypothesis of the sexual division of labor holds that females are assigned work that can be combined with caring for young children. This African woman can process grain with her child on her back, for example.*

subsistence in horticultural versus intensive agricultural populations. (See chapter 8 for a discussion of the distinction between these two systems of cultivation.)

It is fairly well established that women usually do much or most of the garden work in horticultural populations. Of the major tasks involved in growing food using horticultural methods, only two—clearing land for cultivation and, to a lesser extent, preparing the plot for planting by removing natural vegetation and turning over the soil—seem to be almost always done by men. Other tasks, including planting, weeding, guarding, and harvesting, are most often activities of women.

Why do women contribute a relatively large amount of garden labor in horticultural systems? Whether a people practice shifting cultivation, dry land gardening, or some other variety of horticulture, female gardening tasks do not require great strength and are quite compatible with child-care demands. But this statement merely says that women (or, rather, mothers) *can* contribute effectively to subsistence; it does not say why they *will*.

No satisfactory answer has been offered. One suggestion is that in horticultural populations men are frequently absent in trading expeditions or hunting, so women do most gardening by default. For instance, in the Americas before contact with the West, most of the meat that people consumed came from men's hunting, for no large animals had been domesticated outside the Andes. Because men were so occupied with hunting, one of the nearly exclusively male tasks, women were left to garden. Yet we do not know how much of male time hunting usually required, so this suggestion is difficult to evaluate.

Along the same lines, others suggest that men in horticultural societies were so heavily involved in warfare and guarding the settlement against attack that they had little time for cultivation. But warfare was *not* more frequent in horticultural than in intensive agricultural populations, so why should it interfere more with men's ability to grow food in the former? The reason is that so many of the world's intensive agriculturalists were part of large-scale, state-organized societies (chapter 9), which had specialized, standing armies. Among horticulturalists, in contrast, most able-bodied men were expected to be active in defensive and offensive warfare, which detracted from their subsistence activities.

Both of these hypotheses state that since women are able to do most horticultural tasks, and since men are so busy with other things that women cannot do as well, most garden work falls to women. Another possibility is simply that gardening is not much fun—remember the "routine, repetitive" nature of so many women's tasks noted previously. Stronger men/husbands may force weaker women/wives to do such work whenever they can. Essentially, males exploit females by making them do the "drudge work," according to this argument.

Whatever the reason for why females contribute so much to the everyday vegetable food supply among horticulturalists, the importance of women's labor relative to men's tends to decline as cultivation systems become more intensive. ("Intensity" increases as cultivators increase the amount of food they harvest from a given amount of land by putting in more hours of work per acre, by plowing with animal power, by digging irrigation wells and ditches, by gathering dung and spreading it over the fields as fertilizer, and so on—see chapter 8). Women generally contribute much less agricultural labor than men in intensive agricultural systems. Why should this be?

■ *Women generally contribute less labor to direct food production in intensive agricultural societies. One hypothesis for this is that women lack the strength needed to work with the plow. As this photo shows, this hypothesis is questionable.*

One possibility is that the work involved in intensive systems demands more strength and stamina than the work required by horticulture. For instance, using a plow to till the soil might be too heavy a type of work for women. Yet this hypothesis has never been demonstrated to be true (animals provide most of the strength, at any rate). Besides, since plowing is usually done only once or twice a year, there is no reason why men should not handle the plowing while women continue to perform other agricultural tasks.

The relative strength and stamina of the sexes alone is insufficient to account for why women contribute relatively less labor in intensive systems. A number of anthropologists have proposed a more complicated hypothesis. Their ideas are based on studies suggesting that, as cultivation becomes more intensive, two changes occur in women's domestic work loads. First, domestic tasks that women generally perform require more of women's time in intensive systems. Second, in intensive systems, new kinds of tasks emerge that are generally done by women. Both sets of changes—the increased time required for old domestic tasks and the addition of new kinds of work—divert women's time from cultivation, so they work relatively less than men in supplying food.

One such hypothesis was proposed in 1983 by Carol Ember. Using studies comparing how much time men and women spend in food production versus domestic work in horticultural and intensive agricultural societies, she suggested that women generally have significantly more domestic work to perform in intensive agricultural

societies. There are several reasons that women's domestic work load generally increases with increasing intensity. For one thing, about half of all horticulturalists concentrate on root crops (such as yams, potatoes, manioc, taro, and sweet potatoes) rather than cereal crops. In contrast, about 90 percent of all intensive agriculturalists subsist mainly from cereals (such as wheat, rice, corn, oats, barley, and millet).

How could this general difference in the kinds of crops grown affect the kinds of tasks women perform in the two systems? In 1975, Kay Martin and Barbara Voorhies suggested an important implication of this seemingly insignificant difference—again showing us how subtle differences can have major effects on sociocultural systems. The root crops grown more often by horticultural peoples tend to be harvested continuously rather than seasonally. Edible roots can be stored in the ground for relatively long periods, allowing cultivators to harvest them more or less at will (within limits, of course). Cereals (grains), however, are the seeds of cultivated plants, so they mature at about the same time every year. The seeds will fall off and rot (or sprout) unless harvested at the proper time. Therefore, cereals are typically harvested seasonally, dried, and stored for processing and eating the rest of the year. This increases both cooking and processing time—picture the Mexican peasant woman grinding corn to make tortillas, or the Greek woman winnowing, grinding, making flour, and baking bread from wheat. Because, overall, cereals require more labor to process and prepare for eating than roots, and because in almost all societies such domestic tasks are done by females, women tend to devote more hours to domestic work in intensive agricultural societies. They therefore have relatively less time to spend in the fields.

Douglas White, Michael Burton, and Malcomb Dow pursue this line of reasoning. In a 1981 cross-cultural study, they noticed a fairly consistent relationship between crop type and the average length of dry season: the longer the dry season, the more likely cereals rather than roots are to be the main crops of a people. They also found a relationship between crop type and the importance of animal husbandry: domesticated animals are more important to people who grow cereals, since cereal-growers tend to be intensive agriculturalists who use animals to pull plows.

In summary, and in general, most intensive agriculturalists live in regions with a long dry season, grow cereals as an important part of their diet, and keep domesticated animals both for traction and food. How might the association between these factors explain the lower involvement of women in intensive agriculture than in horticulture?

First, consider the possible effects of a long dry season. Because of the lack of rain for many months of the year, the timing of crop planting needs to be adjusted so that the growing plants will have adequate water. Therefore, planting tends to be concentrated during a few weeks of the year; of course, harvesting is later concentrated into a small time period as a result. So the seasonality of agricultural tasks is greater than that of horticultural tasks. There is an increased demand for agricultural laborers who can do a lot of hot, heavy work in a short period that cannot be interrupted by other tasks, that is, for men's rather than women's labor (see previous section).

In contrast, root-growing horticultural peoples living in regions with a short or no dry season, or in which the time of planting is relatively unaffected by climate, tend to spread cultivation tasks out more evenly over the entire year. Gardening is a day-in, day-out activity but also requires less muscle power and is relatively interruptible. So women are able to do it effectively.

Now consider the possible effects on women's time of the keeping of large numbers of domesticated animals used to pull plows, supply meat and dairy products, and fertilize fields in intensive systems. Burton and White cite some evidence that many of the labor burdens involved in keeping domesticated animals are borne by women (as well as children). Women do most of the work of collecting fodder for the animals to eat, of gathering dung, of watering livestock, of milking cows, and several other animal-husbandry tasks. This also tends to divert their labor from direct involvement in agricultural chores, Burton and White believe. (Their evidence that women do most of the care of domesticated animals is weak, however.)

In summary, some cross-cultural researchers suggest that a combination of the following factors explains why women contribute less labor to cultivation in intensive agricultural than in horticultural populations:

- The cereals grown using intensive cultivation methods require more processing time than the root crops of horticultural peoples.
- Cereal-growing intensive agriculturalists tend to live in parts of the world with a long dry season, which increases the advantage of using men's rather than women's labor in the fields.

- Intensive agriculturalists tend to keep more domesticated animals, which directly or indirectly increases the nonagricultural work load of women.

We note here something you may already have noticed; these associations are very generalized. Intensive agriculturalists "tend to" live in regions with a long dry season, domesticated animals are "generally" cared for more by women than by men, and so on. Obviously, these hypotheses are not very precise, and there are serious questions about whether the cross-cultural tests "really" support what those who conduct them claim they support. And, as always, there are numerous exceptions—some specific population may have intensive agriculture without any of the things it is "supposed to" be associated with. Despite these and other problems, these hypotheses are at least plausible; they do not merely restate in fancy language what everyone already knows; and they do have some empirical support in the form of cross-cultural tests. So long as we do not accept them as the final word, as *the truth*, they are useful guides for further research.

Right or wrong, the preceding ideas are a good example of the materialist perspective on humanity, which we introduced in chapter 5. The preceding argument assumes that the way a population exploits its habitat (by horticulture or more intensive methods) greatly affects the kinds of tasks women and men do (given the physical differences between the sexes and the biological fact that women give birth to and nurse children). So the material conditions of life in a certain kind of economy interact with biological differences between women and men to produce an overall pattern of the division of labor along gender lines. (Or so those scholars who proposed these hypotheses believe.)

Does this have any relevance for women's occupational roles in a modern, industrialized society? If it is true that the essential differences between men and women that account for the sexual division of labor in preindustrial populations are (1) male strength (and, perhaps, ability to run fast or long) and (2) the fact that only women bear and nurse children, then this matters for modern women. It matters, first, because advanced technology and machinery have greatly reduced the need for strength and stamina to perform tasks; so there is less of a biological basis for allocating some tasks ("jobs," they have become) exclusively to males. It matters, second, because the economies of Western Europe and North America are increasingly

PEOPLES OF
AUSTRALIA AND OCEANIA

AUSTRALIA The aboriginal peoples of Australia spoke over 300 different languages, which were unrelated to languages anywhere else. The aborigines were foragers, living from the unique animals and plants of the continent. Technology was limited to stone- or bone-tipped spears, boomerangs, stone axes and knives, and a few other tools. Frequent moves limited their architecture to simple brush dwellings and windbreaks. The sparsely populated aborigines lived in small bands, with informal leaders. Their main areas of sociocultural elaboration were their complex social organization, rich ceremonial life, and artistic talents.

OCEANIA Oceania is usually defined as those islands lying east of Wallace's line, the ecological boundary separating Asian flora and fauna from that of the insular Pacific.

MELANESIA Melanesia includes the island groups surrounding New Guinea, the Solomons, the New Hebrides (now Vanuatu), New Caledonia, and Fiji. Two major linguistic groupings were present: Austronesian (also spoken in other regions of the Pacific and Asia) and Papuan (the incredibly diverse languages confined to Melanesia). Some coastal Melanesians relied on fishing, but most were settled horticulturalists, raising root crops and keeping pigs that were exchanged

at enormous feasts. Most peoples lived in well-constructed houses, frequently decorated with carvings and painted designs. A few Melanesians were politically organized as chiefdoms, but most were egalitarian and tribal, with a big-man pattern of leadership.

POLYNESIA The islands lying within the vast triangle with vertices at New Zealand, Hawaii, and Easter island form the sociocultural area known as Polynesia. These brown-skinned, black-haired people all speak closely related Austronesian languages. Living mainly in coastal villages of volcanic islands or on tiny coral atolls, Polynesians depended on fishing, farming root and tree crops, and raising domestic pigs and chickens for their food. Wood was worked with adzes of stone and shell, and clothing was made of bark cloth. With their large double-hulled sailing canoes and open-ocean navigational skills, Polynesians sailed the vast distances separating island groups for trade, migration, and occasionally conquest. Developing out of a common heritage, various island groups elaborated different sociocultural features. Easter island is famous for its huge stone heads. The Maori (of New Zealand) and the Hawaiians developed wood carving to a high art. Everywhere social ranking was strong, but the Tahitians, Hawaiians, and Tongans lived in complex

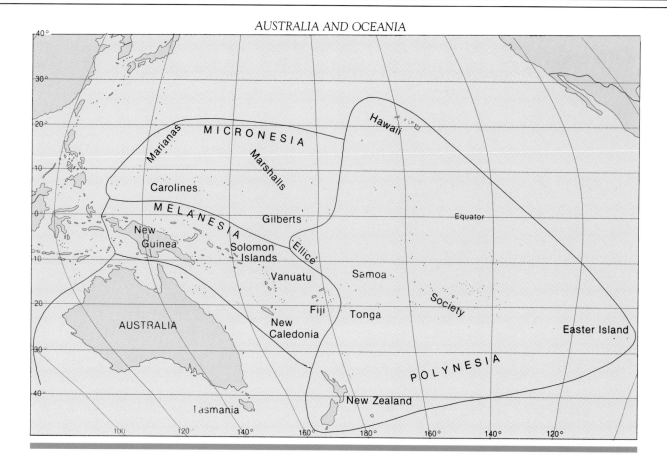

chiefdoms, with marked inequalities between nobles and commoners.

MICRONESIA   Micronesia includes the small and scattered islands of the western Pacific. The main island groups are the Marianas, the Carolines, the Marshalls, and the Gilberts (now Kiribati). Micronesia, with at least nine distinct languages and greater sociocultural diversity, is more diverse than Polynesia. Occupying small volcanic islands and atolls, in traditional times Micronesians lived by horticulture and fishing. Shell adzes were used for canoe and house construction. Fishing technology and methods were diverse and productive. Micronesians are most famous for their highly developed navigational skills and large outrigger sailing canoes, which allowed them to undertake long voyages for purposes of trade and visits. Hereditary rank and a chiefdom political type were found on all island groups.

AUSTRALIA AND OCEANIA TODAY   Over the past two hundred years some Oceanic peoples have been displaced by immigrants from Europe and Asia. Modern Australia and New Zealand are occupied mainly by British immigrants; the surviving Australian aborigines and New Zealand Maori have been relegated to minority status. Native Hawaiians now comprise only 12 percent of the population of Hawaii; people of Asian and Euro-American ancestry constitute the majority. Large French communities exist in New Caledonia and the Society Islands, both overseas territories of France. Over half the population of Fiji is of East Indian ancestry, for large numbers of South Asians were imported to work on British-owned sugar cane plantations in the nineteenth century. The population of most other Pacific islands remains mostly indigenous, although every island has been greatly influenced by economic changes and global political forces.

■ (Above, left) Because of immigration from Asia, America, and Europe, native Hawaiians are now a minority in their islands. This scene of foreign tourists on the beach of Waikiki symbolizes the displacement of the ethnic Hawaiians.

■ (Above) Today many Pacific peoples are self-governing and live in independent nations. These childern are celebrating the independence of Papua New Guinea in 1975.

■ (Left) Micronesians showed great ingenuity in wresting a living from the tiny islands on which most of them lived. This man is roofing a cookhouse with thatch made from leaves.

■ (Above) Most Melanesian societies farmed the land by means of slash-and-burn horticulture.

■ (Left) At one time ranging over the entire continent of Australia, the aborigines are now a minority in their native homeland.

■ (Left) These Tahitians from Tubuai island in the Austral Islands of French Polynesia are dedicating a new crafts center.

Source for creation of this insert: Oliver (1989).

service- and high-tech-oriented; so the biological differences that once mattered a lot need not matter so much (if at all) today. It matters, third, because the birthrate of industrialized nations is lower than that of most preindustrial peoples; so child-care burdens may be lessened for modern women. It matters, fourth, because one reason why some tasks were allocated to women in preindustrial societies was their compatibility with women's child-care duties; but today these duties are delegated to child-care specialists, with no harm to children.

A more general implication arises from the fact that the sexual division of labor shows great, but not unlimited, variability in human populations. In the materialist hypotheses we have discussed, this variability is seen as resulting from the interaction between female-male biological differences and the overall economic conditions of a people. If these hypotheses have merit, then, the sexual division of labor responds to other changes in a peoples' way of life—particularly to changes in their adaptive, productive, and economic systems. That the sexual division of labor in industrialized nations is responding and will continue to respond to similar changes is not surprising. That the long-term development will be toward a decreasing emphasis on gender as a basis for recruitment into tasks is consistent with many anthropological hypotheses about the sexual division of labor. As technological, economic, and demographic changes reduce the importance of male-female differences in the ability to perform most jobs, the gender of the job holder will come to matter less and less.

The Status of Women

Another issue in the anthropological study of gender relationships is how and why the status of women varies across sociocultural systems. By **status of women,** we mean how women and men relate to one another on the basis of the gender difference between them. The overall status of women in a society includes numerous components: the kinds of social positions men and women hold and the roles they perform; the economic importance of and cultural value attached to women's contributions to their families and to society at large; whether or how much women defer to men with whom they have important bonds, such as their husbands and male relatives; the female influence in public and political life; the degree to which women have the right to control their own bodies and to make marital, occupational, and other important decisions for themselves; and so on.

Comparative data on variations in the status of women is relevant for the present and future of modern women, for two reasons. First, if ethnographic information shows that women's status is low to the same degree and in the same ways in most societies, then it may be more difficult to improve women's status in modern nations. Conversely, if there are preindustrial populations in which women have status higher than or equal to men, then our confidence that modern societies can reach the same state is increased.

Second, assuming we find that women's position in societies varies significantly, we may be able to discover why it does so. We might be able to find a key economic, political, domestic, sexual, or religious factor that determines how women are treated and regarded every-

■ *The biological facts that women are on average not as strong as men, get pregnant, and nurse infants, need not limit their work activities in a modern industrial economy. This Swedish assembly line worker lets neither her gender nor her pregnancy keep her from this traditional male job.*

where. If so, then modern feminists will need to work to alter this key factor, and in the long term our societies will develop greater equality between the sexes.

Before proceeding, we need to recognize how difficult it may be to determine "the" status of women in any given society. This difficulty arises because relationships between the sexes are complex and have many dimensions or aspects. For example, many anthropologists who have investigated domestic life (see chapter 10) have reported that women have a great deal of independence and control over child-rearing and domestic activities in most societies. Even in male-dominated societies like traditional Japan and China, the eldest female in a household usually had the right to manage household affairs with a fair degree of autonomy. Yet in China, Japan, and many other societies, women were not allowed to participate in public affairs, had hardly any property of their own, had little say over whom they married, and were clearly subordinate to their fathers and husbands socially and even legally.

So it is misleading to think of women's status as a unitary phenomenon: the way men regard and treat women and the rights of women have many dimensions, and the factors that constitute women's status are not always consistent with one another. Like other kinds of relations, the gender relations of sociocultural systems are complex. This is not surprising: people of other societies are not obliged to arrange their relations between males and females in such a way that modern social scientists can understand and label them with the simple phrase "women's status."

Nonetheless, we shall continue to use this phrase. It serves as a useful shorthand for the overall way women are regarded, the kinds of property and political rights they lack or enjoy, how highly their material and nonmaterial contributions are valued, and so forth. Most important, the phrase is a meaningful one for discussing the degree to which women are subordinate to men, a subject to which we now turn.

■ *Universal Subordination?*

A main question asked by anthropologists interested in gender is whether females are everywhere subordinate to males. Are there populations in which women and men are absolutely equal? Are there societies in which women dominate men?

The answer to the second question is no. Despite the stories we sometimes read or the occasional old adventure movie in which the hero is captured by "amazons," not a single instance of clear female domination over men has ever been found by ethnographers. Matriarchy—rule by women over men—does not exist, nor has it ever existed, to the best of our knowledge. Certainly there have been and are individual women who hold great power, control great wealth, and are held in high esteem. Certainly there are queens, female chiefs, and individual *matriarchs* of families and kin groups. But no instance of *matriarchy*—women as a social category holding power over men as a social category—has been documented.

The first question, of whether societies exist in which men and women are equal, has a more uncertain and complex answer. Even feminist anthropologists who have devoted their careers to studying gender relations do not agree on the answer. On the one hand, some scholars believe that women are never considered to be fully equal to men. They interpret the ethnographic record as showing that an asymmetry always exists between the sexes in one or more areas of life—in sexual freedom, familial relations, participation in religious rituals, political influence, or other realms. Even in domestic life, where women often have relative equality and autonomy, there is almost everywhere a cultural expectation that it is right and proper for husbands to dominate their wives and to make most of the important decisions. In social relations generally, women everywhere are likely to defer to men in a multitude of subtle and not-so-subtle ways—assuming, of course, that other dimensions of their relationship (such as age or class) do not overpower the gender dimension.

Those who believe that male dominance/female subordination is universal point to two fairly well established ethnographic generalizations. One applies to political institutions. In political life, sexual asymmetry almost always exists: in no society on record are the primary political leadership and authority roles regularly performed by females; but in many systems any woman is denied the right to succeed to political offices. In the majority of cases, even kin-group leadership roles are dominated by men. Male elders of the lineage or clan decide how the group's land and other resources are to be used and allocated, how the group's wealth objects are to be disposed of, whether the group is to engage in a battle to avenge a wrong, and so on. (But as we shall soon see, women do sometimes have significant influence over these matters, especially in matrilineal societies.)

The other realm of life in which sexual asymmetry is found is religion. In many societies women are excluded from performing major religious leadership roles and are forbidden to participate in the most important rituals. For example, sometimes the death of a man is blamed on the witchcraft of his wife, and she is cruelly punished for her alleged "homicide." In many New Guinea societies, men believe that their health or masculinity is jeopardized if they come into contact with women's menstrual discharges, so women must seclude themselves during their periods to avoid harming the men. Among some New Guinea people, contact with women is believed to be so polluting to men that husbands actually fear sexual intercourse with their wives and take elaborate ritual precautions to protect themselves from sexual pollution. (Chapter 16 discusses menstrual and sexual pollution in more detail.)

Widespread patterns of intersexual relations such as these led Michelle Zimbalist Rosaldo (1974) to generalize about the universal socioculturally defined superiority of men in these words:

> What is perhaps most striking and surprising is the fact that male, as opposed to female, activities are always recognized as predominantly important, and cultural systems give authority and value to the roles and activities of men. Contrary to some popular assumptions, there is little reason to believe that there are, or once were, societies of primitive matriarchs, societies in which women predominated in the same way that men predominate in the societies we actually know. . . . An asymmetry in the cultural evaluations of male and female, in the importance assigned to women and men, appears to be universal. (19)

According to Rosaldo and some other scholars, then, the activities of males are everywhere regarded as more important than those of females. Women as a social category are everywhere culturally devalued relative to men as a social category. Women are everywhere subordinate to men.

Other scholars interpret the ethnographic record differently. They note that most of the fieldwork and the ethnographies produced until the 1960s were done by men, who were usually uninterested in the females of the societies they studied and who, at any rate, had little access to women's points of view and behind-the-scenes maneuvers. Another possibility is that ethnographers and theorists both are guilty of ethnocentrism in their reporting and thinking. Because of the nature of Euro-American societies, with their inequalities in wealth and power (chapter 14), anthropologists tend to perceive relations of inequality, hierarchy, and domination/subordination even among populations where they are less developed. For instance, when a

wife greets her husband by bowing her head or stays behind him while walking, Western ethnographers may interpret such behaviors as genuine female deference and subordination, when in fact they are merely public shows of politeness.

In short, some scholars think that many fieldworkers have been sexually and culturally biased. Because of this bias, the ethnographic record is not objective; it "records" a universal female subordination not justified by the real world. Note, however, that even those who accuse others of bias may be biased themselves, albeit in another direction!

Those who argue in favor of the existence of societies with female-male equality also cite specific ethnographic cases that they think document their point. The Iroquois, a matrilineal people of northeastern North America, are the most famous ethnographic example of women achieving equality (or is it only relative equality?) with men. Iroquois women produced the corn and other cultivated foods, put them in storage, and largely controlled how they were distributed from the storehouses. Iroquois men were away from their apartments in the longhouse much of the time, engaged in warfare or cooperative hunting expeditions. The matrilineally related women of a longhouse influenced their inmarried husbands' behavior by withholding provisions from their hunting trips and war parties. Only men had the right to hold the most powerful political leadership offices, for only males could be elected to the great council of chiefs. But chiefs were nominated by and represented their matrilineages on the council, and the elderly women of the matrilineage had the most important say about which of their male relatives were nominated. Also, women had a voice in the deliberations of the council itself: they could veto declarations of war and introduce peace-making resolutions.

So who is right? Are women subordinate to men in all societies or not? Certainly, ethnographers have been biased—but does this bias explain their consistent reports of female subordination? Certainly, the Iroquois and other peoples demonstrate that women in some societies have achieved considerable control over their own lives and even over public decision making—but do such cases represent full equality of males and females? Indeed, would we know "full gender equality" if we saw it in a society? What would it look like? Would men and women have to carry out the same kinds of economic tasks before we could say they are equal? Is monogamy necessary, or can a society be polygynous and still qualify? Shall we require that

■ *Iroquois women's control over cultivated foods and their distribution gave them relatively high status.*

women occupy 50 percent of all leadership roles before we say they have equal rights? How should domestic life be organized before we can say that husbands in general do not dominate their wives?

As you can see, many questions must be answered before we can say whether women are everywhere subordinate—not the least of which is how we would know complete gender equality if we were to encounter it!

But perhaps too much weight is given to the issue of universal male dominance. Many anthropologists (especially feminist ones) are prone to think that their discipline must ferret out human populations in which women and men are equal in order for the anthropological data to lend support for the feminist cause. Feminist psychologists, sociologists, historians, biologists, and other scholars likewise have turned to the ethnographic record to support their positions. Their reasoning is that if ethnographic cases can be found in which women have achieved equality, then women will be more likely to be able to achieve equality in the future. Their hope is that there are many such cases. Conversely, their fear is that the ethnographic record shows few or no such cases.

But how much does it matter for the feminist cause if women are universally or nearly universally subordinate? Perhaps it does not matter as much as some think it does. Perhaps what matters most is that women and men are a good deal more equal in some populations than they are in others, which allows us to study the conditions under which future equality is likely to be possible. To argue that because women have always been subordinate they are forever doomed to be subordinate is analogous to many pre-twentieth-century

arguments that humans will never be able to fly. Just because no human society has achieved some state in the past does not mean that none will achieve it in the future. It does not mean that we should give up trying to achieve it today. And it certainly does not mean that late-twentieth-century Euro-American women have achieved about all the equality they are likely to be able to achieve, and therefore ought to shut up and be happy.

■ Influences on Women's Status

What influences the status of women in a human society? No one can generalize about this subject with confidence. Women's status is affected by such a multitude of factors that thus far no one has shown to everyone's satisfaction that any small number of forces are the prime shapers of women's status in all times and places. Here we discuss only a few hypotheses that point to influences that might be most widespread and important.

Women's Contributions to Material Welfare Many materialists argue that women's role in production strongly influences their property rights, their role in public affairs, men's attitudes toward them, their degree of personal freedom, and so on. One hypothesis is that where women produce a sizable proportion of the food, shelter, clothing, and other necessities of existence, their contributions will be recognized and

■ *Many anthropologists think that women's labor as gatherers gives them relative equality with men among foragers. San women gathered most of these nuts that are such an important food to their bands.*

rewarded with influence, property, prestige, dignity, and other benefits. In other words, the sexual division of labor, together with the proportion of valued goods women produce, are strong influences on women's overall status.

Such ideas might apply to some foraging and horticultural people, among whom women's gathering or gardening contributes a sizable amount of resources to their domestic groups. Women's productive labor might give them a status that is closer to equality with men than they have in other forms of adaptation in which their subsistence contributions are not as great.

But everyone's status is "closer to equality" in most hunter-gatherer and many horticultural populations (see chapters 7, 8, 9, and 14). So perhaps the relative equality of women in these two systems of adaptation results not from their importance in subsistence but from something else that "levels out" social inequalities of all kinds. In fact, so far no cross-cultural study has supported the hypothesis that female contribution to subsistence is consistently associated with high female status.

Women's Control over Key Resources A more complex proposal is that women's contribution to production, by itself, is not enough to "earn" them relative equality. It is necessary for women to contribute heavily to material welfare to gain resources, rights, and respect, but this alone is not sufficient. (After all, slaves contributed a lot to production in the Americas and the Caribbean in the eighteenth and nineteenth centuries, but they were not rewarded with social equality!) One specific hypothesis is that women must also own productive resources (land, tools), or have considerable control over the distribution of the products of their labor, or both. If women own productive resources and have a great deal of say over what happens to the goods they produce, then they can have some influence on the activities of men. Overall, this tends to give them more equality. Peggy Sanday found some support for this hypothesis in a cross-cultural study (1973).

This hypothesis seems to account reasonably well for some specific cases. For instance, Iroquois women controlled the production and distribution of important resources. They used this control to nominate their kinsmen to chiefly positions and to influence the public decision making from which they were formally excluded. Likewise, Hopi (see chapter 11) women owned land and had considerable control over the

distribution of its products. Women had relatively high status in both these societies.

Along the same lines, in many West African and Caribbean societies, women are more active than men in market trade in foodstuffs, handicrafts, textiles, and other goods produced by themselves. Market-trading women are sometimes able to transform their independent control over exchangeable resources into more equitable relations with men. Frequently, wives maintain separate income from their husbands, which they are free to expend on themselves and their children. One such group is the Yoruba of Nigeria, whose women formed a trade guild to regulate craft standards and protect the interests of its members. Yoruba women are said to be "quick to divorce their husbands if they find a more advantageous match, and generally difficult to control" (LeVine 1970, 179).

Thus many ethnographic and comparative studies suggest that controlling resources is one way for women to get respect and independence from their husbands, brothers, and other men. This ability to acquire some measure of control over family resources helps account for why many late-twentieth-century wives are demanding and receiving more help from their husbands in housework and child care. Since the 1950s, many married women have left hearth and home for wage employment. Increased female employment stems from many factors, including inflation, widespread cultural desires for an ever-increasing living standard, increasing worries about divorce, and structural changes to a more service-oriented economy. (Some ideas about how these forces led to increases in women's employment and to the women's movement are presented in Box 12.2.) Not only do working wives now have psychological ammunition against their husbands' domestic indolence ("I work forty hours a week just like you do!"), but they also have the wherewithal to back up their demands. With most women now out in the world of work, and with the families of married women now virtually dependent on their income to pay the bills, more women are demanding equal pay for equal work, equal treatment and opportunity in the work place, equal legal rights, and equal respect.

Descent and Postmarital Residence The form of descent and postmarital residence also influences women's overall status. Some scholars have noted that women in matrilineal and matrilocal societies have greater equality in many areas of life. What is it,

ON WOMEN'S LIBERATION

In the late 1960s a social movement organized by and for women got under way in the United States. In the 1970s many thousands of women joined the National Organization for Women, and millions more joined it in spirit by supporting economic and legal equality and an end to all forms of discrimination based on gender. Why did the women's movement occur when it did? Why were so many American women attracted to its goals of equality of opportunity in hiring and promotion, in salaries and wages, in divorce settlements, in domestic chores, and so forth?

One possible answer is women's rising "gender consciousness." The civil rights struggle and the antiwar movement in the 1960s made some women aware of their oppression. These movements also showed women that they could do something about it by organizing other Americans to pressure legislatures and companies, and even amend the Constitution to gain and guarantee equal rights.

No doubt the activism of the 1960s changed the political climate of the country, making women aware of their low status. And no doubt the experience gained by activist women in the 1960s provided them with organizational know-how, which they put to good use in attracting other women to their cause. But political movements are grounded in social and economic problems. People are not attracted to movements in large numbers unless they are dissatisfied.

The major source of discontent in a country such as the United States, in which money and wealth are so highly valued, is economic conditions. We can understand the women's movement, which represented a change in women's consciousness (ideas) about their proper roles, by considering economic circumstances, which changed in a certain way in the 1950s through the 1970s.

In *America Now*, anthropologist Marvin Harris analyzes these economic shifts. They can be reduced to two interrelated overall changes in the past three decades: (1) increased employment of women and (2) alterations in the structure of the American economy.

Roughly 50 percent of single American women have had jobs since the 1940s. But except during the Great Depression and World War II, relatively few married women worked for a wage. In 1947 only 21 percent of married women worked outside the household. Over the next four decades, this percentage rose steadily, to 32 percent in 1960, 42 percent in 1970, 51 percent in 1980, and nearly 60 percent today. Surprisingly, but significantly, the in-crease in the employment rate for women with preschool-aged children has been even greater than the overall rate since 1970: in 1948 only 11 percent of women with children under six were employed, but this number rose to 19 percent in 1960, to 30 percent in 1970, to 45 percent in 1980, and to about 60 percent today. Why did so many women, especially married women with young children, have the desire to find jobs during the past two or three decades? Why were their husbands agreeable to their employment?

Part of the answer is rising consumer expectations, spurred on by advertising that created new desires in the mass market. More important, high rates of inflation in the mid-1960s through the 1970s seriously eroded the purchasing power of a family's income. Prices of housing (both for sale and rent), autos, medical care, education, energy, food, and other necessities skyrocketed. The purchasing power of Average Joe's single paycheck could not keep up with inflation. In fact, the average American family with only the husband employed actually lost real income in some years—between 1969 and 1970, single-earner families lost 6.9 percent in real earnings. To keep up with inflation and achieve the American Dream became impossible for millions of families with a single income.

But getting a job requires that jobs be available, and that the job seeker have the skills to qualify for them. As is well known, the American economy has

---

specifically, about matrilineality and matrilocality that tends to give relatively high status to females? It is *not* that "females rule" in these societies. Generally, men hold positions of both political and domestic authority in matrilineal societies, just as they do in patrilineal and bilateral ones (see chapter 11). The main difference is whom among their relatives men have authority over: their sisters and sister's children in matrilineal systems versus their sons, unmarried daughters, and son's children in patrilineal systems.

But other elements of matrilineality and matrilocality tend to benefit females. Martin Whyte found that women enjoy more authority in domestic matters, have more sexual freedom, and have more worth placed on

undergone important structural changes in the past few decades. Automation, overseas competition, and other factors have resulted in the rise of the so-called *service economy*, and have led to what is sometimes called the *postindustrial economy*. These kinds of jobs became available in vast numbers. Most women who filled jobs beginning in the 1950s became typists, secretaries, receptionists, cashiers, waitresses, file clerks, nurses, retail clerks, teachers, and other people-processing and information-processing jobs (as Harris calls them).

Because these were traditionally women's jobs, male employees were not threatened by female hirees. Because so many women were looking for work, and because married women were not considered the primary source of income for their families, employers could get away with paying them low wages. (In this, the opinions of bosses were reinforced by many husbands, who salvaged their male egos by saying they "let their wife work because she wanted to.") Women were passed over for most promotions, for their bosses often thought women unsuitable for managerial positions, considered female employees liable to resign, and didn't want flak from those male employees who got beat out by women and who would have to take orders from them. So on the job, most women were second-class employees—they earned only 50 to 60 percent of what men made for compar-

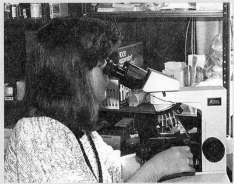

able work, were usually the first laid off, and had little chance of moving up.

This situation might have been more tolerable if so many husbands had not insisted on having the best of both worlds: the wife's paycheck as well as her continued household duties and subordination. As we mentioned in chapter 7, job-holding women in the United States and Europe spend between ten and thirteen hours daily on their jobs and housework combined, as compared to only seven or eight hours daily for men. Large numbers of women were caught in a double bind: underrewarded at work and overworked at home, they were willing to pay attention when the leaders of the feminist movement told them they were exploited by bosses, husbands, and the male sex in general.

This analysis helps to correct a popular misconception about the women's movement—that a small clique of radical feminists succeeded in making large numbers of American women dissatisfied with their so-called traditional roles as homemakers, wives, and mothers. Feminists have been blamed for making housewives feel guilty about their lack of independence, for making women not want to have babies, for making women into hedonists, for making women want to be just like a man, for the high divorce rate, for abortions, and for many other "problems."

But feminists are not to blame. Like all social movements, feminism does indeed promote and channel the direction of change, but it also is a response to other kinds of changes. Feminist leaders did not stir up women who were otherwise happy, nor did they plant ideas into heads that were otherwise empty. Rather, millions of Americans supported the women's movement because changing economic conditions provided women with the opportunity to work, even as the maintenance of their family's living standards required them to leave home. Yet neither their bosses nor their husbands—the one benefiting from their cheap wages, the other from their domestic services—were willing to grant them rewards proportionate to their efforts. ■

Sources: Berch (1982), Harris (1981), United States Bureau of the Census (1989:373–74).

their lives in these societies. Two factors contribute to their equality. First, because it is husbands who go to live with the families of their wives, sisters generally remain with or close to one another throughout their lives. Inmarrying husbands face a relatively cohesive and enduring group of related women. A typical wife thus has her mother, sisters, and perhaps other female relatives around to support her in domestic quarrels. Second, in many matrilineal and matrilocal societies, domestic authority over a married woman is divided between her husband and her brother. Alice Schlegel suggests that this arrangement increases her freedom, because each man acts as a check on the other's attempts to dominate her.

Contrast this situation to patrilineal and patrilocal China before the mid-twentieth century. When a Chinese woman married, she was incorporated as a member of her husband's household. This was symbolized by the fact that she began to pay homage to his deceased patrilineal ancestors rather than to her own. A woman's relationships with her own parents and siblings were sharply curtailed when she married. Her main duties were to work for her husband and his parents, to obey them in all things, and to bear them male heirs. In many respects a new wife was treated as a domestic servant to her father- and mother-in-law: she was given arduous household tasks to perform for most of her waking hours, and she could be berated and even beaten with impunity. Only when she herself bore sons and heirs to her husband's family did her status improve, and only when she herself became a mother-in-law to her sons' wives could she relax a bit. The Confucian social and moral philosophy, which held that women must always be submissive to men, affected the way wives and daughters-in-law were treated. But also important were the social facts that wives were fully incorporated into the households of their husbands' parents and the lines of authority over them were clearly and legally redrawn upon their marriage. A Chinese wife had few viable alternatives to submission to her husband's family, and few sources of social support when she was treated poorly.

Overall Societal Complexity So far, we have discussed ideas that try to account for the variations in women's status synchronically. That is, we have treated societies as if they are frozen in time, and we have looked at what kinds of other sociocultural factors might be associated with variations in women's status. Another approach considers women's status in general evolutionary terms (chapter 5). That approach largely ignores specific societies with their specific variations and asks instead what has happened to women's overall status in the very long term.

Rather than present an overview of existing evolutionary hypotheses, here we concentrate on one. This hypothesis claims that women's overall status has tended to decrease as social complexity has increased (at least until the development of industrialized technology and the profound sociocultural changes that accompanied it). This idea comes mainly from the work of Jack Goody, Ester Boserup, and Martin Whyte, whose ideas we shall sketch and integrate. The following argument is complex, but it is worth the effort to understand it.

Not only is it a fascinating attempt to show how women's place in societies has changed throughout history, but it is yet another example of how alterations in one subsystem affect other subsystems in subtle and unexpected ways.

Recall the strong relationship between cultivation systems and the relative degree of importance of women's labor to subsistence. As the intensity of cultivation increases, women participate less and less in agricultural tasks, for reasons suggested earlier in this chapter. Recall also (from chapter 9) that intensive agriculture is generally associated with societies that are highly stratified, with economies featuring much centralized control, with well-developed craft and other specializations, with marked distinctions between rulers and ruled, and so on. Such large-scale hierarchically organized societies are called *complex* by anthropologists. How does increasing agricultural intensity, together with these other features of complexity, affect the status of women?

Jack Goody provides a hypothesis that makes connections between increasing complexity and the (seemingly unrelated) overall status of women. In a cross-cultural study he compared the predominantly horticultural societies of sub-Saharan Africa with the mainly intensive agricultural societies of Eurasia (Europe, the Middle East, and Asia). In Eurasia, land is relatively scarcer because of higher population densities. It is also more intensively exploited, with plows, irrigation, and fertilization with animal droppings used to increase yields. Because land is scarcer and more productive in Eurasia, there is more competition for it, family wealth and prestige tend to depend more on access to it, and a family has a greater chance of losing it to someone else. Finally, because Eurasian societies are generally more stratified than African societies, in the former there is a real danger of downward mobility for one's children and grandchildren unless access to resources is maintained through the generations. Therefore, in Eurasia, parents are concerned about maintaining their male and female descendants' access to land, since so much else depends on it.

Goody argues that these differences between Africa and Eurasia have important sociocultural consequences. In Africa, land and other property is generally transmitted through males. An African man passes land rights down to his sons; his daughters receive little or no inheritance but rely largely on their husbands to supply them with access to land, cattle, and other productive resources. In Eurasia it is relatively more important that parents make a "good match" for their daughters, meaning that their daughters marry someone of at least equal wealth. So in most Eurasian societies, parents divide property among their daughters as well as their sons in order to maintain their daughters' and daughters' children's access to adequate resources. By giving property to their daughter, parents improve her chances of attracting "the right kind of husband," one with sufficient resources to maintain the social and economic standing of her and her children. Bilateral inheritance thus is typical of Eurasia.

Often, Eurasian daughters receive their inheritance when they marry—that is, as a dowry (chapter 10). Dowries usually include money, jewelry, and household goods rather than land itself. The purpose of a dowry is not to provide a daughter and her children with land but to attract a man with a sizable inheritance of land and other property as her husband. Therefore, dowry is the predominant form of marital transaction in European and Asian societies. In contrast, dowry is practically nonexistent in sub-Saharan Africa, where bridewealth is the predominant form of marital exchange.

All these factors influence patterns of marriage. In horticultural Africa, where female labor is so important to subsistence, men who can pay bridewealth for several wives acquire a critical resource: their wives' labor. But more wives mean more children, which in turn means the need to find spouses for all these children. In a bridewealth society a man acquires wives for his sons partly out of the bridewealth he receives for his daughters. So, unlike dowry, bridewealth tends to "circulate" in a single generation rather than "pass down" to the next. If, in contrast, an African man had to provide all his daughters with dowries, the daughters would become more of an economic liability than an asset to him. So we see how the importance of female labor to subsistence, polygyny, and bridewealth all tend to go together in most African populations; they form a system, each reinforcing the other.

In contrast, Eurasian societies with bilateral inheritance tend to be monogamous. This is because (1) women's labor has less value in accumulating wealth in intensive agricultural systems and (2) it would be difficult for all but the very rich to provide an adequate dowry for the daughters of more than one wife. It is relatively more important for parents to control who their daughters marry, for a bad match could impoverish her and her offspring and lower the wealth and honor of the whole family. A woman therefore has little say about whom she marries. As part of their

effort to control whom their daughters marry, parents place restrictions on their unmarried daughter's relations with males. In the Islamic Middle East and northern India, a woman's virtue strongly reflected on the honor of her whole family, so extreme steps (to Western eyes) were taken to ensure that no question could arise about her virtue: daughters lived secluded lives in the houses of their fathers and had to veil their faces and cover their heads when out in public.

■ What about the Status of Modern Women?

We conclude by pulling together some of the ideas covered in this chapter and suggesting their relevance for women today. Some scholars try to show what has happened to the overall status of women throughout the course of sociocultural evolution. Generally, they believe that women in foraging and many horticultural populations had relative equality with men, especially in matrilineal and matrilocal societies. As agricultural

■ Much evidence suggests that the overall status of women tends to decline as sociocultural complexity increases, at least until the industrial era. In the Islamic Middle East, males exercise great control over their daughters, sisters, and wives. These Bedouin women are required to wear veils because unrelated males are present.

systems grew more intense, the sexual division of labor was affected, and women's labor was pulled out of agriculture and into domestic tasks. A whole set of sociocultural changes accompanied intensification. Goody argues that as stratification increased, there was a greater chance for downward social mobility unless control over productive resources was passed along to the next generation. This led to changes in inheritance and marriage patterns. Together, these "developments" led to the deterioration of women's overall status in more complex societies: women lost the ability to choose their marital partner, a double standard of sexual morality became pronounced, and women had less of a say in domestic matters and less independent property of their own.

This evolutionary trend has been reversed in some countries in the twentieth century, although complexity certainly has continued to increase. Perhaps this reversal is because industrial technology increasingly substitutes for labor and muscle power, reducing the relevance of biological differences for recruitment into economic tasks ("jobs"). Perhaps, as materialists would argue, it is because so many modern married women feel obliged to seek employment in order to maintain the living standards to which they and their spouses have (or would like to) become accustomed. Or perhaps, as idealists might argue, it is all attributable simply to an autonomous cultural change—the development of women's "gender consciousness" of their low status and common interests. (See box 12.2 for a discussion of gender consciousness and the women's movement.)

Whatever the reason, anthropological ideas about gender relations provide modern women with a hope and a warning. The hope derives from the fact that the roles, rights, and restrictions placed on women vary throughout humanity, from place to place and time to time. As we have seen, we do not know whether there has ever been a human population in which women had an overall status equal to men. We can certainly say that women enjoy more equality in some sociocultural systems than in others. So there is reason to think that equality of opportunity and achievement (if not the elimination of all distinctions based on gender, an idea to which some feminists subscribe) is a possible future for womankind.

The materialist hypotheses we have described suggest that the provision of equal economic/employment opportunities for women will be a key factor. It will bring with it improvements for women in other realms of life, such as sexuality, legal equality, participation in political life, and husbands' sharing of child care and housework.

Or will it? This is our warning: Anthropological studies have not yet uncovered the magic key that unlocks the door leading to equality between the sexes. No one thing that feminists can do will inevitably lead to equal treatment for women in the work place, in the household, in the bedroom, and in the voting booth. No one male-dominated institution, chauvinistic attitude, or discriminatory practice that modern societies could change will suddenly and radically improve the position of women in various realms of life. For example, if lawmakers should outlaw sexual discrimination in the work place or make comparable pay for comparable work legally mandatory, it might take decades for the effects to "work through" the sociocultural system and be realized in greater female-male equality. It is possible that passing laws—including amending the "supreme law of the land"—against discrimination on the basis of gender will have little effect on male-female social relations or on male attitudes toward women. So anthropological ideas suggest that modern feminists must continue to work on a broad front to achieve their goals.

Summary

Differences between males and females are everywhere an important basis for recruitment into social groups and roles. Gender is rooted in biological differences between males and females, but sociocultural systems vary in the importance they attach to gender differences. Gender does not matter everywhere to the same degree or in the same way.

Much attention has been given to how and why the sexual division of labor varies cross-culturally. One firm conclusion of this research is that our sexual stereotypes that men are breadwinners and women are caretakers are not based on natural differences between the sexes. Male domination is not rooted in men's supplying the necessities of existence, for women's labor frequently produces much or most of the food supply.

There are certain widespread patterns in the sexual division of labor, as shown in Table 12.1. Three major hypotheses have been offered to explain the broad cross-cultural similarities in the allocation of economic tasks: superior male strength; the depression of fertility that seems to occur when a woman engages in heavy exercise; and the compatibility of a task with care of infants and young children, which is everywhere primarily a female responsibility.

No biological difference can account for the cross-cultural variations in the sexual division of labor. A difference to which much attention has been given is the higher importance of female labor in horticultural populations relative to intensive agriculturalists. Credible hypotheses explain why women's contributions to subsistence decline as intensity increases. The seasonally maturing cereal grains grown by most intensive agriculturalists require seasonally heavy work (done by males), more processing of food before it is eaten (done by females), and more time spent in caring for domesticated animals (done by females). As a result, males spend more time in cultivation, and females experience a greater domestic work load. As technology reduces the importance of biological differences in task performance and as the birth rate declines, gender will matter less for occupational recruitment in industrialized nations.

Another issue in gender studies is the nature and causes of diversity in the status of women. Even specialists in this subject cannot agree on whether ethnographic studies reveal that females are universally subordinate to males. This is mainly because no explicit criteria can be used to judge whether there are populations in which males and females are fully equal. It does seem to be true that females as a social category are never dominant over males as a social category.

A multitude of forces influence women's overall status in a sociocultural system, including their relative contributions to subsistence, their control over key resources, the prevalent pattern of descent and post-marital residence, and overall societal complexity. Studies that document the variability in women's status suggest that greater sexual equality is an achievable goal for modern women, but there may be no single attitude or institution that feminists can alter that will give women equality in all realms of life.

Key Terms

sexual division of labor
strength hypothesis
fertility maintenance
  hypothesis
child-care-compatibility
  hypothesis
status of women

Suggested Readings

■ Boserup, E. *Women's Role in Economic Development.* London: Allen and Unwin, 1970.
  A study concerning the changing role of women in farming societies, including how the intensification of agriculture affects women's status.

■ Buckley, Thomas, and Alma Gottlieb, eds., *Blood Magic: The Anthropology of Menstruation.* Berkeley and Los Angeles: University of California Press, 1988.
  The title of this book speaks for itself.

■ Dahlberg, F., ed. *Woman the Gatherer.* New Haven: Yale University Press, 1981.
  A collection of papers that draws on archaeological and ethnographic data to examine the role of women in foraging societies.

■ Friedl, E. *Women and Men: An Anthropologist's View.* New York: Holt, Rinehart and Winston, 1975.
  A brief study of male and female roles in nonindustrial societies.

■ Margolis, M. *Mothers and Such: American Views of Women and How They Changed.* Berkeley, Calif.: University of California Press, 1984.
  A study examining the historical changes in the status and role of American women.

■ Martin, M. K., and B. Voorhies. *Female of the Species.* New York: Columbia University Press, 1975.
  A comparative study focusing on the relative status of women that examines status differences by studying economic differences between societies.

■ Mead, Margaret. *Sex and Temperament in Three Primitive Societies.* New York: William Morrow, 1963.
  A book originally published in 1935 and based on research in New Guinea societies. The first major attack by an anthropologist on the notion that biological differences explain the differences in roles between males and females. Although dated, it is a highly readable argument that many gender differences that are thought to be biological are in reality cultural.

■ Ortner, Sherry B., and Harriet Whitehead, eds. *Sexual Meanings: The Cultural Construction of Gender and Sexuality.* Cambridge: Cambridge University Press, 1981.
  Contains ten papers, all written from a symbolist theoretical perspective, on gender relations in various societies.

■ Rosaldo, M. Z., and Louise Lamphere, eds. *Women, Culture, and Society.* Stanford: Stanford University Press, 1974.
  A collection of essays by women, examining the role, status, and perceptions of women in various societies.

■ Sanday, Peggy R. *Female Power and Male Dominance.* Cambridge: Cambridge University Press, 1981.

A lengthy and involved cross-cultural study of the factors affecting the status of women and the cultural imagery of females.

■ Schlegel, A., ed. *Sexual Stratification: A Cross-Cultural View.* New York: Columbia University Press, 1977.
Essays on the range of relative statuses of women, with data from a wide range of societies.

■ Tiffany, Sharon W. *Women, Work, and Motherhood.* Englewood Cliffs, N.J.: Prentice-Hall, 1982.

A very short overview that discusses women's place in foraging, pastoral, and cultivating societies.

■ Whyte, M. K. *The Status of Women in Preindustrial Societies.* Princeton, N.J.: Princeton University Press, 1978.
A cross-cultural study examining the status of women in ninety-three societies and attempting to detail the variations in how women are treated and culturally regarded.

THE ORGANIZATION OF POLITICAL LIFE

■ *Contents*

■ (Above) *When we think of law and social control, we usually think of the police.*

very society has some form of political system, meaning those institutions that organize and direct the collective actions of the population. In small societies, political leadership and organization may be informal and even ad hoc. Only when a specific need for leadership arises does some individual assume an overt leadership role. In general, the larger the population, the more formalized the leadership and the more complex the political organization.

Likewise, as mentioned in chapter 3, all societies demand some minimal degree of conformity from their members. All therefore develop mechanisms of social control by which the behaviors of individuals are constrained and directed into acceptable channels. There are always behavioral patterns that are approved or acceptable, and patterns that are disapproved or unacceptable. By means of social control a society encourages normatively proper behavior and discourages unacceptable actions, the objective being the maintenance of harmony and cooperation. The most serious deviations from acceptable behavior, which threaten the cohesiveness of the group, fall under that aspect of social control known as *law*, also discussed in this chapter. It is important to note that in the least organized societies law and political organization exist independently of one another. However, as political organization becomes increasingly formalized and structured, governmental institutions take over legal institutions, until legal institutions become part of the formal political structure.

Forms of Political Organization

When we speak of the political organization of a particular sociocultural system, we are frequently left with the impression that political boundaries and sociocultural boundaries are the same. But the boundaries of a *polity*, or politically organized unit, may or may not correspond with the boundaries of a particular way of life. For example, the Comanche of the Great Plains shared a common language, customs, and ethnic identity, yet politically they were never organized above the local group. Thus, the term *Comanche* refers to a people with a common language and lifeway, who never united to carry out common political activities.

At the other extreme we find highly centralized polities that incorporate several socioculturally distinct peoples. In these instances the political boundary is suprasocietal and multicultural. The United States is unusual in this regard only in the degree of sociocultural heterogeneity that exists in the population. France, though predominantly "French," also includes Bretons and Basques. India has several hundred different ethnic groups. The U.S.S.R., China, Indonesia, and the Philippines also integrate highly diversified populations into a single polity. In fact, every large and most small countries in the world today politically integrate several ethnic groups (see chapter 18).

Political organization falls into four basic forms. From the least to the most complex, these forms are **bands** (**simple** and **composite**), **tribes, chiefdoms,** and **states.** Today, few societies exist that are not integrated into state-level political systems. Thus, to understand societies organized at less complex levels, we have to reconstruct the structure of such societies at an earlier period.

■ *Bands*

As the least complex form, bands were probably the earliest form of human political structure (see chapter 7). As more complex political systems developed, band-level societies were unable to compete for resources. Thus, bands survived until the modern period only in regions of the world with limited natural resources. Most known band-level societies were found in the dry deserts and grasslands of Australia, Africa, and the Americas. A few others lived in the tropical forests of Africa, Asia, and South America, and in the boreal forest and tundra regions of North America and Asia.

Bands consist of a number of families living together and cooperating in economic activities throughout the year. Most frequently, band-level organization was found among peoples with foraging economies, which usually dictated low population densities and high

■ *Band-level political organization survives in only a few isolated regions of the world, such as among the Sau of the Southern African Kalahari desert.*

seasonal mobility. As a result, only a relatively small number of people could stay together throughout the year. Bands ranged in size from only a dozen to several hundred individuals. The adaptive significance of the band's size and seasonal mobility is described in chapter 7. In this chapter we are concerned with leadership statuses and political organization of bands.

The smallest bands, called *simple bands,* were usually no larger than an extended family and were structured as such. Leadership was informal, with the oldest or one of the older male members of the family serving as leader. However, decision making was reached through consensus and involved both adult males and females; simple bands operated as families. Because all members of the band were related either through descent or marriage, they were exogamous units, and members of the band had to seek spouses from other bands. Thus, although an autonomous economic and political unit, every band was by social necessity allied through intermarriage with other bands, usually territorially adjacent ones. Simple bands usually had names, although names may have been informal and may have simply referred to some prominent geographic feature associated with the band's usual territory.

Resource availability influenced the formation of such small groups. Simple bands were often associated with the hunting of nonmigratory game animals, such as deer, guanaco, moose, or small mammals, which occupy a limited territory on a year-round basis and are found either singly or in small herds. The foraging

activities of simple bands usually did not generate any significant surpluses of food, which necessitated the year-round hunting of game animals. Effective hunting of these animals required only a few male hunters who had intimate knowledge of the seasonal shifts in range of these animals within their territory. The game resources of such areas could be exploited most effectively by a small and highly mobile population. In addition, such bands depended on the seasonal collection of wild roots, berries, nuts, and other edible plants, as well as on limited fishing and shellfish collection.

Composite bands consisted of a larger aggregation of families, sometimes numbering in the hundreds. In contrast to simple bands, composite bands encompassed a number of unrelated extended families. Although leadership in composite bands was informal, it was more defined. Such leaders have frequently been called **big men.** Big men did not hold formal offices, and leadership was based on influence rather than authority over band members. **Influence** is merely the ability to convince people that they should act as you suggest. **Authority** is the recognized right of an individual to command another person to act in a particular way. Thus, a big-man leader could not, by virtue of his position, make demands or impose rules on the members of the band; and his decisions were not binding on others. Because big-man status did not involve a formal office, no prescribed process for attaining leadership status existed. A man might emerge as the leader through a variety of personal accomplishments or qualities, such as his proven ability in hunting or warfare, the supernatural powers he possessed, or merely his charisma. There was no set tenure in the position, which was filled by a man until he was informally replaced by some other leader.

Like simple bands, composite bands are frequently nomadic groups that move within a relatively well defined range. However, because of their greater size, composite bands are not as cohesive as simple bands and are politically more volatile. Disputes between families may result in some members joining another band, or even the band splitting into two or more bands.

The formation of composite bands resulted from economic pressures that facilitated or necessitated the cooperation of a larger number of individuals than found in a single extended family. As in the case of simple bands, the behavior of the principal game animals was an important influence. Composite bands were associated with the seasonal hunting of migratory animals that form large herds, such as bison and caribou. Migratory herd animals usually appeared only seasonally in the range of a particular composite band as the herd moved between its summer and winter ranges. Because bison and caribou migrate in herds that sometimes number in the tens of thousands, there was no difficulty in locating the herds on the open grasslands and tundra. Unlike the nonmigratory-animal hunters, who secure game steadily throughout the year, hunters of migratory animals take most of their game only twice a year, usually as the herds pass through their territories during migrations.

Hunting large herds of animals effectively required directing the movements of the herd into situations where large numbers could be slaughtered. Herds might be run over a cliff, into a holding pen, or into a lake, where hunters in boats could kill them. Regardless of the actual method used, all of these strategies required the presence of a larger group of hunters than was available in a simple band. Thus, composite bands were formed to bring together a sufficiently large number of hunters to control the movements of large herds of animals.

The Comanche of the southern Great Plains of the United States illustrate the nature of composite bands. These horse-raising, bison-hunting people were politically autonomous until the Red River War of 1875. During the early and mid-nineteenth century, the Comanche numbered about 6,000 to 7,000, divided between five and thirteen main bands. Comanche bands had only vaguely defined territories, and frequently two or more bands occupied the same general area or had overlapping ranges. Membership in Comanche bands was fluid: both individuals and families could and did shift from one band to another, or a number of families might join together to establish a new band. Some anthropologists have theorized that there were only five major bands, with a varying number of secondary bands appearing and disappearing from time to time.

A band consisted of a number of families, each headed by an older male member who was "peace chief" or "headman." One of these family heads also served as the peace chief for the entire band. There was no formalized method of selecting either the family heads or the head of the band. As the Comanche say, "No one made him such; he just got that way." A Comanche peace chief was usually a man known for his kindness, wisdom, and ability to lead by influencing other men. Although a war record was important,

■ Among the Comanche, "peace chiefs" lead the band villages. Quanah Parker, pictured here, was one of the most famous Comanche peace chiefs.

peace chiefs were not chosen from among the most aggressive or ambitious men. Such men usually remained war chiefs—great warriors who periodically recruited men to raid neighbors—but frequently had little influence outside war and raiding.

A band peace chief was responsible for the well-being of the band. Through a consensus of the family heads, he directed the seasonal movement of the band and the bison hunts. He did have men who voluntarily assisted him. In the morning the peace chief usually sent out two men to scout the area around the camp for the presence of enemy raiding parties. He also sent a crier through the camp periodically to announce plans for the movement of the camp, an upcoming hunt, or some other cooperative activities. During the bison hunts, the peace chief called on a number of men from the camp to police the hunt and restrain overly eager hunters from scattering the herd and thus spoiling the hunt for others.

In an extraordinarily individualistic and egalitarian society, Comanche band leaders had to strive for and maintain consensus. If a dispute arose and a consensus could not be reached, individuals and families were free either to shift residence to another band or even to form a new band under another leader.

Comanche bands were economically and politically autonomous units. Only rarely did two or more bands come together for any unified action, and never did leaders of the bands come together to discuss issues. At the same time there was a very strong consciousness of common identity, of being Comanche. Comanches freely traveled between bands to visit, marry, and even shift residence. There was an informally reached general consensus on whether relations with a particular neighboring group were friendly or hostile. Comanche bands also usually refrained from attacking other Comanche bands, although on occasion some Comanche bands did ally themselves with foreign groups.

Thus, on the band level of political organization, populations are fragmented into numerous independent political units which operate only at the local-group level. These various communities share a common cultural identity and usually attempt to maintain harmonious relations with each other, but they lack any political structure capable of organizing all of the various communities into a single unit for collective actions.

■ Tribes

Tribes differ from bands in that they have formally organized institutions that unite the scattered residential communities, give the society greater cohesiveness, and make possible a more united response to external threats. These institutions are called **sodalities.** Sodalities take various forms: they may be based on large kin groups, such as clans and lineages; on nonkinship units, such as age sets (see chapter 16); or on voluntary associations, such as warrior societies. Regardless of their exact nature, sodalities unify geographically dispersed communities into political units. Although tribal-level societies are usually egalitarian, with leadership dependent in part on the persuasive abilities of individuals, formalized political offices with institutionalized authority exist. Although tribes vary greatly in structure, here we can examine only two tribal-level societies.

The Osage, who formerly occupied the prairie and woodlands of southwestern Missouri, had a tribal structure organized around kinship-based sodalities. Numbering between 5,000 and 6,000, the Osage originally had a mixed horticultural and hunting subsistence base. After the acquisition of horses during the

eighteenth century, the Osage gradually shifted toward an increasing economic dependence on bison hunting.

The Osage were divided into five named villages, each with its own fields and designated hunting territory. Each village contained some members of all twenty-four Osage patrilineal clans. These clans were, in turn, divided between the *Tsi-zhu* (sky) moiety, with nine clans, and the *Hon-ga* (earth) moiety, with fifteen clans. The villages reflected this structure: each village was divided by an east-west street, with Tsi-zhu families living on the north side and Hon-ga families on the south.

Osage political organization was structured in such a manner that the authority over and responsibility for internal and external affairs was divided. Internal village affairs were the realm of the two village *ga-hi'-ge,* or "chiefs." Within each village was a *Tsi-zhu ga-hi'-ge* (sky chief), a formal position that was hereditary within a specific clan of the Sky moiety, and a *Hon-ga ga-hi'-ge* (earth chief), which likewise was hereditary within a specific clan of the Earth moiety. Each chief chose five *a-ki-da,* or "soldiers," to assist him in his duties. Although the position of chief was hereditary, succession was not based on a rule of primogeniture. In fact, any close male relative of a deceased chief theoretically could assume the position. The five soldiers acting in council chose the new chief from among this group of kinsmen.

The responsibility of the chief was internal. Each was responsible for settling disputes within his half of the village. In addition, the two village chiefs led the village hunts, each acting as the leader on alternate days. The chiefs theoretically received all of the game taken on the hunt and divided it among the participating families, with the chiefs taking a larger share because they were responsible for feeding the widows, orphans, and old people in their half of the village. They were also responsible for compensating families for any losses incurred during the days they led the hunt. While hunting, the Osage were frequently attacked by enemy raiders, who killed hunters and took horses. The chief had to compensate the family of any slain hunter and replace any stolen horses. The responsibilities of the two chiefs were identical except in one regard: the sky chief was responsible for entertaining and protecting visitors within the village.

In most matters the chiefs of each village acted independently of the other village chiefs, and it is difficult to determine if any set of chiefs had authority over the others. During at least part of the historic period, the two chiefs from the Upland Forest village were the most influential and were sometimes referred to as the *tribal chiefs*, but their actual authority over the chiefs of the other villages is questionable. While the Osage were still in Missouri, there was little need for direct consultation between the chiefs, because hunting territories were already defined. However, after the Osage moved west and became dependent on bison hunting on the plains, cooperation was needed. Village hunting territories were not defined on the plains, and before the hunts the chiefs from the five villages met in council and agreed on the areas where each village would hunt during that season.

Authority over external affairs, both human and supernatural, was the exclusive realm of the *non-hon-zhin-ga*, or "little-old-men." These men were highly trained ritual leaders who served their respective clans. Each clan had its own set of rituals and ritual knowledge known only by the little-old-men of that clan. Each ritual was divided into twenty-four parts, one for each of the clans. The learning of the clan rituals was a long process, and most individuals were old before completing their initiation. Each village had one or more little-old-men for each clan. Collectively these

men formed a village council, which was responsible for the performance of the village's required rituals and for warfare. To the Osage, warfare was a ritual activity: only a council attended by little-old-men from all twenty-four clans could initiate a war, and then only if representatives of all twenty-four clans agreed. The war ritual required a little-old-man from each clan to perform his clan part to make it complete. From among their own membership the little-old-men chose a *do-don-hon-ga*, or leader for the war party. This leader was chosen not for his military ability but solely for his ritual knowledge. The *do-don-hon-ga* carried the ritual medicine bundles for war and prayed during the actual fighting. The strategy and conduct of the battle were left to eight men chosen to lead the attack. In warfare and religious activities the chiefs and their soldiers played no direct role in their official capacities; these men were only participants if they were also little-old-men.

Any group of little-old-men that included the full representation of the clans symbolically represented the tribe as a whole. Thus, if the little-old-men from one village declared war by performing the war ritual, then all Osage regardless of village affiliation were bound by their action. The villages were thus subordinate to what was seen not as a village action but as a collective action of the clans in regard to external affairs. Among the Osage, then, formalized kinship units—the patrilineal clans—were the sodalities that cut across village boundaries and united the Osage as a unit capable of collective actions.

The Cheyenne of the Great Plains, whose adaptation we discussed in chapter 7, illustrate how an entire tribe can be organized without using kin-based units. Numbering between 3,000 and 3,500 during the early 1800s, the Cheyenne, like the neighboring Comanche, were horse-mounted bison hunters. They were divided into ten main nomadic villages, which averaged between 300 and 350 people. Village membership was not based on kinship, although the members of a particular village were usually related either by blood or by marriage. Village membership was relatively stable, and marriages between villagers were common. In spite of this stability, myths concerning village origins were not well developed, and band names were only nicknames (e.g., Grayhairs, Hairrope Men, Ridge Men, or some other trivial characteristic). Although a particular village usually frequented a certain range, there was no sense of village territoriality. Periodically and seasonally, family camps and subvillage camps broke off from the main village.

■ *An Osage man spent most of his adult life learning the ritual knowledge of his clan in order to become a Little-old-man.*

The only time the entire tribe came together was in early summer, when all of the widely scattered villages gathered into a single camp at a predetermined location. This crescent-shaped encampment stretched for several miles from end to end, with the open portion facing East. Within the tribal encampment every village had a designated location; and while camped together, they performed the great tribal ceremonies (e.g., the Arrow Renewal, the Sun Dance, or the Animal Dance). At least one and possibly two of these rituals were performed, depending on the particular ritual needs of the tribe at that time. Following the performance of the ritual(s), the tribe as a unit staged the great summer bison hunt. After the hunt, the tribe again scattered into smaller village camps.

Politically, the tribe was controlled by the Council of Forty-four and the warrior societies. The Council of Forty-four, which had both political and religious duties, was headed by the Sweet Medicine chief, who was responsible for keeping the Sweet Medicine bundle, a sacred package of sweet grass. Second to him in importance were four other sacred chiefs, each representative of specific supernatural beings. Under these five sacred chiefs were thirty-nine ordinary chiefs.

Chiefs served in their positions for ten years and could not be removed for any reason. Serving as a chief placed a burden on the individuals. Usually chiefs were selected from among the older men, all of whom had war records. However, when an individual was chosen as a chief, he was to act like a chief, not an aggressive warrior. If the man was an officer in one of the warrior societies, he had to resign his position, although he remained a member of the society. A chief was to be generous, kindly, even tempered, and aloof from everyday disputes. In short, he was expected to display ideal human behavior at all times: he was to take care of the poor, settle disputes between individuals, and be responsible for the ritual performances that protected the tribe.

There were five original warrior societies, but this number was not fixed. These were formal voluntary associations of adult males, each with its own style of dress, dances, songs, and set of four leaders. As young warriors, men were recruited by the different societies, until all had joined one or another of the societies. Theoretically there were no status differences between the societies; in actuality, they did vary somewhat in prestige.

The term *warrior societies* is slightly misleading. Each warrior society had four leaders, one of whom served as its head. The heads of the various societies constituted what some call the *tribal war chiefs*. Although this group planned and led attacks on their enemies, the different societies did not fight or operate as military units in battles. In battles men fought as individuals, and members of several societies may have been present in a particular raiding party.

Subordinate to the council of chiefs, the warrior societies cooperated as a group only in the policing of the camps. During the summer tribal encampment, the Council of Forty-four appointed one of the societies as camp police. Later when the villages scattered into separate camps, the members of the council resident in the village appointed one of the warrior societies to police the camp. After being appointed, the warrior society usually carried out its function with little direction from the chiefs. Its members scouted the area around the camp to check for the presence of any enemy raiding parties, corrected young boys involved in any mischief, and intervened in any serious disputes between village members.

But it was during bison hunts that the policing role of the warrior societies became most evident. Successful bison hunts required a strategy that caused the herd to stay together and not scatter; only in this way could the maximum number of animals be killed. Before the hunt, as the village moved into a position near the herd, hunting by individuals was prohibited; and the warrior society in charge of the camp enforced this order. If any man flagrantly violated the order, the society might beat him with whips, shoot his horses, and destroy his tipi. As the hunters gathered on their horses to begin the hunt, the society in charge restrained any overly eager hunters and made certain that every man had an equal opportunity to secure game for his family.

There are two points to be emphasized about the political organization of tribal societies. First, although there were some formalized political and religious offices that bequeathed some limited authority and prerogatives, on the whole tribal societies were basically egalitarian (see chapter 14). Few positions were hereditary, and most leaders were selected on the basis of personal qualities and individual merit.

Second, there was little economic specialization, either individual or regional, among tribes. Except for cooperation in communal hunts, families produced their own food and manufactured their own clothes and other material goods. From an economic perspective, each band or village was virtually a self-contained unit, capable of sustaining itself without support from other communities; therefore, it generally was not economic necessity, convenience, nor efficiency that led to the supracommunity political organization of tribes. Although sodalities unite tribes at a higher level of cohesiveness than bands, sodalities alone are not sufficient to maintain the unity of a group indefinitely. For example, the Osage, Ponca, Omaha, and Kansa share a number of clans in common. Clan members from these different tribes called each other *clan brothers* and marriage between clan members of different tribes was considered incest. Yet, politically these were independent tribes, who on occasion warred against one another and allied themselves with still other groups. At some time in the past, these four tribes were probably a single tribe; thus, the mere existence of sodalities is not sufficient to generate or maintain the cohesiveness of a tribe. It is likely that external military threats, either real or perceived, necessitated the cooperation in warfare of a large group of people and was the major factor that united geographically dispersed communities. Thus, warfare— the existence and activities of hostile human neighbors—was an important force in creating the political integration of separate communities.

■ Chiefdoms

Like tribes, chiefdoms were multicommunity political units. However, unlike tribes, chiefdoms had a formalized and centralized political system. A chiefdom (see chapter 9) was governed by a single chief, who usually served as both political and religious head of the polity. The chief had authority over members of the chiefdom, and the position was often hereditary within a single kin group, which based its chiefly rights on supernatural powers. Thus a chiefdom was not an egalitarian society but a ranked or stratified society (see chapter 14) with access to resources based on inherited status. With authority and power conferred by supernatural beings, governing was not by consensus but by decree.

Chiefdoms were usually associated with horticultural societies in which craft or regional specialization in production had emerged. There was a need for regularized exchanges of goods either between geographically dispersed communities or at times within a single community. This economic exchange was managed through redistribution, with the chief occupying the central position in the flow of goods (see chapter 9).

In earlier historic periods chiefdoms were probably found throughout much of the Old World. However, during more recent periods such political systems were primarily concentrated in Oceania (Polynesia, Micronesia, and Melanesia) and in the Americas (the circum-Caribbean and coastal portions of South America and the Northwestern Coast of North America).

The Polynesian-speaking people of Tahiti, an island in the Southeastern Pacific, illustrate many characteristics typical of a chiefdom. This relatively large, mountainous, volcanic island had a population of about 100,000 at the time of European discovery. Tahiti was divided among about twenty rival chiefs. Although most of these chiefdoms were about the size of the average tribe and significantly smaller than the largest tribes, their political organization differed significantly.

The economy of Tahiti was based largely on farming: taro, breadfruit, coconuts, and yams were the main crops; pigs and chickens were also raised, and fish and other seafoods supplemented the food supply. Food production was sufficient not only to meet the needs of the population but also to produce surpluses for export to other islands. Although sufficient food was produced in all regions, there were significant regional differences in types of food produced because Tahiti varied ecologically.

Tahitian society had at least three, and possibly four, distinct classes, depending on how finely one wishes to divide the units. *Arii,* or chiefs, and their close relatives formed the ruling elite. The arii were divided into two groups: the *arii rahi,* or sacred chiefs, and the *arii rii,* or small chiefs. Under these chiefs were the *raatira,* or subchiefs, and the *manahune,* or commoners. The sacred chiefs were viewed as actually descended from the gods, whereas the commoners were merely created by the gods for their use. The subchiefs were the offspring of intermarriage between the sacred chiefs and commoners, whereas the small chiefs were the products of still later intermarriages between sacred chiefs and subchiefs. Once these four classes were established, class endogamy became the rule.

The sacred chiefs, viewed as gods on earth, evoked both reverence and fear. Whatever the highest ranking sacred chiefs touched became *tabu,* or sacred, and could not be used for fear of supernatural punishment. Such chiefs had to be carried on the back of a servant, lest the ground touched by his feet become tabu. They could not enter the house of another individual, for the same reason. The lifestyle of the chief's family differed from that of other individuals: they had larger and more elaborate houses, the largest canoes, insignia of their rank, and particular clothing.

Unlike in band and tribal-level societies, resources in chiefdoms were individually owned. Land was owned mainly by the chiefs and subchiefs, but ultimate authority rested with the sacred chiefs within the polity. Although sacred chiefs could not withhold the title to lands from the families of subchiefs, they could banish an individual subchief. Crafts were specialized, and craftspeople were attached to particular sacred chiefs and produced goods for them. Communal fishing equipment was made by these craftspeople, and the chiefs regulated their use. Thus, the sacred chiefs directly controlled craft production and communal fishing. The chiefs could make any demands on the property of the subchiefs and commoners. If someone refused, the chief could have the recalcitrant banished or make him or her a sacrificial victim. Theoretically, the sacred chief was the head judicial figure in the polity, but some believe that the chief rarely intervened in disputes between individuals; usually the chief used these powers only against people who challenged his authority.

The sacred chief in each polity was the focal point for redistributive exchanges. Periodically the chief demanded surplus production from all of his subjects for a public redistribution. Such events were associated with a number of different occasions: a rite of passage for a member of the chief's family, the organizing of a military attack, religious ceremonies, or the start of the breadfruit harvest. During such ceremonies the chief distributed the goods collected to all of his subjects.

■ States

Although they had a centralized political system, chiefdoms were still kinship-based structures. Even in Tahiti, the sacred chief's authority rested in large part on his control over families of subchiefs, each of whom had his own inalienable rights to lands—and thus families—of commoners. As a result, the number of people who could be effectively integrated into a chiefdom was limited. In Polynesia most chiefdoms ranged from only a few thousand to 30,000 people. Polities with larger populations require a political structure based on institutions other than kinship.

States, like chiefdoms, have a centralized political structure, but what distinguishes them from chiefdoms is the presence of a bureaucracy. A chiefdom is basically a two-level system: (1) the chiefs (which in Tahiti included the subchiefs), who have varying levels of authority and power, and (2) the commoners, or great mass of the populace. A state has three levels: (1) the ruling elite, (2) a bureaucracy, and (3) the populace.

In states, as in chiefdoms, highest authority and power reside in the ruling elite, the formal political head or heads of the polity. States vary greatly in the types of political leaders present and in the basis for the leaders' authority and power. Leaders in the earliest states were frequently considered to be the descendants of gods, and thus themselves gods on earth. The Inca of Peru (discussed in chapter 9) and the pharaohs of Egypt were leaders who ruled as gods. Other political leaders, although not claiming to be gods, have legitimated their positions with claims of having been chosen by god. Early European kings legitimized their claims to leadership on such a basis; and as English coins still proclaim, the queen rules *Dei gratia*—by the "grace of God." Other states have evolved political leadership that uses strictly secular ideas to justify its power. In countries where leaders are elected by a vote of the populace, rule is legitimated by the internalized acceptance of such ascendance to office. Even strictly secular kingdoms, dictatorships, and oligarchies can, if in power for a sufficient time, have their rule accepted by the populace as "legitimate." We have more to say about legitimation in the next chapter.

Although they differ greatly in political leadership, states all share one characteristic: the presence of a bureaucracy that carries out the day-to-day governing of the polity. In simple terms, a bureaucrat is a person to whom a political leader delegates certain authority and powers. The bureaucrat thus acts on behalf of the political leader. Lacking any inherent authority or powers personally, bureaucrats depend on the continued support of political leaders. The emergence of bureaucracies allowed for both qualitative and quantitative changes in political systems. Using bureaucrats as intermediaries, political leaders could expand the size of their polities both geographically and demographically, while strengthening their political control over the population. Bureaucrats could engineer such expansion without threat of revolution and political fragmentation, because they lacked any personal claims to independent political legitimacy.

The emergence of states increased the complexity of political units, and bureaucracies not only allowed for specialization in governmental functions but also made possible the effective integration of large land areas and population into political units. For example, chiefdoms rarely exceeded 30,000 individuals, whereas modern states such as China may have populations of one billion people. In addition, political units could incorporate multiple ethnic populations.

Social Control and Law

In all societies there are clearly defined rules which govern the relationships between members. However, not all individuals in any society will conform to these rules. There will always be some individuals who will behave in a socially unacceptable manner. Thus, among all peoples there exist formal and informal ways to correct the behavior of individuals. In general, we call these mechanisms social control. One form of social control is called law.

■ Social Control

Social control refers to the diverse ways in which the behaviors of the members of a society are constrained into socially approved channels. All cultures have certain behavioral norms that most people learn and begin to conform to during enculturation. But all societies have individuals who, to one degree or another, deviate from those norms. Violations of norms usually result in sanctions or punishments for the offender, which serve both to correct the behavior of particular persons and to show others the penalties for such deviance. The severity of sanctions and the process by which sanctions are imposed differ greatly, depending on the seriousness culturally attached to the violated norm, the perceived severity of the violation, and to the overall political and legal system of the people.

Children who get into mischief are usually corrected by their parents. In our own society parents may impose sanctions ranging from physically spanking children to verbally scolding to withdrawing privileges such as television viewing or activities with friends. The correcting of children trains individuals in proper behavior at an early age.

The community also applies informal sanctions against individuals—both children and adults—who are not behaving properly. Gossip, or fear of gossip, serves as an important method of social control in most societies. People usually fear the contempt or ridicule

of their peers, so most individuals generally try to conform to acceptable behavioral norms. People attempt to hide behavior that would be the subject of gossip, scandal, and ridicule. Individuals whose known behavior consistently violates social norms may even find themselves ostracized by friends and relatives (the most severe of informal punishments). Informal economic penalties also may be imposed. A family may withdraw economic support in attempts to modify errant behavior of a member.

Often, a wide variety of supernatural sanctions assist in controlling individual behavior, and in some cases these supernatural sanctions are automatically imposed on particular types of behavior. Whether the commission of these acts becomes public knowledge or not, and thus regardless of whether other punishments are inflicted on the individual, the commission still endangers one's immortal soul. However, supernatural sanctions can be more specifically directed. In many societies, including some Christian ones, an individual may place a curse on another person by calling upon a supernatural being to punish that individual. Fear of sorcery or witchcraft (see chapter 15) frequently serves as another important form of social control. Victims are usually people who in some way offended a witch or sorcerer, often through a breach of social norms.

■ Law

Law is the highest level of social control, and legal punishments are usually reserved for the most serious breaches of norms. The question of how law can be distinguished from other forms of social control is not easy to answer. In societies with court systems the distinction is formalized, but in societies without such formalized legal systems the division is not as clear.

E. Adamson Hoebel (1954, 28) defined law in the following way: "A social norm is legal if its neglect or infraction is regularly met, in threat or in fact, by the application of physical force by an individual or group possessing the socially recognized privilege of so acting." Law so defined was and is present in virtually ever society. Leopold Pospisil, building in part on Hoebel's work, defined law as having four attributes: *authority, intention of universal application, obligatio,* and *sanction.*

In a legal action some individual or group must have publicly recognized authority to settle a case or punish a violation. In societies with courts, who has the authority is obvious, but in societies that lack courts the authority becomes less clear. What emerges frequently is an ad hoc authority; that is, because of the peculiarities of the case, a particular individual or group becomes recognized by the community as the authority responsible for its resolution. In some cases the victim himself or herself may be the recognized authority. In the victim's absence (as in the case of murder), the victim's family or clan or kin group may be placed in the role of authority. Such ad hoc authority is discussed later in some of the examples.

Implicit in all legal actions is the intention of universal application, which means that in identical cases the sanction imposed is the same. Although one might argue that no two legal cases have been or will ever be identical, the notion of universal application requires that the law be consistent and thus predictable; the arbitrary imposition of sanctions is not law.

Obligatio refers to the legal relation between two or more living individuals. All individuals are immersed in a complex web of rights and duties, and every individual has both certain rights and certain duties to others. In some cases an individual's rights and the correlative duties of others are well defined; in other cases some ambiguity exists. Most civil legal cases and arguments in our own court system focus on questions about rights and duties. For example, when two drivers argue after a traffic accident, they argue about who was properly exercising rights and who was negligent regarding duties. An act breaches the law only if the abridgment of one's individual rights resulted from another person's failure to perform a legitimate duty.

Whereas Hoebel limited legal sanctions to physical sanctions, Pospisil argued that this definition is too narrow. A legal sanction does not have to be some form of corporal punishment, nor does it have to involve the loss of property. Based on his work with the Kapauku of New Guinea, Pospisil contended that the impact of psychological sanctions can be more severe than that of actual physical punishment. For this reason he stated, "We can define a legal sanction as either the negative behavior of withdrawing some rewards or favors that otherwise (if the law had not been violated) would have been granted, or the positive behavior of inflicting some painful experience, be it physical or psychological" (Pospisil 1958, 268).

The legal institutions of a society consist of two distinct components: (1) **procedural law** and (2) **substantive law.** Procedural law refers to the manner in which a breach of the law is adjudicated or resolved, and it focuses on questions such as the following: Who assumes the role of authority? How is it determined that a breach of the law has taken place? How is the proper sanction determined? Who imposes the sanc-

tion on the offending party? Substantive law, on the other hand, is concerned with defining the types of behavior that are categorized as illegal—in other words, violations of the rights and duties of individuals and the appropriate sanctions to be imposed. Substantive laws—or at least the relative significance of such laws—differ greatly, and thus they are extraordinarily difficult to categorize. For example, some societies have laws against witchcraft. However, witchcraft is not illegal under American law, because we deny the existence of true witchcraft. In many societies adultery is considered a serious crime punishable by death, whereas in other societies adultery is of little consequence and is either ignored or subject to only a small fine.

Although substantive laws vary widely in particulars, they do fall into two main categories: (1) criminal laws and (2) civil laws or torts. Criminal law is concerned with breaches of social norms that are considered to be crimes against the state or against society as a whole. They are handled by the society acting in a collective manner through its legal institutions, such as courts, prosecutors, judges, and police. In contrast, civil laws or torts are breaches of social norms that are considered to affect only an individual or groups of individuals. The society may or may not have formal organized institutions to adjudicate such cases. As we discuss later, not all societies make a distinction between criminal and civil law. In some societies there are only civil laws or torts, even for the more serious breaches of norms, such as murder.

Legal Systems

On the basis of procedural characteristics two main levels of complexity and formality can be defined: (1) **self-help legal systems** and (2) **court legal systems.**

■ Self-Help Systems

Self-help systems, also called *ad hoc systems,* are informal and exist in the absence of any centralized or formalized legal institutions capable of settling disputes. Such systems are associated with band-level societies and most tribal-level societies. In such systems there is only civil law. All legal actions concern only the principal parties and/or their families. The reason for terming the legal procedure in these societies *self-help* will become clear.

Self-help legal systems fall into two main forms: (1) *familial* and (2) *mediator*. In familial systems all actions and decisions are initiated and executed by the families or larger kin groups involved. In mediator systems there is the formal presence of a neutral third party—the mediator—who attempts to negotiate and resolve the dispute peacefully.

In familial systems legal actions are handled by the families involved. A legal offense only indirectly concerns the community as a whole. When an individual and/or family determines that its rights have been violated, the imposition of the proper sanction falls to the plaintiffs; in other words, the offended party assumes the role of authority. Such a system in which the redress of a legal grievance falls to the victim, or in the case of murder to the victim's family, has some problems in implementation, but not as many as one might anticipate. This is not a system of "might makes right." Certainly cases arise in such societies in which the physically (or militarily) weak are victimized by the strong. However, in cases of legal redress there is a collective consensus of the community in support of the victim and usually a recognized means by which even the weakest members of the community can gather support adequate to impose appropriate sanctions on the strongest.

The Comanche exemplify how a familial legal system operated and how victims weaker than their opponents could nonetheless obtain redress. One of the most frequent Comanche offenses was "wife stealing." Older Comanche men were usually polygynous, and some of their wives were significantly younger than their husbands. Among young Comanche men it was considered prestigious, though illegal, to steal the wife of another man. Under Comanche law the injured husband could either demand his wife back or some property, usually horses, in compensation. However, the husband had the responsibility of imposing these sanctions. In such actions the community played no direct role, but a husband could not ignore the loss of a wife. If he did ignore it, the community would ridicule him, and his prestige would decline. Thus, not only did the community support the husband in pressing his claim, but they informally pressured him to act.

In imposing these sanctions the husband was allowed to use whatever physical force was needed, short of actually killing the individual. In cases in which the men involved were physically about equal, the two men met to negotiate and discuss the husband's demands. Behind these negotiations was the potential threat that the husband might physically assault the defendant.

In cases where the husband presented little or no personal threat to the defendant, institutionalized means existed whereby the husband could gain the physical backing needed. Although it lowered his prestige in the community, he could call upon his relatives for support; the husband, with his male relatives present and prepared to support his demands physically, could then negotiate with the defendant. The defendant, however, always had to stand alone. He would not even consider asking his relatives for support because he would lose prestige, and wife stealing was motivated in large part by prestige. Even if he had asked his kinsmen for support, they would not have responded for fear of community ridicule.

In cases where the husband was an orphan or lacked kinsmen to negotiate successfully, another cultural avenue was open: the aggrieved man could call upon any other man he wished to prosecute his case. Usually he called on the assistance of one of the powerful war leaders in the band. Such a request was so prestigious that a war leader could not refuse. At the same time, such a request was demeaning to the man asking for help, and greatly lowered his prestige. As a result, it usually required a great deal of social pressure to force a man to ask for assistance; however, once the request was made, the issue was between the defendant and the war leader alone. On approaching the defendant, the war leader would call out, "You have stolen my wife," and then proceed to exact whatever demands the husband had requested. For his action, the war leader received nothing in payment other than the admiration of the community; the husband received the settlement. Although this process was most commonly used in wife-stealing cases, it could be used for other issues as well. Thus, Comanche legal institutions gave any individual the means to marshal overwhelming physical force in the protection of his rights.

As the Comanche example shows, familial systems often work relatively well in protecting individual rights. However, there are exceptions, and in some situations this system can fail. The Caribou Eskimo illustrates one of the inherent problems. In cases of murder the authority and responsibility for imposing the sanction—execution—fell to the family of the victim. Execution of the murderer was not always immediate. The family might wait years until the opportunity presented itself to kill the murderer with impunity; shooting the man in the back while he was working was considered an ideal situation. For the system to work, however, a relative of the victim had to be left alive to impose the sanction. To prevent being killed himself, a murderer might not stop with the killing of his intended victim, but proceed to kill the entire family as well. For example, a Caribou Eskimo man was rebuffed by the family of a girl he wished to marry. He killed the girl's father, mother, brothers, and sister—a total of seven or eight people—and then took the girl as his wife. Such massacres were thought by many Eskimos to be prudent behavior and sometimes enhanced the prestige of the individual.

The Caribou Eskimo case illustrates the problems with familial systems of law; yet we must remember that all legal systems have defects, and manipulative individuals frequently escape sanctions in all societies. Murderers sometimes escape punishment because of legal technicalities under the American legal system. Also, the fact that an individual may actually enhance his prestige by committing a particular illegal act does not necessarily reflect on the law—after all, American folk heroes include Jesse James and Pretty Boy Floyd.

A more formalized type of legal procedure is found in the mediator system. Under this system disputes are still between individuals and families. The offended party and/or his or her family fills the position of authority. However, a third party is called upon, usually by the offending individual or his or her family, to attempt to negotiate a mutually agreeable solution. The mediator has no authority to impose a settlement. The aggrieved party and/or his or her family must agree to accept the compensation negotiated.

The Nuer, a pastoral tribal society of the Sudan, provide an example of how mediator systems operate. The Nuer live in small villages of related families. Although villages are tied together through lineages and clans, there is no effective leadership above the village level. The only formalized leaders who transcend the local units are individuals called *leopard-skin chiefs*, whose position is indicated by the wearing of a leopard-skin cloak. These men have no secular authority to enforce their judgments, but only limited ritual powers to bless and curse.

The most important function of leopard-skin chiefs is mediating feuds between local groups. The Nuer are an egalitarian, warrior-oriented people. Disputes between individuals frequently result in physical violence, and occasionally men are killed. The killing of a Nuer requires that his kinsmen exact retribution. Any close patrilineal kinsman of the murderer may be

killed in retaliation, but at least initially the kinsmen of the victim attempt to kill the murderer himself. Immediately after committing a murder, the killer flees to the house of a leopard-skin chief. This dwelling is a sanctuary, and as long as the man stays in the chief's house, he is safe. The victim's kinsmen usually keep the house under surveillance to try to kill the murderer if he ventures out.

The leopard-skin chief keeps the murderer in his house until a settlement is arranged. The chief will wait until tempers have cooled, which usually requires several weeks, before he begins to negotiate the case. First, he goes to the family of the murderer to see if they are willing to pay cattle to the victim's family in compensation. Rarely do they refuse, because one of them might be killed in retaliation. After the murderer's family has agreed to pay, the chief proceeds to the family of the victim, offering so many cattle in compensation. Initially the victim's family invariably refuses, saying they want blood, that cattle cannot compensate them for the death of their beloved kinsman. However, the leopard-skin chief persists, usually

■ *The cloak of this Nuer man indicates that he is a Leopard Skin Chief. As such, he is in charge of mediating disputes.*

gaining support of more distant relatives of the victim who also pressure the family to settle. The leopard-skin chief may even threaten to place a curse on the family if they continue to refuse to settle for a payment rather than blood. The family finally agrees and accepts cattle, usually about forty head, as compensation. Even though the matter is formally settled, the killer and his close patrilineal kinsmen will avoid the family of the victim for some years so as not to provoke spontaneous retaliation.

Up to this point we have examined legal systems that operate without a formalized or centralized political structure capable of resolving disputes. In many of these societies law, not subordination to a common set of formal political institutions, defines the boundaries of the society. To see what we mean, consider the Nuer. The Nuer distinguish between a *ter*, or a feud within a Nuer tribe that is a legal action subject to arbitration; a *kur*, or a fight between members of two Nuer tribes that cannot be arbitrated; and a *pec*, or a war with non-Nuer people. Nuer believe that disputes within a tribe should be resolved by legal means (that is, peacefully), whereas disputes between individuals who are not members of the same tribe should be resolved by extralegal means, including organized warfare. Legal processes serve to repair and maintain social relations between families; thus, law serves both to maintain the cohesiveness and to define the boundaries of the society.

The Jívaro, a horticultural and foraging people of eastern Ecuador, illustrate how law defines social boundaries. The Jívaro are best known for their former practice of severing the heads of their enemies and shrinking them to the size of a fist. By the 1950s the Jívaro had been reduced to slightly more than 2,000 people settled in over 200 scattered family households. Such households usually consist of a man, his wife or wives, their children, and possibly a son-in-law or other relatives. These households are grouped into "neighborhoods," which consist of a number of households living within a few miles of one another; the membership of such a neighborhood is poorly defined and fluid. Poor hunting, a dispute with other households, or some other factors might result in a family moving away. Neither corporate kin groups nor formalized leadership positions exist. Except for household heads, there are only a few men called *unta*, or "big," but their informal leadership role is limited and transitory. Politically, the Jívaro are organized at a band level. Although they have only limited political insti-

tutions, the Jívaro have a strong sense of common sociocultural identity and territorial boundaries. Living in adjacent or nearby territories are four other "Jívaroan" groups, who speak mutually intelligible dialects, share the same basic customs, and at times trade with Jívaro households. In spite of their minimal political integration, there is little question about which households are Jívaro and which belong to the other four groups.

With this political organization the methods employed in settlement of disputes define the effective boundaries of the society. Disputes between Jívaros are resolved by legal means, whereas disputes with members of other societies are resolved through extralegal means. Like the Nuer, the Jívaro make a sharp distinction between a **feud** and a war. A feud is the legal means by which a sanction is imposed on another family for the murder of a kinsman. As a legal procedure, a feud proceeds in a manner quite different from a war.

As in most societies, murder is the most serious offense. According to Jívaro beliefs, few deaths are attributable to natural causes; most deaths are the result of physical violence, sorcery, or avenging spirits. Deaths caused by physical violence and witchcraft are considered murders, which have to be avenged by the kinsmen of the deceased. In most cases of physical violence, the murderer is readily identifiable. In cases of poisoning and witchcraft, divination is used to determine the guilty party.

Determination of the guilty party, and whether they are Jívaro or non-Jívaro, affects how the victim's kinfolk avenge the death. If the guilty party is Jívaro, the kinsmen of the victim attack the household of the murderer with the goal of killing the man himself. If they are not successful in finding him, they may kill a male relative of his, even if it is only a small boy. Normally they will not harm women or children, except in cases in which the victim was a woman or a child. Even if they have the opportunity to kill more, only one individual will be killed. This is a legal action, and Jívaro law allows only a life for a life. The head of the victim cannot be taken.

If, on the other hand, the guilty party is determined to be a non-Jívaro, different actions are taken. The relatives of the murdered person attack the household of the guilty party, trying to kill as many people as possible. They attempt to massacre the entire family, with no regard for either sex or age. In some cases, they attack nearby households as well, attempting to kill even more members of the group. This is a war, not a legal action, and the heads of all victims are taken.

The Jívaro, the Nuer, and other peoples who lack centralized and formal political structure nonetheless have definite means of maintaining social control. To those of us who have formal governmental institutions that are supposed to handle our grievances and right the wrongs done to us, self-help systems such as those of the Comanche, Caribou Eskimo, Nuer, and Jívaro look rather anarchic. However, rules govern such systems. Some anthropologists believe, in fact, that the best definition of *society* in self-help systems is those individuals whose vengeance-taking activities are constrained by procedural rules.

■ Court Systems

A number of factors distinguish a *court legal system* from a self-help legal system. First, authority resides not with the victim and/or his or her family but with a formalized institution, the court. The court has the authority and the power to hear disputes and to unilaterally decide cases and impose sanctions if they are deemed warranted. Authority in legal matters is a component of political authority; thus, fully developed court systems can exist only in societies that have centralized formal political leadership, that is, chiefdoms or states. Second, court systems usually operate with formal public hearings, presided over by a judge or judges, with formally defined defendants and plaintiffs. Grievances are stated, evidence is collected and analyzed, and in cases of conflicting evidence oaths or ordeals may be used to determine truthfulness. Finally, only in court systems does one find substantive law clearly divided into criminal law and civil law.

Court systems, in turn, may be divided into three categories; (1) **incipient courts,** (2) **courts of mediation,** and (3) **courts of regulation.** All court systems mediate disputes as well as regulate behavior; however, as societies become increasingly complex, the primary focus of the courts shifts from mediating disputes to regulating behavior. This shift results in a qualitative difference, not only in courts but in the nature of the law itself. Associated with this shift is an increasing codification of the laws. Laws and their associated sanctions become standardized and rigid, and civil laws are steadily transformed into criminal laws. Court systems begin to emerge with the concept of "crime against society"—the need to control individual acts that might endanger the society as a whole, as opposed to acts that threaten only individuals. Herein lies the distinction between criminal law and civil law.

Incipient Court Systems   True court systems can only be found in societies with centralized political systems—chiefdoms or states. However, in some tribal societies are what might best be termed *incipient courts.* Although a tribal-level society, the Cheyenne, as described earlier in this chapter, demonstrate the development of an incipient court system. At times both the Council of Forty-four and the warrior societies assumed the role of de facto judges and courts. The Cheyenne recognized that certain individual actions threatened the well-being of the group and thus had to be controlled. Some of these actions were purely secular, whereas others were religious. Designated warrior societies were formally empowered by the council to enforce secular laws and regulations on the camp members. For example, in preparation for a communal bison hunt, camp members would be told to refrain from independent hunting for some days before the hunt. If the policing warrior society discovered someone hunting illegally, the men present became the de facto judges and court, and immediately imposed sanctions on the offender. Often, such an offender was beaten with whips, his horses were shot, and his tipi was slashed with knives. Other secular criminal violations were handled just as swiftly. The Council of Forty-four was responsible for the religious or sacred well-being of the tribe; thus, any action that endangered the supernatural well-being of the Cheyenne was their concern. The murder of a Cheyenne by another Cheyenne was the most heinous of crimes. Such a crime was said to bloody the sacred arrows, the most sacred of Cheyenne tribal medicine bundles. The arrows were symbolic of Cheyenne success in hunting (their main economic activity) and in warfare. Murder within the tribe polluted the arrows and thus made the Cheyenne vulnerable to their enemies and less successful in their hunting. When a Cheyenne died at the hands of another Cheyenne, the Council of Forty-four became a de facto court. Although there was no formal hearing, the council met and discussed the case: Was it a murder? If so, then the sacred arrows had to be "renewed," or ritually purified. They also decided on the sanction to be imposed—usually exile for a period of years. With the Cheyenne there could be no capital punishment without again polluting the sacred arrows. (See Box 13.1 for further discussion of the Cheyenne system.)

MURDER AMONG THE CHEYENNE

The killing of one Cheyenne by another Cheyenne was not only a "sin" that "polluted" the murderer and endangered the well-being of the tribe, but also a crime against the society. This pollution of the sacred arrows caused the game animals that Cheyenne depended on for their subsistence to shun their hunting territory. A killing of one Cheyenne by another required the ritual purification of the sacred arrows. However, not every killing was considered a criminal act. Upon hearing of a killing within the band, the members of the Council of Forty-four assembled. Exactly how and what they discussed in such cases we shall never know; but the council members had to decide when a killing was to be treated as a murder: Was suicide murder? Was abortion murder? Was a killing ever justifiable? Was drunkenness a mitigating circumstance? If the council determined that a murder had taken place, the chiefs ordered the immediate banishment of the murderer. Such banishment usually included not only the murderer but his or her family, and sometimes friends who went along voluntarily. This banishment usually lasted between five and ten years. During the period of exile, the banished individual usually lived with a friendly group of Arapahos or Dakotas.

The act of a Cheyenne taking his or her own life was not typically considered murder. Several cases are known of Cheyenne women committing suicide for what were considered trivial reasons. Such cases were not considered murder, and as far as can be determined, the sacred arrows were not renewed. In other instances, however, suicide was treated as murder. For example, one mother became infuriated when her daughter eloped with a young man of whom she did not approve. The mother found the girl and beat her with a whip while dragging her home. Inside the tipi the girl seized a gun and shot herself. In another case, a young girl divorced her husband and returned to her parents' home. At some later time, her mother found the girl participating in a young persons' dance and beat her; the girl subsequently hung herself. In both cases the chiefs ruled that the girls were driven to suicide by the actions of their mothers, who were thus considered the murderesses. In both cases the sacred arrows were renewed, and the mothers were banished.

Was a killing ever justifiable? In one case, a man attempted to rape his daughter, who resisted and used a knife to kill her father. The sacred arrows were renewed, but the chiefs did not order the girl banished, nor did the people treat her as a murderess. In another case, a man named Winnebago took the wife of another man, who retaliated by taking one of Winnebago's wives. Winnebago was enraged and killed the second man; the murderer was then banished. After his return from banishment, Winnebago argued

Courts of Mediation   The key difference between court systems is not how the actual legal hearings are conducted, but the manner in which breaches of the law are determined and suitable sanctions imposed. In courts of mediation few laws are codified, and the judges follow few formalized guidelines as to what constitutes a legal violation or the sanction that should be imposed. This is not to say that judges act arbitrarily in these matters, but that they have tremendous latitude in their actions. What they apply is a **reasonable-man model.** Using prevalent norms and values, they ask the question, How should a reasonable individual have acted under these circumstances? To determine this, an individual's actions have to be examined within the social context in which the dispute occurred: What was the past and present relationship between the parties involved? What were the circumstances leading up to the event? Thus, they attempt to examine each case as a unique occurrence. Although some sanctions are imposed as punishments, other sanctions are designed to restore as fully as possible a working, if not harmonious, relationship between the parties involved.

One difficulty in attempting to describe courts of mediation is our limited knowledge of such systems. Polities having courts of this nature were some time ago brought under European colonial rule. Their courts were soon modified by and subordinated to European colonial courts, which were more regulatory in nature. The example we will use is that of the Barotse judicial system, as described by Max Gluckman. The Barotse made up a multiethnic state in southern Africa which at the time of Gluckman's study in the 1940s had been under British rule for forty years. More serious

with and killed a second man, so he was banished again. While living among the Arapaho, Winnebago became involved in a dispute with a Cheyenne named Rising Fire, who knew of Winnebago's murders and therefore shot Winnebago out of fear. Although the facts are unclear, it appears that Rising Fire was not exiled for this killing. Thus, under some circumstances, such as incestuous rape and the fear of a known murderer, the chiefs felt that killing was justifiable. In such instances the sacred arrows had to be renewed, but the killer was not exiled.

Was drunkenness a mitigating circumstance? During a drunken brawl, Cries-Yia-Eya killed Chief Eagle. In another case, during a drunken party Porcupine Bear stabbed Little Creek and then called on his relatives to stab Little Creek as well. They did so and killed Little Creek. Cries-Yia-Eya and Porcupine Bear and his guilty relatives were banished by the chiefs; drunkenness was not a defense for murder.

The chiefs were faced with a second issue regarding Little Creek's killers. After their banishment, Porcupine Bear and his relatives had continued to stay close to the band camp. When the tribe organized a revenge attack on the Kiowas, Porcupine Bear and his relatives kept their distance but followed along with the other Cheyenne. In the attack on the Kiowas, Porcupine Bear and his six relatives distinguished themselves by bravely attacking first and killing about thirty Kiowas. What about war honors for acts of bravery accomplished during banishment? The council ruled that exiles could not receive recognition for their military acts, no matter how courageous they might be. In a sense, during their period of banishment they were not Cheyenne.

Was abortion murder? In one case, a fetus was found near a Cheyenne camp. An investigation by a warrior society discovered that a young girl had concealed her pregnancy. The young girl was banished, but only until after the sacred arrows had been renewed. Thus, the chiefs considered abortion to be a less serious type of murder that required a shorter period of banishment.

The chiefs had to answer many other types of questions concerning murder and banishment. About 1855 one of the chiefs, a member of the Council of Forty-four, killed another Cheyenne. The sacred arrows were renewed, and the chief was banished; but what was to be done about his position on the council? The council ruled that the man could not be removed from office and that he remained a chief even though he could not participate in the council.

From the discussion of these cases emerges some of the reasoning behind Cheyenne legal decisions. The chiefs considered a range of factors in reaching their final determinations. Murder included not merely the cold-blooded killing of one Cheyenne by another; it also included abortion and acts that compelled one to commit suicide. At the same time, the chiefs thought that in particular instances killing was justifiable, but that intoxication at the time was not a mitigating factor. ■

Source: Llewellyn and Hoebel (1941).

---

offenses had been removed by the British from the jurisdiction of this court. However, in spite of these factors, the basic Barotse legal concepts aptly illustrate this type of court system.

The Barotse state had two capitals—a northern capital where the king resided, and a subordinate southern capital ruled by a princess. All villages in the state were attached to one or the other of these capitals. The capitals were identical in structure; each had a palace and a council house. Courts of law were held in the council house.

The titular head of the court was the ruler; however, in practice the ruler was rarely present at trials. In the center at the back of the house was the dais, or raised platform, for the ruler to be seated upon if present. There were three ranked groupings of judges. The highest ranking group of judges were the *indunas*, or "councilors," who sat to the right of the dais. The second highest ranking group was the *likombwa*, or "stewards," who sat to the left. These two groups were divided into senior members, who sat in the front, and junior members, who sat behind. The third group consisted of princes and the husbands of the princesses, who represented their wives. This group sat at a right angle to the likombwa.

A case was introduced by a plaintiff, who was allowed to state his or her grievance at length with no interruption; the defendant was then allowed the same privilege. The statements of witnesses for both sides followed. There were no attorneys for either side; the judges questioned and cross-examined the witnesses. After all of the testimony had been heard, the judges began to give their opinions, starting with the most junior indunas, followed by the others in order of

■ *The British integrated existing native court systems of Africa into their colonial administrations. Here a policeman and a local headman preside over a meeting in Botswana.*

increasing seniority. The last judge to speak was the senior induna, who actually passed judgment on the case, subject to the ruler's approval.

In judging a case, a reasonable-man model was used. However, with the Barotse, the reasonableness of behavior was related to the social and kinship relationships of the individuals involved. Also, a breach of the law usually did not happen in isolation, and many individuals were at fault; so one case frequently led to a number of related cases. In passing judgment and imposing sanctions, the judges considered numerous factors. One of the most important factors was the kinship relationship between parties. The judges attempted to restore the relationship and reconcile the parties—but not without blaming those who had committed wrongs and not without imposing sanctions. The judges' opinions frequently took the form of sermons on proper behavior. As Gluckman (1973, 22) notes, "Implicit in the reasonable man is the upright man, and moral issues in these relationships are barely differentiated from legal issues. This is so even though . . . [they] distinguish 'legal' rules, which the . . . [court] has power to enforce or protect, from 'moral' rules which it has not power to enforce or protect. But the judges are reluctant to support the person who is right in law, but wrong in justice, and may seek to achieve justice by indirect . . . action."

Courts of mediation have great potential for meeting the basic social purpose of the law, which is the maintenance of group cohesiveness. However, there is one serious drawback: such a system is workable only in a culturally homogeneous political unit; that is, it works only if the judges and the parties involved share the same basic norms and values.

Courts of Regulation   In the second millenium B.C., the Code of Hammurabi, the earliest known set of written laws, was created in Babylon. The code covered a variety of laws. One section dealt with physicians. It set the prices to be charged for various types of operations, based on the ability of individuals to pay. It also decreed, among other things, that if a surgeon operated on an individual using a bronze knife, and the patient died or lost his eyesight, the surgeon's hand was to be cut off. The laws defined in the Code of Hammurabi reflect the emergence of regulatory laws. The role of the court was no longer to merely arbitrate disputes and strive for reconciliation but to define the rights and duties of members of an increasingly heterogeneous community.

Courts of regulation were a natural outgrowth of state-level polities, which evolved socially and economically distinct classes and encompassed numerous socioculturally distinct peoples. As relationships between individuals in the population became depersonalized, the law too became increasingly depersonalized. This change in the nature of law was compounded by the political incorporation of diverse peoples who frequently had conflicting cultural norms and values. The use of a reasonable-man model is workable only as long as there is a general consensus on what is "reasonable." In increasingly complex and stratified societies, the possibility of such consensus declined. Mediation of disputes works well in small kinship-based societies, where all parties recognize the need for reconciliation through compromise. In sharply divided societies, however, the need for mediation is not as great, because reconciliation in itself is not seen as a gain. Compromise is viewed only in terms of what is lost. Laws were thus created to bring order and stability to the interactions between individuals, particularly between individuals who were not social equals. With law divorced from social norms and values, justice was no longer simply a moral or ethical issue but came to be viewed in terms of consistency, or precedent.

The separation of law from social norms and values also allowed for the "politicization" of the laws. Laws were created to serve political ends, as various groups vied with one another for the creation of laws that would protect, express, or further their own goals, interests, and values. This situation is particularly evident in multiethnic and religious and economically diverse state-level systems such as that of the United States. Given the cultural pluralism, religious diversity, and economic inequality of the United States, it would be impossible to create a code of laws that could equally protect the interests of all classes and that would be consistent with the norms and values of all groups. As a result, many people find themselves subject to laws and sanctions, many of which they judge either immoral or unethical; at times people find that laws violate their own cultural values. We see this with the Right to Life advocates who think that abortion is murder and thus should be made illegal. We see this with groups who oppose capital punishment on the grounds that the state does not have the right to kill individuals. During the Vietnam War we saw it with the draft resisters who argued that the state did not have the right to order men to fight in a war that they considered immoral. Less obvious is the manner in which numerous ethnic minorities, notably Native Americans, subordinate their cultural norms and values to comply with the legal system. With the emergence of states and courts of regulation, law ceased to be an expression of social norms and values and became their molder.

Summary

In this chapter we discussed two distinct but overlapping sociocultural institutions: political organization and social control. Humans live in cooperative groups. Group action—both in economic and social activities—is a prerequisite for the survival of the population. To be effective, group activities must have leadership and organization, which are the basis for political structure. At the same time, individual differences, conflict, and competition within the group must be controlled and channeled in such a manner that the internal cohesiveness and cooperation of the individual members of the group are maintained—thus the need for social control.

Four major categories of political organization are found: bands, tribes, chiefdoms, and states. Found among foraging societies, the band is the simplest and least formal level of political organization. Two forms of band organization exist: simple bands and composite bands. In simple bands the highest level of political organization is the extended family, with the highest level of political leadership being the heads of the various families. These simple bands are economically self-sufficient and politically autonomous. Because a simple band has as its core a group of related individuals, band members are forced to seek spouses from outside the band; they are exogamous units. Thus, kinship ties through marriage serve as the primary link between bands. Simple bands are most commonly found among foragers who depend on the hunting of game animals that are present in small numbers year-round.

Composite bands are larger than simple bands and include a number of distinct families. Leadership in composite bands is vested in "big men," or informal leaders, who have influence, but not actual authority. Composite bands are most often found among foragers who depend on the hunting of migratory herd animals.

At the tribal level, formal institutions transcend local residence groups and bind the geographically scattered members of the society into a cohesive unit. The key element in tribal societies is sodalities, which may be either kinship based, as in the case of clans, or nonkinship based, as in the case of warrior societies or age grades. Leadership in such groups is more structured, with formal political offices.

Chiefdoms have formal, hereditary leadership with centralized political control and authority. The associated redistributive economic exchange system focused on the chief serves to integrate economically the various communities within the political unit.

The state is the most complex level of political organization. States have centralized power and control, but the key characteristic of a state is the presence of a bureaucracy—individuals acting on behalf of the political elite, thus enabling the centralized power figures to maintain control of a greater number of individuals.

Social control consists of the various methods used to control and channel the behavior of individual members of a society into approved behavior. Law and legal systems are merely the highest level of social control. Law is defined as having four attributes: (1) authority, (2) obligatio, (3) intention of universal application, and (4) sanction. By this definition all societies have law. All legal systems consist of two elements: substantive law is concerned with the types of unacceptable behavior and their associated sanctions, and procedural law is concerned with handling breaches of substantive law and imposing sanctions.

In societies without centralized political systems, legal systems are self-help. In self-help systems the responsibility and authority for determining a breach of the law and imposition of the proper sanction fall to the victim or his or her family (or both). As we discussed, this system is not as arbitrary as we might think. In the case of murder or killing, the result may be a feud between families; but a feud—sharply distinguished from a war—is part of the legal process.

Law in societies with centralized political systems is handled by courts. Court systems, in turn, can usually be categorized as either courts of mediation or courts of regulation. In relatively homogeneous societies, court systems usually take as their primary objective the mediation of disputes between individuals and the restoration of harmonious social relationships. In more heterogeneous groups, courts usually become more regulatory in nature, with formally defined laws and sanctions.

Key Terms

simple bands	law
composite bands	procedural law
tribe	substantive law
chiefdoms	self-help legal systems
state	court legal systems
big men	feud
influence	incipient court systems
authority	courts of mediation
sodalities	courts of regulation
social control	reasonable-man model

Suggested Readings

■ Cohen, R., and Elman Service, eds. *Origins of the State: The Anthropology of Political Evolution.* Philadelphia: Institute for the Study of Human Issues, 1978.
   A collection of essays from various perspectives examining the development of state-level political systems.

■ Fried, Morton. *The Evolution of Political Society.* New York: Random House, 1967.
   A theoretical study that traces the development of political systems from egalitarian societies through ranked to stratified and state-level societies.

■ Hoebel, E. Adamson. *The Law of Primitive Man.* Cambridge, Mass.: Harvard University Press, 1964.
   The first major comparative study of non-Western legal systems. Although somewhat dated, it remains a classic study.

■ Mair, Lucy. *Primitive Government.* Baltimore: Penguin, 1966.
   Concerned exclusively with African peoples, this is an excellent introduction to preindustrial political systems.

■ Newman, Katherine S. *Law and Economic Organization: A Comparative Study of Pre-Industrial Societies.* Cambridge: Cambridge University Press, 1983.
   A cross-cultural analysis of sixty societies to show that legal institutions systematically vary with economic organization.

■ Service, Elman. *Primitive Social Organization: An Evolutionary Perspective.* New York: Random House, 1966.
   Traces the evolution of political systems from bands to chiefdoms.

The following ethnographies are excellent descriptions of political and/or legal systems within particular societies.

■ Barth, Fredrik. *Political Leadership among Swat Pathans.* London: Athlone, 1959.
   A description and theoretical analysis of political life of a people on the Pakistan and Afghanistan border.

■ Fortes, M., and E. E. Evans-Pritchard, eds. *African Political Systems.* London: Oxford University Press, 1940.
   A collection of short descriptions of the political organization of eight different African societies.

■ Gluckman, Max. *The Ideas in Barotse Jurisprudence.* Manchester: Manchester University Press, 1965.

■ _____. *The Judicial Process among the Barotse.* Manchester: Manchester University Press, 1973.
   These two studies of the Barotse of Zambia not only describe a system in a non-Western state but also—and more important— illustrate the legal reasoning used in their court systems.

■ Hoebel, E. Adamson. *The Political Organization and Law–Ways of the Comanche Indians.* American Anthropological Association, Memoir 54, 1940.
   Good description of the political structure and legal system of a band-level society.

■ Kuper, Hilda. *The Swazi: A South African Kingdom.* 2d ed. New York: Holt, Rinehart and Winston, 1986.
   An excellent short ethnography of Swaziland, now an independent nation. Has a good discussion of recent changes.

■ Leach, Edmund. *Political Systems of Highland Burma.* Boston: Beacon, 1965.
   Describes the cyclical political changes of the Kachin.

■ Llewellyn, Karl, and E. Adamson Hoebel. *The Cheyenne Way.* Norman, Okla.: University of Oklahoma Press, 1941.
   One of the best descriptions of the legal system of a tribal society.

■ Meggitt, Mervyn J. *Blood Is Their Argument: Warfare among the Mae Enga Tribesmen of the New Guinea Highlands.* Palo Alto, Calif.: Mayfield, 1977.
   Perhaps the best ethnography ever written about warfare and war-related practices among a preindustrial people.

Chapter 14

SOCIAL INEQUALITY AND STRATIFICATION

■ *Contents*

■ *Inequality is the difference in access to rewards that exist within a society. Families who live in stilt houses along this Colombian river do not enjoy the wealth brought about by the gold taken from it.*

We hold these truths to be self-evident, that all men are created equal, that they are endowed by their creator with certain unalienable Rights . . .

As you can guess by now, whether in fact all "men" are believed to have been created equal depends on which sociocultural system you happened to have been born into. Whether you have certain "unalienable rights," and the nature of these rights, also varies from people to people. In this chapter we consider another dimension of diversity in sociocultural systems, namely, how they vary in regard to the differential allocation of rewards.

Systems of Equality and Inequality

There is great cross-cultural variation in the degree to which relations of **inequality** between individuals exist in a society. *Relations of inequality* refers to the extent to which culturally valued material and social rewards are allocated disproportionately to individuals, families, and other groups.

Before discussing how societies vary in inequality, it will be helpful to consider the different kinds of rewards that exist. They generally are broken down into three categories. The most visible reward is *wealth*, or access to material goods and/or to services performed by others. Another kind of reward is usually called *power*, or the ability to make others do what you want based on coercion, legitimate authority, or informal influence. A final type of reward is *prestige*, or the respect, esteem, and overt approval granted by others to individuals they consider meritorious. Prestige is a social reward, based on judgments about an individual's personal worthiness or the contributions the individual makes to others in the group.

Each of these kinds of rewards varies in detail from people to people. For instance, how individuals and groups acquire power, how the exercise of power is organized, the uses to which power is put, and so forth, vary between societies. Similarly, many Americans tend to admire so-called self-made men, who have supposedly gained wealth and power through their own drive, talent, and effort, whereas such men would be looked down upon as self-centered and ungenerous in other societies. In spite of the diversity, this typology of rewards is quite useful, for in all sociocultural systems the desire for wealth, power, and prestige motivates at least some individuals to "get ahead" of others. But, as we shall see, some ways of life inculcate these motivations more than others. And some societies make it possible for ambitious individuals to acquire wealth, power, and prestige, whereas other societies make it difficult for anyone to accumulate resources and possessions, achieve control over others, and put themselves above their peers socially.

We can classify societies by "how much" inequality they exhibit with respect to wealth, power, and prestige. Imagine a continuum. At one end can be placed societies that feature only slight differences between individuals and groups in access to these rewards. At the other end appear those societies with marked contrasts in access to rewards. In the middle are a myriad of societies that are intermediate between the two extremes: some have contrasts in prestige but lack significant differences in wealth, for example.

Over the decades of ethnographic research, a large body of information has accumulated about inequality in various societies. In 1967, Morton Fried formulated a threefold classification of the kinds and degree of inequality found in diverse human lifeways. He labelled the three basic types of inequality **egalitarian, ranked,** and **stratified.** A description and examples of each type follow.

It is important to understand that these categories are merely points along a continuous spectrum of systems of inequality. It is impossible to pigeonhole all human societies into one of these types, for most fit somewhere in between the three categories. The terms *egalitarian, ranked,* and *stratified* are useful mainly as short descriptions of the kinds and range of variation in inequality found cross-culturally.

It also should be noted that egalitarian-ranked-stratified is almost certainly the temporal order in which the three forms developed. Until ten thousand years ago, practically everyone on earth lived in egalitarian societies. Ranked societies developed in a few areas about then, and a few thousand years later stratification developed in the great civilizations (see chapters 8, 9, and 13 on the economic and political dimensions of chiefdoms and states). Stratified societies in the next four to five thousand years spread throughout most of the world. Today, practically everyone on earth lives in a stratified society—even though some national governments deny the fact!

■ Egalitarian Societies

Egalitarian societies are at the low end of the inequality continuum. There is little noticeable difference in wealth and power between individuals, aside from distinctions based on gender and age. Of course, there are always differences in personality, skill at certain tasks, willingness to work, and other personal qualities. Individuals with attractive personalities, unusual talents, and high diligence may receive the esteem of other members of the group; but in egalitarian societies they are unable to transform their admirable personal qualities into power and possessions, for reasons to be discussed.

Mobile foragers such as the Eskimo, the western Shoshone, the Hadza, and the San (see chapter 7) are highly egalitarian. James Woodburn identified several reasons why such peoples maintain relatively equal access to social rewards. First, and most obviously, effective adaptation demands frequent seasonal movements of the band or camp, and this high rate of mobility inhibits one's ability to accumulate possessions.

Second, among mobile foragers, individuals generally are not tied to specific territories but have the right to live in and exploit the resources of a variety of areas to which they have rights of access because of bilateral kin networks (see chapters 9 and 11). They therefore are free simply to leave and live elsewhere should any other individual attempt to exercise control over their behavior. In fact, interpersonal disputes are among the most commonly reported reasons for the frequent movements of individuals between camps in groups such as the San and Hadza.

Third, the hunting-and-gathering way of life places a great advantage on sharing of food products. This seems to produce a generalized cultural value on generosity and deprecation of one's own abilities and contributions. Sharing on the principle of generalized reciprocity is *expected* behavior—the recipients of what nonegalitarian peoples might consider largesse seem to feel less compelled to make a return. Indeed, there is strong social pressure not to make oneself stand out as worthy of greater rewards. Among the !Kung San, BaMbuti and Hadza foragers, men who boast about their hunting skill are ridiculed or subject to other kinds of informal sanctions.

Fourth, sharp contrasts in wealth usually develop out of differential control of productive resources, but it is difficult in a nomadic foraging adaptation for any individual or group to maintain exclusive access to the natural resources of a territory or over the labor of

■ *Hunter-gatherers are usually egalitarian, partly because their adaptation makes it mutually beneficial to share access to resources and posessions. These Efe pygmies are sharing honey, one of their favorite foods.*

other people for a prolonged period, for reasons discussed in chapter 9.

In sum, if individuals have a range of alternatives about where to acquire what they need to survive, if sharing of products is expected and failure to share is socially punished, and if no one can exercise long-term control over necessary resources, then inequality in access to valued rewards does not have much chance of developing. And if it should develop, it does not have much chance of persisting for very long.

Not all foragers, however, are egalitarian. The Indians of the North American Northwest Coast, for instance, developed a ranked society, for in this area the abundance of anadromous fish and the relative reliability of their occurrence allowed greater sedentariness and territoriality (see chapter 7). Further, not all mobile foragers were as egalitarian as those just discussed.

Many egalitarian people do have leaders. Some individuals serve as leaders of certain kinds of activities because others recognize their special skill at some valuable task or because of special religious or practical knowledge they are believed to possess. Their leadership role, however, is quite informal and generally is limited to the activities in which they have special abilities. And leaders have only influence, not authority. Their influence is derived from their ability to persuade others. Leaders cannot coerce adherence to their decisions, and others may or may not defer to their opinions on some matter. If they do, it is generally because they believe that the leaders' knowledge or skill is superior to their own.

In egalitarian societies, however, leadership does not take the form of political offices for which people compete or to which certain people automatically succeed. In this respect, egalitarian societies contrast with ranked societies, which we now describe.

■ Ranked Societies

In ranked societies there are a fixed number of social positions, generally titles or some kind of formal office, that certain individuals occupy by virtue of birth into families that are culturally considered to have high social status. Certain families, lineages, or clans have the traditional right to have their members hold these titles or offices. High social rank is thus restricted to certain kin groups and is largely or entirely hereditary within those kin groups.

The significance of the fact that rank is mainly hereditary is realized when we contrast ranked with egalitarian societies. In the former, individuals who are born into kin groups culturally defined as lower ranking usually cannot acquire the most valued rewards offered by their societies, regardless of their skill, diligence, ambition, or other personal qualities considered admirable. In the latter, leadership, prestige, and other valued rewards can be attained by almost anyone (often restricted to males, however) regardless of their birth.

In one of the most common types of ranked societies, all kin groups are ranked relative to one another: each group has its own unique rank relative to each and every other kin group. Further, within each kin group, each and every member is ranked relative to all others, usually on the principle of genealogical seniority (elders being superior in rank to younger persons). The most valued positions that bring the highest rewards in prestige, wealth, and power are held by the highest-ranking individuals of the highest-ranking kin group. This way of ranking individuals and kin groups is most well documented for several ancient Polynesian chiefdoms.

In another kind of ranked society the kin groups that make up the population are not ranked relative to one another or are ranked in only a vague and loose way. Within each kin group certain family lines are granted the right to have their oldest members succeed to political offices. Each officeholder, usually called a *chief,* is respected throughout the society but has authority mainly over those in his own group.

An excellent example of this kind of ranking is Tikopia, a tiny Pacific island whose kinship system is described in chapter 11. In the 1920s, Tikopia's 1,200 people were divided into four patrilineal clans, each with its own chief who exercised authority over his clanmates. Each clan, in turn, was divided into several patrilineages, with an average size of about thirty members. Every Tikopian patrilineage had a head, who was believed to be the oldest living male descendant of the man who founded the lineage about four to six generations ago. Alongside this ranking of individuals within a single lineage, the various lineages of a single clan were ranked relative to one another. One lineage of each clan, supposedly the original, "senior" lineage from which the "junior" lineages had budded off, was considered the noble lineage. Members of other lineages of the clan had to defer socially to members of the noble lineage, according to Tikopian standards of etiquette. In addition, the noble lineage of each clan selected one of its members to be the chief of the whole clan.

Chiefs and other members of the noble Tikopia lineages had little more wealth than anyone else. The nobility did receive tribute from other lineages of their clan, but they gave away most of it in the many public activities that they organized and financed through redistribution (see chapter 9). The chief and nobility of each clan had no way to deny access to land and ocean resources to members of other lineages, for each lineage was considered to have inalienable rights to certain pieces of land. The Tikopia nobility, then, received much prestige and token tribute from other islanders, but they did not use this tribute to enrich themselves, and their sphere of power was limited. They were honored, but their wealth and power were not great. It is mainly in this respect that ranked societies contrast with stratified societies.

■ Stratified Societies

Stratified societies are at the high end of the inequality continuum. In general, a society is said to be stratified if

- there are marked inequalities in access to all three kinds of rewards: wealth, power, and prestige;
- this inequality is based primarily on unequal access to productive resources such as the land and tools people need to make their living; that is, a few people control access to the resources others need to survive at culturally acceptable levels;

■ unequal access to rewards has a strong tendency to be heritable throughout the generations, regardless of the personal qualities or aptitudes of individuals.

The last point means that most individuals (and families) do not move very far up or down the social ladder during their lifetimes. Although upward social mobility for individuals and families may be theoretically possible in stratified societies, it is uncommon. This is because peoples' **life chances**—their chances to receive rewards in proportion to their talents, efforts, and so on—are largely determined by the social stratum into which individuals happen to have been born. As in ranked societies, hereditary factors are the main determinant of where one fits into the social hierarchy.

Stratified societies vary, however, in the cultural ideas they have about the possibilities of social mobility. In some, such as North American and other contemporary Western and Western-derived democracies, upward or downward mobility is considered possible, although numerous studies have shown it to be uncommon. In others, especially in preindustrial soci-

■ In stratified societies, one's life chances depend on the class one was born into. This South African child will have much greater difficulty in life than his white countrymen.

eties, one's class membership is culturally considered fixed, often partly because of beliefs that existing inequalities are ordained by supernatural beings.

In stratified societies it is possible to distinguish groups and/or categories of individuals and families on the basis of their relative access to rewards. A social group or category whose members share about the same degree of access to rewards is called a *social stratum.* The two major kinds of strata are **classes** and **castes.**

Two general differences between class and caste systems stand out. First, by definition, castes are endogamous groups: they have cultural norms or laws that require individuals to marry within their caste. As discussed in chapter 10, rules that mandate marriage within one's own group have the effect of maintaining the distinctiveness of the group relative to other groups. This is because there is no possibility of upward mobility through intercaste marriage, and because there are no children who have potentially anomalous group membership. Class societies, however, generally allow an individual to marry someone of a different class, and in fact intermarriage between classes is commonly one avenue of social mobility. It follows from the endogamous nature of caste that one's caste membership is theoretically hereditary: one is born into the caste of one's parents, one marries someone in the same caste, and one's children are likewise born into and remain members of one's own caste. (We say "theoretically" because social reality occasionally differs from cultural norms, in caste societies as in all others.)

Second, caste systems have some kind of prohibition against contact between members of different castes. High-caste members, for example, sometimes believe they will be spiritually polluted should they come into contact with members of other castes. Indeed, they often must perform rituals to cleanse themselves after accidental contacts.

Both of these general differences mean that castes have more permanent membership and more rigid social boundaries than classes. However, this does not mean that it is easy to tell whether some particular stratified society "has" castes or classes. Some societies have elements of both. For instance, some scholars have suggested that black-white relations in the American South were more castelike than classlike until the mid-twentieth century. There was no possibility of upward mobility into the white "caste" for blacks, for no one could overcome the sociocultural stigma of black skin color. Interracial marriage was legally prohibited or culturally taboo, so that the two races were endogamous. Explicit laws against certain kinds of "intercaste" contacts and interactions—known as *segregation laws*—forced blacks to live apart from whites, forbad them to enter certain white business establishments and public restrooms, made them send their children to all-black schools, and so forth.

Castes in Traditional India

The most well known caste system is that of traditional India. India's caste system was quite complex and varied from region to region, so we can present only a generalized picture. There were four main caste categories, or *varnas*. (A varna is not itself a caste.) Each varna was ranked relative to the others in honor and degree of ritual purity, and each was broadly associated with certain kinds of occupations.

The highest varna was the Brahmins, or priests and scholars; next was the varna of nobles and warriors, the Kshatriyas; third were the Vaishas, or merchants and artisans; and ranked lowest were the farmers, craftsmen, and certain other laborers, the Shudras. A fifth category—outside and ranked below the varna—were the untouchables, to whom fell work that was considered polluting to the varna.

The varna (which, incidentally, first arose in the second millenium B.C. when the Aryans invaded and conquered what is now northern India) were the largest, most inclusive categories into which India traditionally was divided. However, the villages in which most people lived were divided into much smaller and specific occupational groupings called *jati* (castes, as the term is usually used). For example, in a particular village the Shudra varna might be represented by several jati with names such as weaver, potter, and tailor. There were thousands of these castes in India, distributed among the many thousands of villages, with each village containing a variable number of castes.

To better understand Indian castes, it is necessary to understand the basic tenets of Hinduism, the traditional religion of India. (Hinduism is incredibly diverse and complex, so here we can present only a simplified depiction of it.) Hindu religion holds that spiritual souls are reborn into different physical bodies at various stages of their existence—this is the doctrine of *reincarnation*. Souls ultimately desire an end to the cycle of earthly birth, death, and rebirth, but to achieve this end each soul must be reborn thousands of times into thousands of bodies, both animal and human. Souls attempt to move up the "ladder" of reincarnation, from lower forms of life to higher ones: from animals to humans (of various ranked castes) to gods.

The particular body (be it human or animal) that a soul is born into depends on how closely that soul adhered to proper standards of behavior in previous lifetimes. For souls that had made it up to human forms in their previous incarnation, these standards include avoidance of activities that Hindus believe are polluting. Among the most polluting activities are handling and working with animal carcasses or the bodies of deceased humans, touching excrement and other waste materials, dealing with childbirth, and eating meat. People who regularly perform these activities are not only polluted themselves, but anyone of a higher caste who comes into physical contact with them likewise becomes polluted and must bathe ritually to cleanse himself or herself. One's present place in society— one's "station in life"—varies with the degree to which one is associated with pure and impure activities. In turn, because of reincarnation, whether one is associated with pure or impure activities depends on one's behavior in previous lives—such as the degree to which one has allowed oneself to become polluted or failed to cleanse oneself.

India's traditional caste hierarchy is so intimately tied up with Hindu doctrines that the two are almost inseparable. First, the caste into which one is born

■ *Hindus regard certain objects and activities as spiritually defiling or polluting. Pollution may be removed by bathing.*

depends on the behavior of one's soul in previous incarnations. People are low caste either because their soul has not yet been through enough lifetimes to have reached a higher form, or because their sins in a previous lifetime merit reincarnation into a low caste. In the present life, people have what they deserve. Thus all "men" were not created equal, in the Hindu world view; it is legitimate and right that some castes have more power and privilege, and more status and wealth, than others.

Second, caste categories are associated with certain occupations. Each village contains a number of castes, most of which are named according to the occupation traditionally performed by their members. Thus a village might include castes of priests, merchants, blacksmiths, potters, tailors, farmers, weavers, carpenters, washers, barbers, leather workers, and "sweepers" (the last refers to those who remove human waste matter from peoples' houses). Just as activities are ranked in Hindu beliefs according to their degree of purity and impurity, so occupations and those who perform them are ranked. Working with animal carcasses is defiling, so leather working is a defiling occupation and leather workers are so polluting as to be untouchable. The same applies to sweeping: people who remove human wastes from houses or spread excrement over village fields are polluted, and their touch pollutes those of higher castes. Therefore, members of the leather working, sweeping, and other castes associated with defiling occupations were traditionally untouch-

able. (Discrimination against people of untouchable ancestry is illegal in modern India, incidentally). Untouchables usually lived in their own special section of the village, separate from members of higher castes. Because they would contaminate temples by their entry, they could not go inside a temple. Their touch contaminated water, so they had to use separate wells. These and other restrictions on their behavior were sometimes extreme, and they were truly "outcastes."

However, members of high-ranking castes such as priests, landowners, warriors, and merchants actually needed the services of low-ranking castes. Again, this is because Hinduism defines some activities essential for life as polluting, so castes who would be defiled by these activities need lower castes to perform these services for them. The bullocks essential for farming died, so someone had to remove dead cattle from the village; Brahmin women gave birth just as other women, so the women of some low-ranking caste had to serve them as midwives, since other Brahmin women would become polluted by so serving; everyone produces feces and urine, so someone must remove these products from the houses of high-caste members lest they pollute their occupants. Accordingly, each caste had its proper role and function in the economic, social, and religious life of the village.

Likewise, each caste had its religiously ordained duties to the other castes. In Hindu beliefs, one's soul is reincarnated into a higher or lower form in succeeding lives partly according to how well one fulfills the obligations of his or her caste in the present life. Leather workers, for instance, cannot do anything to improve their lot in this life; but by faithfully fulfilling their obligations to members of higher castes, their souls will receive higher reincarnations in future bodies.

In much of India (especially in the north), caste membership was the organizational basis for some kinds of economic cooperation. Individual members of the various castes represented in a region were involved in hereditary patron-client relationships with one another known as *jajmani*. A village farmer, for example, might require the services of a blacksmith, carpenter, leather worker, potter, tailor, barber, and other specialized craftsmen or workers. The farmer did not have to search for someone to perform these jobs for him, nor did those who performed these services have to make special deals with other farmers to obtain their livelihood; rather, the farmer and the individual members of the castes who specialized in the appropriate occupation inherited these "contracts" from their

■ *In traditional Hindu India, caste and occupation were broadly associated. This member of the barber caste performed his services for other castes.*

parents. So during the course of the year, the blacksmith fixed the farmer's plow, the leather worker made the shoes for the farmer's family, the barber cut their hair, the washers did their laundry, and so on.

These specialists were not paid each time they performed their tasks. At the end of the agricultural season, when the farmer's grain was harvested, each specialist received a portion of the total harvest. The amount of grain each specialist received was supposedly fixed by tradition: so much would be sent to the temple priests, so much given to the blacksmith, so much to the leather worker, and so on. Each specialist had a jajmani relationship with many other people and acquired food or other goods or services from each of them according to the traditional allotment of the occupation. Many members of a caste inherited the jajmani networks of their parents, which provided them with patrons whom they served and with clients who served them. Individuals of various castes in a village or region thus were involved in economic relationships with one another, exchanging their specialized services or goods for those of other castes.

One should not conclude, however, that intercaste relations were harmonious, nor that the complementary tasks associated with each caste were entirely mutually beneficial. A great deal of friction and outright conflict existed between individual members of different castes. In fact, local castes as a whole group sometimes organized themselves with a council to pursue their common interests. It was even possible for a caste to improve its rank in the local caste hierarchy, despite the normatively unchanging relative position of castes. This was done in several ways, including adopting the customs and prohibitions of a higher caste and "reinventing" the history of one's caste to make it seem that it originally came from a higher varna.

Classes

Class societies may be subdivided into strata—the classes—that have different degrees of access to material goods or control over land, tools, and other kinds of productive resources; have different degrees of control over or access to the public decision-making apparatus of government; and are ranked by esteem or respect from the society at large. We first discuss an unusual example of a preindustrial class system and then consider classes in industrial societies.

■ Preindustrial Class Systems: The Natchez

We already have mentioned some examples of class-stratified preindustrial societies, such as the Inca (chapter 9) and other representatives of the state level of political structure (chapter 13). Here we shall discuss only one additional example.

In the lower Mississippi Valley of North America lived the Natchez, a society of about 5,000 people known to us only through ethnohistorical reconstruction. Until their society was destroyed in a war with the French in 1731, the Natchez had one of the most unusual and interesting class systems of the preindustrial world. Among these horticultural, matrilineal people were two major classes: rulers and commoners. The rulers, in turn, were divided into three ranked social categories: Suns, Nobles, and Honored People.

The highest-ranking member of the Sun rank was the Great Sun. He and his matrilineage were believed to be at the apex of the society, for the Natchez believed that God (the real Sun) had sent the Great Sun and his wife to rule them, giving them their laws and the sacred fire. Because of his divine origin, the Great Sun assumed the attributes of a living god and had great authority over the lives of the people. As the link between humans and God, the Great Sun had ritual duties. Each morning he went to the temple of the sacred fire and blew tobacco smoke toward the rising sun and in the four cardinal directions, to bless the people.

The Great Sun also had wealth and many privileges denied to others. His large house, complete with a wooden throne, sat atop an earthen mound located across the plaza from the temple of the sacred fire. When traveling, he sat on a litter, carried by eight servants. A large number of other servants, who were given to him at his birth by their parents, served his household, hunted for him, and planted his fields. Only he could wear a beautiful headdress made from black and white feathers. He received and redistributed game killed on communal hunts. The first corn harvested from the fields was presented to him. He had substantial political control, for he could order the execution of anyone whose actions offended him.

The Great Sun was a member of the small Sun matrilineage (with between eleven and seventeen members). At the death of a Great Sun, a new Great Sun was chosen from among the male members of this lineage who were "without physical blemish." Other

Suns lived in houses near the residence of the Great Sun. Like him, they had many privileges, including servants whose work freed them from most physical labor and the right to wear fine headdresses that marked their rank. The senior female member of the Sun matrilineage, called White Woman, also was carried around on a litter.

Other members of the ruler class—the Nobles and the Honored People—also had certain privileges. Noble and Honored People males could wear black breechclouts, whereas commoners were allowed to wear only white. Children of the ruling class wore two or three sacred pearls from the temple around their necks, while commoner children went naked. Although all Natchez were tatooed on their faces, rulers were elaborately tatooed on their bodies and limbs as well.

Suns, Nobles, and Honored People filled virtually all positions conferring authority and leadership, including the status of Great War Chief, temple priests, village chiefs, and councilors to the Great Sun. The commoner class was thus excluded from positions carrying privileges and authority.

But—and this next feature was what made this system so unusual—Natchez marriage rules required all rulers to take their spouses from among the commoners. (Since there were many more commoners than nobles, most commoners married one another, however.) If a Sun woman married a commoner man, their offspring became Suns (because of matrilineal descent). But if a Sun man married a commoner woman, their children received the status of Noble. So Nobles were the children of marriages between Sun men and commoner women. When, in turn, a Noble woman married—as she was required to do—a commoner man, their children remained Nobles. But the children of Noble men and commoner women dropped to the status of Honored People, the lowest rank in the ruler class. When an Honored People man married a commoner, their children dropped to the class of commoners, whereas the children of Honored People women remained Honored People. As you can see, in essence children took the rank of their mother if she was in the ruler class; if their father was a ruler and their mother a commoner, their rank was one notch below that of their father. No satisfactory explanation for this unusual (and possibly unique) class system has been offered.

The Natchez class system allowed for the possibility of mobility: the offspring of any commoner who married one of the rulers would rise in class. In addition to interclass mobility by means of marriage, commoner men who distinguished themselves in war could be advanced into the rank of Honored Person, as could their wives and children. Finally, at the death of a Great Sun, a commoner family could become Honored People by offering one of their children as a sacrifice.

■ Industrial Class Systems: The United States

In industrial societies upward mobility between classes is possible through interclass marriage, personal talent and effort, or good luck. In actuality, few individuals rise much higher in the class system than their parents. Members of different classes have differential access to the material resources (income, wealth), social contacts, and cultural knowledge (education, "social graces") that are valued and rewarded in the sociocultural system.

The kind of work one does is often assumed to be the best single overall indication of class membership. (Is this perhaps the reason one of the first questions you ask new acquaintances is, "What kind of work do you do?") Occupation is popularly assumed to be the main determinant of income, and one's income influences so much else: overall lifestyle, the access of one's children to education, the kinds of individuals with whom one associates, the kind of church or club to which one belongs, and so on.

Unfortunately for our desire to make things neat and orderly, there are problems with defining a class of the basis of occupation or any other single criterion. For one thing, different criteria used to define class membership do not always agree. For instance, people do not agree on the prestige of many occupations—attorneys are despised by some but granted high prestige by others. The same applies to politicians, physicians, academicians, police, and numerous other professionals. Further, the degree to which some occupation is respected by the population at large does not always reflect the relative wealth and/or access to power of those who practice it. (See Box 14.1).

So it is often difficult to decide to which class some individual belongs. One way around this ambiguity, favored by some sociologists, is to separate the three kinds of rewards from one another and define a separate class ranking for each reward. We can distinguish classes defined on the basis of prestige (*status groups*, as some call them) and on the basis of income or wealth

OCCUPATIONAL PRESTIGE IN THE UNITED STATES

Sociological studies reveal how highly Americans regard certain occupational categories. Below is a sample of twenty-five occupations, listed from highest to lowest prestige ranking:

- physician
- college professor
- attorney
- stockbroker
- registered nurse
- high school teacher
- social worker
- electrician
- plumber
- police officer
- dental assistant
- carpenter
- welder
- mechanic
- truck driver
- hairdresser
- cashier
- assembly-line worker
- housekeeper
- coal miner
- waitress/waiter
- babysitter
- garbage collector
- janitor
- hotel chambermaid

Apparently, the main influence on how people rank occupational categories is how much formal education is required to assume the occupational role: generally, "brain work" is ranked above "manual work."

The interesting thing about these prestige ranks is that a great many of them do not reflect income levels typical of the occupation. College professors, nurses, teachers, and dental assistants receive significantly higher prestige than plumbers, carpenters, welders, and assembly-line workers. Yet, largely because of unionization of the latter occupations, many of them earn more yearly income than those who do "brain work." This is not a contradiction—for being in a high-prestige professional career offers other, nonmaterial rewards—but it does make it difficult to decide exactly to which "class" some individuals and families belong. ■

Source: Tischler 1990.

(*economic classes*), for instance. The definitions and methods used for ranking the classes obviously depend to some extent on the interest of the social scientist, as well as on the nature of the society under study.

In the United States probably the most widely accepted approach to stratification uses the concept of economic class. Individuals and families are placed into classes based on their wealth. Using wealth as the primary basis of class ranking has four major advantages. First, it is more measurable than other indications of class membership (although, as we discuss later, cash income does not measure it adequately).

Second, wealth is the best single indication of the overall benefits individuals and families are receiving from their citizenship in the nation. Money cannot buy you love, happiness, or many other things, but it can buy you much of what Americans value.

Third, wealth generally (but not completely) matches up with an individual's or family's access to what Marxians call the *means of production* (see chapter 5). That is, high wealth is correlated with ownership of productive resources such as factories, financial institutions, and income-producing real estate. By and large, the richest people in the country own the nation's large businesses. They either built their companies themselves, or their ancestors made fortunes through business activity and passed their ownership along to the present generation.

Fourth, wealth levels broadly determine people's access to political power. Through campaign contributions the wealthy have a greater say in who gets nominated and elected to important offices. Through lobbying efforts the rich enjoy greater influence on the laws and policies of the nation than their numbers warrant. By providing much of the funding for think tanks and other public advisory groups, the wealthy subsidize the expertise of many economists, political scientists, sociologists, and other social scientists who advise government. Many appointed officials in the executive branch of the federal government are members of the elite. Some appointees move back and forth between business and government service regularly. (These generalizations are documented convincingly in William Domhoff's [1983] book *Who Rules America Now?*)

■ *Wealth is quite unequally distributed in the United States. This is the terrace of a mansion that used to be owned by an Oklahoma oil family.*

■ *As this homeless man reminds us, in the United States, great wealth coexists with brutal poverty.*

For these and other reasons, we can learn most about inequality in the United States by focusing our discussion on the distribution of wealth. Most Americans know something about economic inequality in their country. If we consider annual cash income, for example, the poorest fifth of Americans received only 4.6 percent of the nation's total income in 1987, whereas the richest fifth received 43.7 percent (see Table 14.1). This distribution of annual income has been quite consistent over the last thirty or forty years. Year after year, the poorest 20 percent of Americans earn around 5 percent of all the money earned in the country, whereas the richest 20 percent earn over 40 percent. The wealthiest 5 percent of Americans received 17 percent of all income earned in 1987, and this percentage also has altered little over the past thirty years.

That there are poor people in the United States is well known. What is less well known—or at any rate less talked about—is how much of the nation's wealth is owned by a very small minority of its citizens. Middle-income people, and in fact people who are generally considered fairly affluent, own little in comparison with the truly wealthy.

Figures on annual income such as those given in Table 14.1 greatly underestimate the degree of economic inequality in the United States. People's material standards of living are not determined in any simple way by their income, nor is their influence over local, state, and national political decision making. Living standards and political influence are more greatly determined by a person's or family's net worth;

that is, by all assets (property) minus all indebtedness. Assets include property such as savings and checking accounts, stocks and bonds, money market funds, trusts, and cash surrender value of life insurance policies. Assets also include tangible property such as real estate, homes, automobiles, and other personal property, all of which can be assigned a dollar (market) value. The assets a family owns are a much better measure of its wealth than its income. Assets represent stored-up purchasing power: by selling off their assets, individuals and families can acquire additional money.

In 1983 the Federal Reserve Board carried out a study of the assets and liabilities of a random sample of over 4,000 American households. The results of the

■ *Table 14.1* **Distribution of Family Annual Income in the United States, 1987**

PERCENTAGE OF INCOME EARNED BY		AMOUNT EARNED, 1987
Poorest fifth	4.6%	less than $14,449
Second fifth	10.8%	between $14,450 and $25,099
Third fifth	16.9%	between $25,100 and $36,599
Fourth fifth	24.1%	between $36,600 and $52,909
Richest fifth	43.7%	over $52,910
Richest 5%	16.9%	over $86,300

Source: U.S. Bureau of the Census (1989,446).

study were summarized in a 1986 report published by the Joint Economic Committee of the U.S. Congress. The conclusions were later amended, and the following discussion uses the corrected information.

The report divides American families into four categories, defined as follows:

- "Super rich": the 0.5 percent of families with the most wealth
- "Very rich": the next 0.5 percent richest families
- "Rich": the next 9 percent of richest families
- "Everyone else": the rest of the families, or 90 percent of all the nation's families

How much of the nation's privately held wealth is owned by families of these four categories?

- Super-rich families own 24 percent of all assets
- Very rich families own 7 percent of all assets
- Rich families own 35 percent of all assets
- Everyone else owns 34 percent of all assets

The richest 1 percent of Americans thus own 31 percent of the nation's wealth, and the richest 10 percent of Americans own two-thirds of all privately owned assets. The bottom 90 percent of the population has a net worth of only one-third the total wealth under private ownership.

So the ownership of wealth is highly concentrated in the United States. Just as important as the unequal distribution of wealth is the nature of the assets owned by the wealthy and by everyone else. Some kinds of wealth are owned for purposes of producing future wealth for their owners. Super rich families and very rich families together own a remarkably high percentage of these kinds of wealth: 57 percent of public stock, 51 percent of the net worth of corporate assets not publicly traded, and 36 percent of real estate not used as the owner's residence. Adding in the wealth-producing assets of the run-of-the-mill "rich" families, the 10 percent of the most wealthy families in the country own almost 90 percent of the stocks, 91 percent of the non-publicly-traded business assets, and 76 percent of non-owner-occupied real estate. The richest 10 percent of Americans also own 93 percent of the value of all bonds and trusts. Of course, these kinds of wealth produce income continuously for their owners.

Finally, a few hundred Americans are enormously wealthy. Every year *Forbes,* one of the country's leading business magazines, publishes a list and a brief biography of the richest 400 individuals in the United States. In 1986, *Forbes* estimated the net worth of the 400

wealthiest Americans at $156 billion. How much money is this? It was nearly as much as the gross national product of Mexico ($158 billion), a country with a 1986 population of about 80 million. It was more than the U.S. government redistributed to its least affluent citizens in the form of welfare, food stamps, unemployment compensation, housing subsidies, and so forth ($151 billion, excluding social security). It was three-fourths of the 1986 federal budget deficit (around $200 billion).

Maintaining Inequality

The persistence of inequality in stratified societies demands an explanation. As the United States illustrates, typically a small percentage of the population controls most of the wealth and wields a great deal of influence over public affairs. Why does the majority allow them this power and privilege?

One answer is that this question is ethnocentric: even to ask it assumes that the cultural value North Americans supposedly place on human equality is universal, which, of course, it is not. One might argue that we find high degrees of inequality puzzling, especially if wealth and power are largely inherited, because we believe that all people are created equal. But people brought up in other cultural traditions accept inherited inequalities as a normal part of human life.

This response will not suffice. First, it is no response at all: it says merely that not everyone in the world has the same hangups about inequality that we do, but it explains neither our hangups nor why others lack them. Second, there is evidence of widespread conflict between strata in a wide range of stratified societies. Resentment, rebellion, and occasional attempts at revolution occur in stratified societies from all parts of the world (which is not to say that they are universally present). A great many powerless and poor people do not simply accept their place in the social hierarchy, so we need some understanding of why so many others do. Finally, although our knowledge of the history of preindustrial stratification systems is scanty, we know that in a great many societies a conquering militaristic group imposed their rule over the indigenous population of a region. This was true in African states such as Bunyoro and Zulu, in the ancient civilizations of the Americas such as the Aztec and Inca, in China and India, and in many other regions. In many and probably most stratified societies, the lower strata did not consent to their low standing but had it forced upon them.

Another possible explanation of how inequality persists is that members of the highest stratum (hereafter called the *elite*) use their wealth and power to organize an armed force stronger than that of their opposition. If the elite somehow manage to monopolize control over weapons or to organize a loyal army, then they can use coercion and threat to maintain their access to rewards and resources. Armed force, of course, is sometimes used by the elite to put down rebellions, and no doubt the ever-present threat of coercive sanctions does deter resistance to the elite's wealth, prestige, and power.

Yet in most systems of stratification, including even modern military dictatorships, only occasionally do the elite find it necessary to use force. In most preindustrial stratified societies a monopoly over the use of armed force was difficult to achieve, since the military technology was undeveloped and generally available. Besides, use of actual force and the threat of force have disadvantages to the elite itself. Suppose the elite wait for rebellions to occur and then use superior military force to put them down. Even though none succeed, each time a rebellion is suppressed, more hatred and resentment and more awareness of the relative wealth and power of the elite are produced. Increased hatred and awareness caused by suppression can backfire and lead to a greater probability of future rebellion. Notice also that the elite's reliance on oppression to maintain wealth and power reduces or eliminates their honor and esteem, the third major reward offered by stratification, and one which they presumably covet. Further, those who supply the military might—the army, henchmen, thugs, or police—must be paid or otherwise provided for by the elite; this requires resources. The elite can either take these resources from their own wealth, thus reducing it, or they can increase their exploitation of the majority population, thus breeding more hatred and resentment toward themselves. Finally, relying entirely on the loyalty of an army is risky, because their allegiance may change. In sum, armed force alone is costly and risky.

This is not to deny that military might is an important reason why high degrees of inequality are maintained for many generations. We lack the data to be certain, but probably few elites have maintained themselves for many generations without occasionally using the deterrent value of force and periodically suppressing rebellions and dissent. Nonetheless, stratification systems that rely entirely or largely on force seem to be short-lived and unstable and have been replaced by those that use other mechanisms. What other mechanisms are available?

■ Ideologies

We can begin to answer this question by noting yet another reason that inequality rarely persists because of force alone. A single rebellion can have many causes, but a persistent *pattern* of rebellion is caused mainly by the lower strata's perception that they are not receiving their fair share of rewards. Putting down rebellions does nothing to change the reasons why people rebel. The instigators may be sanctioned or eliminated, but the underlying discontent that causes persistent conflict remains. Sooner or later, there will be new instigators who organize new rebellions. Armed force cannot eliminate the perceptions of unfair distribution of rewards that cause rebellions.

One mechanism available to an elite to reduce dissent without coercion is to change the perceptions of the underprivileged about why they are underprivileged. For example, if poor people think it is God's will that they are poor, they are less likely to rebel than if they believe they are poor because of exploitation. Or if they think the elite use their property and power to benefit everyone in the society, then they are less likely to begrudge the elite their rewards. Or if they think that a concentration of property and power is inevitable, because that's just the way life is, they will be less likely to resist. Or if they think that they too can acquire property and power through their own achievements, they are likely to put their effort into improving their own position rather than into causing trouble.

If, to state the general point, members of the lower strata adopt a set of cultural ideas that justifies and legitimizes the rewards received by the higher strata, then they are more likely to try and join the system rather than to beat it. In such beliefs the elite have a powerful, and relatively cheap, tool with which to reduce the amount of opposition to their power and privileges. Further, these ideas increase the prestige of the elite. If people believe that inequality is God's will, or that the activities of the elite benefit all, or that the elite became elite through intelligence and hard work, then the elite deserve the honor and respect of everyone else.

Those beliefs that explain inequality as desirable or legitimate are called **ideologies.** The phrase sometimes used by Marxists for ideology captures the essence of the concept, but you do not need to be a Marxist to appreciate the point. They call it *false consciousness,* meaning that the disadvantaged do not have a true and objective understanding of their sociocultural system and how and why it allocates rewards. When you do not like the ideologies of some sociocultural system, you probably believe the "common people" are brainwashed or just ignorant. But few people can see through the ideologies of their own sociocultural system, or the ideologies would not be effective and perhaps already would have been replaced.

In preindustrial systems of stratification inequality usually is justified with religious ideologies. We are familiar with the notion of the "divine right of kings" from feudal Europe—certainly a handy supernatural mandate for kings and aristocracies! Similar notions are common in non-Western stratified societies. For instance, in Bunyoro, a kingdom in East Africa, the health and welfare of the ruler were mystically associated with the fertility and prosperity of the whole kingdom. Anything that threatened his life was believed a threat to everyone. In many ancient civilizations, such as the Aztec, the Inca, the Japanese, and the Egyptian, the ruler himself was believed to be a divine or semidivine being. In pre-twentieth century China, the emperor was believed to rule because he had the "Mandate of Heaven," meaning that Heaven itself had granted him secular authority over the vast Chinese empire for so long as he ruled it wisely and humanely. In traditional India, as we have seen, Hindu beliefs about reincarnation and pollution were so intertwined with the caste system that they rendered its inequities both explicable and legitimate.

We now look at how religious beliefs justified inequality in another preindustrial stratified society, Hawaii. A Hawaiian paramount chief was literally a son of god—he was believed to be descended from one of the gods of the Hawaiian pantheon through a line of eldest sons. Lesser chiefs, who generally were relatives of the paramount, also included the same deities among their ancestors and likewise had a divine mandate for their wealth and power. The nobility of ancient Hawaii—which included chiefs and their families—were believed to be endowed with a supernatural power or force called *mana* (discussed further in chapter 15). Mana allowed chiefs to curse those who were disloyal of disobedient. Thus, chiefs could call on not only an

In Europe, until a couple of centuries ago, the power, possessions, and prestige of monarchs were reinforced by the religious ideology known as the divine right of kings. This is the Versaille, the former castle of the monarch of France.

armed human force to punish dissenters but also on superhuman forces. Hawaiians also believed that the prosperity of a chiefdom and everyone in it depended on the periodic performance of certain rituals, which only priests had the proper training and supernatural mandate to perform. The elaborate rituals organized and led by the priesthood were financed by the chiefs, who collected tribute from the commoner population for this purpose.

In sum, the Hawaiian religion reinforced and legitimized the power and privilege of the nobility by providing the chiefs with a divine right to rule, with supernatural powers to punish, and with a set of ritual activities that gave them a function to perform that was believed to benefit the whole population. The same general kinds of supernatural mandates are found in other preindustrial stratified societies.

■ Modern Secular Ideologies

What about ideologies in modern industrial societies, most of which are as highly stratified as any in the preindustrial world? Take the contemporary United States, for instance. Certainly the beliefs of the dominant religion in the United States, Christianity, often are said to provide support for the American way of life. The Bible sometimes is claimed to teach that it is okay to be rich—many television evangelists even preach that wealth is a sign of God's blessing to the faithful. In many parts of the country, few politicians win elections without periodic references to God in their speeches.

Still, many American citizens regard themselves as too sophisticated to believe ideologies based on supernatural mandates. Politicians may find it politically expedient to invoke God's name periodically, but few contemporary politicians go far by claiming they are chosen by God. Likewise, the super-rich and very rich generally do not justify their wealth and access to power by invoking supernatural authority. In other words, there is religious reinforcement for American institutions and "basic values," but religious ideologies justifying the wealth and power of particular *individuals* are not as widely accepted (and hence not as powerful) as they are in other societies and in Western civilization a few centuries ago.

This does not imply that industrial societies such as the United States no longer have ideologies, for ideologies do not have to be based on religious beliefs; a **secular ideology** may exist. The three necessary characteristics of an ideology are that

■ it must reinforce inequality by reducing activities that would redistribute wealth and power more equally;
■ it must perform this function by affecting the popular consciousness (cultural ideas), not by threatening physical coercion;
■ it must be believable, based on existing standards of knowledge.

In the first requirement, *activities* refers not just to rebellions against the government but also to legitimate political activities such as demonstrations, to economic activities such as strikes and work stoppages, to attempts to redistribute wealth through influencing government social welfare policies, and so forth. On the third point, an effective ideology must match up with other ideas people have about the world, especially their ideas about how their political and economic systems work. It must make sense and be plausible, or it will be ineffective and (presumably) will not survive.

In other words, there must be a consistency between workable ideologies and other aspects of a sociocultural system. It would not "fit" with most Americans' ideas about how their society works if wealthy individuals claimed a supernatural mandate for their privileged and powerful position, or if a Congressional candidate claimed "God wants me to win this election." They must justify their access to power and wealth in ways that the rest of us find acceptable, or the ideas they put

forward will be ineffective. What are these "other beliefs" with which American ideologies must fit?

Like the citizens of most nations with market economies, most Americans believe that people will not scramble to get an education, work hard on the job, and so forth—that is, will not give their best efforts—unless they have an incentive to do so. To bring out the best in individuals, it is necessary that they be rewarded for their efforts, or at least that they think they have the possibility of being rewarded in the future. Many of us think this is only "human nature." Also, Americans accept it as morally fair and just that, given equal opportunity, people who work the hardest, have the most talent, and are the most ambitious should receive the highest rewards. If the rich and powerful in the United States are to promote an ideology that justifies their position, it must be compatible with these other cultural opinions and values of most Americans.

In the context of this cultural knowledge, many scholars suggest that two major ideas justify the high degree of inequality in the modern United States. First is the idea that our whole society benefits from inequality—because a few are wealthy, everyone else is better off than they would be if wealth were distributed more equally. This is because the possibility of gaining wealth motivates individuals to do their best, and we all win when our fellow citizens perform up to their potentials. Besides, the concentration of wealth is believed necessary to create jobs, from which everyone benefits. Second is the belief that the elite have earned their rewards through their own meritorious qualities and efforts—skill, intelligence, hard work, ambition, willingness to take risks, and other qualities that we consider laudable in an individual.

Some Americans believe these ideas; others do not. (Probably more believe the first idea than the second!) But to the extent that they are believed, these two ideas fit together with Americans' other ideas about how their nation works to legitimize inequality. The first says that inequality is socially necessary and even beneficial. The second says that the present way rewards are distributed is, in general, just. Wealthy and powerful people justify their rewards with these ideas without any recourse to the will of supernatural beings. They do so with ideas that many of us find acceptable according to our cultural premises, because we share the belief in the necessity of incentive, and because we agree in the fairness of greater rewards for greater efforts and talents.

Theories of Inequality

You may or may not personally believe the ideas just summarized. (If you do not believe them, then they are not effective ideologies to you.) Or you may believe that these ideas are a fairly accurate representation of how American society allocates rewards (in which case, you will deny that they are mere ideologies). Your personal opinion depends on your class, your upbringing, your political philosophy, your other ideas about human nature, and so forth.

Are these ideas accurate representations of reality, as some conservatives believe? Or are they ideologies, as many liberals hold? The answer boils down to two questions: (1) Who benefits from inequality? and (2) Do the elite themselves perform any functions for which they deserve to be rewarded with the amount of power and privilege that they actually have?

There is—as usual—disagreement on the answers to these questions. Two distinct political and philosophical views exist. One view is that a high degree of inequality in the final distribution of rewards is necessary, just, and beneficial to all the members of society. Stratification is the only way to provide unequal rewards for unequal talents and efforts. Without such unequal rewards, this view holds, collective mediocrity will result. This is sometimes called the **functional theory of inequality** (see chapter 5 for an overview of the functionalist theoretical perspective).

Another opinion holds that a high degree of inequality is not only unjust but robs the whole society of the benefits of much of its talent, which lies undeveloped in those at the bottom of the social ladder. Stratification and its accompanying ideologies are ways that the privileged and powerful have devised over the generations to ensure the maintenance of their access to resources and the machinery of government. Called the **conflict theory of inequality,** this view holds that stratification preserves the social, economic, and political position of the well-off but offers no benefit to society at large, and indeed is the major source of conflict in class and caste societies.

We now consider each of these theories in more detail.

■ *Functionalist Theory*

Functionalists believe that inequality is functionally necessary if a society is to motivate its most able members to perform its most important roles. A problem faced by any group is recruitment: it must have some effective principles by means of which qualified individuals can be recruited into it. Some jobs or roles require more skill and training than do others. Ordinarily, the more skill and training required to perform a role, the fewer the number of members in the group who are qualified to "do the job," and, all else equal, the more valuable their talent is to the whole group. Functionalists argue that unequal rewards—and the system of stratification that results from them—are an effective way to recruit the most trained individuals with the most scarce talents into the most socially valuable roles. Unless there are rewards for those with the personal qualities that most of us lack, they will have no incentive to put those qualities to work in activities that benefit all of us. Further, inequality is not only advantageous, it also is socially just, in the functionalist view. If society as a whole is to enjoy the fruits of the labor of its small number of well-trained, talented, and hard-working individuals, it is only fair that it reward these individuals with material goods, respect, and control over public decision making.

How can we evaluate this argument? Two objections are possible within the framework of the the the theory itself. First, there is little reason to believe that the high degree of inequality in most stratified societies is needed to ensure that scarce talent is put to its most valuable uses. This is true even in industrialized societies. As an example, how many dollars does it take to motivate a qualified individual to run a major oil or auto company? If the income levels of top oil and auto executives were reduced to, say, $100,000 annually, would we have inferior executives and less well managed and profitable companies? Or would oil and auto workers simply receive a greater slice of the company pie, and the rest of us enjoy lower gasoline and car prices? To broaden the question: Is the *high degree* of inequality empirically found in stratified societies needed to realize the benefits of *some degree* of inequality? Or could some of the wealth now controlled by the rich be redistributed without reducing anyone's incentives to perform critical roles? One objection to the functionalist theory, then, is as follows: Granted that unequal rewards are needed to motivate people, no one knows how unequal the rewards must be. Certainly, no one knows whether the rewards must be as unequal as they actually are in some particular stratified society.

Second, functionalists assume that the system of stratification *effectively* places qualified individuals into important roles. But it is a very large assumption, and perhaps only an ideology, that those who are best able to perform the most important roles are those who usually are recruited into them. In all systems of stratification there is a powerful element of inheritance of wealth, prestige, and power. Assume it is true (and it is not) that all those individuals who acquired their rewards in previous generations did so by performing roles that the rest of the population was willing to reward them for performing. There still is no guarantee that their children and children's children have the same enviable and scarce personal qualities, yet their descendants have a head start. If we think of much of economic, social, and political life as analogous to a race—like a 100-meter dash—then to ensure that the fastest runners finish first, we need to start them all off from the same place. But the tendency for rewards to be inherited is analogous to starting some runners at the starting line, others at the 40-meter mark, and a few at the 80-meter mark; obviously who finishes first and last is not determined mainly by who is the fastest.

Only if a society were able to devise some way of beginning each generation on an equal footing, with truly equal opportunities to compete, would the functionalist theory of inequality be adequate. Of course, no stratified society has ever achieved this condition, partly because the wealthy and powerful would have to consent to such a change, and they have no incentive to do so. In sum, the second objection to functionalism is that stratification is an inefficient way to recruit talented individuals into the most valuable roles, because it virtually ensures unequal life chances or opportunities.

■ Conflict Theory

The conflict theory takes off from objections to functionalism, such as the two just given; but it argues that such objections do not get to the heart of the issue. We could argue endlessly about how much inequality is needed for a society to function effectively, and about whether society A or B presently has more than the required amount. We also could try mightily to institute a system in which wealth is redistributed each generation (say, by high and progressive inheritance taxes); but the well-to-do would find a way around such laws, even if they should allow them to pass, and even if the laws were not impossibly unwieldy. According to the conflict theorists, what the functionalists do not realize—or are trying to cover up with a "theory" of inequality that in fact is only an ideology!—is that stratification is based on the exploitation of the many

by the few. They also ignore the fact that stratification actually creates many problems for a human population.

Conflict theorists claim that stratification is based ultimately on control over the means of production (see chapter 5); that is, over productive resources such as land, technology, and, indirectly, labor. Once some people gain control over these resources—by whatever means—they use their economic power to coerce other people into working for them. The way this coercion operates varies between different kinds of economic systems. In ancient preindustrial states and some chiefdoms, the noble class controlled the land, and the commoners had to provide tribute to the nobility in return for the privilege of using it. In parts of feudal Europe the serfs were tied to their estate and ordinarily could not be denied access to the land they worked, but they still had to contribute a certain number of days of work or a certain proportion of their harvest to their lord per year.

As for the capitalist economic systems, Karl Marx—the "father" of conflict theory—argued that capitalist societies include only two fundamental classes. Members of the capitalist class (or *bourgeoisie*) own the factories and other means of production. Members of the working class (or *proletariat*) have only one thing to sell on the market: their labor. To earn their living, workers must sell their labor to some capitalist. This seems like an equitable arrangement: the capitalists buy the labor they need to operate their capital to sell goods and make profit; the workers get the jobs they need to support their families by selling their time and skills for a wage.

But, Marx noted, the goods the workers produce must be worth more on the market than the workers themselves receive in wages, or there would obviously be no profit for the capitalists. The difference between the amount the capitalists receive for the goods they sell and their costs (including the amount they pay their workers) is *profit*. Thus, although the workers are not fully aware of it, a portion of every one of their workdays is spent in labor for the owners of the equipment they operate to make their living. Because workers do not receive the full market value of what they produce, part of their labor benefits not themselves, but the capitalist who employs them. For this reason, workers are exploited, Marx felt. The notion that the exchange of workers' labor for wages is mutually beneficial is merely an ideology. Sooner or later, the workers will see through the ideologies and realize what the exploiters have been doing to them, and they will rise up and overthrow the ruling (capitalist) class. They will establish a new economic system in which the means of production are owned collectively, by workers themselves, and hence exploitation will disappear.

In one way or another, then, the owners of productive resources exploit the labor of nonowners, according to conflict theorists. Members of the elite class maintain their control over the means of production in spite of their smaller numbers by their control over ideas (i.e., by ideologies), over armed force, and/or over the kinds of laws that are passed and enforced by governmental authority.

Conflict theorists have been criticized for being ideologues themselves, although of a different political persuasion than functionalists. If one wishes to find exploitation in a relationship, one can always do so. Critics of conflict theory claim that the value-laden term *exploitation* does not adequately characterize relations between chiefs or kings and commoners, between lords and serfs, or between capitalists and workers. Conflict theorists ignore the valuable services and/or resources that elite classes perform, such as maintaining social control, organizing the society for the provision of public goods, accumulating productive resources (capital) put aside to increase future production, and so forth.

Many conflict theorists assume it is possible to create a complex social system without unequal rewards. This is a rather romantic view of human nature, according to some critics of the approach. Complex social systems are always hierarchically organized, with centralized leadership of the system's parts (if not of the whole). It is naively romantic to think that leaders who have power over the activities of so many other people will not use this power to benefit themselves, their families, and their friends. Indeed, many critics believe that the functions of leaders, controllers, and organizers are so valuable to society at large that they deserve the rewards they receive.

■ Who Benefits?

Contrasting the two theories, we see that functionalism emphasizes the positive aspects of stratification, whereas conflict theory emphasizes the negative side. Conflict theory points to the costs of stratification not just to those on the bottom of the social ladder but also to society at large. Society loses the undeveloped potential of its less fortunate members and must suffer the periodic violent conflicts (rebellions, revolutions) and/or ongoing disorder (crimes, political dissent) caused by a high degree of unjust inequality and of inherited privilege.

The functionalist and conflict theories imply different philosophical and moral views of inequality, views that have contemporary relevance for industrial societies. The first implies that inequality should be maintained; the second that it should be reduced or even eliminated. The first argues that the best and the brightest naturally gravitate to the top; the second that much goodness and brightness never have a chance to reveal themselves. The first suggests that government get out of the business of redistributing wealth; the second proposes an active government policy to redistribute wealth in order to maximize the chances that hidden genius in the ghettoes will have a chance to manifest itself. Profound issues of social policy are involved.

Does the comparative perspective of anthropology have anything to offer to a solution of this issue? Who does generally benefit from inequality? If we review some of the information given in this chapter, and in chapters 9 and 13, we find that preindustrial elites did indeed perform some vital roles for the whole population, just as functionalists claim. For example, elites often organized labor for the construction and maintenance of public works projects, provided relief to regions struck by famine, and raised a military force to provide for the defense of the political unit. Some kind of central authority may indeed be necessary for such tasks to be coordinated effectively. Cooperative activities require organization; organization generally requires leaders and controllers; leaders and controllers deserve to be rewarded.

On the other hand, preindustrial elites performed some roles that probably were created mainly to maintain their positions as rulers. Thus, their religious functions often were viewed as indispensable to the general welfare by ordinary people, but in fact the rituals they sponsored did not ensure rain nor the fertility of land or women. Their regulation of access to land and other resources might have been necessary, but it was partly because they themselves controlled so many resources that other peoples' access to them had to be "regulated." The social order they helped to maintain benefited everyone, but the elite's power, wealth, and internal political rivalries produced conflicts that otherwise would not have existed.

We see, then, that some of the functions of nobles, lords, and other elite classes in the preindustrial world are useful for the whole population. But other "functions" are imaginary and exist only because of prevailing (usually religious) ideology. Still other "benefits" that the population receives from the elite are beneficial only because of the control of the elite itself over society. The existence of inequality itself produces some societal "needs" that the elite help to meet, and then they claim to deserve rewards for fulfilling the so-called needs.

With the insight gained from this comparative perspective, we can be fairly certain that some of the "functions" carried out by the elite in industrialized nations likewise are imaginary. We also can imagine that some of the "benefits" the rest of the people receive from the roles performed by the elite exist only because the past and present elite class itself has set up our sociocultural system in such a way that their roles are popularly perceived as necessary or beneficial. (To take a provocative and only half-serious example, if there were no such occupation as lawyer, how often do you think you would need one?) It is difficult for insiders to pick out which functions of an elite are and are not needed—after all, most people are enculturated to see these functions as necessary for the general welfare. But with a comparative view of humanity we can see that much of what is needed for the general welfare is relative to time, place, and sociocultural conditions. In turn, such conditions are influenced by those with wealth and power.

Along these same lines, note that many of the institutions we regard as beneficial to all in fact do not benefit everyone to the same degree. A good example of this is our laws regarding the government's protection of private property. Most Americans are enculturated to believe that private property is a basic human right and that the general good requires laws to protect everyone's property. But, as shown previously, the bulk of the private property is owned by a very small percentage of the population in the United States, as in most industrialized nations. It may be true that we all benefit somewhat from the legal safeguarding of our private property, but we do not all benefit equally. For one thing, we differ vastly in the amount of property that needs to be protected. For another, since big thefts are investigated more thoroughly and prosecuted more vigorously than small thefts, the poor receive less protection than the rich.

So who does benefit from the inequality found in stratified societies? The functionalists probably are correct in their assumption that some degree of inequality is needed for motivation. We might also agree that unequal rewards for unequal efforts is a fair and just standard. But we do not know how much inequality is necessary to provide incentives, much less whether some particular stratified society has just the right amount. We do know that power and privilege are partly—and usually largely—inherited in stratified societies and that therefore the present members of the elite class are not automatically more talented and diligent than everyone else. By comparing stratified societies, we see that elites do provide some useful services for the population at large. But we also see that many popular ideas about their functions are ideologies, and that many of their roles are useful only under circumstances that they themselves had a hand in creating.

Probably most of us would benefit from some degree of inequality, if only there were some way to find out what the optimum amount of inequality is for some given sociocultural system, if only there were some way to achieve this optimum initially, and if only there were some way to reset opportunities at equal in future generations. But no known human society has ever achieved this utopia.

Summary

Inequality refers to the degree to which individuals and groups enjoy differential access to socially valuable rewards of wealth, power, and prestige. Fried's typology of egalitarian, ranked, and stratified societies provides a useful description of the range of cross-cultural diversity in inequality.

Most foragers are egalitarian. This is largely because their adaptation makes it difficult for anyone to exercise control over productive resources and the behavior of others. Such adaptive features include high rates of mobility, ability of individuals to choose their band affiliation, a cultural value placed on sharing and the social pressure against making oneself stand out, and the difficulties of maintaining exclusive access to a territory. Leadership is largely situational and informal.

In ranked societies there are a set number of honored positions (chiefs, titles, offices) to which only a small number of people are eligible to succeed. Succession may be determined by genealogical ascription, or membership in a particular kin group may establish a pool of candidates from which one will emerge or be selected. Tikopia illustrates one form of ranking.

Stratified societies are defined by three characteristics: they have marked inequalities in access to all three kinds of rewards, this inequality is based largely on unequal access to productive resources, and the inequality is strongly heritable. One system of stratification is the caste system. Castes are best known from India, where they were intimately associated with the Hindu doctrines of reincarnation and pollution.

Class systems are more common in the preindustrial world and are characteristic of all modern nations. In modern nations the class into which one was born is a strong determinant of one's life chances, although in theory interclass mobility is possible. Assigning a particular family to a particular class is not always easy, but in the United States the best criterion of class membership is wealth. Studies conducted by scholars and by the federal government reveal an enormous disparity in the distribution of wealth, especially if net assets rather than annual cash income are used to measure a family's wealth.

How such highly unequal distribution of rewards persists in stratified societies is puzzling. The mobilization of armed force by the elite is an insufficient explanation. Cultural beliefs that inequality is inevitable, divinely ordained, legitimate, and/or beneficial to society as a whole provide ideologies that justify and reinforce the power and privilege of elite classes. Among preindustrial peoples, religious beliefs were the main form of ideology, as exemplified by ancient Hawaii. In modern countries, ideologies are more secular in orientation, for effective ideologies must be compatible with a peoples' overall cultural ideas about how their society works. In the United States, Americans' ideas about the social and economic usefulness of inequality, about the fairness of unequal rewards for unequal talents and efforts, and about how the well-to-do achieved their wealth may be interpreted as secular ideologies.

The two major theories about inequality are the functional and the conflict theories. Functionalists hold that societies offer unequal rewards to those individuals who have the scarcest talents and who use them to perform the most socially valuable roles. Conflict theorists claim that inequality is based ultimately on control over the means of production, which allows those who own productive resources to exploit those who do not. The two theories imply contrasting views of the nature of inequality. Anthropology's comparative perspective suggests that although elites often do perform valuable services for society at large, many of their "functions" are illusory. Others exist only because past elites have set up the structure of society so that their "services" are necessary. Although functionalists are correct that some degree of inequality is necessary for incentive, we have no way of knowing whether any society has the amount it "needs," nor has any society ever succeeded in establishing the equal opportunity required for the functionalist theory to be correct.

Key Terms

inequality

egalitarian society

ranked society

stratified society

life chances

class

caste

ideology

secular ideology

functional theory of inequality

conflict theory of inequality

Suggested Readings

■ Bendix, Reinhard, and Seymour M. Lipset, eds. *Class, Status, and Power: Social Stratification in Comparative Perspective.* 2d ed. New York: The Free Press, 1966.
    A reader intended primarily for sociologists. Contains many seminal articles, although now dated.

■ Berreman, Gerald D., and Kathleen M. Zaretsky. *Social Inequality: Comparative and Development Approaches.* New York: Academic Press, 1981.
    A collection of papers discussing social inequality in a number of societies.

■ Fried, Morton. *The Evolution of Political Society.* New York: Random House, 1967.
    A well-known book with an extensive discussion of ranking and stratification and how they relate to political organization.

■ Genovese, Eugene. *The Political Economy of Slavery.* New York: Pantheon, 1965.
    A study examining slavery in the United States from a political and economic perspective.

■ Goldman, Irving. *Ancient Polynesian Society.* Chicago: University of Chicago Press, 1970.
    A comparative study of social stratification in a variety of Polynesian islands.

■ Heller, C., ed. *Structured Social Inequality.* New York: Macmillan, 1969.
    A well-balanced collection of papers examining stratification from a variety of perspectives.

Lenski, G. *Power and Privilege.* New York: McGraw-Hill, 1966.

A treatment of stratification comparing the range of inequality in preindustrial and industrial societies. Best known as an attempt to reconcile the functionalist and the conflict perspectives.

Several studies treat the concentration of power and wealth in the United States in great detail.

Domhoff, G. William. *Who Rules America Now?* Englewood Cliffs, N.J.: Prentice-Hall, 1983.

Dye, Thomas R. *Who's Running America? The Conservative Years.* 4th ed. Englewood Cliffs, N.J.: Prentice-Hall, 1986.

Jencks, Christopher, et. al. *Who Gets Ahead? The Determinants of Economic Success in America.* New York: Basic, 1979.

Mills, C. Wright. *The Power Elite.* New York: Oxford University Press, 1956.

RELATIONS WITH THE SUPERNATURAL

Contents

■ *Religious rituals are intended to secure benefits and blessings from supernatural powers. These men are Guatemalan Catholics.*

In this chapter we consider religion, perhaps the most puzzling of all human phenomena. Religion is in one respect different from the other elements of the sociocultural system that we have covered in previous chapters. It is easy to understand the necessity for most sociocultural elements: any human population needs to exploit its environment, to have a family life, to keep track of relatives, to organize decision making, to maintain social control, and the like. But what kinds of individual and group needs and wants are served by religion? This question is one topic of the present chapter.

Anthropologists, as well as other scholars, have long been fascinated by religion, and have written more about it than about any other dimension of human existence. We have many hundreds of volumes describing the forms of religion found among various peoples. Providing an overview of this religious diversity is the second goal of this chapter.

Defining Religion

What is religion? How can we best define it so as to encompass all the diversity of religion found in the human species? Certainly, it is ethnocentric to define religion as "belief in God," for the same reason that it is ethnocentric to define politics as "the activities and organization of a government." Just as some societies have no formal government, so are there societies that lack a belief in any kind of deity, much less in the Judeo-Christian God. We need a definition that can be applied cross-culturally.

The oldest anthropological definition of religion is E. B. Tylor's **animism,** or "belief in spiritual beings" (see chapter 5). Most modern conceptions follow Tylor's lead: they specify that, at the least, all religions include beliefs that some kind of spiritual or supernatural powers exist. But Tylor's definition leaves out much about religion. By expanding on it, we can present an overview of religion in cross-cultural perspective.

■ Supernatural Powers: Beings and Forces

"Beings" are not the only kind of spiritual powers that people believe in. Many religions posit the existence of other kinds of powers that are more like "forces" than "beings." For example, in aboriginal times the peoples of Polynesia believed in *mana,* a diffuse, impersonal, incorporeal force. Mana lent supernatural potency to things, which explained unusual qualities; or to people, which explained unusual success. People and objects could be infused with greater or lesser amounts of mana. Having a lot of mana explained why some chiefs always won battles, why some fishing equipment seemed to work so well, why certain gardens produced such fine crops, and so forth. But mana could be withdrawn by the gods: a chief defeated by a rival in battle had lost his mana, which had been given instead to the victor.

The widespread belief in powers such as mana make it useful to divide supernatural powers into beings and forces. Spiritual *beings* usually are believed to have qualities such as a bodily form, some way of appearing before people, a personality, and a fairly predictable way of responding to human actions. The characteristics people attribute to supernatural beings vary enormously: they can be capricious or consistent, stubborn or reasonable, vengeful or forgiving, amoral or just. Some beings have human origins, such as souls or ancestral ghosts, which reside or resided in a specific individual. Other kinds of beings have nonhuman origins, such as many gods or demons.

Supernatural *forces* likewise are believed to have definite properties, which vary from people to people. Because forces usually have no will of their own—no power to refuse humans who know how to command or manipulate them in the proper manner—they often can be used for either good or evil purposes. In most cases, people believe that supernatural forces can be manipulated by humans who know the proper rites and spells. The manipulation of forces by means of rites and spells, known as *magic,* is discussed later in this chapter.

■ Myths

Belief in the existence of supernatural powers (beings and forces) is only part of religion. Religion also includes **myths**—oral or written stories about the actions and deeds of supernatural powers in the past. Myths frequently tell of the actions of cultural heroes and supernatural powers of long ago. They sometimes explain how the entire universe was created. They may recount how and why people, animals, plants, and natural features originated. Myths commonly explain how a people acquired their tools and customs and how they came to live where they do. They often tell why people should or should not act in certain ways, and what happened to someone in the past who did something people are forbidden to do.

North Americans mostly learn their mythology in formal settings: myths are taught at church, and to a lesser extent at home. (Here we need to emphasize that calling Bible stories "myths" does *not* mean that we regard them as false.) In many societies people learn the mythology of their religion as an ordinary part of enculturation. Elders recount myths in moments of leisure. Myths are repeated regularly on days set aside for religious performances. They are sung or chanted while one is doing daily tasks. The fact that myths are sometimes recounted rather casually does not mean that their importance in a people's way of life is negligible. A people's world view is greatly affected by their mythology.

It has been argued, for example, that the Judeo-Christian mythology makes it easy for North Americans to view nature as something to be conquered and used for their own profit. When God made humans, He gave us "dominion" over nature and told us to "subdue" the earth and its living creatures (see Genesis 1:26–30). He also created us in His own image. When it suits our purposes and interests, we thus have no supernatural mandate to keep us from fouling the water and air, from destroying the habitats of other creatures with dams and other developments, from destroying hills with strip mines, and so forth. According to this argument, if individual Americans have any opinions about the way God wants them to relate to nature, they are more likely to believe that He gave it to humans to exploit than that He wants them to restrict their consumption so that they can preserve it for its own sake or for future generations.

In contrast, we might show more respect for other living things if (like some societies) we had a religious heritage with sacred myths telling that some of us came from bears, some from rabbits, some from whales, and so forth. We might be more reluctant to tear up a mountain for its minerals if we thought that some of us came from a hole in its side. We might hesitate to destroy a forest if the Bible told us explicitly that trees are just as precious to God as humans.

A people's myths—and this is the general point we are trying to make—are more than stories they tell after dark or recite on appropriate occasions. They do more than satisfy idle curiosity and help pass the time. Myths are part and parcel of a peoples' world view: their fundamental conceptions of nature and society and how people ought to relate to the world and to one another. They therefore affect how people behave in their everyday lives.

■ Rituals

All religions share yet a third component. Even though spiritual beings such as gods, ghosts, demons, and devils are otherworldly, people think that they take an interest in the events of this world. They can be asked to intervene favorably in human affairs. And even though supernatural forces have no bodily form, they still can be manipulated to cause good or harmful effects to human bodies. This leads to another component of religion: besides beliefs and myths, religions also prescribe certain behaviors people can use to interact with and influence supernatural powers.

The organized performance of behaviors intended to influence spiritual powers is known as **ritual**. Rituals are always stereotyped: there are definite patterns of speech or movement, or definite sequences of events, that occur in much the same way in performance after performance. In general, people performing rituals want supernatural powers to do things on their behalf: to make someone (or everyone) healthy or fertile, to bring rain, to make the crops grow, to save their souls, to bring back the game, to provide blessings, and so forth. People may pray, worship, make sacrifices, and follow ritual procedures scrupulously to ensure that their gods, their personal spirits, or the ghosts of their dead ancestors intervene favorably in their lives.

Often, the performers of ritual want supernatural powers to harm their enemies in some way: to make them sick or barren, to bring floods or pestilence to their land, to drive the animals out of their territory, to make their spears fly crooked in the upcoming battle, and so forth. Of course, if we can ask supernatural powers to harm our enemies, our enemies may have the same ability; they can cause supernatural harm to us, making us sick or prone to misfortune. So ethnographers commonly report that members of some society believe that many or all illnesses, deaths, and accidents are caused by the supernatural powers of evil or enemy humans. And many kinds of rituals exist whose explicit purpose is to counteract the harm caused by other rituals performed by enemies.

Rituals the world over have symbolic aspects. They often occur in *places* that have symbolic significance to the performers. For example, they may be held where some mythological event occurred, or where the women who founded a matrilineage were born. Rituals often involve the display and manipulation of *objects* that symbolize an event (e.g., the cross), a holy person (statues of Jesus and Mary), a relationship (wedding rings, the symbol of holy matrimony), and a variety of other things. Symbolic significance is usually attached to the *language* and *behavior* of ritual, as in the Christian rituals of worship, hymn singing, prayer, baptism, communion, and confession. (The symbolic places, objects, language, and behaviors used in rituals are sometimes said to be sacred, but our cultural distinction between sacred and profane must be applied with great care in describing non-Western religions.)

Anthropologists often classify rituals on two bases. The first basis is their conscious purposes—the reasons people themselves give for performing them. For example, there are divination rituals, which are performed to acquire information from a supernatural power about the future or about some past event that people have no other way of finding out about. There are also curing, sorcery, sacrificial, and exorcism rituals. There are rituals to renew the world, to make a man out of a boy and a woman out of a girl, and to free the soul from a dead person's body. There are rituals held for single individuals, for kin groups, for people of similar age, for whole societies, and so forth. A few examples of these are discussed in this chapter.

The second basis of classification is when rituals occur—whether they are held on a regular schedule (like Sunday church services) or simply whenever some individual or group wants or needs them (like funerals or prayers for a sick person). If rituals are held regularly (seasonally, annually, daily, monthly, etc.) they are called *calendrical rituals*. *Crisis rituals* are organized and performed whenever some individual or group needs, wants, or asks for them—for purposes of curing, ensuring good hunting or fishing, or other events that happen sporadically or unpredictably.

The three components of all religions, then, are (1) beliefs about the existence and nature of supernatural powers, (2) mythologies about the historical deeds of these powers, and (3) rituals intended to influence these powers to intervene favorably on behalf of the performers. With this conception of religion we can

■ *Crisis rituals are held whenever some event occurs that people believe requires a ritual performance. This funeral of a Buddhist child is an example.*

glimpse the ways in which sociocultural systems vary in their religious dimension. There is diversity in beliefs about the nature of supernatural beings and forces, in what spheres or realms of life their powers extend to, in how they can be requested or commanded to intervene in human affairs, and in who can organize the rituals that make such requests or demands. We consider some of these variations in this chapter.

With this brief and broad overview of human religion in mind, we now look at a few aspects of the anthropological study of religion. A good place to start is with some of the major theoretical orientations offered to understand or explain religion.

Theories of Religion

So far as we know, every society has some kind of religion. The fact that religion is universal is a bit surprising, for two reasons. First—with regard to beliefs and myths—it can never be proven that supernatural powers such as ghosts, gods, devils, demons, angels, souls, mana, and so forth exist at all, much less that myths about them are true. Indeed, from an outsider's ("nonbelievers") perspective, other peoples' religious beliefs and myths often seem irrational. Yet in every society we know about, many, most, or all people believe in supernatural powers and recite myths about their actions. Why?

Second—with regard to rituals—religious behavior is often not effective at achieving the goals the performers have in mind. From an outsider's perspective, rituals seem to be a huge waste of time and resources. For example, when a Trobriand Islander plants a yam garden, he does some things that "work" in the way he thinks they do: he clears the land, removes weeds, and so forth, just as anyone should for success. But a Trobriander believes that acts which many outsiders consider to be superfluous are also necessary for success in gardening. He hires a magician to perform rites and spells that will keep his yams from leaving his garden at night and roaming around, for he knows that other people are performing magic to steal his yams by luring them into their own gardens. We can see what the gardener gets out of the first kind of activity—a yam harvest, if nature cooperates. But what does he get out of the magical rites and spells? How did Trobrianders come to believe that magic is needed?

We can state this second problem another way to see the major puzzling thing about rituals. When the Trobriander clears land, plants a crop, and weeds his garden, his actions are effective in attaining the goal he has in mind—they work in more or less the way he thinks they do. But when the garden magician performs rites and spells to keep his client's yams from being stolen by a neighbor during their nightly wanderings, his actions do not achieve the result he has in mind. Yams do not really roam around; the magic does not really work. (Again, remember that these statements are made from an outsider's perspective.) How then did the Trobrianders get the idea that they do?

Speaking generally, rituals do not work the way the performers imagine they do—the rain does not fall because of the rain dance; the crazy woman is not made sane by exorcizing the devil within her; no spirits enter the body of the medicine man; there were no witches in Salem, Massachusetts, in 1692. Why then do so many people believe in power of ritual?

You may already have thought of possible answers. If rituals do not work in the way the performers believe they do, perhaps they work in some other way. If they do not have the effects people believe they have, they

may have other effects that people find useful or satisfying. As for myths, if they are not accurate historical accounts, perhaps they are symbolic statements that help people categorize reality and give meaning to real-world things and events.

We all have heard people who consider themselves sophisticated and educated say that religious beliefs rest on simple ignorance and superstition—"they believe because they don't know any better." This nonanswer to the question: Why religion? is (or should be) rejected by all anthropologists. Its ethnocentrism is apparent: superstition is something that someone else believes in, but you do not; but many of your own beliefs seem superstitious to others, and possibly many of the accepted scientific truths of the twentieth century will be considered superstitious in the year 2050. Besides, even if we admit that such beliefs and practices are superstitious, we have not explained them. Why does one form of superstition develop in one place, and another form in another place?

Few, if any, modern anthropologists believe that religious beliefs and rituals can be explained as simple delusions. That is, few of us claim that religion results from ignorant folk making mistakes in logic that lead them to perform ritual activities that are a total waste of energy and resources. Practically all of us believe that religion has some kind of positive value to individuals, to society, or both. It is difficult to explain its universality in any other way: How could something that is totally worthless be found among all humanity?

We do not, however, agree on what this positive value is. This leads us to the functions of religion—its useful effects to individuals, to society as a whole, or to some social group within a society. Broadly, social scientists have proposed three types of functions of religion: the **intellectual** (or **cognitive**), the **psychological,** and the **social**.

■ Intellectual/Cognitive Functions

Many scholars believe that human beings actively seek explanations for things and events, for the human mind does not tolerate uncertainty and unanswered questions (or so some believe). According to the cognitive approach, religions perform the function of explaining things and events that would otherwise remain inexplicable. Religion provides a pseudo- or prescientific theory that accounts for the origin of the sun, moon, stars, world, animals, people, and so forth. It allows people to account for and interpret natural and social phenomena and events. As we have seen, this was E. B. Tylor's theory of the origins of animism—people sought explanations for things they saw in dreams and imaginations and mistakenly came to believe in spiritual beings (see chapter 5).

Around the turn of the twentieth century, Sir James Frazer proposed a similar theory. He noticed that "savages" usually believe in some kind of magical power that can be manipulated by people who perform the proper rites and spells. He saw this belief as a prescientific one: people wanted to influence natural occurrences and other people, but they did not understand true scientific cause-and-effect relationships. Believers in magic thought, for example, that a magician could cause harm to people by performing rites and spells on things that were once in contact with their victims, such as hair, nails, feces, or even footprints. Such beliefs had a kind of logic—by doing something to things once in contact with a man, you can do something to him—but the logic was based on false premises. Frazer felt that people gradually realized their logical errors and eventually gained knowledge of true scientific cause and effect. Frazer thus believed that magic and science are alternative world views: each provides people with an intellectual model of the way the world works and a means to manipulate events and people.

The notion that religious beliefs substitute for objective scientific knowledge in so far as they provide explanations for things and events is partially correct, but it is certainly incomplete. Religion does satisfy curiosity about the world, but this is not its only function. "Savages" possess and use practical knowledge just as we do—a Trobriander knows that he must care for his yams as well as perform garden magic. Conversely, many "civilized" and "scientific" folk believe in and practice religion—even many of those who make their living practicing the science for which religion supposedly substitutes. Religious beliefs do not take the place of practical knowledge; in some way that we do not fully understand, they supplement it.

Although few scholars today believe that religion exists because some peoples are the victims of erroneous thought processes, the intellectual approach is by no means passé. Clifford Geertz, a leading modern cultural theorist, holds that religion provides its believers with the assurance that the world is meaningful—that events have a place in the grand scheme of things, natural phenomena have causes, suffering and evil happen to specific individuals for a good reason, and injustices are corrected. Cultural beings (i.e., humans) cannot tolerate events that contradict the basic premises, categories, and world view of their cultural tradition. Yet such events do occur periodically. Because of religion, people are able to maintain their world view in spite of events that seem to contradict it. Religion, Geertz believes, reassures its believers that the world is orderly rather than chaotic, all within the framework of their cultural knowledge.

■ Psychological Functions

The notion that religion helps people cope psychologically (here meaning "emotionally") with times of trouble, stress, and anxiety is a common one. Sicknesses, accidents, misfortunes, injustices, deaths, and other trials and tribulations of life can be handled emotionally if one believes that there is a reason and meaning to them, or that one's troubles can be controlled or alleviated by means of ritual.

One psychological theory holds that humans are unique among animals in that we are aware of our own mortality. The knowledge that we will eventually die produces anxiety and a denial of the finality of death. We invent afterlifes and imagine them to be pleasant to calm our fears. This notion is tainted by ethnocentrism—although belief in life after death is common, a great many people believe that the soul's existence in the other world is greatly inferior to its life in the earthly body. Hardly a "comforting" belief!

In anthropology a well-known psychological theory of religion is that of Bronislaw Malinowski, whom we introduced in chapter 5. Malinowski thought that religion (including magic) serves the valuable function of giving people confidence when they are likely to be unsuccessful in spite of their best efforts. There are always natural phenomena that people cannot control and that constantly threaten to ruin their plans and efforts. Belief in the power of ritual to control these (otherwise uncontrollable) elements instills confidence and removes some of the anxiety that results from the uncertainties of life.

There is little doubt that religion is psychologically useful: it relieves our anxieties, reduces our fears, and generally helps us to cope with life. That religion serves such functions (at least for some people, some of the time) is not subject to dispute. On the other hand, there is little doubt that religious beliefs themselves sometimes increase our anxieties and fears. Consider the Kwaio, a people of the Solomon Islands. Kwaio believe that women are spiritually dangerous to men, so Kwaio wives are expected to take elaborate precautions to avoid polluting their husbands when preparing their food or performing other services for them. If a man dies from illness, his wife is likely to be blamed, and perhaps killed, for her "offense." Just whose "anxieties and fears" are "relieved" by this belief?

■ Social Functions

"Societies need religion to keep people in line," you may have heard people say. The idea here is that religion maintains common values, leads to increased conformity to cultural norms, promotes cohesion and cooperation, promises eternal reward for good deeds and eternal damnation for evil acts, and so forth. Those who champion the social function theory hold that religion exists because of the useful effects it has on human societies: it maintains social order by discouraging individuals from violating the culturally legitimate rights of others and by urging them to perform their proper duties.

Consider the Ten Commandments, for example, which serve as a moral code for Christians and Jews. Two prescribe how people ought to feel and act toward God and other people, and eight proscribe actions—including the five "thou shalt nots" (see Exodous 20:3–17). Note that five of the divinely ordered prohibitions are against the commission of acts that could result in harm to others, such as killing and stealing. God gave us commandments that will, if obeyed, lead to good relations with others, and therefore promote earthly social order. More general Christian moral guidelines are the Golden Rule ("do unto others as you would have them do unto you") and love of one's neighbor (Matthew 19:19), both of which are useful prescriptions for harmonious social life.

Numerous scholars have championed this sociological interpretation of religion. (In fact, if any interpretation can be said to be *the* most popular, this is it.) Because we present several examples of sociological approaches to specific religious phenomena in this chapter, for now we merely discuss why one popular sociological interpretation is unlikely to apply to all religions. This is the idea that religion promotes order and conformity by promising supernatural retribution for immoral or antisocial behavior and by holding out worldly or otherworldly rewards for culturally defined clean living.

Because of their Judeo-Christian heritage—in which eternal reward or damnation is a key belief—Westerners might easily assume that supernatural powers are everywhere believed to be concerned with whether people behave well or poorly in this life. Deities might, for example, reward virtue with earthly wealth and power or with eternal heavenly bliss. Or supernatural powers might punish troublemakers with illness, misfortune, and even death, or with an unpleasant afterlife. Indeed, such beliefs are common.

They are not, however, characteristic of all religions. Many populations have no belief that supernatural powers punish wrongdoers or sinners—in fact, many religions have no concept of sin, in the sense of violations of edicts issued by the supernatural. All peoples have conceptions of morality, of course, but not all believe that supernatural powers apply sanctions against violators of moral standards.

What determines whether a religion does or does not include the belief that deities, ancestors, or other spiritual powers punish and reward people according to the moral worthiness of their actions? According to Guy Swanson's cross-cultural study, the presence or absence of such a belief is related to the degree of inequality in a society: the greater the inequality found in a society, the more likely that society's religion is to include the belief that supernatural powers reward and punish individuals according to how well they behave. There is an especially striking relationship between social classes and supernatural sanctions for morality, as shown by the following cross-cultural tabulation:

SOCIAL CLASSES	SUPERNATURAL SANCTIONS FOR MORALITY	
	Absent	**Present**
Present	2	25
Absent	12	8

According to this study, the religions of class societies are quite likely to include beliefs that supernatural powers reward and punish, the religions of classless societies are much less likely to include such beliefs. This association of a high degree of inequality with the presence of supernatural sanctions may be related to a topic discussed in chapter 14. The power, wealth, and prestige of the "haves" may be reinforced and legitimized if "have nots" believe that spiritual powers punish wrongdoing.

The Sphere of Supernatural Intervention

One cross-cultural variation in religions is the sphere— or the range of human activities and natural occurrences—in which spiritual powers are believed to have an influence. A modern North American Christian is likely to have a relatively narrow conception of the realms of personal and public life in which God intervenes. (This varies with denomination and personal belief, of course.) Most of us do not use divine action to explain the failure of a company, car wrecks, illnesses, great wealth, poverty, or the outcome of elections. We are more likely to blame poor business practices, carelessness, coincidence, poor eating or drinking or exercise habits, and personal skill or laziness for misfortune or success. The same is true for natural occurrences: most of us do not blame God for earthquakes, floods, hurricanes, volcanoes, and other natural disasters, which we attribute to natural forces.

In contrast, in most religions of the preindustrial world, people believe that spiritual powers actively intervene in a wide range of human activities and natural events. Rituals are performed to request or command that their future intervention be favorable or that they remove the effects of their previous malevolent interference. A few examples will illustrate:

■ The matrilineal Ndembu of Zambia attribute a variety of female health problems to the actions of ancestral spirits. Infertility, frequent miscarriages, stillbirths, and other reproductive disorders are explained by the actions of one of the victim's ancestresses, who is punishing the woman for "forgetting her ancestress" or for doing something of which her ancestress disapproves. The cure for the affliction consists of a lengthy ritual designed to make the victim "remember" her dead relative.

■ Some central Canadian Inuit (Eskimo) believe that prolonged inability to find game may be caused by a goddess who is angry over the misconduct of members of the camp. They persuade the goddess to release the game by performing a ritual in which camp members publicly confess their violations.

■ To help them locate caribou, the Naskapi foragers of eastern Canada heated a caribou shoulder blade over a fire until it cracked. They read the pattern of cracks in the scapula, which they believed told them the direction in which to undertake the hunt.

■ The Trobriand Islanders periodically go on long overseas voyages to acquire the shell valuables that are symbols of status and wealth in their culture. They perform magic to induce their trading partner to give a certain valuable to them rather than to someone else. The ocean trip is hazardous because of the possibility of sudden storms, so before they depart the voyagers also perform magic to ensure favorable weather.

■ The Hopi of the American Southwest believe that rainfall is the result of supernatural beings intervening on behalf of humans. These beings, called *kachinas*, live in the peaks of the San Francisco mountains to the southwest of Hopi villages. In the spring and summer, kachinas are thought to come dwell in the villages. During this period Hopi males wearing masks of the kachinas perform a series of ritual dances. While wearing the mask of a specific kachina, the spirit enters the body of the person, and thus the dancer becomes the kachina. By means of the performance of the dances, rain is brought to the Hopi's cornfields.

These brief examples illustrate three areas of human life in which the supernatural is commonly believed to intervene. First, various peoples believe that supernatural powers are responsible for success or failure of many group activities, such as hunting and trading. Second, spiritual beings or forces frequently must be asked to bring about some desired natural event, such as good weather and the return of game. Finally, supernatural powers often are believed to interfere in the lives of individuals, making them ill or poor, or healthy and wealthy. This last kind of intervention is universal, or nearly so, and is an important complex of belief wherever it occurs.

Supernatural Explanations of Misfortune

One occurrence that many peoples attribute to the action of spiritual powers is personal misfortune, including death, illness, and events that we consider

■ *A Hopi kachina performs a ritual dance to influence the spirits to bring rain. The specific activities and events in which supernatural forces are believed to intervene vary from religion to religion.*

accidents. Many beliefs and rituals of various societies are concerned with explaining, preventing, and curing illness and disease. Cross-culturally, two major complexes of beliefs about illness are most common.

First, many peoples believe that sickness is caused by the direct action of some spiritual power. Often, sickness is thought to be brought on by a taboo violation, which some supernatural being or force is punishing. Other societies believe that the ancestral spirits of kin groups cause their members to become ill because of conflict or bad feelings within the group. (We consider ancestral cults later in this chapter.) The same kinds of beliefs may apply to accidents that many Westerners attribute to bad luck or carelessness. Drownings, falls, snakebites, prolonged failure to succeed at some activity—such events are likely to be seen as evidence of unfavorable supernatural intervention. The victim has offended a god or spirit, who brings an "accident" as punishment.

Second, many populations think that all or most illnesses or other misfortunes are caused by the action

of some evil human who is using special supernatural powers against the afflicted person. Belief that certain persons, called *sorcerers* and *witches*, have powers to harm others by mystical means is enormously widespread among humanity. Sometimes, witches and sorcerers are thought to strike randomly and maliciously against individuals who are innocent of any wrongdoing. More commonly, they direct their evil magic or thoughts toward those against whom they have a grudge. Sorcery and witchcraft are among the most fascinating of all religious phenomena—well worth considering in more detail.

■ Sorcery

Sorcery is the performance of rites and spells intended to cause supernatural forces to harm others. In some societies sorcery may be carried out by almost anyone, and the ability to cause harm to an enemy by means of sorcery is learned as an ordinary part of enculturation. Among other peoples sorcery is a more specialized practice: only certain people inherit or otherwise acquire the knowledge of how to recite the spells and perform the rites correctly.

In 1890, Sir James Frazer proposed that magic (including sorcery) is generally based on two kinds of logical premises or assumptions. The first is called the *imitative principle of magic*, which is based on the premise that "like produces like." That is, if some object is like a person, and the sorcerer mutilates the object, the same effect will occur on the person. Voodoo is the most familiar example of imitative magic: an effigy (the so-called voodoo doll) is made of the enemy, some act is performed on the effigy, and the enemy is supposed to experience the same fate. In the case of voodoo the effigy symbolically represents the person, so to harm the effigy is believed to harm the person.

The second kind of logical premise underlying magic and sorcery is called the *contagious principle of magic*, which is based on the assumption that "power comes from contact." That is, things that were once in contact with someone can be used in rites and spells to make things happen to that person. By performing the correct rites and spells on such objects as hair clippings, bodily excretions, nail parings, infant umbilical cords, or jewelry and clothing, harm can be done to one's enemies. In societies in which sorcery rests on the contagious principle, people must be careful to dispose of objects they have been in contact with, lest one of their enemies use them for sorcery. As with the imitative principle, a symbolic identification is made between the objects and the victim. But in the case of the contagious principle, the symbolic equation comes from previous contact rather than from resemblance: by acquiring possession of something once belonging to a person, supernatural power is acquired over that person.

Because sorcery relies on beliefs about the manipulation of supernatural forces, anthropologists consider it part of a society's religious system. Like most aspects of a total sociocultural system, sorcery affects and is affected by other dimensions of life. We shall next consider two of many possible examples of these effects.

Pattern of Accusations   In most societies bad feelings are most likely to occur between individuals and groups who stand in certain relationships to one another—co-wives of a polygynous man, people who have married into a lineage or village and hence are seen as outsiders, brothers who are rivals for a political office, members of other kin groups with whom one group is in conflict, and so forth. In all societies certain kinds of relationships are especially subject to conflict. Which relationships are most likely to be strained varies with the nature of the sociocultural system: in one society brothers-in-law are generally friends and allies, but their interests conflict in another society, for instance.

Sorcerers are generally believed not to strike randomly, but to direct their evil magic against people toward whom they feel hatred, anger, or envy. So when I or my relative becomes ill, or suffers a misfortune, neither of us would suspect just anyone of sorcery. We ask ourselves who has a motive to perform evil magic against one of us: Whose interests have we harmed? Who envies our success? Who will profit from our illness or death? It is these individuals whom we suspect and these individuals whom we are most likely to accuse. But because all sociocultural systems have built-in conflicts and stresses, we are most likely to suspect and accuse individuals with whom we have certain kinds of relationships. So ethnographers frequently report that accusations of sorcery (and witchcraft, to be discussed shortly) tend to be patterned in a society: they reflect the patterned conflicts of interest, disagreements, and so forth that develop because of the relationships in particular forms of social organization.

Sorcery as a Political Weapon   You might imagine that sorcerers everywhere would be despised and punished or killed whenever their practices become public

knowledge. This is not the case, however, at least not everywhere. In many societies there are ambivalent feelings about people widely suspected of practicing sorcery: they may be despised, but they are also feared and respected for their powers. A common strategy on the part of an individual suspected of using sorcery against his enemies is to deny the charge but to leave enough room for doubt that no one is sure that he is not indeed guilty. By this strategy, people will fear his powers enough to give him an advantage in political or other kinds of rivalries. Sorcery (more precisely, fear that one may practice sorcery or be allied with sorcerers) can be used as a political weapon.

A fine example of the use of sorcery as a weapon in political competition is provided by the Abelam, a Papua New Guinea people studied by Anthony Forge. Like most other Melanesians, the Abelam have no hereditary chiefs or other formalized political officials. Rather, leadership is vested in a "big man" (see chapter 13), who achieves prominence through his ability to persuade others to follow his directives. Rivalries between the aspiring big men of a single village are the major focus of political life, and big men use other people's fear of sorcery in their competitions for followers.

The Abelam believe that all deaths not obviously caused by violence result from sorcery carried out by members of an enemy village. Their beliefs are based on the contagious principle; so to perform his deed, an enemy sorcerer must have access to objects (which we shall call here *leavings,* including feces, hair, etc.) that have been in direct contact with his victim. Yet everyone is very careful not to leave their leavings lying about in other villages, so that sorcerers cannot acquire the things necessary to work their powers from the victims themselves. But the Abelam believe that sorcerers are operating against someone in their village almost constantly (why else would people be sick or have other kinds of troubles?). This means that someone in the village must be supplying outside enemies with the bodily secretions or other leavings of his covillagers.

It is the big man in the village, and his rivals, who are thought to be the suppliers. They have secret caches of almost everyone's leavings. Although a big man does not work contagious magic against his own villagemates, he is believed to employ a foreign sorcerer to make his rivals and nonsupporters sick. Should a big man be accused of complicity with an outside sorcerer, he makes a half-denial; that is, he denies the charge but leaves the possibility open. The fear that his cache of leavings will be turned over to an enemy is a major source of power over his rivals and covillagers. In fact, a man who is not suspected of magical complicity with outside enemies has little hope of becoming a powerful big man, for he lacks one of the political weapons essential for success.

■ Witchcraft

Witchcraft is the second explanation that people in many societies give for misfortune. There is no universally applicable distinction between sorcery and witchcraft. Whereas sorcery usually involves the use of rites and spells to commit a foul deed, here we define **witchcraft** as the use of psychic power alone to cause harm to others. Sorcerers manipulate objects; witches need only think malevolent thoughts to turn their anger, envy, or hatred into evil deeds. (Our own language's distinction between the two—witches are female, sorcerers usually male—is not useful cross-culturally.) Many societies believe in the existence of both kinds of malevolent powers that some humans use to harm their enemies, so sorcery and witchcraft are often found among the same people.

Sociocultural systems vary in the characteristics they attribute to witches and in how witches cause harm. A few examples will illustrate some of the diversity:

■ The Navajo associate witches with the worst imaginable sins—witches commit incest, bestiality (sex with animals), and necrophilia (sex with corpses); they change themselves into animals; they cannibalize helpless infants; and so on.

■ The Nyakyusa of Tanzania hold that witches are motivated mainly by their lust for food; accordingly, they suck dry the udders of peoples' cattle and devour the internal organs of their human neighbors while they sleep.

■ The Zande of the southern Sudan believe that witches have under their breastbone an inherited substance that leaves their bodies at night and gradually eats away at the flesh and internal organs of their victims. Witches, as well as their victims, are considered to be unfortunate, for the Zande believe that a person can be a witch without even knowing it. Witches can do nothing to rid themselves permanently of their power, although they can be forced to stop bewitching some particular individual by ridding themselves of antisocial sentiments against their victim.

■ The Ibibio of Nigeria believe that witches operate by removing the spiritual essence (soul) of their enemies and placing it into an animal; this makes the victim sick, and he dies when the witches slaughter and consume the animal. Sometimes Ibibio witches decide to torture, rather than kill, a person. In that case they remove the victim's soul and put it in water or hang it over a fireplace or flog it in the evenings; the afflicted individual will remain sick until the witches get what they want out of him or her.

■ The Lugbara, a people of Uganda, claim that witches—who are always men—walk around at night disguised as rats or other nocturnal animals. They sometimes defecate blood around the household of their victims, who wake up sick the next morning.

Such beliefs, it seems to those who do not share them, are logically outrageous—no one's soul leaves his or her body at night to cavort with other witches, for example. It might seem that these beliefs are socially harmful as well—beliefs in witchcraft, fear of witchcraft, and accusations of witchcraft engender unnecessary conflict and aggression among a people. Finally, the treatment suspected and "proven" witches often receive offends our notions of social justice—as we know from the witch hunts of European and American history, often the truly innocent victims of witchcraft are the accused witches, who are sometimes cruelly executed for crimes they could not have committed.

■ Interpretations of Sorcery and Witchcraft

Anthropologists wonder about why beliefs in witches and sorcery are so widespread, given their seeming logical absurdity, their harmful effects, and the injustices that frequently result from them. Why should so many sociocultural systems independently have developed such beliefs? Why should most of the world's peoples think that some or all of their misfortunes are caused by the supernatural powers of their enemies? What use or value could a human society possibly derive from accusations of witchcraft or sorcery?

Many answers have been offered to these questions. In line with the overall theoretical approaches discussed earlier, the answers fall into two categories: cognitive and sociological. (In the following discussion, for simplicity we use the term *witchcraft* to refer to both witchcraft and sorcery, for the ideas to be presented have been applied to both kinds of beliefs.)

Cognitive Interpretations   The most influential of the various cognitive approaches is that witchcraft explains unfortunate events. The argument is that most people find the idea of coincidence or accident intellectually unsatisfying when some misfortune happens to them or their loved ones, so they search for other causes. Their logic is something like this: I have enemies who wish me harm, and harm just came to me, so my enemies are responsible.

The best example of how people account for misfortune by reference to the actions of witches comes from among the Azande, whose beliefs we just described briefly. The Azande attribute prolonged serious illnesses and many other personal misfortunes to witchcraft. Ethnographer E. E. Evans-Pritchard (1976) describes their beliefs:

> Witchcraft is ubiquitous. . . . There is no niche or corner of Zande culture into which it does not twist itself. If blight seizes the groundnut crop it is witchcraft; if the bush is vainly scoured for game it is witchcraft; if women laboriously bail water out of a pool and are rewarded by but a few small fish it is witchcraft; . . . if a wife is sulky and unresponsive to her husband it is witchcraft; if a prince is cold and distant with his subject it is witchcraft; if a magical rite fails to achieve its purpose it is witchcraft; if, in fact, any failure or misfortune falls upon any one at any time and in relation to any of the manifold activities of his life it may be due to witchcraft. (18)

All this does not mean that the Azande are ignorant of cause and effect and therefore attribute every misfortune to some witch who is out to get them. When a Zande man seeks shelter in a granary, and its roof falls and injures him, he blames witchcraft. But Zande know very well that granary roofs collapse because termites eat the wood that supports them. They do not attribute the collapse of granaries in general to witchcraft; it is the collapse of this particular granary at this particular time with this particular person inside that is caused by witchcraft. Do not granaries sometimes fall, with no one sitting inside them? And do not people often relax in granaries, without the roof falling? It is the coincidence between the collapse and the presence of a particular person—a coincidence that we might consider bad luck—that witchcraft explains.

Another benefit people gain is that witches serve as scapegoats. When things are going poorly, people do not always know why. Witchcraft provides an explanation. It also provides people with a means to do something about the situation: identify, accuse, and punish the witch responsible. If, as is often the case, things still do not improve, there are always other yet-to-be-identified witches! People can blame many of their troubles on witches—evil enemies conspiring against them—rather than on their personal inadequacies or on the failures of their own sociocultural system. Although most of us do not attribute them supernatural powers, evil enemies still are blamed by modern folk for many problems of our nations (see Box 15.1).

Sociological Interpretations   One sociological hypothesis is that witchcraft reinforces the cultural norms and values that help individuals live harmoniously with one another. Every people have cultural notions of how individuals ideally ought to act toward others. Witches typically are the antithesis of these cultural ideals. They act like animals, or actually change themselves into animals. They mate with relatives. They often put on a false front, pretending to be your friend by day while they eat your liver by night. They have no respect for age or authority. They are in league with the forces of evil (in the Judeo-Christian tradition, witches made compacts with the Devil, agreeing to be his servant in return for worldly pleasures.) All the most despicable personal characteristics of individuals are wrapped up in the personality of witches, whom everyone is supposed to hate. So witches symbolize all that is undesirable, wicked, and hateful. Just as one should despise witches, so should one abhor all that they stand for. In short, this argument is that, by providing a hated symbol of the abnormal and the antisocial, the witch strengthens cultural conceptions of normatively approved social behavior.

Another argument is that witches provide an outlet for repressed aggression, and thus beliefs about witches lower the overall amount of conflict in a society. Writing about the Navajo in 1944, Clyde Kluckhohn argued that Navajo culture emphasizes cooperation and maintenance of good relationships between members of the same extended household. Bad feelings do develop within the household, yet Navajo culture leads people not to express them. But pent-up hostilities have an outlet in the form of witches, whom people are allowed to hate and gossip about. Because most people whom the Navajo believe to be witches are members of distant groups, little action is usually taken against them. Solidarity between relatives of the "in-group" is preserved by displacing hostility to people of the "out-group."

any North Americans find great tragedy in the scapegoat function of witches in earlier times and foreign places—innocent people were punished or cruelly put to death as witches. But we should always examine comparable beliefs among ourselves before we feel morally or intellectually superior to others.

Modern societies are too complex for any human mind to comprehend the interaction of all the forces that cause social, political, and economic problems. The most knowledgeable experts and scholars admit they know only a part of the story, and they cannot even agree among themselves on what causes poverty, crime, the so-called decline of the family, voter apathy, and other social problems. Many of us fall into the trap of personifying the reasons for the troubles of our society—rather than

recognizing the complexities of our problems, we simply lay the blame on specific individuals and groups. Is our economy in trouble? Outside powers—for example, the Japanese—are to blame. Is American influence abroad declining? The Soviets—who, like witches, are the "focus of evil in the world," according to a recent American president—are responsible. Is the nation beset by laziness, inflation, incompetence, and moral decay? Social workers, unions, permissive liberals, and the secular humanists are the reason. Johnny and Suzie can't read? Blame their teachers and the colleges that trained them.

It is nearly always incorrect to blame specific individuals and groups for complex social problems. Such problems result from little-understood sociocultural forces, over which particular individuals and groups exert only partial control. Rather than attempting to understand these forces, or at least to appreciate their complexity, it is easier intellectually to personify them, to scapegoat, to witchhunt. We have seen that the Azande and other peoples blame witches for accidents and sickness, two kinds of personal misfortunes for which they have no scientific explanation. Similarly, we find scapegoats for

misfortunes on the societal level, for which we likewise have no explanation.

Our politicians are eager to feed our desire for the simple answer scapegoats provide. By identifying scapegoats, politicians divert responsibility from themselves— foreigners and the other party are to blame. This also increases their reelection chances—what voter wants to hear that the modern world is so complex that candidate Smith does not know how to make our cities safe and all Americans prosperous? And scapegoating makes us feel good about ourselves—the American people and the American system are not at fault after all.

Scapegoating is not harmless, no matter how good it makes us feel. Most Americans know the tragedy of the McCarthy era, when anticommunist sentiment in the country was manipulated by a U.S. senator to further his own career. We know that Jews were the witches of Hitler's Germany, burnt at the stake by the millions. Jews, blacks, Catholics, Communists, and gays serve as witches for certain rightwing organizations in the modern United States. When will our next witchhunt occur, and who will its victims be? ∎

Another hypothesis is that witch beliefs serve as a mechanism of social control. This might work in two ways. First, it is commonly the case that a people believe (abstractly) in the existence of witchcraft but do not know (concretely) which members of their community are witches. This leads individuals to be careful not to make anyone angry, since the offended party may be a witch. Second, it is often the case that individuals who fail to conform to local cultural norms of behavior are most likely to be suspected and accused as witches. People who are always mad at somebody; who carry grudges for prolonged periods; who are known to be envious and resentful of the success of others; who have achieved wealth but selfishly refuse to share it in the culturally accepted manner—such

violators of these and other standards for behavior are frequently believed to be the likely perpetrators of witchcraft. Fear of being accused and punished presumably increases adherence to norms and ideals of behavior. Some cross-cultural studies lend support to this social control hypothesis (see chapter 6).

These are the major ideas that anthropologists have proposed about the benefits people derive from beliefs that witches and sorcerers cause many of their misfortunes. But notice that none of them explain the origin of such beliefs. They all state: "Assuming a people believe in witches or sorcerers (or both), individuals or groups derive positive benefits from these beliefs." Like other functionalist approaches (chapter 5), they state what kinds of rewards individuals or society gains as a *consequence* of beliefs in witches and sorcerers. They do not answer the *causal* question: "Why do some populations develop a belief that misfortune is caused by the supernatural powers of their enemies?" For not all sociocultural systems have such beliefs: some hold that illness is attributable to punishment by ancestors, or violations of a taboo, or divine retribution, or invasion of their bodies by tiny and invisible microorganisms that they themselves have never seen but that experts assure them exist. Anthropologists do not know the answer to this last question; although some suggestive ideas have been offered, none have been systematically tested.

Varieties of Religious Organization

There is no way to present an overview of the great diversity of human religions without some distortion. Just as we oversimplify a given society when we classify it as (for example) horticultural, polygynous, patrilineal, tribal, and egalitarian, so do we simplify when we pigeonhole its religion as (for example) shamanistic or monotheistic. Nonetheless, a typology of religion is useful, for it will give a general picture of religious diversity among humanity.

In his 1966 book *Religion: An Anthropological View*, Anthony Wallace proposed a fourfold classification that we shall adopt. His typology is based on the concept of **cult**. A cult is an organized system of cultural knowledge and practice pertaining to the control over specific supernatural powers. It is important to note that "a cult" is not the same as "the religion" of a people. Rather, religion is a more inclusive concept: a society's religion may include several cults, some of which are devoted to curing, some to controlling weather, some to praying to their ancestors, some to foretelling the future, and so on.

Wallace's classification distinguishes four kinds of cults:

- **Individualistic cults.** Each individual has a personal relationship with one or more supernatural powers, who serve as his or her guardians and protectors. The aid of the powers is solicited when needed for personal goals.
- **Shamanistic cults.** Some individuals—shamans—are believed to have relationships with the supernatural that ordinary people lack. They use these powers primarily for socially valuable purposes, to help (especially cure) others in need. They may also

act on behalf of their band or village to cause supernatural harm to the group's enemies.
- **Communal cults.** The members of some kind of group gather periodically for the performance of rituals that are believed to benefit the group as a whole, or some individual(s) in it. There are no full-time religious specialists, as is also true of individualistic and shamanistic cults.
- **Ecclesiastical cults.** The hallmark of ecclesiastical cults is the presence of full-time religious practitioners who form a religious bureaucracy. The practice of religion is carried out by formal, specialized officials—priests—who perform rituals that allegedly benefit the society as a whole. The priesthood often is supported—and sometimes controlled—by governmental authorities through the mechanism of redistribution (see chapter 9).

Although any given human population usually has more than one of these kinds of cults, the cults are not randomly distributed among the peoples of the world. Rather, there is a rough evolutionary sequence to their occurrence. Many foraging bands and horticultural tribes, such as the Netsilik, San, and Yąnomamö, have only shamanistic cults, and ecclesiastical cults occur only in stratified chiefdoms and states, for example. If we consider the religion of a people to be composed of

■ *This photo of Buddhist monks receiving offerings illustrates religious specialists called* priests.

some number of cults, in general more kinds of cults are found in states than in tribes.

But the evolutionary matching of kinds of cults with kinds of economic and political organizations is only very rough and general. For instance, the aboriginal peoples of Australia had communal cults, although they were foragers and lived in bands. Many tribes of the North American Great Plains had individualistic, shamanistic, and communal cults, although they were primarily foragers.

We now look at some of these varieties of religious organization in more detail.

■ Individualistic Cults

As the term *individualistic* suggests, these kinds of cults feature beliefs and actions focused on the personal relationships supernatural powers establish with specific people. The belief that individuals can ask spiritual beings and forces for aid in their endeavors is found in many religions, but religions emphasize this element to different degrees. Some peoples, such as the Plains Indians of North America, place special emphasis on direct interactions between individuals and the supernatural, to the point that each man sought a special spirit to help him alone. Other religions, such as medieval Catholicism and many other ecclesiastical cults, deemphasize direct contact between individuals and spirits; ordinary folk need intermediaries to mediate between them and the supernatural.

One well-known example of this type of cult is the **vision quest.** It was widespread among Native American peoples, but was especially important for the Great Plains tribes. To the Plains Indians, supernatural powers were dispersed throughout the world. They existed in inanimate objects such as rocks or mountains and in living animals and plants. Human beings required the aid of the supernatural in their lifelong struggle against other people as well as against the natural world—in hunting, in warfare, and in times of sickness or other troubles.

Spiritual power came to individuals in visions. These visions played an important role in the religious life of the plains tribes, for it was through them that men achieved the personal contact with the supernatural that was essential in various endeavors. Occasionally, spiritual powers made contact with individuals for no apparent reason, coming to them as they slept or even as they were walking or riding alone.

More often, however, humans had to seek out these powers through an active search, or a quest intentionally designed to achieve a vision. Young men particularly sought power through vision quests. There were places that supernatural powers were believed to frequent: certain hills, mountains, or bluffs. A young man would go to such a location alone. There he would smoke and fast, appealing to a power to take pity on him. Among one tribe, the Crow, a man might even amputate part of a finger or cut his body to arouse pity. Frequently, the vision would appear on the fourth day, since four was a sacred number to the Crow. Many young men failed at their quest, but others did achieve visions.

The supernatural power that contacted a man and the manner in which it manifested itself varied. Sometimes he only heard the spirit speak to him. Sometimes it came in the form of a dreamlike story. In other instances, it simply materialized in some form before his eyes. It might take the form of a bear, a bison, an eagle, or some other large animal. But even rabbits, field mice, and dogs sometimes appeared.

The power told the man how it would help him. It might give him the ability to predict the future, locate the enemy, find game, become a powerful warrior, or cure illness. It told him the things he would have to do to keep his power—what songs to sing, how to paint his war shield, how to wear his hair, and so forth. It also told the man some things he could not do—for example, if the power came from the eagle, the man might be prohibited from killing "his brother," the eagle. As long as he continued to behave in the prescribed manner, the power would be his supernatural protector, or guardian spirit. It would aid him in his endeavors and give him special powers lacking in other men.

There is no known society in which individualistic cults constitute the entire religion. Even among Plains Indians, in which this kind of cult was unusually well developed, shamanistic and communal cults also existed.

■ Shamanism

A **shaman,** or **medicine man,** is an individual with a special relationship to supernatural powers, which he frequently uses to cure sickness. In many societies (especially among many foraging peoples) the shaman is the only kind of religious practitioner; that is, he practices the only kind of ritual and possesses the only kind of abilities not available to ordinary people.

Shamans usually use their special knowledge to cure people by invoking the aid of supernatural powers. Here, a San Shaman lays hands on a patient to draw out his illness.

speaks to the assembled audience through his mouth. When possessed, the shaman becomes a *medium,* or mouthpiece for the spirits—he may lose control over his actions, and his voice changes quality, for a spirit is speaking through him.

The way in which an individual becomes a shaman varies from people to people. Shamans are usually considered to have knowledge and powers lacking among ordinary folk. They acquire these in three major ways. In some societies they undergo a period of special training as an apprentice to a practicing shaman, who teaches the novice chants and songs and how to achieve the trance state. Often shamans must have endured difficult deprivations, such as prolonged fasting, the consumption of foods culturally considered disgusting, or years of sexual abstinence. Finally, in many societies shamans are people who have experienced some unusual event. For example, they have miraculously recovered from a serious illness or injury, or they claim to have had an unusual dream or vision in which some spirit called them to be its mouthpiece.

In most societies the shaman's major role is curing. Again, how the shaman performs this role varies. By considering an ethnographic example of sickness and curing, we can see shamans in action. We also can use the case to suggest an answer to one of the questions frequently asked about shamanism: How does the belief that shamans have the power to make people well persist, even though many of their clients die?

The Jívaro live in the rain forest of Ecuador (see chapter 13). Jívaro believe that most sickness is caused by the actions of human enemies (rather than by natural causes). Jívaro shamans acquire their power from their control over their personal spirit helpers, which live in their bellies in the form of tiny magical darts. Among the Jívaro, a man becomes a shaman by presenting a gift to an existing shaman, who regurgitates some of his spirit helpers, which the novice swallows. If the novice drinks a hallucinogenic drug nightly for ten days and abstains from sexual intercourse for at least three months—the longer the better—he will acquire the power to transform any small objects (insects, worms, plants, etc.) he ingests into magical darts.

The Jívaro recognize two kinds of shamans: bewitching shamans, who have the ability to make people sick, and curing shamans, who try to make people well by counteracting the evil deeds of bewitching shamans. By ingesting and storing many magical darts in his body, a bewitching shaman can later harm his enemies.

Shamans, however, are rarely specialized practitioners. They carry out their tasks whenever their services are needed, usually in return for a gift or fee; but otherwise they live much as everyone else.

Cross-culturally, shamans are frequently believed to possess several qualities. Typically, they have access to the power of spiritual beings, called *spirit helpers.* The effectiveness of a shaman in curing (or causing harm) is believed to derive from the potency of his spirit helpers and from his ability to contact them and get them to do his bidding. Contact with one's spirit helpers is commonly made by achieving an altered state of consciousness. This altered state (referred to as a *trance*) is reached in a variety of ways: through intake of drugs, ritual chanting, or participation in rhythmic music. Quite often, people believe that one of a shaman's spirit helpers has physically entered (possessed) his body. The spirit takes over his body and

He causes illness by propelling one or more magical darts into the body of his victim; unless the darts are removed by a curing shaman, the victim will die. To effect the cure, a curing shaman first drinks tobacco juice and other drugs, which gives him the power to see into the body of the victim. Once he locates them, the curer sucks out and captures the magical darts; if the cure is successful, the darts return to their owner and the patient recovers.

Obviously, many patients die, which means that curing shamans are often ineffective. How then does the belief that curing shamans really cure persist? The answer is that the Jívaro believe a kind of supernatural battle is waged between the bewitching and the curing shaman. Bewitching shamans have two special spirit helpers. One, called a *pasuk*, looks like an ordinary tarantula to people who are not shamans; the other takes the form of a bird. A bewitching shaman can order his pasuk or spirit bird to remain near the house of the victim, shooting additional magical darts into him as the curing shaman sucks them out. If the victim dies, it may be because the darts shot by the pasuk and spirit bird were too many for the curing shaman to remove. Or, because the supernatural power of shamans varies, it may be because the bewitching shaman has more power than the curing shaman.

Aside from its value as an example of shamanism, the Jívaro illustration shows how beliefs about supernatural causes and shamanistic cures for illness form a logically coherent system. If the patient recovers, the ability of the shaman to cure is confirmed. If the victim dies, this event too is explained ("rationalized," an outsider might say) in terms that are consistent with existing beliefs. Events in the real world—getting better or getting worse, living or dying—cannot falsify the beliefs to the believers.

Faith healers, those shamans of modern times, use similar logical premises. God's power to heal is unquestionable, and faith healers rarely publicly doubt their own calling. If the cancer is not cured, if the blind do not see, if the disabled do not walk away, if the heart patient does not recover, the fault is often with themselves: they had too little faith.

■ Communal Cults

Like shamanism, communal cults have no full-time religious specialists. Although a wide range of people are involved in communal cults, it is quite common for knowledge of the cult's myths and rituals to be limited to only one sex. Rituals organized communally frequently have leaders—often, the elderly, or someone with a special interest in the outcome of some ritual—who manipulate the symbolic objects or who address the supernatural. But the cult leaders are unspecialized—they do not make their living as religious practitioners.

Communal rituals are generally held to intercede with the supernatural on behalf of some group of people, such as a descent group, an age group, a village, or a caste. To illustrate, we consider two widespread kinds of communal rituals organized by descent groups: **ancestral cults** and **totemism**.

Ancestral Cults   Practically all religions hold that people have a spiritual dimension—what we call a *soul*—that lives on after the physical body has perished. Beliefs about the fate of the soul after death vary widely. Some religions—such as Hinduism—believe that it is reincarnated into another person or animal. Others hold that the soul passes into a spiritual plane, where it exists eternally with a community of other souls and has no further effects on the living. Still others believe that souls become malevolent after death, turning into ghosts that cause accidents or sickness, or generally terrifying anyone and everyone.

One of the most common beliefs about the fate of souls after death is that they interact with and affect only particular people—their living descendants. A great many populations hold such beliefs. They usually practice rituals in order to induce the spirits of their deceased ancestors to do favors for them or simply to leave them alone. These beliefs and rituals surrounding the interactions between the living and their departed relatives are called *ancestral cults*. (They are also known as *ancestor worship*, but *worship* is not an accurate term to describe what goes on in many of these rituals!)

The Lugbara, a people of Uganda, illustrate ancestral cults. The patrilineage is an important social group to Lugbara. Its members are subject to the authority of its elders. As the most important members of the lineage, the elderly are expected to oversee the interests and harmony of the entire group. They serve as the guardians of the lineage's morality, although they have no power to punish violations physically.

Lugbara believe that the spirit of a deceased person may become an ancestral ghost of the lineage he belonged to while alive. The ghost's primary activity is to punish his living descendants who violate Lugbara ideals of behavior toward lineage mates. People who fight with their kinsmen (especially a relative older

Ancestral cults involve organized rituals to propitiate the spirits of a kin group's ancestors. At this Tannese funeral, the relatives of the deceased demonstrate their sorrow. The ghost may cause trouble for relatives who do not mourn loudly enough, or long enough.

than oneself), who deceive or steal from their lineage mates, or who fail to carry out their duties toward others are liable to be punished by an ancestral ghost. This sometimes happens because a ghost sees an offense committed and punishes it by causing illness to the offender. More commonly, the ghosts do not act on their own initiative to make someone sick. Rather, the ghosts act upon the thoughts of an elder, who is indignant because of the actions of some member of the lineage. John Middleton (1965) describes Lugbara beliefs about the power of lineage elders to cause illness by invoking ghosts:

> [The elder] sits near his shrines in his compound and thinks about the sinner's behavior. His thoughts are known by the ghosts and they then send sickness to the offender. He 'thinks these words in his heart'; he does not threaten or curse the offender. For a senior man to do this is part of his expected role. It is part of his 'work,' to 'cleanse the lineage home.' Indeed, an elder who does not do so when justified would be lacking in sense of duty toward his lineage. (76)

In this example, we see how elders use beliefs about ancestral ghosts to maintain harmony and cooperation in the lineage. This is a common feature of ancestral cults.

Why do some—but not all—societies have ancestral cults, in which ghosts are believed to punish their descendants who violate cultural prescriptions of right behavior? Like most "why" questions, this one is

controversial. But many anthropologists agree that such beliefs are related to the degree of importance of large kin groups in a society. In general, the greater the importance of kin groups in making public decisions, regulating access to resources, allocating roles, controlling behavior, and so on, the more likely a society is to develop an ancestral cult. This hypothesis has some support from cross-cultural studies, although more research is needed on this possible relationship.

Totemism Totemism, another widespread form of communal cult, is the cultural belief that human groups have a special mystical relationship with natural objects such as animals, plants, and sometimes non-living things. The object (or objects) with which a group is associated is known as its *totem*. Most often, the group is a unilineal kin group, such as a clan. Frequently the totem serves as a name of the group, for example, the Bear clan, the Eagle clan.

The nature of the relationship between the members of the group and its totem varies widely. Sometimes the totem is used mainly for simple identification of the group and its members, much like our surnames. Often there is a mystical association between the group and its totem object: people believe that they are like their totem in some respects. Members of other groups also resemble their totems. In many populations—most notably among some of the aboriginal peoples of Australia—the members of a clan treat their totem like a clanmate, believing that the totem gave birth to their ancestors in a mythical period. The welfare of the clan is associated with the welfare of the totem, so periodically the clan gathers for rituals that ensure the reproduction of its totem.

Despite its many variations, everywhere totemism exists, the totem is a symbol of the group, to a greater or lesser degree. Why are some living things "chosen" as totems rather than others? There are several answers to this question. Perhaps the most influential is that offered by the French structural anthropologist Claude Lévi-Strauss (see chapter 5). He noted that totemic beliefs classify a peoples' social world into kinds of groups. The natural world likewise is divided up into kinds of plants, animals, and other things. In essence, totemic logic posits an association between natural categories ("kinds of things") and social categories ("kinds of people," or groups). According to his argument, particular natural objects are chosen because they are a convenient way to represent (symbolize) kinds of groups and their relationships to one another. As Lévi-Strauss puts it, certain animals are used as totems because they are "good to think"—they have (concrete, constant) properties that provide useful metaphors for conceptualizing and thinking about (abstract, variable) groups and social relationships.

■ *Ecclesiastical Cults*

In chapter 9 we saw that a high degree of specialization generally accompanied the development of civilization. Among New World peoples such as the ancient Incas, Aztecs, Mayans, and Toltecs, and in the Old World cities of ancient Mesopotamia, Egypt, China, Japan, and India, this specialization extended into the religious dimension of sociocultural systems. Rather than organizing rituals on a communal basis—in which a wide range of people controlled and participated in the performance—a formal bureaucracy of religious specialists controlled most public rituals. The religious bureaucracy probably also had a large voice in formulation of the religious laws, which ordered certain kinds of punishments for those who violated them.

These religious specialists are known as **priests**. It is instructive to compare priests with shamans. In addition to their more specialized status, priests differ from shamans in several respects. First, shamans usually perform their ritual functions without aid from other shamans; indeed, as we have seen, many peoples believe that enemy shamans engage in supernatural battles with one another. In contrast, priests are generally organized into a hierarchical priesthood under the sponsorship of a formal government, the state. Second, a priest generally undergoes a lengthy period of special training, for he must master the complex rituals needed to perform his role. Third, the priesthood was at or near the top of the social ladder in the ancient civilizations, so individual priests usually lived much better than the population at large. Fourth, shamans typically perform mainly crisis rituals, whenever some individual requires their services. The rituals at which priests officiate tend to be calendrical—they occur at regular intervals, for the gods that the rituals are intended to appease demand regular praise or sacrifice.

A final difference is especially revealing. With the development of a *priesthood,* there comes to be a strong distinction between "priest" and "layperson." The layperson has little control over the timing and content of religious performances or the content of myths. The population at large relies on the priesthood to keep it in proper relation to supernatural powers. This

■ *Ecclesiastical cults include an organized priesthood, which officiates at rituals usually held in temples. Most religions familiar to Westerners include ecclesiastical cults, as this photo of a Protestant church illustrates.*

creates a sense of spiritual dependence on the priesthood and on the state apparatus that sponsors it, a dependence that reinforced the high degree of stratification found in states.

These state-sponsored cults are called *ecclesiastical* (meaning "of or pertaining to the church") because their priesthood was highly organized and their rituals were usually held in grandiose buildings that served as temples. Generally, the entire ecclesiastical cult was under the control of the government. Officials exacted tribute to finance the construction of temples, the livelihood of the priesthood, the sacrifices that often accompanied state rituals, and other expenses needed to support and organize religious activities on a fantastically large scale.

There is little question that ecclesiastical cults provided a body of myth and belief that supported the domination of the ruling dynasty. (This is not to say, of course, that their function as an ideology totally explains these cults, or that it constitutes their entire significance.) This is seen by the content of the cults' beliefs, myths, and rituals, which almost invariably express the dependence of the entire population on the ruler's well-being and on the periodic performance of rituals. A common belief of official state religions is that the ruler is a god-king—he not only rules by divine mandate but is himself a god or somehow partakes of divine qualities. This was true of most of the ancient civilizations and of the states that developed in sub-Saharan Africa.

Many official rituals of ecclesiastical cults are held to keep the entire polity in beneficial relationship with supernatural beings. For example, the state religion of the ancient Aztec taught that the gods had to be periodically appeased or they would cause the world to end in a cataclysm. To keep the gods' goodwill, the priesthood periodically performed human sacrifice at temples, offering the heart of the victim (usually a war captive) to the deities. The ancient Egyptians believed that their pharaoh would rule in the afterlife—just as in the present world—so when he died, he took much of his wealth, his wives, and his servants into the next world with him.

Ecclesiastical cults everywhere consumed enormous resources in the civilizations, but they did not wipe out other kinds of cults. Common people usually continued to rely on local shamans for curing, to practice magic, to believe in witches and sorcerers, and to worship their ancestors. In China, for example, each household and lineage continued to revere its ancestors while participating in the state religion.

Most Christian denominations—Catholic and the diverse Protestant sects—have an ecclesiastical character. In medieval Europe the authority of the Catholic church was tightly interwoven with the exercise of secular power, although there was often conflict between pope and king. It is only in the last few centuries that the formal alliance between the power of government and the power of God has been broken for any length of time. (Informally and unofficially, religion continues to prop up political systems—God seems always to be on "our side," according to many religious persons in our own and other modern nations.) We should not assume that even this official separation between church and state will necessarily be permanent. As the recent history of Iran suggests, the intermingling of political and ecclesiastical authorities can be reborn even in the modern world.

Revitalization Movements

So far in this chapter we have concentrated on religious phenomena that change only slowly—partly because people often believe that precise performance of rituals and accurate recitations of myths are necessary to control or influence supernatural powers. Further, as we have seen, many existing theories of religion assume it to be a conservative force in sociocultural systems: it keeps people in line, relieves social and psychological conflicts in the present system, and so on.

There are other kinds of religious phenomena, which A. F. C. Wallace called **revitalization movements,** that interest social scientists because they are anything but a conservative force in human life. Revitalization movements aim to create a new sociocultural system, a whole new way of life, to replace present conditions that participants in the movement find intolerable.

Revitalization movements are most likely to occur in a society when three conditions coalesce: (1) rapid change, often caused by exposure to unfamiliar people, customs, and objects; (2) foreign domination, which leads to a sense of sociocultural inferiority, especially common in colonial situations; and (3) the perception of relative deprivation, meaning that people see themselves as lacking wealth, power, and esteem relative to those who dominate them. The movements are especially common in situations of colonialism, but colonialism does not always produce them.

■ *Prophets and Revelations*

Revitalization movements usually originate with an individual—a **prophet**—who claims to have had a dream or vision. Sometimes the prophet says he is a messiah, or savior, sent by a spiritual being to save the world from destruction. In the dream or vision, the prophet received a message—a **revelation**—from a god, an ancestor, or another spiritual power.

Revelations typically include two kinds of information given by the spirit. The first is a statement about what has gone wrong with the world, about why peoples' lives have changed for the worse. Frequently, the introduction of corrupting foreign objects and habits—such as tobacco, alcohol, money, religions, or formal schooling—are blamed for the troubles of today.

Second, prophets' revelations generally include a vision of a new world and a prescription for how to bring it about. In some cases, the message is vague and secular, the prophet claiming that earthly lives will improve if people do (or stop doing) certain things. Quite often, the prophet's preachings are *apocalyptic*: he says that the present world will end at a certain time, and only those who heed his message will be saved. The expulsion or death of foreigners is a frequent theme of apocalyptic visions: foreigners will be drowned in a flood or burned in a fire or swallowed up by an earthquake or killed by the ancestors. Another common theme is the reversal of existing political and economic dominance relations: foreigners will work for us, we will have the wealth instead of them, we will tax them and make laws that they must obey, or some other inversion of the existing structure. Nearly always, the prophets' revelations are *syncretic*, that is, they combine elements of traditional myths, beliefs, and rituals with introduced elements.

Examples from two regions will illustrate prophets, revelations, and the syncretism of revitalization movements.

■ Melanesian Cargo Cults

The area called *Melanesia* in the southwest Pacific has experienced numerous revitalization movements in the twentieth century. Melanesians placed great cultural emphasis on wealth—and the manipulation of the flow of wealth—as the route to becoming a big man or powerful leader. It is therefore not surprising that they were most interested in the material possessions of German, English, French, and Australian colonial powers. Because European wealth was brought to the islands by ship or plane, it became known as *cargo,* and the various movements that sprang up with the aim of acquiring it through ritual means became known as **cargo cults.**

To Melanesians, all Europeans were fantastically wealthy; yet the Melanesians rarely saw them do any work to earn their possessions. The whites who lived in the islands certainly did not know how to make tanks, cars, canned food, radios, stoves, and so forth. In many traditional religions technology was believed to have been made by deities or spirits, so it followed that European objects likewise were made by their God. Further, when the whites living in Melanesia wanted some new object, they simply made marks on papers and placed them in an envelope or asked for the object by speaking into metal things. Some weeks later, the

■ *Some members of the John Frum cargo cult in Tanna, Vanuata perform a ritual march. They await the day that John Frum, their messiah, will return, bringing freedom and wealth. This movement has been in existence for over forty years.*

object was delivered in ships or airplanes. It seemed to appear from nowhere. Surely the goods were made by spirits, and the meaningless acts the whites did to get their spirits to send cargo were rituals. Melanesians therefore believed that they too could acquire this wealth through the correct ritual procedure—which, frequently, they believed the whites were selfishly withholding from them.

Numerous prophets sprang up among diverse Melanesian peoples, each with his own vision or dream, each with his own story for why the Europeans had cargo and Melanesians had none, and each claiming to know the secret ritual that would deliver the goods. Often, the prophet claimed to have received a visit from one of his ancestors or a native deity, who told him that the whites had been lying to people about how to get cargo.

The Garia, of the north coast of Papua New Guinea, illustrate some common themes of cargo cults. Like most other indigenous peoples, the Garia were visited by missionaries. Also, like many other peoples, the Garia initially adopted Christianity for reasons other than those the missionaries had in mind. They assumed that the whites knew the ritual that was the "road to cargo." The missionaries would give it to the "natives" if only the Garia would practice what the missionaries preached: church attendance, monogamy, worship of the true God, cessation of pagan practices such as sorcery and dancing, and so forth. Based on their belief that the missionary lifestyle and rituals held the secret of cargo, many Garia converted to Christianity early in the twentieth century.

But the cargo did not arrive. The Garia grew angry with the missions, for they concluded that the missionaries were withholding the true ritual secret of how to get cargo, in order to deceive the Garia and keep all the wealth for themselves. In the 1930s and 1940s two Garia prophets arose. They told the people that the missionaries had been telling them to worship the wrong gods! God and Jesus both were really deities of the Garia, not of whites. The Europeans knew the secret names of God and Jesus, and asked them for the cargo with secret prayers. All along, Jesus had been trying to deliver the goods to the Garia, but the Jews were holding him captive in heaven. To free Him, the Garia had to perform sacrificial rituals. To show Him how poor they were and to make Him feel sorry for them, they had to destroy all their native wealth objects. If they did these things, Jesus would give the cargo to the ancestral spirits of the Garia, who would in turn deliver it to the living.

■ Native American Movements

Revitalization movements also have occurred among American Indians, whose tragic sufferings at the hands of white traders, settlers, armies, and administrators are known to all twentieth-century Americans. Two movements were especially important, both of which were precipitated by a deterioration of tribal economic, social, and religious life.

Handsome Lake By 1800 the Seneca of New York had lost most of their land to the state, settlers, and land speculators. Whites committed many atrocities against the Seneca in the 1780s and 1790s, partly because they supported the British during the American Revolutionary War. There were also the usual diseases—such as smallpox and measles, which wiped out hundreds of thousands of Native Americans all over the continent—that reduced the tribe to a fraction of its former numbers. Seneca men had previously been proud warriors, hunters, and fur traders, but all of these activities became more difficult because of the loss of land and the presence of whites. The American government waged psychological warfare against them, intentionally corrupting their leaders with bribes and liquor and generally attempting to dehumanize and demoralize them.

Seneca men became victims of alcoholism and drank up most of what little money they could still earn from the fur trade. Neighboring peoples, once subject to the authority of the Seneca and other members of the League of the Iroquois, ridiculed them. A growth in witchcraft accusations increased the internal conflict and divisions of their communities. Many women lost their desire for children and took medicines that caused them to abort or become sterile altogether. A way of life—and indeed a people themselves—was dying.

In 1799 a Seneca man named Handsome Lake lay sick. He was cured by three angels, who also gave him a message from the Creator. Handsome Lake reported that the Creator was saddened by the present life of the people and angry because of their drunkenness, witchcraft, and taking of abortion medicines. The Seneca must repent of such deeds. Handsome Lake had two more visions within the next year. There would be an apocalypse in which the world would be destroyed by great drops of fire, which would consume those who did not heed Handsome Lake's teachings. People could save themselves and delay the apocalypse by publicly confessing their wrongs, giving up sins such as witchcraft and drinking, and returning to the performance of certain traditional rituals.

The apocalypse, of course, did not occur; but Handsome Lake was able to give his teachings a new, more "this worldly," twist between 1803 and his death in 1815. He continued to preach temperance, for the Creator had never intended whiskey to be used by Indians. He taught peace with both whites and other Indians. He urged that the scattered reservations of the Seneca be consolidated, so that the people could live together as one community. Domestic morality must be impeccable: sons were to obey their fathers; divorce (commonplace among the Seneca in aboriginal times) was no longer to be allowed; adultery and domestic quarreling were to cease. Most important, Handsome Lake succeeded in changing the traditional division of labor, in which cultivation of crops was done by women and garden work by men was considered effeminate. Seneca men took up farming and animal husbandry and even fenced their fields and added new crops to their inventory.

The Peyote Religion Peyote is a small cactus that grows in the Rio Grande Valley of Texas and northern Mexico. It produces a mild narcotic effect when eaten. The ritual use of peyote among Mexican Indians predated European conquest. However, its consumption as the central element in a revitalization movement dates only from the last two decades of the nineteenth century.

In 1875 the Southern Plains tribes, the Kiowa and Comanche, lost their land after they were defeated militarily. During their confinement to reservations in southwestern Oklahoma, the Lipan-Apache introduced them to peyote. By the 1880s, the two tribes had made the cactus the center of a revitalization movement. Like many movements, peyotism subsequently spread, reaching about nineteen different Indian groups in Oklahoma by 1899. It ultimately was incorporated as an official church in 1914, with the name Koshiway's First Born Church of Christ. During the early twentieth century, the church spread rapidly to other Indian communities throughout the western United States and Canada. It still exists today as the Native American church.

The peyote movement had no single prophet or leader. Local churches developed their own versions of services and rituals. One early leader was John Wilson, a Caddo/Delaware from western Oklahoma who had learned to use peyote from the Comanche. While eating dinner in the early 1890s, Wilson collapsed. Thinking him dead, his family began preparations for the burial. But Enoch Parker, a Caddo, told the family that he had been told in a vision that Wilson was not dead. Indeed, Wilson revived three days later. He reported that a great Water Bird had sucked the breath and sin out of his body, causing his collapse. Jesus brought him back to life three days later, telling him that his sins had been removed and that he was to

teach the Indian people to believe in God and to use peyote to communicate with Him.

Until his death in 1901, Wilson proselytized the peyote religion among the Osage, Delaware, Quapaw, and other groups. He preached that they needed to believe in God and Jesus, work hard, act morally, and abstain from alcohol consumption. They were to abandon their traditional religious practices, for the spirits that formerly had aided them could be used for evil as well as good purposes. Wilson attracted the greatest number of adherents among the Osage, who combined the use of peyote in worship services with the Christian teachings they had learned in mission schools.

Peyote was not integrated into Christian teachings among all Native Americans who adopted it for ritual use. It did, however, provide meaning and moral direction to Indian life during a period of rapid and generally harmful change. Thousands of Native Americans continue to use it in religious services.

What is the fate of revitalization movements? Many with apocalyptic messages simply disappear when the end of the world does not occur. (Although we must remember that beliefs about the actions of supernatural powers cannot be falsified by actual events, so the failure of the prophecy can always be rationalized.) Other movements were remarkably tenacious. In Melanesia, certain areas saw the rise and fall of numerous prophets, each claiming to have the cargo secret. People followed, again and again, because they had no other acceptable explanation for the existence of cargo, for why whites had it and they lacked it, or for how they could acquire it. Certainly their own worldly efforts—working for Europeans in mines and plantations, growing and selling coffee, copra, cocoa, and so forth—showed no signs of rewarding them with the fantastic wealth that whites enjoyed with virtually no effort. Frequently, cargo cults did not exactly disappear in a region; instead, they transformed into a political movement or party. This was the fate of cargo cults among the Garia, Manus, Tannese, and some Malaitans.

Other movements do not wither away or transform into a more secular, political movement. They retain their religious character, frequently teaching that contentment is to be found within oneself rather than from worldly material things. After his death in 1815, Handsome Lake's exhortations on how to live became codified and still persist as a Native American church—the Old Way of Handsome Lake, also known as the Longhouse religion.

■ *Members of the three Southern Plains tribes are shown here with objects used in peyote rituals. Thousands of Native Americans continue to practice the peyote religion.*

Peyotism also became formally organized. Like many other revitalization movements that give birth to new religions, the adherents of peyotism are thus far largely confined to a single ethnic category: Native Americans. Other movements, however, grow in scale over the centuries. From humble beginnings, they eventually attract millions of believers. They develop a formal organization, complete with priests rather than prophets. Revelations become sacred writings. Beliefs become formal doctrines. Followers and disciples become organized into a church. Most of the major religions of the modern world began as revitalization movements, including Islam, Judaism, and Christianity.

Summary

In comparing religions, it is useful to identify three components that all share: beliefs about the nature of supernatural powers (beings and forces), myths about the past deeds of these powers, and rituals intended to influence them. All known human societies have such beliefs and myths, and practice such rituals, so all have religion.

Religion is universal in spite of the facts that beliefs and myths can never be proven true or false and that rituals are not effective in achieving the goals people have in mind when they perform them. One puzzling thing about religion is what it does for people as individuals or for society as a whole. Various social scientists have proposed that religion performs intellectual/cognitive, psychological, and social functions. No consensus exists about which of these functions are most important. Religion probably fulfills all these kinds of "needs," but none of these functions seems able to explain religion itself, nor the great diversity of human religions.

Religions vary in the range of human activities and natural occurrences in which spiritual powers are believed to intervene. Most religions include a belief that supernatural beings or forces cause or influence group or personal misfortune, such as deaths, illnesses, and "accidents." The malevolent powers of sorcerers and witches are blamed for misfortune in a great many societies. Accusations of sorcery and witchcraft tend to be patterned and to reflect prevalent conflicts and tensions in the organization of society. Those known or suspected of having malevolent powers can use other peoples' belief that they have such powers as a political weapon, for witches and sorcerers are feared as well as despised. Although beliefs in sorcery and witchcraft might seem to be harmful, a number of anthropologists have argued that they have psychological and social functions.

Religions may be classified according to the types of cults they include, although any such classification is inadequate to depict the diversity of the world's religions. Cults may be characterized as individualistic, shamanistic, communal, and ecclesiastical. In a very generalized way there is an evolutionary sequence to cults in that they tend to be associated with different degrees of sociocultural complexity.

Revitalization refers to religious movements that aim to create a new way of life to replace present conditions that are felt to be intolerable. Revitalization movements usually originate with prophets who claim to have received a revelation, which is usually syncretic and often apocalyptic. Twentieth-century Melanesian cargo cults are among the best-studied movements. The Handsome Lake religion among the Seneca of New York and the peyote religion are two of many North American revitalization movements.

Key Terms

animism	communal cults
myths	ecclesiastical cults
ritual	vision quest
intellectual/cognitive functions of religion	shaman (medicine man)
psychological functions of religion	ancestral cults
social functions of religion	totemism
	priests
sorcery	revitalization
witchcraft	movement
cult	prophet
individualistic cults	revelation
shamanistic cults	cargo cults

Suggested Readings

■ Douglas, Mary. *Purity and Danger.* Baltimore: Penguin, 1966. *An innovative and thoughtful study of pollution and taboo beliefs and practices.*

Lehman, Arthur C., and James E. Myers, eds. *Magic, Witchcraft, and Religion*. 2d ed. Palo Alto, Calif.: Mayfield, 1989.

An excellent reader prepared mainly for undergraduates.

Lessa, William, and Evon Vogt, eds. *Reader in Comparative Religion*. 2d ed. New York: Harper and Row, 1979.

A collection of essays that examine religion from a variety of perspectives and introduce students to the range of anthropological ideas concerning the subject.

Lowie, Robert. *Primitive Religion*. New York: Liveright, 1948.

A somewhat dated classic in anthropology that is still interesting reading for students.

Mair, Lucy. *Witchcraft*. New York: McGraw-Hill, 1969.
Excellent introduction to witchcraft and its analysis.

Martin, Brian. *Anthropological Theories of Religion*. Cambridge: Cambridge University Press, 1987.

Swanson, Guy. *The Birth of the Gods*. Ann Arbor: University of Michigan Press, 1960.

A cross-cultural study of religion with a sociological interpretation.

Following is a list of ethnographies that examine religion and religious movements.

Boyer, Dave, and Stephen Nissenbaum. *Salem Possessed*. Cambridge, Mass.: Harvard University Press, 1974.

Historical study of the witchcraft outbreak in 1692 in Salem, Massachusetts. Shows that the accusations closely reflected long-standing lines of conflict in the community.

Evans-Pritchard, E. E. *Witchcraft, Oracles, and Magic among the Azande*. Abridged ed. Oxford: Clarendon, 1976.

An abridgement of the 1937 edition that loses little of the information found in the original. One of the best descriptions of witchcraft among an African people ever written.

Geertz, Clifford. *The Religion of Java*. Glencoe, Ill.: The Free Press, 1960.

One of the great case studies of non-Western religions.

Jorgensen, Joseph. *The Sun Dance: Power for the Powerless*. Chicago: University of Chicago Press, 1972.

An analysis of the historic adoption of the Sun dance by the Ute Indians of Utah.

Keesing, Roger. *Kwaio Religion*. New York: Columbia University Press, 1982.

Study of the religion of a Solomon Island society.

Kluckhohn, Clyde. *Navaho Witchcraft*. Boston: Beacon, 1967.

Well-written study of witchcraft among the Navajo of the Southwest, originally published in 1944.

La Barre, Weston. *The Peyote Cult*. New York: Schocken, 1969.

Originally published in 1938, a book that remains a good introduction to the peyote religion of the Indians of the western United States.

Lindstrom, Lamont. "Cult and Culture: American Dreams in Vanuatu." *Pacific Studies* 4:101–123, 1981.

A history of one Melanesian cargo movement and its contemporary political significance to the people of Tanna, Vanuatu.

Malinowski, Bronislaw. *Coral Gardens and Their Magic*. New York: American Book Company, 1935.

A detailed description of garden magic and horticultural practices in the Trobriand Islands.

Myerhoff, Barbara. *Peyote Hunt: The Sacred Journey of the Huichol Indians*. Ithaca, N.Y.: Cornell University Press, 1976.

An ethnography describing how the Huichol Indians of northern Mexico locate and acquire peyote, which they use in their rituals.

Neihardt, John G. *Black Elk Speaks*. 2d ed. Lincoln: University of Nebraska Press, 1961.

A very popular and readable account of an Ogalala Sioux holy man and an excellent introduction to the religious beliefs and practices of this American Indian people.

Turner, Victor. *The Forest of Symbols*. Ithaca, N.Y.: Cornell University Press, 1967.

Collection of papers on the religion of the Ndembu of Zambia. Turner's descriptions are rich in detail, and his analysis of the meaning of symbols used in rituals has been influential.

Wallace, Anthony F. C. *The Death and Rebirth of the Seneca*. New York: Vintage, 1969.

A highly readable and interesting account of the Longhouse religion, a revitalization movement that first appeared among the Seneca of New York State in the early 1800s.

Worsley, Peter. *The Trumpet Shall Sound: A Study of "Cargo" Cults in Melanesia*. New York: Schocken, 1968.

A comparative study of the origins and development of cargo cults.

Of the numerous studies of religion in contemporary America, these are especially useful.

Chalfant, H. Paul, Robert E. Beckley, and C. Eddie Palmer. *Religion in Contemporary Society*. Palo Alto, Calif.: Mayfield, 1984.

A textbook on the sociology of American religion.

Liebman, Robert C., and Robert Wuthnow, eds. *The New Christian Right: Mobilization and Legitimation*. New York: Aldine, 1983.

Twelve articles analyzing the mobilization of evangelical Christians for the conservative cause.

■ Rochford, E. Burke, Jr. *Hare Krishna in America.* New Brunswick, N.J.: Rutgers University Press, 1985.

■ Stark, Rodney, and William Sims Bainbridge. *The Future of Religion.* Berkeley: University of California Press, 1985.
A theoretical analysis of religious change and diversification, focusing on Protestant denominations in the United States.

Chapter 16

PERSONALITY FORMATION AND THE LIFE CYCLE

■ *Contents*

■ (Above) *Like all peoples, these South Asians classify individuals according to their age. Although chronological age is biologically determined, cultural categories of age, and social roles based on age, vary from people to people.*

nfants begin to interact with other people soon after they are born. Within a single sociocultural system, adults have certain kinds of ideas about how to bring children into the world, how to treat them at various stages of their lives, when to make them assume responsibility for their actions, and so forth. An infant's parents also have social obligations that affect how they interact with their children, if only by reducing the time and energy they devote to their offspring. Because of their ideas about enculturation and their wider social obligations, parents are likely to behave in patterned ways toward their children, as will grandparents, aunts, friends, teachers, and other individuals.

From the beginning of life, then, individuals are influenced by their sociocultural environment. One topic of this chapter is how children's motivations, emotional states, behavior, and so forth are shaped by sociocultural factors—that is, how the formation of personality is affected by the sociocultural system. A related topic is how, in turn, sociocultural systems might be affected by the personalities of their members.

Later in life, individuals pass through a series of changes as they achieve sexual maturity, marry, assume adult responsibilities, have children, and become elderly. As people move though life's various stages, they undergo changes in their activities, obligations, rights, and (to some extent) attitudes and ideas. The changes associated with growing up and aging are referred to as the *life cycle*. Life cycle changes are also discussed in this chapter.

Personality and the Sociocultural System

A child learns how to think, feel, speak, and behave by participating in a sociocultural environment made up of other individuals and the cultural traditions they live by (see chapter 2). Just as no child is genetically identical to any other (except for identical twins), so no two children experience exactly the same social environments during their maturation. Partly because of their different upbringing, individuals develop different personalities as adults. How is the nature of an individual's personality related to the sociocultural system in which he or she is brought up? What subsystems of this sociocultural system are most important in forming an individual's personality? And just how similar are the personalities of individuals raised in the same society? These questions are the concern of this section.

Although every human is the product of many interacting factors, these factors never interact in the same ways during the lives of different individuals. This makes each of us to some extent unique. Still, you are more similar to some people than you are to others in your moods and motivations, emotional responses, attitudes, reactions to situations, perceptions, and the like. You also are more similar to some people than to others in what kinds of behavior you regard as acceptable or normal.

If, for instance, you were to visit the Yąnomamö, the Amazonian people whose marriage alliances we introduced in chapter 11, you would be shocked by some of the things they do. By our standards of "normal," the Yąnomamö—called "The Fierce People" by ethnographer Napoleon Chagnon—are abnormally demanding and aggressive. Slight insults meet with violent responses. Quarreling men duel by engaging in a chest-pounding contest, during which they often put rocks in their hands and take turns beating one another across the chest. Serious quarrels call for clubs, which men use to bash one another on the head; a Yąnomamö man often shaves the top of his head to reveal the scars left from his many club fights. When the members of one village visit another for a feast, an event that supposedly is a manifestation of friendly relations between them, they are on the lookout for treachery, for their hosts are liable to attack and kill them. Husbands beat their wives' heads with clubs, and the wives compare scars among themselves. Fathers encourage their sons to strike them (and anyone else) by teasing and goading, all the while praising the child for his fierceness.

If, on the other hand, you were to visit the Semai, a people of Malaysia, you would be surprised at their refusal to express anger and hostility. Indeed, you might find them *too* docile. One adult should never strike another—"Suppose he hit you back?" they ask.

■ *By most people's standards the Yąnomamö are abnormally aggressive. Here combatants take sides in a club fight.*

With this attitude toward violence, murder is nonexistent or extremely rare—so rare, in fact, that there are no penalties for it. The Semai rarely hit their children—"How would you feel if he or she died?" they say. When children misbehave, the worst physical punishment they receive is a pinch on the cheek or a pat on the hand. The ethnographer Robert Dentan suggests one reason for the nonviolence of the Semai: children are so seldom exposed to physical punishment that when they grow up they have an exaggerated impression of the effects of violence.

Obviously, a Yąnomamö and a Semai react to similar situations in different ways. If one Yąnomamö demands something of another—as it seems they constantly do—and the demand is refused, the asker is likely to fly into a rage, make threats, and sometimes resort to violence. If a Semai fails to grant the request of another, the individual who is refused may experience a psychological state Semai call *punan*. Punan might be translated as "accident proneness," for the Semai think that to make someone unhappy by frustrating their desires increases that individual's chances of having an accident. So (and this is perfectly logical given their beliefs) if you ask me for something and I refuse your request, I have committed an offense against you that could result in your becoming accidentally injured. You, being the victim of the punan caused by my affront, have the right to demand compensation from me!

Yąnomamö and Semai belong to different sociocultural systems, so individuals brought up in one or the other system develop some differences in personality. The study of the relationships between the personality of individuals and the sociocultural systems of societies is one concern of *psychological anthropology.*

■ *What Is Personality?*

What do we mean by personality? According to one of its many possible definitions, *personality* refers "to the internally determined consistencies underlying a person's behavior, to the enduring differences among people insofar as they are attributable to stable internal characteristics rather than to differences in their life situation" (Child, quoted in LeVine 1973, 4). **Personality,** then, consists of those mental processes that make an individual's behavioral reactions to similar events and situations consistent and predictable over time, but different from the reactions other individuals have to similar events and situations. So a Yąnomamö is likely to behave aggressively to a denial of his wishes, whereas a Semai is more likely to become sad and depressed in a similar situation. The differing behavioral reactions of Yąnomamö and Semai individuals are influenced by their differing motivations, attitudes toward other people and the world, emotional responses, cognitive perceptions, and other "stable internal characteristics" of their personalities.

Personality is a product of the complex interaction between an individual's unique biological constitution and total life experiences. An examination of the possible ways in which these two sets of forces interact to fashion a unique human individual is outside the scope of this book. However, anthropologists have tended to focus much more on life experiences than on biological influences. In particular, we are concerned with the effects of how children are enculturated during early childhood on the type of personality they are likely to develop. If enculturation practices differ from society to society, then these differences might be reflected in the personalities of the members of these societies. The early childhood experiences of two Yąnomamö are more likely to be similar to one another's than either's is to the experiences of a Semai, for instance.

■ *Child-Rearing Practices and Personality Formation*

In enculturating their children, people employ certain methods. The phrase **child-rearing practices** refers to how children are nursed, weaned, toilet trained, and nurtured; the kinds of behavior that are punished and rewarded, and how they are punished and rewarded; how much time they spend with various caretakers and how much attention they receive from adults and other family members; and the like.

Child-rearing practices are an important part of any sociocultural system, for it is largely during childhood that individuals acquire the cultural knowledge that influences their behavior throughout their lives. They also are important influences on personality formation. To the extent that children are exposed to similar child-rearing practices, they will tend to develop some common elements of personality.

Societies vary in their child-rearing practices in many ways. Even within a single society, parents and other adults differ in how they teach and otherwise treat children, which is one reason why children develop different personalities. But, overall, there are likely to be some important similarities in how members of a society raise their children, and these child-rearing practices can vary significantly from people to people. Here we can only briefly point out a few of these variations to provide a feeling for some of the various ways children are enculturated in different sociocultural systems.

People in many societies share certain cultural norms about the best way to raise children. For example, members of the same society often agree (roughly) on the proper way to nurse and wean babies, but there is much variability *between* societies in whether people believe that infants should be allowed to nurse whenever they desire or only at certain times of the day. There may also be norms about the proper age of weaning and how it should be accomplished. Reportedly, some Inuit (Eskimo) allowed children to nurse as long as they desired; even ten-year-olds might occasionally be given the breast. Weaning methods likewise vary: some people believe that infants should be allowed to "wean themselves," whereas other mothers coat their nipples with bitter substances to discourage nursing after a certain age.

Norms about disciplining children likewise vary from people to people. In some societies people believe that physical punishment is an integral and necessary part of childhood discipline (as in the saying "spare the rod and spoil the child"). In other societies correcting children's behavior by slapping or beating them is rare. Parents and siblings may cruelly ridicule (by our standards) a child for misbehaving. Or children may be

■ *Age and method of weaning are one important way in which child-rearing practices vary cross-culturally. Most North American mothers wean their children during the first year of life. This four-year-old San child is still given the breast.*

quite indulged until they reach a certain age, after which they are punished severely for their misdeeds. In many Micronesian and Polynesian islands, an infant of either gender is caressed, fondled, played with, and is generally the center of interest of the whole family. Such indulgence and attention continue until a younger sibling is born. Then attention shifts to the newborn, and the child finds herself or himself just another member of a (usually large) family. Prolonged tantrums often result.

In some societies children are threatened by animals, ghosts, spirit beings, and the like (the equivalent of "the boogey man will get if you act like that"). Among the Hopi of the American Southwest, children are threatened by *kachinas*, or masked dancers impersonating spiritual beings whom Hopi believe live in the mountains near their villages (see chapter 15). When a Hopi child seriously misbehaves, parents often get someone to put on a costume (including a frightening mask) of an "ogre" kachina believed to eat children. When the kachina tries to steal the child for misbehaving, the parents come to his or her rescue. Children are so grateful to their parents for saving them that they

■ *Ways of getting children to behave in culturally acceptable ways vary from people to people. This carving of a Hopi ogre* kachina *represents a masked spirit that parents sometimes use to frighten misbehaving children.*

generally accede to their wishes—for a while, anyway. Kachinas also reward "deserving" children by passing out gifts during their dances. Boys are often given a small bow and arrow, whereas girls receive carved wooden figures shaped and painted like the spirits, the kachina doll.

Numerous other differences in child-rearing norms and practices exist between societies. Age and methods of toilet training are diverse. The kind and degree of nurturing vary widely—children are constantly fussed over among one people, left alone more to amuse themselves among others. Youngsters are punished for playing with their genitals in one society but are masturbated by adults in another. Pubescent boys and girls are allowed to associate freely with one another in some societies, but are discouraged or forbidden from doing so in others. Often fathers are hardly involved with their children and in fact are absent much of time, but sometimes men are more or

less equal partners in child care. Caretaking roles vary: in some cases virtually all the care is the responsibility of the mother, but frequently other relatives of the child (e.g., grandparents, uncles, aunts, older siblings) share the duties.

These are only a few of the many ways societies vary in child-rearing norms and practices. Not surprisingly, as a result of these variations, members of different sociocultural systems develop some differences in adult personality. A major question of psychological anthropology is, How are differences in adult personality related to different child-rearing practices? More broadly phrased, How do sociocultural systems affect the personalities of their members?

The answer is not at all simple. Early studies often assumed a one-to-one relationship between personality and sociocultural systems. That is, largely through its child-rearing practices, each sociocultural system was seen as molding the personalities of its members into a certain basic type. It was often believed that "a" culture fashioned the individual personalities of its members into the kinds of persons "it" needed to persist.

The most famous exponent of this approach was Ruth Benedict, whose 1934 book *Patterns of Culture* was enormously influential. Benedict argued that from the vast array of humanly possible cultures, each develops only a limited number of "themes," "patterns," or "configurations" that come to dominate the thinking and responses of its members. These patterns are essentially emotional: each people develop a unique set of feelings and motivations that govern their behavior. Each culture has a conception of an ideal personality type, and these ideals vary from culture to culture (contrast the Yanomamö to the Semai, for instance). Everything about the lifeway of a people reflects and is consistent with the basic pattern of their culture. This meant that the essence of both the culture and the personality of a people could be described in very simple terms—sometimes even by a single word. It also meant that behavior that one people considered crazy or otherwise abnormal would be acceptable, normal, and even ideal among another people.

For instance, Benedict wrote that the Kwakiutl, who live on the Northwest Coast of North America, are individualistic, competitive, intemperate, and egoistic to the point of megalomania. This culture (or is it a personality?) affects Kwakiutl customary behaviors. In aboriginal times they staged ceremonies known as *potlatches* in which one kin group gave away enormous quantities of goods to another. The aim was to shame the rival group, for if it was unable to return the presentations on certain occasions, it suffered a loss of prestige. In fact, to avoid losing prestige, the recipient group was obliged to return gifts of even greater value. Over time, the presentations often snowballed until the members of one group, in their ceaseless quest for prestige, were left destitute (or so Benedict imagined). The whole complex of behavior connected to the potlatch reflects the cultural configuration of the Kwakiutl—so caught up was Kwakiutl culture by the prestige motivation that groups impoverished themselves to achieve this goal. Benedict used the term "Dionysian" to describe the Kwakiutl, after the Greek god known for his excesses.

Benedict contrasted this configuration to the Zuni villagers of the North American Southwest. Zuni control their emotions; they are moderate, modest, stoical, orderly, and restrained in their behavior; they do not boast or attempt to rise above their fellows, but are social and cooperative. This "Apollonian" cultural theme, as Benedict called it, penetrates all of Zuni life. Unlike a Kwakiutl leader, a Zuni man does not seek status; indeed, a leadership role practically has to be forced upon him.

So, according to Benedict, each culture has its unique patterns and themes, which produce images of the ideal personality that vary from culture to culture. One culture's crazed megalomaniac is another culture's ideal person. And culture programs personality more or less completely.

Benedict's approach is not highly regarded today by most psychological anthropologists. Her notion that whole cultures could be described, compared, and contrasted with fairly simple labels that depict their basic emotional patterns is regarded as simplistic. It is invalid to apply single labels to *the* personality type of the members of a sociocultural system, such as that Kwakiutl are Dionysian (given to excesses), whereas the Zuni are Apollonian (moderate in all things). Yet labels comparable to those used by Benedict are common even today. They often take the form of stereotypes that one people have about the "personality" of another. For example, the Japanese are popularly said to have "authoritarian" personalities because they seem to submit to instituted authority more than some other people. Italians are "excitable" to North American perceptions because they seem to be so enthusiastic about love, food, and family and so quick to take offense at slight indiscretions. Similarly, according to

common American stereotypical labels, French are passionate, Irish have bad tempers, Swiss are humorless, Germans are scatological, and Swedes sensual.

In fact, wherever researchers have tried to measure the personality "type" of a people, they have found considerable variability in personality between individuals. Individuals do not share the same personality just because they belong to the same sociocultural system and have experienced similar child-rearing practices and other influences. There is always variability. The best we can do is to identify and describe the **modal personality** of a people, meaning those elements of personality that many or most members of a sociocultural system share, or the type of personality that is most common.

Keeping in mind this variability, there do seem to be some interrelationships between child-rearing practices and modal personality. Here we illustrate these studies by describing one finding, and it is suggestive rather than definitive, like other analyses you have encountered in this book.

On the island of Timor in eastern Indonesia live a people known as the Alor. The Alorese were studied in the 1930s by Cora DuBois, who gave them psychological tests and had the tests interpreted by several psychologists when she returned from the field. The Alorese get most of their food by gardening. Women are responsible for most food production. When a woman gives birth, she devotes most of her attention for several weeks to her newborn, nursing the baby whenever he or she cries and generally nurturing the infant. After only two or three weeks, the mother returns to work almost daily in the family gardens. From early morning until late afternoon the child is left with his or her grandparents, siblings, or other relatives. An Alorese father is often absent, engaged in the borrowing and lending of pigs and other wealth objects that are so important to these people.

During the long hours his or her mother is away, the infant is not suckled, although attempts are made by caretakers to give it premasticated foods to quiet its crying. As the child matures, his or her emotional demands are met only irregularly and by a variety of individuals. Children are not often caressed or praised, and they are frequently teased and lied to. Their demands for attention are often ignored by their caretakers. Weaning is accomplished by pushing the child away from the breast; sometimes a recently weaned child is deliberately provoked by nursing another child, for adults find the child's reaction humorous. All in all, the

Alorese child lives in an uncertain, insecure, and to some degree hostile social environment.

As a result of these childhood experiences, many Alorese develop a personality described as suspicious, antagonistic, uncooperative, prone to violent outbursts of jealousy, and lacking in self-confidence and social responsibility. These features of Alorese modal personality affect adult interpersonal relationships. Relations between husbands and wives, for instance, generally lack intimacy and often are downright hostile.

The Alorese case study suggests that the modal personality of a people is significantly affected by the degree to which parents and other caretakers reject or nurture children. How can we know whether this same relationship between a relatively low degree of nurturing and modal personality type applies elsewhere? And how do we know whether it is the relative neglect of children, rather than some other child-rearing practice, that produces a personality type like that of many Alorese?

One way to investigate such questions is with cross-cultural methods. For a variety of societies we can study their child-rearing practices with respect to the degree of parental and caretaker nurturing they receive and see whether rejection/nurturing tends to have similar effects on modal personality among them. Ronald Rohner has conducted such a study. He found that, generally, parental neglect and lack of affection do produce certain similarities in modal personality: people who experience rejection and neglect in childhood tend to develop personality traits such as hostility, low self-esteem, and emotional instability.

Child-rearing practices seem to be the major link between a sociocultural system and the personalities its members are most likely to develop. The sociocultural system influences how adults raise their children, and child-rearing practices in turn influence modal personality. The Alorese case illustrates how these influences might operate in one society, and many comparative studies like those of Rohner suggest that the same influences might produce the same kind of modal personalities generally.

■ Sociocultural Consequences of Personality Type

So far, we have considered only how modal personality is affected by the sociocultural system of a people. We have ignored the possible effects of personality on the sociocultural system. There is another approach that

tries to describe how personalities and sociocultural systems might *mutually* affect one another. Essentially, it proposes that certain subsystems of a sociocultural system have greater impact on child-rearing practices than other subsystems; that is, some aspects of a lifeway affect the kinds of personalities individuals develop more than other aspects. In turn, because many individuals share certain elements of their personality, they tend to relate in certain patterned ways to other individuals, and they tend to find certain kinds of behaviors and ideas more attractive than others. Modal personality therefore influences other subsystems of the sociocultural system.

According to this approach, then, for purposes of relating sociocultural elements to personality, we divide a sociocultural system into two parts: (1) those subsystems that importantly affect child rearing and hence influence the kind of personality many or most individuals develop and (2) those subsystems that are partly determined by this modal personality.

What about a people's way of life is most likely to have important effects on their child-rearing practices? Again, there is no simple answer. For instance, most people in a society may share ideas about the proper way to bring up children, and these shared ideas about upbringing affect the kind of modal personality that develops.

But some scholars believe it is possible to say more than that "it all depends on people's ideas." We can say more because child-rearing *practices* are affected by more than people's *ideas* about the proper way to raise children—ideas constrain child-rearing practices, but they do not determine them. In Alor, for example, the sexual division of labor leads mothers to abandon their infants for many hours a day, forcing other relatives to assume the caretaking role. In modern North America employed mothers leave their children with babysitters or in day-care centers. Alorese or North American mothers may believe they ought to spend more time with their children, but economic conditions as well as their ideas constrain their child-rearing behavior, and they have other values and motives that conflict with their desire to bring up their children the way they think they "ought to."

John Whiting and Irvin Child have developed the Social Systems Model, which suggests a relationship between the modal personality and the sociocultural system of a people. It is diagrammed in Figure 16.1.

The *maintenance system* is, essentially, those specific elements of human lifeways we have discussed in chapters 7 through 14. It includes how people acquire

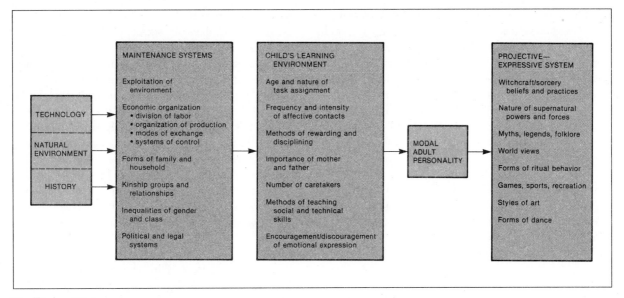

■ *Figure 16.1*
The Social Systems Model

Adapted from "A Model for Psychocultural Research," by John Whiting in *Culture and Infancy*, P. Herbert Leiderman, Steven R. Tulkin, and Anne Rosenfeld, eds. Orlando, Fla.: Academic Press, 1977. Reprinted by permission.

energy and materials from their environment; the organization of production, exchange, and control over resources; the prevalent forms of family and domestic groups; the kinds and sizes of kin groups and the strength and breadth of kinship relations; prevalent inequalities in access to resources and to social rewards; and the organization of political life, legal systems, and warfare. A maintenance system, in short, consists of a people's basic adaptation to nature and how their society is organized to persist, cooperate, allocate rewards, defend itself, and maintain internal order. It is influenced by technology, natural environment, and historical forces.

The maintenance system affects child-rearing practices and the overall learning environment of children: how soon they are made to take on household chores, how and how much they are punished or rewarded, how children interact with their caretakers, and so on. The kinds of personality children develop in turn depends on the total learning environment to which they are exposed, as the Alorese example shows. To the extent that most or many children experience the same learning environment, they will tend to develop similarities in personality as adults, which we have called the *modal personality.*

But the Social Systems Model suggests how modal personality influences a sociocultural system as well as

being influenced by it. Because so many individuals develop similar personalities, they tend to find certain kinds of activities and ideas about the world more attractive (or congenial) than others. For example, they are likely to attribute certain qualities to super-

■ *In the Social Systems Model, the maintenance system affects modal personality. This Burkina-Faso woman keeps her child with her while working. If many of her tasks were incompatible with childcare, her child might be left with other caretakers or be more neglected, and this might affect his or her adult personality.*

natural beings and forces; to find some kinds of games, art styles, and stories more enjoyable to play, view, and hear than others; and to find some kinds of rituals and ceremonies more meaningful than others. Sociocultural elements that are strongly influenced by modal personality are called the *projective-expressive system.*

The Social Systems Model does not "explain" how modal personality types and sociocultural systems are related; rather, it directs our attention to the sociocultural factors that are likely to be most important in the formation of modal personality. It distinguishes these from sociocultural factors that are likely to be strongly influenced by modal personality. It therefore is a useful way to conceptualize the relationship between personality and the sociocultural system.

Age Categories

In all societies, an individual's age makes a difference in the kinds of roles he or she adopts and in the activities he or she performs. Although chronological age is a biological fact, societies vary in how age influences the kinds of statuses and roles people hold. Everywhere, individuals are culturally classified on the basis of their age: infant, child, adult, elderly person, and so forth. People of similar age are often allocated the same kinds of roles. Although all peoples have such age categories, societies vary in the number of categories, the sharpness with which they are defined, their importance relative to other distinctions such as gender and class, and the roles members of the category are expected to adopt.

Like other people, Westerners classify people on the basis of their age. In the United States, we make subdivisions of age categories as needed by the context (e.g., the age category "child" may be divided into infant, toddler, preschooler, first grader, and so on). Many other societies establish more formal and highly organized groups of individuals of similar age, and these age groupings assume quite definite and important rights in and duties to the society as a whole. One such grouping common in the preindustrial world is the *age set association.*

An **age set association** is a permanent, formally organized, named group of males or females, the members of which are recruited on the basis of similar age. It is more common for males to be organized into age sets, although some societies have such organiza-

tions for both males and females. Because age sets include all members of a society of a particular sex and age cohort, they cut across kinship lines and often serve as pantribal sodalities (chapter 13). In many societies age sets take over many functions usually assigned to kin groups and frequently surpass the kin group in relative importance for the individual. If a society has age sets, people usually enter them about or a little after the time they reach sexual maturity. Age sets are found among peoples in North and South America, Melanesia, and Asia. They are especially common in Africa; about 75 percent of all peoples with age sets are African peoples. There are two distinct types of age sets: *cyclical age sets* and *lineal age sets.*

Societies with *cyclical age sets* have a limited number of named associations. Although the same individuals continue to associate with one another throughout their lives, the members move as a group from one association to another in rank or age order. The Hidatsa of the Great Plains are an example of this type of system. Periodically, about every four to six years, all adolescent Hidatsa boys banded together. With the help of their parents they purchased the lowest ranking of the ten age set associations from the members of that association. This lowest-ranking association was called the *Kit-Foxes.* The purchase of the age set gave the new members the sole rights to wear the insignias of this group, as well as to perform its dances and songs. In addition, many rights and duties of the individual members were defined by the association of which they were members. After they themselves sold the lowest-ranking age set, the former members of the Kit-Foxes purchased the rights and privileges of the next highest association, and within a short period all the groups had moved up a step to the next age set. The few surviving old men in the highest-ranking association withdrew from the system after selling their age set, for there was no higher place for them to go within the system. Among the Hidatsa age sets were primarily men's social clubs with limited economic and political significance. However, among the Cheyenne and other Great Plains peoples, these organizations frequently filled the role of camp police.

Lineal age sets offer a contrast. In a lineal age-set system an individual remains a member of the same association throughout his or her life. The Swazi of southern Africa provide an example of lineal age sets. Every five to seven years the king of the Swazi announced that a new age set would be created to include all the adolescent boys in the kingdom. This announcement coincided with the proclamation that the members of what had up to then been the youngest set were now free to marry. The role of the youngest set was to serve as active warriors and thus its members could not be married. Many of them moved to barracks near the royal family, and even those who remained in their home communities were organized into military units. Every association had its own leaders and insignias, and a man belonged to the same age set for his entire life. All sets participated in wars, each as a separate and distinct military unit. Indeed, after English contact age sets were commonly called regiments.

Loyalty was fostered between the members of a given Swazi age set. Whether they were living in a royal barracks or at home, the members of a particular set were expected to work together. All members were equals who ate, worked, and smoked together. They used the terms *brother* or *age mate* in referring to each other. Some anthropologists have argued that age set ties were stronger than kinship ties, and that a man's identity became more closely linked with his age set than his family. Rivalries between age sets were intense, and occasionally fighting broke out between members of different sets, which pitted close relatives against each other.

Age sets illustrate how different sociocultural systems use the principle of age differently to allocate statuses and roles to individuals and even to place them into groups. In a sense, age sets represent one extreme in the use of age as a principle of recruitment—age differences are sharply (although partly culturally) defined, and they become the organizational basis of many cooperative activities. One African people, the Nyakyusa, even used age together with sex to establish residence. Male members of the same age set lived in the same age-based village, bringing their wives to live with them.

Why do some societies have age sets, whereas most do not? Age sets are most commonly found among peoples who lack a centralized political system, yet are frequently engaged in warfare. This correlation has led some anthropologists to suggest that age sets are a means of organizing males for warfare among people who lack formal political leadership and specialized armies. The problem with this explanation is that very often neighboring peoples with equally decentralized political systems and equal frequencies of warfare do not have age sets. Thus these two factors alone cannot explain the presence or absence of age sets, so some other sociocultural factors must also be involved that we have yet to identify.

The Life Cycle

The birth, childhood, physical/sexual maturation, marriage, adulthood, old age, and death of an individual constitute his or her **life cycle.** Each stage in the life cycle carries certain cultural expectations; and as individuals move through these stages, their overall status and role in society change. All societies recognize at least three major distinctions in the life cycle: childhood, adulthood, and old age. These stages serve as a convenient way to organize our discussion of the life cycle, but it is important to recognize that peoples vary in how they conceive of these stages and in how transitions from one to the other are recognized and marked.

Transitions between stages may take place gradually and not be the object of any particular notice, or they may be sharply and formally defined by a rite of passage. A **rite of passage** is a public ceremony or ritual that marks a change in status, usually but not always brought about or related to increasing age. Examples of rites of passage in North America include baptism, graduation ceremonies, weddings, and funerals.

■ *Childhood*

One might think that childhood obviously begins at birth. Actually, the issue is more complex. Like all phases of the life cycle, "child" is a culturally defined category of person as well as a physical state. Childhood may be said to commence only when an individual is accorded "human" or "membership" status within some society, and the time when this happens varies from people to people. Is one given human status at the time of conception, at some period during the mother's pregnancy, at birth, or sometime after birth? As we discussed in chapter 13, all societies have legal systems, which are partly concerned with protecting the individual rights of the members of the society. Societies differ in how and when such rights are conferred on an individual, so the time when childhood begins may be said to vary.

In our own society this question has not been resolved. Members of Right to Life (antiabortion) groups believe that human life, and thus legal protection, begins at the time of conception. From their perspective, abortions constitute murder of a human being. Data from other societies concerning this question reveals a similar lack of consensus. As discussed in Box 13.1, the Cheyenne considered the murder of one Cheyenne by another as the most serious of crimes, and they categorized a woman who had an abortion as a murderer. In contrast, in many societies even birth itself does not automatically convey human status. Infanticide (the killing of infants) has been a widespread practice. Among the Canadian Eskimo, a child, particularly a female child born during the winter, could be placed outside immediately after birth to die of exposure. No stigma was attached to such an act. In ancient Greece, even in Athens itself, parents of sickly or unwanted newborn babies could abandon them along the road to die. Any passerby was free to adopt such an infant or to raise it as a slave to be sold, as in the famous story of Oedipus, the Greek king who unknowingly married his mother. In preindustrial societies with a high infant-mortality rate, the conferring of full human status is sometimes delayed until the period of infancy has passed; thus, the responsibility for providing formal burials for the large numbers of children who die in infancy is avoided. Even in societies in which infanticide is not practiced, the bestowal of full human status is frequently delayed for some period following the birth of a child.

The formal naming of a child is frequently associated with the conferring of human status and is often the first rite of passage. For the Osage, a Native American people whose political organization we discussed in chapter 13, the naming rite was the most important rite of passage: it fully bestowed human status on the individual. Osage parents often waited several months—in the case of a sickly child, possibly over a year—before naming a child. If the child died before acquiring a name, he or she was quietly buried, and the family did not have to observe a year of mourning. After they were convinced that the infant was going to survive, parents began to prepare for a naming ritual. A ritual specialist called a *non-hon-zhinga* (or "little-old-man") from the child's father's clan was chosen leader to organize and direct the ceremony. Little-old-men representing all twenty-four Osage patrilineal clans gathered in the "lodge of mystery," a ritual structure in the village, to hold the ceremony. One at a time the leader gave a trade blanket to all of the little-old-men, each of whom recited a long and complex ritual prayer asking *Wa-kon-tah's* (god's) bless-

ing for the child and outlining the supernatural powers associated with his particular clan. After all twenty-four clan prayers had been recited, the child was handed to each of the little-old-men, who in turn blessed the child. Some anointed the baby with water, others rubbed the child with cedar or touched the child with ground corn. Then the baby was seated on a specially prepared robe in the center of the lodge and given a name belonging to his or her clan by the leader. The giving of this name symbolized the acceptance of the child as a member of a particular clan. The ritual participation of members of the other twenty-three clans indicated the acceptance of the child as an Osage. The ritual ended with the father of the child giving horses and blankets to the main little-old-men and lesser gifts to the other little-old-men. Only after the naming ritual might one say that Osage childhood truly began.

As we discussed earlier in this chapter, childhood is the stage in the life cycle during which the basic elements of the individual's personality are formed and basic norms and values are internalized. It is also a time of socially learning the linguistic, social, and technical skills that will be used later in life. Much social learning comes from the observation and imitation of the behavior of parents, older siblings, grandparents, neighbors, and other members of the community. Other moral lessons are communicated orally, through stories and legends that illustrate the proper behavior and values of the group.

Childhood is also the period when individuals begin acquiring the technical skills they will use in adult life. In most societies the learning of technical skills begins early by our standards, by about the age of five or six years. Simple tasks not demanding great strength are done even earlier—three-year-olds may sweep the house, feed the animals, wash the baby, pick up the yard, run errands, deliver messages, and so forth. In more complex societies, much technical learning takes the form of formal education in schools, where children are instructed by trained specialists. In less complex societies children learn most skills informally by watching and imitating adults and following their instructions. Boys begin spending more time with their fathers and other male relatives, who instruct them in skills and knowledge they will need as men. Among cultivators, children begin going to the fields with their parents and performing minor tasks that are suited to their physical abilities. In herding societies children begin caring for the herds at a young age. For example,

■ *Games help children learn the technical, physical, and social skills of their society.*

among the Navajo, six- and seven-year-old boys and girls begin helping with the herds of sheep and goats. While Navajo boys learn the technical skills needed by males, girls learn the skills of women by imitating their mothers and playing with toy animals. As they become older, they help their mothers by preparing wool for weaving, preparing foods, making clothing, and caring for their younger brothers and sisters.

■ *Becoming an Adult*

An individual usually reaches puberty (sexual maturation) between the ages of about twelve and fifteen. Female sexual maturation is indicated by the menarche, or first menstruation. With boys the physical indicators develop more gradually: increase in body hair, change in voice, development of musculature, and so forth. The onset of sexual maturation necessitates a change in the status of an individual. The biological fact that such individuals are now capable of producing children often means that they bear greater social responsibility. At the same time, however, in some societies these sexually mature individuals are not yet considered fully adult. For example, while a thirteen- or fourteen-year-old boy may be sexually capable of fathering a child, he still usually lacks the strength and stamina, as well as the mastery of technical and social skills, needed to assume the full economic and social responsibilities required of a husband and parent. Sexual maturation precedes full social and physical maturity, and this intermediate period of transition from childhood to adulthood is called *adolescence.*

Adolescence may be a troubled period in the life of an individual. In American society adolescence has been characterized as filled with tension, conflict, rebellion against parents, and extreme moodiness. Some researchers attribute the problems that arise during this period primarily to physiological changes, but others consider sociocultural factors to be the major causes. In the 1920s Margaret Mead examined the question of adolescence in her classic study *Coming of Age in Samoa.* Mead found that adolescence was not a particularly traumatic time in the life of Samoan girls, and she argued that the problems associated with adolescence were the result of sociocultural factors, not physiological changes. In 1983 Derek Freeman challenged Mead's Samoa findings in his book *Margaret Mead in Samoa,* arguing that Samoan adolescents have about as much trouble and conflict as do American teenagers. He went on to suggest that the physiological changes that occur during adolescence have similar effects among all peoples, so this stage of the life cycle is always stressful despite the sociocultural context. Most modern anthropologists would probably contend that the universal physiological changes do create problems for adolescents everywhere, but that these problems are manifested in a variety of ways depending on the sociocultural context.

Not only are there physical changes and the associated intensification of sexual urges, but changes in expected behavior also occur during adolescence. However, although adolescents take on many of the social and legal responsibilities of adulthood, they are not accorded the full prerogatives of adults. For example, in the United States adolescents frequently can be tried and sentenced in an adult court for a criminal offense yet cannot vote in local, state, or national elections; purchase liquor; marry without parental consent; or get a bank loan without a cosigner. Until the voting age was lowered to eighteen in 1971, a male could be drafted into the army before he could vote. Thus in the United States an adolescent has some of the legal obligations of an adult, but still lacks full adult privileges. There are similar disparities in many other societies as well. Among the Cheyenne, older adolescent boys were expected to join war parties and to be daring and aggressive warriors and raiders. Along with adult males they were expected to take part in hunts and help supply food for their family. At the same time they could not hold an official position within the tribe and had to remain silent in the presence of the elders of the tribe.

■ Initiation Rites

The manner in which individuals are incorporated into adulthood and into adult rights and responsibilities varies from people to people. In the United States, the transition to the adult stage of life is marked by rites of passage we call graduation ceremonies (from high school or college): one leaves the status of "student" and (we hope!) becomes an independent, wage-earning adult. In preindustrial societies, the transition from childhood to adulthood is frequently marked by an elaborate set of ceremonies known as **initiation rites.**

Initiation rites often occur around puberty, so they are sometimes called *puberty rites,* although it is important to note that they do far more than simply mark off an individual's sexual maturation. During many rituals, the initiates are educated in the intricate responsibilities of adulthood, being told of the changes that will from then on be expected in their behavior, and often being let in on ritual secrets.

Some societies have initiation rituals for males only, others for females only, and still others for both sexes. But even those societies that hold initiation rites for both males and females almost always have separate ceremonies for each sex. This generalization suggests that an important function of initiation rituals is to incorporate children not just into adulthood, but also into the adult roles and responsibilities culturally appropriate for their gender. In fact, the most common theme of initiation rituals is to make girls into women and boys into men.

Some of the most interesting forms of male initiation rituals occur in the highlands of New Guinea. Before describing them, we must point out that in many of these societies (and there are many hundreds of them) people believe that females can pollute males. Above all else, men fear contact with women's menstrual discharges, which they believe can cause them to sicken and die. Ethnographer Mervyn Meggitt (1970) describes the beliefs of one New Guinea people, called the *Enga,* about women's pollution:

Men regard menstrual blood as truly dangerous. They believe that contact with it or a menstruating woman will, in the absence of counter-magic, sicken a man and cause persistent vomiting, turn his blood black, corrupt his vital juices so that his skin darkens and wrinkles as his flesh wastes, permanently dull his wits, and eventually lead to a slow decline and death. Menstrual blood introduced into a man's food, they say, quickly kills him, and young women crossed in love sometimes seek their revenge in this way. Menstrual blood dropped on the bog-iris plants . . . that men use in wealth-, pig-, and war-magic destroys them; and a man would divorce, and perhaps kill, the wife concerned. (p. 129)

Because of these beliefs that their menstrual discharges are dangerous to their husbands and to other men, among many New Guinea peoples women must remain in seclusion during their periods, either in a menstrual hut away from the main settlement or in a special place in their houses, which men never enter. An Enga woman may do garden work during her period, but only in gardens containing "female crops"; should she enter any garden containing "male crops" such as taro and sugar cane, the crops would die.

These beliefs about feminine contamination have many implications for women's lives. Women must take precautions to avoid accidentally causing injury to their husbands by polluting the food they serve to their husbands. In some New Guinea societies, women must travel on separate paths from men, lest a man unknowingly step on a female secretion and become polluted. A wife is sometimes believed to "murder" her husband by introducing her bodily fluids into his food; occasionally a woman is killed in retaliation if her husband dies suspiciously. Women have to suffer through having their young sons taken away from them by force, for according to beliefs the sons are endangered by continued association with their mothers once they reach a certain age.

Finally, it is common in these societies for husbands and wives to live in separate dwellings. A man's wife or wives has her own house, where she lives with her children. Her husband lives in a separate men's house, together with all the older boys and men of the hamlet or village. By the time they are around ten years old, boys are usually taken away from their mothers—for even contact with one's own mother is dangerous for a boy—and brought to live in the men's house. Male initiation rituals usually begin when a boy is dissociated from the company of his mother and other women and inducted into the men's house.

The details of male initiation vary from people to people in New Guinea. One common goal or cultural rationale of the rituals is to transform a boy into a man: boys do not grow up naturally, but must go through a lengthy series of rituals to give them masculine qualities. Masculine courage, strength, aggressiveness, and independence are desirable not only for the boys themselves but are needed by the group as a whole, for most New Guinea peoples traditionally were heavily involved in warfare with their neighbors and so needed warriors to survive. Another goal of the rituals is to protect boys from feminine contamination: initiates learn ritual procedures that will allow them to have sexual relations in relative safety.

The Awa, a New Guinea people numbering about 1,500 who were studied by Philip Newman and David Boyd, illustrate both themes: "maturation" and "protection." Like many of their neighbors, Awa men believe that if female substances penetrate male bodies, the men will become sick or old before their time—or even pregnant! Beginning in their early teens, boys go through a series of rituals that have five stages and last well into their adult years. When several boys in a region have reached the appropriate age of twelve to fourteen, they are taken from their mothers' houses. They are inducted as a group into the men's house during an intimidating ritual involving food and water restrictions, beating with stinging nettles to toughen them, and rubbing the inside of their thighs with a coarse vine. This is the first stage of their initiation.

In the second stage, about one year later, the boys experience the first cleansing of their bodies from female pollution. At a secluded site in the forest they are forceably bled and made to vomit. The purpose of these acts is to protect their general well-being and promote their physiological maturity by removing female substances from the boys' bodies. Small bundles of sharp-edged swordgrass are jabbed into their nostrils and two small cuts are made in the glans of their penises to bleed out contamination. A vine is looped and thrust down their throats, inducing the vomiting that also cleanses and helps dry out their bodies—for the Awa believe that dessication is necessary for boys to achieve maturity.

The third ritual stage occurs when the males are between eighteen and twenty. They again are purged of female contamination by nose bleeding, penis cutting, and induced vomiting. They also are let in on certain ritual knowledge, known to all adult men but kept secret from women and boys. After they have been through the third stage, the young men are taught why too much contact with women is so dangerous. They learn how menstrual pollution can overstimulate their growth and age them prematurely, and how it is possible for a man to become pregnant. Because they have not yet learned to protect themselves from female substances, they are warned to avoid sexual intercourse altogether until they are married.

About five years later, when the men are in their midtwenties, they go through the "sweat ceremony," which is the fourth stage of initiation. They sit together next to the fire in the men's house and sweat profusely for a week or more. The older men lecture to them about their upcoming responsibilities as husbands and fathers. They are told about how to protect themselves from the dangers of sexual intercourse and are emphatically warned about the evils of adultery. When the men emerge from the men's house after the sweat ceremony, they receive new clothes and body ornaments, including a pair of boar's tusks which they wear in their pierced noses as a symbol of their adult status. After this stage, young women chosen as brides are brought to the hamlet of their future husbands.

The fifth stage—appropriately called the "severe penis cutting"—occurs only a few days later. The young men are again subjected to food and water taboos, to nosebleeding and vomiting, and to penis

■ *Beginning in their early teens, Awa boys participate in a lengthy series of rituals intended to strengthen, protect, and instruct them. This second-stage initiate is having his nose bled to remove harmful female substances from his body.*

cutting. This time, however, canes are driven deep into their noses to cause severe bleeding. Small wedges of flesh are cut from either side of their penises, producing deep gashes in the glans. In fact, at the final stage of initiation, all the adult men present line up and expose their penises to puncture wounds made by tiny stone-tipped arrows. This treatment is held to be necessary periodically to remove harmful female substances that have entered the body through the penis during sexual intercourse. In Awa beliefs, a married man may become pregnant if he has sex too often, has intercourse with a menstruating woman, or penetrates the vagina too deeply causing his penis to contact the blood and water contained in the womb. Womb blood moves up into the man's body and can make him pregnant. He therefore must have the female blood removed by being shot with miniature arrows, which will halt the pregnancy. Once a man has been through the fifth stage, Awa believe that he has been sufficiently strengthened by the hardships of initiation that he is capable of withstanding feminine pollution, although he must continue to undergo ritual bloodletting to maintain his strength and to fight the dangers of male pregnancy.

The Awa illustrate several themes common in male initiation rituals: inducing physical maturation, strengthening and protecting, imparting secret knowledge, and learning the importance of masculine responsibilities. Awa initiation also exemplifies another practice, common not just in New Guinea but around the world: the rituals are almost always painful and traumatic to the boys. They frequently involve scarification, beatings, genital mutilation, tattooing, intimidation by threats and frightful stories, social seclusion, fasting, going without water, and so forth. Usually, these pains and traumas are considered to be necessary to strengthen the boys and prepare them for the rigors of adulthood (see Box 16.1 for one mildly comparable ritual in the United States). Certainly, such ordeals indelibly mark the transition from boy to man in the minds and usually the bodies of the males.

Perhaps the most unusual of all male initiations are found among the Sambia, a New Guinea people of about 2,400 who were studied by Gilbert Herdt. Like the Enga, Awa, and many other peoples of New Guinea, Sambia men fear feminine pollution, especially that associated with female genitalia and menstruation. Males over the age of about ten accordingly live in the men's house and women have to travel on separate trails and retire to menstrual huts during their

■ *Pain and physical mutilation are frequent aspects of male puberty rites. Not only was this Nuer man circumcised, but the six scars across his forehead are the result of deep cuts made during his initiation.*

periods. Like the Awa, Sambia males practice nose-bleeding to rid their bodies of female contaminants.

The Sambia live from horticulture, hunting, and some pig herding. But coping with their human environment, not their natural surroundings, is their main adaptive problem (or was until "tribal" warfare was outlawed by the government). Surrounded by enemies and heavily involved in warfare, the men of a Sambia hamlet have to be constantly prepared to defend their settlement from attack. Their culture therefore places a heavy value on male "strength," meaning in the Sambia context prowess as a warrior, bravery, mental toughness, and spiritual potency. According to Sambia beliefs, a man acquires the strength that is so important in making him a man of consequence, as well as in defending the hamlet, from only one thing: semen. Semen is what hardens a man's muscles, gives him fortitude, makes him fierce in battle, and renders him domineering and aggressive. In short, semen makes men *masculine.*

In the Sambia world view, girls grow up naturally: they develop breasts, reach menarche, and are able to

Box 16.1

LIMINALITY AND BECOMING A SOLDIER

The late anthropologist Victor Turner pioneered the modern study of rites of passage. In his study of initiation rites among the Ndembu of Zambia, Turner noted that the rites have three phases: separation, liminality, and incorporation. These phases correspond to the basic nature of rites of passage: individuals who go through them are separated from their former statuses in society, go through a transition ("liminal") period during which they are "betwixt and between" normal statuses and social categories, and finally are reincorporated into society as a new person with new rights and obligations.

These phases are seen clearly in common cultural themes and behaviors involved in male initiation rituals among numerous peoples. Often the boys are forcibly removed from their homes, a frequent practice being to separate them from the company of women (especially their mothers, who sometimes are expected to mourn as if their sons had died) so they can become real men. The boys are often secluded during the rituals and subjected to tests of their ability to endure pain without crying out. They may have to fast or go without drink for days. Nearly always, some painful operations are performed on their genitals; they may be circumcised or have their penises mutilated in other ways. Scarification of face and body is common, for it is a visible symbol that a male has gone through the proceedings and is entitled to the privileges of manhood. Although sometimes the proceedings last for years, the initiates may have to refrain from eating certain foods or from coming into contact with females or female things, for the period of transition into manhood is regarded as a dangerous time. A simple social structure characterizes the liminal period: the initiates are equal in status and utterly subordinate to the control of the men who are in charge of the proceedings. Typically, the boys are stripped of all possessions, their faces or bodies are painted in an identical way, they are dressed alike, and their heads are shaven, all to make them look alike and to emphasize their common identity.

Modern folk also have rites of passage that serve similar functions: births, graduations, marriages, and deaths are generally marked by some kind of public ceremony signifying the social transitions involved. Baptisms, betrothals, promotions, installations of new public officials, birthdays, and many other ceremonial gatherings also are rites of passage.

But one of our most interesting rites of passage—because of its similarity to the initiation rituals just discussed—is entering military service. Many of the behaviors involved in entering the military are reminiscent of puberty rites.

Basic training is a liminal period—recruits have been separated from civilian life but have not acquired the secret knowledge and skills needed to become a soldier. Recruits are stripped of possessions, their hair is cut, they are issued identical uniforms, they are secluded from most contact with the outside, they all have identical (low) rank that requires complete subordination to sergeants and superior officers, they must undergo arduous trials and perform daring physical feats (such as getting up before sunrise), and they live in a common barracks where they have identical sleeping and eating facilities. In the military, too, the aim is to grind down a boy so that he can be rebuilt into a man (as the Marines used to say). Masculine qualities of courage, toughness, dedication, discipline, and determination are supposed to be instilled. When the recruit has successfully completed his training, he is incorporated into a new group, the military, and acquires a new status (rank and job).

We should not carry the analogy too far—recruits are not operated on (but note that voluntary tattooing used to be fairly common), nor is it necessary for a boy to enter the military to be a real man (although many men who were not in the military are looked down upon by many of those who were). Still, the similarities are striking enough for us once again to see our common humanity with preindustrial peoples. Their behaviors and beliefs may seem strange to us, but often we engage in similar activities that only seem perfectly natural because we are used to them. ■

have babies with no human or supernatural intervention. Little boys, however—who are weak and unmanly because they lack semen—will not grow up unless they undergo a series of initiation rituals. The intention of the rituals is therefore to "masculinize" the boys (in Herdt's words). Because no boy will become a man unless he passes through the six stages of the ritual, all boys are forced to participate.

Sambia initiations are so unusual because of one of their beliefs: although males are born with a repository for semen (a "semen sack") inside their bodies, the male body cannot manufacture semen. The semen sack will remain empty and the boy will never be masculinized unless it is filled up. Filling up the sack of the young boys is what the early stages of the rituals do. During the first stage (ages about seven to ten) and the second stage (ages about eleven to fourteen), the boys perform fellatio on young but sexually mature bachelors and swallow the semen. Swallowing the semen (no anal intercourse occurs) during this *ritualized homosexuality* is the action that begins the masculinization of the boys. During the actual ritual proceedings, which last several days, the boys live together in a forest culthouse, ingesting semen from bachelors (who, of course, have been through the first two initiation stages and so have received their supply of semen, which they are now duty-bound to share).

The boys also are forced to endure nosebleeding. Elders ram sharp cane grasses into their nostrils to release the pollution the young boys have acquired during their years of association with their mothers and other women. The ritual nosebleeding occurs in later stages of the rituals as well, for masculinization requires ridding the body of feminine substances.

Later, during the fourth stage, a man in his late teens or early twenties marries a young girl who has not yet reached sexual maturity. Until she reaches menarche, he does not live with his young wife, but stays in the men's house and continues to donate semen to first- and second-stage initiates. The fifth stage occurs when a man's wife has her first period and goes into menstrual seclusion. Only then, when the man is in his early twenties, does he engage in heterosexual intercourse. In fact, the main goal of the fifth-stage rituals is to teach the man to protect himself from feminine pollution by learning to ritually bleed his own nose. This technique makes it possible for him to minimize the dangers of intercourse with a woman. However, he still engages in homosexual relations in the men's house, and hence is in effect bisexual.

During the fifth stage, then, a man may have sex with his wife. It is likely to be his first heterosexual experience. As mentioned, a man cannot make more semen for himself, and ejaculation will deplete his supply and reduce his masculinity. (Interestingly, sex with a woman is seen as depleting a man's semen much more than homosexual fellatio.) But, it turns out, there is an alternative way for a man to replace his semen. During the fifth stage, he is told of the existence of a certain tree that exudes a milky semen-like sap, hitherto kept secret from him. He learns that by drinking the sap of this tree he can replace the semen that he loses from intercourse. Throughout the rest of his life, he will drink this substance so that he can retain his masculinity even while engaging in sex.

Homosexuality continues in the men's house, even when the formal rituals are not in process. But it is important to realize that homosexual acts are part of a ritual process—the process of masculinization, which can only be achieved by imparting semen. Once masculinization is complete, once a man has fulfilled his obligation to masculinize boys, and once he has learned how to have sex with women without harming himself or reducing his masculinity, homosexuality should end. Its end is marked by the sixth stage of the ritual, which occurs when the man's wife has their first child. The husband moves out of the men's house and in with his wife, and the homosexual and bisexual period of his life is over. Men who continue homosexual relations after going through the sixth and final stage are looked down upon.

Aside from the fact that they illustrate one of the most unusual ways in which boys are made into men through initiation rituals, it is interesting to contrast Sambia notions of homosexuality with our own. Many of us see gay man as the antithesis of masculinity, whereas the Sambia view homosexual relationships as essential in producing men who are quintessentially masculine. Also, we tend to view homosexuality as something a person either "is" or "is not", whereas the Sambia view it as a role that men either "do" or "do not" perform at certain times in their lives. Finally, we tend to see homosexuality as unnatural and even sinful, whereas the Sambia view it as an essential part of growing up and its practice as one of a man's duties to others in his group.

Initiation rites for females are not as common as those for males, but similar themes are apparent where they occur: an emphasis on maturation, instruction in sexuality, reminders of a woman's duties as a wife and

■ *These two Apache girls are being initiated.*

ture socially and physically to assume the responsibilities required of spouses and parents of children. Thus, marriage in most societies is marked ceremonially with a rite of passage—a wedding. Women marry shortly after puberty in many societies, at twelve to fifteen years of age, whereas males in the same societies usually do not marry until their early twenties, or even later in many polygynous societies. This difference in age at marriage means that males usually experience a considerably longer period of adolescence than females.

The importance of marrying and having a family has lessened in Western industrialized societies. In most preindustrial societies, however, the eventual marriage of every individual is expected, and there are relatively few spinsters and bachelors. Why should marriage be so

mother, and so forth. There is a parallel to circumcision among males, known as *cliterectomy,* in which a woman's clitoris is removed. The female also is commonly harassed and frightened during her initiation.

When a girl among the Tucuna Indians of the Amazon has her first menstruation, she is immediately placed in the loft of the large communal dwelling where she lives. She remains there until a special seclusion room next to the dwelling is constructed for her. She stays isolated in this room while preparations for her puberty rite are made. During this period, the older women tell her about the danger from various spirits to which she as a woman is now subject, and they also inform her of what will be expected from her as a wife and mother. The ritual itself involves the presence of forty to fifty masked dancers who imitate spirits that both terrify and instruct her. Toward the end of the ceremony the girl is placed on a tapir hide in the middle of the house, and a group of elderly women slowly pull all of the hair out of her head to the sound of a drum and rattle. The girl has to endure this pain without crying out. Although the Tucuna have an elaborate puberty rite for females, they have no such rite for males.

■ *Adulthood*

At what point is an individual considered an adult? In most societies adult status is assumed with marriage. When people marry, there is at least the implicit assumption that both individuals are sufficiently ma-

■ *It is not uncommon for marital status to be indicated by clothing or hair style. The "butterfly" hair style of this Hopi girl indicates that she is unmarried.*

important for the attainment of adulthood in so many preindustrial societies? For one thing, members of these societies usually regard childbearing as a more central cultural value than we do, so children generally enhance the prestige of their parents. Economic factors are equally important reasons for marriage. Among most preindustrial peoples, some kind of family is the basic economic unit, meaning that family members usually produce and process the food they eat, make the clothing they wear, and construct the dwelling in which they live. As discussed in chapter 12, the sexual division of labor exists everywhere, so each sex requires the goods and services produced by the other. It is mainly through marriage that the full range of technical skills needed for the maintenance of a household is obtained. Generally, a person who does not marry remains a dependent member of someone else's household. Finally, marriage is useful because children provide the only form of economic security available for elderly individuals in most preindustrial societies. More than among ourselves, marriage therefore establishes an individual's rights to essential or valued resources.

With marriage the bride and groom both assume new rights and responsibilities, not only to one another but to their affines as well. Marriage creates new relationships of many kinds: both partners acquire parents- and siblings-in-law; and as the couple have children, they experience considerable new demands on their time and energy. Thus, getting married is not just something people do or are expected to do as they mature physically and socially. Equally important, the new responsibilities the couple assume after they marry force them into social maturity.

◼ Old Age

Gerontology, the study of the elderly, has only recently become an important interest of anthropologists. Part of our interest stems from conditions in our own sociocultural system, in which the elderly are so often seen as a burden, both to their children and to those of us who pay social security taxes. One popular notion is that the neglect of and contempt for the elderly in modern American society is something recent. We sometimes hear or read statements like "The elderly were respected and admired for their wisdom in primitive societies." As we have so often emphasized, however, "primitive" people are enormously diverse in all respects, including the way they regard and treat the elderly.

Among some preindustrial peoples adults who can no longer economically contribute to the family because of age, physical injury, or severe illness become burdens to their kinsmen. As they become dependent on the goodwill of others, their prestige declines rapidly. Among the Comanche, old men were often the victims of pranks by young boys. Sometimes young boys slashed the prized painted buffalo robes of the old men or smeared human excrement on their heads as a joke. As the elderly became increasingly helpless, they were frequently "thrown away" or abandoned by their kinsmen and friends. Little time was spent mourning the death of an old or useless person. Intense mourning was reserved for people who died while still physically in their prime, for only their death constituted a true loss to their community and kinsmen. Among the Inuit of Canada, conditions were even more tenuous, and parricide (the killing of close relatives) was common. The old or infirm who could no longer keep up with the migratory movements of the group were abandoned by their families. In some Eskimo groups an elderly kinsman who was no longer able to travel would be abandoned in a sealed igloo with a little food and a seal-oil lamp for warmth. Further south, in the subarctic forests, the Athabaskan tribes likewise abandoned the elderly. However, animals, particularly wolves, were likely to find the helpless individual before death

◼ *In many societies, advanced age brings increasing prestige and authority, as in this man's homeland of China.*

and attack and kill him or her. To avoid leaving their relatives to such a fate, a family member frequently killed them. Such ethnographic cases are not "typical"—there is no generalization that can be made about *the* treatment of the elderly among preindustrial peoples. They do suffice to show that modern attitudes toward the elderly are not unique.

Other preindustrial peoples come closer to the romantic ideals some of us have about all such peoples: authority over family and community, control of resources, and the respect one receives increase with advancing age. Senior members of the family and community are elevated to positions of leadership. Knowledge and wisdom gained from experience replace physical strength and stamina as the elderly's contribution to the well-being of the family and community.

In the United States old age is defined fairly precisely in terms of years and eligibility for federal entitlements. At sixty-five years of age, an individual becomes eligible to receive full social security benefits and qualifies for federal Medicare and Medicaid programs. Why sixty-five? Certainly the reason is not that people cease being "middle-aged" and become "old" on their sixty-fifth birthday. Many people remain vigorous in mind and body long past our official retirement age. Sixty-five is, in fact, a quite arbitrary designation that goes back to the German chancellor Bismarck, who in 1889 introduced the first social security laws. He decided that sixty-five should be the age at which benefits would be paid, and most other industrial nations have adopted this number. Although American laws have changed so that mandatory retirement was abolished for most occupations in 1986, psychologically many people feel that at sixty-five a person is old regardless of his or her actual physical condition. As a result, over 80 percent of employed Americans retire at about sixty-five.

Of course, old age does not depend solely on chronological age but varies with an individual's personal health and with sociocultural conditions. In many societies physically fit individuals continue to work well beyond the normal age of retirement in American society. Among the Navajo, for example, it is common to find men and women in their seventies and eighties still tending herds of sheep and goats and working alongside their children and grandchildren.

In industrialized societies such as the United States, retired individuals frequently surrender most of their authority and control over economic resources and withdraw from even family decision making. Most are supported partly or entirely through investments, retirement funds, and/or government programs. In extreme instances, individuals physically withdraw from daily contact with their families, moving to retirement communities or to other areas of the country such as California, Arizona, or Florida. Thus, many individuals categorized as elderly are segregated and isolated (sometimes by their own wishes) from younger adults and children, living in their own relatively closed communities. In industrialized societies in general and in the United States in particular, old age is often associated with the inability to maintain a meaningful economic or social role in the community. This in turn frequently results in a loss in self-esteem.

There is no easy explanation for the variations in the treatment of the elderly. One argument is that the elderly receive the greatest respect and authority in those societies in which they control the land, livestock, and other resources of their kin group. Younger members rely on them for use rights to land, and their children (or sister's children, in matrilineal societies) may maximize their chance of a large inheritance by

■ *Among most non-industrial peoples the elderly still play an important if not dominant role in the everyday life of the family. Here two elderly Indonesian women care for their grandchildren in Jakarta.*

acceding to their wishes and deferring to their judgments. In such kin group systems of control (see chapter 9), most everyone who lives long enough will gain the status of elder and the esteem and authority it brings.

Some anthropologists argue that the explanation lies not in economic control per se but in the contrast between literate and nonliterate people. In societies without writing, the elderly become the major repositories of historical, religious, and technical knowledge. They function as the de facto libraries of these societies. Their control of knowledge makes them indispensable to the community and gives them power over its members, thus enhancing their social value and the respect they receive. This might be termed the "knowledge is power" explanation.

Another contributing factor is the rate of change a people are experiencing. In slowly changing societies with relatively stable technologies, knowledge is seen as cumulative, and wisdom as the product of experience. Thus, wisdom is thought to increase with age. The older individuals within the group are viewed as the valued repositories of community wisdom and cultural knowledge, so they are the individuals most capable of making important political and economic decisions. In contrast, industrialization has unleashed rapid and profound changes in the technologies of modern societies, and existing technologies quickly become obsolete. Therefore, we tend to view knowledge not as cumulative, but as ever-changing and transitory; and in our view experience alone does not generate the wisdom necessary for effective decision making. Like yesterday's technology, the elderly are often viewed as obsolete, old-fashioned, and out of step with today's realities. Their ideas and knowledge are thought by many to be antiquated and thus of limited value in decision making. From this perspective, it is not surprising that older individuals are frequently forced out of positions of authority and replaced by younger individuals thought more capable of making the critical leadership decisions.

Summary

Personality refers to those internal, stable mental processes that make a person's reactions to similar events and situations consistent over time but different from the reactions of other people. The kind of personality an individual develops is greatly influenced by the way he or she is brought up, as the Alorese case illustrates. Sociocultural systems differ in their child-rearing practices—in nursing and weaning norms, the degree and methods of discipline, toilet-training practices, nurturing, sexual permissiveness, caretaking roles, and so forth. Therefore, differences in the modal (i.e., typical, or most common) personality found among different peoples are expected. But in any society a wide range of personality types exist, so we cannot correctly characterize "the" personality of a people in any simple way.

The relationship between modal personality and the nature of the sociocultural system is complex, but several attempts have been made to order this complexity. One such attempt is the Social Systems Model. In this model the maintenance systems of a people affect the overall learning environment of children, which results in a tendency for children to develop some important similarities in personality. In turn, individuals with similar personalities tend to develop or find attractive other sociocultural elements, known as the *projective-expressive system.*

The changes that occur in peoples' lives as they mature and age are referred to as *life-cycle changes.* In some populations relative age serves as the recruitment principle for formal groups known as *age sets,* two forms of which are illustrated by the Hidatsa and the Swazi. Most societies lack age sets, but age is everywhere a relevant social characteristic used to allocate roles. This is shown by the fact that transitions from one age category to another are so often marked by formal public ceremonies called *rites of passage.*

Exactly when childhood begins and ends is socioculturally, not biologically, determined. Often, as among the Osage, a naming ritual confers human status to an infant. Childhood is universally a period of intense social learning and of personality formation. Among preindustrial peoples, it is typical for children to begin contributing to the support of their families at a much younger age than among ourselves.

The passage from childhood to adolescence is often accomplished and marked by an initiation ritual, which often involves severe physical and psychological trauma. Both psychological and sociological interpretations of male and female initiation rites have been offered, but no generally accepted theory of their occurrence is available. In preindustrial societies marriage is frequently necessary to attain full adulthood, for marriage tends to create critical rights and obligations between individuals and groups.

Human societies vary enormously in their regard for and treatment of their elderly members. The chronological age at which an individual is considered elderly likewise varies, and our own cultural notion that sixty-five is the age of retirement is largely a historical accident. The degree to which elderly people exercise control over important property and its inheritance seems to be important in how they are regarded. Other influences include the degree of literacy—for among preliterate peoples the elderly serve as a repository of knowledge—and the rate of technological change a people are experiencing.

Key Terms

personality	life cycle
child-rearing practices	rite of passage
modal personality	initiation rite
age set association	

Suggested Readings

■ Barnouw, Victor. *Culture and Personality.* 4th ed. Homewood, Ill.: Dorsey, 1985.
A work that has long been a standard text in psychological anthropology. A well-written introduction to the subject for students.

■ Bernardi, Bernardo. *Age Class Systems, Social Institutions and Policies Based on Age.* New York: Cambridge University Press, 1985.
A comparative study of the significance of age in social institutions.

■ Freeman, Derek. *Margaret Mead and Samoa: The Making and Unmaking of an Anthropological Myth.* Cambridge: Harvard University Press, 1983.
A critique of Margaret Mead's description and analysis of Samoan adolescence. Freeman argues that Mead findings were erroneous and that Samoan girls experience the same kinds of psychological processes as Western girls during their adolescence.

■ Hammond, Dorothy. *Associations.* Reading, Mass.: Addison-Wesley Modular Publications, 14, 1972.
A dated and short study that nevertheless contains a good review of the anthropological literature on age.

■ Leiderman, P. Herbert, Steven R. Tulkin, and Anne Rosenfeld, eds. *Culture and Infancy: Variations in the Human Experience.* New York: Academic, 1977.
A volume of twenty-three articles, mostly dealing with infancy in various sociocultural settings.

■ LeVine, Robert. *Culture, Behavior and Personality.* Chicago: Aldine, 1973.
A provocative text in psychological anthropology.

■ LeVine, Robert, ed. *Culture and Personality.* Chicago: Aldine, 1974.
A book containing twenty-three readings covering most aspects of psychological anthropology.

■ Maretzki, Thomas and Hatsumi. *Taira: An Okinawan Village.* Six Cultures Series, vol. 7. New York: Wiley, 1966.
An in-depth case study of one of the six societies analyzed in Whiting and Whiting (1974).

■ Marsella, Anthony J., George DeVos, and Francis L. K. Hsu, eds. *Culture and Self: Asian and Western Perspectives.* New York: Tavistock, 1985.
Nine articles on cultural conceptions of selfhood in the West, Japan, and China, and in Hinduism and Confucianism. First two chapters are quite good.

■ Mead, Margaret. *Coming of Age in Samoa.* New York: Morrow, 1928.
A highly readable account of adolescent girls in Samoa and one of anthropology's great classics. Few anthropological studies have been more widely read by the general public.

■ Minturn, Leigh, and William W. Lambert. *The Rajputs of Khalapur, India.* Six Cultures Series, vol. 3. New York: Wiley, 1966.
An in-depth case study of one of the six societies analyzed in Whiting and Whiting (1974).

■ Turnbull, Colin. *The Human Cycle.* New York: Simon & Schuster, 1983.
A readable summary of life cycle changes in various populations from all parts of the world.

■ Whiting, Beatrice B., and John W. *Children of Six Cultures: A Psycho-Cultural Analysis.* Cambridge, Mass.: Harvard University Press, 1974.
A comparative psychocultural analysis of children from six different societies around the world, discussing the influence of culture on personality and vice versa.

■ Wilson, M. *Good Company: A Study of Nyakyusa Age-Villages.* Boston: Beacon, 1963.
An interesting and readable account of the unusual age set village organization of the Nyakyusa of East Africa.

Part Four

ANTHROPOLOGY IN THE MODERN WORLD

n the first three parts of this text, you might have gained the impression that anthropologists are concerned largely with people of long ago and far away. To some extent this is an accurate impression—more than any other discipline that deals with humans, anthropology is concerned with the description and analysis of non-Western peoples. But part of the reason for this is our assumption that our comparative, relativistic, and holistic perspectives allow us to better understand what is happening to our own sociocultural system and, indeed, in the world as a whole. We have from time to time suggested some insights on Euro-American societies derived from anthropological theory or ethnographic data. And we have suggested that the economic and political system of the modern world make an understanding of and tolerance for members of other sociocultural traditions increasingly useful. In part 4, our focus shifts explicitly to anthropology's contributions to understanding life in the modern world.

■ (Facing page) *Recent centuries have seen the merging of various cultural traditions. Here we see a traditionally-clothed Nigerian minister reviewing members of the Nigerian police—a force equipped and organized following a modern British plan.*

THE CHANGING HUMAN WORLD

■ *Contents*

■ (Above) *The world has changed
greatly during the post-World War II era.
Former colonial possessions are now
playing an increasingly important role in
international politics. Here we see the
delegation from Swaziland at a meeting
of the United Nations.*

In the preceding chapters we have generally examined sociocultural systems ahistorically. In other words, we have discussed and analyzed them and mapped their geographical distributions without regard to time or historical context. For example, according to our maps, the state of New Jersey is still inhabited by Delaware Indians, and the Great Plains are still home to tipi-dwelling, buffalo-hunting Cheyenne and Comanche. We speak and write of Native Americans' sociocultural systems as if they were frozen in time. Other regions of the world are handled in a similar manner. Our distributional maps in chapters 7 and 8 indicate the geographical distributions of particular modes of adaptation at the time of earliest European contact; thus they are composites of data from the sixteenth through the early twentieth centuries.

When we who are the products of the urban-industrial world look at small farming villages in India, view Masai herding cattle on the plains of East Africa, or watch a movie about the Pygmies of the Ituri forest hunting elephants with spears, we tend to think of these peoples as being unchanged for centuries if not millennia. In their actions, dress, and technology other people may differ greatly from us, and thus all too frequently we assume they have yet to be affected by the massive changes that we know have affected the world. Without questioning, we frequently think of them as having "pristine" or untouched "traditional" sociocultural systems.

Sociocultural Change

Since the late nineteenth century anthropologists have been aware that sociocultural systems are never stable—they are in constant change. Although the process of sociocultural change has been extensively studied by anthropologists, we will only briefly discuss how and why a system changes over time. There are two main processes by which a sociocultural system changes: *innovation* and *diffusion*.

An **innovation** may be anything—from new religious beliefs to a technological change—that is internally generated by members of the society. People are constantly changing what they do and how they do it. In most cases these are minor and imperceptible unconscious changes. In the telling of a myth an individual may delete some part while elaborating another. Individuals may wear their hair differently or paint their face with a new design. In a sense we are all innovators, and sometimes these innovations are adopted by others and become part of the culture and collective behavior of the group. Still other innovations are intentional, as when an individual has an idea about how to do something better or more efficiently. Most innovations consist of the recombining of two or more existing ideas or objects to produce something new. This factor is more evident in technology, since most technological advancements are the result of such recombinations. In our own society, Fulton took a paddle wheel, a steam engine, and a boat and put them together to create a steamboat. Still later, several individuals succeeded in powering a wagon by the use of a gasoline internal combustion engine, and thus the automobile was born.

Diffusion is a second way in which new elements are introduced into a sociocultural system. Diffusion consists of the "borrowing" or adopting of a sociocultural trait from another society. As we will discuss, any category of customs, beliefs, or objects, from religious beliefs and practices to technology, may be diffused from one people to another. The adoption of new traits requires that these traits be integrated into the existing lifeway of the recipient population. In many cases, the form may remain the same while the meaning and function of the trait changes.

Why a group of people adopts or rejects a particular new custom or belief is extraordinarily complex. As a rule, people are receptive to new traits that either enhance their economic well-being or their social survival. Thus, farming peoples are often receptive to new crops that complement their existing crops and new technology that increases their harvest. Societies involved in warfare readily accept more advanced military technology. Still other factors stimulate changes in sociocultural systems. Political and economic domination usually result in the forced introduction of new traits from the dominant society as it restructures the sociocultural systems of dependent peoples to meet new needs and objectives. As we discussed earlier, there is a patterned relationship between the sociocultural system and the natural environment in which it is situated. The displacement and relocation of a people into a different natural environment generates changes in the existing lifeway. Demographic changes—either rapid increases or decreases in population—and their associated changes in relative population densities necessitate changes in the sociocultural system.

History and Anthropology

Frederick Maitland, a historian, commented during the late nineteenth century that anthropology had to be history or it was nothing. Although few if any anthropologists would totally agree with Maitland, anthropologists have for some time realized that history has played an important role in shaping sociocultural systems. However, until recently anthropologists have tended to treat non-Western societies as if they have been static. The importance of change among these peoples was either ignored or minimized. During the early part of this century, ethnographers wrote descriptions of nineteenth-century lifeways using the "ethnographic present," indicative of the "timeless" or static concept of these societies. If any changes had taken place, they were seen as very recent.

It has only been during the last two decades that anthropologists have begun to see the magnitude of the changes that have occurred among even the most technologically unsophisticated peoples over the past few hundred years. Virtually every group of people in the world, no matter how geographically isolated, has directly or indirectly had its lifeway altered to some degree as a result of European expansion and industrialization. In turn, the Europeans were also changed by borrowing and adapting ideas and technology from other peoples in the world. There is not now, nor has there been for several hundred years, a truly pristine society. Not only has the way of life of every people changed, but many societies have become extinct during this period, and numerous new socioculturally distinct populations have come into existence.

The World before 1500

Keeping in mind how and why changes occur in sociocultural systems, we can now briefly outline world history over the past 500 years. In this summary we have two objectives: (1) to provide the reader with some idea of the magnitude and pervasiveness of change within sociocultural systems, and (2) to demonstrate the potential importance of anthropology in the modern world.

The world has experienced phenomenal changes over the past 500 years. Foremost among these changes have been the technological advancements and the harnessing of new sources of energy: coal, petroleum, electricity, and nuclear power. Associated with these advancements has been an explosion in the human population of the earth—from only about 500 to 600 million in 1500 A.D. to over 5 billion today. Not only has the population of the world grown, but there have been major intraregional and interregional population shifts. In the period since 1500, profound sociocultural changes have affected virtually all peoples in the world.

The key cause of these changes has been the economic and political expansion of European populations that began toward the end of the fifteenth century and has served as the major catalyst for these changes. To understand world sociocultural history during this period, we have to trace the history of European expansion and determine how and when it affected the various regions and peoples of the world.

European expansion took place in two rather distinct stages. The first stage can be called the *mercantile phase*. During this period, European traders brought most of the continents of the world into direct trade contact with one another. Some migration and colonization and limited political conquest occurred during the mercantile phase, which began during the 1490s and lasted until the last half of the eighteenth century. The second stage, called the *industrial phase*, encompassed the period of time when European peoples politically conquered almost every region of the world and established a global economic system that they dominated.

Before 1500 A.D. the major world regions were relatively isolated from each other. Most contact was limited to societies that occupied adjacent territories. Trade was minimal, and long-distance trade that existed between Europe and China or Africa rarely involved direct exchange between members of those societies. Trade was managed by intervening groups whose members acted as middlemen. Thus, although Europeans were aware of the existence of places like China, India, and Ethiopia, their knowledge was extremely limited and rarely based on firsthand accounts. Although innovations in technology and sociocultural institutions did diffuse from one center to another, diffusion was slow because direct contact was lacking.

Although the terms *Old World* and *New World* are ethnocentric, this distinction is useful from a sociocultural-historical perspective. The Old World—Europe, Africa, and Asia—did form a unit within which trade and contact, however tenuous and limited, allowed for the spread of technology and institutions. The *New World* is a term usually applied only to the Americas, but it could be applied just as well to Australia and most of Oceania because both of these regions were outside of this exchange network before 1500. Thus, before European expansion the world consisted of two broad geographical regions with peoples who had for much of their history developed technologies and lifeways in isolation from one another.

Reaching from the Ural Mountains west to the Atlantic Ocean, Europe was the smallest of the three Old World continents. Europe also had a relatively small population. In 1450, immediately following a plague that had sharply reduced the population, Europe's total population was estimated at only about 55 million. By 1500 the population had increased but still numbered only about 66 million. Europe was a relatively homogeneous sociocultural region. Although fragmented into numerous small states, it was Christian except for a few peripheral areas, with an economy based on intensive agriculture. The relative sociocultural homogeneity of Europe was in large part the result of a common religion and a highly developed internal trade network, which made it a much more cohesive unit than Asia or Africa.

Africa was significantly less homogeneous. Africa north of the Sahara was an extension of the Islamic core area in the Middle East. South of the Sahara were vast areas of tropical forest, savanna, and desert. The peoples of this region ranged from horticulturalists to pastoralists and foragers (see Figures 7.2 and 8.4). Although before 1500 there were some converts to Islam, most were adherents of so-called tribal religions. States and even multiethnic empires existed in some regions (see Figure 17.1). The Songhai Empire occupied much of the Sudan, reaching from the mouth of the Gambia River eastward to the bend of the Niger and having cities such as Gao and Timbuctu. Further east, around Lake Tchad, was the Kanem-Bornu Empire. To the south were smaller states such as Oyo and Benin. Near the mouth of the Congo River was the Kingdom of Kongo, and to the southwest were the states of Monomatapa and Luba. Along the east coast were the Omani or Arab states like Kilwa and Zanzibar. In the highlands near the horn of Africa was the Christian kingdom of Ethiopia. Little is known about the areas of Africa between these centers before 1500, but in general they were politically fragmented into numerous localized units ranging in complexity from small states and chiefdoms to tribes and band-level societies. Sub-Saharan Africa had a very small population for its geographical size. Population estimates for this period range from as little as 35 million to 100 million, with most estimates in the 35 to 60 million range. Geography tended to isolate sub-Saharan Africa from the rest of the world, relatively speaking. The Sahara on the north served as a partial barrier to contact. The coast offered few good harbors, and most rivers were not suited to boat traffic. As a result, trade between the interior of sub-Saharan Africa and other regions was extremely limited, which probably explains why Africa was one of the least developed regions of the Old World in technology and complexity of political organization.

Asia was the most advanced continent in the Old World in its technological and political development. There were three main centers of Asian development. The Islamic region was centered in western Asia but also included the adjacent portions of southeastern Europe and northern Africa. The Indian subcontinent was socioculturally diverse, with hundreds of distinct ethnic populations. Although predominantly Hindu in religion, the subcontinent also had large numbers of Moslems and Buddhists. Densely populated, having in 1500 a total population of about 100 million, India was politically fragmented into numerous small states. China, with a population well over 100 million, constituted the largest centrally organized political unit in the world and was socioculturally the most homogeneous unit relative to its population size. Thus, India and China each had populations that exceeded the total population of Europe. In addition, numerous small states were scattered throughout southeastern

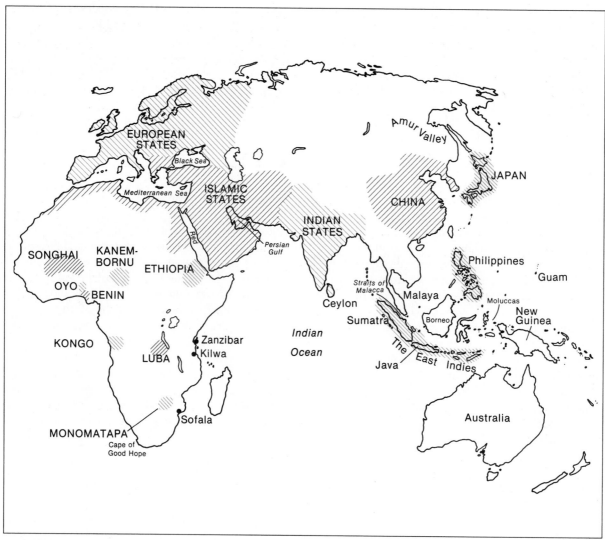

■ *Figure 17.1*
Major States and Regions of Europe, Asia, and Africa (ca. 1500)

Asia and the islands of the East Indies. Although much of Asia was politically organized at the state level, there were still some tribal peoples in the more isolated mountainous regions of the mainland, as well as in the islands of the Indies. In the boreal forests and tundra regions of Siberia, there were scattered tribes of reindeer herders and hunters.

These major population and sociocultural centers of the Old World were connected by a weakly developed trade network. The Mediterranean Sea, a major center of maritime trade, connected the port cities of southern Europe, the Middle East, and North Africa.

Traders sailed through the Straits of Gibraltar to the Atlantic coastal ports of western Europe and into the Baltic Sea to the coastal ports of northern Europe. From the Islamic ports in North Africa, caravans crossed the Sahara Desert to the cities of the Sudan. From the cities of Timbuctu, Gao, Djenne, and others, gold, slaves, ivory, ostrich feathers, cola nuts, and hides flowed northward. The specific nature of the goods that flowed south is not well known, but iron was an important trade item. However, the most significant sociocultural trait that flowed south was the Islamic religion. Most of the Sudanic states were Moslem, and during the fourteenth century Timbuctu had emerged as a major center of Islamic learning.

At the eastern end of the Mediterranean were Islamic ports from which caravans carried goods east. The longest and most important of these routes was the Silk Road, which linked Mediterranean ports with China. As its name implied, the most important item carried west over this route was silk, and western European gold and silver flowed to China in exchange. Other caravan trails linked the Mediterranean ports with cities on the Persian Gulf, from which other maritime traders, primarily Arabs, sailed to India, the East Indies, and even China. Cotton textiles from India as well as highly valued spices were traded west by this land-and-sea route, and gold and silver flowed eastward in exchange. The Islamic religion had also spread by this route and by the twelfth century had found converts as far away as the East Indies.

Along the eastern cost of Africa, Islamic traders from Oman had established trading ports such as Zanzibar and Kilwa, some dating from as early as the eighth century. From these ports Islam found converts among the coastal African societies. Omani traders marketed East African gold, iron ore, camel-hair cloth, slaves, and ivory in India and as far east as China.

Within Asia itself, an active maritime trade existed between China, India, Southeast Asia, and the islands of the East Indies. Of subsequent strategic interest to Europeans was that much of this trade had to pass through the Straits of Malacca, a long and relatively narrow body of water separating the Malay Peninsula (Malaya) from the island of Sumatra (Indonesia).

Before 1492 both the Americas and Oceania were outside this network of trade and sociocultural exchange. The Americas were totally unknown to the peoples of the Old World. Although the westernmost portion of Oceania, primarily New Guinea and Australia, had some sporadic contact with a few peoples of the East Indies, on the whole the societies of Oceania were as unknown to Old World societies as the natives of the Americas.

The natives of the Americas had originally entered the continent as simple foraging societies migrating out of Siberia over a land bridge that connected Asia and North America during the late ice age. After entering the Americas 10,000 to 20,000 years ago, these peoples became isolated from the Old World. The isolation persisted, and they developed sociocultural traditions uninfluenced by changes in the Old World. In some respects, Native American sociopolitical devel-

opment surpassed that of the Old World, but in a few critical areas it lagged behind. Although some Native Americans had learned to work silver, gold, and copper, and in the Andes some bronze, on the whole metallurgy was still in its infancy in the Americas. The impressive temples, buildings, and fortifications of Mesoamerica and Peru were constructed by societies with stone-tool technologies and without wheeled vehicles.

The most important contribution of Native American peoples was the domestication of food plants. In Mesoamerica and western South America, they successfully domesticated a wide range of crops: corn, potatoes, pineapples, papayas, tomatoes, avocados, peanuts, sweet potatoes, and cacao, as well as numerous varieties of beans and squash (see Box 8.1). As a result, at the time of European contact many Native American societies were to some degree dependent on cultivation for their subsistence. Foraging societies were found primarily in those portions of northern North America and southern South America that were not well-suited for cultivation with a preindustrial technology.

Because so many of their peoples were agricultural and had a relatively stable food supply, the Americas had a relatively large population. Recent estimates of the population of the Americas at the time of European contact range from about 80 to 120 million, with about 100 million being the average. This population was not, however, evenly distributed. The main concentrations of population were in Mesoamerica and western South America, where intensive farming was practiced. In these regions large multiethnic empires, such as the Aztec and Inca, had arisen (see Figure 17.2). According to one estimate, Mexico, which was mostly under Aztec domination, had a population of over 25 million. Some estimates of the Inca Empire set the figure as high as 12 million. Adjacent to these empires were other smaller, well-organized states; in Mexico, for example, the Tarascans, the Zapotec, and the city-states of the Maya surrounded the Aztecs. Beyond Mesoamerica and Peru, the two centers of Native American civilization, most farming societies were organized only at a chiefdom or tribal level, and the remaining foraging societies were politically organized as tribes or as simple or composite bands (see chapter 13).

Oceania was composed of the islands of the Pacific Ocean, and Oceanic peoples were divided into four main geographical and sociocultural areas. Micronesia consisted of the mostly small coral atolls of the western

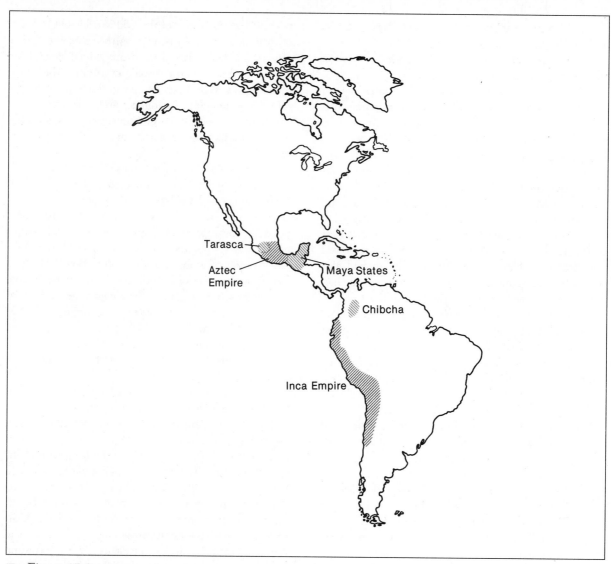

■ *Figure 17.2*
Major Native States of the Americas at Time of European Contact

Pacific. The Polynesian triangle encompassed the islands from New Zealand in the southwest to Hawaii in the north and to Easter Island in the southeast. Melanesia included New Guinea and the large island groups as far east as Fiji. Australia included both Australia and the large island of Tasmania. The peoples of Micronesia, Polynesia, and Melanesia were basically stone-age farming and fishing peoples. On the Polynesian and Micronesian islands societies were organized at the chiefdom level. In contrast, the peoples of Australia and Tasmania were technologically among the least advanced peoples in the world, and they depended solely on foraging for their subsistence.

The World since 1500

With the discovery of the Americas by Christopher Columbus in 1492, and Vasco daGama's successful voyage to India in 1498, the age of European expansion began.

The Initial Expansion of Europe

In population and technological achievement, Europe was not the most developed region of the world during the fifteenth century. Asia had a total population four to five times that of Europe, and in overall technology Asia was ahead of Europe. Compared to the states of Asia, European countries were small. The populations of such soon-to-be-imperial powers as England, Portugal, Spain, and the Netherlands were insignificant in comparison to those of China or the Moghul (Islamic) states of India. Even the Aztec Empire in the Americas may have had a population equal to the total of these four European countries. The major advantage of the European societies was in military technology. Guns, crossbows, iron weapons, armor, and horses gave them significant advantages over the stone-tool military technologies of the peoples of the Americas and Oceania. To a lesser degree, they also enjoyed a military advantage over most peoples of Africa. The same was not true in Asia: on land European armies enjoyed no technological advantage. Only in naval warfare were the Europeans technologically superior to the Asian states. These factors influenced European expansionist policies during the early period and caused the history of contact with Asia, Africa, the Americas, and Oceania to differ significantly. With some exceptions, principally in the Americas, the expansion of Europe during the sixteenth, seventeenth, and eighteenth centuries consisted of the development of maritime mercantile empires, as opposed to actual overseas colonies and territorial empires.

Because European contact took such different forms from one region to the next, it is necessary to examine the history of contact region by region.

Conquest of the Americas In 1492, Columbus discovered a new world inhabited by a numerous people, but a people who still had only an advanced stone-tool technology. Initially, the Spaniards were disappointed in their new discoveries because they failed to find the immense treasures of the Indies they were expecting. On the island of Hispaniola, where they first settled, there were some gold deposits, but most Spanish settlers quickly turned their attention to the development of sugarcane plantations and cattle ranches.

During the first quarter century following its discovery, the New World attracted only a few thousand Spaniards, but they quickly spread over the major islands of the West Indies: Cuba, Jamaica, and Puerto Rico. In 1513, Balboa crossed the narrow Isthmus of Panama and set foot on the shores of the Pacific. In 1519, Hernando Cortez landed on the coast of Mexico and by 1521 had completed the conquest of Tenochtitlán, the capital of the Aztec Empire. Cortez sent gold and silver back to Spain in quantities beyond belief. The discovery of such vast treasures encouraged the migration of others to search for still more wealth and plunder. Between 1532 and 1534 a military expedition led by Francisco Pizarro conquered the Inca Empire and took the wealth of Peru for Spain. By the late 1500s, Spanish expeditions had explored much of the Americas, from the lower Mississippi Valley to the southern Andes and the Amazon Valley, and had located and conquered every major Native American state. In little more than half a century, the Spaniards had conquered the richest and most populous portions of the Americas: the West Indies, Mesoamerica, and Peru. Over half the native population of the Americas had fallen under Spanish political domination.

The Treaty of Tordesillas, signed in 1494, divided the non-Christian world between Spain and Portugal.

■ *Armed with steel weapons and mounted on horses, Spanish conquestadors had little difficulty in conquering Native American groups.*

The easternmost part of South America, Brazil, fell into the Portuguese portion. Although Portugal's area lacked rich gold and silver deposits, the coastal regions of Brazil were well suited for sugarcane plantations. Starting in 1500, Portuguese settlers began colonizing Brazil, and by 1550 there were small settlements scattered along most of the coast.

The Spanish and Portuguese were able to conquer and occupy large portions of the Americas in a surprisingly short time. As the Spanish demonstrated in their conquests of the Aztecs and Incas, their military superiority was so pronounced that small armies numbering in the hundreds were able to vanquish well-organized native armies whose troops numbered in the thousands. Small groups of European troops could move about with near impunity throughout the length of the Americas. Only the lack of manpower limited Spanish and Portuguese expansion and kept them from subjugating all of the Americas. The populations of Spain and Portugal were relatively small, and there were never enough troops or civilians to control such a vast and populous region. Although the conquests of Mexico and Peru stimulated Spanish migration to the New World, the number of immigrants remained relatively small, averaging between one and two thousand a year during the 1500s.

The period of conquest and territorial expansion had virtually ended by 1600, and Spanish settlers turned their attention to exploitation of the West Indies, Mesoamerica, and Peru, where they developed silver and gold mines, ranches, and plantations. The Portuguese contented themselves with coastal Brazil and worked to expand their plantations.

The sociocultural impact of the Spanish and Portuguese was most pronounced in those regions directly under their control. Existing native political organization was either completely replaced or modified and integrated into a colonial government. European technology was introduced—iron tools, plows, cattle, horses, sheep, and so forth—as the existing economic systems were altered or destroyed to meet European needs. Indian labor was used in the mines and on the plantations and ranches that were developed. Missionaries flooded the Americas seeking converts, and they razed temples and other overt signs of the old religions and religious practices. Temples were replaced by Christian churches. In some regions, such as Mexico and Peru, native peoples managed to maintain their languages and Indian social and ethnic identity, but even these societies were given a veneer of Christian customs and beliefs. Even Native American peoples

beyond direct European control were affected. Old World crops, domesticated animals, and tools in limited numbers were diffused to these autonomous populations. In some regions the introduction of European items had revolutionary effects. The horse in particular revolutionized many native societies. On the Great Plains of North America, the adoption of the horse resulted in a sociocultural florescence, and a whole new way of life evolved (see Box 17.1). The adoption of the horse had an equally profound effect on native life on the Gran Chaco and pampas of South America.

As important as these material elements were in altering Native American lifeways, they were not the only causes of change. Old World diseases such as smallpox, measles, influenza, bubonic plague, diptheria, typhus, cholera, malaria, and scarlet fever were the most pervasive agents of change introduced by early Europeans. Isolated as they had been, the natives of the Americas had no natural immunities to these diseases. Because these diseases frequently spread well in advance of European contact, it is impossible to estimate with any exactness the size of the native populations before that contact. The massive population decline caused by European diseases is best documented in regions under direct Spanish and Portugese control. Father Bartolome de las Casas reported that there were 1,100,000 Indians fourteen years of age or older on Hispaniola in 1496. Even the most conservative estimate of the Indian population for the island is 100,000. Regardless of the original population figure, we do know that the native population underwent rapid decline and that by 1535 there were only 500 Indians left on Hispaniola. By the 1550s the Taino and Ciguayo Indians were extinct. Similar declines were reported on the other major islands of the Caribbean: Cuba, Puerto Rico, and Jamaica. In Mexico the decline was also severe but not as devastating. One study places the contact population at 25,200,000 in 1519, with a decline to 16,800,000 by 1532, 2,650,000 by 1568, and 1,075,000 by 1605. Although these estimates are open to question, there is no doubt that Native American societies suffered severe population declines following European contact.

Disease was the major factor in the population decline, but other factors also contributed. As the native populations under their control decreased, the Europeans faced a shortage of available laborers. One answer to this problem was to "recruit" new labor by raiding other Native American groups for slaves. Thus, peoples that were not under direct Spanish or Portuguese control suffered heavy losses from slave raiders

Box 17.1

THE WHITE MAN AND THE PLAINS INDIANS

To the white American public, no group of Indians typifies what Native American life was like more than the Plains Indians: the Cheyenne, the Dakota, the Crow, and Comanche. Thanks in large part to Hollywood, these tipi-dwelling, buffalo-hunting, horse-mounted warriors of the grasslands have come to represent the very essence of "Indianness." When we visualize Indian ways of life of the past, we picture Red Cloud, Black Kettle, Sitting Bull, or some other plains leader dressed in beaded buckskin clothing, wearing a feather "war bonnet," and seated on a horse. What we fail to realize is that Plains Indians in particular, and American Indians in general as we view them, were in large part a product of European contact.

Horses were the primary means of transportation and as such were an integral part of nineteenth-century Plains Indian lifeway. The modern horse was not native to the Americas, but was first brought by the Spanish. It was not until the late 1600s and early 1700s that horses in any numbers became available to the tribes of the Great Plains.

Before horses were available, the open grasslands of the Great Plains held little attraction for American Indians. Not only were bison difficult to hunt for people on foot and armed with only a bow and arrow or spear, but transporting of game any distance over the vast grasslands was physically arduous. Whether food or other material goods, all the possessions of these people had to be carried either on their own backs or those of their dogs. For these reasons, the Plains were inhabited year round by only widely scattered small bands of nomadic foragers. People probably depended more on the collecting of wild food plants than on the vast herds of bison for subsistence. Compared to the farming peoples who lived along the eastern and southwestern margins of the plains, the Plains tribes were materially impoverished and militarily weak. Thus, not surprisingly, before acquiring horses, only a few tribes lived the nomadic life on the plains: the Comanche, Kiowa, Shoshone, a few groups of Apache, possibly the Blackfoot, and a few other smaller tribes. Many of the major tribes later associated with the plains were still farming people.

The horse truly revolutionized life among the Plains tribes. The horse drastically altered the economic base and changed the lifestyle of these peoples. On horseback a hunter armed with bow and arrow could find and kill enough bison within a few months to feed his family for the year. Not only could he kill larger numbers of game animals, but he could pack the meat onto horses and readily transport it vast distances. Horses also allowed for the transporting of increased quantities of material goods. Tipis increased in size, and clothing and other material items became increasingly abundant and elaborate in decoration. For the first time these widely scattered groups could gather together in large camps, sometimes numbering in the thousands, for at least a portion of the year. In short, the horse quickly elevated the Plains tribes from economic poverty to relative prosperity.

The horse also sharply altered the relationship between these peoples and the neighboring farming tribes. The once relatively inoffensive nomads were now transformed into aggressive predatory raiders. The plains tribes were now capable of quickly assembling large parties of horse-mounted warriors who could raid the sedentary farming villages with impunity. The military balance of power had shifted.

In the decades immediately following the acquisition of the horse, the original Plains tribes flourished. Attacks on the neighboring farming peoples had a devastating effect, and many villages were abandoned. It was not long, however, before many cultivators saw both the economic and military advantages derived from being horse-mounted nomadic bison hunters. The Cheyenne and some of the Dakota abandoned the life of settled farmers and moved westward to the Plains to become nomadic tipi-dwelling bison hunters themselves. As they moved onto the plains, they came to challenge directly the original Plains tribes for dominance over critical hunting resources, which intensified warfare. As a result, warfare and the warrior tradition became an integral part of Plains Indian values, social organization, and behavior.

The Plains Indian lifeway as we think of it emerged during the first half of the nineteenth century. Given the diverse origins of the various Plains tribes, they developed a remarkably homogeneous way of life within a short period of time: elaborately equipped tipis, beaded (with European trade beads) clothing, sign language for communication, the Sun Dance, and the emphasis on the male's role as a warrior. It was not until the last half of the nineteenth century that Euro-Americans seriously challenged the Plains Indians for control of the Great Plains, 300 years after they had first begun acquiring horses. Since the Plains peoples were the last major group of tribes to resist Euro-American dominance militarily, it is not surprising that we mistakenly think of them as the "essence of Indianness." ∎

Sources: Ewers (1955), Lowie (1954), and Oliver (1962).

during the sixteenth and seventeenth centuries. It has been estimated that during the first half of the sixteenth century more than 200,000 Indian slaves were taken from Nicaragua and sold in the West Indies. Similar decreases in population caused by slave raiders were common in coastal regions and interior areas beyond European political control. However, enslavement of Native Americans proved to be only a stopgap measure, because these new recruits also died off rapidly from European diseases. New sources of human labor had to be found to fill the expanding vacuum.

Awareness of the rapid and dramatic decline in Native American population is critical to understanding the history of the Americas during the past 500 years. If the Native American societies had maintained their populations, there is little doubt that they would have eventually been able to absorb the relatively small numbers of Europeans who initially conquered them. The history of the Americas could have been similar to the histories of European contact with Africa and Asia, which we will discuss later in this chapter. However,

this decline created a vacuum that was filled by the massive resettling of Old World peoples in the Americas. Neither Spain nor Portugal sent sufficient emigrants to offset the declining Native American population and meet the increasing labor demands of their American colonies. Another source of labor had to be found. This was the genesis of the African slave trade. As early as the 1490s, African slaves had been sent to the island of Hispaniola. During the 1500s and 1600s, ever-increasing numbers of African slaves were sent to the Spanish and Portuguese colonies. By the eighteenth century there were significantly more individuals of African ancestry than European ancestry in these colonies.

During the late sixteenth and early seventeenth centuries, other European powers—namely, England, France, and the Netherlands—began contesting Spanish and Portuguese dominance of the Americas. For the most part, these countries occupied portions of the Americas outside the limits of Spanish and Portuguese control. There were some exceptions. The French, English, and Dutch were able to gain control over some of the small islands in the West Indies. However, the major region of occupation by these European powers became the Atlantic Coast of North America. During the early 1600s, the French, English, and Dutch were able to successfully establish colonies along this coast. The Native American populations in this region had already suffered the devastating effects of Old World diseases. The small, scattered groups of horticulturalists were of little interest to northern Europeans as a source of labor. Unlike the Spanish and Portuguese to the south, these settlers were primarily interested in the land the Indians occupied, and they considered Native Americans to be a hindrance and danger to their settlements, not an economic resource. As these northern European settlers pushed their frontiers into the interior, Native American populations were evicted and forced west. Although there was some enslavement of Native Americans by these colonists, it was not as significant as in the Spanish and Portuguese colonies. Native American slaves were usually sold or traded in the West Indies for African slaves; few were kept in mainland North America. As early as 1619, English colonists in Virginia were purchasing African slaves. The number of African slaves in the French, English, and Dutch West Indies and in English North America increased steadily during the 1600s and 1700s, paralleling the pattern in the Spanish and Portuguese colonies.

■ *To the American public the tipi dwelling, mounted, bison hunting Indians of the Great Plains typify Native American life before the white man. In reality Plains Indian culture as we know it was in large part a product of white contact.*

Although Native Americans were rarely enslaved in the northern European colonies, their labor was used indirectly. Unlike the Spanish and Portuguese, the French, English, and Dutch quickly established trading networks in the interior regions, exchanging cloth, metal tools, guns, and other items of European manufacture for hides and furs. By the mid-1700s most of the Native American societies in North America were in regular commercial contact with these Europeans and dependent upon this trade. By the end of the eighteenth century, virtually every Native American society had been affected by European expansion. Many had already become extinct. Others were under the direct political and economic control of European colonial governments. Even those societies that had been able to retain their autonomy had seen their populations sharply reduced through disease or warfare and their lifestyles changed by the introduction of European material goods and technology. There were no "pristine" societies left in the New World.

Africa South of the Sahara   The Portuguese were the first Europeans to establish contact with African societies south of the Sahara. Portuguese explorers first made contact with sub-Saharan Africans in 1444 and 1445 when their ships made landfall at Cape Verde and the mouth of the Senegal River. Trade quickly followed, and Portuguese explorer-traders steadily expanded farther south down the west coast of Africa. In the 1470s they reached the Gold Coast and found the area so rich in gold that in 1482 they erected a fort at Elmina to protect their trading interest. This fortification was the first of a series of coastal forts that they established to exclude other European powers from the region. By 1488, Portuguese explorers had reached the Cape of Good Hope, the southern extremity of the African continent. Between 1497 and 1499, Vasco da Gama successfully sailed to India and back via the Cape. By the beginning of the fifteenth century, the Portuguese had established the basis for a trading empire that stretched down the western coast of Africa, up the east coast, and all the way to Asia. The problem confronting the Portuguese was strengthening and maintaining their hold against European and Islamic rivals. Trading ports were created along the African coast not only to acquire gold and ivory but also to serve as way stations for ships bound to and from Asia. The major Portuguese centers in Africa became what are today Angola (on the west coast) and Mozambique (on the east coast).

In 1482 the Portuguese discovered one of the largest states in Africa, the Kongo Kingdom, near the mouth of the Congo River. The Portuguese soon developed friendly relations with the Kongo. In 1490 missionaries and a variety of skilled craftsmen were sent to the Kongo. The missionaries soon converted the king and many of the people, and the capital of the kingdom was rebuilt on a European model and renamed Sao Salvador. Many younger Kongo were voluntarily sent to Portugal for formal education.

In 1505 the Portuguese attacked, looted, and virtually destroyed the Omani city of Kilwa. Shortly afterward they occupied the Kilwa port town of Sofala, which became their main base in Mozambique. From this base they usurped the trade with the Monomatapa Empire formerly held by Kilwa.

Although gold and ivory were the primary trade items, early Portuguese traders dealt in other commodities as well: slaves, sea-lion oil, hides, cotton cloth, and beeswax. Slaves eventually emerged as the most valuable trade item of the African coast, and this factor led other European countries to challenge Portuguese control.

Slavery and the slave trade existed in portions of Europe before European expansion. On the Iberian Peninsula in Spain and Portugal, slavery knew no racial or religious boundaries: slaves could be black or white, Christian, Jewish, or Moslem. However, the market for slaves in Europe was limited, and African slaves were transported from Spain by the Spanish to Hispaniola in the 1490s. During the early 1500s, the market for African slaves in the New World expanded rapidly, not only in the Spanish colonies but in the Portuguese colony of Brazil.

The magnitude of the African slave trade cannot be determined with any exactness. We know that the slave trade grew steadily during the sixteenth and seventeenth centuries, reached its zenith during the last decades of the eighteenth century, and ended about 1870. Estimates of the number of African slaves shipped to the Americas range from about 10,000,000 to about 50,000,000, but the actual number was probably closer to the 10,000,000 estimate. Likewise, estimates of the number of slaves taken to the Americas during particular centuries also vary: estimates for the sixteenth century range from 250,000 to 900,000; for the seventeenth century from 1,341,000 to 2,750,000; and for the eighteenth and nineteenth centuries from 6,000,000 to 11,000,000.

The Portuguese became the first major traders of African slaves in the Americas. In the earliest period of

■ *The African slave trade was a direct result of labor shortages in the Americas.*

the trade, slaves were individuals who were already being held as slaves by Africans. However, the number of such people was limited, and as the demand for slaves increased, the Portuguese turned to other methods—in particular, raiding—to acquire them. The expanding demand for slaves changed the relationship of the Portuguese with African societies. The kings of Kongo allowed their subjects to trade slaves to the Portuguese, but they refused to permit them to raid for additional slaves for the trade. As a result, in 1575 the Portuguese mercenaries and African "allies" began systematically to stage slave raids throughout much of central Africa. Finally, in 1660 the Portuguese virtually destroyed the Kongo kingdom in a short war.

In Mozambique the Portuguese also increased their control over trade. Trading posts were built along the Zambezi River, which led to war with the Monomatapa Empire and the subsequent disintegration of that power. In 1629 the king of Monomatapa declared himself a vassal of the king of Portugal.

In the late 1500s the English and French began competing for a share of the African slave trade by marketing slaves in the Spanish colonies. During the early 1600s, with the establishment of French, English, and Dutch colonies in the West Indies, even more traders attempted to tap this lucrative trade. French, English, Dutch, Swedes, and Danes obtained slaves along the west coast of Africa. For the most part, these new traders concentrated on West Africa, where they established their own fortified trading stations and drove the Portuguese out of many posts. The French, English, and Dutch were not just challenging the Portuguese in Africa; they were also competing for the

Asian trade. To reach Asia, they also had to circumnavigate Africa, and they needed ports. In 1652 the Dutch East India Company established a colony of Dutch farmers at the Cape of Good Hope to supply their ships.

By the late 1700s the French, English, Dutch, Portuguese, and Spanish controlled ports scattered along the western coast and much of the eastern coast of Africa. Most of these posts were manned by only a handful of Europeans. Actual European settlements were few and small; the main settlements were the Portuguese colonies in Angola and Mozambique, and the Dutch colony at the Cape. Few Europeans had ever penetrated the interior, and little was known of the inland peoples of Africa. Yet at the same time, the European presence in Africa had produced far-reaching effects on the lives of all Africans through the slave trade and through the introduction of New World food crops.

Slaves were acquired through raiding and warfare, usually in exchange for guns supplied by the Europeans. In Africa the gun trade and the slave trade were inextricably linked. By the early eighteenth century, about 180,000 guns were being traded annually, and by the end of the century that figure had climbed to between 300,000 and 400,000.

The slave-for-gun trade shifted trade networks and disrupted the existing balance of power among the African societies. Some groups, primarily coastal peoples in contact with Europeans, faced the choice of becoming slave raiders and acquiring guns or falling victim to those who opted for raiding. As slave-related warfare escalated, new states sprang up, and there was a concurrent decline in many older states.

In West Africa there was a decline in the power and influence of the old states of Sudan. The Songhai Empire disintegrated, and Kanem-Bornu weakened considerably. At the same time, along the coast of West Africa many small kingdoms and city states—such as Oyo, Aboney, Ashanti, and Benin—were undergoing rapid expansion that was traceable to the slave traffic. In west-central Africa the Kongo kingdom refused to be involved in the slave trade and disintegrated, because the Portuguese supported and encouraged the development of slave-raiding states. Lunda was the largest and most important of these new states.

At the same time that Africa was undergoing this dramatic escalation in warfare, New World crops brought to the continent by Europeans dramatically changed African farming. During the early 1500s, the

Portuguese introduced corn, manioc, sweet potatoes, pineapples, peanuts, papayas, and some lesser crops. The introduction of these new crops, particularly corn and manioc, greatly increased the productivity of farming in Africa. In the savannas and grasslands, corn produced higher yields than native cereal crops, and in the tropical forest regions manioc was superior to existing starchy crops. In portions of West Africa, central Angola, and the northern and southern extremes of the Congo Basin, as well as in portions of eastern Africa, corn became the dominant staple in the diet. Manioc, which was not introduced in portions of the Congo Basin until the late 1800s, spread more slowly than corn. Few details are known about exactly how these New World crops affected African populations. Some researchers have suggested that the introduction of corn resulted in a population explosion that minimized the demographic impact of the slave trade. It is also clear that corn and manioc allowed for the expansion of populations into regions that had hitherto been only sparsely occupied.

Thus, on one hand, the Europeans' quest for slaves had caused an escalation in warfare that had resulted in major losses in population and significant restructuring of African political power. However, the Europeans also introduced new crops that increased and expanded African farming. Although we cannot describe exactly what happened, we can say with certainty that the population of Africa underwent major changes. Basil Davidson (1969, 235) provides an excellent summary of the situation in Africa at the end of the eighteenth century: "By 1800 or soon after there were few regions where many polities, large or small, old or new, had not clearly felt and reacted to strong pressures of transition. Widely varying in form and power though it certainly was, the impact of change had been constantly and pervasively at work."

Europeans in Asia   The Portuguese were the first Europeans to reach Asia by sea: in 1498 Vasco da Gama landed on the coast of India. The Europeans soon learned that Asia offered a situation quite different from what confronted them in the Americas and Africa. The population of Asia far surpassed that of Europe, and Asia was divided into numerous highly developed and militarily powerful states. In almost every aspect of technology, Asian peoples were equal to if not more advanced than Europeans. In economic terms, Asia was a self-sufficient region with only limited interest in outside trade. Although Asia offered such desirable goods as silk, cotton textiles, spices, coffee, tea, porcelain, and so forth for trade, the Europeans had little to offer Asia in exchange other than gold and silver bullion. The Europeans had only one major advantage over Asia: in naval warfare European technology was superior to that of Asia.

Da Gama encountered difficulty in trading Portuguese goods in India, but he managed to trade his cargo and returned home to make a fantastic profit. However, from the outset the Portuguese realized that the only significant role they could play in the Asian trade was as middlemen in the inter-Asian trade. In 1509 they defeated the Egyptian fleet and effectively wrested control of the Indian Ocean trade from Islamic traders. Although they were militarily inferior to the Asians on land, the Portuguese were able, by entering into agreements with local rulers, to establish a series of fortified trading ports along the coast of southern and eastern Asia within fifty years: Diu (India) in 1509; Goa (India), 1510; Malacca (Malaya), 1511; Colombo (Ceylon), 1518; and Macao (China), 1557. Asian goods flowed through these ports and others to European markets in exchange for silver and gold coming from the Americas. However, this trade was extremely limited; during the 1500s the Portuguese trade between Europe and Asia averaged only ten ships annually. Of greater economic importance was the fact that an ever-increasing percentage of the lucrative trade between Asian peoples themselves was being carried by Portuguese merchant ships.

The same treaty that gave Portugal a portion of the Americas (Brazil) gave Spain a portion of Asia (the Philippines). In 1564 the Spanish founded Manila (Philippines). However, unlike the Portuguese trade that flowed westward around Africa, the Spanish ships (called *Manila Galleons*) sailed between Manila and Acapulco, Mexico. From Acapulco goods were transported over land to Vera Cruz, and from there shipped to Spain.

It was not until after 1600 that other European powers began to compete significantly for the trade with Asia. The earliest of these new competitors was the Dutch, who in 1602 organized the Dutch East India Company. By 1605 they had established themselves in a portion of the Moluccas, despite Portuguese opposition. In 1619 they established a base at Batavia (modern Jakarta) on the island of Java. Between 1638 and 1658 they were able to dislodge the Portuguese from Ceylon, and in 1641 they seized Malacca from the Portuguese. With fewer ships and less capital, the English were at a disadvantage relative to the Dutch during the first half of the seventeenth century. Early English attempts to establish trading bases in Asia failed. Their first success came in India (Madras) in 1639. By 1665 they had Bombay, and in 1691, Calcutta. The French were also establishing bases in India during the late 1600s at Chandarnagar and Pondicherry.

While western European maritime powers were active on the southern and eastern coasts of Asia, Russia was expanding by land across northern Asia. Ivan the Terrible fused the Russians into a single centralized state during the 1550s, which allowed them to challenge the powerful Tartar groups to the east. Russian frontier people, the Cossacks, were able to sweep eastward quickly and conquer the small nomadic tribal groups of Siberia. By 1637 the Russians had reached Okhotsk, on the Pacific Coast of Asia. In the 1640s they invaded the Chinese settlements in the Amur valley, only to be defeated by the Chinese Imperial Army in the 1650s. In 1689 Russia and China signed a treaty that permitted trade: the Russians exchanged gold and furs for Chinese tea.

On the whole, the initial European influence on Asian society was not significant. European territorial holdings and populations under direct control were small, usually little more than port cities. The regions most strongly affected by Europeans were the Philippines and the areas in the Indies under Dutch political control. But such regions constituted only a small portion of Asia. Europeans had little effect on Asian economic life; they were little more than a small parasitic group attached to an Asian economic system. The most significant influence on the Asian economy during this period was the introduction of New World crops, the most important of which were corn and sweet potatoes.

Oceania Oceania was the region of the world least affected by the rise of European mercantilism. In 1520, Ferdinand Magellan crossed the Pacific from east to west, and in the process discovered some of the islands. Starting in 1565, the Manila Galleon annually sailed between Acapulco and Manila. However, the galleons stopped only at Guam; other islands were either avoided or unknown to Spanish navigators, who held to the same course for 250 years. As a result, only Guam came under European domination and had any significant direct European contact.

European expansion indirectly exerted an influence on other Oceanic peoples during this period. By some

■ *The Pacific was the last major world region to be contacted by Europeans. This is the first contact of the English explorer, James Cook, with the Hawaiians of Polynesia.*

unknown means, the sweet potato, a Native American crop, was introduced into Melanesia sometime during this period. Capable of being grown at a higher altitude than yams, the sweet potato made possible the growth of native populations in the highlands of New Guinea.

Although Europeans had limited effects on Micronesia (mainly Guam) and Melanesia, Polynesia and Australia appear to have experienced no significant contact with Europeans, and few indirect sociocultural influences during this period.

■ The World and the Industrial Revolution

The industrial revolution began during the waning decades of the eighteenth century with the production of machine-woven cotton textiles in England. By the early nineteenth century the industrial revolution included the production of steel and was spreading to other European countries and the former English colonies in North America, now the United States. The industrial revolution dramatically changed the relationship between European peoples and the other peoples of the world. The technological advances that were associated with industrialization rapidly elevated European peoples to a position of almost absolute military, political, and economic dominance in the world.

As a result, European peoples redrew the political map of the world and restructured the world economy to meet the needs of their new industrial economy. This new European economic system required overseas

■ *The development of textile mills in England was the first stage of the industrial revolution.*

sources of raw materials as well as markets for finished goods. Technological advancements resulted in the construction of larger and faster ships, which meant that maritime commerce was no longer limited to high-cost luxury goods. Sharply lower shipping costs made possible the transportation of massive shipments of basic foodstuffs and raw materials on a global scale. The development of railroads opened the interiors of the continents by lowering the cost of transporting goods to the coastal ports.

During the sixteenth, seventeenth, and eighteenth centuries, global trade and sociocultural exchange had developed. In the nineteenth century there was the incipient evolution of a global economy based on regional economic specialization and the production of commodities for export. As in the earlier period, the effects of this change varied from one portion of the world to another.

The Americas   The Americas were the first region to experience this changed relationship because the Americas were more closely tied politically and economically to Europe. Just as the industrial revolution was beginning in Europe, a political revolution was starting in the Americas. From the English-speaking colonies, this revolution spread to the Spanish-speaking portions of the Americas. By the third decade of the nineteenth century, most areas of mainland America were independent of European political domination. However, these independence movements did not change the status of Native Americans, for the new countries were dominated by Euro-Americans, or in the case of Haiti, Afro-Americans.

Although these new countries had achieved political independence, they maintained economic ties to Europe; and these countries quickly became the major sources of raw materials as well as markets for industrializing Europe. The West Indies and the United States supplied cotton for the textile mills of England, and the Americas—both the English- and the Spanish-speaking countries—served as the earliest major market for finished cotton textiles. The expanding European market for raw materials stimulated economic development and territorial expansion of Euro-American and Afro-American settlements throughout the Americas. This extraordinary economic development and expansion was made possible by an increased relocation of Old World peoples, in particular African slaves. With the initial emphasis of the industrial revolution on the production of plantation crops, such as cotton and sugar, the African slave trade escalated to unprecedented proportions. Of the estimated 10 million plus African slaves brought to the Americas, the vast majority were relocated between 1750 and 1850.

As industrial centers developed in the northeastern United States and as mining, grain farming, and ranching expanded throughout the Americas during the nineteenth century, the need for inefficient slave labor declined. In 1833 slavery was abolished in the British West Indies, and by the 1880s slavery had been abolished throughout the Americas. As the importation of African slaves declined, the migration of Europeans to the Americas increased. It has been estimated that in 1835 there were 18,600,000 individuals of European ancestry in the Americas compared to 9,800,000 people of African ancestry. By 1935 the population of Euro-Americans had jumped to 172,000,000, whereas the number of Afro-Americans had risen to only 36,500,000.

In 1775 the area of Euro-American and Afro-American settlement in North America was for the most part limited to the region east of the Appalachian Mountains (see Figure 17.3). Within a century, however, the territorial limits of these settlements had been pushed across the continent to the Pacific Ocean. During the period of expansion, Native American populations had been quickly defeated militarily and confined to small reservations. A similar pattern of territorial expansion occurred in South America. The grasslands of Argentina had initially attracted few European settlers. In 1880 the territorial limits of Euro-American settlements were approximately the same as they had been in 1590. However, in the late 1800s, Euro-American ranchers swept through the

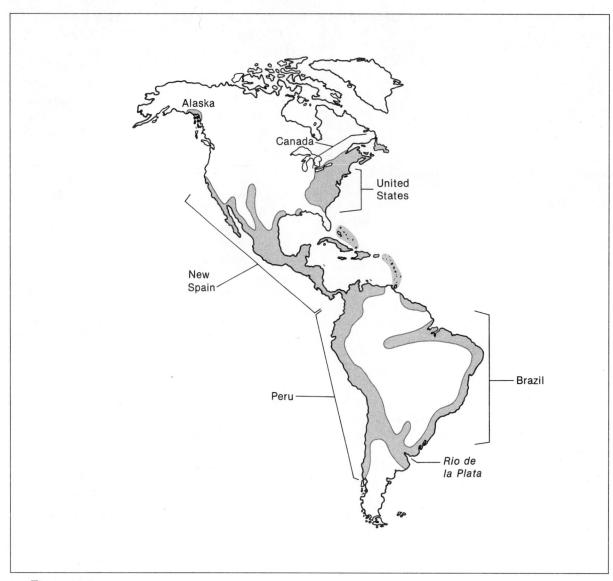

Main Regions of European Settlement or Domination in the Americas (ca. 1800)

pampas and Patagonia, virtually eliminating the Indian population. By the early 1900s autonomous or semiautonomous Native American societies were found only in the Amazon Basin and in a few scattered and isolated pockets in other portions of the Americas.

Africa   The initial impact of European industrialization on Africa was an intensification of the slave trade. However, during the mid-nineteenth century, as the slave trade declined, European economic interest in

Africa changed. Africa had potential as both a supplier of raw materials for industrial Europe and as a market for finished goods. This economic potential could not be realized under existing conditions, however, because the slave trade and resulting warfare had destroyed the political stability of the entire region. If the economic potential of Africa was to be realized, political stability had to be reestablished, transportation systems developed, and the economies restructured to meet European needs. These goals were accomplished through direct military and political intervention by European countries, primarily England, France, Germany, Belgium, and Portugal, who proceeded unilaterally to divide up the peoples and resources of Africa. As late as 1879, European powers claimed only small portions of Africa. The Portuguese had the coastal areas of Angola, Mozambique, and Guinea. The British had Cape Colony, Lagos, Gold Coast, Sierra Leone, and Gambia. The French had only Gabon, Senegal, and a few coastal ports. Twenty years later, virtually all of Africa south of the Sahara, with the exception of Liberia and Ethiopia, was under European rule.

With Africa divided, the European countries concentrated on bringing the peoples of their new territories under political control and economic domination. Colonial administrations supported by European soldiers and native troops soon established their authority. With some exceptions, the imposition of colonial control was accomplished with relatively little bloodshed. However, in German Southwest Africa the Herero War, which lasted from 1904 to 1906, cost the lives of about 100,000 natives; and in German East Africa wars between 1905 and 1906 claimed between 75,000 and 125,000 lives.

As colonial authority was established, the usual policy was to institute a tax system. Taxation of native populations served a dual purpose. The revenues generated were frequently sufficient to cover the cost of the colonial administration and troops. In addition, native populations were forced either to produce marketable exports or to work for European-owned plantations or mines to raise the money for taxes. Thus, taxation forced Africans into the European economic network.

Although exploitation of native populations characterized all European colonies in Africa, it reached its height in the Congo basin. In 1885, King Leopold of Belgium claimed the Congo as "Crown lands," and organized it as the Congo Free State. He then sold concessions to companies, which received sole rights to all land and labor within given tracts. These companies then were able to exploit ruthlessly the resources and native populations within their concessions. Africans were forced to work for the companies, and any resistance was crushed. Murder and mutilation were common. It has been estimated that between 1885 and 1908, when protests from other European powers caused the Belgian government to assume control, as many as eight million Africans were killed, or about half the total population of the Congo.

By the early part of the twentieth century, the authority of Europeans had been established throughout black Africa. The economy of the region was being developed and integrated into the European system. Gold, silver, copper, diamonds, palm oil, rubber, cacao, and other raw materials were flowing back to Europe, while Africa became an expanding market for European manufactured goods. Few Europeans actually immigrated to Africa, except to South Africa, although black Africa had been divided into European colonies. In most regions the actual presence of Europeans was limited to a handful of government administrators, soldiers, missionaries, and entrepreneurs.

Asia   The basic pattern of European political and economic expansion in Asia was similar to that of Africa. However, the magnitude of the population and the presence of an already highly developed economic system tempered much of the European impact. The industrial revolution had resulted in major advances in European military technology, which shifted the balance of power in favor of the Europeans. For the first time, they could successfully challenge even the largest and most powerful Asian states. This change became evident during the mid-1800s. China had successfully resisted making trade concessions to European powers. In the Opium War (1839–1842) with England, and in a second war with England and France between 1856 and 1858, China saw its navy and army badly defeated and was forced to make humiliating land and trading concessions. During the late 1700s and early 1800s, the British East India Company steadily expanded its territorial control in India through manipulation of internal political rivalries and limited localized wars. The crushing of the Sepoy Mutiny (1857–1858) ended any question about English political dominance of India.

By the end of the nineteenth century, much of southern and southeastern Asia had been brought under the control of European colonial governments. England had India, Burma, Malaya, Sarawak, Hong Kong, and Ceylon. The French held Indochina, and the Dutch had extended their control over the Dutch East Indies. Although still politically independent, China, Nepal, Afghanistan, Thailand, Persia (Iran), and most of the Middle Eastern countries were so strongly dominated by various European powers that some historians have called them *semicolonial regions*. Japan stood alone as the only Asian state that truly retained its autonomy.

During the late nineteenth century, as European political control spread over Asia, the economy of the area was steadily modified by various means to meet the needs of industrial Europe. Although Europeans owned and operated plantations, mines, and various industries in some areas, the principal instruments for changing the existing economies were taxes and duties. Taxation encouraged the production of cash crops for export, whereas import and export duties encouraged the production of some goods and commodities and discouraged the production of others. Native industries that would directly compete with European goods were discouraged.

The degree to which the local economy was changed differed greatly from region to region. In some regions there were large-scale developments for the production of critical cash crops, and massive relocations of populations to supply labor were often associated with these developments. Such changes were most characteristic of, but not limited to, territories within the British Empire. Ceylon became a tea-producing colony, whereas Malaya focused on rubber, Burma on rice, and Bengal (India) on jute (hemp for rope). To increase production, additional labor was frequently needed. Indians and Chinese were recruited to work on the rubber plantations in Malaya. Tamil speakers from southern India provided the labor on the tea plantations of Ceylon. Rubber, tea, and hemp flowed to Europe, and Indian immigrants in Burma increased rice production ninefold, a surplus that was in turn shipped to India, Malaya, Ceylon and other plantation regions within the empire to feed the workers.

These comprehensive changes in the political and economic life of Asia were accomplished despite the relatively small number of Europeans actually present in Asia. For example, in India during the mid-1920s Europeans numbered only about 200,000 administrators, soldiers, and civilians, as opposed to a native population of about 320,000,000—a ratio of 1:1,500.

Oceania During the last half of the eighteenth century, French, Russian, and English naval expeditions explored the Pacific, charting and describing the major islands and island groups. These men were soon followed by merchants, colonists, and whalers. In many ways the history of Oceania during the nineteenth century parallels the history of the Americas during the first three centuries after European discovery. The total population of Melanesia, Micronesia, Polynesia, and Australia was estimated at several million at the time of contact. Disease and warfare quickly reduced the population of much of Oceania during the nineteenth century.

In 1785 the English established a penal colony at Botany Bay in Australia and laid the foundation for the Europeanization of portions of Oceania. The pattern of white settlement expansion in Australia, Tasmania, and New Zealand during this period closely followed that of European settlement and occupation of the United States and Canada. The initially small colony of Europeans grew through continued migrations of European settlers. Native populations declined because of disease and warfare, while European settlements expanded, occupying an ever-increasing portion of the land. Surviving native populations were eventually limited to small reserve areas. Numbering about 5,000 at the time of contact, the Tasmanians were extinct within fifty years. During the nineteenth century, the population of native Australians declined from about 300,000 to only 60,000. Tasmania and Australia had become European regions. In New Zealand the native Maori were only slightly more successful in resisting. Numbering only about 100,000 in 1800, by the 1840s the surviving 40,000 Maori were a minority population confined on small reserves.

Aside from Tasmania and Australia, Polynesia (including New Zealand) was the region most affected by Europeans. During the nineteenth century, the indigenous population of these islands declined from 1,100,000 to only 180,000. However, the causes varied significantly from one island group to another. Easter Island was depopulated by Peruvian slave raiders who raided the island in 1842, taking about 1,000 slaves and killing numerous others. Eventually fifteen of these slaves, who were suffering from smallpox, were returned home; this had a deadly effect on the remaining islanders. Among a population that had formerly numbered between 4,000 and 7,000, decline set in, until only 111 Easter Islanders were left by the late nineteenth century. Captain Cook in 1779 estimated the native population of Hawaii at between 300,000 and 400,000. By 1857, only 70,000 native Hawaiians remained. Missionary-entrepreneurs from the United States were able to secure lands for plantations, and as the native population declined, they began importing laborers from Asia to work the fields. This influx of Europeans and Asians reduced the native Hawaiians to a minority population before the end of the nineteenth century. There were major exceptions to these patterns. Although the native populations of Samoa and Tonga declined, there was no significant influx of Europeans, and eventually the native populations of these islands recovered.

The islands of Micronesia also suffered from a population drop during the nineteenth century, declining from about 200,000 to about 83,000. However, these small, scattered islands had little to attract large numbers of Europeans. For the most part, Europeans contented themselves with asserting their political dominance and claiming these islands as possessions. Micronesians were left mostly on their own.

The pattern of contact differed significantly from island to island in Melanesia. Although the German, English, and Dutch politically divided New Guinea and established plantations along the coast, the indigenous population of the island was too vast to be displaced by Europeans. The same was not true in Fiji and New Caledonia. The native population of Fiji decreased from 300,000 to 85,000, and New Caledonia's native population declined from 100,000 to a low of 27,000. In Fiji, English entrepreneurs secured land for sugar plantations and began importing laborers from India, until by the twentieth century the Indians constituted a majority of the population. Mineral wealth attracted European settlers to New Caledonia, which came under French administration. By the twentieth century, the population of the island was about equally native and non-native.

■ European Impact on World Sociocultural Systems

By the start of the twentieth century, European political and economic domination of the world was complete. The four decades from the turn of the century until the start of World War II were, for the relationship between European peoples and non-Western peoples, a period of stability and consolidation. In economic development and world trade, this was a period of relative stagnation (see Table 17.1).

At this point we need to pause and evaluate what had happened to the world's people during the preceding four and a half centuries of European expansion. The demographic and sociocultural changes in the world's population had been profound. Not only had the total world population grown dramatically, but there had also been major dislocations and movements

■ **Table 17.1** Volume of World Trade: 1800–1985

YEAR	VOLUME	YEAR	VOLUME
1800	1	1948	54
1850	5	1953	75
1900	30	1963	142
1913	53	1970	258
1925	43	1975	340
1930	60	1980	450
1938	54	1985	489

Sources: Years 1800 to 1970 adapted from Rostow 1978, 669; 1980 estimate based on The World Bank 1982:11.; 1985 estimate based on The World Bank 1988:191.

of peoples. The lifeways of all peoples had changed, some extensively. What had been the combined effect of demographic shifts and sociocultural change?

In no major region of the world were these vast demographic and sociocultural changes more apparent than in the Americas. The Americas were now home to peoples of three quite divergent origins: Native Americans, Afro-Americans, and Euro-Americans, plus a fewer number of Asian Americans. These peoples, regardless of origin, had a generalized European sociocultural veneer, which was expressed most overtly in religion and language. The vast majority were Christian and most spoke one of three European languages—English, Spanish, or Portuguese. However, underlying this veneer still-significant sociocultural differences were reflected in numerous distinct ethnic and social identities.

The Native American population had suffered severely. Most of their land area had been lost to Euro-Americans and Afro-Americans. Only in a few scattered regions had they remained the majority population, and even in these regions they were politically dominated by Euro-Americans. Many once-distinct Native American groups had virtually vanished, whereas others had been forcibly evicted from their original homelands or had survived as small enclaves within Euro-American and/or Afro-American regions. Massachusetts, Erie, Illinois, Susquehannock, and Biloxi were now only place names instead of independent peoples. A similar fate had befallen the Lucayo, the Ciboney, and the Taino peoples of the West Indies; the Tupinamba tribes of coastal Brazil; and the Ona and Yahgan of Tierra del Fuego, to name only a handful. The Delaware, for example, who originally lived in New Jersey and adjacent portions of New York and Pennsylvania, survived but were forced westward. During the nineteenth century some groups of Delaware were reported living as far west as Oregon and as far south as northern Mexico. By the early twentieth century, scattered communities of Delaware survived in Oklahoma and Ontario. Numerous other native peoples were similarly dislocated.

These movements of peoples into and within the Americas resulted not only in the extinction of many existing native groups, but also in the emergence of new sociocultural systems, and with them new ethnic or social identities. In the West Indies a number of distinct Afro-American traditions emerged. Although basically Christian and speaking either Spanish, French, English, Dutch, or Creole, these Afro-American sociocultural systems combined in varying degrees traits of European and African origin as well as a number of newly innovated localized traits. In mainland North and South America, a host of new Afro-American groups had come into existence. Some societies like the maroon tribes of Surinam and the Gullah people of the Sea Islands of South Carolina have their own distinct languages or dialects (see Box 17.2). Scattered throughout the Americas were innumerable socioculturally distinct rural and urban Afro-American groups without such readily definable boundary markers. In a few cases escaped black slaves became associated with Native American groups and adopted a Native American language and other sociocultural traits; the Black Carib of the West Indies and Central America represent one such case.

As they spread over the Americas, Euro-Americans, like Afro-Americans, developed a multitude of new, regionally distinct sociocultural systems and identities, with varying combinations of European, African, Native American, and newly innovated sociocultural traits.

Contact between Old World peoples and Native Americans also resulted in racial mixture. In most cases, racially mixed individuals were simply absorbed back into one of their parent groups. However, in some cases racial mixture gave rise to still other new sociocultural identities. In Mexico individuals of mixed Spanish and Indian ancestry became the *mestizos*, people who were neither Spanish nor Indian in sociocultural terms. In Canada individuals of mixed French and Indian ancestry become known as the *Metis*, a sociocultural group distinct from both Indians and French.

■ *In the United States Euro-American peoples show significant sociocultural differences. In New Holland, Pennsylvania, a group of Amish men, wearing their traditional straw hats and suspenders, help a friend in a 1978 roof raising.*

To a much lesser degree similar changes occurred in other regions of the world. In South Africa, the Boers, a Euro-African population with a distinct language, had developed into a distinct sociocultural group. Also in South Africa, racial mixing between Europeans and Africans resulted in the emergence of the Cape Coloured as a distinct people. In western Africa repatriated Afro-Americans, known as the *Libero-Americans*, existed as a distinct English-speaking sociocultural group living among and politically dominating the native African peoples of Liberia. In addition, scattered through much of the colonial world were numerous enclaves of peoples who, although retaining their original identities and even languages, in reality constituted "new" sociocultural groups; for example, the East Indian communities in Trinidad, Fiji, and South Africa, and the "overseas" Chinese communities in Hawaii, Malaya, Sarawak, French Indochina, and the Dutch East Indies.

Thus, European expansion generated a wide range of sociocultural changes. By the start of World War II a large number of societies that had existed in 1492 were extinct. Although many societies had vanished, the vast sociocultural changes that took place, together with massive movements of peoples, resulted in the creation of still other new sociocultural traditions and identities. Anthropologists are now just beginning to study these complex historical changes. Many scholars believe that historical studies of sociocultural systems will be one of the major focuses—if not the major focus—of anthropological research in the future.

The World since 1945

Thus far we have discussed the changes in human lifeways as purely a scholarly study. These descriptions may be interesting, but you might be asking, Why is it important to me to understand other peoples? Does insight into other lifeways have any practical value? Does anthropology have any bearing on my life or my future? These are legitimate questions. In this section we hope to show you why anthropology and the understanding of other peoples are important to you as an individual.

World War II was a watershed in world history in that it marked the beginning of a major shift in the direction of sociocultural change. Technological advances have, as we say, "made the world smaller." We can watch the wedding of Prince Andrew and Sara Ferguson live from London on our television sets. On our telephones we can direct dial most major cities in the world and converse with friends or colleagues. Airline travel has put us within two to three days travel time from all but the most remote places on earth.

Technological changes have also increased industrial and agricultural production and greatly increased the social contacts between and economic interdependence of the various countries and regions of the globe. A truly global economic system has evolved. Since 1945 the earth's population has more than doubled; at the same time its geographic distribution is shifting. Finally, the postwar era has seen the end of political colonialism, resulting in the creation of numerous newly independent countries, making the world more politically fragmented. Virtually every country—the United States included—has experienced both major internal economic shifts and demographic ones, as well as significant changes in its external relationships with other countries. These fundamental changes in the economy, population, and political structure of the world make anthropological insights into humanity more important than ever—or so we hope to convince our readers (see Chapter 18 for a discussion of how ethnic groups change).

■ Modern technology has penetrated even the most remote regions of the globe. These Australian aborigines in Arnhemland call relatives to a ceremony using a solar battery-powered shortwave radio.

■ The World Economy

For better or worse, the market principle increasingly integrates the economies of the world into a global economy in which manufactured goods, foodstuffs, and raw materials are marketed worldwide. Thus, the price we pay for a sack of flour in Kansas or a gallon of gasoline in Texas is determined in large part by the world price for wheat and oil. In turn, oil prices are greatly influenced by whether the leaders of OPEC (Organization of Petroleum Exporting Countries) can control the production of its member nations, and thus the world price. The price we pay for a Ford in Detroit is no longer solely influenced by competition from General Motors and Chrysler but also by auto manufacturers in Japan, Scandinavia, and Germany. Foreign imports not only place American auto companies and dealers in competition with foreign companies but also put American auto workers in direct competition with their foreign counterparts. American farmers, oil producers, businesspeople, and workers are now finding that they have to compete on a global level for the prices they can charge for their goods and labor.

Three main factors have been instrumental in the development of this global economic system. First, to varying degrees, the colonial powers economically monopolized their colonies, using them as sources of raw materials as well as markets for their manufactured

Box 17.2

THE GULLAHS AND THE BLACK SEMINOLES

The Gullah people of the Sea Islands and adjacent coastal areas of South Carolina and Georgia are culturally the most distinctive Afro-American population in the United States. In their language and culture, Gullahs have preserved more of their African heritage than other groups. The Gullah language is a creole language based on English, but with many words drawn from several West African languages. Historically it is related to Krio, a language still spoken today in Sierra Leone. African cultural traits permeate many aspects of Gullah culture. In addition to their personal names, individuals have African nicknames, or what they call *basket names*. Some of these names are African personal names: Bala, Salifu, Jah, Fatu, and Jilo. Other names come from African clan names: Kalawa, Koroma, and Marah. Still other names are derived from Sierra Leonean tribal groups: Lim-

ba, Susu, Kissi, and Kono. The Gullahs have retained the African story telling tradition, drawing on African folktales for many of their own stories. The Brer Rabbit stories, immortalized by Joel Chandler Harris in his collections of "Uncle Remus" tales, are the best known of the Gullah stories. Animal tricksters such as Brer Rabbit are a common theme in African storytelling.

Other aspects of Gullah culture also demonstrate their African heritage. Burial customs, such as drumming to announce a death, stopping the funeral party at the cemetery gate to ask the ancestral spirits for permission to enter, breaking bottles and dishes on the grave so that no one else in the family will die, and leaving food on the veranda for the spirit of the deceased, are directly traceable to African practices. Until the early part of this century many aspects of Gullah material culture were African in origin; for example, their basketwork, wooden mortars and pestles for processing rice, carved wooden grave markers and walking sticks, calabash containers, and indigo-dyed cotton blankets. Their rice-based diet and the ways they prepared food strongly reflected their West African heritage. This list is just a sampling of African cultural traits of the Gullahs. A unique set of historical circumstance allowed them to retain more of their African heritage than other Afro-American peoples in the United States.

During the early part of the 1700s, English plantation owners in South Carolina and Georgia discovered that the low-lying tropical islands and coastal areas were ideally suited for the cultivation of rice. Lacking any firsthand knowledge of rice cultivation, these planters began importing large numbers of slaves from the rice-growing areas of West Africa, notably the region around Sierra Leone. In essence these plantation owners transplanted both rice-growing peoples and technology from the west coast of Africa to the coastal region of the southern English colonies.

Fevers and other tropical diseases were prevalent along the low-lying tropical coast and islands. Plantation owners tried to avoid the area, preferring to live inland, where these diseases were not as common. Thus most plantation owners lived for only part of the year on their coastal plantations. The actual running of the plantations was left to a few white managers and trusted slaves, who worked as foremen or "drivers." This arrangement greatly limited direct contact between Europeans and Gullahs. In many ways, their life on the Sea Islands was like their life in Africa. They grew the same crops and used the same technology and material items. Although the ancestors of the Gullahs were drawn from various African groups such as the Mende, Temmne, Limba,

---

goods. With the end of colonialism the export products of these regions could be sold on the world market, and imported goods could be purchased in the same competitive world marketplace. Second, technological improvements in transportation have resulted in a drastic lowering of the cost of transporting ores, metals, manufactured goods, and foodstuffs. Supertankers have been developed for the shipping of oil. The use of containers in transporting and loading has greatly reduced the cost of shipping manufactured goods. Larger and faster cargo planes have revolutionized the

international transportation of lightweight, high-value goods. Geography no longer protects markets nor limits the products produced by a region. Third, international banking and financial institutions have evolved and loaned money to capital-poor Third World nations for economic development, ultimately increasing both the exports and imports of these countries.

These and other changes have stimulated and expanded the volume of world trade. As we have seen, world trade stagnated in the period between World

and others, all had similar sociocultural systems and spoke Krio as a trade language. Because there was no need to learn English, Krio became the language of the group, and the sociocultural traditions of the different groups blended easily together to create a "new" people. When and how they acquired the name *Gullah* is not known. The social isolation of the Gullah people in these coastal areas continued until well after the turn of the twentieth century.

During the late 1700s, many Gullah people escaping from the plantations found refuge in the swamps and forests of what was then Spanish Florida. There they formed small free settlements and survived by growing rice and corn and by hunting. At about the same time, small groups of refugee Creek Indians began moving south and settling in Florida. Eventually these Creek splinter groups became known as the *Seminoles*. Friendly relations developed between the free Gullahs and their more numerous Seminole neighbors. Eventually the free Gullahs adopted much of the Seminole clothing styles and material culture, and even the language, although they never stopped speaking Gullah as well. In turn the Seminoles learned rice cultivation and technology from the Gullah. Although they kept their separate identities and communities, the ever-

growing presence of their common enemy, the Americans, forged a close alliance between the two peoples. Readily distinguishable from other Afro-Americans and closely associated with the Seminoles, the free Gullahs came to be known as the *Black Seminoles.*

In 1819 the United States acquired Florida from Spain, and in 1830 initiated a plan to relocate Native Americans from the east to new areas west of the Mississippi River. The original plan of the federal government was to move the Seminole Indians west, and force the Black Seminoles into slavery. The Seminoles and Black Seminoles joined forces in resisting the plan, and in 1835 war broke out. The war proved to be far longer and more costly than the government had anticipated. It lasted six years, cost the lives of 1,500 American soldiers, and resulted in the capture or surrender of only some of the Seminoles and Black Seminoles. By the end of the war, it had become clear that the Black Seminoles were far too dangerous to be allowed to come into contact with other Afro-Americans. Thus the Black Seminoles were sent west with the other Seminoles to live in the Indian Territory.

In the 1850s a small group of Black Seminoles broke away, left the Indian Territory, and made their way to Mexico. In northern Mexico, they were hired as mercenaries by the government

to fight Comanche and Apache raiders. The Black Seminole community attracted runaway slaves from Texas plantations, and the population grew.

Following the Civil War, the Comanches became a major problem on the plains of Texas. In 1870 the U.S. Cavalry invited the Black Seminoles in Mexico to come to Texas and join the army. Many did, and a cavalry unit known as the *Seminole Negro Indian Scouts* was formed. For valor in their battles with the Comanches, three of these "scouts" were awarded the Congressional Medal of Honor.

Today there are four Gullah-derived groups in the United States and Mexico. The largest, the Gullahs, is in coastal South Carolina and Georgia. Although their exact numbers are not known, about 100,000 Gullah speakers still live in the community. The Black Seminoles, who still live among the Seminoles in Oklahoma, number about 2,000. At Brackettville, Texas, in a small community known as the *scouts*, live the descendants of the cavalry scouts. Finally, at Nacimiento, in the Mexican state of Coahuilla, there is a small community of people called the *Mascogos.* ∎

Source: Opala (1987) and Bateman (1990)

War I and World War II. Following World War II the volume of world trade began once again to expand, until by 1985 it was over nine times the level it had been just before and after the war (refer back to Table 17.1).

Until the 1950s the industrialized regions of the world were concentrated in Europe and North America, with Japan being the only non-Western country that had industrialized to any significant degree. The rest of the world served basically as a source of raw materials and a market for the manufactured goods of

these regions. Since 1960 several "second-wave" industrialized regions have emerged, particularly in Asia: Hong Kong, Taiwan, South Korea, and Singapore. With sophisticated technology and low labor costs, these regions have been able to undercut the prices and invade the markets of the established "first-wave" industrial countries. Initially involved in the production of textiles, clothing, and footwear, these countries have moved steadily into the production of electronics, and in the case of South Korea, into heavy industry— steel, automobiles, and ship building. As a result, the

■ *Today, modern and traditional lifeways often exist side by side. Here in Punjab, India, Sikh farmers in bullock carts travel on a paved road past a modern gasoline station.*

global competition for both raw materials and markets for manufactured goods has intensified.

The changing economic relationship between the United States and the rest of the world over the past forty years illustrates the increasing degree of global interdependence. Just before World War II the United States was what geographer L. Dudley Stamp characterized as a "young nation," meaning that over 50 percent of the U.S. exports consisted of foodstuffs and

raw materials such as oil, raw cotton, wheat and other grains, and tobacco. Imports were dominated by products that did not occur naturally or grow well domestically, notably tropical foodstuffs and raw materials such as rubber, sugar, coffee, and silk. The United States was self-sufficient in most minerals critical for industry, including iron, copper, potassium, coal, and petroleum. Indeed, the United States was an exporter of these items. In turn, American industrial output was more than sufficient to meet domestic needs for most categories of manufactured goods.

The postwar era has seen major shifts in both the kinds and quantities of goods that the United States imports and exports. As the volume of trade has increased, the nature of American imports and exports has changed. From a strategic perspective the most significant change is that the United States now has to rely on other countries for many of the critical raw materials for industries and fuels that it once produced (see Table 17.2). The increasing dependence of Americans on the importation of metals, petroleum, and other raw materials is the result of several factors. The expanding economy of the United States has resulted in an increased consumption of energy fuels and raw materials. At the same time, either domestic energy and raw-material reserves have declined in production, or production cannot be increased to meet demands.

■ *Table 17.2* **Percentage Imported of Selected Minerals and Metals, United States, 1960 to 1986**

MINERALS & METALS	1960	1965	1970	1975	1980	1986	MAJOR SOURCES 1982–1985
Manganese	89	94	95	98	98	100	South Africa, Gabon
Bauxite	74	85	88	91	94	96	Jamaica, Guinea
Cobalt	66	92	98	98	93	85	Zaire, Zambia
Tin	82	80	81	84	79	74	Malaysia, Thailand
Potassium	exp.	7	42	51	65	wh.	Canada, Israel
Titanium	22	9	24	25	32	wh.	Australia, Canada
Petroleum	16	19	22	35	37	36	Mexico, Canada
Iron ore	16	32	30	30	25	33	Canada, Venezuela
Iron and steel	exp.	7	4	9	15	21	Europe, Japan
Vanadium	exp.	15	21	38	35	wh.	South Africa, Canada
Copper	exp.	15	exp.	exp.	14	27	Chile, Canada
Aluminum	exp.	4	exp.	exp.	exp.	26	Canada, Ghana

Note: *exp.* indicates export of surplus production, *wh.* indicates that this figure is officially "withheld to avoid disclosure."

Source: U.S. Bureau of the Census (1980 and 1989).

PEOPLES OF
THE AMERICAS

No region of the globe has changed as dramatically as the Americas over the past five hundred years. The modern peoples of the Americas fall into four overlapping regional groups: Anglo America, Latin America, Afro America, and Native America.

ANGLO-AMERICA   Anglo America includes all those regions and communities whose people speak English as their native language. The main areas are the United States, Canada, Belize, Guyana, and some of the islands of the West Indies. The population is largely European in ancestry, with African, Asian and Native American minorities. The basic sociocultural institutions of these peoples are primarily derived from western Europe. Anglo Americans are predominantly an urban industrialized population.

LATIN AMERICA   Latin America consists of those regions and communities whose people speak Spanish or Portuguese as their native language. This area includes almost all of South America, Central America, Mexico, Cuba, the Dominican Republic, and Puerto Rico as well as some areas of the United States. The basic sociocultural institutions of these peoples are derived primarily from southern Europe. While there are large urban industrial centers in Latin America, much of the population is still rural. The population of Latin America is extremely diverse. In some regions the population is predominately European; other regions have populations that are primarily African or Native American in ancestry.

AFRO AMERICA   Afro America consists of those regions and communities whose people are predominately African in ancestry. The vast majority of Afro Americans would overlap with and be included as parts of Anglo America or Latin America. There are, however, some groups such as the Gullah of South Carolina, the Gurifuna of Belize, and the Saramaka, Djuka, Matawi, Kwinti, Paramaka and Aluku of Suriname who are linguistically and culturally distinct from neighboring populations.

NATIVE AMERICA   Native America includes those regions and communities whose people maintain a social identity as Native American. (In Latin America, there are tens of millions of individuals who are predominately of Native American ancestry, but who are not socially or culturally Native Americans). Surviving only in isolated rural regions, Native Americans are the numerically smallest and politically least powerful of the four major groups. In all countries they are a politically, economically and socially dominated population, and the sociocultural systems of all surviving groups have been strongly influenced by outside forces. Only small groups in South America still retain political autonomy and remain economically unintegrated into the local and national economy.

OTHER PEOPLES   There are several smaller groups in the Americas. There are French speaking peoples in Canada and Haiti. Of more recent origin are Asian communities which are today found scattered in much of Anglo America and Latin America.

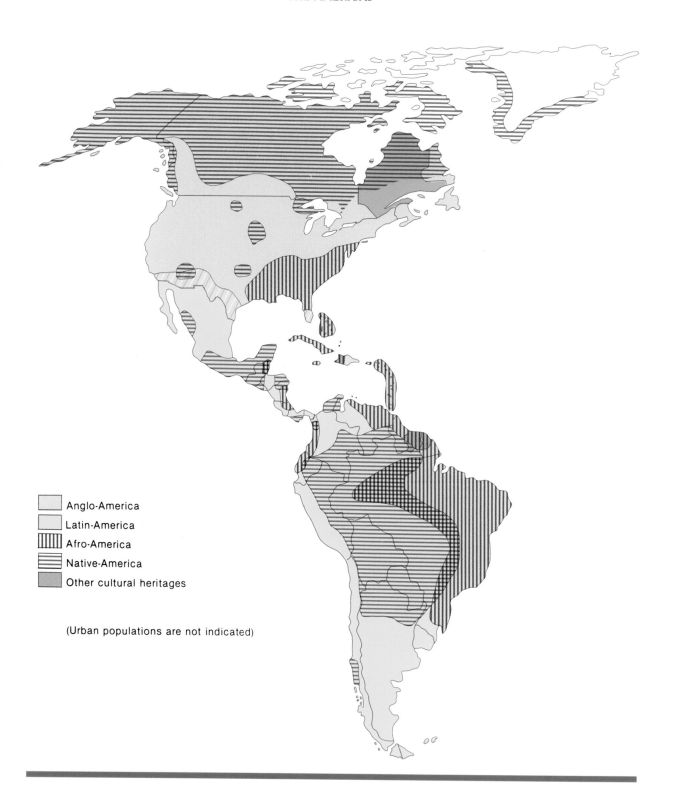

Anglo-America
Latin-America
Afro-America
Native-America
Other cultural heritages

(Urban populations are not indicated)

■ (Above, inset) Native Americans survive as distinct communities mainly in the Amazon Basin and in the highland mountains of Peru and Bolivia. This Amazonian woman is processing a plant.

■ (Above) Afro-Americans live throughout the Americas, including the Caribbean. This is a market in Spanish Town, Jamaica.

■ (Right) In parts of Latin America, over the centuries European catholicism mixed with indigenous Native American traditions to form new and unique religious beliefs and practices. This ritual procession on Good Friday in Antigua, Guatemala, illustrates the mixture of Spanish and Native American influences.

■ (Above) Some Indians of North America spend most of their lives on reservations, whereas others live and work among Anglo-Americans. This Mohawk steelworker lives in New York City, but retains close ties to his relatives on the Caughnawaga Reservation in Canada.

■ (Above, right) The Peruvian Andes is one South American region still peopled mainly by Native Americans. These Quechua are marketing produce in a Peruvian city.

■ (Right) Most Afro-Americans, such as this Jamaican cane worker, are descended from slaves brought to the New World between the sixteenth and nineteenth centuries.

Sources for the creation of this insert: Steward and Faron (1959), Wagley (1968), Wolf and Hansen (1972), Szwed (1970), Kehoe (1981) and Price (1979).

While the United States has become increasingly dependent on foreign sources for basic energy needs and raw materials, the nature of American industry itself has been changing. The American shoe industry is almost gone, replaced by factories in Brazil, Italy, Taiwan, and South Korea. Segments of the American electronics industry have lost out to foreign competition; most television sets, radios, and videocassette recorders are now produced in Japan, Hong Kong, or Singapore. The American garment industry is rapidly losing its domestic market to clothing imported from South Korea, Hong Kong, and Taiwan. The American automobile industry, traditionally the bulwark of the manufacturing economy, has lost a significant portion of its domestic market to imports from Germany, Italy, Sweden, England, France, Japan, South Korea, and Yugoslavia. A similar loss of the domestic market has occurred for the American steel industry. Today the United States depends on foreign sources for much of its basic needs in manufactured goods. To pay for these increased imports, the United States has shifted from being primarily an exporter of raw materials to an exporter of specialized manufactured goods such as aircraft, machinery, chemicals, and vehicles.

These recent changes in the world economic system would not have been possible without the development of international financing, which has made money available to capital-poor nations for economic development. In 1945 the World Bank and the International Monetary Fund were created to help war-ravaged Europe and Japan reestablish their industrial plants. These two institutions have played a pivotal role in the creation of the existing global economic system. The World Bank has been a major conduit for economic-development loans to Third World nations. The World Bank's role in making loan money available to Third World countries has now been supplemented by numerous European, American, and Japanese banking houses that have become international financiers. Some banking practices have adapted to foreign traditions in interesting ways (see Box 17.3).

Loans provided to these capital-poor countries have allowed them to adopt high-cost technology more quickly and increase their economic productivity. With these funds, Third World countries have constructed irrigation projects, expanded and modernized their transportation and communication systems, developed or expanded port facilities, and in some cases developed their own manufacturing industries. In the past decade alone these loans have amounted to hundreds of billions of dollars. An underappreciated consequence of these loans is a stimulation of the exports of industrialized nations, for most of these funds are used to purchase needed technology and equipment from Japan, Europe, and the United States. At the same time, most of the economic development projects funded by these loans have focused on increased production of raw materials needed by these same industrialized countries.

International financing adds another dimension to the increasing interdependence of nations. With Third World countries owing hundreds of billions of dollars in loans to industrial nations through international banks, the citizens of the industrial nations have a very direct vested interest in the economic prosperity of these countries. American banks hold the largest single block of outstanding loans to Third World countries. For example, much of Mexico's national debt of $98 billion (as of 1986) is owed to American banks. A default by Mexico would have a devastating effect on American banks and would result in tremendous financial losses to American investors and, ultimately, the American taxpayers. In speaking of Mexico's loan debts, a Mexican minister for finance noted that when a country's debts are as large as those of Mexico, the country and the banks become in effect partners; that is, the banks cannot afford to let Mexico default. He might have gone a step further and stated that economically speaking, the United States and Mexico are now partners, because the United States government ultimately guarantees these loans.

As discussed in this brief overview, neither the United States nor any other country in the world even approaches economic self-sufficiency. Virtually all peoples are integrated into the global economy. We depend on each other for critical energy fuels, raw materials, and particular categories of foodstuffs and manufactured goods. Without these imports we could not sustain our economy, nor could we even adequately provide food, clothing, and shelter for our population. In turn, other countries depend on us, both as a source for particular manufactured goods and foodstuffs and as a market for their products. Although some countries and regions may be more critical than others because they provide some particular essential goods or resources, all are important in maintaining the present global economic system. In the future the integration and interdependence certainly will become significantly greater. Given that we are all part of the single global system that evolved as a consequence of the expansion of European peoples and ideas, enlightened self-interest as well as humanitarianism demand that

Box 17.3

THE BANKERS AND THE SHEIKS

During the Middle Ages in Europe, the Catholic church through its canon courts declared usury, or the charging of interest on loans, to be un-Christian. Thus, Christians were prohibited from charging interest, and banking in medieval Europe was in the hands of Jews. During the late Middle Ages, Italian Catholics began founding banking houses and by clever semantics were able to circumvent the church laws against usury. An individual would be loaned money, interest free, for an unrealistically short period of time. When the loan was not repaid within this stated time, which it rarely was, the bankers then charged "damages."

The Islamic religion also prohibits usury. However, Islam differs in a number of significant ways from Christianity. The Koran is not merely a book of religious teachings, but is also a codified legal system. Courts in traditional Islamic countries use the Koran as the basis for legal rulings and function as what are sometimes called *Islamic courts*. The Koran prohibits usury by any Moslem.

The law courts in much of the Arab world—Saudi Arabia, Kuwait, Bahrain, and the United Arab Emirates—are Islamic courts. Thirty years ago this fact had little international significance. Relatively poor, these countries had little need for financial transactions and banking institutions. With the discovery of oil and the rapid development of this region starting in the 1960s, a need for such institutions quickly developed. A number of European and American banking houses, such as Citibank and Chase Manhattan, opened Middle Eastern branches. Not only did they manage the vast flow of dollars changing hands through the sale of oil and the purchase of imports, they also began loaning money to local Arab entrepreneurs who organized companies to profit from this economic boom.

Like the medieval Italian bankers, they developed semantic ways of circumventing the Islamic prohibition against usury. The word *interest* was never used in loaning money. Instead these banks charged Islamic borrowers "administrative fees" or "loan initiation discounts." By 1986 it was estimated that the various world banks had between $8 and $9 billion in loans to Saudi Arabian companies alone. This system worked well as long as oil income kept rising and all parties made handsome profits. However, in the 1980s the price of oil began to decline, and in early 1986 the price collapsed, falling from twenty-eight dollars a barrel to (at one point) under ten dollars a barrel.

As their income from oil plunged, governments began to slow payments to government contractors and suppliers. Arab companies with a cash-flow problem quickly fell behind on loan payments to banks. Many Arab businessmen suddenly rediscovered their religion. A flood of Arab companies and individuals quickly took the banks to court, charging them with usury. These courts correctly found the bank guilty of usury under Islamic law.

By the summer of 1986 a number of international banks were cutting back on their Middle Eastern operations. Citibank reduced its offices in Bahrain and the United Arab Emirates; Chase Manhattan closed its Jordanian branch. The issue has yet to be resolved. Western banking practices conflict with Islamic law, yet the oil-rich Arab states need such practices. Arab governments realize this need, but the question remains: How can Western banking institutions be accommodated under Islamic law? ■

---

we understand and respect those with sociocultural heritages different from our own.

■ Demographic Changes

Concurrent with the postwar growth in world trade has been a rapid growth in population, particularly in Latin America, Asia, and Africa. Although the economic development of many of these regions has been significant, economic expansion has not kept pace with population growth. Thus, this population explosion has created extreme economic and/or population pressures in many of the less-developed rural regions of the Third World, contributing to out-migrations of peoples. (Chapter 19 discusses some anthropological insights on population growth.) As we have noted, mass movements of people are not new in history, for migrations of populations came in the wake of European expansion. However, both the nature and geographical direction of population movements since World War II differ from those of earlier periods. These earlier migrations were primarily movements of European and African peoples to the Americas, with secondary waves of European immigrants settling in portions of Oceania, Africa, and Asia, and Asian immigrants being relocated in Asia or resettled in portions of Africa and Oceania. Since 1945 there have been two main patterns of human migration: (1) a worldwide phenomenon of rural-to-urban migration and (2) a migration of Third World peoples to the industrialized countries of Europe and North America.

During the nineteenth and early twentieth centuries the development of major urban centers was associated with industrial economies. Increasing demand for industrial workers had been the primary factor in the growth of cities. In industrialized societies this trend toward urbanization has continued. In addition, major urban centers have emerged in nonindustrialized Third World countries. Just before World War II, approximately 50 percent of the total population of the United States and Europe was urban, compared to only about 8 to 10 percent for Africa and Asia, and 25 percent for Latin America. Today approximately 75 percent of Americans and 70 percent of Europeans are city dwellers. However, the urban population of Asia and Africa has jumped to between 25 percent and 30 percent, and in Latin America it has increased to over 60 percent. The growth rate of urbanization has thus been highest outside Europe and North America. In fact, the world's five most rapidly growing cities are located in nonindustrialized nations: Bandung (Indonesia), Lagos (Nigeria), Karachi (Pakistan), Bogotá (Colombia), and Baghdad (Iraq). In some of these cities the growth rate has been phenomenal. In the 1950s Lagos had a population of only about 350,000; by the early 1980s its population was estimated at about 4,000,000. Similar increases are common in many Latin American, Asian, and African nations. Most Third World cities lack the large industrial complexes capable of employing the great masses of people migrating into them, but their small-scale industries, transportation services, and government jobs, although limited, offer greater economic opportunities than do the overcrowded rural regions of the adjacent countryside.

Most migration has been within countries, but a growing trend has been toward international migration. Most evident has been the migration from the nations of Latin America, Asia, and Africa to the highly industrialized countries of North America and Europe. As their industrial economies expanded during the 1950s and 1960s, many Western European coun-

■ *With almost 40 million people living within a 100-mile radius of the Emperor's palace, Tokyo, Japan is one of the largest and most densely occupied cities in the world.*

tries began experiencing labor shortages. West Germany initiated a "guest-worker" program to actively recruit foreign laborers, first in southern Europe, Italy, and Spain, and later in Yugoslavia and Turkey. Concurrently, French factories began recruiting Arab workers from their then North African colonies, particularly Algeria. In the 1950s England began experiencing an influx of West Indians from its possessions in the Caribbean. In the 1960s a wave of Pakistani and Indian immigrants also settled in England. Other Western European countries also experienced a similar phenomenon, although usually on a smaller scale.

By the early 1970s, when the economic growth of Western Europe began to slow, large non-European communities were well established in most of the major cities. When West Germany ended its guest-worker program in 1974, it had hosted 2.5 million foreign workers, a number equal to over 10 percent of its total labor force. Through various means the West German government tried to repatriate these guest workers and their families, but failed. France, England, and other Western European countries have considered stricter immigration laws to stop the continuing influx of African and Asian workers, but the number of new immigrants is increasing in spite of tighter controls. In

1985 alone it was estimated that 150,000 additional immigrants entered Western Europe. In 1986 Western Europe, out of a total population of 238 million, it was estimated that 16 million were legal immigrants, and an additional 1 million were illegal immigrants, most from Asia and Africa. As a result, Western European countries, which once had relatively homogeneous populations, are now home to a number of culturally and ethnically diverse peoples.

This change in patterns of human migration is equally evident in the United States, a country peopled primarily by Old World immigrants and their descendants. Since World War II, approximately 25 percent of American population growth has been the result of immigration. However, unlike in earlier periods, this new wave of immigrants is being drawn predominantly from Latin America and Asia. The exact number of people involved in this new wave of immigration is impossible to determine, because a considerable number are illegal immigrants and thus are uncounted. Some are political refugees, like the Vietnamese, Cambodians, Laotians, Cubans, Salvadorans, Afghans, and Ethiopians. However, the majority of Latin American, West Indian, Chinese, Asian Indian, Arab, European, and African immigrants are mainly economic refugees.

Although Europe and North America have been the primary destination for most international migrants, other regions with high income, labor shortages, or both have experienced major influxes of immigrants. Many of the oil-rich Arab countries—Libya, Saudi Arabia, Kuwait, Quatar, Oman, and the United Arab Emirates—have recruited foreign workers from India, Pakistan, Bangladesh, and Egypt, and from among Palestinian refugees. Indeed, in some of the smaller of these countries, foreign workers outnumber native Arabs. Thus, the population of the world is in constant flux.

In the not-too-distant past, white missionaries took Christianity and European culture to the peoples of the Americas, Africa, Asia, and Oceania. Although Christian missionary work continues, today we also find Islamic mosques in such cities as Berlin, Paris, London, and New York, and Hindu gurus find converts among European peoples in both Europe and North America. Before World War II small pockets of European peoples were found scattered throughout the cities of Africa and Asia. Today, enclaves of newly arrived Turks, Arabs, Africans, Asians, and Latin Americans are scattered throughout the cities of Western Europe and North America.

This massive migration of peoples has alleviated some of the economic and population pressures in many Third World countries. At the same time, like it or not, it is bringing peoples from extremely diverse sociocultural backgrounds into direct daily contact with one another. We all need to learn tolerance for one another.

■ *Political Fragmentation*

The postwar era has been characterized by increased political fragmentation. Although the precise number varies depending on how one defines an "independent" or "autonomous" country, at the beginning of World War II there were approximately sixty countries in the world. Most of Asia, Africa, and Oceania was divided between European colonial empires. As the era of colonialism came to an end following the war, the number of politically independent countries increased rapidly. Between 1946 and 1980, eighty-eight new countries were carved out of the colonial empires of Europe. Today there are approximately 170 independent countries.

The emergence of these new countries has forever changed the face of global politics. Before the war European leaders, consulting only among themselves, controlled the political destiny of the world's peoples. Even Japan was considered a second-level power. As non-European countries have increasingly emerged as economic and even military powers, non-European leaders have to come to play an ever-expanding role in world politics. (Chapter 18 expands on this discussion of political fragmentation.)

The Consequences of an Interdependent World

The world we live in today is not the world of our parents or our grandparents. This is true at both the individual level and the national level.

For the individual the consequences of recent changes are both direct and indirect. Urbanization is resulting in increased daily contact between individuals from diverse ethnic and sociocultural backgrounds. In cities throughout the world people are finding that employers and employees, customers and vendors, landlords and tenants, doctors and patients—in other words, individuals whose actions affect the quality of their everyday lives—are increasingly individuals with

■ *The Hare Krishna movement and many other non-Western religions have found converts in the United States and Western Europe during the past few decades.*

whom they do not share a common sociocultural heritage. Certainly there has always been diversity in American cities; but when our grandparents thought of ethnic diversity, they thought primarily about the differences between Irish, Italians, Poles, Germans, Russians, Swedes, and so forth. Although there were some sociocultural differences between these groups, they shared a basically common sociocultural tradition. Today these new immigrant groups are from Asia, Africa, Latin America, and the Middle East, people with whom most Americans do not share a common sociocultural tradition. Thus, greater awareness of and tolerance for sociocultural differences are increasingly necessary parts of our lives.

These changes have important consequences at the individual level, but it is at the national level where the consequences of these changes become greatest. First, the economic interdependence of the world's peoples requires a steady flow of manufactured goods, foodstuffs, and raw materials from other countries. Because virtually no region of the world is economically self-sufficient, disruption in the steady flow of this exchange could conceivably have catastrophic economic repercussions. The vulnerability of the United States and its dependence on other countries for critical resources were made clear in 1973 when the Arab oil-producing countries embargoed shipments of oil to the United States for six months in retaliation for

American support of Israel. The result was a major shortage of petroleum products that created lines at gasoline stations throughout the country. The primary threat to this global trade network is political conflict that has the potential to cut trade in particular items. Population pressures and related economic pressures increase the possibilities for political conflict. Whether we wish to view the existing and potential problems of the world in a humanistic way or look at it with pragmatic self-interest, the answers are the same. The turning to desert of portions of Africa and the resulting problems of starvation are not simply African problems; these are problems of the world community. Economic development projects in Latin America or Africa or Asia serve the needs not only of the peoples of these particular regions but also of the global economy.

Certainly we would not argue that tolerance and understanding of sociocultural differences can solve all the world's difficulties. However, many problems in the world today are the result of sociocultural intolerance and misunderstandings. Anthropologists and anthropological theory are well suited to understanding and arbitrating these problems, and to showing why we all ought to show more respect for one another's rights and opinions.

Summary

In this chapter we have outlined worldwide cultural history since 1500, touching on only a few aspects of a very complex subject. The purpose of this approach is twofold: (1) to show the magnitude and pervasiveness of the recent historical changes that underlie existing sociocultural systems and (2) to show the importance of understanding sociocultural differences for living in the modern world.

Worldwide history over the past 500 years falls into three major time categories. First, the discovery of the Americas by Columbus in 1492 initiated a period of rapid change, in that contact allowed for the transferring of Old World technologies, food crops, domesticated animals, diseases, and people to the New World, and vice versa. Although the region most profoundly affected during this period was the Americas, the effects of these changes were global. By the end of this period in the late 1700s, the sociocultural system of virtually every society in the world had been either directly or indirectly affected.

Next, with the advent of the industrial revolution the nature of European contact with non-Western peoples changed from trade to colonialism and political domination. During the nineteenth century, European political domination spread throughout Africa, Asia, and Oceania, until by 1900 it was complete. Colonial powers restructured the economies of their possessions to meet European needs. The colonial period lasted through World War II.

The post–World War II period has been a time of tremendous economic, political, demographic, and sociocultural growth and change. The two important features of this period have been the emergence of a highly interdependent global economic system and the political fragmentation that ensued as the colonial empires were dismantled and "new" countries were created.

There are no "pristine" sociocultural systems among the peoples of the world, nor have there been for some centuries. For social identities and sociocultural systems, the past 500 years have been extremely volatile. Anthropologists are only now beginning to research intensively and gain some appreciation of the magnitude of the changes that have occurred. Virtually every society in the world has experienced major changes in its sociocultural system, some more dramatically than others. In addition to the changes within preexisting societies, numerous societies that existed in 1492 have become extinct, and a host of "new" social identities and associated sociocultural systems have developed. Although this phenomenon has been most prevalent in the Americas with the emergence of numerous new mixed Afro-American, Euro-American, and Native American societies, this phenomenon has also taken place on a lesser scale in other regions. Thus, the old view of non-Western societies and sociocultural systems as unchanging is no longer adequate. The past and present sociocultural system of any society is understandable and explainable only within the context of its history. The growing realization of the significance of the historical context of sociocultural phenomena has opened a major new area of research for anthropologists and has generated an increasing interest in ethnohistoric research.

This expanding historical awareness has also helped to define more clearly the importance and need for anthropology in helping to resolve world problems. During the past half century a rapidly growing economic interdependence between the various nations and regions of the world and a shift in world economic

and political power have taken place. Before World War II, with the exception of Japan, the world was both economically and politically controlled by individuals of European ancestry—people from the United States, England, Germany, France, and so forth. Thus, important decisions were made by a relatively small group of leaders who shared what were basically common sets of values, norms, and beliefs. With European political and economic dominance of the world rapidly waning, this is no longer the situation. In the increasingly complex global political and economic climate of today, important decisions now frequently involve agreements between leaders with quite different sets of cultural values, norms, and beliefs. The economic and political conditions of the world necessitate a far greater degree of cross-cultural understanding and tolerance than ever before in human history.

Suggested Readings

There are numerous excellent historical studies of world history since 1500. The following list includes only studies by anthropologists or those of more general interest.

■ Crosby, Alfred W. *The Columbian Exchange.* Westport, Conn.: Greenwood, 1972.
   An important and readable study by a historian, showing some of the major cultural and demographic effects of contact between the Old World and New World. The study emphasizes the exchange of food plants, animals, and diseases.

■ Mintz, Sidney W. *Sweetness and Power.* New York: Penguin, 1986.
   An interesting study examining the effect of sugar and its production on the course of world history.

■ Stavrianos, L. S. *The World since 1500: A Global History.* 4th ed. Englewood Cliffs, N.J.: Prentice-Hall, 1982.
   A history textbook that is the best and most readable general description available of world history over the past 500 years.

■ Wolf, Eric. *Europe and the People without History.* Berkeley: University of California Press, 1982.
   A study that should become one of the great classics in anthropology, this is the first attempt by an anthropologist to describe and analyze global history since 1400.

In recent decades a host of studies have considered historical changes within the sociocultural systems of particular societies or regions of the world. The following studies are recommended.

■ Ewers, John. *The Horse in Blackfoot Indian Culture.* Smithsonian Institution, Bureau of American Ethnology Bulletin no. 159. Washington, D.C.: U.S. Government Printing Office, 1955.

The best and most complete study of the effects of the horse on an American Indian society.

■ Kelly, Raymond. *The Nuer Conquest.* Ann Arbor: University of Michigan Press, 1985.

An important study of the Nuer from a historical perspective that challenges many of the earlier ahistorical explanations for the development of Nuer sociocultural institutions.

■ Klien, Martin A., ed. *Peasants in Africa: Historical and Contemporary Perspectives.* Sage Series on African Modernization and Development, vol. 4. Beverly Hills, Calif.: Sage, 1980.

A group of essays in which some of the effects of colonialism on native African populations are discussed and analyzed.

■ Krech, Shepard III. *The Subarctic Fur Trade: Native Social and Economic Adaptations.* Vancouver: University of British Columbia, 1984.

A collection of essays examining the effects of the fur trade on the life of the Algonquin and Athabaskan tribes of the Canadian subarctic.

■ Leacock, Eleanor. *The Montagnais "Hunting Territory" and the Fur Trade.* American Anthropological Association Memoir no. 78, 1954.

A study in which the author used ethnohistoric data to challenge the notion that hunting territories among eastern Canadian Indians were pre-European in origin.

■ Leacock, Eleanor, and Nancy Lurie, eds. *North American Indians in Historical Perspective.* New York: Random House, 1971.

A collection of fourteen essays on various North American Indian societies that directly challenges the static notion of American Indian culture.

■ Rosaldo, Renato. *Ilongot Headhunting, 1883–1974: A Study in Society and History.* Stanford: Stanford University Press, 1980.

An excellent cultural historical study of the Ilongot of the Philippines.

■ Sahlins, Marshall. *Islands of History.* Chicago: University of Chicago Press, 1985.

An important, but not very readable, theoretical study of historical anthropology in which the author analyzes a series of historical events in Hawaii, Fiji, and New Zealand. The focus of the study is how native populations interpreted and responded to events of European contact.

■ White, Richard. *The Roots of Dependency: Subsistence, Environment, and Social Change among the Choctaws, Pawnees, and Navajos.* Lincoln: University of Nebraska Press, 1983.

A study by a historian who, by using a dependence model, examines the effects of white contact on three Native American societies.

■ Whitten, Norman E., Jr., ed. *Cultural Transformations and Ethnicity in Modern Ecuador.* Urbana: University of Illinois Press, 1981.

A collection of essays discussing ethnicity and cultural transformations in Indian, white, and black communities of Ecuador.

■ Wolf, Eric. *Sons of the Shaking Earth.* Chicago: University of Chicago Press, 1959.

A very readable sociocultural history of Mexico and Guatemala from prehistoric times to the present.

ETHNICITY IN THE MODERN WORLD

Contents

■ (Above) *Ethnic unrest threatens the political stability of the Soviet Union. Here Lithuanian nationalists demonstrate for independence.*

n the news we regularly hear of conflict in the world. The Irish Republican Army has ambushed a British patrol in Northern Ireland. Sikh separatists assassinated Indira Gandhi, the Prime Minister of India. Tamil guerrillas in Sri Lanka attacked an army post. A Palestinian demonstrator was killed by Israeli soldiers in Gaza. Armenians were attacked by Azerbaijanis in the Nagorno Karabakh region of the Soviet Union. Drought relief efforts in Ethiopia were hampered by fighting between Eritrean rebels and the Ethiopian army. A police station in Spain was bombed by Basque separatists. The Chinese army arrested Tibetan protesters. Lithuania proclaimed its independence from the Soviet Union. Navajo Indians at Big Mountain, Arizona, resisted eviction by federal authorities. These conflicts are not simply results of differences in political ideologies or of economic forces. Rather, they are conflicts between ethnic groups and so involve profound differences in values and desirable lifestyles.

As we discussed in the last chapter, the global trade that has emerged has resulted in an ever-increasing economic interdependence among the peoples of the world. At the same time, ethnic conflicts have escalated and seem likely to increase. With the cooling of the Cold War and relaxing of East-West tensions in the late 1980s, one could argue that ethnic conflict is the most potent political force in the modern world. It threatens not only the political stability of many nations, but possibly the global economy as well.

In this chapter we address several questions: (1) What is an ethnic group? (2) Why is ethnicity such a powerful political force in the modern world? and (3) What has been and can be done to try to resolve ethnic conflicts?

Ethnic Groups

Over the past two decades the terms *ethnic* and *ethnicity* have become part of our everyday vocabulary. We frequently hear and use the terms *ethnic food, ethnic vote, ethnic conflict, ethnic clothes, ethnic neighborhood,* and *ethnic studies.* In the 1960s, anthropologists began studying ethnicity as a distinct social phenomenon, and since that time the literature on ethnicity has proliferated. Part of the increased scholarly interest in ethnic groups came as a result of Nathan Glazer and Daniel Moynihan's study (1963) of ethnic groups in New York City. They found that "In the third generation, the descendants of the immigrants confronted each other, and knew they were both Americans, in the same dress, with the same language, using the same artifacts, troubled by the same thing, but they voted differently, had different ideas about education and sex, and were still, in many essential ways, as different from one another as their grandfathers had been" (13). These findings contradicted the idea of the American "melting pot." Ethnic differences were far more resilient and significant than had been believed.

What is an ethnic group? First it is necessary to realize that all peoples, not just minority populations, have a feeling of ethnicity and an ethnic group identity. In essence an **ethnic group** is a named social category of people based on perceptions of shared racial or national ancestry. Members of the ethnic group see

■ *Protesting treatment of Native Americans, members of the American Indian Movement (A.I.M) occupied Wounded Knee, South Dakota by force in 1973.*

themselves as sharing sociocultural traditions and history that socially distinguish them from other groups. There is in ethnic group identity a strong psychological or emotional component that divides the social world into the categories of "us" and "them." In contrast to social stratification (discussed in chapter 14), which divides and unifies people along a series of "horizontal axes" on the basis of socioeconomic factors, ethnic identities divide and unify people along a series of "vertical axes." Thus ethnic groups, at least theoretically, crosscut socioeconomic class differences, drawing members from all strata of the population.

Before discussing the significance of ethnic differences and conflicts in the modern world, we first need to examine the varying dimensions of ethnic group identity, including (1) the situational nature of ethnic group identity, (2) the attributes of ethnic groups, (3) the fluidity of ethnic group identity, and (4) the types of ethnic groups.

■ The Situational Nature of Ethnic Identity

One of the more complicating aspects of ethnicity is that an individual's ethnic group identity is rarely absolute. A particular individual may assume a number of different ethnic identities depending on the social situation. For example, in the United States an individual may simultaneously be an American, a white American, an Italian-American, and a Sicilian-American. The particular ethnic identity chosen by an individual varies with the social context. While in Europe or among Europeans, he or she would assume an ethnic identity of American in contrast to German, French, or Italian. In the United States, the same individual might assume an identity of white American as opposed to Afro-American or Native American. Among white Americans, the person might take the ethnic identity of Italian-American as opposed to Irish-American or Polish-American. While among Italian-Americans, the individual might identify himself or herself as Sicilian-American as opposed to Italian-Americans whose families came from Rome, Naples, or some other region of Italy.

The situational nature of ethnic identity demonstrates what some have called the **hierarchical nesting** quality of identity. A particular ethnic group forms part of a larger collection of ethnic groups of like magnitude or social significance. In turn these ethnic groups collectively form still another, higher level of ethnic identity, which in turn is nested in still another higher level of ethnic identity. Thus ethnic identity does not simply divide the world into categories of us and them, but into varying hierarchically ranked categories of us and them.

■ The Attributes of Ethnic Groups

Two main attributes help define and identify an ethnic group: (1) an origin myth and/or history, and (2) various ethnic boundary markers.

Origin Myth   It is important to understand that each ethnic group is the product of a unique set of social and historical events. The common or shared historical experiences that unite and distinguish the group from other groups and give it a distinct social identity are part of the group's **origin myth**. By *myth* we do not mean to imply that the historical events did not really happen, or that the group is not what it claims to be. We mean only that the experiences serve as the ideological charter for the group's common identity and provide the members with a sense of being different from other people. Origin myths play an integral part in creating and maintaining ethnic group identity: they define and describe the origin and collective historical experiences of the group.

Not all historical events are equally important. Origin myths make selective references to historical events. Wars and conflicts with other peoples are frequently emphasized since they clearly distinguish us from them. The origin myth imbues the group's members with feelings of distinctiveness and often of superiority in relation to other groups. In many cases, this myth is oral and is transmitted informally from generation to generation. Many myths tell of supernatural forces and beings who created the group and invested them with special status. In other cases, particularly in larger, more sophisticated groups, the origin myth takes the form of a written, purportedly objective history that is formally taught in schools. American history as taught in elementary and high school is not merely the objective, factual history of a geographic region; it is also the story of the American people. Thus it serves as the de facto origin myth of the American ethnic group. Similarly, English, French, Japanese, and Russian history as taught in their schools also serve as the origin myth of those groups.

When you realize that history as taught in schools serves in fact as the collective origin myth of the group, then you realize the significance of including or excluding a particular subgroup of the population. Using American history as an example, we can see how a number of historical events play a critical role in the emergence and definition of a distinctively American ethnic identity. Among these events are the American Revolution, the Constitutional Convention, the Civil War, the westward expansion, and the World Wars. Certain historical groups, such as cowboys and cavalry, are used as embodiments of American ideals and identity. Americans are the descendants of the various peoples who collectively participated in these and other group-defining events. Thus it is not surprising that every American subgroup is sensitive to their portrayal in these events. Thus to Afro-Americans, it is important that American history, as taught in the public schools, acknowledge that the first man to die in the American Revolution was an Afro-American, that Afro-Americans fought as soldiers in the Revolutionary and Civil Wars, that a high percentage of cowboys were Afro-Americans, and that Afro-American cavalrymen played an important part in winning the West. Similarly, the public acknowledgment and recognition that their groups were active participants in some if not all of the major events of American history are equally important for Polish-Americans, Italian-Americans, Irish-Americans, Chinese-Americans, and other immigrants in a nation of immigrants. It is inclusion in the collective origin myth that truly legitimizes a people's status as members of the group.

Ethnic Boundary Markers   Every ethnic group has a way of determining or expressing membership. Overt factors used to demonstrate or denote group membership are called **ethnic boundary markers.** Ethnic boundary markers are important not only to identify the members to each other but also to demonstrate identity to and distinctiveness from nonmembers. Since they serve to distinguish members from all other groups, a single boundary marker is rarely sufficient. A marker that might distinguish one ethnic group from a second group may not distinguish it from still another group. Thus, combinations of markers are commonly used. Differences in language, religion, physical appearance, or particular cultural traits serve as ethnic boundary markers.

As we saw at the end of chapter 4, speech style and language use serve as symbols of personal identity: we send covert messages about the kind of person we are by how we speak. Language therefore frequently serves as an ethnic boundary marker. The native language of an individual is the primary indicator of ethnic group identity in many areas of the world. In the southwestern United States, Hopi and Navajo members are readily distinguished by their language alone. However, just because two populations share a common language does not mean they share a common identity, any more than the fact that two populations speak different languages means they have two distinct identities. For example, the Serbs and Croatians of Yugoslavia all speak Serbo-Croatian. They are, however, distinct and historically antagonistic ethnic groups. Conversely, an individual may be Irish and speak either Gaelic or English as his or her native language. The West German government grants automatic citizenship to all ethnic German refugees from eastern Europe. A difficulty in assimilating these refugees is that many speak only Polish or Russian. Thus one does not have to speak German to be an ethnic German.

Like language, religion may serve as an ethnic boundary marker. The major world religions such as Christianity, Islam, and Buddhism encompass numerous distinct ethnic groups, so that religious affiliation does not always indicate ethnic affiliation. But in many cases, religion and ethnic group more or less correspond. The Jews may be categorized as either a religious or an ethnic group. Similarly, the Sikhs in India constitute both a religious and an ethnic group. In still other situations, religious differences may be the most important marker of ethnic identity. As we mentioned earlier, the Serbs and Croatians speak the same language; the most important distinction between these two groups is that the Serbs are Eastern Orthodox and the Croatians are Catholic. Conversely, the Chinese ethnic identity transcends religious differences: an individual is still Chinese whether he or she is a Moslem, Christian, Taoist, Buddhist, or Maxist atheist.

Physical characteristics, or phenotypes, can also (at times) indicate ethnic identity. It is impossible to identify Germans, Dutch, Danes, and other northern European ethnic groups by their physical characteristics. A similar situation is found in those regions of the world where populations have been in long association with each other. Thus, physical characteristics do not distinguish a Zulu from a Swazi, a Chinese from a Korean, or a Choctaw from a Chickasaw Indian. However, with the massive movements of people, particularly over the past few hundred years, physical characteristics have emerged increasingly as a marker of ethnic identity. Members of the three major ethnic groups in Malaysia—Malays, East Indians, and Chinese—are readily distinguishable by their physical appearance. The significance or lack of significance of physical characteristics in ethnic identity may also vary with the level of ethnic identity. The American identity includes almost the full range of human physical types. However, at a lower level of identity— white American, Afro-American, and Native American—physical characteristics do serve as one marker of ethnic identity. Yet, within these groups physical characteristics alone cannot be the only marker. Some Native Americans physically appear to be white Americans or Afro-Americans, and some Afro-Americans would be identified as white Americans or Native Americans on the basis of physical appearance alone.

A wide variety of sociocultural traits, clothing, house types, personal adornment, food, technology, economic activities, or general lifestyle may also serve as ethnic boundary markers. Over the past 100 years, a rapid homogenization of world material culture, food habits, and technology has erased many of the more overt sociocultural markers. Thus today you do not have to be a Mexican to enjoy tacos, an Italian to eat pizza, or a Japanese to have sushi for lunch. Similarly, you can dine on hamburgers, the all-American food, in Japan, Oman, Yugoslavia, Mexico, or most other countries in the world. Sociocultural traits remain, however, the most important, diverse, and complex category of ethnic boundary markers. For the sake of brevity, we will limit our discussion to one trait—clothing.

Clothing styles have historically served as the most overt single indicator of ethnic identity. In the not-too-distant past, almost every ethnic group had its own unique style of dress. Even today a Scottish-American who wishes to overtly indicate his ethnic identity wears a kilt, while a German-American may wear his *lederhosen*. Similarly, on special occasions Native Americans wear "Indian clothes" decorated with beadwork and ribbonwork. These are not, however, the everyday clothing of these individuals, and they are worn only in social situations in which they wish to emphasize their ethnic identity. In many regions of the world, "ethnic" clothes are still worn every day. One of these regions is highland Guatemala. In that region clothing, particular women's clothing, serves to readily identify the ethnic affiliation of the wearer. Guatemalan clothing styles actually indicate two levels of ethnic identity. If a woman wears a *huipil*, a loose-fitting blouse that slips over the head, it indicates that she is a Native

American. Non-Native American women, called *Ladinas*, dress in western style clothes. The style, colors, and designs on the huipil further identify the particular Native American ethnic group she is from: Nahuala, Chichicastenango, Solola, or one of the other hundred or so Native American groups in highland Guatemala.

■ *Fluidity of Ethnic Groups*

Ethnic groups are not stable groupings of people, for (1) ethnic groups vanish, (2) people move between ethnic groups, and (3) new ethnic groups come into existence.

During the past five hundred years, numerous ethnic groups have vanished. Massachusett, Erie, Susquehannock, and Biloxi were not originally place names, but the names of now-extinct Native American ethnic groups. Still other ethnic groups in Asia, Africa, Oceania, Europe, and the Americas have vanished as well. Extinction of an ethnic group is rarely biological extinction. In most cases the members of one group are merely absorbed into the population of a larger ethnic group. The Tasmanians of Australia are typical of what happened to many smaller ethnic groups. Numbering at most 5,000 when the British began colonizing the island of Tasmania in 1802, the population was so ravaged by wars and massacres that only a handful existed by 1850, and the Tasmanians as a viable ethnic group had ceased to exist. In 1869 the last full-blooded Tasmanian man died and in 1888 the last full-blooded woman died. However, even today mixed-blood descendants of the Tasmanians can be found among the Australian population.

Both individuals and communities can and do move between ethnic groups. During the sixteenth and seventeenth centuries, French Protestants, called *Huguenots*, fled persecution in France and settled in large numbers in England and the English colonies in North America. These people quickly became absorbed into the English population. Over the past two hundred years Americans have absorbed numerous immigrant populations.

Ethnogenesis refers to the emergence of a new ethnic group. Ethnogenesis occurs in two main ways: (1) a portion of an existing ethnic group splits away and forms a new ethnic group, and (2) members of two or more existing ethnic groups fuse, forming a new ethnic group.

Probably the most common cause of ethnogenesis is the division of an existing ethnic group. At one time the Osage, Kansa, Omaha, Ponca, and Quapaw Indians of the central United States were a single ethnic group. The origin myths of these peoples tell how at different times portions broke away until there were five distinct groups. In the 1700s, small groups of Creek Indians began moving south into Florida, where they eventually developed a distinct identity as the Seminole. Similarly, as Bantu-speaking peoples spread through central and southern Africa, they became separated, and new ethnic groups formed. As the Spanish Empire in the Americas disintegrated during the early 1800s, new regional ethnic identities (such as Mexican, Guatemalan, Peruvian, Chilean, and so on) began emerging among the Spanish-speaking peoples in that region. In 1652 the Dutch began settling near the Cape of Good Hope in southern Africa. Eventually these people developed their own distinctive dialect of Dutch, called *Afrikaans,* and their own identity, Boers.

In other cases, members of two or more ethnic groups fuse and a new ethnic identity emerges. In England the Angles, the Saxons, and the Jutes fused and became known as the English. The original white American ethnic group was not the result of a split among the English people, but rather the result of a fusion of English, Dutch, German, Scots, Irish, French-Huguenots, Scots-Irish, and other European settlers residing on the coast of North America. Most Afro-American groups in the Americas are the result of the fusion of numerous distinct African groups. Intermarriage between French traders and Native Americans in Canada resulted in the emergence of the Metis. Under their leader Louis Riel, the Metis in 1870 rebelled against the government of Canada. Similarly, in South Africa the Cape Coloured, people of mixed Dutch and Khoikhoi ancestry, are socially and politically distinct from both whites and Africans. The Cape Coloureds are an excellent example of how new ethnic categories often arise as a result of economic forces and political mobilization (see Box 18.1).

Fluidity also exists in ethnic group status. An ethnic minority may over time establish a distinct homeland and evolve into a new ethnic nationality. As we discuss later in this chapter, an ethnic nationality may become assimilated by another ethnic nationality and become an ethnic minority of that group.

■ Types of Ethnic Groups

From our discussion and examples so far, it should be apparent that the term *ethnic group* covers a range of

■ *Afrikaner extremists in South Africa protest the movement for shared power with Black Africans.*

social groupings. In general, ethnic groups fall into two main categories: nationalities and minorities.

An **ethnic nationality** is an ethnic group with a feeling of **homeland,** a geographic region over which they have exclusive rights. Implicit in this concept is the assumption of an inherent right to political autonomy and self-determination. In contrast, the term **ethnic minority** refers to any subnational ethnic group. Ethnic minorities make no claim to rights over a distinct and separate homeland, nor to political sovereignty or self-determination. An ethnic minority sees itself as a dependent and politically subordinate subset of a nationality.

Although it is easy to define the difference between ethnic nationalities and ethnic minorities, it is sometimes far more difficult to classify particular groups as either a nationality or minority. The ethnic groups in the United States demonstrate some of the difficulties in classification. With some ethnic groups, there is no doubt about their classification. Italian-Americans, German-Americans, Polish-Americans, Scottish-Americans, and Irish-Americans are all ethnic minorities. At a higher level of identity, the same is true for Afro-Americans. None of these groups today demands a distinct and separate geographical homeland within the United States. Hence they are ethnic minorities, who together with many other groups collectively constitute the American ethnic nationality.

There are other ethnic groups within the United States whose status is not as clear. What is the status of Native American groups such as the Navajo, the Hopi,

Box 18.1

THE EMERGENCE OF COLOURED ETHNICITY IN SOUTH AFRICA

Mary Howard
Ohio Wesleyan University

An American tourist who spends an afternoon window-shopping in one of Johannesburg's downtown malls might be startled to come upon numerous shops filled with African handicrafts of the finest quality from every part of the African continent. Why, this tourist may ask, would white South Africans who decorate their homes with these artifacts be so taken with what they call "Africanity"? A pronounced interest in African ethnicity seems strange in a system that legitimizes racism and oppresses people of African origin. Not only are ethnic categories rigidly regulated by the state, but separate national identities distinct from that enjoyed by the White minority have also been imposed on people of African origin. This is called *apartheid,* or "separate development." People of European ancestry are supposed to develop industrial lifestyles, while people of African ancestry are forced by law to develop within their own tribal areas where they are expected to maintain traditional lifestyles.

The system of apartheid developed out of early twentieth century events and laws, but it was not legally implemented until the Afrikaner-dominated Nationalist party came to power in 1948. Afrikaners are the offspring of Dutch settlers who originally came to South Africa in 1652. They conquered the African inhabitants and later came into conflict with the British over political hegemony for South Africa's gold and diamond mines. Afrikaners were originally fundamentalist Christian farmers who even today maintain an origin myth based on a biblical interpretation that views blacks as the errant descendants of Ham, in need of control and salvation. This view legitimizes a position of superiority over nonwhite peoples. The emergence of the Afrikaner ethnic identity—which includes a distinct language with Dutch, German, French, Malay, Portuguese, English and African elements—is itself a response to nineteenth-century industrialism and British imperialism. Often referred to as the "White Tribe of South Africa," Afrikaner people believed ethnic solidarity to be the keystone for an Afrikaner nation and control over South Africa's mineral resources, urban industries, and African labor.

British colonists who first arrived in 1820 were less identified with mobilization for independence and the creation of a distinct South African nation. Instead, their interests lay in maintaining ties with Britain to secure their economic self-interest. The Afrikaners (also known as the *Boers*) were defeated by British troops in the Boer War of 1899–1902, and the Union of South Africa was formed in 1910.

Afrikaners gained control of Parliament in the 1948 elections. They enacted legislation that (1) classified every person according to race; (2) established *Bantustans,* or homelands, for people classified as black; (3) restricted people into group areas outside the industrial centers, which were divided along racial lines; (4) developed job classifications that maintained white privilege; (5) began a pass system for influx control of black labor so that migration and settlement of Africans around urban areas would occur only when corporations could use their work; and (6) instituted a vast array of security legislation that has resulted in numerous declarations of emergency, arrests, tortures, and murders of black protesters. This legalized segregation is what is meant by apartheid.

The arbitrary racial divisions created by the Race Classification Act of 1950 are white, Asian, Bantu, and coloured [*sic*]. Japanese businessmen were recently given "honorary white" status for sound economic reasons, which was soon followed by a similar shift in the status of people of Chinese ancestry. Presently, 17 percent of the population (about 5.5 million) are whites who are themselves split into two groups—the original Dutch Afrikaner settlers and the more recent British immigrants. Eight hundred thousand people are Asian descendants of the Indian laborers who first came to South Africa in 1860. The majority population (16 to 17 million) are classified as Bantu-speaking black Africans from such indigenous groups as Swazi, Tswana, Sotho, Zulu, Ndebele, and Xhosa. No black is considered a citizen of South Africa and no black can vote for the South African government. Instead, every black person is supposed to be a citizen of his or her "nation," or one of the ten Bantustans that loosely corresponds to each individual's ethnic origins.

Like most Native American reservations, land allocated to the Bantustans is of poor quality and far from resources and urban centers. Over 70 percent of South Africa's population are supposed to live in these areas, which make up only 13 percent of all South African territory. This has had disastrous consequences for the health and well-being of the majority of black South Africans, whose infant and child mortality rate in the Bantustans and incidence of tuberculosis in the black townships rivals the very poorest nations in the world. In contrast, whites enjoy the world's highest living standard, based largely on rich mineral resources mined by a cheap and oppressed black labor pool. These injustices have resulted in the formulation of numerous black resistance movements, such as the African National Congress, which have been struggling for an end to white minority rule even before the beginning of the twentieth century.

Caught between black and white conflict are about 5.5 million people presently classified as coloured. They are the result of over 400 years of close proximity of the "races" in spite of various legislation against interracial sexual relationships and marriage. The emergence of the official racial category coloured is closely related to the "divide and conquer" objectives of the ruling white class, while coloured self-identity was in part a product of ethnic mobilization to maintain or improve relative social positions. The fluidity of ethnic identity boundaries is especially apparent in the case of South Africa's Cape Town coloured population. These boundaries have constantly shifted in response to political, social and economic circumstances, as the following brief history testifies.

Until the turn of the twentieth century, the term *coloured* referred to all non-Europeans. At the time there had been a definite class of poor whites, and ethnic divisions were blurred by class divisions in areas where poor whites and coloured lived together. Many of the coloured were artisans, skilled laborers, and petty traders. Some were able to achieve advanced education and a relatively high standard of living. During the Victorian era, when notions of social Darwinism and eugenics reached South Africa, upper-class whites developed humanitarian concerns about poor whites and saw miscegenation as a peril to the survival of white supremacy. These concerns resulted in extensive improvements in the working and living conditions for poor whites, while coloured people began to be seen as a sign of the dangers of racial contamination. Coloureds became regarded as the illegitimate offspring of a mixing of European "civilization" and African "savagery," although many of them

were better off and more educated than poor whites. However, because of their claim to European ancestry, coloureds were thought to be superior to Africans. Coloureds therefore had little to gain from an identification with Africans and "passing for white" remained a possible escape route for many lighter-skinned Coloureds.

A 1901 urban plague epidemic forced segregation of whites away from impoverished rat-infested areas in the cities. Coloureds resisted forced removal from their urban homes and formed an African Peoples Organization that excluded Africans. This organization sought to advance their economic interests and to gain assurance that the segregation measures then being imposed on Africans would not be extended to coloureds. By 1905 the coloured ethnic identity in the Western Cape Province was established. This identity was the result of white efforts to maintain their own privileges combined with coloured efforts to maintain their distinctiveness from oppressed blacks.

When the Nationalist party came to power in 1948, racial categories were reconstituted into the four present groupings. Even more effort was placed on uniting all Afrikaners, regardless of class. In 1950, with the passage of restrictive legislation such as the Immorality Act (which forbad sexual relations and marriage between the races) and the Group Areas Act (which forced people of each race classification to live in governmentally designated areas), light-skinned coloureds could no longer easily pass for white. Instead, the Nationalist party tried to foster in the coloureds a sense of distinct ethnic pride in being coloured and to prepare them for segregated relocation into coloured townships. Afrikaners also stripped coloureds of direct representation in Parliament so that neither their proximity nor their votes would constitute a threat to white rule. These actions disenfranchised the coloureds from whites and fed into a growing

identification with the African struggle, even though understandably their participation was not always welcomed by blacks.

In efforts to co-opt coloured interests with white economic power, the government did not compel coloureds to carry passes, nor did it regulate them with influx control legislation. The Nationalist party also enacted an employment preference policy that favored Coloureds so that "passing for coloured" became as important to Africans as "passing for white" had once been for coloured.

An unrelenting assault on black squatter settlements during the 1950s, 1960s, and 1970s kept alive coloured fears of being relocated. Eventually such fears were realized when residents of District Six in Capetown were forced to relocate outside the city. This event intensified the ambiguity many coloured people felt in choosing between participation in the white system to prevent further impoverishment or in the black struggle to eliminate a racist regime.

In 1981 a tricameral parliamentary system was introduced that gave coloureds and Asians a vote, but only in matters pertaining to their own affairs. Most of them, to protest the exclusion of blacks, boycotted the referendum that endorsed the changes. However, this token representation has served to further fragment coloured opposition to the blatantly racist policies of South Africa. Many coloureds are now very visible in nonracial liberation organizations composed of persons from all four classifications. In the wake of the release of Nelson Mandela from prison, the hopes of South Africans opposed to apartheid have risen, but the fragmentation sown by long-standing purposeful efforts to align some disenfranchised members to the system while exploiting the rest seems destined to result in violence. Such is the legacy of European colonialism in South Africa. ■

Source: Goldin (1987).

the Crow, the Cheyenne, the Cherokee, and the Osage, to name only a few? These groups have a concept of homelands within the United States. They also have histories quite distinct from that of other Americans. In recent years, they have been asserting increased political sovereignty and self-determination within their reservations (homelands). Although there is disagreement, many Native American individuals and groups still see themselves as distinct nationalities. Some question also exists as to the status of Spanish-speaking peoples in the southwestern United States. Texas, New Mexico, Arizona, and California were parts of Mexico until the mid-nineteenth century. Should the Spanish-speaking population within this region be considered an ethnic minority or an ethnic nationality? Many Hispanics of New Mexico see themselves as a separate people distinct from both Mexicans and other Americans, whom they call "Anglos." Others see themselves as a distinct nationality living in what is rightfully the Mexican homeland, a region they call "Atzlan." Still other individuals see themselves as Americans who are of Mexican or Spanish ancestry.

The distinction between nationality and ethnic minority is important because of their different political implications. As we shall see, the demands of minorities for equal rights and treatment have long been a source of conflict. But the demands of nationalities for independence and sovereignty in a region carved out of an existing country create a political time bomb.

The Problem of Stateless Nationalities

It is difficult for most Americans to understand the causes and bitterness of ethnic conflict in other parts of the world. We think of *nationality* and *nation* as being one and the same. An American is any person who is a citizen of the United States. Most of us think of ourselves as Americans first, and secondarily as Irish-, Italian- or Chinese-Americans. This mind-set about the meaning and significance of ethnicity is due mainly to our history as a nation of immigrants—with the exception of Native Americans, immigrants renounced their claims to their national homelands when they came to the New World. For the most part, the ethnic groups in the United States are minorities, not nationalities. Thus, from our common perception

of the meaning of ethnic group as any minority population, a Yugoslavian is a person from Yugoslavia, a Nigerian is a citizen from Nigeria, and so forth. Falsely equating country of origin with ethnic nationality, we tend to see all ethnic groups as ethnic minorities, and we view ethnic conflicts in other regions of the world as if they are comparable to conflicts between ethnic minorities within the United States. Ethnic problems within a country are thought to be the result of social or economic discrimination—resolvable and reparable by reforms—and their political significance is minimized. However, the ethnic conflicts in most countries are not between ethnic minorities, but between ethnic nationalities.

The ethnic conflicts in Northern Ireland and in Israel/Palestine have proved particularly bitter. In 1922, following several centuries of British colonial domination and periodic rebellions by the native Irish, the Irish Free State (now the Republic of Ireland) was established. However, not all of Ireland was given independence. In the seventeenth century, to control the Irish, the British evicted Irish farmers from the northernmost portion of the island and colonized the region with Scottish Presbyterians, who became known as the *Scots-Irish*. The Scots-Irish did not identify themselves as Irish and had no desire to become part of an independent Ireland. Recognizing the wishes of the Scots-Irish, at independence the British partitioned the island. The northern six counties became Northern Ireland and remained part of the United Kingdom. Many Irish did not and do not accept the legality of this partitioning of Ireland. To them Northern Ireland is part of the Irish homeland and thus should be part of the Republic of Ireland. Since 1968 the Irish Republican Army, a secretive guerrilla army that is illegal in the Republic of Ireland, has been actively waging a war with the object of reuniting Northern Ireland with the Republic of Ireland. Since 1968, bombings, ambushes, and assassinations have claimed the lives of over 2,200 people, and no end appears in sight. The news media frequently report the problems in Northern Ireland as conflict between the British and Irish, or between Catholic and Protestants; in reality it is neither. The root of the problem is the conflicting claims of two rival and hostile nationalities: the Irish and the Scots-Irish. The Scots-Irish have emerged over the past 400 years as a distinct nationality who claim the northern part of Ireland as their homeland. Many Irish see the area as an integral and inalienable part of the Irish homeland.

■ *British soldiers in Belfast, Northern Ireland pass a building which was destroyed in fighting with the Irish Republican Army.*

As a result, there is no way to resolve this conflict to the satisfaction of both groups, and so the conflict continues.

After an absence of almost 2,000 years, the Jews began returning to their historic homeland in Palestine in 1882. During the early twentieth century Jewish settlements in Palestine grew, and in 1948 the state of Israel was unilaterally proclaimed by the Jewish settlers. For the past 40 years, conflict between Israelis and Palestinians has been constant, varying only in the intensity and form of violence. The problem is similar to that in Northern Ireland, in that two nationalities—Israelis and Palestinians—claim the same geographical region as their legitimate homeland. As in Northern Ireland, most of us understand the conflict as being caused by disagreements and hatred between religious groups—Jews and Muslims. And as in Northern Ireland, it is impossible to resolve this conflict to the satisfaction of both nationalities, so conflict between Israelis and Palestinians continues with no resolution in sight.

These two conflicts vividly illustrate the strength of nationalist sentiments. In both cases, we see groups of educated, rational human beings who are willing to sacrifice their lives and economic well-being in unending conflicts for what they consider to be their nationality's legitimate rights.

Such conflict between rival nationalities is more common in the modern world than most of us realize. To understand the magnitude or potential magnitude of this problem, one need only realize that the world is divided into only about 170 countries and between 3,000 and 5,000 distinct ethnic nationalities. As a result, the populations of most countries encompass a number of distinct nationalities. China officially recognizes 56 distinct nationalities. The Soviet Union has about 100 different nationalities. Some estimates are as high as 300 ethnic nationalities in Indonesia. Ethiopia has at least 70 different nationalities. Only a handful of countries are peopled by members of a single nationality and are thus ethnically homogeneous.

The ethnic nationality problem is further complicated because present political boundaries frequently divide members of a nationality and their historic homeland. For example, Hungarians are found not only in Hungary, but large numbers also live in the adjacent portions of Romania and Yugoslavia. Somalis live not only in Somalia but also in the adjacent Ogaden portion of Ethiopia. Thus the world is filled with ethnic groups who do not fully recognize the legitimacy of "their" central government and who aspire or may potentially aspire to have political autonomy.

For the most part the nationality problems in most countries were not created by the nationalities themselves. The present political boundaries for most of the world are legacies of European colonialism and expansion (see chapter 17). During the nineteenth century, the European powers divided most of the geographical regions and peoples of the world among themselves. In 1884–85, at the Berlin Conference, European leaders sat at a table and with pens and pencils drew lines on a map of Africa, dividing the resources and peoples of that continent among themselves. Through this agreement, the English, French, Germans, Belgians, and other European powers assumed sovereignty over lands they had never traveled and over peoples who had never seen a white man. Nor was Africa the only continent to have boundaries imposed by Europeans. The national boundaries of most of the world were drawn by Europeans for their own interest, with little regard for the interest of any indigenous peoples or the boundaries of the ethnic groups affected. As a result, most European colonial possessions were a polyglot of ethnic groups, many of whom had long histories of hostilities toward one another. In other instances an ethnic group found its land and people divided between two or more European colonies. To make matters worse, colonial powers frequently moved people from one colony to another to supply labor, introducing still other ethnic groups to new areas. For example the British settled Indian laborers in Burma,

Malaya (Malaysia), Fiji, Sri Lanka, Kenya, Uganda, South Africa, Trinidad, and British Guiana.

The end of the colonial period did not end the ethnic conflicts in the world, but only signaled the beginning of the problems. As European powers granted independence to their colonies, they made little attempt to redefine political boundaries. In most cases these newly independent countries had precisely the same boundaries and ethnic composition as the former colonies. Because these political divisions were imposed by European military power, some scholars have termed these former colonies **artificial countries** (see Figure 18.1). In most cases, the basic colonial administrative and governmental structure was main-

tained after independence; the major departure from the colonial period was that native officials replaced European officials. However, not all ethnic groups were equally represented in these new governments, and most former colonies quickly came under the domination of one or two of the more powerful ethnic groups. Thus in many instances, European domination was replaced by domination by one or another "native" ethnic group. With this in mind, the political problems endemic in much of the Third World become more comprehensible.

India is a prime example of ethnic unrest in the postcolonial period. Consisting of several hundred distinct ethnic groups as well as major religious divi-

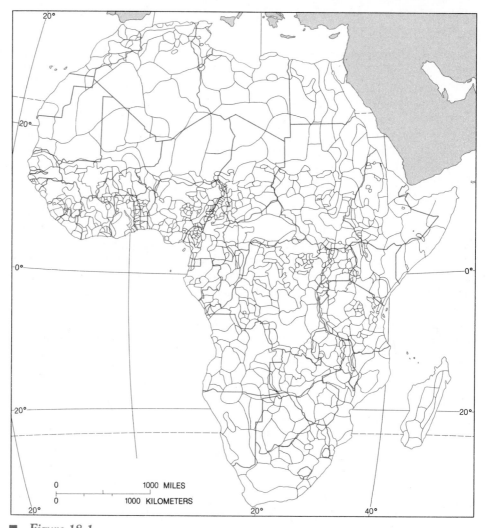

■ *Figure 18.1*

Ethnic Groups and National Boundaries in Africa The boundaries of most African countries do not correspond with the territories of ethnic groups.

sions, India did not exist—and never existed—as a unified country before British domination (see Figure 18.2). As independence approached in the 1940s, hostilities between rival Moslem and Hindu factions became so intense that British officials decided that a unified, independent India was an impossibility. They decided that India had to be divided into two countries: India (predominantly Hindu) and Pakistan (predominantly Moslem). The borders of these new countries were drawn by the British. The problem was the lack of clear geographical boundaries separating these groups; in many regions the populations were mixed Hindu and Moslem. An East Pakistan and a West Pakistan were carved out on either side, separated by 1,000 miles of what was to be India. Following the official announcement of the boundaries, massive migrations began as millions of Muslims and Hindus found themselves on the wrong sides of the boundary. These migrations were stimulated by fanatics on both sides, who massacred Muslims living in what was to become India and Hindus in what was to be Pakistan. Some estimate that as many as 1,000,000 people were killed in these riots. The grant of actual independence to the two countries in 1947 made the situation worse because neither side was satisfied with their geographical boundaries. The new Indian army occupied the largely Moslem region of Kashmir, and war quickly broke out between the two countries. The first India-Pakistan war ended in 1949, with Kashmir occupied by India. In 1990, the demands of Moslems in Kashmir for

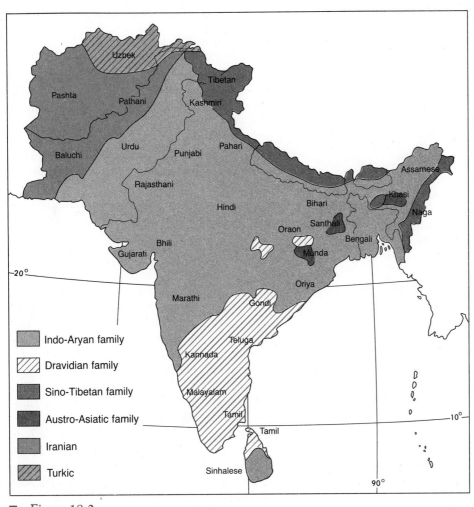

■ *Figure 18.2*

Language Regions of South Asia Some of the ethnic boundaries of India are reflected by these language regions.

Troops of the Indian Army still actively patrol the potentially explosive border with Pakistan.

Murdered by her Sikh bodyguards, Prime Minister Indira Gandhi of India, shown here at her funeral, was a victim of Sikh separatists.

a separate nation again brought violence to the world's largest democracy.

The creation of two separate states out of British India addressed—but did not solve—only one of the region's problems. Immediately after independence, the Naga people in India's easternmost Assam province revolted and demanded an independent Nagaland. This Naga secessionist movement is still active, and for 40 years periodic bloody clashes have occurred between Naga rebels and Indian authorities. More recently a Sikh separatist movement emerged, demanding an independent homeland in Punjab. The violent tactics of the Sikh nationalists resulted in the Indian army attacking the holiest Sikh religious shrine, the Golden Temple in Amritsar, in 1984. Later that year two Sikhs assassinated Indira Gandhi, the Prime Minister of India, causing more violence between Sikhs and Hindus. Since 1986 problems have arisen in West Bengal with the Gurkhas, who also want a separate autonomous homeland.

Pakistan has also experienced ethnic difficulties. Although both Pakistans were Moslem, there were major ethnic differences between the two. East Pakistanis were predominantly Bengalis. West Pakistan was more heterogeneous ethnically, but dominated by Urdu-speaking peoples. Although West Pakistan had a smaller population, the capital was located there after independence in 1947, and the Urdu peoples gained dominance in the government and the military. In West Pakistan a separatist movement emerged among the Baluchi, who sought an independent Baluchistan. However, it was with the Bengalis in East Pakistan that

the major conflict emerged. Although the Bengalis were economically exploited and discriminated against by the Urdu, it was not until the government attempted to impose the Urdu language in the schools of East Pakistan that the situation came to a head. In 1971 the East Pakistanis revolted and, after a short but bloody war aided by India, succeeded in establishing the state of Bangladesh.

Similar secessionist movements have occurred and are still occurring throughout the old colonial world:

- Burma includes a dozen or more distinct ethnic groups. Immediately after independence from Britian in 1948, Karen and Shan peoples declared their freedom from Burma and revolted. Other ethnic groups soon followed the lead of the Karen and Shan. Today, over 40 years later, the Burmese army is involved in an inconclusive war with secessionist armies of ten different ethnic groups.
- Within weeks after the Congo (now Zaire) became independent in 1960, Katanga Province declared its independence and remained autonomous until 1963, when it was militarily reoccupied.
- In 1960 Nigeria became independent. In 1967 the Ibos, seeing Nigeria increasingly controlled by the Yoruba and Hausa peoples, seceded and established the Republic of Biafra. Three years of bloody war followed, before the Ibos were militarily overwhelmed.
- Burundi became independent in 1962, and political conflict developed between the Tutsi and Hutu; in

1972 this conflict culminated in the slaughter of about 200,000 Hutu.

■ In 1952 the former Italian colony of Eritrea was federated with Ethiopia. Since 1961 Oromo (Eritrean) separatists have waged a war of independence against Ethiopia.

Nationalist separatist movements are also active in the southern Sudan, the island of Mindanao in the Philippines, and in Sri Lanka—just to name a few of the most important movements. Certainly, it is facile to lay all the blame on colonialism for these and other conflicts in the postcolonial era. But it is undeniable that violence between ethnic nationalities, each believing its political and territorial claims are legitimate, is one of colonialism's most unfortunate and long-lasting legacies.

Not all of the ethnic conflicts have been or are confined to the old colonial world. For example, the Kurds (who live in the mountainous regions of Turkey, Iraq, Iran, Syria, and the Soviet Union) have had an active separatist movement since the 1960s (see Figure 18.3). At different times they have fought the Turks, the Iraqis, and the Iranians. In 1950 China invaded and occupied Tibet, a region that the Chinese consider part of China. A Tibetan revolt in 1959 was crushed, but conflict is again escalating as Tibetan Buddhists seek political autonomy under the Dalai Lama, their spiritual leader. Even in Europe, Basque separatists periodically attack police stations and other government facilities in their struggle for independence from Spain and France.

This is only a sampling of armed nationalist conflicts. Nationalist movements are difficult to defuse. In most cases the recognized national governments lack the military resources to totally defeat them. Even when a government has overwhelming resources, such as the British in Northern Ireland, rural or urban guerrilla wars are difficult to win decisively. As a result, few separatist movements have been extinguished. In many cases, the central governments have adopted policies of geographical containment and lessening of direct conflict. A graphic example of this approach is in Western Sahara, which was formerly Spanish Sahara. In the early 1970s, Spain committed itself to a policy of independence and self-determination for its colony. However, in 1976, before independence was achieved, Morocco occupied the northern portion of

■ In 1967, the Ibos of eastern Nigeria seceded, forming their own separatist county of Biafra. Here, young Ibos, some armed with only clubs, train to fight the Nigerian Army.

■ Tibetan refugees living in India protest the 1987 executions of two Tibetans by Chinese authorities.

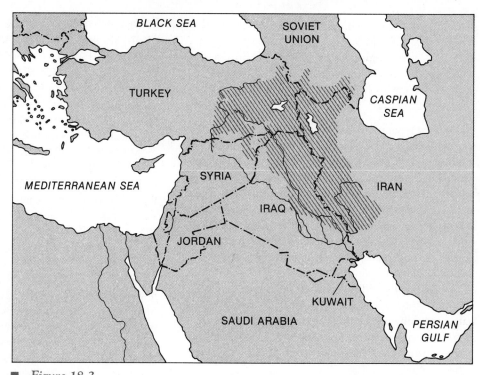

■ *Figure 18.3*

Kurdistan The Kurdish area and the proposed boundaries of an independant state of Kurdistan.

the region, claiming it was historically part of Morocco. In 1979 Morocco occupied the southern portion of the region. The Spanish did not resist the Moroccan occupation. However, the local Sahrawi population rejected Moroccan domination, formed the Polisario Front, and initiated a guerrilla war. Unable to defeat the guerrillas, but yet unwilling to withdraw, the Moroccan government partitioned the region with a 2,500-kilometer-long sand "wall" that was equipped with electronic devices to detect movements; the purpose of the wall was to separate the portion Morocco controlled from the area they did not control. In 1989 the Moroccan government agreed to a referendum sponsored by the United Nations, but the status of Western Sahara has yet to be resolved. Almost yearly the number of unresolved ethnic conflicts increases, and the number of peoples and regions affected widens. By some estimates, there are approximately 120 ongoing armed conflicts in the world today, and about 75 to 80 percent of these conflicts would be classified as nationalist movements.

Central governments as a whole have been unsuccessful in achieving total military victories over separatist groups, but nationalist separatist groups themselves have rarely been successful in achieving political victories. Except for Bangladesh, no separatist state has received international recognition in the postcolonial period. Such recognition is not based on military success. The Oromo (the so-called Eritrean rebels) have militarily defeated the Ethiopian army and created what is a de facto independent state. Yet they are not formally recognized by any other country, even those who supported them in the war. African leaders oppose such recognition because they have similar ethnic problems within their own countries and the recognition of Eritrea would encourage separatist rebellions at home.

This situation is not unique to Africa. In chapter 1, article 1 of the Charter of the United Nations, the right of a people to self-determination is recognized. However, the United Nations also recognizes the sovereignty and territorial integrity of the existing states. A new central government that comes into power by revolution may be granted recognition, but the United Nations refuses to recognize a secessionist rebellion, no matter how successful. The one exception has been Bangladesh. Thus both formal and informal agreements are made among the existing countries of the world to maintain the present political status quo.

Resolving Ethnic Conflict

How can such deep-rooted conflicts be resolved? The most obvious solution is to divide the country, giving the dissatisfied nationality their land and independence and allowing them to establish their own country or merge with another country. However, central governments have always been highly reluctant to surrender their territorial claims. As Burma, Ethiopia, the Sudan, and many other countries have shown, they would rather fight a long, destructive, and inclusive war than officially recognize the independence of a rebellious nationality. This stance is taken partly because governments fear setting a precedent. As a result, most ethnic conflicts have been resolved—and future solutions will most likely have to be sought—within the existing political structure.

Historically, such internal solutions to ethnic issues have taken two forms: (1) sociocultural homogenization of the population through the elimination of rival ethnic groups, and (2) the political accommodation of ethnic groups.

■ Homogenization

Homogenization involves the attempt to eliminate a particular ethnic group or groups within a country or some region. **Sociocultural homogenization** has historically taken three main forms: (1) genocide, (2) relocation, or (3) assimilation.

Genocide is the most radical strategy in that it involves a deliberate and systematic attempt to physically destroy the members of an unwanted ethnic group and thus extinguish the group. The objective may be to totally destroy the group, or merely to reduce their numbers and lessen their threat. Genocide may be part of official government policy (as in Nazi Germany) or may take the form of spontaneous acts by individual members of the dominant group (as white atrocities against Native Americans). Regardless of the objective and degree of formality, the result is the same: the slaughter of men, women, and children of the targeted ethnic group.

When we think of genocide, we usually think of the attempted extermination of the Jews and Gypsies by the Germans during the 1930s and World War II. Far from being unique, historically this strategy has been used by many different dominant groups against minorities and nationalities. The Turks instituted a policy of systematic slaughter of Armenians during the early years of this century. During the nineteenth century, English settlers in Tasmania slaughtered most of the Tasmanian population. English, French, Spanish, and Portuguese settlers periodically massacred Native American groups. In American history, genocide began with the slaughter of the Pequots of Connecticut in 1637 and ended with the massacre of over 150 Sioux Indians at Wounded Knee, South Dakota, in 1890. Even today atrocities occur against Native American groups in portions of Latin America (see the Epilogue).

Relocation involves the forced resettlement of an ethnic group in a new location. Sometimes the unwanted group is forced outside the boundaries of the country, becoming what today we term *refugees*. In other cases, an ethnic group is forcibly moved to a new area within the boundaries of the state, where it is assumed that they will pose less of a problem. Following World War II, the boundaries of much of eastern Europe were redrawn. That portion of Germany located east of the Oder River was given to Poland, and seven million German residents were forcibly evicted. At the same time, Czechoslovakia evicted almost three million resident Germans from their homes (see Figure 18.4). After independence many east African countries expelled many East Indians, who had settled there during the colonial period. In American history, Native Americans were regularly relocated as the frontier moved west, thus "solving" the Indian problem for white settlers and the American government. The largest and best known of these relocations occurred in the 1830s, when the Five Civilized Tribes were forced to move (along the so-called Trail of Tears) from their homes in the southeastern states to what is today

■ *Following World War II, millions of ethnic Germans living in Poland and Czechoslovakia were forced from their homes.*

■ *Figure 18.4*

Relocation of Ethnic Germans after World War II. Direction arrows indicate the transfer, eviction, or flight of ethnic Germans. Figures are in thousands of people.

Oklahoma. Most indigenous tribes of the United States experienced similar resettlement programs. A few years ago the Ethiopian government announced a plan to resettle 1,500,000 people from Eritrea and Tigre provinces in the central part of the country. This relocation would have removed the support population for the secessionist guerrillas in the region. A lack of money and international protest stopped the project.

Assimilation is the sociocultural absorption of one ethnic group by another, dominant one. Assimilation may be total, in which the ethnic identity of one group is totally lost; or partial, in which one ethnic group assumes a subordinate identity and is reduced to the status of an ethnic minority. Assimilation may either be forced or passive.

Forced assimilation occurs when the government adopts policies designed to deliberately and systematically destroy or change the ethnic identity of a particular group. The ultimate objective is usually the total absorption of the group into the dominant ethnic group. A key target of forced assimilation policy is the elimination of ethnic boundary markers: language, religion, modes of dress, and any sociocultural institution that readily distinguishes the population. If these boundary markers are destroyed, the group loses much of its social cohesiveness. For example, until very recently the Bulgarian government pursued a policy that was designed to assimilate their Turkish population. Turks were not free to practice their Islamic religion, and they were forced to speak Bulgarian in public and adopt Bulgarian names.

One of the best examples of forced assimilation was the United States' Indian policy in the last part of the nineteenth and early twentieth centuries. Federal Indian policy attacked Native American ethnic identity from several directions. Reservation lands, which were owned communally, were broken up, and the land was allotted (deeded) to individual members of the tribe. The objective was to destroy community or village life. Ceremonies, such as the Sun Dance and peyote religion, were frequently made illegal. Traditional or hereditary tribal leaders were not recognized, and tribal governments were either dissolved or reorganized along an American political model. Individuals who worked for the government were commonly forced to cut their hair and wear "citizens" (western style) clothes. Native American children were taken from their families and placed in boarding schools, where they were forbidden to speak their native language, had their hair cut, were made to dress in citizens' clothes, were taught Anglo-American technical skills, and were in general indoctrinated with Anglo-American Christian values and attitudes.

Assimilation need not be the result of a conscious official policy to solve an "ethnic problem" by incorporating the population into the sociocultural mainstream. Another form, called **passive assimilation,** occurs without any formal planning or political coercion. Unless strong social barriers prevent assimilation, social and economic forces frequently result in more dominant ethnic groups absorbing the members of less powerful groups with whom they are in contact. The dominant ethnic group does not necessarily have to be the larger; but it must be the most socially prestigious and economically powerful group. Many of

■ *Overt ethnic boundary markers are usually the main targets of forced assimilation policies. Here we see the same Native American before and after attending an Indian school founded by the government.*

the governments in Latin America have historically followed a laissez-faire policy toward Native American groups. Guatemala has not had a policy of forced assimilation. In Guatemala, the primary differences between Ladinos and Native Americans are not biological, but social and cultural, and individuals who are ethnically identified as Native Americans are socially and economically discriminated against. As a result, more ambitious and educated Native Americans have frequently abandoned their native languages, dress, and lifestyles (ethnic boundary markers) and reidentified themselves as Ladinos. During the past hundred years, the Native American population in Guatemala has decreased from about 75 percent of the total population to less than 50 percent; passive assimilation is the primary cause of this decrease.

■ *Accommodation*

The alternative to homogenization is some form of political and sociocultural accommodation. By accommodation we mean the formal recognition and support of ethnic group identities and sociocultural differences. The central government does not attempt to create a homogenous population, but works within a framework of ethnic and cultural differences. Some multinationality countries have adopted this strategy. For instance, Canada has two main nationalities: Anglo-Canadians (English speaking) and French-Canadians (French speaking). Both English and French are official languages in Canada. Belgium has two main national groups: the Flemish (Dutch) and the Walloons (French). Like Canada, Belgium recognizes these two official languages without recognizing these ethnic groups as political divisions. However, in other countries, ethnic group identity does provide the basis for internal political divisions. The Soviet Union has over 100 different nationalities within its population, 23 of which number over 1,000,000 members. The U.S.S.R. has a rather complex political structure, which gives official recognition to most of its ethnic nationalities (see Figure 18.5). Thus the largest nationalities—the Russians, the Armenians, the Azerbaijanis, the Byelorussians, the Estonians, the Georgians, the Kazakhs, the Kirgiz, the Latvians, the Lithuanians, the Moldavians, the Tajiks, the Turkmen, the Ukrainians, and the Uzbeks—have their own republics. Ten of the fifteen Soviet republics are further divided into "autonomous" areas for smaller ethnic nationalities. The Russian Soviet Federated Socialist

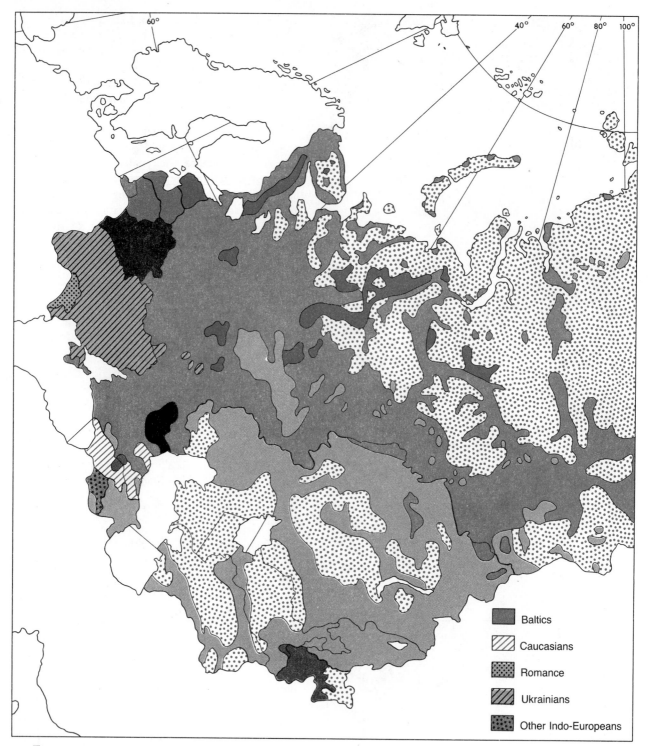

■	Baltics
▨	Caucasians
▦	Romance
▧	Ukrainians
▩	Other Indo-Europeans

■ *Figure 18.5*

Major Ethnic Regions of the Soviet Union The following regions include several ethnic groups. Baltics include Latvians and Lithuanians. Caucasians include Georgians, Avars, Aguls, Dargins, and Laks. Finno-Ugians include Estonians, Finnish, Komis, Saams, and Mordvins. Mongolians include Buryats and Kalmyks. Turkic include Azerbaijanis, Kazakhs, Tartars, Turkmans, Uzbeks, and Yakuts.

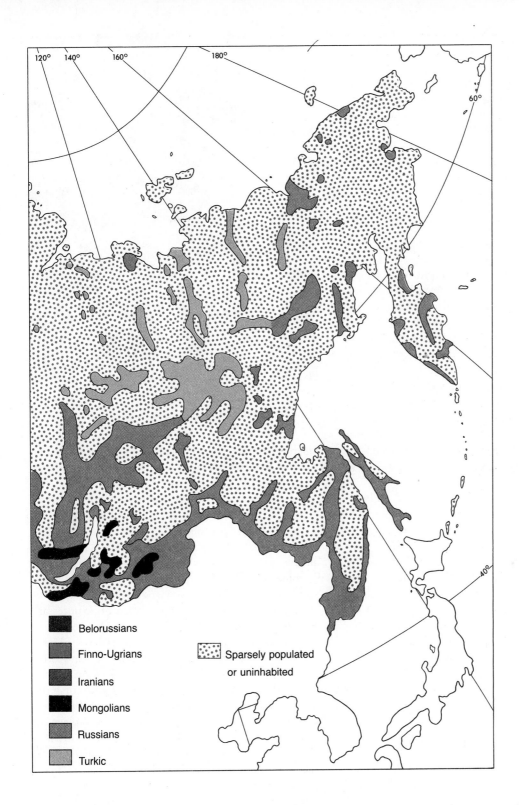

■	Belorussians
▨	Finno-Ugrians
▨	Iranians
■	Mongolians
▨	Russians
▨	Turkic

⦂	Sparsely populated or uninhabited

Republic (the largest republic) has political subdivisions for non-Russians, called *Autonomous Soviet Socialist Republics*, *Autonomous Oblasts* (regions), and *Nationality Okrugs* (districts). For example, the Chukchi and Evenk have Nationality Okrugs, whereas the Yakut, Tuva, and Tartar have Autonomous Soviet Socialist Republics with the Russian Republic. These nationality areas are not set aside exclusively for the use of the members of a particular nationality: members of other nationalities may live there as well. Ethnic Russians—the dominant and largest ethnic group—are found living in most of the other republics.

■ *Resolution?*

Setting aside moral issues for the moment, we can now examine the effectiveness of these strategies for resolving ethnic conflict. Genocide has eliminated certain ethnic problems, particularly with smaller groups. It was effective in Tasmania, and one has only to list the extinct native groups in the Americas to see that this strategy can work very well in eliminating small ethnic rivals to the dominant nationality. However, with larger ethnic groups it is rarely effective since many, if not most, survive. The history of massacres becomes part of the origin myth of the group, and strengthens group cohesiveness by intensifying the feeling of us versus them. Genocide often worsens conflict by intensifying the ethnic consciousness and the determination of the survivors.

Relocation was only occasionally successful. Relocation was successful with Native American groups in the eastern portion of the United States—at least, it worked for the Anglo-Americans. However, 400 years after the Irish were evicted from Northern Ireland, the Irish Republican Army is fighting to "reclaim" the lost homeland. The Jews were expelled from Jerusalem in the first century A.D., and eventually became dispersed throughout much of Europe, North Africa, and the Middle East. But over the past 100 years they have succeeded in returning to Israel and reclaiming their homeland. Like genocide, the history of the relocation becomes part of the origin myth of the group, and the idea of reclaiming the lost homeland can serve to strengthen the group identity and cohesion.

Assimilation—whether passive or forced—is not always effective. There is no question that throughout history smaller groups have been absorbed by larger groups. However, assimilation is usually a slow and uncertain process. As we discussed, in Guatemala Native Americans have slowly declined as a percentage of the total population over the past 100 years. We

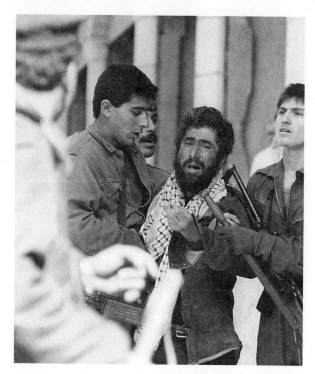

■ *An Israeli Army patrol arrests a Palestinian shortly after a demonstration in Gaza.*

might therefore assume that passive assimilation has proved effective in this case. However, considering absolute rather than relative population, we find that the Native American population actually increased from 1,000,000 to about 4,000,000 during the same period. The main problem with passive assimilation, then, is that population growth often creates new members as fast as or faster than former members become assimilated. Another problem is that many minorities do not want to give up their ethnic identity; if they did, forced assimilation would not be necessary. The forced assimilation policies in the United States were equally unsuccessful in regard to Native Americans. Loss of language, material culture, and other cultural institutions that functioned as ethnic boundary markers did not destroy ethnic identity or group cohesiveness, because new cultural institutions and ethnic boundary markers soon emerged to replace the old. From a population of only about 250,000 in 1890, the Native American population of the United States has risen to over 1,500,000 today, and the major political demands are for greater tribal sovereignty and self-determination on Native American lands.

So genocide, relocation, and forced or passive assimilation may be effective to a greater or lesser degree, but each under most circumstances does not truly resolve ethnic problems. More often they postpone the formulation of workable policies, and are even counterproductive—they worsen rather than alleviate conflicts. Besides these "pragmatic" considerations, genocide and forced assimilation are so morally abhorrent that few modern governments would admit to pursuing such policies. Relocation likewise poses ethical dilemmas; most groups are moved against their will, and some other nationality must be relocated to make room for the migrants. In the modern world, there is nowhere to relocate to without violating some other group's rights. Finally, as we have seen, passive assimilation is usually slow and its result uncertain: many nationalities and minorities wish to maintain their identities and refuse to give up their claims.

That leaves accommodation as the only remaining practical and ethically acceptable solution. To be sure, attempts by governments of multinationality countries to accommodate sociocultural differences and nationalistic aspirations of their minorities have also had mixed results. Belgium has been relatively stable politically for the 160 years of its existence. The same, however, cannot be said about some other countries. In the 1960s a serious separatist movement developed among the French-Canadians in Quebec. In the 1976 elections, Parti Quebecois, the separatist party, won control of the government of Quebec and the following year made French the offical language of the province. In 1980 the voters of Quebec rejected a referendum on the question of separation. Although rejected, separa-tion from Canada was supported by 40 percent of the voters in Quebec. Although the ethnic republics within the Soviet Union are officially autonomous and may, under the constitution, unilaterally withdraw from the union, political reality is far different. The U.S.S.R. is a Russian-dominated state, and the ethnic republics are more akin to administrative regions than separate states.

The fragility of the union of Soviet republics is shown by recent events. In the Caucasus, violence has erupted between the Christian Armenians and Islamic Azerbaijanis, some of the latter demanding unity with their ethnic brothers in Iran. In the Baltic region, Estonians, Lithuanians, and Latvians are demanding independence from the "union." In central Asia, the Kazakhs, Uzbeks, Turkmen, and other Muslim nationalities threaten Soviet Unity. What may be in store for the U.S.S.R. is indicated by the case of another multinationality, Socialist country, Yugoslavia (see Box 18.2, which illustrates the complex difficulties of holding a "multinational nation" together).

Armed with hunting rifles, Armenians in the Nagorno Karabakh region of the Soviet Union prepare for battle with the Azerbaijanis.

Rene Levesque, leader of the French separatist party in Quebec, addresses party workers in 1976.

Box 18.2

ETHNICITY AND POLITICS IN YUGOSLAVIA

Yugoslavia is one of the larger countries in the world without a dominant nationality. In spite of attempts to create a national identity, only a small fraction of the population identifies itself as Yugoslavian. The country is a collection of eight different nationalities (Serbs, Croatians, Slovenians, "Moslems," Montenegrins, Macedonians, Hungarians, and Albanians) who speak five different languages (Serbo-Croatian, Slovene, Macedonian, Hungarian, and Albanian), who follow three religions (Catholic, Eastern Orthodox, and Islam), and use two official alphabets (Latin and Cyrillic). Five of these ethnic groups are found only within Yugoslavia, and three of the groups have ethnic ties to other countries: the Hungarians with Hungary, the Albanians with Albania, and the Macedonians with their close linguistic and cultural kinsmen the Bulgarians. As a result, Yugoslavia has no ethnic majority; the largest nationality, the Serbs, constitutes only 36 percent of the total population.

The cultural and ethnic diversity is partially the result of, as well as a causal factor in, the political conflict and instability of that portion of the Balkans. The Balkans have long been a region of contact and conflict between Europe and Asia, and between Christianity and Islam. The history of the region has been one of cultural and political domination by outside forces emanating from the east or west. During the medieval period, the Catholic Church (Rome) and the Eastern Orthodox Church (Constantinople) and their associated political states competed for the souls and political allegiance of the region's inhabitants. In 1453 the Ottoman Turks conquered Constantinople and invaded the Balkans. For over three hundred years the armies of Christendom and Islam fought for control. Except for Montenegro and a few coastal areas, most of the region fell under Turkish control. All of these competing outside groups left their sociocultural imprint and redefined the ethnic groups of the region. For example, the Serbo-Croatian–speaking peoples split into three rival ethnic groups: the Serbs (Eastern Orthodox), the Croatians (Catholic), and the Moslems (Islamic).

Localized nationalist uprisings and wars against Turkish domination were frequent. It was, not however, until Turkish power began to wane during the nineteenth century that any revolts were successful. In 1878 the Serbs succeeded in regaining their independence. However, most of the former Turkish dominion soon fell under the control of still another outside power, the Austro-Hungarian Empire. Protesting Austrian occupation of Bosnia-Herzegovina, in June 1914 a nationalist shot and killed Archduke Ferdinand. This incident was the catalyst that brought about the First World War.

During the war, the Central Powers (Germany and Austria) invaded and occupied Serbia and Montenegro. Following the war, the Austro-Hungarian Empire was dismantled. Slovenia, Croatia, Bosnia-Herzegovina, and portions of Hungary were joined with Serbia and Montenegro to create the new Kingdom of Serbs, Croats, and Slovenes (in 1929 the name was changed to Yugoslavia) and Prince Peter of Serbia was named the first king. This construct was a totally new state, in that never before had all the varied peoples of this region been placed together in a single independent country. This new country was an artificial political creation of the Allied Powers rather than an entity created by internal forces. The centralized government of this new country was controlled by the Serbians, which meant that in effect the Allied Powers had created a greater Serbia.

It did not take the other nationalities in Yugoslavia long to realize that Serbian domination was no different than domination by the Turks or Austro-Hungarians. Peter died in 1921 and was succeeded by Alexander. King Alexander came into increasing conflict with the other ethnic groups, particularly the Croatians. In 1928 the Croatians unilaterally established their own parliament in Zagreb. The king responded by abolishing all parliaments, all political parties, and ignoring Croatian demands for autonomy. In 1934 Alexander was assassinated by a Macedonian working with Croatian revolutionaries.

Germany and Italy invaded Yugoslavia in 1941, and in only ten days overran the country. The Germans and Italians found local support for their invasion, particularly among the Croatian separatists. As a reward, an "independent" Republic of Croatia was created by the Germans and Italians. Croatian military units, called the *Ustashi*, were formed to assist the German and Italian armies in their occupation of other portions of Yugoslavia. Two guerilla armies quickly formed to oppose the Germans and Italians and their Ustashi allies: (1) the Chetniks, who were predominantly Serbians and royalists; and (2) the Partisans, who were a multiethnic force led by a half Slovene and half Croatian communist by the name of Josip Broz, who was usually called by his nickname "Tito." The result was an extraordinarily bloody, three-sided war that pitted the Chetniks and the Partisans against each other as well as the Germans, Italians, and the Ustashi. In four years of fighting, approximately 1,700,000 Yugoslavians were killed out of a total population of only about 18,000,000. In percentage killed, Yugoslavia suffered more than any other country in Europe during the war. Before the war's end, Tito and his nationalist communists had prevailed, virtually eliminating the Chetniks and liberating most of the countryside from German and Italian control and thereby preventing military occupation by the Russians or any other allied army.

In 1945 Tito was elected president of a war-ravaged country deeply divided by bitter ethnic rivalries and hatreds. Recognizing the impossibility of forging a highly centralized and cohesive state out of Yugoslavia, Tito attempted to create a political structure that would accommodate ethnic differences and minimize the possibility of ethnic conflict. The country was divided into six autonomous republics: Serbia, Slovenia, Croatia, Macedonia, Montenegro, and Bosnia-Herzegovina. Within the Republic of Serbia were large Hungarian and Albanian populations. Thus

within Serbia two autonomous provinces were established, Vojvodina for the Hungarians and Kosovo for the Albanians (see Figure 18.6). What Tito created was a federation, with a weak central government and most governmental powers vested in the autonomous republics and provinces. Thus each of the major nationalities had its own locally autonomous government.

This system worked well under Tito. Although the central government was relatively weak, Tito himself was not. In 1963 he had himself elected president for life and ruthlessly eliminated any opposition to him or his government. In the early years of his presidency he suppressed royalists and various nationalist groups. Most of the surviving Chetnik leaders were executed.

Following Tito's death in 1980, power fell to a central committee, composed of representatives of the six republics and two autonomous provinces. The office of president became more symbolic and was rotated among the members of this committee, and problems began to arise.

In 1981 Albanians in Kosovo province rioted, demanding separation from Serbia and the creation of a new republic. Two major problems arose in attempting to meet the demands of Albanian separatists: (1) although the Albanians were the majority ethnic group in Kosovo, there was also a sizeable Serbian minority; and (2) the Kosovo region was the original homeland of the Serbs. The ethnic composition of the region had changed because the Islamic Albanians had a higher birthrate than the Orthodox Serbs. Serb leaders had no intention of politically surrendering the Kosovo region to the Albanians. Throughout the 1980s,

conflict in Kosovo escalated. A number of bloody riots occurred, and many Serbs fled the province. These riots served to rekindle Serbian nationalism and their historic hostility toward the Albanians. In March of 1989, the Republic of Serbia took control of the local administration, courts, and police in Kosovo and began arresting Albanian leaders. In essence the Serbians unilaterally abolished the autonomous status of the province and reintegrated it into the Republic of Serbia. More radical Albanian leaders are now calling for separation from Yugoslavia and union with Albania.

The unilateral suppression of the Albanians by the Serbs has created tension with other republics. Not only are the Serbs the largest ethnic group, but the national capital of Yugoslavia, Belgrade, is also the capital of Serbia. Members of other ethnic nationalities, who have frequently accused the Serbs of acting as if Yugoslavia were "their" country, feel threatened by any growth in Serbian political power. Thus, not surprisingly, the republics of Slovenia and Croatia have voiced strong opposition to Serbian actions in Kosovo and Serbian nationalism. To make matter worse, the Yugoslavian economy is rapidly deteriorating, inflation is rampant, and unemployment is growing. Slovenia is the most prosperous of the republics, and many Slovenians want to establish a less socialistic economic structure. These factors in turn create envy and resentment among the nationalities of the other republics. There is a distinct possibility that Yugoslavia again will be "Balkanized" and torn apart by the historically hostile nationalities that constitute the population of the country. ■

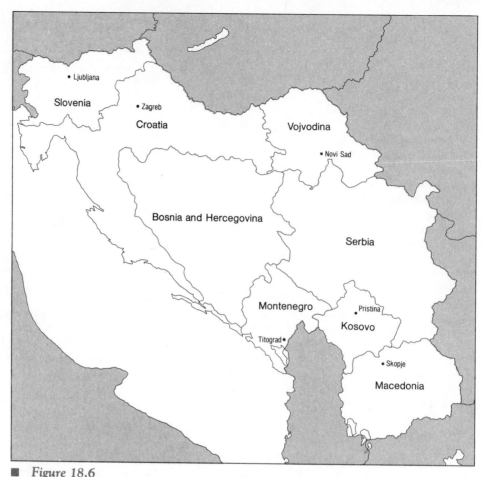

■ *Figure 18.6*

Republics and Autonomous Provinces of Yugoslavia The individual republics and autonomous provinces more or less correspond with the territories of major ethnic groups.

We hope that enough has been said to make this important point: in the modern world, both practical and ethical considerations suggest that accommodation of ethnic nationalities is the only viable and moral solution to problems of ethnic demands and conflicts. The sooner the economically and politically dominant nationality of a country—be they Russians, Mandarins, Latinos, Serbs, or WASPS—accept this reality, the quicker solutions will be forthcoming.

On the other hand, it is clear that such accommodation is inherently difficult to achieve. As we said earlier, ethnic nationalities believe that they have an inherent right to self-determination and autonomy within their homelands, and these beliefs often conflict with the aspirations of other nationalities and with the wishes of the dominant majority or ruling elite. The unity of a country is often more fragile than people

know. This is because the current political map of our planet is more an artifact of colonialism, expansionist conquests, world wars, and violent revolutions than of voluntary, peaceful amalgamation of separate peoples. As recent events in the Soviet Union, Romania, Yugoslavia, South Africa, India, and numerous other countries show, members of many nationalities await only the political or military opportunity to assert their claims.

This political reality has important implications for everyone, including those of us who live in nations whose own unity is in no immediate danger. The major threat to international peace and stability is not likely to come from conflicts between economic systems or political ideologies of existing superpower nation-states. Rather, the chief danger is ethnically generated conflict within nations. If eastern Europe, or the Soviet Union, or India, or some other major region should erupt in ethnic violence and be in danger of breaking apart, what will and should our reaction be? Should and can we stay neutral? Shall we simply see these conflicts as us versus them—will one side become "freedom fighters," the other "dictators"? Shall we send arms to the Armenians or to the Uzbeks in their nationalist struggle, or ought we to uphold the Soviet government's claims to territorial sovereignty? Should we support the separatist Muslims in Kashmir (northern India) or the official government of India? If we support one side or the other, why? (do we know?), and what form should our support take?

The danger is that most of us do not know enough to make intelligent decisions about these issues—indeed, most of us have never even heard of the Uzbeks, the Kazakhs, the Turkmen, the Kirghiz, and other Soviet nationalities. Nor do we have any factual basis for evaluating the legitimacy of nationalist claims. Isn't it worth the effort to find out?

Summary

In this chapter we have discussed the nature of ethnic groups and their significance in the world. Every individual, not just members of minority populations, belongs to an ethnic group and has an ethnic identity. An ethnic group is a named social grouping of people based on what is perceived as being shared ancestry, sociocultural traditions, and history. Ethnic group identity divides the world into categories of "us" and "them."

An individual's ethnic group identity is rarely absolute, but changes with social context. An individual may assume various hierarchically ranked identities. This characteristic is called the *hierarchical nesting quality* of identity.

There are two main attributes of an ethnic group. Every ethnic group has an origin myth or "history" that describes the common or shared historical experiences that created the group. Every ethnic group also has ethnic boundary markers that make its members identifiable. Ethnic boundary markers may include language, religion, physical characteristics, and other cultural traits such as clothing, house types, personal adornment, food, and so on.

There are two distinct types of ethnic groups. An ethnic nationality is an ethnic group with a feeling of homeland, and the inherent right to political autonomy. An ethnic minority is any subnational ethnic group. An ethnic minority does not have a feeling of a separate homeland nor of an inherent right to political autonomy.

Much of the conflict in the world today is between ethnic nationalities. There are between 3,000 and 5,000 ethnic nationalities in the world, but only about 170 separate countries. Most countries in the world are multinationality countries, and much conflict is the result of nationalities wanting to establish their own independent countries.

There is no simple or easy solution to ethnic conflict. Genocide, relocation, and forced assimilation are not only immoral, but history shows that they rarely solve ethnic problems. Passive assimilation is a slow and uncertain process. Attempts by governments of multinationality states to accommodate cultural differences and nationalistic aspirations are not always successful. Ethnic conflict is and will be a major destabilizing factor in world politics for some time to come. So far, the citizens and even governments of militarily powerful Western nations have not come to grips with the threat of nationalism.

Key Terms

ethnic group	artificial countries
hierarchial nesting	sociocultural
origin myth	homogenization
ethnic boundary	genocide
markers	relocation
ethnogenesis	forced assimilation
ethnic nationalities	passive assimilation
homeland	accommodation
ethnic minorities	

Suggested Readings

■ Bodley, John. *Victims of Progress.* 2d ed. Palo Alto: Mayfield Publishing, 1982.
  A very readable book that is a good overview of tribal peoples in the modern world, with emphasis on how they are being destroyed by industrial civilization.

■ Carmack, Robert, ed. *Harvest of Violence.* Norman: University of Oklahoma Press, 1988.
  This collection of twelve original essays is concerned with the war in Guatemala during the late 1970s and early 1980s,

and how the war effected and involved the native Maya communities.

■ De Vos, George and Lola Romanusci-Ross, ed. *Ethnic Identity: Cultural Continuities and Change*. Palo Alto: Mayfield Publishing, 1975.

A collection of fourteen important essays (with a conclusion) covering a variety of ethnic issues. A number of European, Asian, African and American ethnic groups are examined.

■ Eder, James F. *On the Road to Tribal Extinction: Depopulation, Deculturation, and Adaptive Well Being Among the Batak of the Philippines*. Berkeley: University of California Press, 1987.

During the twentieth century the Batak have become increasingly integrated into the Philippine economy. This has had far-reaching effects on the Batak sociocultural system, and has resulted in an erosion of their ethnic identity.

■ Foster, Charles, ed. *Nations Without States*. New York: Praeger, 1980.

This collection of essays covers ethnic conflict and nationalist movements among western European peoples such as the Scots, Welsh, Basques, Brittons, Corsicans, and Catalans.

■ Friedlander, Judith. *Being Indian in Hueyapan*. New York: St Martin, 1975.

An excellent and readable study of Native American identity in rural Mexico.

■ Grobsmith, Elizabeth. *Lakota of the Rosebud*. New York: Holt, Rinehart and Winston, 1981.

This is one of the best studies available on a contemporary Native American community in the United States.

■ Handler, Richard. *Nationalism and the Politics of Culture in Quebec*. Madison: University of Wisconsin Press, 1988.

An excellent introduction to French Canadian nationalism. This text examines the growth and changes in nationalism in terms of ideology.

■ Horowitz, Donald. *Ethnic Groups in Conflict*. Berkeley: University of California Press, 1985.

This study examines ethnic conflict on a global basis. It has a good discussion of theory of conflict, examples of conflict, and strategies for conflict reduction.

■ International Work Group for Indigenous Affairs. *The Naga Nation and Its Struggle against Genocide*. Copenhagen: International Work Group for Indigenous Affairs, No. 56, 1986.

A survey of the historical background and contemporary problems of the Naga people of India, who have had an separatist movement for over forty years.

■ Verdery, Katherine. *Transylvania Villagers: Three Centuries of Political, Economic, and Ethnic Change*. Berkeley: University of California Press, 1983.

The Romanian region of Transylvania is occupied by German, Hungarian and Romanian peoples. This study examines the social, political, and economic changes which have affected three nationalities and their relationships with one another over the past three hundred years.

Chapter 19

ANTHROPOLOGY AND TWO WORLD PROBLEMS

■ *Contents*

Population Growth
Consequences of Population Growth
Costs and Benefits of Children: North
  America
Costs and Benefits of Children: LDCs

World Hunger
Scarcity or Inequality?
Is Technology Transfer the Answer?
Comparative Perspectives on Food
  and Energy

■ (Above)*These Ethiopian refugees illustrate two of the greatest threats to human welfare today: population growth and hunger.*

For all our fascination with other ways of reckoning kinfolk, exchanging goods, relating to the supernatural, and the like—in short, with alternative ways of being human—modern anthropologists do have an interest in the application of our discipline to contemporary problems. There is, in fact, a subfield devoted specifically to bringing anthropological perspectives and knowledge to bear on the solutions to real-world problems. *Applied anthropologists*, as its practitioners call themselves, often serve as temporary consultants or permanent employees with some private or government agency. Their services are likely to be especially valuable whenever their employer needs expertise on some particular sociocultural community, wants firsthand fieldwork carried out on some specific problem about which information is lacking, or needs to determine the impact of some large-scale project on an indigenous population.

Our purpose in this chapter, however, is not to provide an overview of how relevant anthropology is. Rather, we shall examine in some detail the kinds of insights anthropologists offer to two specific problems of worldwide importance: population growth and world hunger. We address these particular problems because (1) there are many popular misconceptions about them, and (2) anthropological perspectives and ethnographic fieldwork have contributed to their understanding.

Before proceeding, a word of warning: of all the chapters in this text, this one is likely to be the most controversial. Both population growth and hunger affect hundreds of millions of people directly (and, indirectly, all of us). It therefore is not surprising that numerous explanations have been offered for them, and numerous policies proposed for their solution. We can only summarize a small segment of scientific opinion on these two problems—just enough, in fact, to make anthropological insights on them comprehensible.

Both problems also involve powerful political ideologies and opinions. Left- and right-wingers stack up on the various sides of these issues in fairly predictable ways. If we seem to lean to the left, it is partly to encourage our readers to stand a bit straighter the next time they hear someone bemoan the "fact" that "those ignorant people are breeding themselves into starvation" or that "a strong dose of modern technology will cure world hunger."

Population Growth

One of the most important worldwide problems of modern times is the phenomenal increase in the earth's population. Many people who know little about this subject believe that human numbers have been increasing steadily for millenia. We who live in the twentieth century just happen to live in a time when our numbers have finally reached a critical point, and threaten to exceed the capacity of the earth to support them.

In fact, today's high population growth rates are a recent phenomenon, at least on a global level. Around 10,000 years ago, before the development of cultivation and civilization, there were probably under ten million people on earth. Around the time of Christ, there were about 250 to 300 million. By the mid-nineteenth century, there were one billion. By 1930 human numbers had reached two billion; by 1960, three billion; by 1974, four billion; by 1986, five billion. To drive home the point that high rates of worldwide population growth are historically recent, note that it took the human population two or three hundred thousand years to number one billion, approximately eighty years to reach two billion; thirty years to reach three billion; fourteen years to reach four billion; and only twelve years to reach five billion. By the year 2000 the human population will probably increase to six billion.

It is therefore only in the last hundred years that the earth's population has been increasing at high rates. What has changed in the last century that accounts for this increase?

If we exclude the effects of migration, the rate of growth of a population depends on its excess of births over deaths, that is, on its fertility and mortality rates. So population growth is caused by some combination of falling death rates and rising birthrates. (See below for definitions of these and other terms used in this section.)

Population Terminology

birthrate (crude birthrate): number of births per 1,000 people per year

death rate (crude death rate): number of deaths per 1,000 people per year

infant mortality rate: number of deaths of children under the age of one per 1,000 children under the age of one per year

One possible cause of population growth is the increased supply of food made possible by modern technology, which could lower mortality, raise fertility, or both. But contrary to many people's beliefs, improved nutrition is not an important cause of recent population growth. It is most unlikely that rural people in the lesser developed countries (or LDCs), where most of the growth is occurring, eat better than they did, say, a century ago. Further, countries in which there is widespread malnutrition generally have among the fastest growth rates. For example, the lowest income countries of sub-Saharan Africa have the highest percentages of undernourished people of any continent. The poorest residents of nations such as Ethiopia, Mali, Chad, and Mozambique suffer more from hunger than any people in the world. Yet the populations of the lowest income African nations grew at an average annual rate of 2.8 percent between 1980 and 1986. If this rate continues, these countries will double their populations in only 25 years. In contrast, the citizens of the industrialized market economies (all of Western Europe, plus Canada, the United States, Japan, Australia, and New Zealand) are the most well nourished people on earth. Yet their populations increased at an average annual rate of only 0.6 percent between 1980 and 1986. So the mere fact that a population eats well does not mean that its women will have more children; indeed, in the modern world it is the relatively more malnourished women who tend to have the most babies. Some factors other than better nutrition are contributing to worldwide population growth.

Demographers (experts who describe and analyze human populations) generally agree that improvements in public health and medical care are the main reason for twentieth-century population growth. Vaccinations against smallpox, typhoid, yellow fever, cholera, and other diseases that are often fatal have lowered death rates. The spread of diseases such as dysentery and tuberculosis has been reduced by drugs and public health measures. Pesticide sprayings have reduced the numbers of mosquitoes and other insects that carry malaria and bubonic plague. Physicians and other medical personnel carry scientific treatments for illness into most parts of the world.

Improved public health and medicine affect population growth by reducing mortality: more infants survive into adulthood, or more adults live longer, or both. The former is probably the most important way in which medical science has reduced mortality, for the infant mortality rate in almost all LDCs began to decline significantly after World War II. Both infant mortality and death rates continue to fall today. For example, in the lowest income countries of sub-Saharan Africa and southeast and south Asia, infant mortality rates fell from 150 to 106 between 1965 and 1986. Between them, China and India have 40 percent of the world's people. In China, the infant mortality rate fell from 90 to 34 between 1965 and 1986; in India, it fell from 151 to 86. Overall death rates have likewise fallen. Between 1965 and 1986, crude death rates fell in the lowest income countries of Africa and Asia from 21 to 15, in China from 10 to 7, and in India from 20 to 12.

■ *High birth rates combined with sharply lowered death rates have caused unprecedented worldwide population growth in the twentieth century. Although still young, this Kenyan mother already has six children.*

In comparison, all developed industrial market economies have infant mortality rates of around 10 and crude death rates of around 9. People in the developed countries (DCs) of Western Europe, North America, and Oceania also live longer—our female life expectancy at birth is around seventy-nine, as compared to only fifty for sub-Saharan Africa.

So, despite medical progress, the LDCs lose far more of their infants and children to malnutrition and disease; they generally have higher crude death rates; and their life expectancies are lower. Nevertheless, their populations are growing at an average of about 2 percent (closer to 3 percent in sub-Saharan Africa and the Middle East), whereas the developed countries' overall rate of population increase is well under 1 percent.

The reason, of course, is that the developed industrial countries of Western Europe, North America, and Oceania have lower birthrates than do the LDCs. An average Japanese, British, or North American woman has 1.7 children during her lifetime, whereas an average Nigerian woman has 6.9 children; a Kenyan, 7.9; a Pakistani, 6.0; and an Indian, 4.4. In the developed countries, birthrates fell a few decades after death rates began to decline significantly in the mid-nineteenth century, so that today their populations are fairly steady. In the LDCs, birthrates have also fallen in the past two decades, but their rate of decline has not kept up with falling death rates, so that today their populations continue to grow. Of the LDCs with populations over fifty million, only China has achieved a significant decline in its birthrate, which fell from 39 to 19 (or 51 percent) between 1965 and 1986. In the same period, most other populous LDCs have experienced declines of around 25 percent.

In summary, population growth has accelerated rapidly in the last century. Worldwide progress in medicine and public health, not greater availability of food, is mainly responsible. It is occurring mainly in the LDCs today, because birthrates are not falling as fast as death rates.

What insights do anthropologists offer on this complex problem? We answer this question by first considering the adverse effects of population growth.

■ Consequences of Population Growth

Some people believe that humankind is irrationally breeding itself into mass starvation. Whether or not this possibility comes to pass, many undesirable effects do follow from high population growth rates. Some consequences are global—they affect everyone on earth, regardless of whether they live in an overpopulated region. For example, it has been suggested that the cutting of large amounts of tropical forest for cultivation to feed more people may have significant impacts on the earth's climate, raising its temperature enough to affect ecosystems and agriculture in unknown ways.

Americans already know one way population growth in one country, Mexico, affects our own nation—thousands of Mexicans cross the border in pursuit of the jobs and income that their nation cannot provide, due partly to population growth. Dense and growing population aggravates resource scarcity in Central American countries such as El Salvador and Guatemala, contributing to discontent, political instability, and even civil war.

For such practical as well as humanitarian reasons, we all should care about worldwide population growth, for it threatens the whole world ecologically, economically, and politically. However, the issue here is not the global consequences of population growth but its adverse effects on those very people and nations who are having "too many children." What are some of these consequences?

Population growth contributes to environmental problems. More people consume more resources of all kinds, so the production of food, wood, minerals, energy, and clean water will have to grow. In turn, this increased exploitation of nature means environmental deterioration—pollution, soil erosion caused by overgrazing and more intensive land use, habitat destruction for other living things, deforestation, urban sprawl, and so forth are accelerated by increasing numbers of people.

Economic problems also are magnified in countries with high population growth. The higher the population growth rate, the more children as a proportion of the total population will be alive, so the country must devote more of its resources to education and other things that "unproductive" children require.

Finally, many social and political problems are related to overpopulation. To escape rural poverty, many people born on farms migrate to cities, where they add to crime rates, produce housing shortages, create problems of sewage disposal and water supply, and so on. Increases in human numbers contribute to political conflicts, insurrections, and civil wars, as different ethnic groups, regions, classes, and parties compete for their slice of a shrinking pie.

■ *One consequence of population growth is rural to urban migration. This contributes to urban problems of overcrowding, substandard housing, and provision of adequate services, as we see in this apartment building in the slums of Cairo.*

Enough has been said to make the point: population growth is harmful to most LDCs. And, indeed, most governments have policies designed to curb fertility through educating couples in family planning and providing them with contraceptive devices to prevent conception. For example, realizing the probable disastrous long-term effects of continued population growth, in the late 1970s the Chinese government initiated a policy of allowing a family to have only two children. In the 1980s, a controversial one-child policy was instituted. Women apply for a child-bearing permit for the right to bear their only child, and those who become pregnant for a second time are subjected to intense social, political, and economic pressure to have abortions. Yet, in spite of the policies of their governments and the harmful effects of population growth, citizens of the LDCs continue to have large families, often rejecting birth control even when it is widely and freely available.

This seems to be a paradox. An average North American family is able to afford more children than an average Nigerian family. We have more money to house, feed, clothe, educate, and otherwise provide for our children. Yet we have only two or three, whereas the Nigerian family has six or seven. And this is the most puzzling thing about high fertility: it continues in spite of its adverse consequences for those very nations who are experiencing it and whose citizens are causing it—the LDCs.

Why do these people continue to have so many children? Are Indians, Nigerians, and El Salvadorans too ignorant to realize that they cannot afford to support so many children? Can't they see the strain that all these children put on their nation's educational, health, and agricultural systems? Don't they realize that when all these people grow up, their economies will have to supply jobs for them? Isn't the refusal of couples in these countries to practice birth control even when condoms, pills, and IUDs are available a perfect example of their backwardness and ignorance?

Not at all.

■ Costs and Benefits of Children: North America

We North Americans have no trouble seeing ourselves as making conscious choices to create our own family sizes. We decide whether or not to get pregnant based on how we weight our desire for children against the conditions of our personal lives. Our choices about how many children to have are made under certain constraints. One constraint is our cultural ideas (norms) about the proper and socially acceptable number of children. Some of us want more children than others, but most of us would agree that eight is too many. So we fear that people will laugh at us or call us "baby machines" or think us socially irresponsible or foolish if we have "too many."

North American cultural norms surrounding family size are important, of course, but they are not the only factors that influence the number of children we have. (Besides, the norm of family size itself responds to other conditions.) Other factors influencing our reproductive choices include

■ *Occupational and spatial mobility.* Many young couples do not know where they will be or how they will be earning a living in the next few years. They want children someday but are too unsettled and lack the income to start their family right away. If most couples postpone pregnancy until their mid-twenties or thirties, a lower completed average family size results than if most women begin childbearing earlier.

■ *Women's employment.* Many modern women want a career of their own and perceive that numerous children will interfere with this goal. A husband may want four children, but the wife wants her career, so they settle for two.

■ *Monetary costs.* Children are an economic liability to most couples in a twentieth-century industrial society. Many bills—for food, housing, doctors, clothing, transportation, insurance, education, day care, and babysitting—increase with the number of children. So when a young couple read in a newspaper that it costs over $100,000 to raise a child, not including college, they decide that one or two is quite enough. Nor are children likely to contribute much economically to their parents as they grow older—retirement plans, social security, and recently IRAs are expected to provide most of the income of the elderly.

■ *Social burdens of children.* Modern society offers numerous social and recreational outlets, which serve as alternatives to devoting one's time and energy to children. A couple may know some friends who have hardly left their house since their baby was born, and they have no desire to be so tied down.

None of this implies that North American couples always have the number of children they choose. Some have an "accident," and wind up with more children than they want or with a child sooner than they had planned. And the preceding considerations to some extent are class and race biased—they apply more to well-educated middle-income whites than to low-income blacks and Hispanics, for example. But we do make reproductive choices, and the result of them—barring infertility and so forth—is that we generally have about the number of children we desire. (Couples who want two kids only rarely wind up with four, for instance, even allowing for unplanned pregnancies.)

There are other factors that North American couples consider, of course. But notice one overall feature of the constraints just listed: they are all things that will affect the deciding couple personally. Thoughts of, we're too unsettled, we can't both pursue our careers fully, we will have less money to spend on ourselves, we won't be able to go out as often—these are the general kinds of influences people consider. They consider the benefits and costs of having or not having children, or of having so many and not more children, to *themselves.* Generally, they do not worry much about

whether their children will increase the burden on the American educational system, or increase the unemployment rate twenty years in the future, or contribute to society's expenditures on public waters and sewers, or overload the nation's farmlands. That is, they do not generally concern themselves with the *societal consequences* of their reproductive decisions. They do what they think is best for themselves.

■ Costs and Benefits of Children: LDCs

Curiously, although we know we make reproductive decisions, many of us think people in the LDCs do not do so. They seem to us to reproduce blindly, perhaps because "their culture values children," so they "have no choice." And, also curiously, although most of us do not take the societal consequences of our reproductive choices into account, for some reason we expect people in the LDCs to be more altruistic.

Part of our error comes from our failure to put ourselves in their shoes—to grasp the conditions of their lives that lead them to bear more children than we do. Just because children are an economic liability in a highly mobile, industrialized, urbanized, monetarized society does not mean that they are a liability everywhere. Many demographers argue that rural people in the LDCs have high fertility not because their culture leads them to like children but because children are economically useful. Village-level ethnographic studies conducted since the 1960s suggest that children do indeed offer a variety of material benefits to their parents in the LDCs.

One study was done by Indian anthropologist Mahmood Mamdani, who analyzed why a family planning program failed to reduce the birthrate in seven Indian villages. The villagers, it seemed, accepted the birth control pills offered by the staff of the program, but many did not take them. The reaction of the program's administrators was like that of many outsiders when local people do not respond in the way experts believe they should: they blamed the ignorance and conservatism of the local people. To the experts, the benefits of lowered fertility seemed obvious. The amount of land available to village families was already barely adequate, so by reducing the size of their families, villagers could stop the fragmentation of land that was impoverishing them each generation.

The village's parents did not see it that way. They believed it was to their benefit to have many children—especially sons. Most advantages revolved around having extra labor to work the family land—labor for which they did not have to pay. By having many sons, villagers also hoped to send one or more of them to the city, where they would earn cash that the family could use to buy more land. Acquiring more land—rather than having fewer children—was the way individual village families believed they could best solve their personal resource-scarcity problems.

Children offer similar benefits to their parents in other LDCs. On the densely populated Indonesian island of Java, parents do not have to wait for their children to grow up to acquire the benefits of their labor. Children aged six to eight spend three to four hours daily in tending livestock, gathering firewood, and caring for their younger siblings. By the time they are fourteen, girls work almost nine hours a day in child care, food preparation, household chores, handicrafts, and other activities. Most of the labor of children does not contribute directly to their family's cash income or food supply, so it is easy to see how outsiders might conclude that children are unproductive. However, children accomplish many household-maintenance tasks that require little experience and skill, which frees the labor of adult family members for activities that do bring in money or food. Ethnographer Benjamin White suggests that large families are more successful economically than small families in Java.

Similar findings have been reported by ethnographers working in rural Nepal, Bangladesh, Samoa, and the Philippines. Unlike suburban and urban North Americans, farming families in the LDCs use much of the time of even young children productively. As children grow older, they are used to diversify the economic activities of a household, earning cash themselves or performing subsistence work that frees their parents for wage labor. In many regions adult children migrate to a city or to a developed country, where they send cash back to their parents and siblings. Such remittances make up 50 percent of the total cash income of Western Samoans and also are important in Ghana, Nigeria, Burkina Faso, India, Mexico, and much of the Middle East.

In most parts of the world children also serve as the major source of economic support in their parents' old age, for rural villagers lack pension plans and social security. In many parts of India parents prefer to bear two or three sons in order to ensure themselves of having one adult son to live with them, in case one son dies or moves elsewhere.

In addition to the value of children's labor, remittances, and old age security, many other factors encourage families in the LDCs to have many children, including

- relatively high rates of infant mortality, which encourage parents to have "extra" children to cover possible deaths of their offspring;
- extended families, which spread out the burden of child care among other household members, thus reducing it to individual parents;
- low monetary cost of children compared to ourselves, partly because many necessities (such as housing and food) are produced by family labor rather than purchased; and
- the fact that the labor tasks women are commonly assigned are not as incompatible with childcare as wage employment.

Such factors mean that children are perceived (probably correctly) as both more valuable and less costly than they are among ourselves. We should not assume that couples in the LDCs are too ignorant to understand the costs of having many children or to appreciate the benefits of small families. Nor should we think that they are prisoners of their "traditional cultural values," which have not changed fast enough to keep up with changing conditions. We should rather assume that they make reproductive decisions just as we do. We should seek to understand the economic and other conditions of their lives that lead them to *want* many

Rather than being a financial burden as in industrialized nations, the labor of children is often an important economic asset to rural families in the LDCs. These young farm boys from Peru are carrying maize to their homes.

children. We then will understand why the simple availability of family planning advice and contraception so often has little effect on fertility—ignorance and lack of birth control technology were not the problems in the first place.

As we have seen, rising human numbers certainly contribute to the resource shortages faced by the LDCs today. One of the resources in shortest supply is one of the things people cannot do without: food. Most North Americans see malnutrition and overpopulation as two sides of the same coin. In the popular view, the "fact" that there are "too many people" in the world is the major reason that there is "too little food to go around." And the solution to world hunger is "more food," that is, increased production by the application of modern mechanized agricultural methods. In the next section, we shall try to convince you that neither the problem ("too many people") nor the solution ("more production through better technology") is this simple. (Box 19.1 argues that "too much consumption" is a greater cause for alarm than "too many people" for resource depletion of many kinds.)

World Hunger

Records and benefit concerts organized by popular singers in the mid-1980s dramatized the problem of world hunger. Nearly a billion people are malnourished to some degree. Children under the age of five are hit especially hard, dying either from malnutrition itself or from illnesses that well-nourished children could fight off.

A popular tale is that "there have always been people starving," that "humans have been struggling to find enough food since time began." Anthropology offers no certainties on this issue, but the weight of the ethnographic evidence suggests that widespread, serious malnutrition of the kind commonly found in Africa and southern Asia today was rare in the preindustrial world, at least until the development of states (see chapters 9 and 13). There were seasons of food shortage—times of the year when foods were scarce and people did not eat all they would have liked to or had to eat foods they did not especially like. There were years of hardship—times when heat, rainfall, disease, or other natural forces reduced the harvest of wild or cultivated foods and led to hunger. But severe hunger—year-in and year-out malnutrition and all it means for human health, vigor, and happiness—seems to have been uncommon.

■ *The scarcity explanation of hunger holds that there is an absolute shortage of productive land relative to the number of people who need food. When drought, plant disease, insect infestations, or other natural disasters occur, large numbers of malnourished people face starvation. These people are refugees from the drought in the Sahel of northern Africa.*

In this section we discuss twentieth-century conditions that have contributed to the (perhaps unprecedented) scale of worldwide malnutrition. We examine some of the problems of trying to feed the world with mechanized agricultural methods. And, of course, we suggest some anthropological insights on the problem.

■ *Scarcity or Inequality?*

Two major explanations are commonly offered for hunger and starvation in the LDCs. The first is the one most people believe. It holds that hunger is mainly caused by too many people chasing too few resources. Poor countries like India, Bangladesh, Mali, Ethiopia, and El Salvador simply have too many people to be supported adequately by their land area, this argument runs. With so many people on the edge of starvation, natural disasters such as drought reduce food production enough to lead to massive famine. So the periodic outbreaks of starvation in these already overpopulated countries have natural causes: the famines in Bangladesh in the 1960s, in the Sahel in the early 1970s, and in Ethiopia in the 1980s were all caused by lack of rain, for example.

According to this explanation, hunger and starvation are caused by overpopulation combined with natural disasters. Overpopulation creates chronic under-

WHOSE "POPULATION" IS TOO LARGE?

As we have discussed, one consequence of the growing world population is environmental deterioration and depletion of the earth's resources. More people mean more consumption of energy, more forests removed to cultivate land and provide living space, more minerals and other raw materials exhausted, and so on.

So far, so true. But this is not far enough. Fossil fuels, forests, minerals, water, and other resources can be depleted either because there are more people or because some people grow more affluent and consume them at a growing rate. Contrary to popular belief, population growth is not the major reason for the rapid exhaustion of global resources and is not the cause of most environmental problems. The high and growing standards of living of the developed countries are more responsible for the depletion of global resources than are the increasing populations of the LDCs.

This point is most conveniently made for energy consumption, which is a good measure of overall resource consumption. The amount of energy a person consumes can be expressed in kilocalories, and since we know how many kilocalories are locked up in a kilogram of oil, we can compare energy consumption using kilograms of oil equivalent. According to the World Bank's *World Development Report*, an average citizen of an industrial market economy consumed about 4,952 kilograms of oil equivalent in 1986. An average citizen of a low-income sub-Saharan African country consumed only 66 kilograms of oil equivalent. The 1986 per capita energy consumption of some familiar countries is given in the following list. Note that the six developed countries have far higher energy consumption than the eight LDCs.

Ethiopia, 21	Mexico, 1,235
Bangladesh, 46	France, 3,640
Kenya, 100	United Kingdom, 3,802
India, 208	West Germany, 4,464
Peru, 478	Soviet Union, 4,949
China, 532	United States, 7,193
Brazil, 830	Canada, 8,945

These figures on per capita energy consumption can be used to show how much more important high standards of living are than high population growth rates as a cause of worldwide resource depletion. An American family of four consumed 29,000 kilograms of oil equivalent in 1983. An average Mexican family of six consumed 7,410; a Chinese family of five consumed 2,660; an Indian family of six consumed 1,248; a Kenyan family of ten consumed 1,000; a Bangladesh family of eight consumed a mere 368. The small American family used 3.9 times more energy than the larger Mexican family; 11 times more than the Chinese family; 23 times more than the Indian family; 29 times more than the Kenyan family, and 79 times more than the Bangladesh family.

Who needs to limit what in the interest of preserving the earth's resources for future generations? ∎

∎ *Resource depletion and other environmental problems are caused by high levels of consumption in the developed countries as well as by increasing numbers of people in the LDCs. This is a Texas oil refinery—which countries use the greatest amount of oil per capita?*

Source: World Bank 1988, 240–1, 276–277.

nourishment, which turns into periodic outbreaks of starvation when crop diseases, insect pests, or droughts inevitably strike. This argument holds that food, water, land, and other life-sustaining resources are absolutely scarce—that is, there is simply not enough food, land, or water to go around in a country or region. We therefore call it the **scarcity explanation of hunger.**

The major alternative to the scarcity explanation may be called the **inequality explanation of hunger.** It holds that resources are not in fact absolutely scarce—that is, there is enough productive capacity in the land of practically every nation to feed its people an adequate diet. The reason for hunger is not overpopulation, drought, or any other natural catastrophe that reduces the availability of food for people. At least, these factors are not the main ones responsible for hunger. Instead, the reason is unequal access to land, water, and other resources required to feed people. Some people are poor because of the way their national economy, and the international economy as a whole, allocates resources, according to the inequality explanation.

In essence, this economy allocates resources on the basis of ability to pay, rather than on need. For example, if wealthy North American consumers want coffee and sugar, they have the ability to pay for it. So wealthy and politically powerful landowners in Central America will devote their land to coffee and sugarcane plantations, for these crops bring the most profit. These products will be exported, and the profits generally will be invested in enterprises that bring the

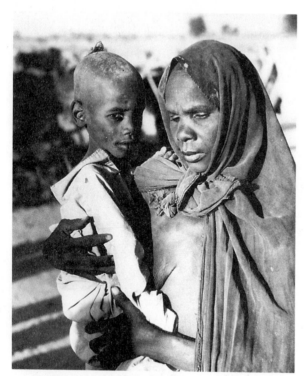

■ The inequality explanation of hunger holds that the global economy allocates food-producing resources on the basis of ability to pay rather than need. This mother probably lacks access to the land needed to feed her hungry child.

greatest future returns, regardless of the need of Central American peasants for farmland to feed their families.

As is often the case with competing explanations for some phenomena, these two are not really alternatives. Scarcity explanations are correct to the extent that, all else equal, the amount of land available per capita is reduced by population growth. Likewise, the amount of food available is reduced if drought, insects, or other natural disasters reduce yields or force some land to be taken out of production. It is hard to see how these statements could be wrong.

But they could be right and still tell only part of the story. The hunger story is more complex than "too many people," or "not enough rain." Hunger is created by human institutions as much as by natural conditions. For example, at a growth rate of 3 percent a year, a population will double in less than twenty-five years. Does this mean that in twenty-five years everybody will have only half the amount of food? Of course not. Land that formerly was underused will be brought into fuller production, more labor-intensive methods of cultivation can bring higher yields per acre, people can eat less meat, and so on. People will adjust their cultivation methods, work patterns, eating habits, and other behaviors to the new conditions.

Or rather, they will adjust if they have access to the resources they need to do so. And this is a large part of the problem in many LDCs: it is not *just* that there are too few resources but that too few people own or control the resources available. In their books *Food First* and *World Hunger: Twelve Myths*, Francis Moore Lappé and Joseph Collins question what they call "the myth of scarcity." They claim that every nation could provide an adequate diet for its citizens if its productive resources were more equitably distributed. For example, in Bangladesh, supposedly a prime example of an overpopulated country, grain was actually exported during the height of the famine of the 1960s!

A further discussion of the evidence that inequality is as important as scarcity in explaining hunger around the world is outside the scope of this text. Here we can only examine briefly one country, El Salvador, in which anthropologist William Durham analyzed in detail the scarcity versus the inequality explanation of hunger and other manifestations of poverty.

Durham notes that El Salvador appears to be a perfect example of the scarcity explanation of hunger and poverty. In 1892 the country had a population of about 700,000; by 1983, over five million people were living there, giving a population density of about 650 per square mile. (To compare with two countries generally considered overpopulated, China's 1983 density was under 300 and India's under 600. The United States' density is about 65.) Indications of El Salvador's overpopulation include widespread deforestation; widespread erosion and environmental devastation caused by intensive cultivation of marginal lands; and declining food production per capita, accompanied by a marked increase in food imports since about 1950. These characteristics are exactly what we would expect to find in a country whose population has outgrown its land resources.

But a closer look reveals that population growth is only part of the reason for the poverty of most of El Salvador's people. Although it is true that production of basic foods (notably maize, beans, and rice) has declined since 1950, total agricultural production has kept pace with population increase. Food production per capita has declined not because the country's land has become filled up with people, but because much of the land that could be used for food is in fact planted in export crops (coffee, cotton, sugar). By the 1960s land devoted to exports averaged over 40 percent of all the land under cultivation in the country. Almost as much land was devoted to coffee as to maize, the principal food crop for El Salvador's rural peasants.

Producing coffee rather than food might not be so bad, for by selling coffee the peasantry can earn money, which they can then use to buy food. But most of the coffee is not produced by peasants, notwithstanding North American coffee drinkers' images of Juan Valdez making a better life for his family by "selling only the finest beans."

To see why, we must first understand that land ownership in El Salvador is quite unequally distributed. Almost half the farms are under one hectare (2.5 acres) and are worked by peasant families mainly for daily subsistence. Only 1.5 percent of the farms are over fifty hectares, and these 1.5 percent of all "farmers" hold nearly half the total farmland of the country. This concentration of land in the hands of a wealthy minority goes back to the colonial era, and so is not a recent development. But it has worsened: in 1950, 39 percent of El Salvador's agriculturally active population was landless or land-poor (owned less than 1 hectare); in 1971 the proportion of landless or land-poor people had risen to 51 percent.

Now most of the food in El Salvador is produced by small farmers. Farms of less than five hectares account for only 16 percent of all the agricultural land in the country, yet they produce 58 percent of El Salvador's maize. Conversely, large farms of over 100 hectares own 48 percent of all the productive land, yet they produce only 19 percent of the maize. As for coffee, the 85 percent of small farmers who own less than five hectares of land produce only 8 percent of the coffee. The 0.9 percent of farms over 100 hectares produce 51 percent of the coffee, most of which is exported. In short, unless Juan Valdez is a large landowner, he is not likely to produce enough coffee beans to escape poverty.

Durham also presents evidence indicating that the larger the size of a farm, the more likely its land is to be underutilized. Small farmers use their land more fully: farmers with less than one hectare cultivate 81 percent of their land annually, whereas farmers with more than fifty hectares cultivate less than 35 percent of their land. Nearly half the land of farms over fifty hectares was used for grazing, mainly of cattle. We already have seen why this is an inefficient way to use land that is cultivable (Box 7.1) if farmers are interested in maximizing the amount of food produced on an area of land. (If farmers are interested in maximizing the amount of money they can earn from the land, then cattle may be the most efficient use, because wealthy El Salvadoran urbanites and North American fast-food chains can afford to pay for beef.)

Durham concludes his analysis of hunger and poverty in El Salvador with two points:

> First, we find that food is scarce not because the land is incapable of producing enough for the resident population, but rather because large areas have been underutilized or dedicated to the production of export crops. Second, we find that land is scarce not because there is too little to go around, but rather because of a process of competitive exclusion by which the small farmers have been increasingly squeezed off the land—a process due as much to . . . land concentration as to population pressure. (1979, 54)

There is no denying that population growth contributes to the hunger and poverty that victimize the peasantry of El Salvador and many other LDCs. But neither should we conclude that "too many people" is *the* problem, or that the scarcity explanation is sufficient. Population growth always occurs within a political and economic context, and this context greatly influences the degree to which poor people can adjust to it.

The combination of population growth and increasing land concentration is doubly devastating. Even if they manage to hang on to their land, the poor will tend to get poorer if their numbers grow. If their increased poverty makes it necessary for them to borrow from the wealthy, to sell part of their land to raise cash, or to work for low wages to make ends meet, they are likely to grow poorer still. This "double crunch" is precisely the experience of the rural poor in many LDCs.

Still, to use a popular metaphor, a rising tide raises all ships. Income and assets are unequally distributed in the DCs as well, yet most DCs have raised the nutrition levels of their poor through poverty programs made possible by technological progress. True, as farm productivity has grown, people have benefited unequally, but everyone has in fact benefited. Can't increased productivity made possible by capital investment in modern technologies solve the world hunger problem?

■ Is Technology Transfer the Answer?

A commonly proposed solution for world hunger is to apply modern scientific know-how and technology to areas in which agriculture is still technologically underdeveloped. This solution seems simple: thanks to agricultural machinery, plant breeding, modern fertilizers, pest-control methods, advances in irrigation technology, and so on, the developed countries have solved the nutrition problem for most of their people. We have developed science and technology and applied it to agriculture. The LDCs need only adopt our know-how and technology to solve their hunger problems. In this view, the main thing hungry countries need is a transfer of our technology.

There are many problems with the **technology-transfer solution.** We can touch on only a few. First, as we saw in our discussion of shifting cultivation in chapter 8, many of the methods developed for application in temperate climates fail miserably when transported to the tropics, where most hungry people live. This is largely because of the profound differences between tropical and temperate soils and climatic conditions.

Second, many experts doubt that so-called high-tech solutions to food problems are appropriate to economic conditions in the LDCs. Generally, labor is much more available than capital in these nations, so to substitute technology (machinery, herbicides, artificial fertilizers, etc.) for labor is to waste a plentiful factor of production in favor of a scarce one. Besides, those who need to increase production the most—the poorest farmers—are those who can least afford new technology. And

borrowing money for new investments involves risks, for many small farmers who borrow from rich landowners lose their land if they default.

Third, although it seems paradoxical, it may not be in the interest of poor farmers for land to become *too* productive. In countries such as Mexico many poor families get all or part of their food and cash by renting marginal lands from wealthy landowners. When technological improvements raise yields, the landlord may decide to use the land for cash crops, and the poor will be forced off the land altogether. On the Indonesian island of Java, many rural peasants do not own enough land to feed their families, so they must seek short-term work in the fields of rich landowners. When "green revolution" crop varieties were introduced to west Java in the 1960s, big landowners used the wealth made possible by increased yields to purchase tractors and rice-milling machines. Richard Franke argues that this reduced rural wages and forced some poor farmers into the cities.

Fourth, new technologies often come as a package deal. For instance, new crop varieties usually require large amounts of water, pesticides, and fertilizers to do well. Small farmers must adopt the whole expensive package for success. The expense, combined with the logistics of long-term supply of each element of the package in countries with uncertain transportation and political regimes, makes many farmers wary of innovations.

Fifth, agricultural experts from the developed world often report problems of "resistance" by peasant farmers. Peasants sometimes cling tenaciously to their traditional crops, varieties, and methods of cultivation even when genuine improvements are made available to them. This famed cultural conservatism of peasants seems downright irrational to many technical experts.

But some anthropologists who have conducted village-level fieldwork offer an alternative interpretation of peasant resistance to change. Living in intimate contact with local people, fieldworkers sometimes are able to perceive problems the way peasants do. Subsistence farmers barely feeding their families cannot afford to drop below the minimum level of food production it takes to survive. Traditional crops and varieties give some yield even when uncontrollable environmental forces are unfavorable, for over the generations they have adapted to local fluctuations of climate, disease, and pests. The new ones might not fare as well. Because the consequences of crop failure are more severe for a poor subsistence farmer than for a well-off commercial farmer, they minimize risks by using tried and true crop varieties and methods. Peasant cultural conservatism thus may be a sound strategy, given the conditions of peasant lives.

For these and a multitude of other reasons varying from region to region, a simple diffusion of modern agricultural methods from us to them is often unworkable and unfeasible. But there is another and even more compelling reason why our technical solutions are probably inappropriate to the rest of the world. A comparative perspective on the world's food systems suggests that the application of modern technologies is not just often unworkable and unfeasible—it may also be undesirable and even impossible. Why?

■ Comparative Perspectives on Food and Energy

Briefly, the reason is energy. If the way North Americans acquire their daily sustenance was exported around the world, the world would have little energy for anything else. In chapter 8 we noted that the major feature of mechanized agriculture, as we called our own system of cultivation, is the substitution of inanimate sources of energy for the energy of human labor needed to create and maintain an artificial community of domesticated plants. In Box 8.2 we showed that food-production systems can be compared on the basis of (1) their **labor efficiency,** or the number of calories of food energy obtained per unit of human labor, and (2) their **energetic efficiency,** or the number of food calories obtained ("output") per calorie of energy "input." Energetic efficiency incudes as an input the energy of human labor, tool making, fuels, animals, fertilizers, and so on. It includes as an output the energy of the food produced.

We need to note that using energy output/input ratios as a measure of efficiency is not entirely satisfactory, because foods have varying amounts of protein, vitamins, and minerals, as well as of energy. However, calories are the only available comparative measure of how much nutritive value is locked up in a wide variety of foods. In the following discussion, *calories output* should be interpreted to mean roughly "the amount of food produced."

To see the enormous difference between the labor efficiency of mechanized agriculture and the preindustrial systems described in chapter 8, we compare the approximate number of calories obtained per hour of labor actually spent producing food. As shown in Table 19.1, for example, North American rice grown using mechanized methods is 150 to 250 times more labor efficient than tropical rice grown under shifting cultivation; maize grown in North America is roughly 130 times more labor efficient than maize grown in the tropics using horticultural methods.

■ *Table 19.1* Labor Efficiencies of Preindustrial and Mechanized Agriculture

	LABOR EFFICIENCY	
CULTIVATION SYSTEM	Kcal./ Man Hour[a]	Kcal./ Kcal. Labor[b]
Preindustrial systems		
Swidden dry rice	2,600–4,500	17–30
Other tropical horticulture	6,000–7,200	40–48
Intensive wet rice, China	9,600	64
Mechanized agriculture		
Rice, U.S.A.	670,000	4,467
Maize, U.S.A.	900,000	6,000
Cereals, United Kingdom	730,000	4,867

[a]Number of calories locked up in the food produced per hour of farm labor.
[b]Number of calories contained in the food produced per calorie of energy expended by the farm laborer. The figures in the column assume that a farm laborer expends a mean of 150 calories per hour of work.

Sources: Calculated from data in Leach (1976) and Pimentel and Pimentel (1979).

■ *Modern mechanized agriculture is highly productive, both per farm worker and per acre. This is because of inputs such as manufactured herbicides and pesticides.*

Table 19.1 contains only data on the labor that food producers actually spend working in the swidden plot, rice field, or modern farm; that is, it includes only "on-farm" labor. The labor spent making tools, producing fertilizers, and other activities needed to produce crops is not included in the table, nor is the time spent processing, preparing, and cooking the harvest. The significance of these omissions will become apparent later.

Table 19.1 documents the much-praised productivity of mechanized agriculture—one person working on a mechanized farm produces much more food than a preindustrial farmer. This high level of labor efficiency on the modern farm means that one farm worker produces enough food to feed roughly sixty to seventy people in the United States and Great Britain. The same is true, as we like to brag, about yields per acre using mechanized methods—new crop varieties, chemical fertilizers, proper irrigation, and other technical inputs produce remarkable yields, which potentially means that more people can be supported from an acre of land than ever before in human history.

Those who champion the export of modern technology as a means to allay hunger in other nations point to numbers like these. Unfortunately, other numbers paint a more pessimistic picture of the possibilities of solving the world food crisis by diffusing our mechanized methods to "backward peoples."

No farming method can produce something out of nothing. If modern methods conserve labor and have

high yields per acre, something other than labor and land are being put into our food system to gain our outputs. These somethings, of course, are fertilizers, pesticides, herbicides, water, tractors, and so forth. Technology substitutes for labor and makes land more productive—this is what we mean by *mechanization*.

But energy is required to manufacture and operate farm equipment, to produce and apply fertilizers and chemicals that control pests and weeds, and so on. Electricity and fossil fuels (oil, natural gas, and coal) are used at various stages of production. It is not just farmers and land that produce our food—it is farmers plus land plus wood plus steel plus energy plus a multitude of other materials. In fact, the energy of human labor (farm workers) is only a fraction of 1 percent of the total energy required to produce our food. We obviously must treat nonhuman energy as an input to food production in mechanized agriculture. (Nonhuman energy is also an input for preindustrial cultivation systems, but there human-labor energy represents a high percentage of the total energy input.)

How much energy does mechanized agriculture require? A lot. Several studies in the 1970s documented that food production in Great Britain and the United States is enormously energy intensive.

To consider the United States first, David Pimentel and his associates estimated the amount of energy

■ *These mechanical harvesters add to the productivity of farm land and farm labor, but they and other agricultural machinery require a large input of energy. Could this energy-intensive technology be the solution to the world food problem?*

consumed in producing various crops. From these figures they made estimates of total energetic efficiency, that is, the ratio of the energy contained in the harvested crop (energy output) to the total energy required to produce it (energy input) using mechanized agriculture. For example, in 1975 corn (maize) had an energetic efficiency of about 2.9, meaning that 2.9 calories of corn were harvested for every calorie of energy used to manufacture, apply, and operate the fertilizers, pesticides, machinery, and so forth used in corn production. If you compare this 2.9 ratio for *total* energetic efficiency to the 6,000 ratio for *labor* efficiency for corn given in Table 19.1, you can see the degree to which inanimate energy substitutes for labor in mechanized agriculture. To give a better feeling for how much energy is required, Pimentel and associates estimated that to raise one acre of corn in the United States in 1970 required the energetic equivalent of eighty gallons of gasoline. We pay a price for our productivity—our farms use prodigious amounts of energy.

This is not the end of the agricultural energy story. The ratio of 2.9 makes it appear that we still come out ahead, getting almost three calories of food from each calorie of total energy we use in production. In fact, we come out way behind—it takes more energy to produce our food than we get out of the food. Why? Partly because most of the agricultural output of our country is fed to livestock, which spend much of their eating lives in feedlots rather than open rangeland. As

mentioned in Box 7.1, over 90 percent of the grains, legumes (especially soybeans), and other vegetable protein produced by American farmers was fed to livestock in 1975. We consumed this vegetable protein indirectly, in the form of milk, eggs, poultry, pork, beef, and other animal products. But in passing it through the bodies of animals, we lost most of it to their respiration and wastes.

So the total energetic efficiency of our farm production is low because we use energy-intensive methods to cultivate our crops and because we feed so many of our crops to livestock. But we still have not discussed the other energy it takes to get our food from farm or feedlot to our dinner tables. And we don't just mean transportation. Much of our food is processed. It is refined (e.g., sugar, flour), canned, frozen, cut up, and placed in containers. The steel, aluminum, glass, paper, plastics, and other products used in processing and packaging take energy to produce. We buy almost all our food in commercial stores and restaurants, where more energy is consumed in freezing, cooling, and cooking it. When we take it home, we store much of it in our electric-powered refrigerators before we cook it on our electric or gas stoves.

In short, between the time the food leaves the farm and enters our mouths, more energy is used to transport, process, package, preserve, and prepare it. En-

■ A lot is done to most of our food between the time it leaves the farm and enters our mouth. It is processed, frozen, canned, and packaged. These inputs must also be counted as part of our entire food system, and they too require considerable energy inputs.

■ A major reason for the low energetic efficiency of modernized food systems is that so much land is devoted to producing food that is fed to livestock on feedlots like this one.

ergy experts Carol and John Steinhart estimated the amount of energy used by our total *food system*, that is, in all the various energy inputs on farms, in processing, and in commercial and home refrigeration and cooking. They found that on-farm inputs (energy consumed before the crop leaves the farm) are only 25 percent of the total energy expended in our entire food system. The remaining 75 percent was divided about equally between processing and home or commercial uses. For 1970 the Steinharts concluded that about nine calories of energy (input) are required to get one calorie of food (output) into our mouths. This gives an energy output/input ratio of 1:9, or 0.11.

Now we shall consider Great Britain. In 1976, Gerald Leach estimated the overall energetic efficiency of British mechanized agriculture. He found that about three calories of energy were needed by British farmers to produce one calorie of food energy. As in the United States, the major reason for this low efficiency is the cultivated crops fed to livestock. Only 13 percent of Britain's cultivable land is planted in crops that are fed directly to people; the remaining 87 percent produces wheat, barley, oats, and other forms of fodder for sheep, cattle, pigs, and poultry. Considerable energy and land savings could be made in both the United States and Great Britain if we ate less meat, eggs, and milk, or if our ranchers, hog farmers, and poultry producers reduced the amount of time livestock spend in feedlots.

Leach also estimated the amount of energy required to transport, process, package, sell, refrigerate, and cook food in Great Britain. He concluded that the overall energetic efficiency of Great Britain's food system is about 0.14: seven calories of energy are required to get one calorie of food energy into British mouths.

The energy required to run our food system is a significant proportion of the total energy we consume for all household and industrial purposes (e.g., heating and cooling homes and buildings, producing steel and lumber). Eric Hirst found that the American food system used about 12 percent of the national energy supply in 1963, and the proportion increased to 16 percent in the 1970s, according to David and Marcia Pimentel. Similarly, Leach estimated that putting food on British tables required almost 16 percent of the total energy consumed in that country.

An interesting implication of these energy studies is that they show why one of the great benefits of mechanized agriculture is not as great as it is presumed to be. One American or British farm worker produces enough to feed about sixty to seventy people. This high productivity allows most workers to seek employment in other industries. Has this productivity ended man's necessity to work endlessly to feed himself and his family?

Not quite. For one thing, in most human societies "man's" labor has been far from endless. As we discussed in chapters 8 and 9, only with the development of stratified civilizations did most people begin to spend long hours producing food, and then partly because so much of their work fed someone else!

For another thing, food industry workers in a mechanized system are not limited to those employed on farms. The people who transport, process, and sell food must be counted as employed in the food system, as should those who manufacture the equipment, packaging, and other materials used. For Great Britain, Leach estimates that 13 percent of the 1968 employed population was involved in food, directly or indirectly. An average worker in the entire food industry supplied enough food for only about eight—not sixty— people. No comparable estimates exist for the United States,

■ *Mechanized agriculture is enormously labor efficient if we count only farm workers. But efficiency falls significantly if we also count the producers of farm machinery, herbicides and pesticides, and other direct inputs. If we include food processors, butchers, wholesalers, retailers, and the like, a significant proportion of the labor force is employed in the food system.*

but Pimentel's group believe that about 20 percent of the American work force are employed in food or food-related industries. True, energy-intensive production methods save considerable farm labor. Yet we eliminate much of the savings by increased employment in food processing, transporting, distributing, and manufacturing farm machinery and other inputs. "Yesterday's farmer is today's canner, tractor mechanic and fast-food carhop," as Steinhart and Steinhart (1974, 79) say.

This information should interest all of us. Knowing that at least half the energy used on-farm is wasted because it is fed to livestock might affect our eating habits. Aside from the personal health benefits of reducing red-meat consumption, patriots could save their nations considerable energy by eating more protein-rich vegetable foods and less beef. Knowing that almost 40 percent of the energy required to put food on our tables is used in processing, packaging, and transporting might encourage us to forgo energy-intensive frozen and canned foods in favor of fresh vegetables and fruit.

However, our present purpose—and the reason we began this discussion of the energy requirements of our food system—is to show why mechanized agriculture cannot feed the world. Table 19.2 contains a comparison of the energy output/input ratios for horticulture, intensive agriculture (using draft animals), and mechanized agriculture (using artificial fertilizers, machinery, fuels, insecticides, and so forth). It shows only the energy used on-farm, including human labor, seeds, tools, fertilizers, and animal or machine power if relevant; the energy needed for transporting, processing, packaging, cooking, and other "after-farm" activities is not included.

As evident from the data in Table 19.2, preindustrial cultivators have energy-efficiency ratios on the order of about 15–50:1, depending on crop, local conditions, and specific methods. Mechanized agriculture has output/input ratios of around 2–4:1. So preindustrial cultivation systems use seven to ten times less energy per amount of food produced.

The energy of food processing (e.g., grinding corn into tortillas) and preparation (e.g., cooking) is not included in the ratios of Table 19.2, because to our knowledge no studies exist that take these energy inputs into account in preindustrial systems. As we have seen, in the food systems of the United States and Great Britain, the after-farm energy inputs make up a high proportion of the total energy in our food system, greatly lowering its overall efficiency to about 0.11 and 0.14. If we wish to compare total food systems, we

■ **Table 19.2** Comparative Energetic Efficiencies, On-Farm Inputs Only

CULTIVATION SYSTEM	CROP	O/I RATIO[a]
Horticulture[b]		
Tsembaga (Papua New Guinea)	Mixed roots	18
Southeast Asia, Tanzania	Rice	14–23
Africa (various regions)	Mixed roots	23–61
Africa, Mexico, Guatemala	Maize	14–38
Intensive agriculture[c]		
Chinese village (1935–1937)	Wet rice	41
Mexico, Guatemala	Maize	4–5
Mechanized agriculture[d]		
Great Britain, U.S.	Maize	2–3
Great Britain, U.S.	Wheat	2–3
California, Japan	Rice	1.5–2.5
United States	Sorghum	2
United States	Soybean	4

[a]Energy output/input ratio, or energetic efficiency, defined as the calories of food produced per calorie of energy input.
[b]In this table we define horticulture as the absence of the animal-powered plow. In all the systems included, human labor constituted over 90% of the total energy inputs.
[c]Defined as systems including significant energy inputs derived from animals. In Mexican and Guatemalan corn farming, oxen provided about five times more energy inputs than human labor, which explains the low O/I ratio.
[d]Inputs include mainly energy used to manufacture machinery, herbicides, pesticides, and fertilizers; to power equipment and transportation; and to dry grain. Human labor is an insignificant (far less than 1%) input to all except rice produced in Japan, where human labor is 11% of the total energy input.

Sources: Leach (1976); Pimentel and Pimentel (1979).

must lower the ratios for preindustrial cultivators to make the comparison with our own food system meaningful. Because most of the energy input of horticulturalists and intensive agriculturalists is in the form of human labor, lowering the ratios by 50 percent seems reasonable. This would give total energetic efficiencies of around 7–25:1 for the preindustrial systems. (Lowering the ratios by two-thirds still gives ratios of 5–17:1. Lowering them by 90 percent—a preposterous adjustment—still means that 1.5 to 5 calories of food energy are produced for every calorie of total energy input in preindustrial food systems.)

Compare these output/input ratios to the food systems of the United States and Great Britain. Instead of 7–25:1, our ratios are about 0.11:1 (U.S.) and 0.14:1

(G.B.). Preindustrial food systems are probably about 50 to 200 times more energetically efficient than the modern food systems some people wish to replace them with!

Consider what these low efficiencies mean for the possibilities of feeding the world using good old American (and British) know-how. If the rest of the world adopted the food system of Great Britain, Leach (1976, 31) says the annual global energy bill would be "40% of global fuel consumption in 1972." Steinhart and Steinhart (1974, 82) say that to feed India's people "American style" would "require more energy than India now uses for all purposes." Pimentel and Pimentel (1979, 8–9) point out that the U.S. food system requires more energy per capita than is "expended per capita in developing countries for all energy-consuming activities including food production." They also calculate that to feed the world a diet as high in animal protein as that of the United States, using petroleum as the source of energy, would exhaust the earth's petroleum reserves in only eleven years.

To conclude, it is unlikely that mechanized agricultural methods can be transferred to very many of the LDCs as the major solution to their hunger problems. This is not to suggest that these countries should abandon modern agricultural technology because of its high energy costs and return to the cultivation methods of their ancestors. It is to say that modern agricultural technologies carry high energy costs (not to mention other environmental costs), and that these costs must be balanced against the benefits. There is, in fact, a middle ground, in which modern methods are used selectively and adapted to local environmental and sociocultural conditions.

At any rate, to claim that hunger can be eliminated by applying modern technological inputs is to assume that the food crisis is caused mainly by people not producing enough food. That is, it is to assume that the scarcity explanation accounts for most of the malnourishment and outright starvation in the world. But, as we have seen, the unequal distribution of productive land, water, and other food-producing resources is also an important cause of world hunger. Solving the food crisis is likely to require more than "more productivity" or even "more production." It may also require profound changes in the ownership and control over productive resources in the LDCs and—most likely—in the world economy as a whole.

There is an old saying that those who want to spread Western agricultural technologies around the globe are fond of quoting: "Give a boy a fish and you'll feed him for a meal; teach a boy to fish and you'll feed him for a lifetime." In other words, "we" need to teach "them" how to grow food, rather than simply being generous with our food aid. However well-meaning this sentiment may be, much evidence suggests that most hungry people already know how to fish, and that their unsophisticated bamboo rods can serve them quite adequately. What they need most is access to a productive pond.

In these last three chapters we have discussed the changes that have occurred in the world over the past five hundred years, and some of the problems of the modern world. Our global economic system has evolved more rapidly than our social identities and political systems. The related issues of population growth and economic development are far more complex than most people realize. The modern world is both interdependent and volatile. All peoples in the world are dependent minorities, with different values, norms, beliefs, and aspirations. All peoples are ethnocentric and all peoples believe that their values, norms, and beliefs are correct. Even if we (whoever we are) wished to change the peoples of the world and remold them in our image, we could not. The true challenge of humanity's future is not to "conquer" the universe, but to conquer ourselves. We must learn to respect the rights of other peoples, and accept them as they are, not as we might like them to be. Only by recognizing these differences and working within the framework of these differences can we, the people of the world, solve the political, demographic, economic, and environmental problems confronting us all.

Summary

This chapter provides anthropological insights on two contemporary world problems: population growth and hunger. High rates of worldwide population growth are a recent phenomenon. High growth rates are caused mainly by advances in medicine and vaccines and widespread improvements in public heath facilities. These advances have reduced death rates and increased life spans in most countries, but in underdeveloped regions birthrates are still relatively high.

Population growth has many unfavorable consequences for those very nations that are experiencing it. It contributes to serious environmental problems, low economic productivity, urban sprawl and shantytowns, political conflicts, and even war. This is the main paradox of population growth: the high fertility of a country's citizens is mainly responsible for it, yet their high fertility contributes to many of their nation's problems.

But having many children is not a simple product of ignorance or irrational cultural conservatism. The fertility rate is a response to the overall economic conditions and sociocultural climate in a country. This is shown by how North American couples choose how many children to have. Our low fertility is a rational response of couples to the conditions of our personal lives. In deciding how many children they want, most modern couples consider the personal, not the societal, costs and benefits of children.

High fertility in the LDCs likewise is a consequence of the overall economic and social environment that constrains reproductive behavior. Ethnographic studies suggest that children are a net economic asset rather than a liability in the rural areas of the Third World. Children are productive family members at a young age. They seek jobs with local people, supplementing the family income. When older, they go to the cities or to foreign countries and send money back home. They provide old-age security for their parents. Under such conditions, high fertility exists because large families are beneficial.

Population growth is popularly believed to be the major cause of world hunger. This is the scarcity explanation of hunger, which holds that overpopulation results in chronic malnutrition and periodic massive starvation. The alternative is the inequality explanation. It holds that land and water resources are in fact adequate to provide an adequate diet for the whole world. Hunger is caused by the way the local and world economies allocate resources—on the basis of ability to pay rather than need. Durham's study of El Salvador illustrates that the two explanations are compatible: population growth contributes to hunger by increasing the scarcity of food-production resources, yet prevalent inequalities in access to productive resources aggravate the scarcity and prevent people from adjusting to it.

Technology transfer is the best viable solution to hunger in the LDCs, according to many. But there are numerous obstacles to exporting modern methods and machinery; reasons to think that a simple transfer of technology will not work well in the tropics; many cases in which such a transfer has harmed the poorest families; and good reasons to think such a solution is undesirable and perhaps impossible. The most basic reason is that modern mechanized agriculture requires prodigious amounts of energy. Although mechanized agriculture is enormously labor efficient, its energetic efficiency is much lower than that of preindustrial cultivation systems. Ethnographic studies suggest that preindustrial food systems are about 50 to 200 times more energetically efficient than our own. Given these comparisons of energy requirements, it is difficult to envision how modern mechanized agriculture could solve the world food crisis.

Key Terms

scarcity explanation of hunger

inequality explanation of hunger

technology-transfer solution

labor efficiency

energetic efficiency

Suggested Readings

■ Bodley, John H. *Anthropology and Contemporary Human Problems.* Menlo Park, Calif.: Cummings, 1976.
   A good place to start in glimpsing the relevance of anthropology to modern problems. Provides insights on war, poverty and hunger, and environmental destruction.

■ Foster, George M. *Traditional Societies and Technological Change,* 2d ed. New York: Harper and Row, 1973.
   A basic introduction to applied anthropology, although most of its ideas are now considered old-fashioned.

■ Franke, Richard W., and Barbara H. Chasin. *Seeds of Famine: Ecological Destruction and the Development Dilemma in the West African Sahel.* Montclair, N.J.: Allanheld, Osmun, 1980.
   A well-documented study of the Sahelian drought and famine, arguing that planners and the international economy were as much responsible as natural disasters.

■ Gupte, Pranay. *The Crowded Earth: People and the Politics of Population.* New York: Norton, 1984.
   Overview of the social, economic, and political dimensions of population growth and control.

■ International Bank for Reconstruction and Development. *World Development Report 1990.* New York: Oxford, 1990.
   One of the World Bank's annual reports on the state of the world economy. The statistical tables in the back of the report provide a wealth of information on population, economic growth and trade, international debt, health, and education.

■ Lappé, Frances Moore, and Joseph Collins. *Food First: Beyond the Myth of Scarcity.* New York: Ballantine, 1977.

■ _____. *World Hunger: Twelve Myths.* New York: Grove, 1986.

Two books that argue against the scarcity explanation of hunger and provide evidence and analysis in favor of the inequality explanation.

■ Leach, Gerald. *Energy and Food Production.* Guildford, Surrey: IPC Science and Technology Press, 1976.

A comprehensive yet brief study of energy use in the food system of the United Kingdom.

■ Pimentel, David, and Marcia Pimentel. *Food, Energy and Society.* New York: Wiley, 1979.

A study of the energy requirements of producing various crops, livestock, and fish in the United States. Processing and transportation energy uses are also estimated.

■ Wrigley, E. A. *Population and History.* New York: McGraw-Hill, 1969.

Traces the history of human population, concentrating on Europe.

■ Wrong, Dennis. *Population and Society.* New York: Random House, 1977.

A short text on demography.

THE SURVIVAL OF INDIGENOUS PEOPLES

■ Contents

■ (Above) *The caption on this print reads: "An Indian Welcome on Charles River." Encounters between Native Americans and Euro-Americans led to the biological extinction, relocation, assimilation, and reservation confinement of most of the indigenous peoples of the Americas.*

419

Throughout this book we have emphasized the sociocultural diversity of humanity. How much of this diversity will persist into the future? Since 1500, as Westerners have spread themselves and their way of life around the world, non-Western technologies, economic systems, kinship and marriage forms, political organizations, and religious traditions have been destroyed deliberately or have withered and died. We doubt that the human species will ever become socioculturally uniform. But there is less sociocultural diversity in the twentieth century than there was in the nineteenth; if present trends continue, there will be still less in the twenty-first century.

We conclude *Humanity* with a discussion of the disappearance of preindustrial ways of life. We also close as advocates for the rights of native peoples to preserve their sociocultural systems, if that is their choice.

The Fate of Indigenous Peoples

Indigenous peoples are the people who lived in a region at the time of its contact with outsiders more powerful than themselves. In the past, these outsiders usually were members of the colonizing Western nations, such as Spain, Portugal, France, Germany, Holland, England, and the United States (see Chapter 17). As the Western variant of civilization advanced across the earth beginning in the fifteenth century, its agents often committed horrendous atrocities against indigenous peoples of the Americas, Africa, and Asia. Dozens of cases of genocide are historically documented, but probably dozens of others have gone unreported.

One example is the fate of the indigenous people of Tasmania, a large island off the coast of Australia. Between 1803, the year of initial British settlement, and 1876, the entire indigenous population of Tasmania was wiped out, most of them by deliberate killing. The main reason for the slaughter was that white settlers wanted to use the land for grazing sheep, but many Tasmanians were hunted down for no higher motive than sport.

When the German government formed its "protectorate" of Southwest Africa in 1884, several hundred thousand pastoralists were grazing their cattle in the region. German settlers, who wanted to establish ranches and farms of their own, dispossessed the indigenous Herero peoples of their land. By the turn of the century, German soldiers had massacred hundreds of Herero. Those who remained were reduced to poverty by cattle diseases and unscrupulous white traders. When the Herero revolted en masse in 1904, German soldiers put down the revolt by force of arms and by poisoning a few waterholes. By the end of the revolt only 20,000 Herero remained, eking out an existence on the arid, marginal lands left to them.

To a large extent, these and numerous other horrors were rationalized by cultural attitudes prevalent at the time: Some people (always the colonialists, of course) are more advanced than others and so are better able to use land and other resources for the greater good of humankind. Indigenous peoples were seen as standing in the way of progress and so could be pushed aside with minimal damage to the colonial powers' moral scruples. A German official justified the actions of his countrymen against the Herero with these words:

> The native tribes must withdraw from the lands on which they have pastured their cattle and so let the White man pasture his cattle on these self-same lands. If the moral right of this standpoint is questioned, the answer is that for people of the culture standard of the South African Natives, the loss of their free national barbarism and the development of a class of workers in the service of and dependent on the Whites is primarily a law of existence in the highest degree. For a people, as for an individual, an existence appears to be justified in the degree that it is useful in the progress of general development. By no argument in the world can it be shown that the preservation of any degree of national independence, national prosperity and political organization by the races of South West Africa would be of greater or even of equal advantage for the development of mankind in general or the German people in particular than that these races should be made serviceable in the enjoyment of their former territories by the White races. (quoted in Bodley 1982, 55)

So racism, ethnocentrism, and social Darwinist ideas about the inevitability and desirability of progress provided the cultural justification for many atrocities during the colonial era.

The most well known examples of extermination and attempted extermination of indigenous peoples occurred against the Indians of North America. The sad history of white atrocities against the original Americans began early. As one instance, in 1637, in Mystic, Connecticut, settlers killed at least 300 Pequot children, women, and men by burning their village and shooting the Indians as they fled the blaze. The survivors were sold as slaves to planters in the West Indies. White Americans also intentionally gave poisoned flour and blankets infected with smallpox to Indians.

Perhaps the worst atrocities occurred in the nineteenth century, with the large-scale settling of the Great Plains. In an attempt to destroy the Plains Indians' source of food and force them onto reservations, white hunters killed off the great herds of bison. As Euro-Americans moved into a region occupied by Native Americans, the U.S. government often relocated the surviving members of the tribe, sometimes moving them vast distances under adverse conditions. The most famous is the movement of the Cherokee from North Carolina to Oklahoma in the 1830s, a forced migration that became known as the Trail of Tears, for over one-fourth of the tribe died during the trek.

Further west, in California, untold thousands of Indians already had died in the seventeenth and eighteenth centuries because of early Spanish atrocities and introduced diseases. More deaths were to come after the 1849 gold rush. Unprotected by the federal government, between 1849 and 1880 the California Indian population dropped from 100,000 to 20,000 because of ruthless exploitation and the killing of Indians as sport by Anglo settlers.

The final, and most famous, massacre of Native Americans was the 1890 attack on a Sioux settlement at Wounded Knee, South Dakota. In previous decades, the Sioux had lost most of their traditional hunting lands and been confined to small reservations. They subsisted mainly on provisions supplied by the U.S. government, for the bison (upon which they and other Native Americans of the plains formerly depended for meat) had been driven nearly extinct. Under the leadership of Sitting Bull, many Sioux were practicing the Ghost Dance, a revitalization movement (see Chapter 15) that many Plains Indians believed would revive their dead, bring back the bison, and rid their lands of whites. Because part of the Ghost Dance doctrine was that special "ghost shirts" would protect Indian warriors from the bullets of white soldiers, the ritual was seen as a military uprising by many U.S. officials. In December, 1890, the Seventh Cavalry surrounded a Sioux encampment at Wounded Knee and ordered the men to turn in their rifles. Gunfire was exchanged and fighting immediately escalated. In the end, nearly 200 Sioux, at least 60 of them women and children, were killed.

It was not just physical bodies that were destroyed. In most cases, those who survived the violence, the expropriation of their territory, and the disease were forced or encouraged to deliberately abandon their traditional way of life—a policy called *assimilation* (see chapter 18). In the United States and South Africa, indigenous peoples were moved to small reservations far away from their ancestral homelands, where their way of life was almost guaranteed to wither and die. Thus, even those indigenous peoples who survived often saw their sociocultural systems collapse.

These historical events are deeply saddening—all the more so because they are much less talked about today than similar atrocities committed by European residents against one another, such as Hitler's attempt to wipe out the Jews of Europe. But at least such things do not happen today—right? Wrong. Today's more "enlightened" governments have not eliminated such excesses—in some cases, it is doubtful that they are even trying to.

Modern governments in Latin America, Africa, and parts of Asia face serious economic, political, and social problems—problems that were created by the history of their incorporation into the worldwide economic and political system. Many governments—including those democratically elected—are under pressure from their dominant ethnic group to pursue policies that lead to the displacement or assimilation of the indigenous peoples whose territories lie within their national boundaries. In many countries aspiring to modernization, indigenous people living in remote, "undeveloped" regions are forced to move aside in the interest of what the dominant ethnic group sees as the "greater good" of their nations.

Sometimes this "greater good" consists of opening up undeveloped areas to settlers. Indonesia has long had a plan to resettle peasants from overpopulated Java onto its outer islands, now claimed to be underpopulated (whatever that means) by indigenous shifting cultivators. Although often considered a modernized nation, Brazil has some of the poorest people in the world living in its northeastern area. It also is one of the few countries left with a frontier—the vast tropical rain forest of Amazonia. In the 1970s Brazil constructed highways intended to open up Amazonia to resettlement and to mineral, timber, grazing, and agricultural exploitation. Some of the resulting atrocities and destruction of the lifeways of the Amazonian Indians are recounted in Shelton H. Davis's *Victims of the Miracle*.

One people who are threatened by the opening up of Brazil's Amazonian frontier is the Yąnomamö, mentioned in chapters 10 and 16. Until the early 1970s, most of the approximately 9,000 Yąnomamö were relatively isolated from outside influences. In 1974, the Brazilian government constructed a road through the southern part of Yąnomamö territory. Workers involved in forest clearing and road building introduced new diseases such as influenza and measles, and in some regions as many as half of the Yąnomamö died from epidemics. Dirt airstrips constructed during the 1980s also made Indian territory accessible to Brazilian gold prospectors. In the late 1980s, thousands of gold seekers—most of them impoverished—poured into the area in search of wealth. By early 1990, as many as 45,000 prospectors had invaded Yąnomamö traditional lands and extracted gold worth an estimated one billion dollars.

The government's National Indian Foundation (FUNAI) is charged to protect Brazil's Native Ameri-

■ *In many countries, indigenous peoples are facing loss of their cultural identity as the nations in which they live find "more productive" uses for their lands and resources. These Xavante of Brazil, here about to depart for a day's gathering, may not be around as a distinct sociocultural group for much longer.*

can peoples and territories from invasion and plunder, but it has been unable to control violence against the Yąnomamö and other indigenous groups. Brazil's former president announced plans to evacuate the miners using military aircraft, forcibly if necessary. But the prospectors protested the policy and threatened guerilla-style resistance, leading the government to reverse its position early in 1990. New president Fernando Collor de Mello ordered the landing strips destroyed in March of 1990, to reduce future access. But it may already be too late for the Yąnomamö, who have already lost rights to 70 percent of their territory in Brazil. Deaths caused by new diseases and violence are almost certain to continue.

Another common justification for the neglect of the territorial rights of indigenous peoples is the desire to improve a country's balance of trade. The Philippines, Indonesia, Zaire, and other countries earn foreign exchange by leasing rights to harvest timber from their tropical hardwood forests to multinational companies, although much of the "unexploited" forest is needed as fallow by indigenous shifting cultivators. Debts owed to foreign banks and international lending agencies encourage some nations to open up their hinterlands to resource development, pushing their indigenous inhabitants aside. In countries such as Brazil, Mexico, and Argentina, minerals, cattle, timber, vegetables, coffee, and other exports are sold to Europe and North America to earn foreign exchange to help pay off international debts.

As these and numerous other cases show, it is still considered legitimate by many to take land from those who have lived on it for centuries. Racism and social Darwinism are not as fashionable as official justifications as they once were. But new rationalizations exist for the forced removal and exploitation of the territories of indigenous peoples: "developing" the whole country; solving "national problems" by providing lands to peasants and making payments on debts owed to American banks and international lending institutions; and making the countries' products "competitive" in international markets.

Fortunately, the indigenous people who remain in living sociocultural communities are learning to protect themselves through political action. In increasing numbers, indigenous peoples around the world are fighting attempts to dispossess them of their access to traditional territories and resources. Many are resisting efforts to assimilate them into the sociocultural mainstream of their nations. They are publicly objecting to racist and ethnocentric attitudes about their beliefs and customs.

One people who are resisting are the Kayapó. In the 1980s the government of Brazil sought World Bank funding for the construction of two enormous hydroelectric dams on Amazon River tributaries. Eighty-five percent of the land that would have been flooded belongs to one or another indigenous Indian population. Organized by leaders of the Kayapó tribe, members of twenty-nine Brazilian Indian groups protested the dams. In early 1988, two Kayapó leaders traveled to Washington with anthropologist Darrell Posey to speak against the project to officials of the World Bank and to U.S. Congressional authorities. When the World Bank deferred action on the loans, Brazil brought charges against the three protestors under a law that forbids "foreigners" from engaging in political activity harmful to the nation. The courage and sophistication of the Kayapó and other members of threatened communities illustrate how indigenous peoples are organizing themselves to acquire the political power to fight various "developments."

In early 1990, the Colombian national government recognized the land rights of various indigenous tribes to half of the Colombian Amazon. Supposedly, the territory will belong to the Indian communities forever and sale to outsiders is prohibited. Whether the government's motives are entirely humanitarian or part of an effort to control illegal drug trafficking and left-wing guerillas is not clear, but this is a hopeful sign for Colombia's Amazonian peoples.

■ *Today, indigenous people are organizing themselves politically to resist further encroachments on their resources and ways of life, as illustrated by this aboriginal rights group in Brisbane, Australia.*

Why Should We Care?

Despite the increased political sophistication of indigenous peoples around the world, and the protests of concerned citizens in many countries, there is no doubt that preindustrial ways of living are in danger of extinction. Even if the people themselves survive the onslaughts of lumbering, mining, damming, grazing, and building, their sociocultural systems are liable to disappear. Most people would agree that genocide is a crime of the highest degree. But destruction or radical alteration of a way of life is another matter—is it not possible that indigenous people themselves would be better off if they joined the sociocultural mainstream of their nations?

Yes, many tribal peoples do want to acquire formal education, get jobs, improve their living standards, and generally "modernize" their societies. It is obviously true that no one has any right to deny them this opportunity, if that is the free choice they make. But it is also true that many indigenous lifeways are overwhelmed by forces that are not of their peoples' own making and over which the people themselves have no control. It is not that most indigenous peoples are given the opportunity to weigh carefully the options available to them, so that they make informed choices about whether it is best for them to preserve or modernize their ways of life. Today, as in the past, more often their traditions are disappearing because powerful national governments wish to open up their territory, or because private entrepreneurs or corporations wish to exploit their resources.

Anthropologists are especially concerned with the rights of indigenous peoples, for several reasons. First, because of our interest in human sociocultural diversity, we are more aware of what has happened to non-Western lifeways in the past several centuries than are most people. Second, we tend to identify with indigenous peoples, partly because so many of us have worked among them. Third, our professional training tends to give us a relativistic outlook on the many ways of being human, so we can appreciate other peoples' customs and beliefs as viable alternatives to our own. Finally, the fieldwork experience often affects our attitudes about our own societies—deep immersion into other sociocultural traditions leaves some of us not so sure about our commitment to our own.

Whether one is an anthropologist or not, one can appreciate the rights of any group of people to have their lives, property, and resources secure from domination by powerful outsiders. The most important factors in considering the rights of indigenous peoples to be left alone are ethical ones. Do not people everywhere have the right to live their lives free from the unwanted interference of those more powerful and wealthy than themselves? Does any government, regardless of its "problems," have the right to dispossess people from land they have lived on and used for centuries? Is the demand of citizens in Japan, Europe, North America, or anywhere else for wood, minerals, meat, electricity, or other products a sufficient justification for relocating a people or taking land away from them? (Our American readers who follow politicians' statements about "human rights violations" in other countries might wonder why they have so little to say about the rights of indigenous peoples. Is it because they recognize the connection between our own high living standards and the exploitation of resources on the lands of indigenous peoples in places like South America and Southeast Asia?)

Surely, most of us can agree on the answers to such questions. Ethical concerns for the social and material welfare of indigenous people, combined with a respect for other ways of being human, are the primary reasons for granting them their rights to survive as living sociocultural communities. But if the ethical arguments alone are not compelling, there are other arguments for why indigenous lifeways should survive. These arguments are analogous to those of ecologists worried about the extinction of natural species.

Plants and animals live in communities, and the species that make up a community are interrelated. Again and again, removal of one species has been shown to affect other species of the community, often in harmful ways. Ecologists tell us that the maintenance of ecological communities may depend on a certain minimum level of species diversity. Each species therefore is important to other species besides itself. Further, when a plant or animal becomes extinct, the information carried in its genes likewise disappears. This lost information may have practical value to humanity—in the treatment of disease, for example. So each species contains information that may be valuable to humans, and we may be unable to recover this information once it is lost.

Analogously, the long-term welfare of all humanity may be jeopardized by the reduction in the sociocultural diversity of our planet. And we do not mean merely that our lives will be less rich if there are no "natives" left to appear on new National Geographic Society TV specials. We mean something far more important. Information is encoded in any sociocultural system—culture itself is a socially transmitted system of knowledge, you will recall from chapter 2—and this information may be useful to all humankind.

It is difficult for many citizens of industrialized nations to believe that we have anything to learn from preindustrial peoples. We think that preindustrial technologies cannot compete with the genius of modern science and technology. For example, when an international agency offers health care to a rural African community, it assumes that it is providing a service that the people could not otherwise provide for themselves, given their knowledge and available resources. More often than not, this assumption is correct.

Yet it does not follow that indigenous people have nothing to teach us. Although our technologies are in some ways more productive and effective, traditional technologies may work as well or better at solving peoples' problems and are usually less costly besides. True, modern medicine allows physicians to save lives that formerly would have been lost—but are there other "native" treatments used by indigenous peoples that we do not yet know about? Granted, mechanized agriculture produces far more food per acre and per farmworker than preindustrial cultivation systems—but at what cost to the environment and to future generations? Yes, we live longer and fewer of our children die in infancy—but how does the quality of our longer lives compare to those of other peoples? To be sure, we have higher material standards of living—but can our high consumption levels continue indefinitely, and are we happier just because we have more goods?

In short, indigenous peoples have some quite practical things to teach us. We conclude this book with just a small sample of the some of the benefits industrialized peoples have already gained from indigenous lifeways, beginning with medical treatments.

■ Medicines We Have Learned

The medical knowledge of indigenous peoples provides one practical reason why we should care about the preservation of their lifeways. Preindustrial peoples around the world use the plants that occur naturally in their habitats to treat medical ailments. Their "primitive remedies" often have genuine medical value. In fact, we originally learned about many of the most important drugs we use today from preindustrial peoples.

We can only provide a few examples of the useful medicines discovered by preindustrial peoples that now have worldwide significance. Numerous other instances may be found in the text *Medical Botany* by Walter H. Lewis and Memory P. F. Elvin-Lewis.

Malaria remains a debilitating, although usually not fatal, sickness in tropical and subtropical regions. Its main treatment is quinine, a component of the bark of the cinchona tree. Europeans learned of the value of quinine in the seventeenth century from Peruvian Indians.

The Madagascaran periwinkle has long been used in folk medicine to treat diabetes. Researchers first became interested in the plant as a substitute for oral insulin, but it seems to have little value for this purpose. However, during the course of their investigation, scientists discovered that extracts from periwinkle yielded dramatic successes in treating childhood leukemia, Hodgkin's disease, and some other cancers. Drugs based on the plant—notably vincristine and vinblastine—remain the major treatments for these otherwise fatal diseases.

Muscle relaxants are important drugs to surgeons. A popular one is curare, made from the chondodendron tree. Taken in large amounts, curare can paralyze the respiratory organs and lead to death. This property was recognized by South American Indians, who used it as arrow poison for hunting birds, monkeys, and other game, and from whom medical science learned of the drug's value.

The ancient Greeks and several North American Indian tribes used the bark of willows for relief from pain and fever. In the nineteenth century, scientists succeeded in artificially synthesizing the compound that today we call *aspirin.*

There is no way of knowing how many plants used by surviving indigenous peoples could prove to be medically effective. The potential is great. According to pharmacologist Norman Farnsworth, about one-fourth of all prescribed drugs in the United States contain active ingredients extracted from higher plants. The world contains about 250,000 species of higher plants. Less than fifty of these plants contain chemical compounds that are approved by the Food and Drug Administration. Many more plant-derived compounds remain to be discovered and tested for their effectiveness. Almost certainly, some of them will be valuable.

Preindustrial peoples already have done some of this work for botanists and medical scientists. Through centuries of trial and error they discovered that certain plants were effective remedies for local sicknesses and diseases. Shall we allow this culturally transmitted knowledge to be lost? If we do, how many millions of dollars will we have to spend to rediscover it? And meanwhile, how many people will suffer and die?

◼ *Adaptive Wisdom of the "Natives"*

Many preindustrial peoples have lived in and exploited their natural environments for centuries. Over their history, they have selected those crops and varieties that grow and yield well in the conditions of their local habitat. They have learned to control insect pests and diseases that attack the plants on which they depend, and to do so without the need for expensive and often polluting artificial chemicals. They often have learned how to make nature work for them with minimum deterioration of their environments. They have, in short, incorporated much adaptive wisdom into their cultural traditions.

This is not to say that "primitive" peoples always lived in harmony with their environments. Such opinions are part of civilized humanity's image of the noble savage, to which we referred in chapter 1. This romantic image reflects our desire for an existence that contrasts with our own more than it represents the realities of preindustrial peoples' relations with nature. Still, given the variety of existing sociocultural systems, there certainly are adaptive lessons to be learned from surviving indigenous peoples. Following are a few possible benefits that all humanity might gain by preserving the ecological knowledge of indigenous peoples.

Preservation of Crop Varieties   In all cultivation systems, natural selection operates in the fields. Like wild plants, domesticates are subject to drought, disease, insects, and other natural elements, which select for the survival of individual plants best adapted to withstand these hazards. In addition, domesticates are subject to human selection. For example, crop varieties most susceptible to drought or local diseases are harvested in smaller quantities than drought-and disease-resistant varieties. Perhaps without knowing it, the cultivator replants mainly those varieties best adapted to survive the onslaughts of drought and local diseases. This process of "tuning" of plant varieties to the local environment, with all its hazards and fluctuations, goes on automatically so long as the domesticates harvested

self-sufficiency, smaller communities, more personal and enduring social relations, and "more humane," "more moral" values. No anthropologist can tell you whether life is better or worse in preindustrial communities; indeed, we cannot agree on the meaning of *better*. We do know that humanity is diverse. We know that this diversity means that human beings—ourselves included—have many alternative ways of living meaningful and satisfying lives.

At any rate, the high value we place on material things is at least in part a cultural value. It is therefore relative and variable, meaning that it will change should the circumstances of our lives change. Anthropology teaches us that much of what we want we want only because we have learned to want it. Should our economies become capable of producing less, and should others around us consume less, we shall learn to want less, to lower our consumption expectations. We probably shall not be less (or more!) happy as a result. If we are willing to see the wants of peoples of the past and present as relative to time, place, and circumstances, perhaps it is time we view our own possible future from the same perspective.

Perhaps a people themselves are the only ones qualified to judge the quality of their lives, to decide what it will take to lend meaning and dignity to their existence. We hope to have convinced you that there are many ways of being human. We hope you have learned to appreciate some of the alternative ways of living experienced by various human populations. And we hope you will agree that some of these alternatives are worth preserving, both in their own right and for the long-term well-being of all humanity.

Summary

As European influences and industrial economies swept the world during the last few centuries, the lives of indigenous peoples were dramatically altered. Many tribal groups have disappeared altogether due to deliberate genocide or introduced diseases. Many others are threatened with relocation, reduction of their traditional lands and resources, and loss of their sociocultural autonomy through assimilation.

Rationalizations for policies harmful to the interests of indigenous peoples have changed since the colonial era, but many modern governments continue to violate their rights. Common official justifications for such violations include resettling people from overpopulated to "underpopulated" areas; lumbering and mining operations; developing energy resources; producing crops and livestock for internal and external markets; improving trade balances; and paying off debts owed to international lending agencies and multinational banks.

As a result of these and other pressures, the lifeways of many surviving preindustrial peoples are in danger of destruction. Ethical considerations alone are a sufficient reason for why these peoples should be allowed to remain in their communities, on their traditional lands, living in the ways of their ancestors, if that is their choice. Pragmatic considerations also are important, for these people still retain a vast body of knowledge—knowledge that is of great potential value to all humanity.

Science already has adopted several important medicines and treatments from indigenous peoples. Many other plants with medical value probably will be discovered, if the tropical forests and the cultural knowledge of their indigenous inhabitants last long enough.

Adaptive wisdom is also to be found in the traditions of indigenous peoples. Land races of important crops still survive and might contain genetic materials from which useful foods might someday be bred. Crops that today are used primarily by indigenous peoples—such as amaranth, quinoa, tepary bean, and the winged bean—might eventually have worldwide significance. Nonfood plants used by indigenes are also important, as insecticides, oils, fibers, and other products.

Finally, indigenous people provide us with alternative sociocultural models that should reduce our anxieties about the likelihood of eventual decline in our material living standards. The diversity of the human species shows that we can live meaningful and wholly satisfying lives in the future without the technologies and huge quantities of consumer goods we now consider necessary to our economic welfare. The remaining preindustrial lifeways allow us to see that there is more than one narrow road to personal fulfillment, sociocultural health, and national dignity and prestige.

Suggested Readings

■ Bodley, John. *Victims of Progress.* 2d ed. Palo Alto, Calif.: Mayfield, 1982.
   A very readable book that is a good overview of tribal peoples in the modern world and how they are being destroyed by industrial civilization.

■ Davis, Shelton H. *Victims of the Miracle: Development and the Indians of Brazil.* Cambridge: Cambridge University Press, 1977.
  A study discussing economic development in Brazil and the resulting destruction of Indian communities.

■ Harrison, Paul. *The Greening of Africa,* London: International Institute for Environment and Development, 1986.
  Shows how indigenous cultivation systems and scientific ecological principles can be integrated to alleviate Africa's food shortages.

■ International Work Group for Indigenous Affairs, comp. *The Naga Nation and Its Struggle against Genocide.* International Work Group for Indigenous Affairs Document no. 56. Copenhagen, 1986.
  A survey of the historical background and contemporary problems of the Naga peoples of India, who have had an independence movement for over forty years.

■ Jorgensen, Joseph, ed. *Native Americans and Energy Development II.* Washington D.C.: Anthropology Resource Center, 1984.
  An excellent collection of papers examining energy development and American Indian communities.

■ Paine, Robert. *Dam a River, Damn a People?* Copenhagen: International Work Group for Indigenous Affairs, 1982.
  A study discussing the effects of a hydroelectric project in Norway on the indigenous Lapp, or Sami, population.

■ Scudder, Thayer. *No Place to Go: Effects of Compulsory Relocation on Navajos.* Philadelphia: ISHI, 1982.
  A study containing a short history of the Navajo-Hopi land dispute, together with a study of the effects of removal on the Navajo families.

■ Weyler, Rex. *Blood of the Land: The Government and Corporate War Against the American Indian Movement.* New York: Vintage, 1982.
  A polemical attack on the U.S. and Canadian governments and corporate development of Indian resources.

The best sources of information concerning contemporary problems among indigenous peoples are the newsletters, bulletins, pamphlets and monographs published by various support organizations such as the following:

Anthropology Resource Center, 59 Temple Place, Suite 444, Boston, Mass. 02111.

Cultural Survival Inc., 11 Divinity Avenue, Cambridge, Mass. 02138.

International Work Group for Indigenous Affairs, Fiolstraede 10, DK-1171, Copenhagen K. Denmark.

GLOSSARY

A

accommodation   The creation of social and political systems that provide for and support ethnic group differences.

acculturation   The sociocultural changes that occur whenever members of two cultural traditions come into contact.

adaptation   Process by which organisms develop physical and behavioral characteristics allowing them to survive and reproduce in their habitats.

affines   In-laws, or people related by marriage.

age set association   A formally organized and named group including all males or females of about the same age.

ambilineal descent   Form of descent in which individuals trace their major kinship connections through either (but not both) of their parents.

ambilineal descent group   A kin group formed using ambilineal descent as the principle of recruitment.

ancestral cults   A type of communal cult centered around rituals performed to influence a kin group's ancestors.

animism   Belief in spiritual beings.

apocalyptic revelation   A revelation in which the prophet predicts the end of the world.

arbitrariness (conventionality)   Refers to the fact that the meanings of words and other kinds of symbols have no inherent or necessary relationship to the physical properties of the symbols themselves.

archaeology   The investigation of the lifeways of people in the prehistoric past through excavation of their material remains.

artificial countries   Multinationality countries created by external powers. Usually applied to former colonies.

assimilation   The merging of the members of one sociocultural system into another, with the consequent abandonment of the former group's customs and beliefs.

authority   The recognized right of an individual to command another to act in a particular way; legitimate power.

avunculocal residence   Couples live with or near the mother's brother of the husband.

B

balanced reciprocity   The exchange of goods considered to have roughly equal value; social purposes usually motivate the exchange.

band   A small foraging group with flexible composition that migrates seasonally.

big men   Political leaders who do not occupy formal offices and whose leadership is based on influence, not authority.

bilateral descent   Kinship system in which individuals trace their kinship connections equally through both parents.

bilocal residence   Postmarital residence is with either the wife's or the husband's parents, according to choice.

biological determinism   The idea that biologically inherited differences between individuals or populations are important influences on differences between them in ways of behaving and thinking.

biome   A large geographic region with similar climate, vegetation, and soils throughout.

biopsychological functionalism   A variety of functionalism that assumes that sociocultural elements exist to fulfill the physical and psychological needs of individuals.

bound morpheme   A morpheme that is attached to a free morpheme to alter its meaning.

brideservice   Custom in which a man spends a period of time working for the family of his wife.

bridewealth   Custom in which a prospective groom and his relatives are required to transfer goods to the relatives of the bride to make the marriage valid.

C

cargo cults   Melanesian revitalization movements in which prophets claimed to know secret rituals that would bring wealth (cargo).

carrying capacity   The maximum number of people a region can support, given its resources and the way humans exploit them.

caste   Stratification system in which membership in a stratum is in theory hereditary; strata are endogamous; and contact or relations between members of different strata are governed by explicit laws, norms, or prohibitions.

chiefdoms   Centralized political systems with authority vested in formal, usually hereditary, offices or titles; exchange in such systems is often organized by redistribution.

chiefly control   Economic system in which control over resources resides in the holders of formal titles.

child-rearing practices   Methods by which infants and children are nurtured, supported, and enculturated.

child-care compatibility hypothesis   The hypothesis that some economic tasks are assigned to women mainly because they are most compatible with pregnancy, nursing, and child care.

civilization   A form of society in which many people live in cities.

clan (sib)   A named unilineal descent group, some of whose members are unable to trace how they are related, but who still believe themselves to be kinfolk.

class   System of stratification in which membership in a stratum can theoretically be altered, and intermarriage between strata is allowed.

cognitive anthropology (ethnoscience)   Specialty within cultural anthropology that studies the principles by which people classify the natural and social world.

communal cults   Cults in which the members of a group cooperate in the performance of rituals intended to benefit all.

comparative perspective   The insistence by anthropologists that valid hypotheses and theories about humanity be tested with data from a wide range of sociocultural systems.

composite bands   Autonomous (independent) political units consisting of several extended families that live together for most or all of the year.

conflict theory of inequality   Theory holding that stratification benefits mainly the upper stratum and is the cause of most social unrest and other conflicts in human societies.

consanguines   "Blood" relatives, or people related by birth.

constraints   Factors and forces that affect decision making and strategizing.

consultant (informant)   A member of a society who provides information to a fieldworker, often through formal interviews or surveys.

controlled historical comparisons   A methodology for testing an hypothesis using historic changes in societies.

court legal systems   Systems in which authority for settling disputes and punishing crimes is formally vested in a single individual or group.

courts of arbitration   Court systems in which sanctions imposed are designed more to restore harmonious relations between parties than to punish.

courts of regulation   Court systems that use codified laws, with formally prescribed rights, duties, and sanctions.

cross-cultural comparisons   A methodology for testing an hypothesis using a sample of societies drawn from around the world.

cross cousins   Offspring of siblings of different sex.

cult   Organized practices and beliefs pertaining to interactions with and control over supernatural powers.

cultivation   Planting, caring for, and harvesting domesticated plants.

cultural anthropology   The subfield that studies the way of life of contemporary and historically recent human populations.

cultural materialism   A modern theoretical orientation holding that natural resources, overall environment, technology, population size and density, and other material things are the major influence on sociocultural systems and sociocultural change.

cultural relativism   (1) The notion that we should not judge the behavior of other peoples using the standards of our own sociocultural system; (2) the notion that each lifeway is unique and so must be analyzed on its own terms.

culture   (as used in this text) The socially transmitted, shared system of knowledge characteristic of some human group.

culture shock   The feeling of uncertainty and anxiety an individual experiences when placed in a strange sociocultural setting.

D

descent   The tracing of kinship relationships back to previous generations.

descent group   A group whose members believe themselves all to be descended from a common ancestor.

dialect   A regional or subcultural variant of a language.

diffusion   The spread or transmission of sociocultural elements from one people to another.

diffusionism   A theoretical orientation, popular around the turn of the century, that studied the spread of sociocultural traits from one region to another; assumed that most sociocultural features are "borrowed" rather than independently invented.

displacement   Ability of language users to converse about things remote in time and space, including things that do not exist and events that never occurred.

distribution   The relative share of income, property, and resources possessed and consumed by individuals or groups in a society.

division of labor   The patterned assignment of specific productive and economic activities (tasks) to individuals and groups in a society.

domestic group   Individuals, usually relatives, who reside together a in single household.

domestication   The process by which people control the distribution, abundance, and biological features of certain plants and animals, in order to increase their usefulness to humans.

double descent   Form of descent in which individuals receive certain rights and duties through their mothers and other rights and duties through their fathers.

dowry   Custom in which the family of a woman transfers property or wealth to her upon her marriage.

dry land gardening   A type of horticulture in which aridity is the major problem that cultivators face.

E

ecclesiastical cults   Highly organized cults in which a full-time priesthood performs rituals believed to benefit believers or the whole society; occur in complex societies.

economic system   Patterned and organized behaviors by which people produce, distribute, and consume material goods.

egalitarian society   Form of society in which there is little inequality in access to culturally valued rewards.

enculturation   The transmission (by means of social learning) of cultural knowledge to the next generation.

endogamous rules   Marriage rules requiring individuals to marry some member of their own social group or category.

energetic efficiency   The number of calories of energy obtained per calorie of total energy input.

ethnic boundary markers   Any overt characteristics that can be used to indicate ethnic group membership.

ethnic group   A named social grouping of people based on perceptions of shared ancestry, sociocultural traditions, and common history that socially distinguish that group from other groups.

ethnic nationalities   An ethnic group with a feeling of a discrete homeland and an inherent right to political autonomy and self-determination.

ethnogenesis   The creation of a new ethnic group identity.

ethnocentrism   The attitude or opinion that the morals, values, and customs of one's own way of life are superior to those of other peoples.

ethnographic methods   Research methodologies used to describe a contemporary or historically recent sociocultural system.

ethnography   A written description of the way of life of some human population.

ethnohistory   The reconstruction of the past through the study of written documents.

ethnological methods   Research methodologies used to test hypotheses about the causes of or relationships between sociocultural phenomena using a sample of societies.

ethnology   The comparative analysis of sociocultural systems.

exchange   Transfer of goods or rights to goods between individuals or groups.

exogamous rules   Marriage rules prohibiting individuals to marry a member of their own social group or category.

extended family   A group of related nuclear families.

extended household   A group of nuclear families that live together.

F

factors of production   The labor, technology, and natural resources used in producing goods.

fertility maintenance hypothesis   The hypothesis that females do not usually perform strenuous tasks because such tasks may decrease their child-bearing potential.

feud   A method of dispute settlement in self help legal systems involving multiple but balanced killings between members of two or more kin groups.

fieldwork   Ethnographic research that involves observing and interviewing the members of a society to describe their contemporary way of life.

foragers (hunter-gatherers)   Populations that rely on wild (undomesticated) plants and animals for their food supply.

forced assimilation   The social absorption of one ethnic group by another ethnic group through the use of force.

form (rule) of descent   How a people trace their descent from previous generations.

free morpheme   A morpheme that can be used alone.

functional theory of inequality   Theory holding that stratification is a way to reward individuals who contribute most to society's well-being.

functionalism   Theoretical orientation that analyzes sociocultural elements in terms of their useful effects to individuals or to the whole sociocultural system.

G

general evolution   Leslie White's approach to sociocultural change, which holds that improvements in technology and energy capture power sociocultural development.

generalized reciprocity   The giving of goods without expectation of a return of equal value at any definite future time.

genocide   The deliberate attempt to eliminate the members of an ethnic category or sociocultural tradition.

gift exchange   In regard to marital exchanges, custom whereby the relatives of the bride and groom give objects reciprocally.

grammar   Total system of linguistic knowledge that allows the speakers of a language to send meaningful messages and hearers to understand them.

group marriage   Several women and several men are married to one another simultaneously.

H

hierarchical nesting   The idea that an ethnic group is frequently part of a larger collection of ethnic groups, which together constitute a higher level of ethnic identity.

historical materialism   Karl Marx's theory that sociocultural changes are caused by development of the forces of production and the conflicts resulting from the opposed interests of classes.

historical particularism   The theoretical orientation holding that each sociocultural system is the unique product of all the influences to which it was subjected in its past.

holistic perspective   The assumption that any aspect of a way of life is integrated with other aspects, so that no aspect can be understood in isolation.

homeland   A geographical region over which a particular ethnic group feels it has exclusive rights.

horticulture   A method of cultivation in which hand tools powered by human muscles are used and in which land use is extensive.

I

idealism   A contemporary theoretical orientation holding that perceptions and classifications of natural and social reality, values, world views, and other kinds of cultural knowledge are partly or wholly independent of material conditions.

ideational definition of culture   The view (used in this book) that culture is most usefully conceptualized as shared and socially learned knowledge.

ideology   Ideas and beliefs that legitimize and thus reinforce existing inequalities in stratified societies.

incest taboo   Prohibition against sexual intercourse between certain kinds of relatives.

independent invention   The development of similar ideas or behavior among two or more peoples who have never had contact with one another.

indigenous people   Those who occupied a region at the time of its contact with colonial powers or the outside world.

individualistic cults   Cults based on personal relations between specific individuals and specific supernatural powers.

inequality   Degree to which individuals, groups, and categories differ in their access to rewards.

inequality explanation of hunger   Notion that modern hunger is not caused by absolute scarcity but by the unequal distribution of resources and how these resources are used.

influence   The ability to convince people they should act as you suggest.

initiation rite (puberty rite)   A rite held to mark the sexual maturity of an individual or a group of individuals of the same sex.

innovation   The creation of a new sociocultural trait by combining two or more existing traits.

intellectual/cognitive functions of religion   The notion that religious beliefs provide explanations for puzzling things and events.

integration   The intermeshing and fitting together of the various elements of a sociocultural system.

intensive agriculture   A system of cultivation in which plots are planted annually or semiannually; usually uses irrigation, natural fertilizers, and (in the Old World) plows powered by animals.

interpretive anthropology   The contemporary theoretical orientation that analyzes elements of sociocultural systems by explicating their meanings to people and understanding them in their local context.

K

key consultant (informant)   A member of a society who is especially knowledgeable about some subject, and who supplies information to a fieldworker.

kin group   A group of people who culturally conceive themselves to be relatives, cooperate in certain activities, and share a sense of identity as kinfolk.

kin-group control   An economic system in which rights of access to productive resources are acquired through membership in a domestic or kin group.

kin terms   The words (labels) that an individual uses to refer to his or her relatives of various kinds.

kindred   All the bilateral relatives an individual recognizes.

kinship terminology   The way a people classify their relatives into labeled categories, or into "kinds of relatives."

L

labor efficiency   Number of calories of energy obtained per time unit of human labor.

law   A kind of social control characterized by the presence of authority, intention of universal application, obligation, and sanction.

levirate   Custom whereby a woman marries a male relative (usually a brother) of her deceased husband.

lexicon   The words that occur in a language.

life chances   An individual's opportunities to achieve rewards proportional to his or her talents, diligence, and other valued personal qualities.

life cycle   The changes in expected activities, roles, rights and obligations, and social relations individuals experience as they move through culturally defined age categories.

limited-purpose money   Money that may be used to purchase only a few kinds of goods.

lineage   A unilineal descent group larger that an extended family whose members can actually trace how they are related.

linguistics   The scientific study of language.

M

market   Exchange by means of buying and selling, using money.

marketplace   Location where buyers and sellers meet for the purpose of acquiring goods and making money.

market principle   Term used to describe exchanges of goods and services at a price determined by supply and demand.

marriage alliances   The strong relationships between families, domestic groups, or kin groups by virtue of intermarriage between their members.

materialism   The theoretical orientation holding that the main influence on human ways of life is how people acquire resources from their environment.

matrilineal descent   Form of descent in which individuals trace their primary kinship relationships through their mothers.

matrilocal residence   Couple live with or near the wife's parents.

mechanized agriculture   Cultivation system in which inanimate sources (oil, gas, electricity) provide the major energy inputs to farms.

modal personality   Within a single society, those personality elements that are most common.

monogamy   Each individual is allowed to have only one spouse at a time.

morpheme   A combination of phonemes that conveys a standardized meaning.

morphology   The study of the units of meaning in language.

multimedia potential   Property of language that allows messages to be communicated through many mediums, including sound waves and written symbols.

multipurpose money   A money that can be used to purchase a very broad range of goods and services.

myths   Stories that recount the deeds of supernatural powers in the past.

N

natural selection   Charles Darwin's theory that competition, predation, disease, and other natural forces favor the survival and reproduction of the most fit individuals in a population.

negative reciprocity   Exchange motivated by the desire to obtain goods, in which the parties try to gain all the material goods they can.

neolocal residence   Couples establish a separate household apart from both the husband's and wife's parents.

nomadism   Seasonal mobility, often involving migration to high-altitude areas during the hottest and driest parts of the year.

nonunilineal descent   Descent forms in which neither the mother's nor the father's line receives consistent emphasis; includes bilateral and ambilineal descent.

norm   Shared ideals and/or expectations about how certain people ought to act in given situations.

O

origin myth   The collective history of an ethnic group that defines which subgroups are part of it and its relationship to other ethnic groups.

P

paleoanthropology   The study of the biological evolution of the human species.

parallel cousins   Offspring of siblings of the same sex.

participant observation   The main technique used in conducting ethnographic fieldwork, involving living among a people and participating in their sociocultural system.

passive assimilation   The voluntary social absorption of one ethnic group by another ethnic group.

pastoralism   Adaptation in which the needs of domesticated animals for naturally occurring pasture and water greatly influence the settlement and movements of herders.

patrilineal descent   Form of descent in which individuals trace their most important kinship relationships through their fathers.

patrilocal residence   Couples live with or near husband's parents.

patterns of behavior   The behavior that most people exhibit when they are in certain culturally defined situations.

patterns of cooperation   Recurrent ways in which many people coordinate their labor to make some task or activity more efficient or successful.

peasants   Rural people who are integrated into a larger society politically and economically.

personality   Mental processes that make an individual's reactions to similar events and situations stable and predictable, but different from the reactions of other individuals.

phoneme   The smallest unit of sound recognized as distinctive in a language.

phonology   The study of the sound system of language.

physical anthropology   The subfield that studies the biological aspects of humankind.

pluralistic   Nations or societies that contain many subcultures.

polyandry   One woman is allowed to have multiple husbands.

ploygamy   Multiple spouses.

polygyny   One man is allowed to have multiple wives.

postmarital residence pattern   Where a newly married couple go to live after their marriage.

priest   A kind of religious specialist, often full-time, who officiates at the rituals of ecclesiastical cults.

primatology   The study of primates, including monkeys and apes.

procedural law   The structured manner in which a breach of the law is adjudicated or resolved.

production   Activities that transform the energy and raw materials in the environment into want-satisfying goods.

productivity   Property of language that allows its speakers to send an infinite number of novel messages.

prophet A person who claims to have dreams or visions in which he or she received a message from a supernatural power.

psychological functions of religion The emotional satisfications people derive from religion.

R

ranked society Society in which there are a fixed number of statuses (e.g., titles, offices) that carry prestige, and only certain individuals are eligible to attain these statuses.

reasonable man model A model used in legal reasoning that basically asks, How should a reasonable individual have acted under these circumstances?

recall ethnography Attempt by ethnographers to reconstruct events, customs, and beliefs of the recent past by interviewing informants.

reciprocity The transfer of goods for goods between two or more individuals or groups.

recombinable elements Property of language by which the total grammatical system is composed of phonemes and morphemes that can be combined in various rule-governed ways to convey diverse meanings.

redistribution The collection of goods or money from a group, followed by a reallocation to the group by a central authority.

relocation The forced removal of the members of a particular ethnic group from one geographical region to another.

revelation A message that a prophet claims to have received from a supernatural power.

revitalization movement A religious movement explicitly intended to create a new way of life for a society or group.

rights of access How rights to exploit or use particular resources are allocated to individuals and groups.

rite of passage A public ceremony or ritual recognizing and marking a transition from one group or status to another.

ritual Organized and stereotyped symbolic behaviors intended to influence supernatural powers.

S

scarcity explanation of hunger Holds that there is not enough land, water, and other resources to feed all the people of a country or region an adequate diet.

secular ideology An ideology that does not rely on the will of supernatural powers but justifies inequality on the basis of its societywide benefits.

self-help (ad-hoc) legal systems Informal legal systems in societies without centralized political systems, in which authorities who settle disputes are defined by circumstances of the case.

semantic domain A class of things or properties that are perceived as alike in some fundamental respect; hierarchically organized.

sexual division of labor The kinds of productive activities (tasks) that are assigned to women versus men in a sociocultural system.

shaman (medicine man) Part-time religious specialist who uses his special relation to supernatural powers for curing members of his group and harming members of other groups.

shamanistic cults Cults in which special individuals (shamans) have relationships with supernatural powers that ordinary people lack.

shifting cultivation (slash-and-burn, swidden) Type of horticulture, most common in the tropics, in which short periods of cultivation of a plot alternate with long periods of fallow.

simple bands Autonomous or independent political units, often consisting of little more than an extended family, with informal leadership vested in one of the older family members.

social control Mechanisms by which the behavior of individuals is constrained and directed into acceptable channels, thus maintaining conformity.

social Darwinism A social and political philosophy holding that biological characteristics explain and justify inequalities of wealth and power between individuals and populations.

social distance The degree to which cultural norms specify that two individuals or groups should be helpful to, intimate with, or emotionally attached to one another.

social functions of religion The effects of religion on maintaining the institutions of society as a whole.

social homogenization The attempt to create a single ethnic group in a particular geographical region.

social learning The process of learning by means of imitating or communicating with others.

society A territorially distinct and largely self-perpetuating group whose members have a sense of collective identity and who share a common language and culture.

sociobiology The scientific discipline that studies the biological basis of social behavior in animals and humans.

sociocultural system   The way of life of a human population, especially their social relationships, behavioral patterns, and the knowledge and ideas they share.

sociolinguistics   Specialty within cultural anthropology that studies how language is related to the sociocultural system, especially the social uses of speech.

sodalities   Formal institutions that cross-cut communities and serve to unite geographically scattered peoples; may be based on kin groups (clans or lineages) or on non-kin-based groups (age grades or warrior societies).

sorcery   The performance of rites and spells for the purpose of causing harm to others by supernatural means.

sororate   Custom whereby a man marries a female relative of his deceased wife.

specific evolution   Julian Steward's evolutionary approach, which holds that many aspects of a population's way of life result from adaptation to its local environment.

state   A centralized, multilevel political unit characterized by the presence of a bureaucracy that acts on behalf of the ruling elite.

state control   Multilevel, hierarchical control system in which commands and some goods flow to lower levels and food, other goods, and/or labor are rendered as tribute or tax by the common people.

status of women   How women are treated and regarded because of their gender, particularly the degree to which females are subordinant to males, participate equally in valued activities, and are allowed access to important positions and other rewards.

stereotype   A preconceived mental image of a category or group of persons that biases the way they are perceived and how their behavior is interpreted.

strategizing   The mental process of planning and choosing among alternative course of action to attain goals.

strategy   Behavior that results from individuals choosing between alternatives.

stratified society   Society with marked and usually heritable differences in access to wealth, power, and prestige; inequality is based mainly on unequal access to productive resources.

strength hypothesis   The hypothesis that many widespread patterns in the sexual division of labor are explained by superior male strength.

structural functionalism   The variety of functionalism that assumes that sociocultural features serve to fulfill the needs of societies for orderly relations, minimal conflict, conformity, and so on.

structuralism   A modern theoretical orientation that assumes that ways of life are the product of unconscious mental processes.

subculture   Cultural differences characteristic of members of various ethnic categories, regions, religions, and so forth within a single society.

substantive law   Refers to the actual types of behavior that are categorized as illegal, together with the appropriate sanctions imposed.

surplus   The amount of food (or other goods) a worker produces in excess of the consumption of herself or himself and his or her dependents.

symbols   Objects, behaviors, and so forth whose culturally defined meanings have no necessary relation to their inherent qualities.

syntax   The rules by which morphemes and words are combined into sequences to form meaningful sentences.

T

technology-transfer solution   Notion that developing nations can best solve their hunger problems by adopting the technology and production methods of modern mechanized agriculture.

tone languages   Languages in which changing voice pitch within a word alters the entire meaning of the word.

totemism   A form of communal cult in which all members of a kin group have mystical relations with one or more natural objects from which they believe they are descended.

trial-and-error learning   The process of learning by means of experimenting with behaviors and repeating only those behaviors that bring a net return.

tribe   Autonomous political unit encompassing a number of distinct, geographically dispersed communities that are held together by sodalities.

tribute   The rendering of goods (typically including food) to an authority such as a chief.

U

uniformitarianism   The geological theory that features of the earth result from imperceptible, steady, gradual processes.

unilineal descent   Descent through "one line," including patrilineal, matrilineal, and double descent.

unilineal descent group   A group of relatives all of whom are related through only one sex.

unilineal evolution   The nineteenth-century theoretical orientation that held that all human ways of life pass through a similar sequence of stages in their development.

universal grammar   Noam Chomsky's idea that at a deep level the grammar of all languages exhibits certain fundamental similarities.

V

values   Shared ideas or standards about the worthwhileness of goals and lifestyles.

vision quest   The attempt to enlist the aid of supernatural powers by intentionally seeking a dream or vision.

W

Whorf-Sapir hypothesis   The idea that language profoundly shapes the perceptions and world view of its speakers.

witchcraft   The use of psychic powers to harm others by supernatural means.

world view   The way a people interpret reality and events, including how they see themselves as relating to the world around them.

REFERENCES

Chapter 1

Perspectives of Cultural Anthropology
The zoologist who tried to explain why humans are allegedly pair-bonded is Morris (1967).

Chapter 2

What Is Culture?
Tylor's definition of culture is from Tylor (1871, 1).

A Formal Definition of Culture
The distinction between trial-and-error learning and social learning is from Boyd and Richerson (1985). See Hart and Pilling (1979) on Tiwi marriage.

Components of Cultural Knowledge
The symbolism of the Ndembu "milk tree" is discussed in Turner (1967). The Hanunóo plant classification example is taken from Conklin (1957). The information on Navajo witchcraft comes from Kluckhohn (1967). Reichel-Dolmatoff (1971) describes the role of the Tukano shaman in getting the spirit of the animals to release game for hunters.

Culture and Behavior
Brinkerhoff and White (1985, 309) report on the American adultery rate.

Chapter 3

Sociocultural Systems and Genetic Differences
The material on lactase deficiency was taken from Harris (1985, 130–53).

Sociocultural Systems and Humankind's Common Biological Heritage
The criticisms of sociobiology appear in Montagu (1980) and Barlow and Silverberg (1980). Lorenz (1966) is one who suggests that human aggression has an instinctual basis. Geertz (1973, chapter 3) discusses why humans are incomplete organisms unless they acquire cultural knowledge.

Two Channels of Transmission
Boyd and Richerson's (1985) important book analyzes the implications of the fact that genes and culture are inherited through two distinct processes: biological reproduction and social learning.

Social Learning Again
The advantages of relying on social learning rather than genes to acquire behavior are discussed in Pulliam and Dunford (1980).

Chapter 4

Some Properties of Language
From Hockett (1960).

Grammar
The examples on Thai aspiration and Nupe tones are from Fromkin and Rodman's (1988) excellent text. We thank our colleague Lamont Lindstrom for the Tannese example illustrating syntax.

Universal Grammar
The information used in the discussion of child language acquisition is from Aitchison (1985), Fromkin and Rodman (1988), and Moskowitz (1985). The interview with Noam Chomsky was conducted by Gliedman (1985).

And What about Culture?
Tyler (1969) provided the American farmer's classification of livestock.

Language and Sociocultural Systems
On color terms, see Berlin and Kay (1969). We consulted Frank and Anshen (1983) and Lakoff (1975) in preparing the material on sexist usages in American English.

The Social Uses of Speech
See Farb (1974) and Trudgill (1983) on male and female speech and on Javanese "levels" of speech. Chagnon (1983) discusses the Yąnomamö name taboo. We thank Kathryn Meyer of Ohio Wesleyan University for help with the example of Japanese honorifics.

Chapter 5

Nineteenth-Century Origins
Unilineal evolutionary theory is best known from the works of Tylor (1865, 1871) and Morgan (1877).

Historical Particularism (ca. 1900–1940)
The best source on Boas is a collection of his articles (1966). See Harris (1968) for a critique of particularism and cultural relativism generally.

Functionalism (ca. 1920–1950)
Biopsychological functionalism is set forth in Malinowski (1960). Radcliffe-Brown (1922, 1965) presents the structural-functional theory.

Later Evolutionary Approaches
On general evolutionism, see L. White (1949, 1959). Specific evolutionism is derived from Steward (1955).

Modern Materialist Approaches
On dialectical materialism, see Marx (1967, 1970). Cultural materialism is described in Harris (1977, 1979, 1985).

Modern Idealist Approaches
See Lévi-Strauss (1963a, 1963b, 1966) on structuralism. Good sources on interpretive anthropology are Geertz (1973, 1980) and Shweder and Levine (1984).

Chapter 6

Ethnographic Methods
The life of Ishi is discussed in Theodora Kroeber's (1963) biography. The Walapai ethnography is listed under Alfred Kroeber (1935). The discussion of how to evaluate a particular historical account was influenced by Naroll (1962). See also Hickerson (1970) on ethnohistoric methods. Sahlins (1981) discusses the Hawaiian interpretation of Captain Cook's visit. See Fogelson (1989) for a discussion of interpretation of historical events. The discussion of suicide in the Trobriand Islands is derived from Malinowski (1926). The problems of collecting genealogies among the Yąnomamö are recounted by Chagnon (1983, 18–20).

Ethnological Methods
The cross-cultural test of the sorcery and social control hypothesis is from B. Whiting (1950). See Adams (1982 and 1988) for an excellent example of what can be done with historical data. Data on matrilineal and patrilineal societies are from Bailey (1989).

Chapter 7

Biomes
Based on Ehrlich, Ehrlich, and Holdren (1977, 144–59).

Foragers
On Hadza, see Woodburn (1968). On Cheyenne see Hoebel (1978). On Netsilik, see Balikci (1970). On the Western Shoshone, see Steward (1938, 1955). On San band organization, see Lee (1979). The material on the Northwest Coast Indians was taken from Ferguson (1984), Piddocke (1965), and Suttles (1960, 1962, 1968). The data on time spent in foraging among the !Kung San comes from Lee (1968, 1969, 1979). The information on labor time in industrialized nations is compiled by Minge-Klevana (1980). Eaton and Konner (1985) summarize the probable diet of prehistoric foragers. More comparative information on work hours among foragers is found in Sahlins (1972) and Cohen (1977).

Chapter 8

The Advantages of Domestication
Information on plant and animal domestication is from Fagan (1986).

Cultivation
On the advantages and disadvantages of cultivation, see Cohen (1977).

Horticulture
See Bradfield (1971) on dry land gardening among the Western Pueblo. Material on shifting cultivation is from Geertz (1963), Conklin (1957), Rappaport (1968), Freeman (1970b), and Ruddle (1974). The process of intensification is best described in Boserup (1965).

Intensive Agriculture
Differences between extensive and intensive agriculture are set forth in Boserup (1965) and Grigg (1974). Material on intensive agriculture in the New World is drawn from our general knowledge and from Donkin (1979). Quantitative data on the labor requirements of intensive agriculture are found in Boserup (1965, 1970), C. Ember (1983), and Minge-Klevana (1980). Geertz (1963) describes Javanese wet rice, and Grigg (1974) discusses how continued high productivity in wet rice paddies is possible. The Sinhalese material is from E. Leach (1968). E. Wolf (1966) is a good source on peasants. On peasant revolts, see E. Wolf (1969).

Pastoralism
Porter (1965) discusses the subsistence risk reduction benefit of pastoralism. Schneider (1981) shows the negative relation between the distribution of the tsetse fly and cattle pastoralism in Africa. On the Basseri, see Barth (1961). A short source on the Karimojong is Dyson-Hudson and Dyson-Hudson (1969).

Chapter 9

Exchange
The three forms of exchange are presented in Sahlins (1972). Malinowski (1922) describes Trobriand *wasi*. The Maring discussion is from Rappaport (1968) and Peoples (1982). Alkire (1977) and Sahlins (1958) describe tribute

in Micronesia and Polynesia, respectively. See Neale (1976) on money. Schneider (1981) describes some African monies. Pospisil (1978) discusses the uses of Kapauku money. Bohannon (1955) describes Tiv exchange spheres. On Philippine *suki*, see W. Davis (1973). Mintz (1961) discusses Haitian *pratik*.

Control in Economic Systems

Dyson-Hudson and Smith (1978) present a model of territoriality. The description of kin-group control is greatly adapted from Sahlins (1972). Chiefly control is taken from Service (1962, 1975) and Fried (1967). Moore (1958) provided much of the information on the Inca.

Chapter 10

Marriage: Definitions and Functions

The material on Nayar marriage is from Gough (1959).

Incest Prohibitions

The "marry out or die out" theory was proposed by Tylor (1888). The "familiarity breeds disinterest" idea was first proposed by Westermarck and is discussed in his 1926 book. Empirical support for Westermarck's hypothesis is given in A. Wolf (1970; on Taiwan), Shepher (1971; on Israeli kibbutz), and McCabe (1983; on Lebanon). A recent summary of work on the incest taboo is Shepher (1983).

Marriage: A Cross-Cultural Perspective

Inuit (Eskimo) polyandry is described by Kupferer (1988). Goldstein (1987) describes Tibetan polyandry and its advantages to husbands and the wife. The 50 percent American divorce rate is reported in Brinkerhoff and White (1985, 302–3). Chagnon (1983) discusses the importance of marriage alliances among the Yąnomamö. Kuper (1963) describes Swazi bridewealth. See Lee (1976) on San brideservice. Kosraen gift exchange at weddings is discussed in Peoples (1985). See Goody and Tambiah (1973) and Harrell and Dickey (1985) on dowry.

Postmarital Residence Patterns

The frequencies of different residence patterns are as reported in Pasternak (1976, 44). Among those who have discussed the influences on residence patterns are Ember and Ember (1971, 1972), Goody (1976), and Pasternak (1976), but none of them should be held responsible for the ideas presented in this section.

Family and Household Forms

Murdock (1949) showed how forms of postmarital residence produce various forms of the family and household. Pasternak, Ember, and Ember (1976) suggest an economic hypothesis for why extended families exist.

Chapter 11

Descent

The material on the Ashanti is taken from Basehart (1961) and Rattray (1929). Data on the frequencies of various forms of descent are from Divale and Harris (1985). The description of the functions of Tikopian lineages and clans is drawn from Firth (1936, 1965). See Eggan (1950) on Hopi matrilineality. Freeman describes the ambilineal system of the Iban. Kosraen bilateral kinship is discussed in Peoples (1985). The material in the subsection "Influences on the Form of Descent" is drawn from many sources, including Aberle (1961); Divale (1974); Divale and Harris (1976); C. Ember (1974); Ember and Ember (1971); and Ember, Ember, and Pasternak (1974).

Systems of Classifying Relatives

Aberle (1961) and Pasternak (1976) are sources of statistical information on the correlation between form of descent and terminological systems.

Chapter 12

The Sexual Division of Labor

Table 12.1 was put together from data in Murdock and Provost (1973). On female hunting among BaMbuti pygmies and Agta, see Turnbull (1962) and Estioko-Griffin (1986), respectively. On the possibility that strenuous exercise inhibits ovulation, see Graham (1985). The child-care compatibility hypothesis is from Brown (1970a). The discussion of why female contributions to subsistence tend to decline with intensification uses information in C. Ember (1983); Martin and Voorhies (1975); Boserup (1970); Burton and White (1984); and White, Burton, and Dow (1981).

The Status of Women

The general discussion relies on Quinn (1977), Whyte (1978), Sacks (1982), Leacock (1978), and Rosaldo and Lamphere (1974). The Iroquois information is from Brown (1970b). The idea that women's control over key resources tends to carry over into high overall status is discussed in Sanday (1973, 1981). Schlegel (1972) and Whyte (1978) discuss why matrilineality and matrilocality tend to give females high status, all else equal. The information on Chinese wives is from our general knowledge and Margery Wolf (1972). The material on the effects of overall societal complexity on women is synthesized from Goody (1976), Boserup (1970), Whyte (1978), and Sacks (1982).

Chapter 13

Forms of Political Organization

The definitions and ideas concerning political structure were influenced by Steward (1955), Service (1962), Cohen and Service (1978), Krader (1968), and Fried (1967). Ethnographic examples were taken from the following sources: Comanche from Hoebel (1940) and Wallace and Hoebel (1952), Osage from Bailey (1973, 1980), and Tahiti from Goldman (1970).

Social Control and Law

For the basic definition of law as well as many of the concepts about legal systems, we relied upon Hoebel (1954),

Pospisil (1958), Fallers (1969), Bohannan (1968), Newman (1983), and Gluckman (1972, 1973). Ethnographic examples were taken from the following sources: Comanche from Hoebel (1940), Cheyenne from Llewellyn and Hoebel (1941), Nuer from Evans-Pritchard (1940), Jivaro from Harner (1973a), and Barotse from Gluckman (1972, 1973).

Chapter 14

Systems of Equality and Inequality
The classification of societies into egalitarian, ranked, and stratified was proposed by Fried (1967). Woodburn (1982) discusses the reasons for the egalitarianism among foragers. The material on Tikopia is from Firth (1936). Berreman (1959) noted the similarity of race relations in the American South to a caste system.

Castes in Traditional India
The Indian caste system and its relationship to Hinduism are discussed in Dumont (1980), Hiebert (1971), Mandelbaum (1971), and Tyler (1973).

Classes
Natchez stratification is covered in Swanton (1946). Material from the subsection on American stratification is from Domhoff (1983), Hurst (1979), the U.S. Bureau of the Census (1989), and the Joint Economic Committee (1986).

Maintaining Inequality
The Hawaiian religion is described in Valeri (1985).

Theories of Inequality
The functionalist theory was first proposed by Davis and Moore (1945). Conflict theory goes back to Marx (1967, original 1867), but a clearer version appears in Marx (1975). Dahrendorf (1959) and Lenski (1966) discuss conflict theory.

Chapter 15

Theories of Religion
The Trobriand magic example is from Malinowski (1954). Frazer's intellectual theory is from Frazer (1963). Geertz (1965) argues that religion provides meaning. Malinowski (1954) argued that magic and religion serve to alleviate anxieties during times of stress and uncertainty. Kwaio pollution is described in Keesing (1982). The cross-cultural study indicating the association between supernatural punishment and inequality is from Swanson (1960, 166).

The Sphere of Supernatural Intervention
Ethnographic data are from Turner (1967; Ndembu), Rasumssen (1979; Eskimo), Moore (1957; Naskapi), Malinowski (1922; Trobriands), and Frigout (1979; Hopi). The distinction between imitative and contagious magic is from Frazer (1963). The witchcraft examples are from Kluckhohn (1967; Navaho), Wilson (1951; Nyakyusa), Evans-

Pritchard (1976; Zande), Offiong (1983; Ibibio), and Middleton (1965; Lugbara). Kluckhohn (1967) hypothesizes that Navaho witchcraft reduces overt hostilities.

Varieties of Religious Organization
Wallace (1966) formulated and named the kinds of cults. The vision quest material is from Lowie (1954, 1956). Harner (1973b) describes Jivaro shamanism. Middleton (1965) describes the Lugbara ancestral cult. The idealist interpretation of totemism is from Lévi-Strauss (1963b).

Revitalization Movements
An excellent general description of cargo cults is in Worsley (1968). Lawrence (1964) describes the Garia cults. On Handsome Lake's movement among the Seneca, see Wallace (1969). Stewart (1980) describes peyotism among Native Americans.

Chapter 16

Personality and the Sociocultural System
The description of the Yąnomamö is from Chagnon (1983). The Semai material is taken from Dentan (1968). Irvin Child's definition of personality, which we use here, appears in LeVine (1973, 4). The configurational or thematic approach to culture and personality was elegantly stated in Benedict (1934). DuBois (1944) describes Alorese child-rearing practices and their effects on adult personality. Rohner (1975) conducted the cross-cultural test of the notion that parental rejection during childhood tends to be associated with certain adult personality traits. The Social Systems Model of the relation between personality and the sociocultural system comes from the work of Kardiner (1945) and is modernized and explicitly formulated by Whiting (1977).

Age Categories
The information on Hidatsa age sets is from Lowie (1954). Material on the Swazi is from Kuper (1963). Hanson (1988) discusses the idea that age sets function as mechanisms for organizing warfare in decentralized societies.

The Life Cycle
The Cheyenne concept of abortion is from Llewellyn and Hoebel (1941). See Jenness (1932) and Hoebel (1954) for a discussion of Eskimo infanticide. The description of the Osage child-naming rite is based on LaFlesche (1928). The material on whether Samoan young women do or do not experience all the stresses and strains typical of American adolescents is based on Mead (1928) and Freeman (1983). The information on New Guinea beliefs about feminine pollution and male initiation rituals is taken from Meggitt (1970–Enga), Newman and Boyd (1982–Awa), and Herdt (1987–Sambia). The data on the Tucuna girl's puberty rite are from Ninuendaju (1948). Wallace and Hoebel (1952) provided the information on the treatment of the elderly among the Comanche. On the Eskimo treatment of the

elderly, see Hoebel (1954). Data on abandonment and parricide among subarctic peoples are drawn from Vanstone (1974) and Jenness (1932). Robertson (1987:335) reports the history of the now-customary American retirement at age sixty-five.

Chapter 17

Sociocultural Change

The concepts of innovation and invention are from Barnett (1953). Foster (1962) has a good discussion of why particular changes are accepted or rejected by a society.

The World since 1500

The most important single source of data used was Stavrianos (1982). Secondarily, information was drawn from E. Wolf (1982) and—for the period from the fifteenth through the eighteenth centuries—from Braudel (1979a, 1979b). Data on the changing magnitude of world trade were obtained from Rostow (1978), and data on the economies of particular countries were from Stamp (1973), and The World Bank (1982). Information on the general effects of Old World contact on Native American populations was drawn primarily from Crosby (1972). Data on the demographic effects of contact on Native American populations are from Dobyns (1976). For more specific information on historic changes among North American Indians, see Leacock and Lurie (1971). More specific historical data on Africa and the African slave trade were from Davidson (1961, 1969) and Oliver and Fage (1962). Data on the effects of New World cultigens on Africa are based primarily on Miracle (1966, 1967). Statistics on foreign workers in Europe were drawn from Zanker (1986) and data on foreign debt came primarily from Russell (1986). Information on slave raids on Easter Island is taken from Goldman (1970) and Heyerdahl (1958). Statistics on the number of Europeans in India during the 1920s is from Mayo (1927).

Chapter 18

There is a vast body of literature in anthropology and sociology on ethnicity and related issues. Our ideas on the nature and significance of ethnicity have been most strongly influenced by the studies of Frederick Barth (1958 and 1969), Joan Vincent (1974), Bud B. Khlief (1979), Nathan Glazer and Daniel Moynihan (1963 and 1975), John Bennett (1975), Robert E. Norris (1990), Joseph Himes (1974), DeVos and Romanusci-Ross (1975), Ronald Cohen (1978), Sol Tax (1967), Edward Spicer (1961), Bernard Nietschmann (1989), Donald Horowitz (1985), and Richard Jackson and Lloyd Hudman (1990). For discussions of international legal and political issues, see Gudmundur Alfredsson (1989) and Lee Swepton (1989). For additional data concerning particular ethnic groups and historical events, we have drawn on a number of sources:

Charles Foster (1980), John Bodley (1982), Joseph Opala (1987), Eric Wolf (1982), L. S. Stavrianos (1982), Basil Davidson (1968), Robert Carmack (1988), Alice B. Kehoe (1981), John T. McAlister (1973), Dale Eickelmen (1989), Richard Handler (1988), and Richard Price (1979) as well as basic reference sources, current news reports, discussions with colleagues and even with students from Saudi Arabia, Oman, Bangladesh, Indonesia, and Malaysia. In addition, one of the authors spent the summer of 1988 in Yugoslavia and the summer of 1989 in Guatemala collecting data on ethnic identity and conflict.

Chapter 19

Population Growth

The data on world population growth are from Ehrlich, Ehrlich, and Holdren (1977, 182–3). Information on population numbers, mortality rates, birthrates, and growth rates from modern nations is taken from the tables compiled in the statistical Annex of World Bank (1988). The economic interpretation of high fertility in seven Indian villages was given by Mamdani (1973). Data on large Javanese and Nepalese families appear in B. White (1973) and Nag, White, and Peet (1978). Nardi (1981, 1983) and Shankman (1976) discuss the importance of remittances. Freed and Freed (1985) discuss why Indian couples feel they need more than one son.

World Hunger

The inequality explanation of hunger is stated and defended in laypersons' terms in Lappé and Collins (1977, 1986). The El Salvadoran data are reported and analyzed in Durham (1979). The discussion of the effects of the "green revolution" on Javanese peasants is from Franke (1974). Johnson (1971) discusses risk minimization among peasants. The quantitative data on the labor and energetic efficiency of various food systems are compiled from information given in Pimentel et al. (1973, 1975, 1980), Hirst (1974), G. Leach (1976), Pimentel and Pimentel (1979), and Steinhart and Steinhart (1974).

Epilogue

The Fate of Indigenous Peoples

Germany's policies toward the Herero are discussed in Bodley (1982). Kehoe describes the Wounded Knee incident (1989). S. Davis (1977) discusses the impact on indigenous tribes of Brazil's efforts to develop the Amazon Basin. Specific material on the plight of the Yąnomamö is from Newsweek magazine (April 9, 1990:34) and from the Commission for the Creation of the Yąnomami Park (1989a, b), published in Cultural Survival Quarterly. The experiences of the Kayapó are recounted by T. Turner (1989).

Why Should We Care?

The examples of medicines we have learned about from indigenous peoples are taken from Lewis and Lewis (1977).

Farnsworth (1984) argues that many more plants will be discovered to have medical uses. A good discussion of the insights of "traditional medicine" is in Fabrega (1975). The discussion of the erosion of the genetic diversity of major food crops is from our general knowledge and Harlan (1975). The material on amaranth is from Sokolov (1986). An informative discussion of the many uses of tropical forest plants is Myers (1984). Gentry and Wettach (1986) report on the oil-bearing vine among the Campa.

BIBLIOGRAPHY

Aberle, David F.

1961 "Matrilineal Descent in Cross-cultural Perspective." In Matrilineal Kinship, edited by David M. Schneider and Kathleen Gough, 655–727. Berkeley: University of California Press.

Adams, Richard N.

1982 Paradoxical Harvest. Cambridge: Cambridge University Press.

1988 "Energy and the Regulation of Nation States." Cultural Dynamics 1:46–61.

Aitchison, Jean

1985 "Predestinate Grooves: Is there a Preordained Language 'Program'?" In Language: Introductory Readings, edited by Virginia P. Clark, Paul A. Eschholz, and Alfred F. Rosa, 90–111. New York: St. Martin's Press.

Alfredsson, Gudmundur

1989 "The United Nations and the Rights of Indigenous Peoples." Current Anthropology 30:255–59.

Alkire, William H.

1977 An Introduction to the Peoples and Cultures of Micronesia. 2nd ed. Menlo Park, CA.: Cummings.

Allen, Michael

1984 "Elders, Chiefs, and Big Men: Authority Legitimation and Political Evolution in Melanesia." American Ethnologist 11:20–41.

Ardrey, Robert

1961 African Genesis. London: Collins.

1966 The Territorial Imperative. New York: Atheneum.

Avery, Robert B., Gregory E. Elliehausen, and Arthur B. Kennickell

1987 "Measuring Wealth with Survey Data: An Evaluation of the 1983 Survey of Consumer Finances." Paper presented at the 20th Congress of the International Association for Research on Income and Wealth, Rocca di Papa, Italy.

Bailey, Garrick

1973 Changes in Osage Social Organization: 1673–1906. University of Oregon Anthropological Papers, no. 5.

1980 "Social Control on the Plains." In Anthropology on the Great Plains, edited by W. Raymond Wood and Margot Liberty. Lincoln: University of Nebraska Press.

1989 "Descent and Social Survival of Native Horticultural Societies of the Eastern United States." Paper presented at the American Anthropological Association meetings, Washington, D.C.

Balikci, Asen

1970 The Netsilik Eskimo. Garden City, N.Y.: Natural History Press.

Barlow, George W. and James Silverberg, eds.

1980 Sociobiology: Beyond Nature/Nurture? Boulder, Colo.: Westview Press.

Barnett, Homer

1953 Innovation: The Basis of Cultural Change. New York: McGraw-Hill.

Barth, Fredrik

1958 "Ecologic Relationships of Ethnic Groups in Swat, North Pakistan." American Anthropologist 60:1079–89.

1961 Nomads of South Persia. Boston: Little, Brown and Company

1969 Ethnic Groups and Boundaries. Boston: Little, Brown and Company.

Basehart, Harry W.

1961 "Ashanti." In Matrilineal Kinship, edited by David Schneider and Kathleen Gough, 270–97. Berkeley: University of California Press.

Bateman, Rebecca

1990 "Africans and Indians: A Comparative Study of the Black Carib and Black Seminole." Ethnohistory 37:1–24.

Benedict, Ruth

1934 Patterns of Culture. Boston: Houghton Mifflin Company.

Bennett, John, ed.

1975 "The New Ethnicity: Perspectives from Ethnology." 1973 Proceedings of the American Ethnological Society. St. Paul, Minn.: West Publishing Co.

Berch, Bettina

1982 The Endless Days: The Political Economy of Women and Work. San Diego: Harcourt, Brace, Jovanovich.

Berlin, Brent, and Paul Kay

1969 Basic Color Terms—Their Universality and Evolution. Berkeley: University of California Press.

Berreman, Gerald D.

1959 "Caste in India and the United States." American Journal of Sociology 66:120–127.

Bertelsen, Judy S. ed.

1977 Nonstate Nations in International Politics: Comparative System Analyses. New York: Praeger.

Blalock, H. M., Jr.

1962 "Occupational Discrimination: Some Theoretical Propositions." Social Problems 9:240–247.

Boas, Franz

1966 Race, Language and Culture. New York: Free Press (original 1940).

Bodley, John H.

1982 Victims of Progress. 2nd ed. Palo Alto, CA: Mayfield Publishing Company.

Bohannon, Paul

1955 "Some Principles of Exchange and Investment Among the Tiv." American Anthropologist 57:60–70.

1968 Justice and Judgement Among the Tiv. London: Oxford University Press.

Boserup, Ester

1965 The Conditions of Agricultural Growth. Chicago: Aldine.

1970 Woman's Role in Economic Development. New York: St. Martin's.

Boyd, Robert and Peter J. Richerson

1985 Culture and the Evolutionary Process. Chicago: University of Chicago Press.

Bradfield, Maitland

1971 The Changing Pattern of Hopi Agriculture. Royal Anthropological Institute of Great Britain and Ireland Occasional Paper, no. 30. London: Royal Anthropological Institute.

Braudel, Fernand

1979a The Structures of Everyday Life: Civilization & Capitalism 15th–18th Century, Vol. 1, New York: Harper & Row.

1979b The Wheels of Commerce: Civilization & Capitalism 15th–18th Century, Vol. 2, New York: Harper & Row.

Brinkerhoff, David B. and Lynn K. White

1985 Sociology. St. Paul: West Publishing Company.

Brown, Judith K.

1970a "A Note on the Division of Labor by Sex." American Anthropologist 72:1073–1078.

1970b "Economic Organization and the Position of Women among the Iroquois." Ethnohistory 17:131–167.

Burton, Michael L. and Douglas R. White

1984 "Sexual Division of Labor in Agriculture." American Anthropologist 86:568–583.

Callender, Charles, and Lee M. Kodrens

1983 "The North American Berdache." Current Anthropology 24:443–90.

Carmack, Robert, ed.

1988 Harvest of Violence. Norman: University of Oklahoma Press.

Chagnon, Napoleon A.

1983 Yąnomamö: The Fierce People. 3rd ed. New York: Holt, Rinehart and Winston.

Coakley, Jay J.

1978 Sport in Society. St. Louis: C. V. Mosby.

Cohen, Mark Nathan

1977 The Food Crisis in Prehistory. New Haven and London: Yale University Press.

Cohen, Ronald

1978 "Ethnicity: Problem and Focus in Anthropology." In Annual Review of Anthropology vol. 7, 1978, edited by Bernard Siegal. Palo Alto: Annual Reviews Inc.

Cohen, Ronald, and Elman Service

1978 Origins of the State: The Anthropology of Political Evolution. Philadelphia: Institute for the Study of Human Issues.

Cohen, Ronald, and John Middleton, eds.

1970 From Tribe to Nation in Africa. Scranton, Penn.: Chandler Publishing Company.

Commission for the Creation of Yanomami Park (CCPY)

1989a "The Threatened Yanomami." Cultural Survival Quarterly 13:45–46.

1989b "Brazilian Government Reduces Yanomami Territory by 70 Percent." Cultural Survival Quarterly 13:47.

Conklin, Harold C.

1957 Hanunoó Agriculture. FAO Forestry Development Paper, no. 12. Rome: Food and Agriculture Organization of the United Nations.

Crosby, Alfred W.

1972 The Columbian Exchange. Westport, Conn.: Greenwood.

Dahrendorf, Ralf

1959 Class and Class Conflict in Industrial Society. Berkeley: University of California Press.

Davidson, Basil

1961 The African Slave Trade: Precolonial History 1450–1850. Boston: Atlantic-Little, Brown.

1969 Africa in History. New York: Macmillan.

Davis, Kingsley, and Wilbert E. Moore

1945 "Some Principles of Stratification." American Sociological Review 10:242–49.

Davis, Shelton H.

1977 Victims of the Miracle. Cambridge: Cambridge University Press.

Davis, William G.

1973 Social Relations in a Philippine Market. Berkeley: University of California Press.

DeMallie, Raymond J.

1983 "Male and Female in Traditional Lakota Culture." In The Hidden Half: Studies of Plains Indian Women, edited by Patricia Albers and Beatrice Medicine, 237–65. Lanham Md.: University Press of America.

Denig, Edwin Thompson

1961 Five Indian Tribes of the Upper Missouri, edited by John Ewers. Norman: University of Oklahoma Press.

Dentan, Robert Knox

1968 The Semai: A Nonviolent People of Malaya. New York: Holt, Rinehart and Winston.

DeVos, George, and Lola Romanusci-Ross, eds.

1975 Ethnic Identity: Cultural Continuities and Change. Palo Alto: Mayfield Publishing Co.

Divale, William T.

1974 "Migration, External Warfare, and Matrilocal Residence." Behavior Science Research 9:75–133.

Divale, William T., and Marvin Harris

1976 "Population, Warfare, and the Male Supremacist Complex." American Anthropologist 78:521–38.

Dobyns, Henry F.

1976 Native American Historical Demography: A Critical Bibliography. Bloomington: Indiana University Press.

Domhoff, G. William

1983 Who Rules America Now? Englewood Cliffs, N.J.: Prentice-Hall, Inc.

Donkin, Robin

1979 Agricultural Terracing in the Aboriginal New World. Tucson: University of Arizona Press.

Douglas, Mary

1966 Purity and Danger. Middlesex, England: Penguin.

DuBois, Cora

1944 The People of Alor. Minneapolis: University of Minnesota Press.

Dumont, Louis

1980 Homo Hierarchicus: The Caste System and Its Implications. Chicago and London: University of Chicago Press.

Durham, William H.

1979 Scarcity and Survival in Central America. Stanford CA: Stanford University Press.

Dyson-Hudson, Rada, and Eric Alden Smith

1978 "Human Territoriality: An Ecological Reassessment." American Anthropologist 80:21–41.

Dyson-Hudson, Rada, and Neville Dyson-Hudson

1969 "Subsistence Herding in Uganda." Scientific American 220:76–89.

Eaton, S. Boyd, and Melvin Konner

1985 "Paleolithic Nutrition: A Consideration of Its Nature and Current Implications." The New England Journal of Medicine 312:283–89.

Edwards, Harry

1971 "The Myth of the Racially Superior Athlete." The Black Scholar 3:16–28.

1973 Sociology of Sport. Homewood, IL: Dorsey Press.

Eggan, Fred

1950 Social Organization of the Western Pueblos. Chicago: University of Chicago Press.

Ehrlich, Paul R., Anne H. Ehrlich, and John P. Holdren

1977 Ecoscience: Population, Resources, Environment. San Francisco: W. H. Freeman.

Eickelman, Dale F.

1989 The Middle East: An Anthropological Approach. Englewood Cliffs, N.J.: Prentice-Hall, Inc.

Ember, Carol

1974 "An Evaluation of Alternative Theories of Matrilocal Versus Patrilocal Residence." Behavior Science Research 9:135–149.

1983 "The Relative Decline in Women's Contribution to Agriculture with Intensification." American Anthropologist 85:285–304.

Ember, Melvin and Carol R. Ember

1971 "The Conditions Favoring Matrilocal Versus Patrilocal Residence." American Anthropologist 73:571–594.

1972 "The Conditions Favoring Multilocal Residence." Southwestern Journal of Anthropology 28:382–400.

Ember, Melvin, Carol R. Ember, and Burton Pasternak

1974 "On the Development of Unilineal Descent." Journal of Anthropological Research 30:69–94.

Estioko-Griffin, Agnes

1986 "Daughters of the Forest." Natural History 95:36–43.

Evans-Pritchard, E. E.

1940 The Nuer. Oxford: Clarendon.

1976 Witchcraft, Oracles, and Magic among the Azande, abridged edition. Oxford: Clarendon Press.

Ewers, John

1955 The Horse in Blackfoot Indian Culture. Bureau of American Ethnology, Bulletin 159, Washington, D.C., U.S. Government Printing Office.

Fabrega, H., Jr.

1975 "The Need for an Ethnomedical Science." Science 189:969–75.

Fagan, Brian M.

1986 People of the Earth. Boston: Little, Brown and Company.

Fallers, Lloyd A.

1969 Law Without Precedent. Chicago: University of Chicago Press.

Farb, Peter

1974 Word Play. New York: Alfred A. Knopf.

Farnsworth, Norman R.

1984 "How Can the Well Be Dry When It Is Filled with Water?" Economic Botany 38:4–13.

Farrer, Claire

1987 "The 1931 Mescalero Apache Field Project: Review and Response in Reconstructing the Past." Anthropology Newsletter 28:3–4.

Ferguson, R. Brian

1984 "A Reexamination of the Causes of Northwest Coast Warfare." In Warfare, Culture, and Environment, edited by R. Brian Ferguson, 267–328. Orlando, Florida: Academic Press.

Figler, Stephen K.

1981 Sport and Play in American Life. Philadelphia: Saunders College Publishing.

Firth, Raymond

1936 We, The Tikopia. Boston: Beacon Press.

1965 Primitive Polynesian Economy. New York: Norton.

Fogelson, Raymond D.

1989 The Ethnohistory of Events and Nonevents. Ethnohistory 36:133–47.

Foster, Charles R., ed.

1980 Nations Without a State: Ethnic Minorities of Western Europe. New York: Praeger.

Foster, George

1962 Traditional Cultures: and the impact of technological change. New York: Harper & Row.

Frank, Francine and Frank Anshen

1983 Language and the Sexes. Albany: State University of New York Press.

Franke, Richard W.

1974 "Miracle Seeds and Shattered Dreams in Java." Natural History 83:10–18, 84–88.

Frankel, O. H., and Michael E. Soule

1981 Conservation and Evolution. Cambridge: Cambridge University Press.

Frazer, Sir James George

1963 The Golden Bough, abridged edition. Toronto: The Macmillan Company (original 1911–1915).

Freed, Stanley A., and Ruth S. Freed

1985 "One Son Is No Sons." Natural History 94:10–15.

Freeman, Derek

1970a "The Iban of Western Borneo." In Cultures of the Pacific, edited by Thomas G. Harding and Ben J. Wallace, 180–200. New York: Free Press.

1970b   Report on the Iban. London School of Economics Monographs on Social Anthropology, no. 41. London: Athlone Press.

1983   Margaret Mead and Samoa. Cambridge, Mass.: Harvard University Press.

Fried, Morton

1967   The Evolution of Political Society. New York: Random House.

Frigout, Arlette

1979   "Hopi Ceremonial Organization." In Southwest, edited by Alfonso Ortiz, 564–76. Handbook of North American Indians, vol. 9. Washington, D.C.: Smithsonian Institution.

Fromkin, Victoria, and Robert Rodman

1988   An Introduction to Language. 4th ed. New York: Holt, Rinehart and Winston.

Gentry, Alwyn H. and Richard H. Wettach

1986   "Fevillea—a New Oil Seed from Ancient Peru." Economic Botany 40:177–85.

Geertz, Clifford

1963   Agricultural Involution. Berkeley: University of California Press.

1965   "Religion As a Cultural System." In Anthropological Approaches to the Study of Religion, edited by Michael Banton. Association of Social Anthropologists Monographs, no. 3. London: Tavistock Publications.

1973   The Interpretation of Cultures. New York: Basic Books.

1980   Negara. Princeton, N.J.: Princeton University Press.

Gliedman, John

1985   "An Interview With Noam Chomsky." In Language: Introductory Readings, edited by Virginia P. Clark, Paul A. Eschholz, and Alfred F. Rosa, 366–75. New York: St. Martin's Press.

Gluckman, Max

1972   The Ideas in Barotse Jurisprudence. Manchester: Manchester University Press.

1973   The Judicial Process Among the Barotse. Manchester: Manchester University Press.

Glazer, Nathan, and Daniel P. Moynihan

1963   Beyond the Melting Pot. Cambridge: Harvard University Press.

Glazer, Nathan, and Daniel P. Moynihan, eds.

1975   Ethnicity: Theory and Experience. Cambridge: Harvard University Press.

Goldman, Irving

1970   Ancient Polynesian Society. Chicago: University of Chicago Press.

Goldin, Ian

1987   "The Reconstitution of Coloured Identity in the Western Cape." In The Politics of Race, Class, and Nationalism in Twentieth Century South Africa, edited by Shula Marks and Stanley Trapido, 156–81. Reading, MA: Longman Group UK Limited.

Goldstein, Melvyn C.

1987   "When Brothers Share a Wife." Natural History 96(3):38–49.

Goodenough, Ward H.

1961   "Comment on Cultural Evolution." Daedalus 90:521–28.

Goody, Jack

1976   Production and Reproduction. Cambridge: Cambridge University Press.

Goody, Jack, and S. J. Tambiah

1973   Bridewealth and Dowry. Cambridge: Cambridge University Press.

Gough, E. Kathleen

1959   "The Nayars and the Definition of Marriage." Journal of the Royal Anthropological Institute 89:23–34.

Graham, Susan Brandt

1985   "Running and Menstrual Dysfunction: Recent Medical Discoveries Provide New Insights into the Human Division of Labor by Sex." American Anthropologist 87:878–82.

Grigg, David

1974   The Agricultural Systems of the World. Cambridge: Cambridge University Press.

Grove, A. T.

1971   Africa South of the Sahara. Oxford: Oxford University Press.

Handler, Richard

1988   Nationalism and the Politics of Culture in Quebec. Madison: University of Wisconsin Press.

Hanson, Jeffery R.

1988   Age-Set Theory and Plains Indian Age-Grading: A Critical Review and Revision. American Ethnologist 15:349–64.

Harlan, Jack R.

1975   "Our Vanishing Genetic Resources." Science 188:618–21.

Harner, Michael J.

1973a   The Jivaro. Garden City, NY: Doubleday-Anchor.

1973b   "The Sound of Rushing Water." In Hallucinogens and Shamanism, edited by Michael J. Harner, 15–27. London: Oxford University Press.

Harrell, Stevan, and Sara A. Dickey

1985   "Dowry Systems in Complex Societies." Ethnology 24:105–120.

Harris, Marvin

1968   The Rise of Anthropological Theory. New York: Thomas Y. Crowell.

1977   Cannibals and Kings. New York: Random House.

1979   Cultural Materialism. New York: Vintage Books.

1981   America Now. New York: Simon and Schuster.

1985   Good To Eat. New York: Simon and Schuster.

Hart, C. W. M. and Arnold R. Pilling

1979   The Tiwi of North Australia. New York: Holt, Rinehart, and Winston.

Hassrick, Royal B.

1964   The Sioux: Life and Customs of a Warrior Society. Norman: University of Oklahoma Press.

Herdt, Gilbert

1987   The Sambia: Ritual and Gender in New Guinea. New York: Holt, Rinehart and Winston.

Heyerdahl, Thor

1958   Aku-Aku. Chicago: Rand McNally & Company.

Hickerson, Harold

1970   The Chippewa and Their Neighbors: A Study in Ethnohistory. New York: Holt, Rinehart and Winston.

Hiebert, P. G.

1971   Konduru: Structure and Integration in a Hindu Village. Minneapolis: University of Minnesota Press.

Himes, Joseph S.

1974   Racial and Ethnic Relations. Dubuque, Ia.: Wm. C. Brown Company.

Hirst, Eric

1974   "Food-Related Energy Requirements." Science 184:134–38.

Hockett, Charles D.

1960   "The Origin of Speech" Scientific American 203:88–96.

Hoebel, E. Adamson

1940   The Political Organization and Law-ways of the Comanche Indians. American Anthropological Association, Memoir 54.

1954   The Law of Primitive Man. Cambridge: Harvard University Press.

1978   The Cheyennes. 2d ed. New York: Holt, Rinehart and Winston.

Horowitz, Donald L.

1985   Ethnic Groups In Conflict. Berkeley: University of California Press.

Hurst, Charles E.

1979   The Anatomy of Social Inequality. St. Louis: C. V. Mosby.

Jackson, Richard, and Lloyd E. Hudman.

1990   Cultural Geography: People, Places and Environment. St. Paul, Minn.: West Publishing Company.

Jenness, Diamond

1932   The Indians of Canada. Ottawa: National Museum of Canada.

Johnson, Allen W.

1971   "Security and Risk-Taking Among Poor Peasants: A Brazilian Case." In Studies in Economic Anthropology, edited by George Dalton, 143–50. American Anthropological Association Special Publication, no. 7. Washington, D.C.: American Anthropological Association.

Joint Economic Committee

1986   The Concentration of Wealth in the United States: Trends in the Distribution of Wealth Among American Families.

Kammer, Jerry

1980   The Second Long Walk, The Navajo-Hopi Land Dispute. Albuquerque: University of New Mexico.

Kardiner, Abram

1945   The Psychological Frontiers of Society. New York: Columbia University Press.

Keesing, Roger M.

1976   Cultural Anthropology: A Contemporary Perspective. New York: Holt, Rinehart and Winston.

1982   Kwaio Religion. New York: Columbia University Press.

Kehoe, Alice B.

1981   North American Indians: A Comprehensive Account. Englewood Cliffs, N. J.: Prentice-Hall, Inc.

1989   The Ghost Dance. New York: Holt, Rinehart and Winston.

Khlief, Bud B.

1979   Language as Identity: Toward an Ethnography of Welsh Nationalism. Ethnicity 6 (4): 346–57.

Kluckhohn, Clyde

1967   Navaho Witchcraft. Boston: Beacon Press.

Kolb, Abert

1971   East Asia. London: Methuen and Co. Ltd.

Krader, Lawrence

1968   Formation of the State. Englewood Cliffs, N.J.: Prentice-Hall.

Kroeber, Alfred, ed.

1935   Walapai Ethnography. American Anthropological Association, Memoir No. 42.

Kroeber, Theodora

1963   Ishi in Two Worlds: A Biography of the Last Wild Indian in North America. Berkeley: University of California Press.

Kuper, Hilda

1963   The Swazi: A South African Kingdom. New York: Holt, Rinehart and Winston.

Kupferer, Harriet J.

1988   Ancient Drums, Other Moccasins: Native North American Cultural Adaptation. Englewood Cliffs, N.J.: Prentice-Hall, Inc.

La Flesche, Francis

1928   "The Osage Tribe: Two Versions of the Child-Naming Rite." 43rd Annual Report of the Bureau of American Ethnology, 1925–1926, 23–164. Washington, D.C.: Government Printing Office.

Lakoff, Robin

1975   Language and Woman's Place. New York: Harper & Row.

Lappé, Frances Moore

1982   Diet for a Small Planet. New ed. New York: Ballantine Books.

Lappé, Frances Moore, and Joseph Collins

1977   Food First. New York: Ballantine Books.

1986   World Hunger: Twelve Myths. New York: Grove Press.

Lawrence, Peter

1964   Road Belong Cargo. Manchester: Manchester University Press.

Leach, E. R.

1968   "The Sinhalese of the Dry Zone of Northern Ceylon." In Economic Anthropology, edited by Edward E. LeClair, Jr., and Harold K. Schneider, 395–403. New York: Holt, Rinehart and Winston (original 1960).

Leach, Gerald

1976   Energy and Food Production. Guildford: IPC Science and Technology Press for the International Institute for Envrionment and Development.

Leacock, Eleanor

1978   "Women's Status in Egalitarian Society: Implications for Social Evolution." Current Anthropology 19:247–75.

Leacock, Eleanor, and Nancy Lurie, eds.

1971   North American Indians in Historical Perspective. New York: Random House.

Lee, Richard B.

1968   "What Hunters Do for a Living, or, How to Make Out on Scarce Resources." In Man the Hunter, edited by Richard B. Lee and Irven DeVore, 30–48. Chicago: Aldine.

1969   "!Kung Bushman Subsistence: An Input–Output Analysis." In Environment and Cultural Behavior, edited by Andrew P. Vayda, 47–79. Garden City, N.Y.: Natural History Press.

1979   The !Kung San. Cambridge: Cambridge University Press.

Lenski, Gerhard E.

1966   Power and Privilege. New York: McGraw-Hill.

LeVine, Robert A.

1970   "Sex Roles and Economic Change in Africa." In Black Africa, edited by John Middleton, 174–80. London: MacMillan.

1973   Culture, Behavior and Personality. Chicago: Aldine.

Levinson, David, and Martin J. Malone

1980   Toward Explaining Human Culture. New Haven, Conn.: HRAF Press.

Lévi-Strauss, Claude

1963a   Structural Anthropology. New York: Doubleday.

1963b   Totemism. Boston: Beacon.

1966   The Savage Mind. Chicago: University of Chicago Press.

Lewis, Oscar

1941   Manly-hearted Women Among the South Piegan. American Anthropologist 43:173–87.

Lewis, Walter H., and Memory P. F. Elvin-Lewis

1977   Medical Botany. New York: John Wiley and Sons.

Linton, Ralph

1937   "The One Hundred Percent American." The American Mercury 40:427–29.

Lipsky, George

1962   Ethiopia: Its People, Its Society, Its Culture. New Haven: Human Relations Area Files Press.

Medicine, Beatrice

1983   "'Warrior Women': Sex Role Alternatives for Plains Indian Women." In Hidden Half: Studies of Plains Indian Women, edited by Patricia Albers and Beatrice Medicine, 267–75. Lanham, MD.: University Press of America.

Little, Michael A., and George E. B. Morren, Jr.

1976   Ecology, Energetics, and Human Variability. Dubuque, Iowa: Wm. C. Brown Company.

Llewellyn, Karl and E. Adamson Hoebel

1941   The Cheyenne Way. Norman: University of Oklahoma.

Lorenz, Konrad

1966   On Aggression. New York: Harcourt, Brace, and World.

Lowie, Robert H.

1954   Indians of the Plains. Garden City, N.Y.: American Museum of Natural History.

1956   The Crow Indians. New York: Holt, Rinehart and Winston (original 1935).

Malinowski, Bronislaw

1922   Argonauts of the Western Pacific. New York: E. P. Dutton and Company, Inc.

1926   Crime and Custom in Savage Society. London: Rutledge and Kegan Paul.

1954   Magic, Science and Religion. Garden City, N.Y.: Doubleday and Company, Inc.

1960   A Scientific Theory of Culture and Other Essays. New York: Oxford University Press (original 1944).

Mamdani, Mahmood

1973   The Myth of Population Control: Family, Caste and Class in an Indian Village. New York: Monthly Review Press.

Mandelbaum, David G.

1970   Society In India. 2 vols. Berkeley: University of California Press.

Martin, M. Kay, and Barbara Voorhies

1975   Female of the Species. New York: Columbia University Press.

Marx, Karl

1967   Capital. Volume 1. New York: International Publishers (original 1867).

1970   A Contribution to the Critique of Political Economy. New York: International Publishers (original 1859).

1975   Wages, Price and Profit. Peking: Foreign Languages Press (original 1898).

Mayo, Katherine

1927   Mother India. Harcourt, Brace & Company.

McAlister, John T., ed.

1973   Southeast Asia: The Politics of National Integration. New York: Random House.

McCabe, Justine

1983   "FBD Marriage: Further Support for the Westermarck Hypothesis of the Incest Taboo?" American Anthropologist 85:50–69.

McVey, Ruth T., ed.

1962   Indonesia. New Haven, Conn.: Human Relations Area Files Press.

Mead, Margaret

1928   Coming of Age in Samoa. New York: Morrow.

Meggitt, Mervyn

1970   "Male-Female Relationships in the Highlands of Australian New Guinea." In Cultures of the Pacific, edited by Thomas G. Harding and Ben J. Wallace, 125–43. New York: Free Press.

Middleton, John

1965   The Lugbara of Uganda. New York: Holt, Rinehart and Winston.

Minge-Klevana, Wanda

1980   "Does Labor Time Decrease with Industrialization? A Survey of Time-Allocation Studies." Current Anthropology 21:279–98.

Mintz, Sidney W.

1961   "Pratik: Haitian Personalistic Economic Relationships." Proceedings of the American Ethnological Society, 54–63. Seattle: University of Washington Press.

Miracle, Marvin P.

1966   Maize in Tropical Africa. Madison: University of Wisconsin.

1967   Agriculture in the Congo Basin. Madison: University of Wisconsin.

Montagu, Ashley

1980   Sociobiology Examined. New York: Oxford University Press.

Moore, Omar Khayyam

1957 "Divination—A New Perspective." American Anthropologist 59:69–74.

Moore, Sally Falk

1958 Power and Property in Inca Peru. New York: Columbia.

Morgan, Lewis Henry

1877 Ancient Society. New York: World Publishing.

Morris, Desmond

1967 The Naked Ape. New York: Dell.

Moskowitz, Breyne

1985 "The Acquisition of Language." In Language: Introductory Readings, edited by Virginia P. Clark, Paul A. Eschholz, and Alfred F. Rosa, 45–73. New York: St. Martin's Press.

Murdock, George Peter

1949 Social Structure. New York: The Free Press.

1959 Africa: Its People and Their Culture History. New York: McGraw-Hill.

1967 Ethnographic Atlas. Pittsburgh: University of Pittsburgh Press.

Murdock, George P., and Caterina Provost

1973 "Factors in the Division of Labor By Sex: A Cross-Cultural Analysis." Ethnology 12:203–225.

Myers, Norman

1985 The Primary Source: Tropical Forests and Our Future. New York: W. W. Norton and Company.

Nag, Moni, Benjamin N. F. White, and R. Creighton Peet

1978 "An Anthropological Approach to the Study of the Economic Value of Children in Java and Nepal." Current Anthropology 19:293–306.

Nardi, Bonnie

1981 "Modes of Explanation in Anthropological Population Theory." American Anthropologist 83:28–56.

1983 "Goals in Reproductive Decision Making." American Ethnologist 10:697–714.

Naroll, Raoul

1962 Data Quality Control—A New Research Technique. New York: The Free Press.

Neale, Walter C.

1976 Monies in Societies. San Francisco: Chandler and Sharp.

Newman, Katherine S.

1983 Law and Economic Organization: A Comparative Study of Pre-Industrial Societies. Cambridge: Cambridge University.

Newman, Philip L., and David J. Boyd

1982 "The Making of Men: Ritual and Meaning in Awa Male Initiation." In Rituals of Manhood: Male Initiation in Papua New Guinea, edited by Gilbert Herdt, 239–85. Berkeley and Los Angeles: University of California Press.

Nietschmann, Bernard

1988 "Third World War: The Global Conflict Over the Rights of Indigenous Nations." Utne Reader (Nov./Dec.):84–91.

Ninuendju, Curt

1948 "The Tucuna." In Handbook of South American Indians, vol. 3, edited by Julian Steward, 713–25. Handbook of South American Indians: The Tropical Forest Tribes. Bureau of American Ethnology Bulletin 143. Washington, D.C.: U.S. Government Printing Office.

Norris, Robert E.

1990 World Regional Geography. St. Paul, Minn.: West Publishing Company.

Offiong, Daniel

1983 "Witchcraft Among the Ibibio of Nigeria." African Studies Review 26: 107–24.

Oliver, Douglas L.

1989 Oceania: The Native Cultures of Australia and the Pacific Islands. Honolulu: University of Hawaii Press.

Oliver Roland, and J. D. Fage

1962 A Short History of Africa. Baltimore: Penguin.

Oliver, Symmes C.

1962 Ecology and Cultural Continuity as Contributing Factors in the Social Organization of the Plains Indians. University of California Publications in American Archaeology and Ethnology 48(1).

Opala, Joseph

1987 The Gullah. Freetown, Sierra Leone: United States Information Service.

Pasternak, Burton

1976 Introduction to Kinship and Social Organization. Englewood Cliffs, N.J.: Prentice-Hall, Inc.

Pasternak, Burton, Carol R. Ember, and Melvin Ember

1976   "On the Conditions Favoring Extended Family Households." Journal of Anthropological Research 32:109–23.

Peoples, James G.

1982   "Individual or Group Advantage? A Reinterpretation of the Maring Ritual Cycle." Current Anthropology 23:291–309.

1985   Island in Trust. Boulder, Colo.: Westview Press.

Piddocke, Stuart

1965   "The Potlatch System of the Southern Kwakiutl: A New Perspective." Southwestern Journal of Anthropology 21:244–64.

Pimentel, David, *et al.*

1973   "Food Production and the Energy Crisis." Science 182:443–49.

1975   "Energy and Land Constraints in Food Protein Production." Science 190:754–61.

1980   "The Potential for Grass-Fed Livestock: Resource Constraints." Science 207:843–48.

Pimentel, David, and Marcia Pimentel

1979   Food, Energy and Society. New York: John Wiley and Sons.

Porter, Philip W.

1965   "Environmental Potentials and Economic Opportunities—A Background for Cultural Adaptation." American Anthropologist 67:409–20.

Pospisil, Leopold

1958   Kapauku Papuans and Their Law. Yale University Publications in Anthropology, no. 54.

1978   The Kapauku Papuans of West New Guinea. 2d ed. New York: Holt, Rinehart and Winston.

Price, Richard, ed.

1979   Maroon Societies: Rebel Slave Communities in the Americas. Baltimore: Johns Hopkins University.

Pulliam, H. Ronald, and Christopher Dunford

1980   Programmed to Learn. New York: Columbia University Press.

Quinn, Naomi

1977   "Anthropological Studies on Women's Status." Annual Review of Anthropology 6:181–225.

Radcliffe-Brown, A. R.

1922   The Andaman Islanders. Cambridge: Cambridge University Press.

1965   Structure and Function in Primitive Society. New York: Free Press.

Rappaport, Roy

1968   Pigs for the Ancestors. New Haven: Yale University Press.

Rasmussen, Knud

1979   "A Shaman's Journey to the Sea Spirit." In Reader in Comparative Religion, edited by William A. Lessa and Evon Z. Vogt, 308–11. New York: Harper & Row.

Rattray, R. S.

1929   Ashanti Law and Constitution. London: Oxford University Press.

Reichel-Dolmatoff, Gerardo

1971   Amazonian Cosmos. Chicago: University of Chicago Press.

Robertson, Ian

1987   Sociology. 3d ed. New York: Worth.

Robinson, Harvey

1967   Monsoon Asia: A Geographical Survey. New York: Praeger.

Rohner, Ronald P.

1975   They Love Me, They Love Me Not: A Worldwide Study of the Effects of Parental Acceptance and Rejection. New Haven, Conn.: HRAF Press.

Rosaldo, Michelle Z., and Louise Lamphere, eds.

1974   Women, Culture, and Society. Stanford: Stanford University Press.

Rostow, W. W.

1978   The World Economy: History and Prospect. Austin: University of Texas.

Ruddle, Kenneth

1974   The Yukpa Autosubsistence System: A Study of Shifting Cultivation and Ancillary Activities in Colombia and Venezuela. Berkeley: University of California Press.

Russell, George

1986   "Easing into an Era." Time (July 14). 44–5.

Sacks, Karen

1982   Sisters and Wives. Urbana: University of Illinois Press.

Sahlins, Marshall

1958   Social Stratification in Polynesia. Seattle: University of Washington Press.

1972   Stone Age Economics. New York: Aldine Publishing Company.

1981   Historical Metaphors and Mythical Realities: Structure in the Early History of the Sandwich Island Kingdom. Ann Arbor: University of Michigan Press.

Sanday, Peggy R.

1973   "Toward a Theory of the Status of Women." American Anthropologist 75:1682–1700.

1981   Female Power and Male Dominance. Cambridge: Cambridge University Press.

Sapir, Edward

1964   "The Status of Linguistics as a Science." In Edward Sapir, edited by David G. Mandelbaum, 65–77. Berkeley: University of California Press (original 1929).

Schlegel, Alice

1972   Male Dominance and Female Autonomy. New Haven, Conn.: HRAF Press.

Schneider, Harold K.

1981   The Africans. Englewood Cliffs, N.J.: Prentice-Hall.

Scudder, Thayer

1982   No Place To Go: Effects of Compulsory Relocation on Navajos. Philadelphia: ISHI.

Service, Elman R.

1962   Primitive Social Organization: An Evolutionary Perspective. New York: Random House.

1975   Origins of the State and Civilization. New York: W. W. Norton.

Shankman, Paul

1976   Migration and Underdevelopment: The Case of Western Samoa. Boulder, Colo.: Westview Press.

Shepher, Joseph

1983   Incest: A Biosocial View. New York: Academic Press.

1971   "Mate Selection Among Second Generation Kibbutz Adolescents and Adults: Incest Avoidance and Negative Imprinting." Archives of Sexual Behavior 1:293–307.

Shweder, Richard A., and Robert A. LeVine, eds.

1984   Culture Theory: Essays on Mind, Self, and Emotion. Cambridge: Cambridge University Press.

Sokolov, Raymond

1986   "The Good Seed." Natural History 95:102–105.

Spicer, Edward, ed.

1961   Perspectives in American Indian Culture Change. Chicago: University of Chicago Press.

Stamp, L. Dudley

1973   A Commercial Geography. 9th ed. London: Longman.

Stavrianos, L. S.

1982   The World Since 1500: A Global History. 4th ed. Englewood Cliffs, N.J.: Prentice-Hall.

Steinhart, Carol, and John Steinhart

1974   Energy: Sources, Use, and Role in Human Affairs. North Scituate, Mass.: Duxbury Press.

Steward, Julian H.

1938   Basin-Plateau Sociopolitical Groups. Bureau of American Ethnology Bulletin 120.

1955   Theory of Culture Change. Urbana, IL: University of Illinois Press.

Steward, Julian, and Louis Faron

1959   Native Peoples of South America. New York: McGraw-Hill.

Stewart, Omer C.

1980   "The Native American Church." In Anthropology on the Great Plains, edited by W. Raymond Wood and Margot Liberty, 188–96. Lincoln, Neb.: University of Nebraska Press.

Suttles, Wayne

1960   "Affinal Ties, Subsistence, and Prestige among the Coast Salish." American Anthropologist 62:296–305.

1962   "Variations in Habitat and Culture on the Northwest Coast." In Man In Adaptation: The Cultural Present, edited by Yehudi A. Cohen, 128–41. Chicago: Aldine.

1968   "Coping with Abundance: Subsistence on the Northwest Coast." In Man the Hunter, edited by Richard B. Lee and Irven DeVore, 56–68. Chicago: Aldine.

Swanson, Guy

1960   The Birth of the Gods. Ann Arbor: University of Michigan Press.

Swanton, John R.

1946   The Indians of the Southeastern United States. Bureau of American Ethnology Bulletin, no. 137. Washington, D.C.

Swepton, Lee

1989   Indigenous and Tribal Peoples and International Law: Recent Developments. Current Anthropology 30:259–64.

Szwed, John F., ed.

1970   Black America. New York: Basic Books.

Tax, Sol, ed.

1967   Acculturation in the Americas. New York: Cooper Square Publishers.

Tischer, Henry L.

1990   Introduction to Sociology. 3d ed. Fort Worth, Tex.: Holt, Rinehart and Winston.

Trudgill, Peter

1983   Sociolinguistics. Middlesex, England: Penguin.

Turnbull, Colin M.

1962   The Forest People. New York: Simon and Schuster.

Turner, Terence

1989   "Kayapo Plan Meeting to Discuss Dams." Cultural Survival Quarterly 13:20–22.

Turner, Victor

1967   The Forest of Symbols. Ithaca, NY: Cornell University Press.

Tyler, Stephen A., ed.

1969   Cognitive Anthropology. New York: Holt, Rinehart and Winston.

Tyler, Stephen A.

1973   India: An Anthropological Perspective. Pacific Palisades, Calif.: Goodyear Publishing Company.

Tylor, Edward B.

1865   Researches into the Early History of Mankind and the Development of Civilization. London: J. Murray.

1871   Primitive Culture. London: J. Murray.

1888   "On a Method of Investigating the Development of Institutions, Applied to Laws of Marriage and Descent." Journal of the Royal Anthropological Institute 18:245–72.

United States Bureau of the Census

1980   Statistical Abstract of the United States 1980. Washington, D.C.

1989   Statistical Abstract of the United States 1989. Washington, D.C.

Valeri, Valerio

1985   Kingship and Sacrifice: Ritual and Society in Ancient Hawaii. Chicago and London: University of Chicago Press.

Van den Berghe, Pierre

1979   Human Family Systems. New York: Elsevier.

Vanstone, James W.

1974   Athapaskan Adaptations: Hunters and Fishermen of the Subarctic Forest. Chicago: Aldine.

Vincent, Joan

1974   The Structuring of Ethnicity. Human Organization 33:375–79.

Waddell, Eric

1972   The Mound Builders. Seattle: University of Washington Press.

Wagley, Charles

1968   The Latin American Tradition: Essays on the Unity and the Diversity of Latin American Culture. New York: Columbia University Press.

Wallace, Anthony F. C.

1966   Religion: An Anthropological View. New York: Random House.

1969   The Death and Rebirth of the Seneca. New York: Vintage Books.

Wallace, Ernest, and E. Adamson Hoebel

1952   The Comanches: Lords of the South Plains. Norman: University of Oklahoma.

Westermarck, Edward

1926   A Short History of Marriage. New York: MacMillan.

Weyler, Rey

1982   Blood of the Land. New York: Vintage Books.

White, Benjamin N. F.

1973   "Demand for Labor and Population Growth in Colonial Java." Human Ecology 1:217–36.

White, Douglas R., Michael L. Burton, and Malcolm M. Dow

1981   "Sexual Division of Labor in African Agriculture: A Network Autocorrelation Analysis." American Anthropologist 83:824–49.

White, Leslie

1949   The Science of Culture. New York: Grove Press.

1959   The Evolution of Culture. New York: McGraw-Hill.

Whiting, Beatrice

1950   Paiute Sorcery. Viking Fund Publications in Anthropology 15. New York.

Whiting, John W. M.

1977   "A Model for Psychocultural Research." In Culture and Infancy, edited by P. Herbert Leiderman, S. R. Tulkin, and A. Rosenfield, 29–49. New York: Academic Press.

Whitworth, John McKelvie

1975   God's Blueprints: A Sociological Study of Three Utopian Sects. Boston: Rutledge and Kegan Paul.

Whyte, Martin King

1978   The Status of Women in Preindustrial Societies. Princeton, N.J.: Princeton University Press.

Wilson, Edward O.

1975   Sociobiology: The New Synthesis. Cambridge: Harvard University Press.

Wilson, Monica

1951   Good Company. Oxford: Oxford University Press.

Wolf, Arthur P.

1970   "Childhood Association and Sexual Attraction: A Further Test of the Westermarck Hypothesis." American Anthropologist 72:503–15.

Wolf, Eric

1966   Peasants. Englewood Cliffs, N.J.: Prentice-Hall.

1969   Peasant Wars of the Twentieth Century. New York: Harper and Row.

1982   Europe and the People Without History. Berkeley: University of California Press.

Wolf, Eric R., and Edward C. Hansen

1972   The Human Condition in Latin America. New York: Oxford University Press.

Wolf, Margery

1972   Women and the Family in Rural Taiwan. Stanford, Calif.: Stanford University Press.

Woodburn, James

1968   "An Introduction to Hadza Ecology." In Man the Hunter, edited by Richard B. Lee and Irven DeVore, 49–55. Chicago: Aldine.

1982   "Egalitarian Societies." Man 17:431–51.

World Bank

1982   World Development Report 1982. New York: Oxford.

1988   World Development Report 1988. New York: Oxford.

Worsley, Peter

1968   The Trumpet Shall Sound. New York: Schocken Books.

Zanker, Alfred

1986   "Europe's Immigration Battles." U.S. News and World Report (March 31). 25–27.

PEOPLES, REGIONS, AND NATIONS INDEX

Java, 405, 410
  see also Javanese
Javanese, 61–62
  see also Java
Jivaro, 262–263, 305–306

Kapauku, 160
Karimojong, 148–149, 150
Kayapo, 423
Kongo Kingdom, 351, 352
Kosrae, 49, 52, 189, 213
!Kung San, 120–122, 124, 271
  see also San
Kurds, 385
Kwakiutl, 320-321
  see also Northwest Coast

Libero-Americans, 360
Lugbara, 300, 306–307

Maori, 358
Maring, 135, 140, 155–156
Masai, 147
Melanesia, 159, 310, 312
  see also Oceania
Micronesia,
  see also Oceania
Metis, 360, 377

Naga, 384
Naskapi, 297
Natchez, 276–77
Native Americans,
  before 1500, 345
  European conquest of, 347–351,
    355–56
  domestication of crops by,
    128–29
  impact of Europeans on, 359–60
  in United States, 376, 377, 380,
    387–88, 392, 421
  see also Brazil, Colombia, Guate-
    mala, and Plains Indians
Navajo, 25, 99, 186, 300, 301, 327,
  334
Nayar, 174, 176–177
Ndembu, 23, 297
Netsilik Eskimo, 119–120
  see also Imuit
Nigeria, 384, 403

Northwest Coast tribes, 122–123,
  271
Nuer, 174, 261–62
Nyakyusa, 300, 325

Oceania,
  before 1500, 345–346
  impact of Europeans upon, 354,
    358–359
Omani, 345, 351
  see also Arabs
Oneida Community, 183
Osage, 99, 253–254, 312, 326
  see also Plains Tribes

Pakistan, 383–384
Palestinians, 381
Plains Indians,
  impact of European upon, 349,
    421
  religion of, 304, 311-12
  sex roles among, 228–29
Polynesia,
  see Oceania
Philippines, 162–163, 353
Pueblos, 99
  see also Western Pueblos

Sambia, 330–332
Samoans, 327
San, 139, 240
  see also !Kung San
Scots-Irish, 380–381
Semai, 317–318
Seneca, 311
  see also Iroquois
Serbs, 375, 394–395
Shoshone, 118, 271
  see also Western Shoshone
Sikhs, 375, 384
Sinhalese, 139, 140
Sioux, 228
  see also Plain Indians
Soviet Union, 389–390
Swazi, 188, 324–325

Tahitians, 256–257
  see also Oceania
Taiwanese, 180
Tasmanians, 358, 376, 420

Tibetans, 185–186, 385
Tikopia, 208–209, 272
Tiv, 160
Tiwi, 19
Trobrianders, 97, 154–55, 294, 297
Tucuna, 333
Tukano, 25
Turks, 387, 388

United States,
  and world trade, 361–66
  black athletes in, 36–37
  class system in, 277–80
  costs benefits of children in,
    403–04
  redistribution in, 157–58
  kinship in, 198
  family in, 212
  ethnic groups in, 373, 374–75,
    376, 377–80
  food system of, 411–16
  secular ideologies in, 282–84
  witches in, 302
  becoming a soldier in, 331
  old age in, 335
  "one hundred percent Ameri-
    can," 20
  women's liberation in, 242–43
  see also Native Americans,
    Oneida Community, and Afro-
    Americans

Western Pueblos, 133–34
Western Sahara, 385–386
Western Shoshone, 120
  see also Shoshone

Yana, 60, 93
Yanomamö, 62, 95, 186–187, 188,
  317–318, 422
Yoruba, 241
Yugoslavia, 394-395
  see also serbs and croations
Yukaghir, 60
Yukpa, 135

Zulu, 62, 187
Zuni, 321
  see also Western Pueblos

NAME INDEX

Aberle, David, 214
Adams, Richard, 81
Agar, Michael, 106
Allen, Michael, 104
Ardrey, Robert, 35

Bainbridge, Wm. S., 315
Balikci, Asen, 12, 126
Barash, David, 42
Barclay, Harold B., 30
Barnouw, Victor, 337
Barrett, Richard A., 30
Barth, Fredrik, 147, 150, 268
Beckley, Robert E., 314
Belshaw, Cyril, 170
Bendix, Reinhard, 288
Benedict, Ruth, 8, 77, 320–321
Berlin, Brent, 58, 64
Bernardi, Bernardo, 337
Berreman, Gerald, 288
Bicchieri, M. G., 125
Blesdoe, Caroline, 195
Boas, Franz, 8, 33, 76–77, 89
Bodley, John, 397, 417, 428
Bohannon, Paul, 90, 160, 170, 195
Boserup, Ester, 244, 247
Boyd, David, 329
Boyer, Dave, 314
Briggs, Jean, 107
Brown, Judith, 233
Buckley, Thomas, 247
Burton, Michael, 235, 236

Carmack, Robert, 397
Chagnon, Napoleon, 95, 224, 317

Chalfant, H. Paul, 314
Chasin, Barbara H., 417
Child, Irvin, 322
Chomsky, Noam, 53–54, 85
Clark, Virginia, 64
Cohen, R., 268
Cohen, Yehndi, 125, 150
Collins, Joseph, 408, 418
Colson, Elizabeth, 224
Crosby, Alfred, 370

Dahlberg, F., 247
Dalton, George, 170
Darwin, Charles, 7, 32, 71–72
Davidson, Basil, 353
Davis, Shelton, 422, 429
Davis, William, 162, 170
Denton, Robert, 318
DeVore, Irven, 125
DeVos, George, 337, 398
Dias, May, IV, 150
Domhoff, William, 278, 289
Douglas, Mary, 86–87, 170, 313
Dow, Malcomb, 235
DuBois, Cora, 321
Durham, William, 408, 409, 417
Dye, Thomas R., 289
Dyson–Hudson, Neville, 149
Dyson–Hudson, Rada, 149, 163

Eder, James, 398
Eggan, Fred, 224
Elvin–Lewis, Memory P. F., 425
Ember, Carol, 215, 235
Ember, Melvin, 215

Escholz, Paul, 64
Estioko–Griffin, Agnes, 231
Evans–Pritchard, E. E., 150, 224, 268, 301, 314
Ewers, John, 371

Fagan, Brian, 12
Farb, Peter, 12, 64
Farnsworth, Norman, 425
Fernea, Elizabeth, 107
Firth, Raymond, 208, 224
Ford, Daryll, 224
Forge, Anthony, 299
Fortes, M., 268
Foster, Charles, 398
Foster, George M., 150, 417
Fox, Robin, 223
Franke, Richard, 410, 417
Freeman, Derek, 327, 337
Freilich, Morris, 107
Fried, Morton, 268, 270, 287, 288
Friedl, E., 247
Friedlander, Judith, 398
Fromkin, Victoria, 12, 64
Frazer, James, 295, 298

Gamst, Frederick, 30
Geertz, Clifford, 17, 30, 38, 88, 90, 150, 295, 314
Genovese, Eugene, 288
Gentry, Alwyn, 427
Glazer, Mark, 90
Glazer, Nathan, 373
Gluckman, Max, 264, 266, 268
Golde, Peggy, 107

Goldman, Irving, 288
Goodale, Jane C., 195
Goodenough, Ward, 17, 27, 30
Goody, Jack, 195, 244–245, 246
Gottlieb, Alma, 247
Gough, Kathleen, 224
Gould, Steven Jay, 42
Grigg, D. B., 137
Grobsmith, Elizabeth, 398
Gupte, Pranay, 417

Hammond, Dorothy, 337
Handler, Richard, 398
Hanks, Lucien M., 151
Harner, Michael J., 151
Harris, Marvin, 83, 86–87, 90
Harrison, Paul, 429
Hart, C. W. M., 224
Hatch, Elvin, 90
Heller, C., 288
Herdt, Gibert, 330
Heyerdahl, Thor, 75
Hickerson, Nancy, 64
Hockett, Charles, 44
Hoebel, E. Adamson, 126, 258, 268
Holmberg, Allan, 126
Honigman, John, 90
Horowitz, Donald, 398
Howell, Nancy, 124
Hsu, Francis L. K., 337
Hunter, David E. K., 12
Hutton, James, 71
Hymes, Dell, 64

Isherwood, Baron, 170

Jencks, Christopher, 289
Jenness, Diamond, 126
Jochim, Michael, 125
Jorgensen, Joseph, 314, 429
Jurmain, Robert, 12

Kamin, Leon J., 42
Kay, Paul, 58, 64
Keesing, Roger, 17, 223, 314
Kelly, Raymond, 371
Kinsey, Alfred, 186

Klien, Martin, 371
Kluckhohn, Clyde, 12, 301, 314
Konner, Melvin, 124
Krech, Shepard III, 371
Kroeber, Alfred, 77, 93
Kuper, Hilda, 268
Kurzeil, Edith, 90

LaBarre, Weston, 314
Lakoff, Robin, 60
Lambert, William W., 337
Lamphere, Louise, 247
Lappé, Frances Moore, 116, 408, 418
Leach, Edmund, 268
Leach, Gerald, 414, 416, 418
Leacock, Eleanor, 371
Leclair, Edward E., 170
Lee, Richard, 121, 124, 125, 126
Lehman, Arthur C., 314
Leiderman, P. Herbert, 337
Lenski, G., 289
Lessa, William, 314
LeVine, Robert, 337
Lévi-Strauss, Claude, 85, 89, 90, 307-308
Lewis, Oscar, 229
Lewis, Walter, 425
Lewontin, R. C., 42
Liebman, Robert C., 314
Liebow, Elliot, 12
Lindstrom, Lamont, 314
Linton, Ralph, 17, 18, 20
Lipset, Seymour, 288
Little, Michael, 150
Llewellyn, Karl, 268
Lorenz, Konrad, 35
Lowie, Robert, 77, 314
Lyell, Charles, 71

Mair, Lucy, 268, 314
Maitland, Frederick, 342
Malinowski, Bronislaw, 12, 78, 89, 96–97, 195, 295, 314
Mamdani, Mahmood, 404
Maretzki, Hatsumi, 337
Maretzki, Thomas, 337
Margolis, M., 247
Marsella, Anthony J., 337
Martin, Brian, 314
Martin, Kay, 235, 247
Marx, Karl, 80, 82–83, 89, 285

Maybury–Lewis, David, 107
McCabe, Justin, 180
McCurdy, David W., 12
Mead, Margaret, 8, 77, 247, 327, 337
Meggitt, Mervyn, 268, 328
Middleton, John, 195, 307
Mills, C. Wright, 289
Minturn, Leigh, 337
Mintz, Sidney, 162, 370
Morgan, Lewis Henry, 73, 76, 80, 89, 216
Morren, George, 150
Morris, Desmond, 35
Moynihan, Daniel, 373
Murdock, George, 103, 195
Myerhoff, Barbara, 314
Myers, James E., 314

Nash, Manning, 171
Neale, Walter C., 171
Needham, Rodney, 195
Neihardt, John, 314
Nelson, Harry, 12
Netting, Robert, 125
Newman, Philip, 329
Newman, Katherine, 268
Nissenbaum, Stephen, 314
Norbeck, Edward, 30

Ortner, Sherry, 247

Paine, Robert, 429
Palmer, C. Eddie, 314
Pasternak, Burton, 224
Pelto, H. Gretal, 106
Pelto, Perti, 106
Pilling, Arnold, 224
Pimentel, David, 412, 413, 414, 416, 418
Pimentel, Marcia, 414, 416, 418
Posey, Darrell, 423
Pospisil, Leopold, 160, 258–259
Potter, Jack, 150
Powdermaker, Hortense, 107

Rabinow, Paul, 107
Radcliffe-Brown, A. R., 78–79, 85, 89, 224

SUBJECT INDEX

abiotic environment, 111, 121
accomodation, 389, 392, 393, 396
adaptation, 81, 83, 111–151, 129,
    145, 147, 214
      see also domestication; foragers
address terms, 60
adolescence, 327
adulthood, 333–4
affines, 173, 191
age,
      see life cycle
age categories, 324–325
age set association, 324–325
    cyclical, 324
    lineal, 324–325
age sets, 253
aggression, 34–5, 38
alliances, 165
    among Maring, 155–156
    among Yanomamö, 186–187
    see also marriage alliances
ambilineal descent, 202, 205
    groups, 211–213
ancestral cults, 306–307
animism, 74, 291, 295
anthropological thought, 68–90
    see also specific theoretical orien-
      tations
anthropology, *passim*
    defined, 2
    development of, 70–72
    subfields of, 2–5
apartheid, 378–379
applied anthropologists, 10–11,
    400
arbitrariness, 45
archaeology, 3–4
artificial countries, 382

assimilation, 388, 392, 421
authority, 251, 259, 260, 261, 263
avunculocal residence, 190, 191, 194
    explained, 211

balanced reciprocity, 154–6, 157, 165
band control, 163–164, 168–169
bands, 120–2, 131
    among Western Shoshone, 120
    among !Kung San, 120–2
    inequality in, 271
    political organization of, 250–
      253
    see also foragers
barter, 156
behavior, 17–8, 39–40, 54, *passim*
    culture and, 28
    patterns of, 18, 29, 111
big man, 299–300, 160, 251
bilateral descent, 202, 204–205, 214
bilateral kinship
    among !Kung, 122
    in Kosrae, 213
bilocal residence, 190–191, 194
biological determinism, 33–34
    see also genes
biological differences, 3
    see also genes
biomes, 111–113(map), 114, 118,
    124, 131
biopsychological functionalism, 78
biotic environment, 111
bound morphemes, 51
brideprice,
    see bridewealth
brideservice, 188–189

bridewealth, 184, 188
    and status of women, 245
British East India Company, 357

calendrical rituals, 293, 308
cargo cults, 310–311
carrying capacity, 128, 137
castes, 174, 181, 273–276
    among Nayar, 176–177
cattle, 128, 139, 143, 348, 409
    among Masai, 147
    among Nuer, 261–262
    among Karimojong, 148–149
    among Tiv, 160
    in Africa, 133, 146, 188, 244
    in India, 116
    in North America, 116
change, *passim*
    process of, 341–342
    importance of, 342
chiefdoms, 165–166, 168–169, 263,
   272
    compared to states, 166–167
    in Hawaii, 282
    in Tahiti, 256–257
    see also chiefly control
chiefly control, 168
chiefs
    among Basseri, 148
    among Iroquois, 239
    among Osage, 253–4
    among Cheyenne, 255
    and redistribution, 158–159
    see also chiefdoms, chiefly
      control
child-care compatibility hypothesis, 233

historical materialism, 82–83
historical particularism, 75–77
historical studies, 92–95
  see also ethnohistory
holism, 6, 74
holistic perspective, 79
homeland, 377, 379, 380
homogenization, 387–389
honorifics (Japanese) 62
horses, 128, 136, 139, 143, 348
  among Cheyenne, 119, 255
  among Osage, 253
  and military success, 347
  impact on Plains Indians, 349
  on Great Plains, 188
horticulture, 131–6, 140, 215, 256
  and status of women, 241, 245
  and sexual division of labor,
    234–236
  efficiency of, 411(table),
    415(table)
  distribution of, 131–132
  and matrilineal descent, 215
  see also dry land gardening; shift-
    ing cultivation
household, 164, 191
household forms, 191–194
human nature, 34–5
hunger, 401
  see also world hunger
hunter-gatherers, 116–126
  see also foragers
hunting, 251–252, 253–255
  and the sexual division of labor,
    231–232

idealism, 83–88, 246
  objections to comparative studies
    by, 105
  versus materialism, 84–85
ideologies, 281–283, 285, 286, 287
  religious, 282
  secular, 282–283
imitative principle of magic, 298
inbreeding avoidance, 179, 180–181
  see also incest taboo
incest prohibitions,
  see incest taboo
incest taboo, 176, 177–181
incipient court systems, 263
inclusive fitness, 35
independent invention, 74

indigenous peoples, 419–429
  adaptive wisdom of, 425–427
  medical knowledge of, 424–
    425
  relocation of, 420–423
individualistic cults, 303, 304
industrial phase, 342, 354–359
industial revolution, 354
  impact on Africa, 356–357
  impact on the Americas, 355–
    356
  impact on Asia, 357–358
  impact on Oceania, 358–359
inequality, 164, 165, 239, 269–289
  and religious beliefs, 296–297
  maintenance of, 280–283
  theories of, 284–287
inequality explanation of hunger,
  407–410
influence, 251
informant,
  see consultant
initiation rites, 328–333
innovation, 341, 343
integration, 18, 73, 79
intellectual/cognitive functions of religion, 294–295
intensification
  and sociocultural evolution, 83
  and status of women, 244–6
intensive agriculture, 131, 135, 137–
  143, 168
  and sexual division of labor,
    233–236
  and sociocultural systems, 139–
    143
  and status of women, 244–245
  distribution of, 138(map)
  efficiency of, 411(table),
    415(table)
intensive land use, 130, 131, 136,
  137
interpretive anthropology, 85–88
Iroquois kinship terminology, 217–
  218(diagrammed), 221
Islam
  and banking in the Middle East,
    366
  see also Moslems

jajmani, , 275–276
Jews, 84, 86–87

key consultant, 99, 100
key informant,
  see key consultant
kin group control, 164–165
kin groups, 133, 164–165, 176, 181,
  205, 211, 256, 324
  among Yanomamo, 187
  and ancestral cults, 306–307
  as sodalities, 253
  defined, 173, 199
  in ranked societies, 272
  see also descent, groups; kinship
kin terms, see kinship terminology
kindred, 213
kinship, 198–224
  as a semantic domain, 57–58
  significance of, 198–199
  variations in, 199–200
  see also descent
kinship terminology, 24, 215–222
  determinants of, 219, 221–222
  varieties of, 216–222
  see also names of specific systems

labor, 114, 115
  and herding, 147, 148
  in cultivation, 130–131
  in horticulture, 132–136
  in intensive agriculture, 128,
    137, 139
  in market economies, 161
  inputs and outputs, 140
  of women, 234–237, 241, 242–
    243, 244–246
  systems of control over, 163–168
labor, division of,
  see division of labor
labor efficiency, 140, 411–413
lactase, 34
land races, 426
language, 28, 43–64
  and gender, 60–62
  and sociocultural systems, 56–59
  and culture, 54–56
  as an ethnic boundary marker,
    375
  children's acquisition of, 52–53
  properties of, 44–46
  and social learning, 40–41
law, 250, 258–9, 287
  defined, 258
  see also legal systems

leadership, 250–258, 271
  among Iroquois, 239
  and women, 238
legal systems, 102, 259–267
leopard-skin chiefs, 261–262
levirate, 187
lexicon, 46, 58
life chances, 273
life cycle, 317, 325–326
liminal period, 331
  see also rites of passage
limited-purpose money, 160
lineages, 206–207, 272
linguistics, 4, 44, 85
  see also language

magic, 291, 294, 295, 297
malnutrition,
  see world hunger
mana, 282, 291
marital exchanges, 187–189
market, 153, 156, 159–163, 241
market economy, 161–162
market principle, 161
marketplace, 161–163
marriage, 174–5, 180, 245
  among Natchez, 277
  among Nayar, 176–177
  and adulthood, 333–334
  functions of, 175–176
  variations in, 181–189
marriage alliances, 186–187
materialism, 82–83, 88, 113
  and sexual division of labor,
    236–237
  and status of women, 240–246
  versus idealism, 84–85
matriarchy, 211, 239
matrilineal descent, 105–106, 201,
  202(diagrammed), 204, 214
  among Natchez, 276–277
  among Hopi, 209–210
  among Iroquois, 239
  groups, 205–207
matrilocal residence, 190–191, 192, 215
  among Hopi, 209
  and status of women, 241–243
mechanized agriculture, 131, 140, 141
  efficiency of, 411–416
mediator legal systems, 261–262
medical anthropologists, 10
medicine man,
  see shamanistic cults

mercantile phase, 342, 347–354
methods, 92–107
migration, 383
  rural-to-urban, 367
  international, 367–368
  see also population, relocation of
modal personality, 321–324
moieties, 207
  among Osage, 253–354
money, 156, 159, 162, 163
  among Kapauku, 160
  among Tiv, 160
monogamy, 182
  and status of women, 245
monotheism, 74
morphemes, 51
morphology, 50–51
Moslems, 84, 86–87, 343–5, 383,
  384
  see also Islam
multimedia potential, 44–45
multipurpose money, 160
myths, 207, 291–292, 293–4, 308–
  309

name taboo, 62
natural selection, 71, 111, 425–426
negative reciprocity, 156
neolocal residence, 190–191, 192
New World crops, 129
  impact on Asia, 354
  impact on Africa, 352–353
nomadism, 143
nonunilineal descent, 202
  groups, 211–213
norms, 182, 266, 267, 296, 301
  and behavior, 21, 23, 27–29
  and child-rearing practices, 319–
    320
  and social control, 258, 259
  defined, 21
  of kin relations, 199
nuclear family, 120, 164, 173, 176,
  177, 181, 212

old age, 334–336
Old World crops, 129
Omaha kinship terminology, 218,
  219(diagrammed), 222
organization, 122, 132, 148, 199, 286
  see also production, organization of

origin myth, 392
  of ethnic groups, 374–375, 378

paleoanthropology, 3
parallel cousins, 204
  in kinship terminology, 217–222
participant observation, 94, 96
  see also fieldwork
passive assimilation, 388–389, 392–
  393
pastoralism, 129, 143–149, 214
  and social organization, 147–149
  benefits and costs of, 146
  descent forms and, 214
  distribution of, 144–145(map)
patrilineal descent, 105–106,
  201(diagrammed), 202–4, 214
  among Tikopia, 208–209
  groups, 206–207
  in China, 244
patrilocal residence, 190–191, 192
  in China, 244
patterns of cooperation, 115, 132
peace chief, 252
peasants, 141–143, 421
  alleged conservatism of, 410–411
  in Inca state, 167–168
  markets among, 161–163
peripheral markets, 161
personality, 317–324
  child-rearing practices and, 318–
    322
  defined, 318
  sociocultural consequences of,
    322–324
peyote religion, 311–313
phonemes, 48–50
phonological system, 47–48, 54
phonology, 47–50
  variations in, 49–50
phratries, 207
physical anthropology, 2–3
physical characteristics
  as ethnic boundary markers,
    375–376
pigs, 138, 188
  among Maring, 155–156
  in Middle East, 86–87
plow, 128, 131, 133, 136, 143
pluralistic societies, 21
political organization, 141, 249–268
  female subordination in, 238

Text Photo Credits Continued

237 J. Rohr/United Nations; 240 UR Historical Pictures Service; 240 LR R. Lee/ Anthro-Photo; 243 Courtesy of James Peoples; 245 Lila Abu-Lughod/ Anthro-Photo; 249 Garrick Bailey; 251 R. Lee/Anthro-Photo; 252 Courtesy of the Thomas Gilcrease Institute of American History of Art, Tulsa, Oklahoma; 254 Garrick Bailey; 261 J.F.E. Bloss/Anthro-Photo; 266 Anthro-Photo; 269 United Nations/John Littlewood; 271 Irven DeVore/Anthro-Photo; 273 United Nations; 274 United Nations/ Doranne Jacobson; 275 M. Etter/Anthro-Photo; 279 UL Courtesy of James Peoples; 279 UR Bob Daemmrich/The Image Works; 282 Courtesy of Garrick Bailey; 290 Norman Prince; 293 Ettes/Anthro-Photo; 298 Jo Mora

Photograph Collection, Special Collections Library, Northern Arizona University; 303 United Nations; 305 Irven DeVore/ Anthro-Photo; 307 Courtesy of Lamont Lindstrom; 308 Courtesy of James People; 310 Courtesy of Lamont Lindstrom; 312 Courtesy of the Thomas Gilcrease Institute of Amer. History of Art Tulsa, Oklahoma; 316 United Nations; 318 Chagnon/ Anthro-Photo; 319 Iven DeVore/Anthro-Photo; 320 Garrick Bailey and James People; 323 United Nations; 327 United Nations; 329 David Boyd; 330 J.F.E. Bloss/Anthro-Photo; 333 UL M. Etter/ Anthro-Photo; 333 LR Jo Mora Photograph Collection, Special Collections Library, Northern Arizona University; 334 United

Nations; 335 United Nations; Andrea Brizzi; 338 United Nations; 340 United Nations/Y. Nagata; 347 Historical Pictures Service; 350 Jo Mora Photograph Collection, Special Collections Library, Northern Arizona University; 352 Historical Pictures Service; 354 Historical Pictures Service; 355 Historical Pictures Service, Chicago; 360 UPI/Bettmann Newsphotos; 361 Irven DeVore/Anthro-Photo; 364 United Nations; 367 Bettmann Newsphotos; 369 UPI/Bettmann Newsphotos; 372 Bettmann Newsphotos; 373 Bettmann Newsphotos; 377 AP/Wide World Photos, Inc.; 381 Bettmann Archive; 384 UL Bettmann Archive; 384 UR Bettmann Archive; 385 LL Bettmann Archive; 385 LR Bettmann Archive;

387 AP/Wide World; 389 UL Smithsonian Institute; 389 LL Smithsonian Institute; 392 AP/Wide World; 393 LL Bettmann Archive; 393 LR AP/Wide World; 399 Bettmann Newsphotos; 401 UPI/Bettmann Newsphotos; 403 United Nations/Photo by B. P. Wolff; 405 United Nations/A. Jongren; 406 United Nations/Rick Grunbaun; 407 United Nations/John Isaac; 408 United Nations/John Isaac; 412 UL UPI/Bettmann Newsphotos; 412 LR UPI/Bettmann Newsphotos; 413 LL James Smith; 413 LR UPI/Bettmann Newsphotos; 414 UPI/ Bettmann Newsphotos; 419 Historical Picture Service; 422 Maybury-Lewis Anthro-Photo; 423 Irven DeVore/Anthro-Photo

Insert Photo Credit

Sub-Saharan Africa opener: Peacock/Anthro-Photo; **page 3:** (*top*) Koons/Anthro-Photo; (*middle*) DeVore/Anthro-Photo; (*bottom*) Anthro-Photo; **page 4:** (*top*) Austen/TSW-Click (Chicago); (*middle*) Jenike/Anthro-Photo; (*bottom*) Koons/Anthro-Photo.

Asia opener: Le Garsmeur/TSW-Click (Chicago); **page 3:** (*top*) Edwards/TSW-Click (Chicago); (*middle*) Calder/TSW-Click (Chicago); (*bottom*) TSW-Click (Chicago); **page 4:** (*top*) Abu-Lughod/ Anthro-Photo; (*middle*) Williams/H. Armstrong Roberts; (*bottom*) Stiven/TSW-Click (Chicago).

Australia and Oceania opener: Muller/Woodfin Camp & Associates; **page 3:** (*top*) Courtesy of Jim Peoples; (*middle*) Anthro-Photo; (*bottom*) Courtesy of Jim Peoples; **page 4:** (*top*) Austen/TSW-Click (Chicago); (*middle*) Lamont Lindstrom; (*bottom*) Vicki Lockwood.

The Americas opener: Bertsch/H. Armstrong Roberts; **page 3:** (*top*) H. Armstrong Roberts; (*middle*) Krubner/H. Armstrong Roberts; (*bottom*) Koene/H. Armstrong Roberts; **page 4:** (*top*) H. Armstrong Roberts; (*middle*) Courtesy of Garrick Bailey; (*bottom*) Barrett/H. Armstrong Roberts.

Map Credits

Map 7.1, pages 112–113: Figure 14–7 from *Fundamentals of Ecology,* Third Edition by Eugene P. Odum, copyright © 1971 by Holt, Rinehart and Winston, Inc., reprinted by permission of the publisher.